# THE SHIPS AND AIRCRAFT OF THE U.S. FLEET

# THE SHIPS AND AIRCRAFT OF THE U.S. FLEET

ELEVENTH EDITION

BY NORMAN POLMAR

NAVAL INSTITUTE PRESS
ANNAPOLIS, MARYLAND

Frontispiece: A Hawkeye E-2 prepares for takeoff aboard the
USS Enterprise (CVN-65). (Charles H. Vickery, Jr.)

To the Memory of
M. Henri Le Masson,
Naval Authority *Par Excellence*

# Contents

# Foreword

This Eleventh Edition of *Ships and Aircraft* describes the U.S. Navy of the late 1970s—its ships, aircraft, personnel, sensor and weapon systems, and organization. The scope and depth of the book have been expanded considerably over previous editions because of the complexity of the contemporary U.S. Fleet, and to compensate for the limitations of other reference works in this field. However, an effort has been made to retain the "flavor" of the earlier works of this series which were edited by the late James C. Fahey from 1939 until 1965.

An effort has been made in this edition to trace the development of the U.S. Navy over the past two decades to provide an understanding of how the current Fleet was developed. Also, by reference to the U.S. five-year defense program, an effort is made to show the probable future development of the Fleet.

Related to this approach, the sections on submarines, aircraft carriers, cruisers, destroyers, frigates (formerly ocean escorts), command ships, and amphibious ships list all ships in those categories since 1945. Thus, when taken together with Fahey's classic Victory Edition (1945) of *Ships and Aircraft,* the reader is provided with a complete listing of all U.S. Navy ships of those categories, from the beginning of the century through the present.

In general, the information in this edition is current through late 1977. Forthcoming changes in ship status are indicated by "bullets" (●). Standard abbreviations and terms are used throughout, with all explained in the Glossary and Ship Classifications sections, which are located in the front of this edition.

The author is in debt to many individuals for their guidance and their contributions to this effort, most especially Mr. Frank Uhlig, Jr., of the U.S. Naval Institute, Dr. Norman Friedman, Dr. Dominic A. Paolucci, Ing. Stefan Terzibaschitsch, and Mr. Arthur Davidson Baker III.

Others who have contributed to this effort include: Rear Adm. David M. Cooney, Chief of Navy Information (CHINFO); Robert Carlisle, Comdr. Robert K. Lewis, Jr., Lt. Edward A. Shackelford, William Lanc, Anna Urband, Evelyn Jutte, and Bocky Walker of CHINFO; Capt. Stuart D. Landersman, Commander Destroyer Squadron 23; Richard C. Bassett and Eleanor Prentiss of the Naval Sea Systems Command; Comdr. Ronald Black of the Information Directorate of the Department of Defense; Comdr. Abe Greenberg of the USS SCHOFIELD; Comdr. George E. Sullivan of the USS PAUL F. FOSTER; Vice Adm. James H. Doyle, Capt. Henry C. Mustin, Capt. William Sommerville, and Comdr. Robert Chancy of the Office of the Chief of Naval Operations; Lt. Michael Baun of the USS TARAWA; Larry Manning of the Military Sealift Command; Stewart Nelson of the Office of the Oceanographer of the Navy; James Murray of the Philadelphia Naval Shipyard; Dolph M. Veatch, Editor of *Surface Warfare*; Kohji Ishiwata, Editor of *Ships of the World*; Dr. Jurgen Rohwer, Editor of *Marine-Rundschau*; Comdr. Rosario Rausa, Editor of *Naval Aviation News*; Robert Zink of the Navy's Dahlgren Laboratory; CWO Joseph Greco, Elizabeth Segedi, and Leo Loftis of Coast Guard Headquarters; Golbert Rector of Aerojet General Corp.; Eugene Costello of Sikorsky Aircraft Corp.; Dent Williams of Rockwell International; R. G. Elwell of Falcon Jet Corp.; Dave Walsh, Fred Kneif, and Joseph Barbetta of Grumman Aerospace Corp.; Steve Shapiro of RCA; Gny. Sgt. Steven C. Wyatt of the 4th Marine Aircraft Wing; Lt. Comdr. Dale W. Swisher of the Naval Air Training Command; Lt. E. A. Sharp, formerly of U.S. Naval Forces Philippines; and to photographers Dr. Giorgio Arra, Robert L. Lawson, John Mortimer, Russ Egnor, and Ron Wright; and Bill McClay of the Naval Institute, who got the grammar right.

Alexandria, Virginia                                            Norman Polmar

# THE SHIPS AND AIRCRAFT OF THE U.S. FLEET

# 1 State of the Fleet

The U.S. Navy has entered the last quarter of the twentieth century with a Fleet that is modern and, in many respects, highly capable. Almost all of the Navy's active aircraft carriers, cruisers, and destroyers are of post-World War II construction; all frigates, amphibious ships, and submarines are less than 20 years old. The Harpoon anti-ship missile has entered service and during the next few years will be deployed in large numbers on surface ships, submarines, and aircraft. Under development is the long-range Tomahawk cruise missile, an extremely versatile offensive weapon, and the Aegis electronic system, which could revolutionize fleet air defense.

However, the Fleet has been severely reduced in size: virtually all of the World War II-era aircraft carriers, cruisers, and destroyers have been discarded, while new construction programs have not kept pace with the reductions. Most significantly, the U.S. Navy seems to suffer from the lack of a clear sense of purpose and direction.

Part of the problem stems from the fact that the Department of Defense and the Navy have worked at cross-purposes, without understanding each other's goals. For example, the Department of Defense accords high priority to rapid reinforcement of the Central Front in the event of a NATO–Warsaw Pact conflict. However, Navy planning and force development emphasizes the establishment of antisubmarine barriers across "choke points" through which Soviet submarines can transit, and the formation of heavily escorted convoys. Both of these operations are more effective in a long war than a short one, in which it would be vital to reinforce NATO forces in Europe rapidly—possibly in a matter of days. Furthermore, most authorities agree that a Soviet assault in Europe will seek to capture its objectives in a few days, since the Soviets could not sustain a lengthy offensive.

Also, even though it has been more than a decade since the dramatic sinking of the Israeli destroyer ELATH by Soviet missiles launched from Egyptian missile boats, the U.S. Navy does not have a viable shipboard Anti-Ship Missile Defense (ASMD) system, and an effective jamming/decoy capability is only now entering the Fleet. In offensive systems, too—despite the decline in the number of carriers, the increasing Soviet surface fleet, and limited effectiveness of existing U.S. missiles in the surface-to-surface role—the Navy's development lags behind its needs. The Harpoon anti-ship missile did not become operational until 1977 (and then only in limited numbers), and the longer-range, more-capable Tomahawk missile is even further behind in deployment.

Similarly, there is a need for gunfire support ships to provide shore bombardment for amphibious landings. The U.S. Navy's only active guns larger than 5-inch caliber are the three 6-inch guns in one cruiser-flagship. The long-delayed 8-inch Major Caliber Light-Weight Gun (MCLWG) has been scheduled for installation in missile cruisers and, at some future date, refitting in the large SPRUANCE-class (DD 963) destroyers. However, it is unlikely that an Aegis missile cruiser would operate in a shore bombardment role, away from a carrier task force where the cruiser's Anti-Air Warfare

2 STATE OF THE FLEET

(AAW) capabilities are needed. Similarly, the Spruance-class destroyers will be too important for Antisubmarine Warfare (ASW) to remain off a beachhead in the gunfire support role. Besides, these ships are too large, too expensive, and, with "tender" bow sonar domes, too vulnerable to risk exposing them to the tactical and navigational hazards of coastal waters.

These and other problems demonstrate the U.S. Navy's lack of cohesive direction in its development of the Fleet. The reasons for this situation are many and beyond the scope of this book, which is concerned with the current and future state of the ships and aircraft of the Fleet. However, in brief, contributing factors to these problems include the rapid rotation of officers in most Navy assignments, the increasing cost of military hardware and personnel, and the failure of the Department of Defense and to some extent the Administration, the Congress, and the public to understand the current importance of the sea to the political, economic, and military goals of the United States.

In numbers of ships, the Fleet has declined to below the pre-Vietnam force levels of the early 1960s. Indeed, depending upon one's criteria, the statement could be made that the active Fleet is smaller than at any time since 1939. However, the many ships assigned to the Naval Reserve Force and Military Sealift Command confuse this comparison.

Nevertheless, the numbers of active warships, amphibious ships, patrol combatants, and minesweepers are significantly less than at any time since before the Korean War erupted in 1950. Further, it appears unlikely that the force levels will increase significantly during the next decade. The DX/DXG program of the 1960s was an attempt to provide large numbers of surface combatants to compensate for the retiring of the last World War II-era destroyers. But only 30 Spruance-class antisubmarine destroyers are being built, less than half of the DX/DXG plan. Now the Oliver Hazard Perry-class (FFG 7) frigates are proposed as a means of providing the large numbers of ships. However, these ships are extremely limited in certain capabilities, and the long-range planning for these ships has been cut from an original schedule of 56 units in the Fiscal Year 1978–1982 shipbuilding programs to only 40 ships.

During the mid-1970s the U.S. Navy's leadership called for an active Fleet of 600 ships in the 1980s (excluding NRF and MSC) as the minimum to meet Navy requirements. It appears unlikely that the Navy will even be able to obtain an active Fleet of 500 ships during the next decade, or, in the 1990s, maintain even 400 active ships. The last ten shipbuilding programs (FY 1969–1978) have averaged only 12½ ships per year actually constructed (more were authorized). Attributing a 30-year nominal life to ships, this rate of construction will support an active Fleet of no more than 400 ships.

Figure 1 indicates the Department of Defense/Navy five-year shipbuilding plan with the actual Congressional approvals listed for FY 1978. The air-capable DD 963 variant was added by Congressional edict to the FY 1978 program, hence there is no DOD/Navy acquisition plan for this type of ship. Subsequent to the five-year plan being issued, Secretary of Defense Harold Brown has

stated that he does not intend to proceed with construction of the LSD 41 and MCM programs. This would reduce the five-year program from an annual average of 27 ships to about 20. The FY 1979 program request calls for only 15 ships.

Figure 2 indicates the U.S. Fleet force level trends over the past two decades.

### FIGURE 1. FIVE-YEAR SHIPBUILDING PLAN OF 1977

| | | FY 1978 Actual | FY 1979 Actual | FY 1979 Plan | FY 1980 Plan | FY 1981 Plan | FY 1982 Plan |
|---|---|---|---|---|---|---|---|
| CVV | Aircraft Carriers | — | — | 1 | — | 1 | — |
| CGN 42 | Guided Missile Cruisers | — | — | 1 | — | 1 | 1 |
| DDG 47 | Guided Missile Destroyers | 1 | — | — | 2 | 3 | 3 |
| DD 963AC | Air-Capable Destroyers | 1 | — | ? | ? | ? | ? |
| FFG 7 | Guided Missile Frigates | 8 | 8 | 8 | 8 | 8 | 8 |
| FFGX | Advanced Frigates | — | — | — | — | 1 | 1 |
| SSBN 726 | FBM Submarines | 2 | 1 | 1 | 2 | 1 | 2 |
| SSN 688 | Attack Submarines | 1 | 1 | 1 | 1 | 2 | 2 |
| LSD 41 | Dock Landing Ships | — | — | 1 | — | 2 | 3 |
| MCM | Mine Countermeasure Ships | — | — | 1 | 6 | 6 | 6 |
| AD | Destroyer Tenders | — | 1 | 1 | 1 | — | — |
| T-AGOS | Ocean Surveillance Ships | — | 3 | 3 | 5 | 4 | — |
| AO | Oilers | 2 | — | 4 | 2 | 2 | 2 |
| AOE | Fast Combat Support Ships | — | — | — | 1 | — | — |
| AR | Repair Ships | — | — | 1 | — | — | 1 |
| T-ARC | Cable Ships | — | 1 | 1 | 1 | — | — |
| T-ASR | Submarine Rescue Ships | — | — | — | 2 | 2 | — |
| T-ATF | Fleet Tugs | 3 | — | 2 | — | — | — |
| | | 18 | 15 | 26 | 32 | 32 | 29 |

### FIGURE 2. U.S. FLEET FORCE LEVELS

| | 1960 | 1964 | 1968 | 1972 | 1976 | 1978 | (Change) |
|---|---|---|---|---|---|---|---|
| Active Ships | 812 | 917 | 976 | 654 | 476 | 462 | (−350) |
| Aircraft Carriers | 23 | 24 | 23 | 17 | 13 | 13 | (−10) |
| Cruisers | 14 | 28 | 34 | 28 | 26 | 28 | (+14) |
| Destroyers | 226 | 213 | 221 | 131 | 69 | 73 | (−153) |
| Frigates | 41 | 40 | 50 | 66 | 64 | 65 | (+24) |
| FBM Submarines | 2 | 21 | 41 | 41 | 41 | 41 | (+39) |
| Attack Submarines (nuclear) | 8 | 19 | 33 | 56 | 64 | 73 | (+65) |
| Attack Submarines (diesel) | 103 | 85 | 72 | 38 | 10 | 7 | (−96) |
| Amphibious Ships | 113 | 133 | 157 | 77 | 62 | 63 | (−50) |
| Patrol Combatants | 4 | 6 | 9 | 16 | 8 | 3 | (−1) |
| Mine Ships | 81 | 85 | 84 | 31 | 3 | 3 | (−78) |
| Auxiliary Ships | 197 | 263 | 251 | 153 | 116 | 93 | (−104) |
| Active Naval Aircraft | 8863 | 8391 | 8491 | 6752 | 5752 | 5317 | (−3,546) |

NOTES: Active ships do not include ships operated by the Naval Reserve Force, Military Sealift Command, or academic institutions.
Active aircraft include Marine Corps, Naval Air Reserve, and Marine Air Reserve.

# 2 Future Ship Classes

The Department of Defense's Five-Year Shipbuilding Program proposes the construction of nine new classes of ships in FY 1979–1982. The FY 1978 budget, approved in mid-1977, also initiates the air-capable variant of the SPRUANCE-class (DD 963) destroyers. That design is described in the main body of this edition because it has been approved by the Congress.

In addition, the proposed "baseline" VSTOL Support Ship (VSS) is included in this section. Although not formally proposed in the current Five-Year Shipbuilding Program, earlier five-year plans proposed several ships of this class. The current Navy interest in VSTOL aircraft and Congressional support for this ship makes it highly probable that a VSS class will be started during the next few years.

**Aircraft Carriers: CVV Design**

| | |
|---|---|
| Displacement: | ~44,000 tons light |
| | ~50,000 tons standard |
| | ~58,000 tons full load |
| Length: | 850 feet (259 m) wl |
| | 900 feet (274.3 m) oa |
| Beam: | 121 feet (36.9 m) |
| Extreme width: | 245 feet (74.7 m) |
| Draft: | 35 feet (10.7 m) |
| Propulsion: | steam turbines; 134,000 shp; 2 shafts |
| Boilers: | 4 1,200-psi |
| Speed: | ~27 knots |
| Complement: | ~2,100 |
| Air wing: | ~1,370 |
| Aircraft: | 50–55 |
| Catapults: | 2 steam C13-1 |
| Elevators: | 2 deck edge |
| Missiles: | IPDMS launchers |

The CVV has been proposed as a lower-cost alternative to nuclear-propelled aircraft carriers in an effort to maintain 12–13 "flattops" in the Fleet through the 1990s. The CVV concept violates Title VIII of the Defense Appropriations Act of 1975 which states that all "major combatant vessels for the strike forces of the U.S. Navy" shall have nuclear propulsion.

Classification: CVV is a planning classification. Previously the classification CVX was applied to this concept.

Cost: Cost estimates in 1977 for two CVV-type ships were approximately $2.5 billion for their design and construction. However, these were highly tentative estimates.

Engineering: The CVV would be the first twin-screw "fleet" carrier constructed for the Navy since the WASP (CV 7) was completed in 1940. The new ship would, however, be slower than the WASP, which had a rated speed of 29.5 knots with 75,000 shp.

**VSTOL Support Ships**

| | |
|---|---|
| Displacement: | ~22,000 tons full load |
| Length: | 750 feet (228.6 m) oa |
| Beam: | 87 feet (26.5 m) |
| Extreme width: | |
| Draft: | 24 feet (7.3 m) |
| Propulsion: | 4 gas turbines; ~90,000 shp; 2 shafts |
| Speed: | 28 knots |
| Complement: | |
| Air wing: | |
| Aircraft: | ~26 { 4 VSTOL fighter/strike aircraft / 16 large ASW helicopters / 6 LAMPS helicopters |
| Catapults: | none |
| Elevators: | 2 |
| Missiles: | IPDMS launchers |

The VSS concept evolved from the never-approved Sea Control Ship (SCS) proposed for construction in the early 1970s. (The SCS would have been a 14,300-ton ship with a speed of 26 knots; it would have embarked 3 VSTOL aircraft and 15–16 helicopters.)

Classification: VSS is a planning classification. It was used, in part, to avoid the complications of Title VIII legislation requiring nuclear propulsion for aircraft carriers. The ship probably would be designated CVS or CVH when built.

Engineering: The VSS is believed to be the world's largest warship currently being considered for gas-turbine propulsion. The British VTOL carrier INVINCIBLE is a gas-turbine ship (19,500 tons) while the largest Soviet gas-turbine ships are the 9,000-ton-plus "Kara" ASW cruisers.

### Nuclear-propelled Guided Missile Cruisers: Improved "Virginia" Class

| | |
|---|---|
| Displacement: | 12,000 tons full load |
| Length: | 585 feet (178.3 m) oa |
| Beam: | 63 feet (19.2 m) |
| Draft: | |
| Propulsion: | steam turbines; 2 shafts |
| Reactors: | 2 pressurized-water D2G |
| Speed: | 30+ knots |
| Complement: | |
| Helicopters: | 2 LAMPS |
| Missiles: | 2 twin Mk 26 Mod 2(?) launchers for Tartar/ Standard-MR SAM (128?) |
| | 8 Harpoon SSM cannisters Mk 141 (2 × 4) |
| | 8 Tomahawk SSM cannisters (2 × 4) |
| Guns: | 1 5-inch (127-mm) 54 cal DP Mk 45 (1 × 1) |
| | or 1 8-inch (203-mm) 55 cal Mk 71 (1 × 1) |
| | 2 20-mm Phalanx CIWS Mk 15 (2 × 1) |
| ASW weapons: | ASROC fired from forward Mk 26 launcher |
| | 6 12.75-inch (324-mm) torpedo tubes Mk 32 (2 × 3) |
| Radars: | SPS-49 air search |
| | SPS-55 surface search |
| | (4) SPY-1A phased array |
| Sonars: | SQS-53 bow-mounted |
| | SQR-19 TACTAS(?) |
| Fire control: | 1 Mk 86 gun FCS |
| | 4 Mk 99 missile FCS |
| | 1 SPQ-9 radar |

The Navy's failure to gain Administration or Congressional approval for the strike cruiser (CSGN) concept has led to development of the "improved" VIRGINIA-class cruiser. This ship is intended to provide Aegis-equipped, nuclear-propelled escorts for nuclear carriers.

The basic VIRGINIA-class hull, power plant, and weapons would be employed in this class with the Aegis radar and fire control system. The VIRGINIA superstructure would be altered considerably to accommodate the fixed-antenna SPY-1A radar "faces" and total ship displacement would increase by about 1,000 tons.

The FY 1978 budget provided $187 million for advanced procurement of nuclear components and for design studies for the ship, with construction funds proposed for FY 1979. Three other ships of this class are planned. With subsequent Aegis installation in the four VIRGINIA-class ships, they would provide two Aegis cruiser escorts for each of the four nuclear carriers.

### Advanced Frigates

The Navy plans to begin construction in the early 1980s of an advanced frigate class (FFGX) as a follow-on to the PERRY class (FFG 7). Specific characteristics of the FFGX have not yet been determined.

The ship probably will have an SES (Surface Effects Ship) configuration if the 3,000-ton SES test ship is successful (see Chapter 12). The ship will have facilities for one or more helicopters and probably for fixed-wing VSTOL aircraft.

### Dock Landing Ships

Eight dock landing ships (LSD) are proposed for construction to replace the THOMASTON-class (LSD 28) ships constructed in the 1950s. Current Navy planning calls for an improved version of the ANCHORAGE class (LSD 36). However, there is major interest in adapting high-speed (circa 30-knot) commercial ships of the LASH or SEABEE design for this class. Under the more conventional approach the Navy proposes to construct the LSD 41 at a cost of $230 million.

### Mine Countermeasure Ships

| | |
|---|---|
| Displacement: | 1,640 tons full load |
| Length: | ~265 feet (80.7 m) oa |
| Beam: | ~40 feet (12.2 m) |
| Draft: | ~11½ feet (3.5 m) |
| Propulsion: | 2 gas turbines; 2 shafts |
| Speed: | 18 knots (sustained) |
| Complement: | |
| Guns: | |
| Radars: | SPS-55 surface search |
| Sonars: | SSQ-14 mine detection (in early ships) |
| | SMS (in later ships) |

Nineteen mine countermeasure ships (MCM) are planned to provide a deep-ocean capability for countering advanced Soviet mines. The estimated cost of the 19-ship program is $1.16 billion, with the lead ship costing $60 million. The ships will be fitted with improved deep-moored sweep equipment, including two-ship towed sweep devices.

Aircraft: The ship will not have helicopter support facilities, but only a vertical replenishment unloading area.

Electronics: The MCM will have the SSN-2 precise navigation

system for plotting areas cleared of deep-moored or bottom-moored mines.

Sonar: A deep-mode version of the current SQQ-14 mine-hunting sonar will be provided until the advanced Ship Mine-hunting Sonar (SMS) is available in the middle to late 1980s. The MCM will have a center well for lowering the mine-detecting sonars.

Artist's conception of the Mine Countermeasures Ship (MCM)

### Ocean Surveillance Ships

The Navy plans to construct a class of 12 ocean surveillance ships (T-AGOS) to expand and refine its capability to conduct acoustic surveillance. The existing seafloor Sound Surveillance System (SOSUS) provides such a capability in selected areas. However, in other areas the mobile T-AGOS using a Surface Towed Array Surveillance System (SURTASS) will be employed.

The surveillance ships will be large tug-type craft and they will be operated by the Military Sealift Command with civilian crews.

The first three ships are proposed for funding in FY 1979 at a cost of $98 million.

### Repair Ships

A new class of repair ships (AR) is planned to replace the venerable VULCAN class (AR 5). Those ships have already seen up to 35 years of service and cannot adequately support modern warships. The first of five new ARs is proposed in the FY 1979 program at a cost of $299 million.

### Cable Repair Ships

Similarly, the Navy's three cable repairing ships (ARC) are dated and only marginally effective. Two will be modernized to extend their useful service lives by 10–15 years. To meet Navy and other requirements for supporting seafloor communications and surveillance systems, the Navy plans two new cable ships, both of which would be operated by MSC with civilian crews. The first ship is proposed for funding in FY 1979 at a cost of $191 million.

### Submarine Rescue Ships

Four additional submarine rescue ships (ASR) are planned, in part to replace the surviving World War II-era CHANTICLEER-class (ASR 7) ships. These will be tug-type ships with advanced diving systems installed. Unlike the recently completed PIGEON-class (ASR 21) ships, the new units will not be able to operate the Deep Submergence Rescue Vehicle (DSRV). (The ships would be able to service a DSRV brought into the area by another surface ship or submarine, and would have some rescue capability employing the McCann submarine rescue chamber.)

### Nuclear-propelled Research Submersible

A second nuclear-propelled research submersible has been proposed by Admiral H. G. Rickover, USN (Ret.), Deputy Commander for Nuclear Propulsion in the Naval Sea Systems Command. This submersible would be constructed of HY-130 steel and would have a greater depth capability than the existing NR-1. The term HTV for Hull Test Vehicle has been used with this program to avoid association with the NR-1 program, which has been criticized for high costs and operational limitations. During 1976, Admiral Rickover requested $130 million for construction of the NR-2/HTV; however, construction had not been approved when this page went to press.

Neither the NR-1 nor NR-2 have been listed in a formal shipbuilding plan or assigned an SCB number. (See Chapter 20 for a description of the NR-1.)

# 3 Fleet Organization

The U.S. Navy's operational forces—ships, submarines, aircraft, and Marine units—are simultaneously under two organization systems: administrative and tactical.

The administrative organization is based on "type" categories; thus, similar units are grouped together to facilitate training, overhaul and repair, logistics, and other aspects of readiness. The so-called "type commanders" have essentially no operational role.

Under the type commanders are the various wings, flotillas, groups, squadrons, and divisions of ships, submarines, and aircraft. In addition, the Marine Corps' combat forces are assigned to the Navy for operational control, and the Commanding Generals of the Fleet Marine Forces (FMF) are type commanders.

The administrative organizations are similar for the U.S. Atlantic and Pacific Fleets. Some administrative unit commanders also serve as tactical commanders; however, the tactical organizations of the Atlantic and Pacific Fleets differ significantly. The principal tactical components of the Atlantic Fleet are the Second Fleet in the Atlantic and the Sixth Fleet in the Mediterranean. In the Pacific the numbered fleets are the Third Fleet in the eastern Pacific and the Seventh Fleet in the western Pacific. In addition to their U.S. missions, both Atlantic-area fleets have NATO responsibilities.

The fleets' principal operating groupings are organized into task forces, with the Commander Task Force (CTF) designation based on numbered fleet designation. When appropriate, subgroupings are designated as task groups (e.g. CTG-60.2) and as task units (e.g. CTU-60.2.1). In Tables 1 and 2 the major task forces are listed under their respective fleets, although they are not all continually in existence. Rather, some task forces are activated only when specific units are assigned.

In the following tables stars are used to indicate the grades of their commanding officers: ★★★★ for admiral, ★★★ for vice admiral or lieutenant general (Marine Corps), ★★ for rear admiral or major general (Marine Corps), and ★ for brigadier general (Marine Corps). (The U.S. Navy does not use the rank of commodore in peacetime.) Note that the Commander Submarine Force, Pacific Fleet is a rear admiral while his counterpart in the Atlantic is a vice admiral. The latter is due primarily to a larger number of strategic missile submarines in the Atlantic Fleet (three squadrons compared to one in the Pacific Fleet). In addition, admirals serve as the "unified" commanders of all U.S. military forces in the Atlantic and Pacific regions, in the positions of Commander-in-Chief Atlantic and Commander-in-Chief Pacific, respectively.

**Table 1**
## COMMANDER-IN-CHIEF ATLANTIC FLEET[a] (★★★★)
### ADMINISTRATIVE

| | |
|---|---|
| Commander Naval Surface Force (★★★) | Norfolk, Va. |
| Cruiser-Destroyer Group 2 | Charleston, S.C. |
| Destroyer Squadron 4 | Charleston, S.C. |
| Destroyer Squadron 6 | Charleston, S.C. |
| Destroyer Squadron 20 | Charleston, S.C. |
| Cruiser-Destroyer Group 8 (★★) | Norfolk, Va. |
| Destroyer Squadron 2 | Norfolk, Va. |
| Destroyer Squadron 10 | Norfolk, Va. |
| Destroyer Squadron 22 | Norfolk, Va. |
| Destroyer Squadron 26 | Norfolk, Va. |
| Cruiser-Destroyer Group 12 (★★) | Mayport, Fla. |
| Destroyer Squadron 12 | Mayport, Fla. |
| Destroyer Squadron 14 | Mayport, Fla. |
| Destroyer Squadron 24 | Mayport, Fla. |
| Destroyer Squadron 28 (NRF) | Newport, R.I. |
| Destroyer Squadron 30 (NRF) | Philadelphia, Pa. |
| Destroyer Squadron 34 (NRF) | Charleston, S.C. |
| Amphibious Group 2 (★★) | Norfolk, Va. |
| Amphibious Squadron 2 | Norfolk, Va. |
| Amphibious Squadron 4 | Norfolk, Va. |
| Amphibious Squadron 6 | Norfolk, Va. |
| Amphibious Squadron 8 | Norfolk, Va. |
| Mine Squadron 12 (NRF) | Charleston, S.C. |
| Mine Division 121 (NRF) | Charleston, S.C. |
| Mine Division 123 (NRF) | Charleston, S.C. |
| Mine Division 125 (NRF) | Charleston, S.C. |
| Mine Division 126 (NRF) | Charleston, S.C. |
| Naval Special Warfare Group 2 | Norfolk, Va. |
| Coastal River Squadron 2 | Little Creek, Va. |
| Coastal River Division 22 | New Orleans, La. |
| Service Squadron 2 | Mayport, Fla. |
| Service Squadron 4 | Norfolk, Va. |
| Service Squadron 6[b] | Naples, Italy |
| Service Squadron 8 | Little Creek, Va. |
| Commander Submarine Force[c] (★★★) | Norfolk, Va. |
| Submarine Development Group 2 | Groton, Conn. |
| Submarine Group 2 (★★) | Groton, Conn. |
| Submarine Group 6 (★★) | Charleston, S.C. |
| Submarine Group 8[d] (★★) | La Maddalena, Italy |
| Submarine Squadron 2 | Charleston, S.C. |
| Submarine Squadron 4 | Charleston, S.C. |
| Submarine Squadron 6 | Norfolk, Va. |
| Submarine Squadron 10 | New London, Conn. |
| Submarine Development Squadron 12 | |
| Submarine Squadron 14 | Holy Loch, Scotland |
| Submarine Squadron 16 | Rota, Spain |
| Submarine Squadron 18 | Charleston, S.C. |
| Commander Naval Air Force[c] (★★★) | Norfolk, Va. |
| Carrier Group 2[f] (★★) | Naples, Italy |
| Carrier Group 4 (★★) | Norfolk, Va. |
| Carrier Group 6 (★★) | Mayport, Fla. |
| Carrier Group 8 (★★) | Norfolk, Va. |
| Commanding General Fleet Marine Force[g] (★★★) | Norfolk, Va. |
| Second Marine Division (★★) | Camp Lejeune, N.C. |
| Second Marine Aircraft Wing (★★) | Cherry Point, N.C. |
| Force Troops (★) | Camp Lejeune, N.C. |

Notes: Location of ashore headquarters of home ports for principal ships are listed.

a. Also Commander-in-Chief Atlantic (unified command of all U.S. air, land, sea (forces); Supreme Allied Commander Atlantic (NATO); CinC Western Atlantic Area (NATO)

b. Also CTF-63

c. Also Submarine Operations Advisor/Poseidon Operations Advisor to CinCLant and SACLant; Commander Submarines Western Atlantic (NATO); Commander Submarine Activities Atlantic

d. Also Commander Submarines Mediterranean; CTF-64; CTF-69

e. Only carrier groups are listed; see Chapter 22 for aviation units

f. Also CTF-60

g. FMF is a type command, but not administratively under the Atlantic Fleet

### TACTICAL

| | |
|---|---|
| Commander Second Fleet/Joint TF-122[a] | Norfolk, Va. |
| Commander Sixth Fleet[b] (★★★) | |
| CTF-60 Attack Carrier Striking Force (★★) | |
| CTF-61 Amphibious Force | |
| CTF-62 Landing Force[c] | |
| CTF-63 Service Force | |
| CTF-64 FBM Submarine Force[d] | La Maddalena, Italy |
| CTF-65 Special Contingency Force | |
| CTF-66 Area ASW Force | |
| CTF-67 Maritime Surveillance and Reconnaissance Force[e] | Naples, Italy |
| CTF-68 Special Operations Force | |
| CTF-69 Submarine Force | |

a. Also Commander Striking Fleet Atlantic (NATO)

b. Also Commander Striking and Support Forces Southern Europe (NATO); the Commander Sixth Fleet's flagship is based at Gaeta, Italy; the Deputy Commander Striking and Support Forces Southern Europe is ashore at Naples

c. A reinforced Marine battalion embarked in TF-61

d. Also CTF-69 and Submarine Group 8

e. Also Commander Fleet Air Mediterranean; Commander ASW Force Sixth Fleet

**Table 2**
## COMMANDER-IN-CHIEF PACIFIC FLEET[a] (★★★★)
### ADMINISTRATIVE

| | | | |
|---|---|---|---|
| Commander Naval Surface Force/CTF-53 (★★★) | Coronado (San Diego), Calif. | Destroyer Squadron 17 | San Diego, Calif. |
| Cruiser-Destroyer Group 1 (★★) | San Diego, Calif. | Destroyer Squadron 27 (NRF) | Long Beach, Calif. |
| Destroyer Squadron 5 | San Diego, Calif. | Cruiser-Destroyer Group 5 (★★) | San Diego, Calif. |
| Destroyer Squadron 13 | San Diego, Calif. | Destroyer Squadron 9 | San Diego, Calif. |
| Destroyer Squadron 23 | San Diego, Calif. | Destroyer Squadron 21 | San Diego, Calif. |
| Cruiser-Destroyer Group 3 (★★) | San Diego, Calif. | Destroyer Squadron 31 | San Diego, Calif. |
| Destroyer Squadron 7 | San Diego, Calif. | Destroyer Squadron 37 (NRF) | Seattle, Wash. |

| | |
|---|---|
| Surface Group Western Pacific (★★) | Subic, Philippines[b] |
| Destroyer Squadron 15 | Yokosuka, Japan |
| Surface Group Mid-Pacific | Pearl Harbor, Hawaii |
| Destroyer Squadron 25 | Pearl Harbor, Hawaii |
| Destroyer Squadron 33 | Pearl Harbor, Hawaii |
| Destroyer Squadron 35 | Pearl Harbor, Hawaii |
| Service Squadron 5 | Pearl Harbor, Hawaii |
| Amphibious Group 1[c] (★★) | Okinawa |
| Amphibious Group Eastern Pacific (★★) | San Diego, Calif. |
| Amphibious Squadron 1 | San Diego, Calif. |
| Amphibious Squadron 3 | San Diego, Calif. |
| Amphibious Squadron 5 | San Diego, Calif. |
| Amphibious Squadron 7 | San Diego, Calif. |
| Naval Special Warfare Group 1 | Coronado (San Diego), Calif. |
| Coastal River Squadron 1 (NRF) | Coronado (San Diego), Calif. |
| Coastal River Squadron 11 (NRF) | Vallejo, Calif. |
| Mine Squadron 5 (NRF) | Long Beach, Calif. |
| Mine Division 51 (NRF) | Long Beach, Calif. |
| Mine Division 52 (NRF) | San Francisco, Calif. |
| Mine Division 53 (NRF) | Seattle, Wash. |
| Mine Division 54 (NRF) | San Diego, Calif. |
| Service Group 1 | Oakland, Calif. |
| Service Squadron 1 | San Diego, Calif. |
| Service Squadron 3 | Vallejo, Calif. |
| Commander Submarine Force/CTF-57 (★★) | Pearl Harbor, Hawaii |
| Submarine Development Group 1 | San Diego, Calif. |
| Submarine Group 5 | San Diego, Calif. |
| Submarine Group 7[d] | Yokosuka, Japan |
| Submarine Squadron 1 | Pearl Harbor, Hawaii |
| Submarine Squadron 3 | San Diego, Calif. |
| Submarine Squadron 7 | Pearl Harbor, Hawaii |
| Submarine Squadron 15 | Guam |
| Commander Naval Air Force/CTF-58[e] (★★★) | North Island (San Diego), Calif. |
| Carrier Group 1 (★★) | North Island (San Diego), Calif. |
| Carrier Group 3 (★★) | North Island (San Diego), Calif. |
| Carrier Group 5[f] (★★) | Cubi Point, Philippines |
| Carrier Group 7 (★★) | Alameda (San Francisco), Calif. |
| Commanding General Fleet Marine Force/CTF-51 (★★★) | Honolulu, Hawaii |
| First Marine Aircraft Wing (★★) | Camp Pendleton, Calif. |
| Third Marine Division (★★) | Okinawa |
| First Marine Brigade (★) | Kaneohoe, Hawaii |
| First Marine Aircraft Wing (★★) | Iwakuni, Japan |
| Third Marine Aircraft Wing (★★) | El Toro, Calif. |
| Force Troops (★) | 29 Palms, Calif. |

a. Also Naval Component Commander, U.S. Pacific Command
b. All assigned ships are homeported in Yokosuka, Japan
c. Also CTF-76; no ships are permanently assigned
d. Also CTF-74; the only ship permanently assigned is the transport submarine GRAYBACK (SS 574) based at Subic.
e. Only carrier groups are listed; see Chapter 22 for aviation units
f. The carrier MIDWAY (CV 41) assigned to Carrier Group 5 and her embarked squadrons are based at Yokosuka

## TACTICAL

| | |
|---|---|
| Commander Third Fleet/CTF-30 (★★★) | Ford Island (Pearl Harbor), Hawaii |
| Commander Seventh Fleet[a] (★★★) | |
| CTF-70 Command Force Seventh Fleet | |
| CTF-71 Special Contingency Force | |
| CTF-72 Patrol and Reconnaissance Force[b] | Kamiseya, Japan |
| CTF-73 Logistic Support Force[c] (★★) | Subic, Philippines |
| CTF-74 Submarine Force[c] | Yokosuka, Japan |
| CTF-75 Cruiser-Destroyer Force (★★) | |
| CTF-76 Amphibious Force[d] | Okinawa |
| CTF-77 Carrier Striking Force[e] | Cubi Point, Philippines |
| CTF-78 Support Forces Ashore[f] | |
| CTF-79 Fleet Marine Force Seventh Fleet[g] (★★) | Okinawa |

a. The Seventh Fleet flagship OKLAHOMA CITY (CG 5) is based at Yokosuka
b. Also Commander Patrol Wing 1
c. Also Commander Submarine Group 7
d. Also Amphibious Group 1
e. Also Commander Carrier Group 5
f. "Tactical" grouping of commanders of U.S. naval forces in the Marianas (TG-78.4), Philippines (TG-78.5), Japan (TG-78.6), Korea (TG-78.7); all rear admirals
g. Elements of Third Marine Division and First Marine Aircraft Wing

## MILITARY SEALIFT COMMAND

In addition to the above fleet organization, the Navy operates the Military Sealift Command (MSC) to provide ocean transportation and support special projects of all of the armed services and other government agencies. The Commander MSC, a rear admiral, is responsible as a "fleet commander" to the Chief of Naval Operations and to the Office of the Secretary of Defense for ocean transportation.

All MSC ships are civilian-manned with Civil Service crews, or are operated by commercial contractors. About 160 Navy personnel serve in MSC ships to provide security for nuclear weapons or operate communications equipment.

MSC ships have the prefix USNS (U.S. Naval Ship) instead of USS, have T- hull designations, and can be identified by blue-and-gold funnel markings.

The MSC ships currently in service include point-to-point cargo ships (T-AK, T-AKR, T-AO), underway replenishment ships (T-AF, T-AO), fleet tugs (T-AF), Polaris/Poseidon tender resupply ships (T-AK), and special project ships (T-AG, T-AGM, T-AGOR, T-AGS, T-ARC). The special project ships support a variety of Navy, Defense, and NASA research and surveillance programs.

In addition, MSC charters privately owned U.S. merchant ships to carry defense cargo. Almost 95 percent of all U.S. military material sent overseas is moved in this manner.

## NAVAL RESERVE FORCE

The Naval Reserve operates a large number of surface ships and small craft as well as several aircraft wings and squadrons which comprise the Naval Reserve Force (NRF). In addition, there are several reserve construction battalions ("seabees"), and administrative and other specialized reserve units. The Chief of Naval Reserve is a vice admiral.

There are 58 ships operated by the NRF with composite active duty and reserve crews: 29 destroyers, 3 amphibious ships, 22 minesweepers, and 4 fleet tugs. These ships are organized into the following units:

Destroyer Squadrons 27, 28, 30, 34, 37
Mine Squadrons 5 (containing Mine Divisions 51, 52, 53, 54), and 12 (containing Mine Divisions 121, 123, 126)

An exception is the attack transport FRANCIS MARION (LPA 249) which is assigned to Amphibious Group 2, an active Navy unit.

The numerous NRF small craft are manned by reserves and are assigned to:

Coastal River Squadrons 1, 2
Coastal River Division 11
Assault Craft Unit 2

The reserve aviation organization is described in Chapter 22, on pages 248–57.

A nuclear-propelled task force in port: The aircraft carrier NIMITZ (CVN 68), guided missile cruisers SOUTH CAROLINA (CGN 37) and CALIFORNIA (CGN 36), and, forward of the CALIFORNIA and barely visible, the attack submarine L. MENDEL RIVERS (SSN 686). (1975, U.S. Navy)

# 4 Personnel

The U.S. Navy in mid-1978 has 536,000 officers and enlisted men and women on active duty, plus 192,000 officers and enlisted men and women in the Marine Corps. (This is a decline from the Vietnam War peak of 765,400 Navy and 307,300 Marine personnel.)

Navy personnel strength is divided into the following major categories:

Strategic Forces. Strategic missile submarines and related support, and command, control, communications ($C^3$): 20,900.

General Purpose Forces. Warships (except SSBNs), naval air forces, direct support: 245,700.

Auxiliary Forces. Intelligence, $C^3$, research and development, support to other nations: 29,600.

Mission Support Forces. Support to reserves, support bases, forces support training: 62,600.

Central Support Forces. Medical support (including Marine Corps), individual training, logistics, support to federal agencies: 83,300.

Individuals. Transients, patients, trainees and students, midshipmen: 93,800.

The total Navy personnel strength consists of 63,277 officers (3,741 women) and 472,700 enlisteds (20,091 women). While total personnel strength has been relatively stable since about 1972 (including the number of woman officers), the number of enlisted women in the Navy has increased some 400 percent. A lessening of the legal restrictions on women serving aboard ship or undertaking combat duties could lead to greater increases. If women are not permitted to serve aboard a large number of ships, the problems of rotating male officers and sailors from shipboard assignments to shore duty will continue to be a problem as the increasing number of women in the Navy take up the shore billets. This, in turn, will further aggravate the recruiting of male sailors.

The all-volunteer armed forces policy has made recruiting more difficult for the Navy. In general, however, the Navy has been able to meet most of its requirements—with the major exception of the shortage of officers for nuclear-propelled submarines. Because of the critical shortage of nuclear-submarine officers, those available have been given extended and continuous assignments at sea; the resulting family separation and other hardships further aggravate the situation. A goal of 60 percent nuclear-submarine officer retention (154 officers) was established for Fiscal Year 1977, but the actual retention rate was only 38 percent (98 officers).

Coupled with the difficulties in recruiting numbers, there has been a problem in the quality of men recruited, as evidenced by the Navy in 1977 recording the highest desertion rate in its history.

# 5 Glossary

| | |
|---|---|
| AA | Antiaircraft |
| AA | Atlantic (Fleet) Active |
| AAM | Air-to-Air Missile |
| AAW | Anti-Air Warfare |
| Academic | Navy-owned ship operated by academic or research institution |
| AR | Atlantic Reserve (Fleet) |
| ASM | Air-to-Surface Missile |
| ASMD | Anti-Ship Missile Defense |
| ASROC | Antisubmarine Rocket |
| ASW | Antisubmarine Warfare |
| Beam | extreme width of hull |
| Boilers | psi indicates pounds-per-square-inch pressure at full power |
| BPDMS | Basic Point Defense Missile System |
| Catapults | flush, flight-deck catapults in aircraft carriers |
| CIWS | Close-In Weapon System |
| Complement | number of personnel to provide full battle-station manning and one-in-three watch-manning on a sustained basis; O = officers, EM = enlisted men |
| DASH | Drone Antisubmarine Helicopter |
| Displacement | *Light* (ship) is displacement of the ship and all machinery without crew, provisions, fuel, munitions, all other consumables, and aircraft<br>*Standard* is displacement of the ship fully manned and equipped ready for sea, including all provisions, munitions, and aircraft, but without fuels<br>*Full load* is displacement of the ship complete and ready for service in all respects, including all fuels |
| DP | Dual-Purpose (for use against air and surface targets) |
| Draft | maximum draft of ship at full load, including fixed projections below the keel, if any (e.g., sonar domes) |
| ECM | Electronic Countermeasures |
| Elevators | aircraft-capable elevators in aircraft carriers |
| EW | Electronic Warfare |
| Extreme width | maximum width at or about the flight deck, including fixed projections, if any (e.g., gun "tubs") |
| FBM | Fleet Ballistic Missile |
| FCS | Fire Control Systems |
| Flag | special accommodations for fleet or task force commander and his staff; lesser division or squadron commanders and their staffs are included in the ship's complement |
| FY | Fiscal Year; from 1 October of the calendar year until 30 September of the following year. (Since 1976; previously from 1 July until 30 June.) S in |

|  |  |
|---|---|
|  | front of an FY number indicates a supplemental authorization |
| GL | Great Lakes |
| Guns | mount or turret arrangement is indicated in parentheses; e.g., (2 × 3) indicates two triple turrets |
| IO | Indian Ocean |
| IPDMS | Improved Point Defense Missile System |
| IW | Inland Waters |
| LAMPS | Light Airborne Multi-Purpose System |
| lbst | pounds of static thrust |
| Length | wl indicates length on waterline (this is the length between perpendiculars in naval practice); oa indicates length overall |
| LVT | Landing Vehicle, Tracked (amphibious tractor) |
| MarAd | Maritime Administration |
| MCLWG | Major Caliber Light-Weight Gun |
| Missiles | number of launchers and tubes or rails are indicated; e.g., 2 twin launchers indicates two launchers with twin launching rails; number of missiles carried in the launcher or magazine are indicated in parentheses |
| Mk | Mark |
| Mod | Modification |
| MR | Maritime (Administration) Reserve |
| MSC | Military Sealift Command (A indicates Atlantic; P indicates Pacific); formerly Military Sea Transportation Service (MSTS) |
| n. mile | nautical mile |
| NRF | Naval Reserve Force (A indicates Atlantic; P indicates Pacific) |
| NTDS | Naval Tactical Data System |
| OSP | Offshore Procurement (ship built overseas with U.S. funding) |
| PA | Pacific (Fleet) Active |
| PR | Pacific Reserve (Fleet) |
| Propulsion | designed shaft horsepower (shp) is indicated; bhp is brake horsepower for diesel engines; and ihp is indicated horsepower for reciprocating engines |

|  |  |
|---|---|
| Radars | radars associated with fire control systems are listed under Fire control |
| Reactors | first letter of reactor designation indicates platform (A = Aircraft carrier, C = Cruiser, D = frigate [DL] or cruiser, S = Submarine); numeral indicates reactor design by specific manufacturer; and second letter is manufacturer (C = Combustion Engineering, G = General Electric, W = Westinghouse). |
| SAM | Surface-to-Air Missile |
| SCB | Ships Characteristics Board's sequential numbering of all Navy ship designs reaching advanced planning; numbered in a single series from 1947 (SCB-1 NORFOLK CLK 1/DL1) through 1964 (SCB-252 FLAGSTAFF PGH1); from 1964 on, numbered in blocks: 001–099 cruisers, 100 carriers, 200 destroyers/frigates, 300 submarines, 400 amphibious, 500 mine warfare, 600 patrol, 700 auxiliary, 800 service craft, 900 special purpose; e.g., SCB-400.65 was the AGC/LCC of FY 1965 |
| SLBM | Submarine-Launched Ballistic Missile |
| SLCM | Sea-Launched Cruise Missile (formerly Submarine-Launched Cruise Missile) |
| Speed | maximum speed unless otherwise indicated |
| SSM | Surface-to-Surface Missile |
| SUBROC | Submarine Rocket |
| TACAN | Tactical Aircraft Navigation (shipboard homing beacon) |
| TACTAS | Tactical Towed Array Sonar |
| 3-D | three-dimensional radar |
| TRA | Training |
| Troops | designed accommodations; O = officers, EM = enlisted men |
| UNREP | Underway Replenishment |
| VERTREP | Vertical Replenishment |
| VSTOL | Vertical Short Take-Off and Landing |

# 6 Ship Classifications

All U.S. Navy ships and small craft, with a few specific exceptions, are classified by type, and by sequence within that type. The list of classifications (Secretary of the Navy Instruction 5030) is issued periodically, updating a system that was begun in 1922.

In late 1977 the Chief of Naval Operations directed that a new system of naval ship classifications be developed to further the understanding of U.S. ship types and missions, and for comparisons with Soviet ship types. The major categories being contemplated with preliminary sub-types are listed below; further sub-types will indicate role (for carriers), weapons, and propulsion, much the same as the current scheme.

**Warships**

Aircraft Carriers

Conventional Take-Off and Landing (CTOL)
Vertical/Short Take-Off and Landing (VSTOL)
Helicopter

Surface Combatants

Battleships
Cruisers
Destroyers
Frigates

Submarines

Attack (torpedo and cruise missile)

Ballistic Missile
Auxiliary

**Other Combatant Ships**

Patrol Combatants
Amphibious Warfare Ships
Mine Warfare Ships

**Auxiliaries**

Mobile Logistic Ships
Support Ships

**Combatant Craft**

Patrol Craft
Amphibious Warfare Craft
Mine Warfare Craft

**Support Craft**

Service Craft

Listed below are those classifications on the current list, dated 6 January 1975. In addition, several quasi-official listings are used by the Navy to indicate new types of ships which have not yet been authorized. Examples include the VSS for VSTOL Support Ship and CVV for VSTOL aircraft carrier.

The arrangement within the official listing of categories and subcategories is alphabetical by symbol. Letter prefixes are used to indicate:

E—prototype ship or craft in an experimental or developmental status

T—ship assigned to the Military Sealift Command (formerly Military Sea Transportation Service)

F—ship being constructed for a foreign government

The suffix letter N is used to denote nuclear propulsion in ships. For service craft, N indicates a non-self-propelled version of a similar self-propelled unit. The letter X is used as a suffix to indicate new designs or concepts (e.g. CVNX, ARX), but it does not appear in the official list of classifications.

## Warships

### Aircraft Carriers

| CV | Aircraft Carrier |
|---|---|
| CVA | Attack Aircraft Carrier |
| CVAN | Attack Aircraft Carrier (nuclear) |
| CVN | Aircraft Carrier (nuclear) |
| CVS | ASW Aircraft Carrier |

### Surface Combatants

| BB | Battleship |
|---|---|
| CA | Heavy Cruiser |
| CG | Guided Missile Cruiser |
| CGN | Guided Missile Cruiser (nuclear) |
| DD | Destroyer |
| DDG | Guided Missile Destroyer |
| FF | Frigate |
| FFG | Guided Missile Frigate |
| FFR | Radar Picket Frigate |

### Patrol Combatants

| PG | Patrol Combatant |
|---|---|
| PHM | Patrol Combatant Missile (hydrofoil) |
| PCE | Patrol Escort |

### Command Ships

| CC | Command Ship |
|---|---|

### Submarines

| SS | Submarine |
|---|---|
| SSN | Submarine (nuclear) |
| SSBN | Fleet Ballistic Missile Submarine (nuclear) |
| SSG | Guided Missile Submarine |

## Amphibious Warfare Ships

| LCC | Amphibious Command Ship |
|---|---|
| LFR | Inshore Fire Support Ship |
| LHA | Amphibious Assault Ship (general purpose) |
| LKA | Amphibious Cargo Ship |
| LPA | Amphibious Transport |
| LPD | Amphibious Transport Dock |
| LPH | Amphibious Assault Ship |
| LPR | Amphibious Transport (small) |
| LPSS | Amphibious Transport Submarine |
| LSD | Dock Landing Ship |
| LST | Tank Landing Ship |

## Mine Warfare Ships

| MCS | Mine Countermeasures Ship |
|---|---|
| MSC | Minesweeper, Coastal (non-magnetic) |
| MSO | Minesweeper, Ocean (non-magnetic) |

## Patrol Craft

| CPC | Coastal Patrol Boat |
|---|---|
| CPIC | Coastal Patrol and Interdiction Craft |
| PB | Patrol Boat |
| PCF | Patrol Craft (Fast) |
| PCH | Patrol Craft (hydrofoil) |
| PGH | Patrol Gunboat (hydrofoil) |
| PTF | Fast Patrol Craft |

## Landing Craft

| AALC | Amphibious Assault Landing Craft |
|---|---|
| LCM | Landing Craft, Mechanized |
| LCPL | Landing Craft, Personnel, Large |
| LCPR | Landing Craft, Personnel, Ramped |
| LCU | Landing Craft, Utility |
| LCVP | Landing Craft, Vehicle, Personnel |
| LWT | Amphibious Warping Tug |

## Mine Countermeasures Craft

| MSB | Minesweeping Boat |
|---|---|
| MSD | Minesweeper, Drone |
| MSI | Minesweeper, Inshore |
| MSM | Minesweeper, River (converted LCM-6) |
| MSR | Minesweeper, Patrol |

## Riverine Warfare Craft

| ASPB | Assault Support Patrol Boat |
|---|---|
| ATC | Mini Armored Troop Carrier |
| PBR | River Patrol Boat |
| SWAM | Shallow Water Attack Craft, Medium |
| SWAL | Shallow Water Attack Craft, Light |

## SEAL* Support Craft

| LCSR | Landing Craft Swimmer Reconnaissance |
|---|---|
| LSSC | Light SEAL Support Craft |
| MSSC | Medium SEAL Support Craft |
| SDV | Swimmer Delivery Vehicle |

* SEAL = Sea, Air, Land Teams; Navy counter-guerrilla units which can be "inserted" by small craft or submarines, helicopter or parachute, or by land.

**Mobile Inshore Undersea Warfare (MIUW) Craft**

| | |
|---|---|
| MAC | MIUW Attack Craft |

**Auxiliary Ships**

| | |
|---|---|
| AD | Destroyer Tender |
| ADG | Degaussing Ship |
| AE | Ammunition Ship |
| AF | Store Ship |
| AFS | Combat Store Ship |
| AG | Miscellaneous |
| AGDS | Auxiliary Deep Submergence Support Ship |
| AGFF | Frigate Research Ship |
| AGEH | Hydrofoil Research Ship |
| AGER | Environmental Research Ship |
| AGF | Miscellaneous Command Ship |
| AGHS | Patrol Combatant Support Ship |
| AGM | Missile Range Instrumentation Ship |
| AGMR | Major Communications Relay Ship |
| AGOR | Oceanographic Research Ship |
| AGP | Patrol Craft Tender |
| AGS | Surveying Ship |
| AGSS | Auxiliary Submarine |
| AH | Hospital Ship |
| AK | Cargo Ship |
| AKL | Light Cargo Ship |
| AKR | Vehicle Cargo Ship |
| ANL | Net Laying Ship |
| AO | Oiler |
| AOE | Fast Combat Support Ship |
| AOG | Gasoline Tanker |
| AOR | Replenishment Oiler |
| AP | Transport |
| APB | Self-propelled Barracks Ship |
| AR | Repair Ship |
| ARB | Battle Damage Repair Ship |
| ARC | Cable Repairing Ship |
| ARG | Internal Combustion Engine Repair Ship |
| ARL | Landing Craft Repair Ship |
| ARS | Salvage Ship |
| AS | Submarine Tender |
| ASR | Submarine Rescue Ship |
| ATA | Auxiliary Ocean Tug |
| ATF | Fleet Ocean Tug |
| ATS | Salvage and Rescue Ship |
| AVM | Guided Missile Ship |
| CVT | Training Aircraft Carrier |
| SES | Surface Effects Ship |

**Service Craft**

| | |
|---|---|
| AFDB | Large Auxiliary Floating Dry Dock (non-self-propelled) |
| AFDL | Small Auxiliary Floating Dry Dock (non-self-propelled) |
| AFDM | Medium Auxiliary Floating Dry Dock (non-self-propelled) |
| APL | Barracks Craft (non-self-propelled) |
| ARD | Auxiliary Repair Dry Dock (non-self-propelled) |
| ARDM | Medium Auxiliary Repair Dry Dock (non-self-propelled) |
| DSRV | Deep Submergence Rescue Vehicle |
| DSV | Deep Submergence Vehicle |
| IX | Unclassified Miscellaneous |
| NR | Submersible Research Vehicle (nuclear) |
| YAG | Miscellaneous Auxiliary (self-propelled) |
| YC | Open Lighter (non-self-propelled) |
| YCF | Car Float (non-self-propelled) |
| YCV | Aircraft Transportation Lighter (non-self-propelled) |
| YD | Floating Crane (non-self-propelled) |
| YDT | Diving Tender (non-self-propelled) |
| YF | Covered Lighter (self-propelled) |
| YFB | Ferryboat or Launch (self-propelled) |
| YFD | Yard Floating Dry Dock (non-self-propelled) |
| YFN | Covered Lighter (non-self-propelled) |
| YFNB | Large Covered Lighter (non-self-propelled) |
| YFND | Dry Dock Companion Craft (non-self-propelled) |
| YFNX | Lighter (special purpose) (non-self-propelled) |
| YFP | Floating Power Barge (non-self-propelled) |
| YFR | Refrigerated Covered Lighter (self-propelled) |
| YFRN | Refrigerated Covered Lighter (non-self-propelled) |
| YFRT | Covered Lighter (range-tender) (self-propelled) |
| YFU | Harbor Utility Craft (self-propelled) |
| YG | Garbage Lighter (self-propelled) |
| YGN | Garbage Lighter (non-self-propelled) |
| YHLC | Salvage Lift Craft, Heavy (non-self-propelled) |
| YM | Dredge (self-propelled) |
| YMLC | Salvage Lift Craft, Medium (non-self-propelled) |
| YNG | Gate Craft (non-self-propelled) |
| YO | Fuel Oil Barge (self-propelled) |
| YOG | Gasoline Barge (self-propelled) |
| YOGN | Gasoline Barge (non-self-propelled) |
| YON | Fuel Oil Barge (non-self-propelled) |
| YOS | Oil Storage Barge (non-self-propelled) |
| YP | Patrol Craft (self-propelled) |
| YPD | Floating Pile Driver (non-self-propelled) |
| YR | Floating Workshops (non-self-propelled) |
| YRB | Repair and Berthing Barge (non-self-propelled) |
| YRBM | Repair, Berthing and Messing Barge (non-self-propelled) |
| YRDH | Floating Dry Dock Workshop (Hull) (non-self-propelled) |
| YRDM | Floating Dry Dock Workshop (Machine) (non-self-propelled) |
| YRR | Radiology Repair Barge (non-self-propelled) |
| YRST | Salvage Craft Tender (non-self-propelled) |
| YSD | Seaplane Wrecking Derrick (self-propelled) |
| YSR | Sludge Removal Barge (non-self-propelled) |
| YTB | Large Harbor Tug (self-propelled) |
| YTL | Small Harbor Tug (self-propelled) |
| YTM | Medium Harbor Tug (self-propelled) |

YW      Water Barge (self-propelled)
YWN     Water Barge (non-self-propelled)

## MARITIME ADMINISTRATION CLASSIFICATIONS

The U.S. Maritime Administration classifies its ships by their design characteristics. This classification scheme is included in *Ships and*

*Aircraft* because of the large number of Maritime Administration (previously Maritime Commission) ships which remain on the Navy list in the amphibious warfare and auxiliary ship categories. (During World War II escort aircraft carriers and patrol frigates also were built to Maritime Commission designs.)

*Explanation of symbols:*

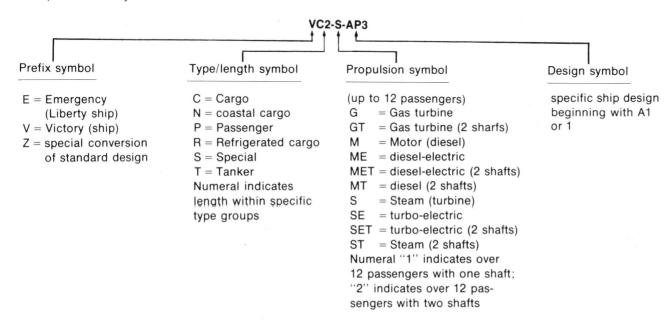

**VC2-S-AP3**

| Prefix symbol | Type/length symbol | Propulsion symbol | Design symbol |
|---|---|---|---|
| E = Emergency (Liberty ship) | C = Cargo | (up to 12 passengers) | specific ship design beginning with A1 or 1 |
| V = Victory (ship) | N = coastal cargo | G = Gas turbine | |
| Z = special conversion of standard design | P = Passenger | GT = Gas turbine (2 sharfs) | |
| | R = Refrigerated cargo | M = Motor (diesel) | |
| | S = Special | ME = diesel-electric | |
| | T = Tanker | MET = diesel-electric (2 shafts) | |
| | Numeral indicates length within specific type groups | MT = diesel (2 shafts) | |
| | | S = Steam (turbine) | |
| | | SE = turbo-electric | |
| | | SET = turbo-electric (2 shafts) | |
| | | ST = Steam (2 shafts) | |
| | | Numeral "1" indicates over 12 passengers with one shaft; "2" indicates over 12 passengers with two shafts | |

# 7 Submarines

The principal types of submarines in service with the world's navies are strategic missile submarines and attack submarines. The former are armed with Submarine-Launched Ballistic Missiles (SLBM) while the latter are armed with torpedoes and increasingly with guided (cruise) missiles. In addition, there are specialized submarines used for troop-carrying and research activities. This section lists strategic missile submarines first, followed by the attack submarines and then specialized submarines; the listings within a class are arranged by hull-number sequence.

## STRATEGIC MISSILE SUBMARINES

The U.S. Navy operates 41 ballistic missile submarines (SSBN). All are nuclear-propelled, 16-tube submarines completed between 1960 and 1967, built partly in response to the Soviet achievements in space and weapons technology during the late 1950s. These submarines have been updated with improved missile-launch and communication systems, and rearmed with improved missiles. The 41 submarines carry a total of 656 SLBMs. A class of larger SSBNs to be armed with Trident missiles is under construction. The first submarine of this class, the Ohio, is to be completed in 1979–1980, and Ohio-class submarines have been authorized in all shipbuilding programs from FY 1974 onward. These submarines each have 24 tubes for the Trident SLBMs.

| Type | Class/Ship | Active | Bldg. | Res. | Comm. | SLBMs |
|------|-----------|--------|-------|------|-------|-------|
| SSBN 726 | Ohio | — | 5 | — | 1979– | 24 Trident I |
| SSBN 616 | Lafayette | 31 | — | — | 1963–1967 | 16 Poseidon C-3 |
| SSBN 608 | Ethan Allen | 5 | — | — | 1961–1963 | 16 Polaris A-3 |
| SSBN 598 | George Washington | 5 | — | — | 1959–1961 | 16 Polaris A-3 |

## ATTACK SUBMARINES

The U.S. Navy in 1978 has in service approximately 70 nuclear-propelled attack submarines (SSN) plus six diesel-electric attack

| Type | Class/Ship | Active | Bldg. | Res. | Comm. | Notes |
|------|-----------|--------|-------|------|-------|-------|
| SSN 688 | Los Angeles | 5 | 26 | — | 1976– | Deep-diving; armed with SUBROC/Mk 48 torpedoes |
| SSN 685 | Lipscomb | 1 | — | — | 1974 | |
| SSN 671 | Narwhal | 1 | — | — | 1969 | |
| SSN 637 | Sturgeon | 37 | — | — | 1967–1975 | |
| SSN 594 | Permit | 13 | — | — | 1962–1968 | |
| SSN 597 | Tullibee | 1 | — | — | 1960 | no longer first-line |
| SSN 587 | Halibut | — | — | 1 | 1960 | research submarine |
| SSN 586 | Triton | — | — | 1 | 1959 | |
| SSN 585 | Skipjack | 5 | — | — | 1959–1961 | high-speed; first-line |
| SSN 578 | Skate | 4 | — | — | 1957–1959 | no longer first-line |
| SSN 575 | Seawolf | 1 | — | — | 1957 | research submarine |
| SSN 571 | Nautilus | 1 | — | — | 1954 | no longer first-line |
| SS 580 | Barbel | 3 | — | — | 1959 | |
| SSG 577 | Growler | — | — | 1 | 1958 | guided-missile configuration |
| LPSS 574 | Grayback | 1 | — | — | 1958 | transport submarine |
| AGSS 569 | Albacore | — | — | 1 | 1953 | research submarine |
| SS 563 | Tang | 3 | — | — | 1952 | to be transferred to Iran |
| AGSS 563 | Tang | 1 | — | — | 1951 | research submarine |
| AGSS 555 | Dolphin | 1 | — | — | 1968 | research submarine |

submarines (SS). In addition, one transport submarine (LPSS) and two auxiliary submarines (AGSS) are in active service. (These numbers do not include three diesel-electric submarines that were to be stricken during FY 1978.)

Additional SSNs are under construction, with an attack submarine force of 90 units planned for the early 1980s. The last of the diesel-electric submarines will have been phased out by that time, and no additional non-nuclear submarines are being planned. The Navy, however, will continue to construct LOS ANGELES-class SSNs into the 1980s.

The amphibious transport submarines and research-auxiliary submarines are officially classified as amphibious warfare ships and auxiliary ships, respectively. They are listed in this section for the reader's convenience. The Navy's Deep Submergence Vehicles (DSV) are listed separately with the NR-1 (the Navy's nuclear-propelled research submersible).

Names: The first U.S. submarine, the HOLLAND (SS 1), completed in 1900, was named for her Irish-born inventor. Subsequent submarines were named for fish and other marine life until letter-number names (e.g., A-3) were assigned to all existing submarines on 17 November 1911. Marine-life names were reintroduced in the early 1930s for "fleet" boats (some units were named retroactively).

Beginning in 1958 the 41 Polaris/Poseidon strategic missile submarines were named for "distinguished Americans who were known for their devotion to freedom."

The name source for attack submarines was changed in 1973 to members of Congress; then in 1974 the names of American cities were used (a source which previously provided names for cruisers and, more recently, for amphibious cargo ships and large replenishment ships). The use of state names was introduced in 1976 for the Trident SSBNs; that source had before been used for battleships and, in the recent past, for guided missile cruisers.

## (14) NUCLEAR-PROPELLED STRATEGIC MISSILE SUBMARINES: "OHIO" CLASS

| Number | Name | FY/SCB | Builder | Laid down | Launch | Commission | Status |
|---|---|---|---|---|---|---|---|
| SSBN 726 | OHIO | 74/304 | General Dynamics (Electric Boat) | 10 Apr 1976 | 1978 | 1979 | Bldg. |
| SSBN 727 | MICHIGAN | 75/304 | General Dynamics (Electric Boat) | 4 Apr 1977 | 1979 | 1980 | Bldg. |
| SSBN 728 | . . . . . . . . | 75/304 | General Dynamics (Electric Boat) | | 1980 | 1981 | Bldg. |
| SSBN 729 | . . . . . . . . | 76/304 | General Dynamics (Electric Boat) | | 1980 | 1981 | Bldg. |
| SSBN 730 | . . . . . . . . | 77/304 | General Dynamics (Electric Boat) | | 1980 | 1982 | Bldg. |
| SSBN 731 | . . . . . . . . | 78/304 | | | | | Planned |
| SSBN 732 | . . . . . . . . | 78/304 | | | | | Planned |
| SSBN 733 | . . . . . . . . | 78/304 | | | | | Planned |
| SSBN 734 | . . . . . . . . | 79/304 | | | | | Planned |
| SSBN 735 | . . . . . . . . | 80/304 | | | | | Planned |
| SSBN | . . . . . . . . | 80/304 | | | | | Planned |
| SSBN | . . . . . . . . | 81/304 | | | | | Planned |
| SSBN | . . . . . . . . | 82/304 | | | | | Planned |
| SSBN | . . . . . . . . | 82/304 | | | | | Planned |

Displacement:

| | 18,700 tons submerged |
|---|---|
| Length: | 560 feet (170.7 m) oa |
| Beam: | 42 feet (12.8 m) |
| Draft: | 35½ feet (10.8 m) |
| Propulsion: | steam turbines; 1 shaft |
| Reactors: | 1 pressurized-water S8G |
| Speed: | |
| | 20+ knots submerged |
| Complement: | 150 (14 O + 136 EM) |
| Missiles: | 24 tubes for Trident C-4 SLBM |
| Torpedo tubes: | 4 21-inch (533-mm) amidships |
| Sonars: | BQQ-6 bow-mounted |
| Fire control: | 1 Mk 98 missile FCS |
| | 1 Mk 118 torpedo FCS |

The OHIO-class submarines are the largest undersea craft known to have been constructed by any nation. They are more than twice the displacement of the preceding LAFAYETTE class, and are significantly larger than the Soviet SLBM submarines of the "Delta II/III" classes completed from 1973 onward. However, there are reports of a Soviet "Typhoon"-class SSBN under construction which is of about the same size as the OHIO class.

The final number of Trident SLBM submarines to be built has not yet been determined. Initial planning provided for ten units; now 14 submarines are planned for funding through FY 1982.

Cost: The FY 1978-program submarines have an estimated average cost of $889 million.

Design: These submarines have a relatively conservative design with an improved LAFAYETTE-class arrangement incorporating the bow dome sonar and amidships torpedo tubes of the later attack submarines. These are the only 24-tube strategic missile submarines. Previous U.S. and foreign SSBNs have had no more than 16 tubes.

Reactors: The S8G has an estimated "core life" of nine years.

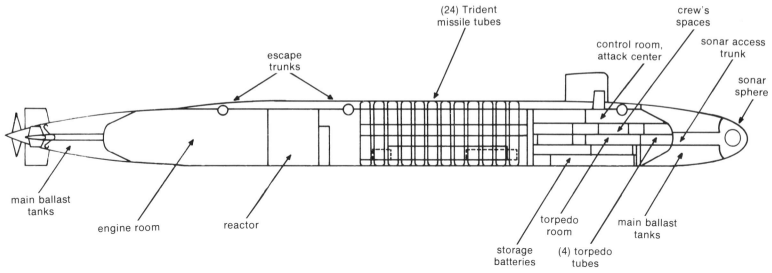

Line drawing of the OHIO-class submarine

Artist's concept of OHIO (U.S. Navy)

**31 NUCLEAR-PROPELLED STRATEGIC MISSILE SUBMARINES: "LAFAYETTE" CLASS**

| Number | Name | FY/SCB | Builder | Laid down | Launched | Commissioned | Status |
|---|---|---|---|---|---|---|---|
| SSBN 616 | LAFAYETTE | 61/216 | General Dynamics (Electric Boat) | 17 Jan 1961 | 8 May 1962 | 23 Apr 1963 | **AA** |
| SSBN 617 | ALEXANDER HAMILTON | 61/216 | General Dynamics (Electric Boat) | 26 June 1961 | 18 Aug 1962 | 27 June 1963 | **AA** |
| SSBN 619 | ANDREW JACKSON | 61/216 | Mare Island Naval Shipyard | 26 Apr 1961 | 15 Sep 1962 | 3 July 1963 | **AA** |
| SSBN 620 | JOHN ADAMS | 61/216 | Portsmouth Naval Shipyard | 19 May 1961 | 12 Jan 1963 | 12 May 1964 | **AA** |
| SSBN 622 | JAMES MONROE | S61/216 | Newport News | 31 July 1961 | 4 Aug 1962 | 7 Dec 1963 | **AA** |
| SSBN 623 | NATHAN HALE | S61/216 | General Dynamics (Electric Boat) | 2 Oct 1961 | 12 Jan 1963 | 23 Nov 1963 | **AA** |
| SSBN 624 | WOODROW WILSON | S61/216 | Mare Island Naval Shipyard | 13 Sep 1961 | 22 Feb 1963 | 27 Dec 1963 | **AA** |
| SSBN 625 | HENRY CLAY | S61/216 | Newport News | 22 Oct 1961 | 30 Nov 1962 | • 20 Feb 1964 | **AA** |
| SSBN 626 | DANIEL WEBSTER | S61/216 | General Dynamics (Electric Boat) | 28 Dec 1961 | 27 Apr 1963 | 9 Apr 1964 | **AA** |
| SSBN 627 | JAMES MADISON | 62/216 | Newport News | 5 Mar 1962 | 15 Mar 1963 | 28 July 1964 | **AA** |
| SSBN 628 | TECUMSEH | 62/216 | General Dynamics (Electric Boat) | 1 June 1962 | 22 June 1963 | 29 May 1964 | **AA** |
| SSBN 629 | DANIEL BOONE | 62/216 | Mare Island Naval Shipyard | 6 Feb 1962 | 22 June 1963 | 23 Apr 1964 | **AA** |
| SSBN 630 | JOHN C. CALHOUN | 62/216 | Newport News | 4 June 1962 | 22 June 1963 | 15 Sep 1964 | **AA** |
| SSBN 631 | ULYSSES S. GRANT | 62/216 | General Dynamics (Electric Boat) | 18 Aug 1962 | 2 Nov 1963 | 17 July 1964 | **AA** |
| SSBN 632 | VON STEUBEN | 62/216 | Newport News | 4 Sep 1962 | 18 Oct 1963 | 30 Sep 1964 | **AA** |
| SSBN 633 | CASIMIR PULASKI | 62/216 | General Dynamics (Electric Boat) | 12 Jan 1963 | 1 Feb 1964 | 14 Aug 1964 | **AA** |
| SSBN 634 | STONEWALL JACKSON | 62/216 | Mare Island Naval Shipyard | 4 July 1962 | 30 Nov 1963 | 26 Aug 1964 | **AA** |
| SSBN 635 | SAM RAYBURN | 62/216 | Newport News | 3 Dec 1962 | 20 Dec 1963 | 2 Dec 1964 | **AA** |
| SSBN 636 | NATHANAEL GREENE | 62/216 | Portsmouth Naval Shipyard | 21 May 1962 | 12 May 1964 | 19 Dec 1964 | **AA** |
| SSBN 640 | BENJAMIN FRANKLIN | 63/216 | General Dynamics (Electric Boat) | 25 May 1963 | 5 Dec 1964 | 22 Oct 1965 | **AA** |
| SSBN 641 | SIMON BOLIVAR | 63/216 | Newport News | 17 Apr 1963 | 22 Aug 1964 | 29 Oct 1965 | **AA** |
| SSBN 642 | KAMEHAMEHA | 63/216 | Mare Island Naval Shipyard | 2 May 1963 | 16 Jan 1965 | 10 Dec 1965 | **AA** |
| SSBN 643 | GEORGE BANCROFT | 63/216 | General Dynamics (Electric Boat) | 24 Aug 1963 | 20 Mar 1965 | 22 Jan 1966 | **AA** |
| SSBN 644 | LEWIS AND CLARK | 63/216 | Newport News | 29 July 1963 | 21 Nov 1964 | 22 Dec 1965 | **AA** |
| SSBN 645 | JAMES K. POLK | 63/216 | General Dynamics (Electric Boat) | 23 Nov 1963 | 22 May 1965 | 16 Apr 1966 | **AA** |
| SSBN 654 | GEORGE C. MARSHALL | 64/216 | Newport News | 2 Mar 1964 | 21 May 1965 | 29 Apr 1966 | **AA** |
| SSBN 655 | HENRY L. STIMSON | 64/216 | General Dynamics (Electric Boat) | 4 Apr 1964 | 13 Nov 1965 | 20 Aug 1966 | **AA** |
| SSBN 656 | GEORGE WASHINGTON CARVER | 64/216 | Newport News | 24 Aug 1964 | 14 Aug 1965 | 15 June 1966 | **AA** |
| SSBN 657 | FRANCIS SCOTT KEY | 64/216 | General Dynamics (Electric Boat) | 5 Dec 1964 | 23 Apr 1966 | 3 Dec 1966 | **AA** |
| SSBN 658 | MARIANO G. VALLEJO | 64/216 | Mare Island Naval Shipyard | 7 July 1964 | 23 Oct 1965 | 16 Dec 1966 | **AA** |
| SSBN 659 | WILL ROGERS | 64/216 | General Dynamics (Electric Boat) | 20 Mar 1965 | 21 July 1966 | 1 Apr 1967 | **AA** |

| | |
|---|---|
| Displacement: | 6,650 tons light |
| | 7,250 tons standard |
| | 8,250 tons submerged |
| Length: | 425 feet (129.5 m) oa |
| Beam: | 33 feet (10.1 m) |
| Draft: | 31½ feet (9.6 m) |
| Propulsion: | steam turbines; 15,000 shp; 1 shaft |
| Reactors: | 1 pressurized-water S5W |
| Speed: | ~20 knots surface |
| | ~30 knots submerged |
| Complement: | 145 (17 O + 128 EM) |
| Missiles: | 16 tubes for Poseidon C-3 SLBM |
| Torpedo tubes: | 4 21-inch (533-mm) bow |
| Sonars: | BQR-7 |
| | BQR-15 towed array |
| | BQR-19 |
| | BQS-4 |
| Fire control: | 1 Mk 88 missile FCS |
| | 1 Mk 113 Mod 9 torpedo FCS |

The LAFAYETTES are the largest class of nuclear-propelled ships, except for the STURGEON class (37 units) and the Soviet "Yankee" class SSBNs (34 units).

Class: These submarines are enlarged versions of the preceding ETHAN ALLEN class. Four additional submarines of this class were proposed for the FY 1965 ship building program, but were not built. The last 12 submarines are officially referred to as the BENJAMIN FRANKLIN class (see design note below).

Cost: The first units cost approximately $109 million.

Design: These submarines are enlarged versions of the previous ETHAN ALLEN class. The last 12 units have quieter machinery than their predecessors. The DANIEL WEBSTER has bow-mounted diving planes instead of sail-mounted planes.

Missiles: The first eight submarines initially deployed with the Polaris A-2 missile and the 23 later units with the Polaris A-3 missile. All were converted during 1970–1977 to the Poseidon missile (see table). Ten submarines of this class are scheduled to be refitted with the Trident C-4 missile, beginning in 1979. The FRANCIS SCOTT KEY is scheduled for modification beginning in late 1978 to serve as test submarine for the Trident SLBM.

Reactors: The nuclear cores installed in these submarines during the late 1960s and early 1970s can provide approximately 400,000 miles of steaming.

**"LAFAYETTE"-CLASS POSEIDON CONVERSIONS** (SCB-353)

| Number | FY | Shipyard | Start | Complete |
|---|---|---|---|---|
| SSBN 616 | 1973 | Electric Boat | Oct 1972 | Nov 1974 |
| SSBN 617 | 1973 | Newport News | Jan 1973 | Mar 1975 |
| SSBN 619 | 1973 | Electric Boat | Mar 1973 | Aug 1975 |
| SSBN 620 | 1974 | Portsmouth NSYd | Feb 1974 | Mar 1975 |
| SSBN 622 | 1975 | Newport News | Jan 1975 | July 1977 |
| SSBN 623 | 1973 | Puget Sound NSYd | June 1973 | June 1975 |
| SSBN 624 | 1974 | Newport News | Oct 1973 | Oct 1975 |
| SSBN 625 | 1975 | Electric Boat | Apr 1975 | July 1977 |
| SSBN 626 | 1975 | Electric Boat | Nov 1975 | Sep 1977 |
| SSBN 627 | 1968 | Electric Boat | Feb 1969 | June 1970 |
| SSBN 628 | 1970 | Newport News | Nov 1969 | Feb 1971 |
| SSBN 629 | 1968 | Newport News | May 1969 | Aug 1970 |
| SSBN 630 | 1969 | Mare Island NSYd | Aug 1969 | Feb 1971 |
| SSBN 631 | 1970 | Puget Sound NSYd | Oct 1969 | Dec 1970 |
| SSBN 632 | 1969 | Electric Boat | July 1969 | Nov 1970 |
| SSBN 633 | 1970 | Electric Boat | Jan 1970 | Apr 1971 |
| SSBN 634 | 1971 | Electric Boat | July 1970 | Oct 1971 |
| SSBN 635 | 1970 | Portsmouth NSYd | Jan 1970 | Sep 1971 |
| SSBN 636 | 1971 | Newport News | July 1970 | Sep 1971 |
| SSBN 640 | 1971 | Electric Boat | Feb 1971 | May 1972 |
| SSBN 641 | 1971 | Newport News | Feb 1971 | May 1972 |
| SSBN 642 | 1972 | Electric Boat | July 1971 | Oct 1972 |
| SSBN 643 | 1971 | Portsmouth NSYd | Apr 1971 | Aug 1972 |
| SSBN 644 | 1971 | Puget Sound NSYd | Apr 1971 | July 1972 |
| SSBN 645 | 1972 | Newport News | July 1971 | Nov 1972 |
| SSBN 654 | 1972 | Puget Sound NSYd | Sep 1971 | Feb 1973 |
| SSBN 655 | 1972 | Newport News | Nov 1971 | Mar 1973 |
| SSBN 656 | 1972 | Electric Boat | Nov 1971 | Apr 1973 |
| SSBN 657 | 1972 | Puget Sound NSYd | Feb 1972 | Apr 1973 |
| SSBN 658 | 1973 | Newport News | Aug 1972 | Dec 1973 |
| SSBN 659 | 1973 | Portsmouth NSYd | Oct 1972 | Feb 1974 |

The DANIEL WEBSTER maneuvering at the New London Submarine Base (actually in Groton, Conn.) with the assistance of two harbor tugs. The WEBSTER is the only U.S. SSBN with bow-mounted diving planes. All four British SSBNs have bow-mounted planes while the modern Soviet and (five) French SSBNs follow the U.S. style. (1975, U.S. Navy)

The strategic missile submarine MARIANO G. VALLEJO at sea off the Virgin Islands. The submarine's hull number has been painted out in preparation for a deterrent patrol. SSBNs normally deploy for 60-day patrols, but from the mid-1970s onward these have been broken up on occasion by selected port visits. "Blue" and "Gold" crews alternate on patrols. (1974, U.S. Navy, John E. Hudson)

## 5 NUCLEAR-PROPELLED STRATEGIC MISSILE SUBMARINES: "ETHAN ALLEN" CLASS

| Number | Name | FY/SCB | Builder | Laid down | Launched | Commissioned | Status |
|--------|------|--------|---------|-----------|----------|--------------|--------|
| SSBN 608 | ETHAN ALLEN | 59/180 | General Dynamics (Electric Boat) | 14 Sep 1959 | 22 Nov 1960 | 8 Aug 1961 | **PA** |
| SSBN 609 | SAM HOUSTON | 59/180 | Newport News | 28 Dec 1959 | 2 Feb 1961 | 6 Mar 1962 | **PA** |
| SSBN 610 | THOMAS A. EDISON | 59/180 | General Dynamics (Electric Boat) | 15 Mar 1960 | 15 June 1961 | 10 Mar 1962 | **PA** |
| SSBN 611 | JOHN MARSHALL | 59/180 | Newport News | 4 Apr 1960 | 15 July 1961 | 21 May 1962 | **PA** |
| SSBN 618 | THOMAS JEFFERSON | 61/180 | Newport News | 3 Feb 1961 | 24 Feb 1962 | 4 Jan 1963 | **PA** |

| | |
|---|---|
| Displacement: | 6,955 tons standard |
| | 7,900 tons submerged |
| Length: | 410½ feet (125.1 m) oa |
| Beam: | 33 feet (10.1 m) |
| Draft: | 30 feet (9.1 m) |
| Propulsion: | steam turbines; 15,000 shp; 1 shaft |
| Reactors: | 1 pressurized-water S5W |
| Speed: | ~20 knots surface |
| | ~30 knots submerged |
| Complement: | 140 (12 O + 128 EM) |
| Missiles: | 16 tubes for Polaris A-3 SLBM |
| Torpedo tubes: | 4 21-inch (533-mm) bow |
| Sonars: | BQS-4 |
| | BQR-15 towed array |
| | BQR-19 |
| Fire control: | 1 Mk 84 missile FCS |
| | 1 Mk 112 Mod 1 torpedo FCS |

The ETHAN ALLEN was the first U.S. ballistic missile submarine design. The previous GEORGE WASHINGTON class was modified from an SSN design, incorporating many features of this class.

Class: Note the non-sequential hull number of the THOMAS JEFFERSON.

Design: These submarines incorporate certain construction features of the PERMIT-class attack submarine.

Missiles: The submarines initially were armed with the Polaris A-2 missile. All five were later modified to fire the Polaris A-3 missile. This class and the previous GEORGE WASHINGTON-class SSBNs could not be fitted to carry the larger Poseidon missile without extensive hull modification.

JOHN MARSHALL (1967, U.S. Navy)

THOMAS JEFFERSON (1976, U.S. Navy, PH1 A. E. Legare)

## 5 NUCLEAR-PROPELLED STRATEGIC MISSILE SUBMARINES: "GEORGE WASHINGTON" CLASS

| Number | Name | FY/SCB | Builder | Laid down | Launched | Commissioned | Status |
|---|---|---|---|---|---|---|---|
| SSBN 598 | GEORGE WASHINGTON | S58/180A | General Dynamics (Electric Boat) | 1 Nov 1957 | 9 June 1959 | 30 Dec 1959 | **PA** |
| SSBN 599 | PATRICK HENRY | S58/180A | General Dynamics (Electric Boat) | 27 May 1958 | 22 Sep 1959 | 9 Apr 1960 | **PA** |
| SSBN 600 | THEODORE ROOSEVELT | S58/180A | Mare Island Naval Shipyard | 30 May 1958 | 3 Oct 1959 | 13 Feb 1961 | **PA** |
| SSBN 601 | ROBERT E. LEE | 59/180A | Newport News | 25 Aug 1958 | 18 Dec 1959 | 16 Sep 1960 | **PA** |
| SSBN 602 | ABRAHAM LINCOLN | 59/180A | Portsmouth Naval Shipyard | 1 Nov 1958 | 14 May 1960 | 11 Mar 1961 | **PA** |

| | |
|---|---|
| Displacement: | 6,000 tons standard |
| | 6,700 tons submerged |
| Length: | 381⅔ feet (116.3 m) oa |
| Beam: | 33 feet (10.1 m) |
| Draft: | 29 feet (8.8 m) |
| Propulsion: | steam turbines; 15,000 shp; 1 shaft |
| Reactors: | 1 pressurized-water S5W |
| Speed: | ~20 knots surface |
| | ~30 knots submerged |
| Complement: | 140 (12 O + 128 EM) |
| Missiles: | 16 tubes for Polaris A-3 SLBM |
| Torpedo tubes: | 6 21-inch (533-mm) bow |
| Sonars: | BQS-4 |
| | BQR-19 |
| Fire control: | 1 Mk 84 missile FCS |
| | 1 Mk 112 Mod 1/2 torpedo FCS |

The GEORGE WASHINGTON-class submarines were the first undersea craft in the West to be armed with ballistic missiles. They were predated by the Soviet diesel-electric "Zulu-V" class (1956) and nuclear-propelled "Hotel" class (1960); the GEORGE WASHINGTON-class submarines, however, carry more and longer-range missiles than these Soviet submarines.

Class: These submarines were "converted" during construction from SKIPJACK-class attack submarines. The FY 1958 supplemental shipbuilding program, signed by the President on 11 February 1958, provided for the immediate construction of three SSBNs. In anticipation of this action, the Navy had shortly before ordered that two attack submarines be redesigned as missile submarines; they were the SCORPION (SSN 589) and the then-unnamed SSN 590; these were completed as the GEORGE WASHINGTON and PATRICK HENRY, respectively. Two additional submarines of this class were authorized in the FY 1959 program.

Design: The redesign of the SKIPJACK class provided for the addition of almost 130 feet in length to accommodate two rows of eight missile tubes, auxiliary machinery, and missile fire control and inertial navigation systems.

GEORGE WASHINGTON (U.S. Navy)

**5 + 26 NUCLEAR-PROPELLED ATTACK SUBMARINES: "LOS ANGELES" CLASS**

| Number | Name | FY/SCB | Builder | Laid down | Launched | Commissioned | Status |
|--------|------|--------|---------|-----------|----------|--------------|--------|
| SSN 688 | LOS ANGELES | 70/303 | Newport News | 8 Jan 1972 | 6 Apr 1974 | 13 Nov 1976 | **AA** |
| SSN 689 | BATON ROUGE | 70/303 | Newport News | 18 Nov 1972 | 26 Apr 1975 | 25 June 1977 | **AA** |
| SSN 690 | PHILADELPHIA | 70/303 | General Dynamics (Electric Boat) | 12 Aug 1972 | 19 Oct 1974 | 25 June 1977 | **AA** |
| SSN 691 | MEMPHIS | 71/303 | Newport News | 23 June 1973 | 3 Apr 1976 | 1977 | |
| SSN 692 | OMAHA | 71/303 | General Dynamics (Electric Boat) | 27 Jan 1973 | 21 Feb 1976 | 1977 | |
| SSN 693 | CINCINNATI | 71/303 | Newport News | 6 Apr 1974 | 19 Feb 1977 | 1978 | Bldg. |
| SSN 694 | GROTON | 71/303 | General Dynamics (Electric Boat) | 3 Aug 1973 | 9 Oct 1976 | 1978 | Bldg. |
| SSN 695 | BIRMINGHAM | 72/303 | Newport News | 26 Apr 1975 | 29 Oct 1977 | 1978 | Bldg. |
| SSN 696 | NEW YORK CITY | 72/303 | General Dynamics (Electric Boat) | 15 Dec 1973 | 18 June 1977 | 1978 | Bldg. |
| SSN 697 | INDIANAPOLIS | 72/303 | General Dynamics (Electric Boat) | 19 Oct 1974 | 30 July 1977 | 1979 | Bldg. |
| SSN 698 | BREMERTON | 72/303 | General Dynamics (Electric Boat) | 8 May 1976 | 1978 | 1979 | Bldg. |
| SSN 699 | JACKSONVILLE | 72/303 | General Dynamics (Electric Boat) | 21 Feb 1976 | 1978 | 1979 | Bldg. |
| SSN 700 | DALLAS | 73/303 | General Dynamics (Electric Boat) | 9 Oct 1976 | 1978 | 1979 | Bldg. |
| SSN 701 | LA JOLLA | 73/303 | General Dynamics (Electric Boat) | 16 Oct 1976 | 1978 | 1979 | Bldg. |
| SSN 702 | PHOENIX | 73/303 | General Dynamics (Electric Boat) | 30 July 1977 | 1979 | 1980 | Bldg. |
| SSN 703 | BOSTON | 73/303 | General Dynamics (Electric Boat) | 1978 | 1979 | 1980 | Bldg. |
| SSN 704 | BALTIMORE | 73/303 | General Dynamics (Electric Boat) | 1978 | 1979 | 1980 | Bldg. |
| SSN 705 | . . . . . . . . | 73/303 | General Dynamics (Electric Boat) | 1978 | 1979 | 1980 | Bldg. |
| SSN 706 | . . . . . . . . | 74/303 | General Dynamics (Electric Boat) | 1978 | 1980 | 1981 | Bldg. |
| SSN 707 | . . . . . . . . | 74/303 | General Dynamics (Electric Boat) | 1979 | 1980 | 1981 | Bldg. |
| SSN 708 | . . . . . . . . | 74/303 | General Dynamics (Electric Boat) | 1979 | 1980 | 1981 | Bldg. |
| SSN 709 | . . . . . . . . | 74/303 | General Dynamics (Electric Boat) | 1979 | 1980 | 1981 | Bldg. |
| SSN 710 | . . . . . . . . | 74/303 | General Dynamics (Electric Boat) | 1979 | 1981 | 1982 | Bldg. |
| SSN 711 | . . . . . . . . | 75/303 | Newport News | 1977 | 1979 | 1980 | Bldg. |
| SSN 712 | . . . . . . . . | 75/303 | Newport News | 1978 | 1980 | 1981 | Bldg. |
| SSN 713 | . . . . . . . . | 75/303 | Newport News | 1979 | 1980 | 1982 | Bldg. |
| SSN 714 | . . . . . . . . | 76/303 | Newport News | 1979 | 1980 | 1982 | Bldg. |
| SSN 715 | . . . . . . . . | 76/303 | Newport News | 1980 | 1981 | 1983 | Bldg. |
| SSN 716 | . . . . . . . . | 77/303 | | | | | Bldg. |
| SSN 717 | . . . . . . . . | 77/303 | | | | | Bldg. |
| SSN 718 | . . . . . . . . | 77/303 | | | | | Bldg. |
| SSN 719 | . . . . . . . . | 78/303 | | | | | Auth. |
| 2 SSNs | . . . . . . . . | 79/303 | | | | | Planned |
| 1 SSN | . . . . . . . . | 80/303 | | | | | Planned |
| 2 SSNs | . . . . . . . . | 81/303 | | | | | Planned |
| 1 SSN | . . . . . . . . | 82/303 | | | | | Planned |

Displacement:  6,000 tons standard
6,900 tons submerged
Length:  360 feet (109.7 m) oa
Beam:  33 feet (10.1 m)
Draft:  32⅓ feet (9.85 m)
Propulsion:  steam turbines; ~30,000 shp; 1 shaft
Reactors:  1 pressurized-water S6G
Speed:
30+ knots submerged
Complement:  127 (12 O + 115 EM)

Missiles:  (see notes)
Torpedo tubes:  4 21-inch (533-mm) amidships
ASW weapons:  SUBROC
Mk 48 torpedoes
Sonars:  BQQ-5 bow-mounted
BQS-15
Fire control:  1 Mk 113 Mod 10 torpedo FCS in SSN 688-699;
Mk 117 in later units

These are large, "high-speed" submarines developed to counter the fast Soviet undersea craft constructed since the late 1960s. The lead submarine of this class went to sea eight years after the first unit of the Soviet "Victor" class (1968), which is similar in several respects to the LOS ANGELES class.

Class: All U.S. attack submarines constructed through at least the FY 1982 program will be of this class; under current planning this would mean a total of at least 39 units.

Cost: The estimated cost of the submarines in the FY 1978 program is $343.1 million per unit. Some earlier submarines of this class cost approximately $380 million.

Design: These submarines displace about half again as much as the previous STURGEON class, the additional size being required for the larger nuclear propulsion plant and improved sonar and machinery-quieting features.

Missiles: The torpedo-tube-launched Harpoon and Tomahawk cruise missiles can be carried by these submarines when those weapons are available.

Reactors: These submarines are estimated to have an initial nuclear core life of 10 to 13 years.

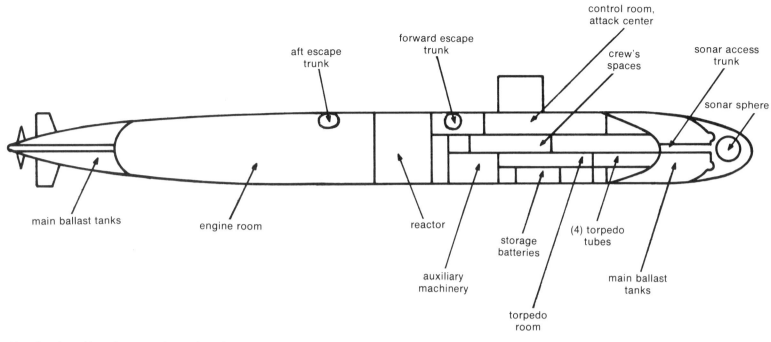

Line drawing of LOS ANGELES-class submarine

The LOS ANGELES, lead submarine of the latest class of U.S. Navy undersea craft and the first U.S. submarine ever named for a city. The LOS ANGELES is faster and has improved sonar capability compared to her predecessors, but those attributes have been achieved by tremendous increases in size and cost, with no increase in armament. (1976, Newport News)

### 1 NUCLEAR-PROPELLED ATTACK SUBMARINE: "GLENARD P. LIPSCOMB"

| Number | Name | FY/SCB | Builder | Laid down | Launched | Commissioned | Status |
|--------|------|--------|---------|-----------|----------|--------------|--------|
| SSN 685 | GLENARD P. LIPSCOMB | 68/302 | General Dynamics (Electric Boat) | 5 June 1971 | 4 Aug 1973 | 21 Dec 1974 | **AA** |

Displacement: 5,800 tons standard
6,480 tons submerged
Length: 365 feet (111.3 m) oa
Beam: 31¾ feet (9.7 m)
Draft:
Propulsion: turbine-electric drive (General Electric); 1 shaft
Reactors: 1 pressurized-water S5Wa
Speed:
~25 knots submerged
Complement: 120 (12 O + 108 EM)

Missiles: (see notes)
Torpedo tubes: 4 21-inch (533 mm) amidships
ASW weapons: SUBROC
Mk 48 torpedoes
Sonars: BQQ-2 bow-mounted
Fire control: 1 Mk 113 Mod 8 torpedo FCS

The LIPSCOMB was constructed to evaluate a Turbine-Electric Drive (TED) propulsion plant; speed was sacrificed to reduce machinery noises. The TULLIBEE, constructed over a decade earlier, was a similar effort to replace steam turbines with turbine-electric drive. No additional submarines with this propulsion system are planned. The LIPSCOMB is considerably larger than contemporary steam-turbine submarines.

Cost: Construction cost was approximately $200 million.

Fire control: The Mk 117 torpedo fire control system will be installed during a future overhaul.

Missiles: Torpedo-tube-launched Harpoon and Tomahawk cruise missiles can be carried in the LIPSCOMB.

Sonars: The BQQ-2 sonar system will be upgraded to the BQQ-5 configuration during a future overhaul.

GLENARD P. LIPSCOMB (1974, General Dynamics/Electric Boat)

The one-of-a-kind GLENARD P. LIPSCOMB at high surface speed. Modern attack submarines are optimized for underwater operation and are faster submerged than when surfaced. The LIPSCOMB, named for a late member of the Congressional Joint Committee on Atomic Energy, is often referred to as the "Lipscomb fish" in the Fleet. (1974, General Dynamics/Electric Boat)

## 1 NUCLEAR-PROPELLED ATTACK SUBMARINE: "NARWHAL"

| Number | Name | FY/SCB | Builder | Laid down | Launched | Commissioned | Status |
|--------|------|--------|---------|-----------|----------|--------------|--------|
| SSN 671 | NARWHAL | 64/245 | General Dynamics (Electric Boat) | 17 Jan 1966 | 9 Sep 1966 | 12 July 1969 | **AA** |

| | |
|---|---|
| Displacement: | 4,450 tons standard |
| | 5,350 tons submerged |
| Length: | 314 feet (95.7 m) oa |
| Beam: | 38 feet (11.6 m) |
| Draft: | 26 feet (7.9 m) |
| Propulsion: | steam turbines; ~17,000 shp; 1 shaft |
| Reactors: | 1 pressurized-water S5G |
| Speed: | ~20 knots surface |
| | ~30 knots submerged |
| Complement: | 120 (12 O + 108 EM) |
| | |
| Missiles: | (see notes) |
| Torpedo tubes: | 4 21-inch (533-mm) amidships |
| ASW weapons: | SUBROC |
| | Mk 48 torpedoes |
| Sonars: | BQQ-2 bow-mounted |
| Fire control: | 1 Mk 113 Mod 6 torpedo FCS |

The NARWHAL was constructed to evaluate the natural-circulation S5G reactor plant in an attack submarine. Weapons, sensors, and other features are similar to those of the STURGEON-class submarines, with which the NARWHAL is listed for force-level and deployment considerations.

Fire control: The Mk 117 torpedo fire control system will be installed during a future overhaul.

Missiles: Torpedo-tube-launched Harpoon and Tomahawk cruise missiles can be carried in the NARWHAL when those weapons are available.

Sonars: The BQQ-2 sonar system will be modified to the BQQ-5 configuration during a future overhaul.

NARWHAL (1969, General Dynamics/Electric Boat)

## 37 NUCLEAR-PROPELLED ATTACK SUBMARINES: "STURGEON" CLASS

| Number | Name | FY/SCB | Builder | Laid down | Launched | Commissioned | Status |
|--------|------|--------|---------|-----------|----------|--------------|--------|
| SSN 637 | STURGEON | 62/188A | General Dynamics (Electric Boat) | 10 Aug 1963 | 26 Feb 1966 | 3 Mar 1967 | **AA** |
| SSN 638 | WHALE | 62/188A | General Dynamics (Quincy) | 27 May 1964 | 14 Oct 1966 | 12 Oct 1968 | **AA** |
| SSN 639 | TAUTOG | 62/188A | Ingalls SB Corp | 27 Jan 1964 | 15 Apr 1967 | 17 Aug 1968 | **PA** |
| SSN 646 | GRAYLING | 63/188A | Portsmouth Naval Shipyard | 12 May 1964 | 22 June 1967 | 11 Oct 1969 | **AA** |
| SSN 647 | POGY | 63/188A | Ingalls SB Corp | 4 May 1964 | 3 June 1967 | 15 May 1971 | **PA** |
| SSN 648 | ASPRO | 63/188A | Ingalls SB Corp | 23 Nov 1964 | 29 Nov 1967 | 20 Feb 1969 | **PA** |
| SSN 649 | SUNFISH | 63/188A | General Dynamics (Quincy) | 15 Jan 1965 | 14 Oct 1966 | 15 Mar 1969 | **AA** |
| SSN 650 | PARGO | 63/188A | General Dynamics (Electric Boat) | 3 June 1964 | 17 Sep 1966 | 5 Jan 1968 | **AA** |
| SSN 651 | QUEENFISH | 63/188A | Newport News | 11 May 1965 | 25 Feb 1966 | 6 Dec 1966 | **PA** |
| SSN 652 | PUFFER | 63/188A | Ingalls SB Corp | 8 Feb 1965 | 30 Mar 1968 | 9 Aug 1969 | **PA** |
| SSN 653 | RAY | 63/188A | Newport News | 1 Apr 1965 | 21 June 1966 | 12 Apr 1967 | **AA** |
| SSN 660 | SAND LANCE | 64/188A | Portsmouth Naval Shipyard | 15 Jan 1965 | 11 Nov 1969 | 25 Sep 1971 | **AA** |
| SSN 661 | LAPON | 64/188A | Newport News | 26 July 1965 | 16 Dec 1966 | 14 Dec 1967 | **AA** |
| SSN 662 | GURNARD | 64/188A | Mare Island Naval Shipyard | 22 Dec 1964 | 20 May 1967 | 6 Dec 1968 | **PA** |
| SSN 663 | HAMMERHEAD | 64/188A | Newport News | 29 Nov 1965 | 14 Apr 1967 | 28 June 1968 | **AA** |
| SSN 664 | SEA DEVIL | 64/188A | Newport News | 12 Apr 1966 | 5 Oct 1967 | 30 Jan 1969 | **AA** |
| SSN 665 | GUITARRO | 65/300 | Mare Island Naval Shipyard | 9 Dec 1965 | 27 July 1968 | 9 Sep 1972 | **PA** |
| SSN 666 | HAWKBILL | 65/300 | Mare Island Naval Shipyard | 12 Dec 1966 | 12 Apr 1969 | 4 Feb 1971 | **PA** |
| SSN 667 | BERGALL | 65/300 | General Dynamics (Electric Boat) | 16 Apr 1966 | 17 Feb 1968 | 13 June 1969 | **AA** |
| SSN 668 | SPADEFISH | 65/300 | Newport News | 21 Dec 1966 | 15 May 1968 | 14 Aug 1969 | **AA** |
| SSN 669 | SEAHORSE | 65/300 | General Dynamics (Electric Boat) | 13 Aug 1966 | 15 June 1968 | 19 Sep 1969 | **AA** |
| SSN 670 | FINBACK | 65/300 | Newport News | 26 June 1967 | 7 Dec 1968 | 4 Feb 1970 | **AA** |
| SSN 672 | PINTADO | 66/300 | Mare Island Naval Shipyard | 27 Oct 1967 | 16 Aug 1969 | 29 Apr 1971 | **PA** |
| SSN 673 | FLYING FISH | 66/300 | General Dynamics (Electric Boat) | 30 June 1967 | 17 May 1969 | 29 Apr 1970 | **AA** |
| SSN 674 | TREPANG | 66/300 | General Dynamics (Electric Boat) | 28 Oct 1967 | 27 Sep 1969 | 14 Aug 1970 | **AA** |
| SSN 675 | BLUEFISH | 66/300 | General Dynamics (Electric Boat) | 13 Mar 1968 | 10 Jan 1970 | 8 Jan 1971 | **AA** |
| SSN 676 | BILLFISH | 66/300 | General Dynamics (Electric Boat) | 20 Sep 1968 | 1 May 1970 | 12 Mar 1971 | **AA** |
| SSN 677 | DRUM | 66/300 | Mare Island Naval Shipyard | 20 Aug 1968 | 23 May 1970 | 15 Apr 1972 | **PA** |
| SSN 678 | ARCHERFISH | 67/300 | General Dynamics (Electric Boat) | 19 June 1969 | 16 Jan 1971 | 17 Dec 1971 | **AA** |
| SSN 679 | SILVERSIDES | 67/300 | General Dynamics (Electric Boat) | 13 Oct 1969 | 4 June 1971 | 5 May 1972 | **AA** |
| SSN 680 | WILLIAM H. BATES | 67/300 | Ingalls (Litton) | 4 Aug 1969 | 11 Dec 1971 | 5 May 1973 | **AA** |
| SSN 681 | BATFISH | 67/300 | General Dynamics (Electric Boat) | 9 Feb 1970 | 9 Oct 1971 | 1 Sep 1972 | **AA** |
| SSN 682 | TUNNY | 67/300 | Ingalls (Litton) | 22 May 1970 | 10 June 1972 | 26 Jan 1974 | **AA** |
| SSN 683 | PARCHE | 68/300 | Ingalls (Litton) | 10 Dec 1970 | 13 Jan 1973 | 17 Aug 1974 | **PA** |
| SSN 684 | CAVALLA | 68/300 | General Dynamics | 4 June 1970 | 19 Feb 1972 | 9 Feb 1973 | **AA** |
| SSN 686 | L. MENDEL RIVERS | 69/300 | Newport News | 26 June 1971 | 2 June 1973 | 1 Feb 1975 | **AA** |
| SSN 687 | RICHARD B. RUSSELL | 69/300 | Newport News | 19 Oct 1971 | 12 Jan 1974 | 16 Aug 1975 | **AA** |

| | |
|---|---|
| Displacement: | 3,640 tons standard |
| | 4,650 tons submerged |
| Length: | 292⅙ feet (89.0 m) oa |
| Beam: | 31⅔ feet (9.65 m) |
| Draft: | 29⁵/₁₂ feet (8.9 m) |
| Propulsion: | steam turbines; ~15,000 shp; 1 shaft |
| Reactors: | 1 pressurized-water S5W |
| Speed: | ~20 knots surface |
| | ~30 knots submerged |
| Complement: | 120 (12 O + 108 EM) |
| Missiles: | (see notes) |
| Torpedo tubes: | 4 21-inch (533-mm) amidships |
| ASW weapons: | SUBROC |
| | Mk 48 torpedoes |
| Sonars: | BQQ-2 bow-mounted; except BQQ-5 in SSN 647, 660, 665, 672, 678 |
| | BQS-8/12 in SSN 637–639, 646–653, 660–664; BQS-13 fitted in later units |
| Fire control: | 1 Mk 113 Mod 6 torpedo FCS through SSN 677; Mod 8 in SSN 678–683; Mod 10 in SSN 684, 686–687 |

This is the largest class of nuclear-propelled ships in the West, followed by the 34 SSBNs of the Soviet "Yankee" class.

Builders: The POGY was begun by the New York Shipbuilding Corporation, Camden, New Jersey; the contract was terminated on 5 June 1967 and the unfinished submarine was towed to the Ingalls yard for completion under a contract awarded on 7 December 1967.

Design: These are improved PERMIT-class submarines. Their sail-mounted diving planes are rotated to the vertical plane for breaking up through ice during polar operations.

Fire control: The Mk 117 torpedo fire control system will be installed in this class during future overhauls.

Missiles: Torpedo-launched Harpoon and Tomahawk cruise missiles can be carried in these submarines when those weapons become available.

Sonars: The BQQ-2 sonar system in these submarines is being upgraded to the BQQ-5 configuration during overhauls; five submarines were modified through mid-1977.

The RICHARD B. RUSSELL, the last of 37 STURGEON-class SSNs. In the view the RUSSELL's hull number is visible on the bow and sail, and the full name is spelled out on the sides, amidships; for some operations they will be painted out. The light "spots" on the bow and amidships are flush-fitting submarine sunk marker buoys. (1975, Newport News)

The RICHARD B. RUSSELL at high speed. Note officers atop sail structure; the deck is too slick at high speeds unless men use safety lines hooked into track running aft from sail. (1975, Newport News)

BILLFISH (1977, Giorgio Arra)

**13 NUCLEAR-PROPELLED ATTACK SUBMARINES: "PERMIT" CLASS**

| Number | Name | FY/SCB | Builder | Laid down | Launched | Commissioned | Status |
|--------|------|--------|---------|-----------|----------|--------------|--------|
| SSN 594 | PERMIT | 58/188 | Mare Island Naval Shipyard | 16 July 1969 | 1 July 1961 | 29 May 1962 | **PA** |
| SSN 595 | PLUNGER | 58/188 | Mare Island Naval Shipyard | 2 Mar 1960 | 9 Dec 1961 | 21 Nov 1962 | **PA** |
| SSN 596 | BARB | 58/188 | Ingalls SB Corp | 9 Nov 1959 | 12 Feb 1962 | 24 Aug 1963 | **PA** |
| SSN 603 | POLLACK | 59/188 | New York SB Corp | 14 Mar 1960 | 17 Mar 1962 | 26 May 1964 | **PA** |
| SSN 604 | HADDO | 59/188 | New York SB Corp | 9 Sep 1960 | 18 Aug 1962 | 16 Dec 1964 | **PA** |
| SSN 605 | JACK | 59/188 | Portsmouth Naval Shipyard | 16 Sep 1960 | 24 Apr 1963 | 31 Mar 1967 | **AA** |
| SSN 606 | TINOSA | 59/188 | Portsmouth Naval Shipyard | 24 Nov 1959 | 9 Dec 1961 | 17 Oct 1964 | **AA** |
| SSN 607 | DACE | 59/188 | Ingalls SB Corp | 6 June 1960 | 18 Aug 1962 | 4 Apr 1964 | **AA** |
| SSN 612 | GUARDFISH | 60/188 | New York SB Corp | 28 Feb 1961 | 15 May 1965 | 20 Dec 1966 | **PA** |
| SSN 613 | FLASHER | 60/188 | General Dynamics (Electric Boat) | 14 Apr 1961 | 22 June 1963 | 22 July 1966 | **PA** |
| SSN 614 | GREENLING | 60/188 | General Dynamics (Electric Boat) | 15 Aug 1961 | 4 Apr 1964* | 3 Nov 1967 | **AA** |
| SSN 615 | GATO | 60/188 | General Dynamics (Electric Boat) | 15 Dec 1961 | 14 May 1964 | 25 Jan 1968 | **AA** |
| SSN 621 | HADDOCK | 61/188 | Ingalls SB Corp | 24 Apr 1961 | 21 May 1966 | 22 Dec 1967 | **PA** |

| | |
|---|---|
| Displacement: | 3,750 tons standard (except SSN 613–615, 3,800 tons) |
| | 4,300 tons submerged (except SSN 605, 4,500 tons; SSN 613–615, 4,600 tons) |
| Length: | 278½ feet (84.9 m) oa (except SSN 605, 296¾ (89.5); SSN 613–615, 292⅙ (89.1)) |
| Beam: | 31¾ feet (9.6 m) |
| Draft: | 25⅙ feet (7.6 m) |
| Propulsion: | steam turbines; ~15,000 shp; 1 shaft |
| Reactors: | 1 pressurized-water S5W |
| Speed: | ~20 knots surface |
| | 20 knots submerged |
| Complement: | 120 (12 O + 108 EM) |
| Missiles: | (see notes) |
| Torpedo tubes: | 4 21-inch (533-mm) amidships |
| ASW weapons: | SUBROC |
| | Mk 48 torpedoes |
| Sonars: | BQQ-2 bow-mounted (see Sonar notes) |
| Fire control: | 1 Mk 113 Mod 6 torpedo FCS |

These submarines established the standard for later U.S. Navy nuclear-propelled attack submarines, having a deep-diving capability, advanced sonar systems, and the SUBROC antisubmarine rocket.

Builders: The GREENLING and GATO were launched by the Electric Boat yard in Groton; they were then towed to the Quincy yard (Massachusetts) for completion to a modified design.

Class: Originally called the THRESHER class, they became generally known as the PERMIT class after the accidental loss of the lead submarine with all hands (129 men) on 10 April 1963.

Design: The FLASHER, GREENLING, and GATO were delayed for completion to a modified design incorporating additional Submarine Safety (SUBSAFE) features. The JACK's design incorporates a modified power plant (see below).

Engineering: The JACK has an inner propeller shaft fitted within an outer, sleeve-like shaft to provide counter-rotating propellers; also fitted with counter-rotating turbines without reduction gears. Both features seek to reduce operating noises. These features provide a ten-percent increase in power efficiency, but no increase in speed; they have not been used in later submarines.

Fire control: The Mk 117 torpedo fire control system will be installed in this class during future overhauls.

Missiles: Torpedo-tube-launched Harpoon and Tomahawk cruise missiles can be carried in these submarines.

Names: The names of three submarines were changed during construction: SSN 595, ex-POLLACK; SSN 596, ex-POLLACK, ex-PLUNGER, and SSN 603, ex-BARB.

Sonars: The BQQ-2 sonar system in these submarines is being upgraded to the BQQ-5 configuration during overhauls; one unit was modified through mid-1977.

POLLACK (1977, Giorgio Arra)

The BARB running in a heavy sea. The "E" painted on her sail structure indicates excellence in Fleet competitions. The lead ship of this class, the THRESHER, was the world's first nuclear-propelled submarine to be lost at sea. Two others have gone down since, the USS SCORPION (1967) and a Soviet November-class SSN (1970). (U.S. Navy)

### 1 NUCLEAR-PROPELLED ATTACK SUBMARINE: "TULLIBEE"

| Number | Name | FY/SCB | Builder | Laid down | Launched | Commissioned | Status |
|--------|------|--------|---------|-----------|----------|--------------|--------|
| SSN 597 | TULLIBEE | 58/178 | General Dynamics (Electric Boat) | 26 May 1958 | 27 Apr 1960 | 9 Nov 1960 | **AA** |

Displacement: 2,317 tons standard
2,640 tons submerged
Length: 273 feet (83.2 m) oa
Beam: 23⅓ feet (7.1 m)
Draft: 21 feet (6.4 m)
Propulsion: turbo-electric with steam turbines (Westinghouse); 2,500 shp; 1 shaft
Reactors: 1 pressurized-water S2C
Speed: ~15 knots surface
15+ knots submerged
Complement: 87 (7 O + 80 EM)
Torpedo tubes: 4 21-inch (533-mm) amidships
ASW weapons: torpedoes
Sonars: BQQ-2 bow-mounted
BQG-4 PUFF
Fire control: 1 Mk 112 Mod 1 torpedo FCS

The TULLIBEE was designed as a small hunter-killer submarine intended to operate off enemy ports and in narrow waterways, just as were the smaller diesel-electric submarines of the SSK 1 class. The construction of further units was halted in favor of the larger and more versatile PERMIT class.

Design: This was the first U.S. submarine to have bow-mounted sonar with the torpedo tubes fitted amidships, and angled out at about ten degrees from the centerline. This sonar arrangement, followed in all later SSNs, places the acoustic detection equipment in the best position with respect to ship movement and machinery noises.

Engineering: The nuclear power plant is smaller than that in other U.S. submarines, with turbo-electric drive used in place of conventional steam turbines with reduction gear, in an effort to reduce machinery noises.

TULLIBEE (1968, U.S. Navy)

**5 NUCLEAR-PROPELLED ATTACK SUBMARINES: "SKIPJACK" CLASS**

| Number | Name | FY/SCB | Builder | Laid down | Launched | Commissioned | Status |
|--------|------|--------|---------|-----------|----------|--------------|--------|
| SSN 585 | SKIPJACK | 56/154 | General Dynamics (Electric Boat) | 29 May 1956 | 26 May 1958 | 15 Apr 1959 | **AA** |
| SSN 588 | SCAMP | 57/154 | Mare Island Naval Shipyard | 22 Jan 1959 | 8 Oct 1960 | 5 June 1961 | **PA** |
| SSN 590 | SCULPIN | 57/154 | Ingalls SB Corp | 3 Feb 1958 | 31 Mar 1960 | 1 June 1961 | **PA** |
| SSN 591 | SHARK | 57/154 | Newport News | 24 Feb 1958 | 16 Mar 1960 | 9 Feb 1961 | **AA** |
| SSN 592 | SNOOK | 57/154 | Ingalls SB Corp | 7 Apr 1958 | 31 Oct 1960 | 24 Oct 1961 | **PA** |

| | |
|---|---|
| Displacement: | 3,075 tons standard |
| | 3,500 tons submerged |
| Length: | 251¾ feet (76.7 m) oa |
| Beam: | 31½ feet (9.6 m) |
| Draft: | 28 feet (8.5 m) |
| Propulsion: | steam turbines (Westinghouse in SSN 585; General Electric in others); ~15,000 shp; 1 shaft |
| Reactors: | 1 pressurized-water S5W |
| Speed: | ~20 knots surface |
| | 30+ knots submerged |
| Complement: | 112 (10 O + 102 EM) |
| Torpedo tubes: | 6 21-inch (533-mm) bow |
| ASW weapons: | torpedoes |
| Sonars: | BQS-4 (modified) |
| Fire control: | 1 Mk 101 Mod 20 in SSN 585; Mod 17 in other units |

The SKIPJACK-class submarines combine nuclear propulsion with the high-speed, "tear-drop" hull of the experimental submarine ALBACORE. They are the fastest submarines propelled by the S5W reactor plant (later S5W submarines are larger and have more "wetted surface"). The SKIPJACKS remain first-line submarines, although they lack advanced sonar and SUBROC capabilities.

Class: The SCORPION (SSN 589) was accidentally lost with all hands (99 men) in May 1968 while some 400 miles southwest of the Azores.

Cost: Approximately $40 million per submarine.

Design: This class formed the basis for the U.S. fleet ballistic missile submarines (SSBN) constructed during the late 1950s and 1960s; see GEORGE WASHINGTON class for details.

SCAMP (1976, Giorgio Arra)

The SCAMP, second ship of the highly successful SKIPJACK class, at anchor in Hong Kong. These were the first high-speed SSNs; later U.S. submarines can dive deeper, are quieter, and have better sonars, but are slower and have fewer torpedo tubes. The SKIPJACKS were the last of several post-war classes to have same-letter names. (1976, Giorgio Arra)

## 1 NUCLEAR-PROPELLED RESEARCH SUBMARINE: "HALIBUT"

| Number | Name | FY/SCB | Builder | Laid down | Launched | Commissioned | Status |
|--------|------|--------|---------|-----------|----------|--------------|--------|
| SSN 587 | HALIBUT | 56/137A | Mare Island Naval Shipyard | 11 Apr 1957 | 9 Jan 1959 | 4 Jan 1960 | PR |

| | |
|---|---|
| Displacement: | 3,850 tons standard |
| | 5,000 tons submerged |
| Length: | 350 feet (106.6 m) oa |
| Beam: | 29½ feet (8.9 m) |
| Draft: | 21½ feet (6.5 m) |
| Propulsion: | steam turbines (Westinghouse); 2 shafts |
| Reactors: | 1 pressurized-water S3W |
| Speed: | 15.5 knots surface |
| | 15+ knots submerged |
| Complement: | 120 (12 O + 108 EM) |

| | |
|---|---|
| Missiles: | removed |
| Torpedo tubes: | 6 21-inch (533-mm) (4 bow + 2 stern) |
| ASW weapons: | torpedoes |
| Sonars: | BQS-4 |
| Fire control: | 1 Mk 101 Mod 12 torpedo FCS |

The HALIBUT was designed and constructed as a guided missile submarine (SSGN) to launch the Regulus strategic attack missile; after that weapon was removed from service the HALIBUT was reclassified as an attack submarine (SSN) on 25 July 1965. She subsequently served as a research submarine until decommissioned on 30 June 1976. In the latter role the HALIBUT's forward missile hangar was modified for research equipment, a ducted bow thruster was provided for precise control and maneuvering, and facilities were installed aft for carrying submersibles.

Class: No additional submarines of this class were planned. An improved Regulus-armed SSGN class was planned, but those submarines were reordered as PERMIT-class submarines.

Design: The HALIBUT has a large hangar faired into her forward hull (capable of storing two Regulus II or five Regulus I missiles). In her SSGN configuration a trainable launcher was fitted between the hangar and sail structure.

Engineering: Reactor plant is similar to the SKATE-class SSNs with lower speed because of her hull shape and larger size. The HALIBUT originally was ordered as a diesel-electric submarine, but on 27 February 1956 the Navy announced that she would be provided with nuclear propulsion.

HALIBUT (1970, U.S. Navy)

The HALIBUT in San Francisco Bay. A deep submergence vehicle is on her fantail, "mated" to the submarine's aftermost hatch to permit crewmen to pass between the two while they are submerged. In the objective area the HALIBUT could launch and recover the vehicle while remaining at depth. After several years of research work the unique HALIBUT was laid up. (1970, U.S. Navy)

## 1 NUCLEAR-PROPELLED ATTACK SUBMARINE: "TRITON"

| Number | Name | FY/SCB | Builder | Laid down | Launched | Commissioned | Status |
|---|---|---|---|---|---|---|---|
| SSN 586 | TRITON | 56/132 | General Dynamics (Electric Boat) | 29 May 1956 | 19 Aug 1958 | 10 Nov 1959 | AR |

Displacement:    5,940 tons standard
6,670 tons submerged
Length:    447½ feet (136.3 m) oa
Beam:    37 feet (11.3 m)
Draft:    24 feet (7.3 m)
Propulsion:    steam turbines (General Electric); ~34,000 shp; 2 shafts
Reactors:    2 pressurized-water S4G
Speed:    27 knots surface
20+ knots submerged
Complement:

Torpedo tubes:    6 21-inch (533-mm) (4 bow + 2 stern)
ASW weapons:    torpedoes
Sonars:    BQS-4
Fire control:    1 Mk 101 Mod 11 torpedo FCS

The TRITON was designed and constructed as a radar picket submarine (SSRN) to provide early warning of aircraft attacks against a carrier task force. With the end of the radar picket program, the TRITON was reclassified as an SSN on 1 March 1961 and employed in general submarine operations until decommissioned on 3 May 1969 and placed in reserve. The TRITON was the longest U.S. submarine to be constructed until the OHIO-class SSBNs were built, almost two decades later.

Design: The TRITON is designed for high-speed surface operations. A large, retractable search radar antenna was fitted in the sail structure; in addition, a large Combat Information Center (CIC) is provided, as well as extensive communication equipment.

Engineering: This is the U.S. Navy's only two-reactor submarine, with a total shp not approached until the LOS ANGELES-class SSNs were built. The Soviet "Yankee" and "Delta" classes of SSBNs may have two-reactor plants.

Reactors: The TRITON's nuclear fuel cores were replaced from July 1962 to March 1964 after 2½ years of operation, during which time the submarine steamed more than 110,000 miles.

TRITON (U.S. Navy)

**4 NUCLEAR-PROPELLED ATTACK SUBMARINES: "SKATE" CLASS**

| Number | Name | FY/SCB | Builder | Laid down | Launched | Commissioned | Status |
|--------|------|--------|---------|-----------|----------|--------------|--------|
| SSN 578 | SKATE | 55/121 | General Dynamics (Electric Boat) | 21 July 1955 | 16 May 1957 | 23 Dec 1957 | **AA** |
| SSN 579 | SWORDFISH | 55/121 | Portsmouth Naval Shipyard | 25 Jan 1956 | 27 Aug 1957 | 15 Sep 1958 | **PA** |
| SSN 583 | SARGO | 56/121 | Mare Island Naval Shipyard | 21 Feb 1956 | 10 Oct 1957 | 1 Oct 1958 | **PA** |
| SSN 584 | SEADRAGON | 56/121 | Portsmouth Naval Shipyard | 20 June 1956 | 16 Aug 1958 | 5 Dec 1959 | **PA** |

| | |
|---|---|
| Displacement: | 2,570 tons standard |
| | 2,861 tons submerged |
| Length: | 267⁷/₁₂ feet (81.5 m) oa |
| Beam: | 25 feet (7.6 m) |
| Draft: | 21 feet (6.4 m) |
| Propulsion: | steam turbines (Westinghouse); ~15,000 shp; 2 shafts |
| Reactors: | 1 pressurized-water S3W in SSN 578 and SSN 583; S4W in SSN 579 and SSN 584 |
| Speed: | 15.5 knots surface |
| | 20+ knots submerged |
| Complement: | 108 (9 O + 99 EM) |
| Torpedo tubes: | 8 21-inch (533-mm) (6 bow + 2 stern) |
| ASW weapons: | torpedoes |
| Sonars: | BQS-4 |
| Fire control: | 1 Mk 101 Mod 19 torpedo FCS in SSN 578 and SSN 584; Mod 15 in SSN 579 and SSN 583 |

This class was the first U.S. effort to develop a production-model nuclear-propelled submarine. They are no longer considered first-line submarines and soon will reach the end of their effective service life.

Engineering: The nuclear plant of the SKATE class is similar to that of the NAUTILUS, but simplified with improved operation and maintenance. Differences between the S3W and the S4W are primarily in plant arrangement.

Reactors: The SKATE was provided with a new fuel core in early 1961 after three years of operation, during which time she steamed 120,862 miles.

SWORDFISH (1970, U.S. Navy)

## 1 NUCLEAR-PROPELLED RESEARCH SUBMARINE: "SEAWOLF"

| Number | Name | FY/SCB | Builder | Laid down | Launched | Commissioned | Status |
|--------|------|--------|---------|-----------|----------|--------------|--------|
| SSN 575 | SEAWOLF | 52/64A | General Dynamics (Electric Boat) | 15 Sep 1953 | 21 July 1955 | 30 Mar 1957 | **PA** |

Displacement: 3,720 tons standard
4,280 tons submerged
Length: 337½ feet (102.9 m) oa
Beam: 27¾ feet (8.4 m)
Draft: 22 feet (6.7 m)
Propulsion: steam turbines (General Electric); ~15,000 shp; 2 shafts
Reactors: 1 pressurized-water S2Wa
Speed: 19 knots surface
20+ knots submerged
Complement: 120 (12 O + 108 EM)

Torpedo tubes: 6 21-inch (533-mm) bow
ASW weapons: torpedoes
Sonars: BQS-4
Fire control: 1 Mk 101 Mod 8 torpedo FCS

The SEAWOLF was the world's second nuclear-propelled submarine. She was developed as a competitive prototype with the NAUTILUS, to evaluate an alternative reactor plant. She is no longer considered a first-line submarine and has been engaged in research activity since 1969. She was refitted to carry submersibles.

Engineering: As built, the SEAWOLF was fitted with the liquid-metal (sodium) S2G reactor plant. After two years of limited operations the SEAWOLF reactor plant was shut down in December 1958 and a modified NAUTILUS-type reactor plant was installed. The submarine was recommissioned on 30 September 1960.

Reactors: On her initial S2G reactor fuel core the SEAWOLF steamed 71,611 miles during a two-year period. The pressurized-water reactor core was replaced for the first time during an extended overhaul from May 1965 to August 1967, with the SEAWOLF having steamed more than 161,000 on her original S2Wa core.

SEAWOLF (1974, William Whalen, Jr.)

## 1 NUCLEAR-PROPELLED ATTACK SUBMARINE: "NAUTILUS"

| Number | Name | FY/SCB | Builder | Laid down | Launched | Commissioned | Status |
|--------|------|--------|---------|-----------|----------|--------------|--------|
| SSN 571 | ●NAUTILUS | 52/64 | General Dynamics (Electric Boat) | 14 June 1952 | 21 Jan 1954 | 30 Sep 1954 | **AA** |

Displacement: 3,530 tons standard
              4,040 tons submerged
Length:       319⁵/₁₂ feet (97.36 m) oa
Beam:         27½ feet (8.4 m)
Draft:        22 feet (6.7 m)
Propulsion:   steam turbines (Westinghouse); ~15,000 shp; 2 shafts
Reactors:     1 pressurized-water S2W
Speed:        18 knots surface
              20+ knots submerged
Complement:   120 (12 O + 108 EM)

Torpedo tubes:  6 21-inch (533-mm) bow
ASW weapons:    torpedoes
Sonars:         BQS-4
Fire control:   1 Mk 101 Mod 6 torpedo FCS

The NAUTILUS was the world's first nuclear-propelled submarine (preceding the first Soviet nuclear-propelled surface ship, the LENIN, and the "November"-class submarines by about five years). The NAUTILUS got underway on nuclear power for the first time on 17 January 1955. She is no longer considered a first-line submarine; after an extensive overhaul and modification in 1972–1974 she has been partially employed in communications research.

Design: The NAUTILUS and the five succeeding nuclear attack submarines have conventional-submarine hull forms, based on the German Type XXI and later U.S. GUPPY programs (see TANG-class listing). Although designed and constructed to evaluate nuclear propulsion in an actual ship platform, the NAUTILUS is a fully armed and combat-capable submarine, unlike the unarmed submarines ALBACORE and DOLPHIN, also built to evaluate new concepts.

Reactors: During her first two years of operation the NAUTILUS steamed 62,562 miles on her initial reactor core; she was refuelled beginning in April 1957 and steamed 91,324 miles on her second core; again refuelled May 1959–August 1960, travelling approximately 150,000 miles on her third core. She was refuelled again during overhaul from January 1964–May 1966, and again during overhaul from August 1967–December 1968.

NAUTILUS (1975, General Dynamics/Electric Boat)

NAUTILUS (1975, General Dynamics/Electric Boat)

## 3 ATTACK SUBMARINES: "BARBEL" CLASS

| Number | Name | FY/SCB | Builder | Laid down | Launched | Commissioned | Status |
|--------|------|--------|---------|-----------|----------|--------------|--------|
| SS 580 | BARBEL | 56/150 | Portsmouth Naval Shipyard | 18 May 1856 | 19 July 1958 | 17 Jan 1959 | **PA** |
| SS 581 | BLUEBACK | 56/150 | Ingalls SB Corp | 15 Apr 1957 | 16 May 1959 | 15 Oct 1959 | **PA** |
| SS 582 | BONEFISH | 56/150 | New York SB Corp | 3 June 1957 | 22 Nov 1958 | 9 July 1959 | **PA** |

| | |
|---|---|
| Displacement: | 2,145 tons standard |
| | 2,895 tons submerged |
| Length: | 219½ feet (66.9 m) oa |
| Beam: | 29 feet (8.8 m) |
| Draft: | 28 feet (8.5 m) |
| Propulsion: | 3 diesels (FM); 4,800 bhp |
| | 2 electric motors (GM); 3,150 shp; 1 shaft |
| Speed: | 15 knots surface |
| | 25 knots submerged |
| Complement: | 78 (8 O + 70 EM) |
| Torpedo tubes: | 6 21-inch (533-mm) bow |
| ASW weapons: | torpedoes |

| | |
|---|---|
| Sonars: | BQS-4 |
| Fire control: | 1 Mk 101 Mod 20 torpedo FCS |

These were the last diesel-electric combat submarines to be constructed for the U.S. Navy. They are expected to remain in service until the early 1980s.

Design: The BARBEL class has the "tear-drop" or modified spindle-hull design best suited for high-speed underwater operation. The design was tested in the research submarine ALBACORE. As built these submarines had bow-mounted diving planes; these were later fitted instead to the sail structure.

BONEFISH (1969, U.S. Navy)

## 1 GUIDED MISSILE SUBMARINE: "GROWLER"

| Number | Name | FY/SCB | Builder | Laid down | Launched | Commissioned | Status |
|--------|------|--------|---------|-----------|----------|--------------|--------|
| SSG 577 | GROWLER | 55/161 | Portsmouth Naval Shipyard | 15 Feb 1955 | 5 Apr 1957 | 30 Aug 1958 | **PR** |

| | |
|---|---|
| Displacement: | 2,540 tons standard |
| | 3,515 tons submerged |
| Length: | 317$^{7}$/$_{12}$ feet (96.8 m) oa |
| Beam: | 27$^{1}$/$_{6}$ feet (8.3 m) |
| Draft: | 19 feet (5.8 m) |
| Propulsion: | 3 diesels (FM); 4,600 bhp |
| | 2 electric motors (Elliott); 5,600 shp; 2 shafts |
| Speed: | 20 knots surface |
| | ~12 knots submerged |
| Complement: | 88 (10 O + 78 EM) |
| Missiles: | (see notes) |
| Torpedo tubes: | 6 21-inch (533-mm) (4 bow + 2 stern) |
| ASW weapons: | torpedoes |
| Sonars: | BQS-4 |
| Fire control: | 1 Mk 106 Mod 13 torpedo FCS |

The GROWLER was one of two conventionally propelled submarines built to carry the Regulus missile; her near-sister submarine the GRAYBACK has been converted to a transport submarine.

The GROWLER operated in the strategic-missile attack role from her completion until she was decommissioned on 25 May 1964 and placed in reserve. Plans to convert the GROWLER to a transport were halted because of rising ship-conversion costs.

Design: These were originally ordered as attack submarines of the DARTER class. The GRAYBACK and GROWLER were reordered in 1956 as missile submarines; their hulls were extended approximately 50 feet, and two cylindrical hangars (each 70 feet long and 11 feet high) were superimposed on their bows. They were also fitted with a launching rail located between the hangars and the sail structure, and with the necessary navigation and fire control equipment.

Missiles: As SSGs, the GRAYBACK and GROWLER were designed to carry two Regulus II strategic attack guided or "cruise" missiles; however, development of that missile was halted and from 1959 to 1964 these submarines each made nine "deterrent" patrols in the western Pacific carrying four Regulus I missiles.

The GROWLER, laid up in reserve, is the only guided missile submarine on the Navy's list. She was to have undergone conversion to a transport submarine, as did her near-sister GRAYBACK; however, Vietnam War requirements forced dropping of the project. The new Harpoon and Tomahawk missiles will be fired from SSN torpedo tubes. (U.S. Navy)

## 1 ATTACK SUBMARINE: "DARTER"

| Number | Name | FY/SCB | Builder | Laid down | Launched | Commissioned | Status |
|---|---|---|---|---|---|---|---|
| SS 576 | ●DARTER | 54/116 | General Dynamics (Electric Boat) | 10 Nov 1954 | 28 May 1956 | 20 Oct 1956 | Str. FY 1978 |

Displacement: 1,720 tons surface  
2,388 tons submerged  
Length: 268⁷/₁₂ feet (81.9 m) oa  
Beam: 27¹/₆ feet (8.3 m)  
Draft: 19 feet (5.8 m)  
Propulsion: 3 diesels (FM); 4,500 bhp  
2 electric motors (Elliott); 4,500 bhp; 2 shafts  
Speed: 19.5 knots surface  
14 knots submerged  
Complement: 87 (8 O + 79 EM)  

Torpedo tubes: 8 21-inch (533-mm) (6 bow + 2 stern)  

ASW weapons: torpedoes  
Sonars: BQS-4  
BQG-4 PUFF  
Fire control: 1 Mk 106 Mod 11 torpedo FCS  

The DARTER was built to an improved TANG-class design. This design was superseded by the improved BARBEL class before additional units could be constructed. The DARTER is to be stricken during FY 1978.

Class: The GRAYBACK and GROWLER were to have been of this class; both were completed as guided missile submarines.

DARTER (1967, Giorgio Arra)

## 1 AMPHIBIOUS TRANSPORT SUBMARINE: "GRAYBACK"

| Number | Name | FY/SCB | Builder | Laid down | Launched | SSG Comm. | LPSS Comm. | Status |
|--------|------|--------|---------|-----------|----------|-----------|------------|--------|
| SS 574 | GRAYBACK | 52/161 | Mare Island Naval Shipyard | 1 July 1954 | 2 July 1957 | 7 Mar 1958 | 9 May 1969 | **PA** |

| | |
|---|---|
| Displacement: | 2,670 tons standard |
| | 3,650 tons submerged |
| Length: | 334 feet (101.8 m) oa |
| Beam: | 30 feet (9.1 m) |
| Draft: | 19 feet (5.8 m) |
| Propulsion: | 3 diesels (FM); 4,500 bhp |
| | 2 electric motors (Elliott); 5,600 shp; 2 shafts |
| Speed: | 20 knots surface |
| | ~12 knots submerged |
| Complement: | 88 (10 O + 78 EM) |
| Troops: | 67 (7 O + 60 EM) |
| Torpedo tubes: | 8 21-inch (533-mm) (6 bow + 2 stern) |
| ASW weapons: | torpedoes |
| Sonars: | BQS-4 |
| | BQG-4 PUFF |
| Fire control: | 1 Mk 106 Mod 12 torpedo FCS |

The GRAYBACK and GROWLER were built as guided missile submarines (see latter listing for notes). The GRAYBACK operated in the strategic-missile attack role from her completion until she was decommissioned on 25 May 1964. She was subsequently converted to a transport submarine.

Classification: She was originally commissioned as a guided missile submarine (SSG). During her subsequent conversion she was listed as a transport submarine (APSS), but was formally changed to an LPSS on 30 August 1968. The GRAYBACK was reclassified as an attack submarine (SS) on 30 June 1975 for administrative purposes, but retained her transport configuration.

Conversion: The GRAYBACK was converted to a transport submarine at the San Francisco Bay Naval Shipyard (Mare Island),

from November 1967 to May 1969. She was lengthened (from 322⅓ feet) and fitted to berth and mess troops; her missile hangars were modified to "lock out" swimmers and six Swimmer Delivery Vehicles (SDV). Sail-structure height was increased and a PUFF sonar system was installed during her conversion. The conversion was No. 350.65 under the new SCB scheme.

Marines on GRAYBACK (1975, U.S. Marine Corps)

GRAYBACK (1968, U.S. Navy)

## 2 ATTACK SUBMARINES: "SAILFISH" CLASS

| Number | Name | FY/SCB | Builder | Laid down | Launched | Commissioned | Status |
|---|---|---|---|---|---|---|---|
| SS 572 | ● SAILFISH | 52/84 | Portsmouth Naval Shipyard | 8 Dec 1953 | 7 Sep 1955 | 14 Apr 1956 | Str. FY 1978 |
| SS 573 | ● SALMON | 52/84 | Portsmouth Naval Shipyard | 10 Mar 1954 | 25 Feb 1956 | 25 Aug 1956 | Str. FY 1978 |

Displacement:  2,625 tons standard
3,168 tons submerged
Length:  350½ feet (106.7 m) oa
Beam:  30 feet (9.1 m)
Draft:  18 feet (5.5 m)
Propulsion:  4 diesels (FM); 6,000 bhp
2 electric motors (Elliott); 8,200 shp; 2 shafts
Speed:  19.5 knots surface
14 knots submerged
Complement:  87 (8 O + 79 EM)

Torpedo tubes:  6 21-inch (533-mm) bow
ASW weapons:  torpedoes
Sonars:  BQS-4
BQG-4 PUFF
Fire control:  1 Mk 106 Mod 21 torpedo FCS

These submarines were built as radar pickets with large air-search radars and elaborate control centers. Along with older converted submarines and the nuclear-propelled TRITON, they were to provide warning of approaching aircraft to surface task forces. When the submarine radar picket program was abandoned in the late 1950s these submarines were employed as attack units. Both submarines were to be stricken during FY 1978.

Classification: Originally commissioned as radar picket submarines (SSR), both were changed to SS on 1 March 1961. The SALMON was reclassified as an auxiliary submarine (AGSS) on 29 June 1968 for use as test and evaluation submarine for the Deep Submergence Rescue Vehicle (DSRV), but when that program was delayed the SALMON was reclassified as SS on 30 June 1969.

Design: The hull form is designed for high surface speed in operations with surface forces. These were the largest non-nuclear submarines to be constructed for the U.S. Navy except for three "boats" completed from 1928–1930, the ARGONAUT (SM 1), and the NARWHAL class (SS 167–168).

SALMON (1976, Giorgio Arra)

SALMON (1977, Giorgio Arra)

**1 RESEARCH SUBMARINE**
**3 ATTACK SUBMARINES**    "TANG" CLASS

| Number | Name | FY/SCB | Builder | Laid down | Launched | Commissioned | Status |
|---|---|---|---|---|---|---|---|
| AGSS 563 | ●TANG | 47/2A | Portsmouth Naval Shipyard | 18 Apr 1949 | 19 June 1951 | 25 Oct 1951 | **PA** to Iran 1982 |
| SS 565 | ●WAHOO | 48/2A | Portsmouth Naval Shipyard | 24 Oct 1949 | 16 Oct 1951 | 30 May 1952 | **PA** to Iran 1980 |
| SS 566 | ●TROUT | 48/2A | Electric Boat Co, Groton | 1 Dec 1949 | 21 Aug 1951 | 27 June 1952 | **AA** to Iran 1979 |
| SS 567 | GUDGEON | 49/2A | Portsmouth Naval Shipyard | 20 May 1950 | 11 June 1952 | 21 Nov 1952 | **PA** |

| | |
|---|---|
| Displacement: | 2,100 tons standard |
| | 2,700 tons submerged |
| Length: | 287 feet (87.5 m) oa |
| Beam: | 27$\frac{1}{6}$ feet (8.3 m) |
| Draft: | 19 feet (5.8 m) |
| Propulsion: | 3 diesels (FM); 4,500 bhp |
| | 2 electric motors (see notes); 5,600 shp; 2 shafts |
| Speed: | 16 knots surface |
| | 16 knots submerged |
| Complement: | 87 (8 O + 79 EM) as SS |
| | |
| Torpedo tubes: | 8 21-inch (533-mm) (6 bow + 2 stern) |
| ASW weapons: | torpedoes |
| Sonars: | BQS-4 |
| | BQG-4 PUFF in SS 565 and SS 567 |
| Fire control: | 1 Mk 106 Mod 18 torpedo FCS |

The six units of the TANG class were the first submarines constructed for the U.S. Navy in the post-World War II period. The TANG is now employed in acoustic research. Three submarines of this class are scheduled for transfer to Iran after overhauls.

Class: The TRIGGER (SS 564) was transferred to Italy on 10 July 1973, and the HARDER (SS 568) to Italy on 15 March 1974.

Classification: The TANG was reclassified as a research submarine (AGSS) on 30 June 1975.

Conversion: The TANG was converted to an acoustic research submarine at the Mare Island Naval Shipyard from July 1975 to mid-1976.

Design: This class incorporates the hull form, large batteries, streamlined superstructure, and snorkel breathing device of the German Type XXI advanced submarines; these features also were incorporated into 52 World War II-era submarines under the GUPPY program (for Greater Underwater Propulsive Power).

Engineering: As built, the submarines of this class were 269$\frac{1}{6}$ feet long; when the TANG, TROUT, and WAHOO had their original diesels replaced, they had to be lengthened by 9 feet; all were subsequently lengthened to 287 feet. There are Elliott electric motors in the TANG, General Electric in the WAHOO and TROUT, and Westinghouse in the GUDGEON.

The WAHOO, one of three diesel-electric submarines scheduled for transfer to the Iranian Navy. The three small "fins" are sonar domes for the BQG-4 fire control system. The WAHOO will be overhauled from mid-1978 through the end of 1979, after which she probably will go to Iran. The TROUT is shown being overhauled at the Philadelphia Naval Shipyard. (1975, U.S. Navy, PH3 C. Velasquez)

TROUT (1976, U.S. Navy)

ALBACORE (U.S. Navy)

## 1 RESEARCH SUBMARINE: "ALBACORE"

| Number | Name | FY/SCB | Builder | Laid down | Launched | Comissioned | Status |
|--------|------|--------|---------|-----------|----------|-------------|--------|
| AGSS 569 | ALBACORE | 50/56 | Portsmouth Naval Shipyard | 15 Mar 1952 | 1 Aug 1953 | 5 Dec 1953 | AR |

| | |
|---|---|
| Displacement; | 1,500 tons standard |
| | 1,850 tons submerged |
| Length: | 210½ feet (64.2 m) oa |
| Beam: | 27⅓ feet (8.3 m) |
| Draft: | 18½ feet (5.6 m) |
| Propulsion: | 2 diesels (GM); 1,500 bhp |
| | 1 electric motor (Westinghouse); 15,000 shp; 1 shaft |
| Speed: | 25 knots surfaced |
| | 33 knots submerged |
| Complement: | 52 (5 O + 47 EM) |

Torpedo tubes: none

The ALBACORE was built to the so-called "tear-drop" or modified spindle-hull configuration to serve as a hydrodynamic test vehicle. At the time of her completion the ALBACORE was the fastest submarine afloat. The basic hull form was later incorporated in the BARBEL-class conventional submarines and all nuclear submarines beginning with the SKIPJACK.

After extensive testing in several configurations, the ALBACORE was decommissioned on 1 September 1972 and was then placed in reserve.

Design: The ALBACORE underwent several modifications after completion to test various configurations. (Her original length was 203¾ feet.) During the Phase III modification from November 1960 to August 1961 she was fitted with a new stern, with four stern planes arranged in an "X," a dorsal rudder, a new bow sonar dome, and a series of ten hydraulic "dive breaks" encircling the hull amidships; Phase IV modifications from December 1962 to March 1965 provided her with a high-capacity silver-zinc battery and contra-rotating propellers, revolving around the same shaft. Major modifications were SCB-182 and −182A.

## 1 RESEARCH SUBMARINE: "DOLPHIN"

| Number | Name | FY/SCB | Builder | Laid down | Launched | Commissioned | Status |
|--------|------|--------|---------|-----------|----------|--------------|--------|
| AGSS 555 | DOLPHIN | 61/207 | Portsmouth Naval Shipyard | 9 Nov 1962 | 8 June 1968 | 17 Aug 1968 | **PA** |

Displacement:  800 tons standard
               930 tons submerged
Length:        152 feet (46.3 m) oa
Beam:          $19^5/_{12}$ feet (5.9 m)
Draft:         18 feet (5.5 m)
Propulsion:    2 diesels (Detroit)
               1 electric motor (Elliott); 1,650 shp; 1 shaft

Speed:         12+ knots submerged
Complement:    24 (3 O + 21 EM); 4 to 7 scientists

Torpedo tubes: removed
Sonars:        (see notes)

The DOLPHIN is an experimental deep-diving submarine. Reportedly, she has operated at greater depths than any other operating submarines.

Design: The DOLPHIN has a constant-diameter pressure hull with an outside diameter of approximately 15 feet and hemisphere heads at both ends. An improved rudder design and other features permit maneuverability without the use of conventional submarine diving planes; there are built-in safety systems which automatically surface the submarine in an emergency, and there are few pressure-hull penetrations (e.g., only one access hatch). An experimental torpedo tube that was originally mounted was removed in 1970.

Engineering: Submerged endurance is approximately 14 hours; her endurance at sea is about 14 days.

Sonar: Various experimental sonars have been fitted in the DOLPHIN. Her original bow sonar, which had four arrays that could be extended at 90° angles to the submarine's bow-stern axis, have been removed.

DOLPHIN (U.S. Navy)

## POST-WORLD WAR II SUBMARINE PROGRAMS

United States submarine construction during World War II reached hull number SS 550 (with hulls SS 526–550 being cancelled). SS 551–562 were not used in the immediate post-war programs; subsequently five of these numbers were assigned, two of them to U.S.-financed, foreign-built submarines (Offshore Procurement). The last wartime submarine on the Navy Register was the transport submarine SEALION (LPSS 315), decommissioned and laid up in 1970, and stricken on 15 March 1977.

All post-war U.S. submarines have been numbered in the same series except for three small hunter-killer submarines (SSK) and three training submarines (SST), which are in separate series.

| | | |
|---|---|---|
| SS 551 | BASS (ex-K 2/SSK 2) | stricken 1 Apr 1965 |
| SS 552 | BONITA (ex-K 3/SSK 3) | stricken 1 Apr 1965 |
| SS 553 | (KINN) | Norway OSP 1964 |
| SS 554 | (SPRINGEREN) | Denmark OSP 1964 |
| SS 555 | DOLPHIN | |
| SS 556–562 | Not used | |
| SS 563–568 | TANG class | |
| AGSS 569 | ALBACORE | |
| AGSS 570 | completed as SST 1 | |
| SSN 571 | NAUTILUS | |
| SSN 572–573 | SAILFISH class | |
| SSG 574 | GRAYBACK | to LPSS 574 |
| SSN 575 | SEAWOLF | |
| SS 576 | DARTER | |
| SSG 577 | GROWLER | |
| SSN 578–579 | SKATE class | |
| SS 580–582 | BARBEL class | |
| SSN 583–584 | SKATE class | |
| SSN 585 | SKIPJACK | |
| SSRN 586 | TRITON | to SSN 586 |
| SSGN 587 | HALIBUT | to SSN 587 |
| SSN 588–592 | SKIPJACK class | |
| SSN 593 | THRESHER | sunk 1963 |
| SSN 594–596 | PERMIT class (ex-THRESHER class) | |
| SSN 597 | TULLIBEE | |
| SSBN 598–602 | GEORGE WASHINGTON class | |
| SSN 603–607 | PERMIT class | |
| SSBN 608–611 | ETHAN ALLEN class | |
| SSN 612–615 | PERMIT class | |
| SSBN 616–617 | LAFAYETTE class | |
| SSBN 618 | ETHAN ALLEN class | |
| SSBN 619–620 | LAFAYETTE class | |
| SSN 621 | PERMIT class | |
| SSBN 622–636 | LAFAYETTE class | |
| SSN 637–639 | STURGEON class | |
| SSBN 640–645 | LAFAYETTE class | |
| SSN 646–653 | STURGEON class | |
| SSBN 654–659 | LAFAYETTE class | |
| SSN 660–670 | STURGEON class | |
| SSN 671 | NARWHAL | |
| SSN 672–684 | STURGEON class | |
| SSN 685 | GLENARD P. LIPSCOMB | |
| SSN 686–687 | STURGEON class | |
| SSN 688–725 | LOS ANGELES class | |
| SSBN 726–735 | OHIO class | |

### HUNTER-KILLER SUBMARINES

| | | | |
|---|---|---|---|
| SSK 1 | BARRACUDA (ex-K 1) | Comm. 1951 | to SST 3 |
| SSK 2 | BASS (ex-K 2) | Comm. 1951 | to SS 551 |
| SSK 3 | BONITA (ex-K 3) | Comm. 1952 | to SS 552 |

These were small (1,000-ton, 196-foot) hunter-killer submarines, intended to lie in wait to attack Soviet submarines off foreign ports and in narrow waterways. Several hundred were to have been produced in time of war. Originally assigned K-number "names," they were given fish names in 1955. The BASS and BONITA were reclassified as SS in 1959 for training; the BARRACUDA was changed to SST in 1959 for training.

### TRAINING SUBMARINES

| | | | |
|---|---|---|---|
| SST 1 | MACKEREL (ex-T 1) | Comm. 1953 | stricken 31 Jan 1973 |
| SST 2 | MARLIN (ex-T 2) | Comm. 1953 | stricken 31 Jan 1973 |
| SST 3 | BARRACUDA (ex-K 1/SSK 1) | | stricken 1 Oct 1973 |

The SST 1–2 were small (310-ton, 133-foot) training submarines. The MACKEREL was ordered as AGSS 570. Originally assigned T-number "names," they were given fish names in 1956.

DOLPHIN (U.S. Navy)

# 8 Aircraft Carriers

The U.S. Navy in 1978 operates ten conventional (CV) and three nuclear-propelled aircraft carriers (CVN). These are large, multi-mission ships which can operate from 80 to 95 aircraft. All have been designed since World War II, except for two MIDWAY-class ships which were completed in 1945 and 1947 and have since been extensively modernized.

One additional nuclear carrier is under construction, thus providing for a carrier force of eight conventional and four nuclear ships in the mid-1980s. At that time the FORRESTAL, the first U.S. carrier constructed after World War II, will be 30 years old. A program known as SLEP (Service Life Extension Program), to be begun in the early 1980s, will extend the service life of the post-war carriers by 10 to 15 years. It is anticipated that the SLEP modernization will require 28 months; thus, with a 12-carrier force only 11 CV/CVNs could be available at any given time, because there will always be one carrier being modified under SLEP.

Classification: Into the 1970s two principal types of aircraft carriers were in service: attack aircraft carriers (CVA/CVAN) and ASW aircraft carriers (CVS), classifications dating from 1952–1953. The last ASW carrier was decommissioned in 1974. With the phase-out of the CVS-type ships, their squadrons of fixed-wing ASW aircraft and helicopters were integrated into CVA/CVAN air wings. With assignment of these aircraft and provision of a Tactical Support Center (TSC) to direct ASW operations several ships were reclassified as multi-mission carriers (CV). However, on 30 June 1975 all other active CVA/CVANs were changed to CV/CVN, whether or not they had the ASW aircraft and the appropriate support facilities. Included in the latter change were the three MIDWAY-class ships and two HANCOCK-class ships, none of which would have ASW capability. The CV/TSC is to be installed in all 12 post-war carriers by 1979.

Names: The Navy's first aircraft carrier, the LANGLEY (CV 1), was named for an aviation pioneer who proposed a flying machine for naval use in 1898. Subsequently, aircraft carriers were named for older warships (RANGER, INTREPID) and battles (MIDWAY, SARATOGA). The FRANKLIN D. ROOSEVELT was named for the 32nd President, who died in office in 1945; the FORRESTAL for the first Secretary of Defense, who died immediately after leaving office in 1949; and the JOHN F. KENNEDY for another President who died in office in 1963. All subsequent ships have been named for public persons who died in private life, except for the CARL VINSON, the first U.S. Navy ship named for a living American since about 1800. (Mr. Vinson, a member of the House of Representatives from 1914 to 1965, was a long-time advocate of American naval power.)

**AIRCRAFT CARRIERS**

| Type | Class/Ship | Active | Bldg. | Reserve | Comm. | Aircraft |
|------|-----------|--------|-------|---------|-------|----------|
| CVN 68 | NIMITZ | 2 | 1 | — | 1975– | ~95 |
| CVN 65 | ENTERPRISE | 1 | — | — | 1961 | ~90 |
| CV 63 | KITTY HAWK | 4 | — | — | 1961–1968 | ~85 |
| CV 59 | FORRESTAL | 4 | — | — | 1955–1959 | ~85 |
| CV 41 | MIDWAY | 2 | — | — | 1945–1947 | ~75 |
| CV/CVA/CVS | HANCOCK | — | — | 4 | 1943–1950 | ~45–80 |
| CVS | Mod. ESSEX | — | — | 2 | 1943–1944 | ~45 |
| CVT 16 | LEXINGTON | 1 | — | — | 1943 | — |

**2 + 1 NUCLEAR-PROPELLED AIRCRAFT CARRIERS: "NIMITZ" CLASS**

| Number | Name | FY/SCB | Builder | Laid down | Launched | Commissioned | Status |
|--------|------|--------|---------|-----------|----------|--------------|--------|
| CVN 68 | NIMITZ | 67/102 | Newport News | 22 June 1968 | 13 May 1972 | 3 May 1975 | **AA** |
| CVN 69 | DWIGHT D. EISENHOWER | 70/102 | Newport News | 14 Aug 1970 | 11 Oct 1975 | 18 Oct 1977 | **AA** |
| CVN 70 | CARL VINSON | 74/102 | Newport News | 11 Oct 1975 | 1979 | 1981 | Bldg. |

Displacement: 81,600 tons standard
81,400 tons full load
93,400 tons combat load
Length: 1,040 feet (317 m) wl
1,092 feet (332.8 m) oa
Beam: 134 feet (40.8 m)
Extreme width: 252 feet (76.8 m)
Draft: 37 feet (11.3 m)
Propulsion: steam turbines; ~260,000 shp; 4 shafts
Reactors: 2 pressurized-water A4W
Speed: 30+ knots
Complement: 3,131 (142 O + 2,989 EM)
Air wing: 2,627 (304 O + 2,323 EM)

Aircraft: ~95
Catapults: 4 steam C13-1
Elevators: 4 deck edge
Missiles: 3 8-tube Sea Sparrow launchers Mk 25 BPDMS
Radars: SPS-10 surface search
SPS-43A air search
SPS-48 3-D search
SPS-58 threat warning
Fire control: 3 Mk 115 missile FCS

These are the world's largest warships. Three ships originally were proposed in the mid-1960s as replacements for the MIDWAY-class carriers. These ships have been delayed by labor shortages at the shipyard and delays in the supply of certain nuclear components. The NIMITZ was seven years from keel-laying to commissioning, compared to less than four years for the earlier, eight-reactor ENTERPRISE.

Classification: The NIMITZ and EISENHOWER were ordered as attack aircraft carriers (CVAN); they were changed to multi-mission (attack and ASW) aircraft carriers (CVN) on 30 June 1975. The VINSON was ordered as CVN.

Cost: The NIMITZ cost an estimated $1.881 billion in FY-1976 dollars; the later ships will cost in excess of $2 billion each. The FY 1977 budget provided $350 million to fund long-lead components for the CVN 71; these funds were not released by the Ford or Carter Administrations.

Design: These ships are similar in general arrangement to the KITTY HAWK class with respect to flight deck, elevator, and island-structure arrangement. Full-load displacement is the maximum load for entering port; "combat load" is with maximum amount of aviation fuel and ordnance that can be loaded at sea.

Reactors: These carriers have only two reactors, compared with eight in the first nuclear carrier, the ENTERPRISE. The initial nuclear cores in these ships have an estimated life of at least 13 years of normal operation (estimated 800,000 to one million miles).

The NIMITZ at sea with only a pair of test aircraft on the ship's broad flight deck. The NIMITZ-class design is similar to that of the KITTY HAWK, with two deck-edge elevators forward of the island superstructure and one aft; the fourth elevator is on the starboard quarter. The island, lacking conventional exhaust stacks or the SPS-32/33 "billboard" antennas of the ENTERPRISE, is small. (1975, U.S. Navy, PH1 Harold Phillips)

Striking power at sea: The nuclear-propelled aircraft carrier with her air wing of almost 100 high-performance aircraft provides a highly flexible, mobile, and capable weapons system. The NIMITZ, shown here with the nuclear propelled missile cruiser SOUTH CAROLINA (CGN 37), is the first of a class of the largest warships ever built (1975, U.S. Navy, PH1 Richard B. Clinton)

The NIMITZ with Carrier Air Wing 8 (AJ) on board. F-4 Phantom fighters are parked on the starboard quarter; fiscal limitations led to deploying the ship initially with Phantoms; later refitting is planned to provide support for the more-complex F-14 Tomcats. About one-half of the air wing can be accommodated in the hangar, with the remainder parked on the flight deck with enough clear area remaining to land or launch aircraft. (1975, U.S. Navy, JO1 Chris Christensen)

## 1 NUCLEAR-PROPELLED AIRCRAFT CARRIER: "ENTERPRISE"

| Number | Name | FY/SCB | Builder | Laid down | Launched | Commissioned | Status |
|--------|------|--------|---------|-----------|----------|--------------|--------|
| CVN 65 | ENTERPRISE | 58/160 | Newport News | 4 Feb 1958 | 24 Sep 1960 | 25 Nov 1961 | **PA** |

Displacement: 75,700 tons standard
89,600 tons full load
Length: 1,040 feet (317 m) wl
1,123 feet (342.3 m) oa
Beam: 133 feet (40.5 m)
Extreme width: 257 feet (78.3 m)
Draft: 35¾ feet (10.9 m)
Propulsion: steam turbines (Westinghouse); ~280,000 shp; 4 shafts
Reactors: 8 pressurized-water A2W
Speed: 30+ knots
Complement: 3,061 (147 O + 2,914 EM)
Air wing: 2,627 (304 O + 2,323 EM)

Aircraft: ~90
Catapults: 4 steam C13
Elevators: 4 deck edge
Missiles: 2 8-tube Sea Sparrow launchers Mk 25 BPDMS
Radars: SPS-10 surface search
SPS-12 air search
(4) SPS-32 fixed-array air search
(4) SPS-33 fixed-array 3-D search
SPS-58 threat warning
Fire control: 2 Mk 115 missile FCS

The ENTERPRISE was the world's second nuclear-propelled surface warship (preceded by the cruiser LONG BEACH). She is exceeded in size only by the NIMITZ-class carriers.

Class: The Congress provided $35 million in the FY 1960 budget to order long-lead nuclear components for a second nuclear-propelled carrier; however, the Eisenhower Administration deferred the project. The next nuclear carrier, the NIMITZ, was not ordered until 9½ years after the ENTERPRISE.

Classification: Originally an attack aircraft carrier (CVAN); changed to multimission aircraft carrier (CVN) on 30 June 1975.

Cost: The ENTERPRISE cost $451.3 million.

Design: Constructed to a modified KITTY HAWK design, the ENTERPRISE has a distinctive island superstructure because of her eight fixed array "billboard" radars, and because she has no smokestack.

Missiles: As built, the ENTERPRISE has neither missiles nor guns (except saluting battery); she was fitted with Sea Sparrow point-defence in late 1967. She is scheduled for eventual installation of three NATO Sea Sparrow Mk 29 missile launchers.

Reactors: After three years of operation, during which she steamed more than 207,000 miles, the ENTERPRISE's reactors were refueled during an overhaul from November 1964 to July 1965; the second set of cores provided about 300,000 miles of operation. A third set, which were installed from October 1969 to January 1971 are expected to fuel the ship for an estimated 10 to 13 years.

The ENTERPRISE at anchor in Hong Kong with planes of Carrier Air Wing 14 (identification letters NK). (1976, Giorgio Arra)

The ENTERPRISE was the U.S. Navy's first nuclear-propelled carrier; the second, the NIMITZ, was not completed until 14 years later. Note the distinctive shapes of her F-14 Tomcats parked around the after flight deck. The Tomcats' wings do not fold but sweep back for flight-deck parking. The ENTERPRISE was the first carrier to deploy with Tomcats. (1975, U.S. Navy, PH1 James Lumzer)

The ENTERPRISE about to replenish at sea. Nuclear-propelled ships require periodic replenishment of provisions, munitions, spare parts, and, in the case of carriers, aviation fuels. Moving into position off her starboard beam are the ammunition ship SHASTA (AE 33) and frigate BAGLEY (DE 1069). The Navy's shortage of destroyers has forced the employment of less capable frigates with carriers. (1974, U.S. Navy, PH3 Don Redden)

## 4 AIRCRAFT CARRIERS: "KITTY HAWK" CLASS

| Number | Name | FY/SCB | Builder | Laid down | Launched | Commissioned | Status |
|--------|------|--------|---------|-----------|----------|--------------|--------|
| CV 63 | KITTY HAWK | 56/127 | New York SB Corp | 27 Dec 1956 | 21 May 1960 | 29 Apr 1961 | **PA** |
| CV 64 | CONSTELLATION | 57/127A | New York Naval Shipyard | 14 Sep 1957 | 8 Oct 1960 | 27 Oct 1961 | **PA** |
| CV 66 | AMERICA | 61/127B | Newport News | 9 Jan 1961 | 1 Feb 1964 | 23 Jan 1965 | **AA** |
| CV 67 | JOHN F. KENNEDY | 63/127C | Newport News | 22 Oct 1964 | 27 May 1967 | 7 Sep 1968 | **AA** |

| | |
|---|---|
| Displacement: | 60,100 tons standard CV 63–64 |
| | 60,300 tons standard CV 66 |
| | 61,000 tons standard CV 67 |
| | 80,800 tons full load |
| Length: | 990 feet (301.8 m) wl |
| | 1,062½ feet (323.9 m) oa CV 63 |
| | 1,072½ feet (326.9 m) oa CV 64 |
| | 1,047½ feet (319.3 m) oa CV 66–67 |
| Beam: | 129½ feet (39.5 m) CV 63–64 |
| | 130 feet (39.6 m) CV 66–67 |
| Extreme width: | 249 feet (75.9 m) CV 63–64, 66 |
| | 252 feet (76.8 m) CV 67 |
| Draft: | 35¹¹/₁₂ feet (10.9 m) |
| Propulsion: | steam turbines (Westinghouse); 280,000 shp; 4 shafts |
| Boilers: | 8 1,200-psi (Foster Wheeler) |
| Speed: | 30+ knots |
| Complement: | ~2,900 (137 O + 2,765 EM) |
| Air wing: | ~2,500 (290 O + 2,200 EM) |
| Aircraft: | 85 |
| Catapults: | 4 steam C13 in CV 63–64; 3 C13 and 1 C13-1 in CV 66–67 |
| Elevators: | 4 deck edge |
| Missiles: | 2 twin launchers for Terrier SAM Mk 10 Mod 3/4 in CV 63–64, 66 |
| | 3 8-tube Sea Sparrow launchers Mk 25 BPDMS in CV 67 |

| Radars: | CV 63–64 | CV 66 | CV 67 |
|---------|----------|-------|-------|
| | SPS-10B | SPS-10F | SPS-10F |
| | SPS-30 | SPS-30 | SPS-37A |
| | SPS-37A | SPS-39 | SPS-48 |
| | SPS-39 | SPS-43A | |
| Sonars: | SQS-23 bow-mounted in CV 66 | | |
| Fire control: | CV 63–64 | CV 66 | CV 67 |
| | 4 Mk 76 Mod 1 | 3 Mk 76 Mod 3 | 3 Mk 115 |
| | 4 SPG-55A | 3 SPG-55B | |

These are improved FORRESTAL-class carriers. Construction of the KENNEDY was delayed because of debates over whether the ship should have conventional or nuclear propulsion.

Class: The KENNEDY is officially considered a separate, one-ship class. These ships often are grouped with the FORRESTAL class in force-level discussions.

Classification: All four ships were originally attack aircraft carriers (CVA); two ships were changed to multi-mission (attack and ASW) aircraft carriers (CV) when modified to operate ASW aircraft (the KITTY HAWK on 29 April 1973 and KENNEDY on 1 December 1974); the CONSTELLATION and AMERICA were changed to CV on 30 June 1975, prior to modifications.

Cost: Construction costs were: the KITTY HAWK $265.2 million, the CONSTELLATION $264.5 million, the AMERICA $248.8 million, and the KENNEDY $277 million.

Design: These ships are larger than the FORRESTAL class and have a different flight-deck arrangement; the later ships have two elevators forward of the island structure (instead of one in the FORRESTALs) and the port-side elevator is on the stern quarter (rather than on the forward end of the angled deck, as on the FORRESTAL class).

Missiles: Three ships have large Terrier launchers, with Mk 10 Mod 3 launchers on the starboard quarter and Mk 10 Mod 4 on the port quarter. They were expected to be removed and replaced by NATO Sea Sparrow point-defense launchers.

Sonar: The AMERICA and KENNEDY have bow sonar domes, but sonar is fitted only in the AMERICA—the only active U.S. carrier with sonar (also fitted in laid-up ESSEX-class ASW carriers).

The JOHN F. KENNEDY during flight operations in the North Sea. An A-6 Intruder is about to touch down. Note the squared-off stack, angled out to starboard in an attempt to divert hot exhaust fumes from the landing pattern. U.S. carriers have their hull numbers in large numerals on both sides of the island and on the forward flight deck. (1972, U.S. Navy, LT Rodney Moen)

## 4 AIRCRAFT CARRIERS: "FORRESTAL" CLASS

| Number | Name | FY/SCB | Builder | Laid down | Launched | Commissioned | Status |
|--------|------|--------|---------|-----------|----------|--------------|--------|
| CV 59 | FORRESTAL | 52/80 | Newport News | 14 July 1952 | 11 Dec 1954 | 1 Oct 1955 | **AA** |
| CV 60 | SARATOGA | 53/80 | New York Naval Shipyard | 16 Dec 1952 | 8 Oct 1955 | 14 Apr 1956 | **AA** |
| CV 61 | RANGER | 54/80 | Newport News | 2 Aug 1954 | 29 Sep 1956 | 10 Aug 1957 | **PA** |
| CV 62 | INDEPENDENCE | 55/80 | New York Naval Shipyard | 1 July 1955 | 6 June 1958 | 10 Jan 1959 | **AA** |

| | |
|---|---|
| Displacement: | 59,650 tons standard CV 59 |
| | 60,000 tons standard CV 60–62 |
| | 78,000 tons full load |
| Length: | 990 feet (301.8 m) wl |
| | 1,039 feet (316.7 m) CV 59–61 |
| | 1,046½ feet (319.0 m) CV 62 |
| Beam: | 129½ feet (38.5 m) |
| Extreme width: | 252 feet (76.8 m) CV 59–60, 62 |
| | 260 feet (79.2 m) CV 61 |
| Draft: | 37 feet (11.3 m) |
| Propulsion: | steam turbines (Westinghouse); 260,000 shp in CV 59, 280,000 shp in |
| | CV 60–62; 4 shafts |
| Boilers: | 8 615-psi (Babcock & Wilcox) CV 59 |
| | 8 1,200-psi (Babcock & Wilcox) CV 60–62 |
| Speed: | 33 knots |
| Complement: | ~2,865 (135 O + 2,730 EM) |
| Air wing: | ~2,400 (290 O + 2,100 EM) |
| Aircraft: | 85 |
| Catapults: | 2 steam C7 and 2 steam C11 in CV 59–60; 4 C7 in CV 61–62 |
| Elevators: | 4 dock odgo |
| Missiles: | 2 8-tube Sea Sparrow launchers Mk 25 BPDMS in CV 59–60 |
| | 2 8-tube NATO Sea Sparrow launchers Mk 29 IPDMS in CV 61–62 |
| Radars: | SPS-10 surface search |
| | SPS-30 height-finding |
| | SPS-43A air search |
| Fire control: | 2 Mk 91 missile FCS in CV 61–62 |
| | 2 Mk 115 missile FCS in CV 59–60 |

These were the first U.S. aircraft carriers constructed after World War II. (The only other nation to build fixed-wing aircraft carriers after the war was France, which completed the smaller CLEMEN-CEAU and FOCH in 1961 and 1963, respectively; however, Britain completed several carriers that had been started during the war years.)

Classification: The FORRESTAL and SARATOGA were ordered as large aircraft carriers (CVB); they were reclassified as attack aircraft carriers (CVA) in October 1952. Two ships were changed to multi-mission (attack and ASW) aircraft carriers (CV) when modified to operate ASW aircraft—the SARATOGA on 30 June 1972 and INDEPENDENCE on 28 February 1973; the FORRESTAL and RANGER were changed to CV on 30 June 1975, prior to modifications.

Cost: Construction costs were: the FORRESTAL $188.9 million, the SARATOGA $213.9 million, the RANGER $173.3 million, and the INDEPENDENCE $225.3 million.

Design: These ships incorporated many design features of the aborted carrier UNITED STATES (CVA 58). They were originally designed as axial (straight) deck ships; the FORRESTAL was modified during construction to the angled-deck design. As built, the FORRESTAL had two pole masts; the second mast was removed in 1967. Details differ (the first two ships have enclosed fantails).

Guns: All ships of this class were completed with eight 5-inch/54 cal DP Mk 42 single guns, fitted on sponsons. Forward sponsons were removed because of damage in heavy seas; after sponsons were removed as BPDMS installed (except the RANGER retained forward sponsons after removal of guns).

Missiles: After 5-inch guns were removed and BPDMS provided from 1967 to 1974, with the RANGER being provided a NATO Sea Sparrow system in 1977.

The first of the super carriers, the FORRESTAL, seen underway in the Mediterranean. Under current planning, about 1981 the FORRESTAL will begin a two-year modernization known as SLEP (for Service Life Extension Program) which should add 10 to 15 years to the carrier's nominal 30-year life. That could permit operation into the year 2000. (1975, U.S. Navy, PH2 James P. Kiser)

The Saratoga at sea with only six F-4 Phantoms on her broad flight deck. Note the forward position of her island superstructure, with one elevator forward and two aft, compared to later carrier classes. Her starboard elevator is at the forward edge of the angled deck. The dome at the after end of her island houses Carrier Controlled Approach (CCA) radar. (1975, U.S. Navy, PH1 Donald Deverman)

Saratoga (1975, U.S. Navy, PH1 Donald Deverman)

**2 AIRCRAFT CARRIERS: "MIDWAY" CLASS**

| Number | Name | Builder | Laid down | Launched | Commissioned | Status |
|--------|------|---------|-----------|----------|--------------|--------|
| CV 41 | MIDWAY | Newport News | 27 Oct 1943 | 20 Mar 1945 | 10 Sep 1945 | **PA** |
| CV 43 | CORAL SEA | Newport News | 10 July 1944 | 2 Apr 1946 | 1 Oct 1947 | **PA** |

| | |
|---|---|
| Displacement: | 51,000 tons standard CV 41 |
| | 52,500 tons standard CV 43 |
| | ~64,000 tons full load |
| Length: | 900 feet (274.3 m) wl |
| | 979 feet (298.4 m) oa |
| Beam: | 121 feet (36.9 m) |
| Extreme width: | 238 feet (72.5 m) |
| Draft: | 35⅓ feet (10.8 m) |
| Propulsions: | steam turbines (Westinghouse) |
| | 212,000 shp; 4 shafts |
| Boilers: | 12 565-psi (Babock & Wilcox) |
| Speed: | 33 knots |
| Complement: | 2,645 (116 O + 2,529 EM) in CV 41 |
| | 2,637 (116 O + 2,521 EM) in CV 43 |
| Air wing: | 1,946 (222 O + 1,724 EM) in CV 41 |
| | 1,738 (201 O + 1,537 EM) in CV 43 |
| Aircraft: | ~75 |
| Catapults: | 2 steam C13 in CV 41; 2 steam C11 in CV 43 |
| Elevators: | 3 deck edge |
| Guns: | 3 5-inch (127-mm) 54 cal DP Mk 39 (3 × 1) |
| Radars: | SPS-10 surface search |
| | SPS-30 height finding |
| | SPS-43 air search |
| Fire control: | 1 Mk 37 Mod 62 gun FCS |
| | 2-3 Mk 56 Mod 41/46 gun FCS |

These ships were the largest constructed by the U.S. Navy during World War II and were the first U.S. warships designed with a beam too great to permit transit through the Panama Canal locks (110 feet). The CORAL SEA is in a reduced commission status without an air wing assigned, and will not normally deploy overseas.

Class: Three additional ships of this class were planned; the CVB 44 was cancelled on 1 November 1943 and CVB 56–57 were cancelled on 28 March 1945. None had been laid down.

The FRANKLIN D. ROOSEVELT (CVB/CVA/CV 42 of this class was decommissioned and stricken on 1 October 1977.

Classification: The MIDWAY-class ships were completed as large aircraft carriers (CVB), reclassified as attack aircraft carriers (CVA) in October 1952, and changed to multi-mission aircraft carriers (CV) on 30 June 1975, although they are not fitted to operate ASW aircraft.

Design: These ships were designed to provide greater aircraft capacity and better armor protection than the earlier carriers. Their original standard displacement was 45,000 tons and full load was approximately 60,000 tons.

Guns: As built, these ships mounted 18 5-inch guns (14 in the CORAL SEA), arranged on both sides at main deck level, below flight deck. Secondary gun armament of 84 40-mm AA guns and 28 20-mm AA guns provided at completion were subsequently replaced by 3-inch AA guns in twin mounts. Guns were removed during overhauls and modernizations, leaving the present minimal 5-inch battery.

Modernization: Both of these ships have been extensively modernized, receiving enclosed (hurricane) bows, angled flight decks, and strengthened flight decks; elevators were rearranged and strengthened. The MIDWAY underwent her most extensive modernization in 1966–1970.

Names: The second ship originally was named CORAL SEA; she was renamed after death of President Franklin D. Roosevelt on 12 April 1945. The third ship was then named the CORAL SEA.

The CORAL SEA during a ship's training exercise off the California coast. The only plane on her deck is a C-1 COD cargo aircraft. As built, these ships could operate 137 World War II-era aircraft, of which the largest were 7½-ton TBM/TBF Avengers. Subsequent modernizations have considerably changed their appearance and enabled them to operate 35-ton A3D/A-3 Skywarriors. (1971, U.S. Navy)

The MIDWAY resting at anchor in a Far Eastern port. She is the only U.S. carrier ever homeported overseas, having been based at Yokosuka, Japan, since 1973. Plans to also base a carrier in Piraeus, Greece, were dropped for political reasons. The MIDWAY has an RA-3B Skywarrior from Fleet Air Reconnaissance Squadron 1 parked forward of her island; the other planes are from her own Carrier Air Wing 5. (1977, Giorgio Arra)

The MIDWAY at sea shortly after her last major modernization, from 1966 to 1970. All three ships of this class differ considerably in flight deck and island configurations. The MIDWAY has a pole mast with lattice supports forward to support an SPS-30 radar antenna; The ROOSEVELT and CORAL SEA have thick pylon masts. (1971, U.S. Navy)

**7 AIRCRAFT CARRIERS: "HANCOCK" and MODERNIZED "ESSEX" CLASSES**

| Number | Name | Builder | Laid down | Launched | Commissioned | Status |
|--------|------|---------|-----------|----------|--------------|--------|
| CVS 11 | INTREPID | Newport News | 1 Dec 1941 | 26 Apr 1943 | 16 Aug 1943 | AR |
| CVS 12 | HORNET | Newport News | 3 Aug 1942 | 29 Aug 1943 | 29 Nov 1943 | PR |
| CVT 16 | LEXINGTON | Bethlehem Steel Co | 15 July 1941 | 26 Sep 1942 | 17 Feb 1943 | **TRA** |
| CVS 20 | BENNINGTON | New York Navy Yard | 15 Dec 1942 | 26 Feb 1944 | 6 Aug 1944 | PR |
| CVA 31 | BON HOMME RICHARD | New York Navy Yard | 1 Feb 1943 | 29 Apr 1944 | 26 Nov 1944 | PR |
| CV 34 | ORISKANY | New York Navy Yard | 1 May 1944 | 13 Oct 1945 | 25 Sep 1950 | PR |
| CVS 38 | SHANGRI-LA | Norfolk Navy Yard | 15 Jan 1943 | 24 Feb 1944 | 15 Sep 1944 | AR |

| | |
|---|---|
| Displacement: | ~33,000 tons standard except |
| | 33,250 tons standard CV 34 |
| | 39,000 tons full load CVT 16 |
| | 40,000 tons full load CVS 12, 20 |
| | 42,000 tons full load CV 11, 34, 38 |
| | 44,700 tons full load CVA 31 |
| Length: | 820 feet (249.9 m) wl |
| | 890 feet (271.3 m) oa CV 12, 20, 34 |
| | 894½ feet (272.6 m) oa CV 11, 16, 31, 38 |
| Beam: | 103 feet (30.8 m) except |
| | 106½ feet (32.5 m) CV 34 |
| Extreme width: | ~195 feet (59.5 m) |
| Draft: | 31 feet (9.4 m) |
| Propulsion: | steam turbines (Westinghouse); 150,000 shp; 4 shafts |
| Boilers: | 8 565-psi (Babcock & Wilcox) |
| Speed: | 30+ knots |
| Complement: | ~2,090 (110 O + 1,980 EM) in CV/CVA |
| | ~1,615 (115 O + 1,500 EM) in CVS |
| | ~1,440 (75 O + 1,365 EM) in CVT |
| Air wing: | ~1,185 (135 O + 1,050 EM) in CV/CVA |
| | ~800 in CVS |
| Aircraft: | ~70–80 in CV/CVA |
| | ~45 in CVS |
| Catapults: | 2 steam C11 except 2 hydraulic H-8 in CVS 12, 20 |
| Elevators: | 3 elevators (2 deck edge + 1 centerline) |
| Guns: | 4 5-inch (127-mm) 38 cal DP Mk 24 (4 × 1); 2 guns in CV 34; removed from CVT 16 |
| Radars: | SPS-10 surface search |
| | SPS-12 air search in CVT 16 |
| | SPS-30 height-finding except CVT 16 |
| | SPS-43A air search |
| Sonars: | SQS-23 bow-mounted in CVS 12, 20 |
| Fire control: | 1 Mk 37 Mod 20/21 gun FCS except 2 in CV 34; none in CVT 16 |
| | 2-3 Mk 56 Mod 43 gun FCS, except removed from CV 34, CVT 16 |

These ships are the survivors of the ESSEX class constructed during World War II; five units which have been extensively modernized are known as the HANCOCK class, while the less updated HORNET and BENNINGTON are considered the modernized ESSEX class. All except the LEXINGTON are in reserve; the BENNINGTON was decommissioned on 15 January 1970; the HORNET on 26 June 1970; the BON HOMME RICHARD on 2 July 1971; the SHANGRI-LA on 30 July 1971; the INTREPID on 15 March 1974; and the ORISKANY on 30 September 1976. The LEXINGTON remains in commission as a training carrier based at Pensacola, Florida.

Aircraft: When active the ASW carriers operated air groups of two fixed-wing squadrons (with S-2 Trackers) and one helicopter squadron (with SH-3 Sea Kings), plus various detachments. No aircraft are assigned to the LEXINGTON in the CVT role, and she has no maintenance facilities.

Class: Twenty-four ESSEX-class ships were completed (CV 9–21, 31–34, 36–40, 45, 47); two started ships were cancelled at the end of World War II (CV 35, 46), while six units not yet begun were cancelled on 27 March 1945 (CV 50–55).

Classification: All ships were designated CV when built; all were reclassified as attack aircraft carriers (CVA) in October 1952; five of the above ships changed to ASW aircraft carriers (CVS): the HORNET on 27 June 1958, the BENNINGTON on 30 June 1959, the INTREPID on 31 March 1962, the LEXINGTON on 1 October 1962, the SHANGRI-LA on 30 June 1969; the LEXINGTON was again changed to a training carrier (CVT) on 1 January 1969; the ORISKANY was changed to multi-mission aircraft carrier (CV) on 30 June 1975.

Design: Original standard displacement was 27,100 tons and full-load displacement 33,000 tons. Construction of the ORISKANY was suspended from 1947 until the start of the Korean War in 1950; she was completed to a modified design.

Guns: As built these ships each had 12 5-inch guns, 68 to 72 40-mm AA guns, and 52 20-mm AA guns, except the ORISKANY, which was built with 8 5-inch guns and 28 3-inch AA guns. Those ships in commission after World War II had their AA guns removed in favor of 28 3-inch AA guns. Subsequently, the latter were removed during overhaul and modernization, until only the minimal 5-inch battery remained.

Modernization: All of these ships have been extensively modernized, receiving enclosed (hurricane) bows, angled flight decks, strengthened decks, etc.; their elevators have been rearranged and strengthened.

Sonar: SQS-23 sonar was fitted to several ASW carriers during modernization.

## POST-WORLD WAR II AIRCRAFT CARRIER PROGRAMS

U.S. World War II aircraft carrier construction programs reached hull number CVB 57 (a cancelled MIDWAY-class ship). The "heavy" aircraft carrier UNITED STATES (CVA 58) was ordered on 10 August 1948 from Newport News; laid down on 18 April 1949 and cancelled on 23 April 1949. She was to have displaced 65,000 tons standard, 80,000 tons full load; her length was 1,090 feet overall with flush deck (i.e., no angled deck and a retracting control station); she was designed with conventional steam-turbine propulsion.

The Bon Homme Richard during an UNREP evolution with the large oiler-ammunition ship Sacramento (AOE 1) and destroyer Thomason (DD 760). The 44 aircraft on her flight deck represent just over half of her air wing. The deck-edge elevator aft of the "Bonnie Dick's" island is folded upward to facilitate replenishment. Just aft of the island are two A-3 Skywarriors. (1969, U.S. Navy)

The last active ESSEX/HANCOCK-class carrier is the LEXINGTON, employed for basic training in carrier landings and takeoffs. She has no aircraft maintenance or rearming capability. She will be replaced before the end of the decade in the CVT role by the CORAL SEA and in the 1980s by the MIDWAY. The "Lex"—known as the "Blue Ghost" during World War II—is based at Pensacola, Fla. (U.S. Navy, PH2 Burns Palmer)

The BON HOMME RICHARD entering San Diego after an eight-month deployment to the Western Pacific. Her air wing has already flown ashore; an H-46 Sea Knight and a UH-2 Sea Sprite helicopter are on her flight deck. At the far left is an auxiliary submarine, going to sea from the Point Loma submarine complex. (1968, U.S. Navy)

Four ESSEX/HANCOCK-class carriers in line: From left, the SHANGRI-LA, YORKTOWN (CVS 10), ESSEX (CVS 9), and RANDOLPH (CVS 15). This group, laid up at Bayonne, New Jersey, may have been the last "division" of these ships to be assembled; during World War II as many as 16 sometimes operated together in Task Force 38/58. (1976, U.S. Navy, LT(jg) John James)

# 9 Battleships

The United States is the world's only nation to retain battleships, with the four ships of the IOWA class laid up in reserve. All four ships were in combat in the Pacific during the latter years of World War II and again in the Korean War. The NEW JERSEY was reactivated in 1968 and saw action in the Vietnam War; after one combat deployment to Vietnam, she was mothballed for the third time in 1969. The IOWA and WISCONSIN are at the Philadelphia Naval Shipyard, the NEW JERSEY and MISSOURI at the Bremerton Naval Shipyard.

Names: U.S. battleships have almost exclusively been named for States of the Union.

**4 BATTLESHIPS: "IOWA" CLASS**

| Number | Name | Builder | Laid down | Launched | Commissioned | Status |
|--------|------|---------|-----------|----------|--------------|--------|
| BB 61 | IOWA | New York Navy Yard | 27 June 1940 | 27 Aug 1942 | 22 Feb 1943 | AR |
| BB 62 | NEW JERSEY | Philadelphia Navy Yard | 16 Sep 1940 | 7 Dec 1942 | 23 May 1943 | PR |
| BB 63 | MISSOURI | New York Navy Yard | 6 Jan 1941 | 29 Jan 1944 | 11 June 1944 | PR |
| BB 64 | WISCONSIN | Philadelphia Navy Yard | 25 Jan 1941 | 7 Dec 1943 | 16 Apr 1944 | AR |

| | | | |
|---|---|---|---|
| Displacement: | 45,000 tons standard | Radars: | SG-6 surface search except removed from BB 62 |
| | 59,000 tons full load | | SPS-6 air search |
| Length: | 860 feet (262.1 m) wl | | SPS-8A height-finding except none in BB 62 |
| | 887¼ feet (270.4 m) oa except BB 62, 887⁷/₁₂ feet | | SPS-10 surface search in BB 62 |
| Beam: | 108¹/₆ feet (33 m) | | SPS-53 in BB 62 |
| Draft: | 38 feet (11.6 m) | Fire control: | 4 Mk 37 Mod 8/9/10 gun FCS |
| Propulsion: | steam turbines (General Electric in BB 61, 63; Westinghouse in BB 62, 64); 212,000 shp; 4 shafts | | 2 Mk 38 Mod 4/5 gun directors |
| | | | 1 Mk 40 Mod 1 gun director |
| Boilers: | 8 565-psi (Babcock & Wilcox) | | 1 Mk 51 Mod 2 gun director |
| Speed: | 33 knots | | 2 Mk 63 Mod 6 gun FCS |
| Complement: | ~2,860 as designed; 1,626 (70 O + 1,556 EM) in BB 62 during her Vietnam deployment, 1968–1969 | | |

| | |
|---|---|
| Guns: | 9 16-inch (406-mm) 50 cal Mk 7 Mod 0 (3 × 3) |
| | 20 5-inch (127-mm) 38 cal DP Mk 28 Mod 0/10 (10 × 2) |
| | several 40-mm AA Mk 2 (? × 4), except removed from BB 62 |

The four IOWAs were the last U.S. battleships to be constructed. (Two foreign ships were completed later, the British VANGUARD in 1946, and French JEAN BART in 1952.) In size and firepower the IOWAs were exceeded only by the Japanese battleships YAMATO and MUSASHI (~70,000 tons full load, with nine 18.1-inch guns).

After World War II three ships were mothballed in 1948–1949, while the MISSOURI was retained in reduced commission as a training ship. All four ships returned to full service in 1950–1951 for the Korean War; all were decommissioned between 1953 and 1958. The NEW JERSEY was commissioned for the third time on 6 April 1968 for the Vietnam War; she was subsequently decommissioned on 17 December 1969.

Aircraft: These ships were built with provision for three float-planes to conduct scouting and gunfire spotting, with two catapults fitted on the fantail. The catapults were removed, and helicopters were embarked, during the Korean War.

Armor: Armor was provided to protect vital areas of the ships from the enemy's 16-inch guns. The Class A steel armor belt tapers vertically from 12.1 inches to 1.62 inches; there is a lower armor belt aft of the No. 3 main battery turret which is 13.5 inches to protect the propeller shafts. Turret faces are 17 inches, turret tops are 7.25 inches, turret backs are 12 inches, barbettes have a maximum armor of 11.6 inches, second deck armor is 6 inches, and the three-level conning tower sides are 17.3 inches with roof armor of 7.25 inches.

Class: Six ships of this class were ordered; the ILLINOIS (BB 65) was cancelled on 12 August 1945 when 22 percent complete; construction of the KENTUCKY (BB 66) was halted after the war and she was cancelled on 22 January 1950 when 73.1 percent complete.

Cost: The MISSOURI cost $114,485,000; the other ships cost slightly less.

Guns: As built, these ships mounted 80 40-mm AA guns and 60 (BB 61–61) or 49 (BB 63–64) 20-mm AA guns. The 20-mm weapons were removed after World War II and the number of 40-mm guns successively reduced; all were removed from the NEW JERSEY by 1968 with only a few remaining in the other ships.

Electronics: When recommissioned in 1968 the NEW JERSEY was fitted with additional electronic warfare equipment (note modified conning tower).

The world's last active battleship, the NEW JERSEY, fires one of her 16-inch guns during a fire mission in the Vietnam War. She can easily be distinguished from her sister ships by the EW "ears" added to the forward tower during her 1968 reactivation. Note that only the No. 2 turret is trained toward the target and only one barrel is elevated (1969, U.S. Navy)

The NEW JERSEY going to sea after reactivation in 1968. She retained some of the circular ''tubs'' for 40-mm gun mounts, but those and her lighter 20-mm weapons all had been removed. Plans to replace the quad forties with twin 3-inch/50 caliber gun mounts were never executed. (1968, U.S. Navy)

Probably the most famous U.S. battleship, the MISSOURI (to starboard), rides at anchor with her sister ship IOWA in a Far Eastern port during the Korean War. The IOWA is taking aboard 5-inch cartridge cases from small craft. Both ships have lost their stern catapults, all 20-mm AA guns, and some of their quad 40-mm AA guns. (1952, U.S. Navy)

# 10 Cruisers

All active U.S. Navy cruisers are guided missile ships intended primarily to provide defense for aircraft carriers against air, missile, and submarine attacks. Three are fitted to serve as fleet flagships.

In 1978 the Navy had 27 guided-missile cruisers in active service: 7 nuclear-propelled ships (CGN) and 20 conventional ships (CG), plus one ship (the BELKNAP) being rebuilt. Two additional nuclear cruisers of the VIRGINIA class are under construction. Except for one nuclear ship and three older, converted cruisers, all large "destroyer-type" ships were formerly designated as "frigates" in the U.S. Navy (DLG/DLGN); they have no armor, accommodations for fleet commanders, etc.

The two VIRGINIA-class cruisers will be completed by the early 1980s, when the three oldest ships will be ready for retirement.

In addition to the active cruisers, there are seven World War II-era cruisers in reserve. As indicated below, with the exception of one converted CLEVELAND-class cruiser with three 6-inch guns, all 6-inch (light) and 8-inch (heavy) cruisers are laid up in reserve. The 3-inch guns are being removed from the active cruisers because they have limited effectiveness and require a great deal of maintenance. Eventually the Harpoon anti-ship missile will be fitted in the active cruiser force.

In the following table AAW indicates Talos/Terrier/Standard-ER/MR surface-to-air missile systems; ASW indicates ASROC and SQS-23/26/63 sonar; Hel. indicates that ships of that class are fitted with a helicopter hangar; and Guns indicates the largest caliber installed.

**CRUISERS**

| Type | Class/Ship | Active | Bldg. | Res. | Comm. | AAW | ASW | Hel. | Guns |
|------|-----------|--------|-------|------|-------|-----|-----|------|------|
| CGN 38 | VIRGINIA | 2 | 2 | — | 1976– | √ | √ | √ | 5-inch |
| CGN 36 | CALIFORNIA | 2 | — | — | 1974–1975 | √ | √ | — | 5-inch |
| CGN 35 | TRUXTUN | 1 | — | — | 1967 | √ | √ | √ | 5-inch |
| CG 26 | BELKNAP | 9 | — | — | 1964–1967 | √ | √ | √ | 5-inch |
| CGN 25 | BAINBRIDGE | 1 | — | — | 1962 | √ | √ | — | removed |
| CG 16 | LEAHY | 9 | — | — | 1962–1964 | √ | √ | — | removed |
| CG 10 | ALBANY | 2 | — | — | 1945–1946 | √ | √ | √ | 5-inch |
| CGN 9 | LONG BEACH | 1 | — | — | 1961 | √ | √ | — | 5-inch |
| CG 4 | Conv. CLEVELAND | 1 | — | 2 | 1944–1945 | √ | — | — | 6-inch |
| CA 139 | DES MOINES | — | — | 3 | 1948–1949 | — | — | √ | 8-inch |
| CA 73 | SAINT PAUL | — | — | 1 | 1945 | — | — | √ | 8-inch |
| CA 70 | CANBERRA | — | — | 1 | 1943 | — | — | — | 8-inch |

Classification: Most of the currently active guided missile cruisers previously were classified as guided missile frigates (CG/CGN 16–40, formerly DLG/DLGN 16–40). They were changed to the cruiser classifications on 30 June 1975. At that time the surviving guided missile light cruisers (CLG) were changed to CG; this change was confusing in that the "light" had indicated a 6-inch gun battery, which has been retained. The ten COONTZ-class (ex-DLG 6) ships were reclassified as guided missile destroyers (DDG) although they have Terrier/Standard-ER missile systems and other "cruiser" features.

Names: U.S. cruisers traditionally have been named for American cities. In 1971 the name source was changed to states, with the CALIFORNIA being named for the home state of then-President Richard Nixon (three years later, attack submarines were assigned American cities as their source). Frigate-to-cruiser classification changes of 1975 introduced "person" names to the cruiser ranks.

**2 + 2 NUCLEAR-PROPELLED GUIDED MISSILE CRUISERS: "VIRGINIA" CLASS**

| Number | Name | FY/SCB | Builder | Laid down | Launched | Commissioned | Status |
|---|---|---|---|---|---|---|---|
| CGN 38 | VIRGINIA | 70/246 | Newport News | 19 Aug 1972 | 14 Dec 1974 | 11 Sep 1976 | **AA** |
| CGN 39 | TEXAS | 71/246 | Newport News | 18 Aug 1973 | 9 Aug 1975 | 10 Sep 1977 | **AA** |
| CGN 40 | MISSISSIPPI | 72/246 | Newport News | 22 Feb 1975 | 31 July 1976 | 1978 | Bldg. |
| CGN 41 | ARKANSAS | 75/246 | Newport News | 17 Jan 1977 | | 1980 | Bldg. |

| | |
|---|---|
| Displacement: | 11,000 tons full load |
| Length: | 585 feet (178.3 m) oa |
| Beam: | 63 feet (19.2 m) |
| Draft: | 29½ feet (9.0 m) |
| Propulsion: | steam turbines; 2 shafts |
| Reactors: | 2 pressurized-water D2G |
| Speed: | 30+ knots |
| Complement: | 442 (27 O + 415 EM) |
| | |
| Helicopters: | 2 LAMPS |
| Missiles: | 2 twin Mk 26 Mod 0/1 launchers for Tartar/Standard-MR SAM (68) |
| Guns: | 2 5-inch (127-mm) 54 cal DP Mk 45 (2 × 1) |
| ASW weapons: | ASROC fired from forward Mk 26 launcher |
| | 6 12.75-inch (324-mm) torpedo tubes Mk 32 (2 × 3) |
| Radars: | SPS-40B air search |
| | SPS-48A 3-D search |
| | SPS-55 surface search |
| Sonars: | SQS-53A bow-mounted |
| Fire control: | 1 Mk 86 Mod 5 gun FCS |
| | 1 Mk 74 Mod 5 missile FCS |
| | 1 Mk 116 Mod 1 ASW FCS |
| | 2 SPG-51D radar |
| | 1 SPG-60 radar |
| | 1 SPQ-9A radar |

The first three ships of the VIRGINIA class were considerably behind schedule because of shipyard labor shortages and disagreements between the U.S. Government and the shipyard.

Class: Proposals for a fifth ship of this class (CGN 42) in the FY 1976 budget were not approved by the Congress. The strike cruiser (CSGN) design was substituted in subsequent budget requests. Early planning provided for at least 11 ships of this class to provide, along with earlier ships, four nuclear-propelled escorts for each of the four nuclear carriers. Subsequently, the FY 1980 program reintroduces the CGN 42 hull number as an "improved" VIRGINIA-class ship fitted with the Aegis electronics system.

Classification: CGN 38–40 were originally classified as frigates. (DLGN 38–40); they were changed to cruisers on 30 June 1975.

Design: These ships are of an improved CALIFORNIA class, the principal differences being the substitution of the Mk 26 ASROC for separate launchers in the earlier class, and the fitting of a helicopter hangar and elevator into the stern. These were the first U.S. combatants constructed after World War II to have the latter feature.

Electronics: These ships are designed to use the Aegis radar/fire control electronics system, including the fixed-antenna SPY-1A radars. Aegis probably will be fitted in these ships during a major overhaul, possibly during a modernization at mid-service life.

VIRGINIA (1976, Giorgio Arra)

The VIRGINIA at sea on builder's trials. While similar in size and appearance to the previous CALIFORNIA class, the later ship's Mk 26 missile launchers are vastly superior. Also, the CALIFORNIA is configured for eventual Aegis conversion and she has a stern helicopter hangar serviced by an elevator. (1976, Newport News)

TEXAS (1977, U.S. Navy, PH2 Thomas J. Baroody)

## 2 NUCLEAR-PROPELLED GUIDED MISSILE CRUISERS: "CALIFORNIA" CLASS

| Number | Name | FY/SCB | Builder | Laid down | Launched | Commissioned | Status |
|--------|------|--------|---------|-----------|----------|--------------|--------|
| CGN 36 | CALIFORNIA | 67/241 | Newport News | 23 Jan 1970 | 22 Sep 1971 | 16 Feb 1974 | **AA** |
| CGN 37 | SOUTH CAROLINA | 68/241 | Newport News | 1 Dec 1970 | 1 July 1972 | 25 Jan 1975 | **AA** |

| | |
|---|---|
| Displacement: | 10,150 tons full load |
| Length: | 596 feet (181.7 m) oa |
| Beam: | 61 feet (18.6 m) |
| Draft: | 31½ feet (9.6 m) |
| Propulsion: | 2 steam turbines; 2 shafts |
| Reactors: | 2 pressurized-water D2G |
| Speed: | 30+ knots |
| Complement: | 540 (28 O + 512 EM) |
| | |
| Missiles: | 2 single Mk 13 Mod 3 launchers for Tartar/Standard-MR SAM (80) |
| Guns: | 2 5-inch (127-mm) 54 cal DP Mk 45 (2 × 1) |
| ASW weapons: | 1 8-tube ASROC launcher Mk 16 |
| | 4 12.75-inch (324-mm) torpedo tubes Mk 32 (4 × 1 fixed) |
| Radars: | SPS-10 surface search |
| | SPS-40 air search |
| | SPS-48 3-D search |
| Sonars: | SQS-26CX bow-mounted |
| Fire control: | 1 Mk 11 Mod 13 weapons FCS |
| | 2 Mk 74 Mod 2 missile FCS |
| | 1 Mk 86 Mod 3 gun FCS |
| | 1 Mk 114 Mod 23 ASW FCS |
| | 4 SPG-51D radar |
| | 1 SPG-60 radar |
| | 1 SPQ-9A radar |

These ships were the first results of an effort to produce sufficient numbers of nuclear-propelled surface escorts to screen the planned force of nuclear-propelled aircraft carriers. No additional ships were constructed because of the subsequent VIRGINIA-class design.

Class: A third ship of this class was authorized in FY 1968, but construction was deferred because of rising costs and development of the VIRGINIA class.

Classification: Both ships originally were classified as guided-missile frigates (DLGN); they were changed to cruisers on 30 June 1975.

Cost: Estimated costs were $200 million for the CALIFORNIA and $180 million for the SOUTH CAROLINA.

Design: These ships have a large helicopter landing area aft, but no hangar or support facilities. Their SCB number is part of the new SCB series (technically 241.65).

The SOUTH CAROLINA entering port Note the "single-arm" Mk 13 missile launcher, and ASROC reload structure and launcher aft of the forward 5 inch gun mount. The two ships of this class also differ from the later VIRGINIA class by having their after 5-inch gun mount on the 01 level vice main deck. (1975, U.S. Navy, PH2 Robert Edmonson)

CALIFORNIA (1976, U.S. Navy, JO2 R. Leonard)

## 1 NUCLEAR-PROPELLED GUIDED MISSILE CRUISER: "TRUXTUN"

| Number | Name | FY/SCB | Builder | Laid down | Launched | Commissioned | Status |
|--------|------|--------|---------|-----------|----------|--------------|--------|
| CGN 35 | TRUXTUN | 62/222 | New York SB Corp | 17 June 1963 | 19 Dec 1964 | 27 May 1967 | **PA** |

Displacement: 8,200 tons standard
9,200 tons full load
Length: 564 feet (117.9 m) oa
Beam: 58 feet (17.7 m)
Draft: 31 feet (9.4 m)
Propulsion: steam turbines; ~60,000 shp; 2 shafts
Reactors: 2 pressurized-water D2G
Speed: 30+ knots
Range: 150,000 n. miles at full speed
Complement: 510 (41 O + 467 EM)

Helicopters: 1 SH-2 LAMPS
Missiles: 1 twin Mk 10 Mod 7 launcher for Terrier/Standard-ER SAM (60)
Guns: 1 5-inch (127-mm) 54 cal DP Mk 42 (1 × 1)
ASW weapons: ASROC fired from missile launcher
4 12.75-inch (324-mm) torpedo tubes Mk 32 (4 × 1 fixed)
Radars: SPS-10 surface search
SPS-40 air search
SPS-48 3-D search

Sonars: SQS-26 bow-mounted
Fire control: 1 Mk 11 Mod 1 weapons FCS
2 Mk 76 Mod 4 missile FCS
1 Mk 68 Mod 8 gun FCS
1 Mk 114 Mod 12 ASW FCS
1 SPG-53A radar
2 SPG-55B radar

The TRUXTUN was the U.S. Navy's fourth nuclear-propelled surface warship. The ship was requested by the Navy as one of seven oil-burning frigates in the FY 1962 program; however, the Congress directed that one unit be nuclear-propelled.

Classification: Originally classified as a guided missile frigate (DLGN); changed to cruiser (CGN) on 30 June 1975.

Design: The TRUXTUN was built to a modified BELKNAP-class design, with the gun and missile-launcher arrangement reversed; distinctive lattice masts replace "macks" of the oil-burning ships.

The one-of-a-kind TRUXTUN. She is named for Captain Thomas Truxton [sic], first commanding officer of the sail frigate CONSTELLATION (1797) and a hero of the War of 1812. The TRUXTUN has the same weapons, sensors, and electronics as the fossil-fuel BELKNAP-class ships, but with the arrangement of gun and missile launcher reversed. (1977, Giorgio Arra)

## 9 GUIDED MISSILE CRUISERS: "BELKNAP" CLASS

| Number | Name | FY/SCB | Builder | Laid down | Launched | Commissioned | Status |
|--------|------|--------|---------|-----------|----------|--------------|--------|
| CG 26 | BELKNAP | 61/212 | Bath Iron Works Corp | 5 Feb 1962 | 20 July 1963 | 7 Nov 1964 | **AA** |
| CG 27 | JOSEPHUS DANIELS | 61/212 | Bath Iron Works Corp | 23 Apr 1962 | 2 Dec 1963 | 8 May 1965 | **AA** |
| CG 28 | WAINWRIGHT | 61/212 | Bath Iron Works Corp | 2 July 1962 | 25 Apr 1964 | 8 Jan 1966 | **AA** |
| CG 29 | JOUETT | 62/212 | Puget Sound Naval Shipyard | 25 Sep 1962 | 30 June 1964 | 3 Dec 1966 | **PA** |
| CG 30 | HORNE | 62/212 | San Francisco Naval Shipyard | 12 Dec 1962 | 30 Oct 1964 | 15 Apr 1967 | **PA** |
| CG 31 | STERETT | 62/212 | Puget Sound Naval Shipyard | 25 Sep 1962 | 30 June 1964 | 8 Apr 1967 | **PA** |
| CG 32 | WILLIAM H. STANDLEY | 62/212 | Bath Iron Works Corp | 29 July 1963 | 19 Dec 1964 | 9 July 1966 | **AA** |
| CG 33 | FOX | 62/212 | Todd Shipyard Corp | 15 Jan 1963 | 21 Nov 1964 | 28 May 1966 | **PA** |
| CG 34 | BIDDLE | 62/212 | Bath Iron Works Corp | 9 Dec 1963 | 2 July 1965 | 21 Jan 1967 | **AA** |

| | |
|---|---|
| Displacement: | 6,570 tons standard |
| | 7,930 tons full load |
| Length: | 547 feet (166.7 m) oa |
| Beam: | 54¾ feet (16.7 m) |
| Draft: | 28¾ feet (8.7 m) |
| Propulsion: | steam turbines (GE in CGN 26–28, 32, 34; De Laval in CG 29–31, 33); 85,000 shp; 2 shafts |
| Boilers: | 4 1,050-psi (Babcock & Wilcox in CG 26–28, 32, 34; Combustion Engineering in CG 29–31, 33) |
| Speed: | 33 knots |
| Range: | 7,100 n. miles at 20 knots |
| Complement: | 418 (31 O + 387 EM) |
| | |
| Helicopters: | 1 SH-2 LAMPS |
| Missiles: | 1 twin Mk 10 Mod 7 launcher for Terrier/Standard ER SAM (60) |
| | 2 quad Mk 141 tubes for Harpoon SSM |
| Guns: | 1 5-inch (127-mm) 54 cal DP Mk 42 (1 × 1) |
| ASW weapons: | ASROC fired from missile launcher |
| | 6 12.75-inch (324-mm) torpedo tubes Mk 32 (2 × 3) |
| Radars: | SPS-10F surface search |
| | SPS-40 air search in CG 29, 31–34 |
| | SPS-43 air search in CG 26–28, 30 |
| | SPS-48 3-D search |
| Sonars: | SQS-26 bow-mounted |

| | |
|---|---|
| Fire control: | 1 Mk 11 Mod 0 weapons FCS |
| | 1 Mk 68 Mod 8 gun FCS |
| | 2 Mk 76 Mod 4/6 missile FCS |
| | 1 Mk 114 Mod 9/12 ASW FCS |
| | 1 SPG-53A radar |
| | 2 SPG-55B radar |

These are "single-end" guided missile cruisers, the final oil-burning AAW screening ships for carrier task forces. The nuclear-propelled TRUXTUN has the same weapons and sensors.

The BELKNAP was severely damaged by a collision with the carrier JOHN F. KENNEDY (CV 67) in the Ionian Sea on 22 November 1976 (with eight killed in the BELKNAP); she is being rebuilt at the Philadelphia Naval Shipyard through 1978.

Classification: Originally classified as guided missile frigates (DLG 26–34); they were changed to cruisers (CG) on 30 June 1975.

Guns: The two 3-inch Mk 34 single guns mounted in "tubs" amidships are being removed from these ships.

Missiles: The Fox was fitted in 1977 with a twin Tomahawk SSM launcher for combat tests.

Torpedoes: The Mk 32 tubes are fitted in the amidships superstructure. The two Mk 25 torpedo tubes originally fitted in the stern have been removed.

STERETT with quad Harpoon SSM launchers in place of 3-inch guns (1977, Giorgio Arra)

The WILLIAM H. STANDLEY at sea. The BELKNAP-class ships have one less missile launcher and three-quarters of the magazine capacity of the previous class (part of which must be devoted to ASROC weapons); however, the BELKNAPs have a 5-inch gun (aft), helicopter facilities, and larger sonar. The single 3-inch gun mounts shown amidships in this view have been removed. (1975, U.S. Navy)

The BAINBRIDGE is the smallest nuclear-propelled surface warship. Although originally classified as a "destroyer-type" ship (DLGN), the BAINBRIDGE has not met the long-standing U.S. Navy operational requirement for a nuclear-propelled destroyer. These views show the BAINBRIDGE after an extensive AAW modernization in 1974–1976. The ship now has a large amidships structure and a new pole mast atop the after lattice mast. The 3-inch twin gun mounts aft of the boat davits have been removed. (1977, U.S. Navy)

## 1 NUCLEAR-PROPELLED GUIDED MISSILE CRUISER: "BAINBRIDGE"

| Number | Name | FY/SCB | Builder | Laid down | Launched | Commissioned | Status |
|--------|------|--------|---------|-----------|----------|--------------|--------|
| CGN 25 | BAINBRIDGE | 56/189 | Bethlehem Steel Co (Quincy) | 15 May 1959 | 15 Apr 1961 | 6 Oct 1962 | **PA** |

Displacement: 7,600 tons standard
8,580 tons full load
Length: 550 feet (167.6 m) wl
565 feet (172.5 m) oa
Beam: 58 feet (17.7 m)
Draft: 29 feet (7.9 m)
Propulsion: steam turbines; ~60,000 shp; 2 shafts
Reactors: 2 pressurized-water D2G
Speed: 30+ knots
Range: 90,000 n. miles at full speed
Complement: ~480 (32 O + 437 EM)
Missiles: 2 twin Mk 10 Mod 5/6 launchers for Terrier/Standard-ER SAM (80)
Guns: 2 quad Mk 141 Mod 0 tubes for Harpoon SSM being installed
2 20-mm AA Mk 67 (2 × 1)
ASW weapons: 1 8-tube ASROC launcher Mk 16
6 12.75-inch (324-mm) torpedo tubes Mk 32 (2 × 3)
Radars: SPS-10D surface search
SPS-37 air search
SPS-39 3-D search
Sonars: SQS-23 bow-mounted
Fire control: 1 Mk 7 Mod 0 weapon FCS
2 Mk 63 Mod 28 gun FCS
2 Mk 76 Mod 1 missile FCS
1 Mk 111 Mod 6 ASW FCS
2 SPG-50 radar
2 SPG-55B radar

The BAINBRIDGE was the U.S. Navy's third nuclear-propelled surface ship. She differs from the later TRUXTUN in being a "double-end" missile ship, and in not having a helicopter-support capability.

Classification: Originally classified as a guided missile frigate (DLGN), she was reclassified as a cruiser on 30 June 1975.

Cost: Estimated construction cost was $163.6 million.

Guns: The two 3-inch Mk 33 twin gun mounts previously mounted in "tubs" amidships were removed in 1976; they were replaced by single-barrel 20-mm guns.

BAINBRIDGE (1977, U.S. Navy)

BAINBRIDGE (1977, U.S. Navy)

## 9 GUIDED MISSILE CRUISERS: "LEAHY" CLASS

| Number | Name | FY/SCB | Builder | Laid down | Launched | Commissioned | Status |
|--------|------|--------|---------|-----------|----------|--------------|--------|
| CG 16 | LEAHY | 58/172 | Bath Iron Works Corp | 3 Dec 1959 | 1 July 1961 | 4 Aug 1962 | **PA** |
| CG 17 | HARRY E. YARNELL | 58/172 | Bath Iron Works Corp | 31 May 1960 | 9 Dec 1961 | 2 Feb 1963 | **AA** |
| CG 18 | WORDEN | 58/172 | Bath Iron Works Corp | 19 Sep 1960 | 2 June 1962 | 3 Aug 1963 | **PA** |
| CG 19 | DALE | 59/172 | New York SB Corp | 6 Sep 1960 | 28 July 1962 | 23 Nov 1963 | **AA** |
| CG 20 | RICHMOND K. TURNER | 59/172 | New York SB Corp | 9 Jan 1961 | 6 Apr 1963 | 13 June 1964 | **AA** |
| CG 21 | GRIDLEY | 59/172 | Puget Sound Bridge & DD Co | 15 July 1960 | 31 July 1961 | 25 May 1963 | **PA** |
| CG 22 | ENGLAND | 59/172 | Todd Shipyards Corp | 4 Oct 1960 | 6 Mar 1962 | 7 Dec 1963 | **PA** |
| CG 23 | HALSEY | 59/172 | San Francisco Naval Shipyard | 26 Aug 1960 | 15 Jan 1962 | 20 July 1963 | **PA** |
| CG 24 | REEVES | 59/172 | Puget Sound Naval Shipyard | 1 July 1960 | 12 May 1962 | 15 May 1964 | **PA** |

| | |
|---|---|
| Displacement: | 5,670 tons standard |
| | 7,800 tons full load |
| Length: | 533 feet (162.5 m) oa |
| Beam: | 55 feet (16.8 m) |
| Draft: | 24½ feet (7.4 m) |
| Propulsion: | steam turbines (GE in CG 16–18, De Laval in CG 19–22, Allis-Chalmers in CG 23–24); 85,000 shp; 2 shafts |
| Boilers: | 4 1,050-psi (Babcock & Wilcox in CG 16–18, Foster Wheeler in CG 19–24) |
| Speed: | 32 knots |
| Range: | 8,000 n. miles at 20 knots |
| Complement: | ~415 (37 O + 414 EM) |
| Missiles: | 2 twin Mk 10 Mod 5/6 launchers for Terrier/Standard-ER SAM (80) |
| Guns: | removed |
| ASW weapons: | 1 8-tube ASROC launcher Mk 16 |
| | 6 12.75-inch (324-mm) torpedo tubes Mk 32 (2 × 3) |
| Radars: | SPS-10 surface search |
| | SPS-43 air search (except SPS 49 in CG 19) |
| | SPS-48 3-D search |
| Sonars: | SQS-23 bow-mounted |

| | |
|---|---|
| Fire control: | 1 Mk 11 Mod 2 weapon FCS |
| | 2 Mk 63 Mod 28 gun FCS |
| | 4 Mk 76 Mod 5/6 missile FCS |
| | 1 Mk 114 Mod 20 ASW FCS |
| | 2 SPG-50 radar |
| | 2 SPG-55B radar |

These are "double-end" missile ships; they are the smallest cruisers in the U.S. Fleet.

Classification: Originally classified as guided missile frigates (DLG 16–24), they were reclassified as cruisers (CG) on 30 June 1975.

Design: These ships introduced the "mack" structure combining masts and exhaust stacks into a streamlined structure; this was subsequently adopted for U.S. cruiser, destroyer, frigate, and amphibious command ship designs.

Guns: The two 3-inch Mk 33 twin gun mounts in "tubs" amidships are being removed from these ships.

The HARRY E. YARNELL, a "double-end" cruiser seen off Genoa. The ship is optimized for AAW with no helicopter and an SQS-23 in place of an SQS-26 sonar. The two 3-inch twin gun mounts, shown here abaft the after missile directors, have been removed because of high maintenance requirements and limited effectiveness. (1972, Giorgio Arra)

GRIDLEY (1976, Giorgio Arra)

GRIDLEY (1976, Giorgio Arra)

HALSEY (1977, Giorgio Arra)

## 2 GUIDED MISSILE CRUISERS: "ALBANY" CLASS

| Number | Name | Builder | Laid down | Launched | CA Comm. | CG Comm. | Status |
|---|---|---|---|---|---|---|---|
| CG 10 | ALBANY | Bethlehem Steel Co (Quincy) | 6 Mar 1944 | 30 June 1945 | 15 June 1946 | 3 Nov 1962 | **AA** |
| CG 11 | CHICAGO | Philadelphia Navy Yard | 28 July 1943 | 20 Aug 1944 | 1 Jan 1945 | 2 May 1964 | **PA** |

| | |
|---|---|
| Displacement: | 13,700 tons standard |
| | 17,500 tons full load |
| Length: | 664 feet (202.4 m) wl |
| | 673 feet (205.3 m) oa |
| Beam: | 70 feet (21.6 m) |
| Draft: | 27 feet (8.2 m) |
| Propulsion: | steam turbines (GE); 120,000 shp; 4 shafts |
| Boilers: | 4 565-psi (Babcock & Wilcox) |
| Speed: | 32.5 knots |
| Complement: | ~1,000 (60 O + 940 EM) |
| Flag: | 68 (10 O + 58 EM) |
| | |
| Helicopters: | utility helicopter in CG 11 |
| Missiles: | 2 twin Mk 12 Mod 1 launchers for Talos SAM (92) |
| | 2 twin Mk 11 Mod 1/2 launchers for Tartar SAM (80) |
| Guns: | 2 5-inch (127-mm) 38 cal DP Mk 24 (2 × 1) |
| ASW weapons: | 1 8-tube ASROC launcher Mk 16 |
| | 6 12.75-inch (324-mm) torpedo tubes Mk 32 (2 × 3) |
| Radars: | SPS-10C surface search |
| | SPS-30 height-finding in CG 11 |
| | SPS-43A air search |
| | SPS-48 3-D search |
| Sonars: | SQS-23 |
| Fire control: | 1 Mk 6 Mod 1/2/3 weapon FCS |
| | 2 Mk 56 Mod 43 gun FCS |
| | 4 Mk 74 Mod 1 missile FCS |
| | 2 Mk 77 Mod 2/3 missile FCS |
| | 1 Mk 111 Mod 9 ASW FCS |
| | 4 SPG-49B radar |
| | 4 SPG-51C radar |
| | 4 SPW-2B radar |

These ships were fully converted to "double-end" missile cruisers from conventional heavy cruisers; the ALBANY originally was of the OREGON CITY class (CA 122), and the CHICAGO formerly of the BALTIMORE class (CA 68). The FALL RIVER (CA 131), originally scheduled for conversion to CG 12, was replaced by the COLUMBUS, now stricken.

Aircraft: The CHICAGO retains her stern hangar and elevator; these were removed from the ALBANY during CG conversion.

Class: The COLUMBUS (CG 12, ex-CA 74), the third conversion of this class, was laid up in reserve in 1975 and stricken on 9 August 1976.

Conversion: During their missile conversion these ships were stripped down to their main deck, with all their guns and existing superstructure removed. The new superstructure is largely aluminum, with a large "mack" structure combining masts and exhaust stacks. Conversion was SCB-173.

Guns: After their conversion to missile ships these ships were not fitted with guns; they subsequently were fitted with single, open-mount 5-inch guns to provide minimal defense against low-flying subsonic aircraft and small-boat attacks.

Missiles: The original CG design provided for these ships to carry the Regulus II strategic cruise missile. After cancellation of that program in 1958 plans were developed to arm these ships with eight Polaris SLBMs; however, these weapons were not installed.

The three ALBANYs were the most extensively reconstructed cruisers of the dozen U.S. missile conversions. The ALBANY-class ships retained virtually nothing above the main deck during their CG conversion. The ALBANY was modernized (SCB-002) in 1967–1968, being fitted with NTDS, improved fire control systems, and other AAW features. (1975, Giorgio Arra)

**1 NUCLEAR-PROPELLED GUIDED MISSILE CRUISER: "LONG BEACH"**

| Number | Name | FY/SCB | Builder | Laid down | Launched | Commissioned | Status |
|--------|------|--------|---------|-----------|----------|--------------|--------|
| CGN 9 | LONG BEACH | 57/169 | Bethlehem Steel Co (Quincy) | 2 Dec 1957 | 14 July 1959 | 9 Sep 1961 | **PA** |

| | |
|---|---|
| Displacement: | 14,200 tons standard |
| | 17,350 tons full load |
| Length: | 721¼ feet (219.8 m) oa |
| Beam: | 73¼ feet (22.3 m) |
| Draft: | 29 feet (8.8 m) |
| Propulsion: | steam turbines (GE); ~80,000 shp; 2 shafts |
| Reactors: | 2 pressurized-water C1W |
| Speed: | 30+ knots |
| Range: | 90,000 n. miles at 30 knots |
| | 360,000 n. miles at 20 knots |
| Complement: | 1,060 (60 O + 1,000 EM) |
| | |
| Missiles: | 2 Twin Mk 10 Mod 1/2 launchers for Terrier/Standard-ER SAM (120) |
| | 1 twin Mk 12 Mod 0 launcher for Talos SAM (46) |
| Guns: | 2 5-inch (127-mm) 38 cal DP Mk 30 (2 × 1) |
| ASW weapons: | 1 8-tube ASROC launcher Mk 16 |
| | 6 12.75-inch (324-mm) torpedo tubes Mk 32 (2 × 3) |
| Radars: | SPS-10 surface search |
| | SPS-12 air search |
| | (4) SPS-32 fixed-array air search |
| | (4) SPS-33 fixed-array 3-D search |
| Sonars: | SQS-23 bow-mounted |
| Fire control: | 1 Mk 6 Mod 0 weapon FCS |
| | 2 Mk 56 Mod 43 gun FCS |
| | 4 Mk 76 Mod 1 missile FCS |
| | 1 Mk 77 Mod 4 missile FCS |
| | 1 Mk 111 Mod 5 ASW FCS |
| | 2 SPG-49B radar |
| | 4 SPG-55A radar |
| | 2 SPW-2B radar |

The LONG BEACH was the first U.S. cruiser to be constructed since World War II, the first nuclear-propelled surface warship, and the first warship to be built with guided missiles as the main battery.

Classification: The LONG BEACH was ordered as a guided missile light cruiser (CLGN 160) on 15 October 1956, reclassified as a guided missile cruiser (CGN 160) on 6 December 1956, and re-numbered CGN 9 on 1 July 1957.

Cost: Estimated construction cost was $332.9 million.

Design: The LONG BEACH was initially proposed as a large destroyer or "frigate" of some 7,800 tons (standard displacement); subsequently her design was enlarged to accommodate additional missile systems to take maximum advantage of the benefits of nuclear propulsion.

Engineering: The C1W reactors in the LONG BEACH are essentially the same as the A2Ws in the aircraft carrier ENTERPRISE (CVN 65). After having steamed more than 167,700 miles on her initial reactor cores, the LONG BEACH was refueled during an overhaul from August 1965 to February 1966.

Guns: As built the LONG BEACH had no guns; subsequently she was fitted with two 5-inch guns to provide minimal defense against attacks by subsonic aircraft or small craft.

Missiles: The original LONG BEACH design provided for the ship to carry the Regulus II strategic cruise missile and, after cancellation of that program in 1958, the Polaris SLBM. Neither weapon was installed (see ALBANY class).

Modernization: The LONG BEACH will undergo an extensive mid-life modernization during the late 1970s; proposals to provide her with the Aegis radar/fire control system have been dropped, since it was felt that she does not have enough service life left to justify the expenditure. Mk 26 missile launchers for the Standard-ER/SM-2 will be installed during modernization.

LONG BEACH (1967, U.S. Navy)

The LONG BEACH was the world's second nuclear-propelled surface ship, being completed two years after the Soviet nuclear icebreaker LENIN. The LONG BEACH has two Terrier SAM launchers forward; the first launcher has a two-ring, 40-missile magazine and the second, with additional height available, has a four-ring, 80-missile magazine. The long-range Talos missile launcher is aft. (U.S. Navy)

LONG BEACH (*Ships of the World*)

## 3 GUIDED MISSILE CRUISERS: CONVERTED "CLEVELAND" CLASS

| Number | Name | Builder | Laid down | Launched | CL Comm. | CLG Comm. | Status |
|--------|------|---------|-----------|----------|----------|-----------|--------|
| CG 5 | OKLAHOMA CITY | Cramp Shipbuilding (Philadelphia) | 8 Mar 1942 | 20 Feb 1944 | 22 Dec 1944 | 7 Sep 1960 | **PA** |
| CG 6 | PROVIDENCE | Bethlehem Steel Co (Quincy) | 27 July 1943 | 28 Dec 1944 | 15 May 1945 | 17 Sep 1959 | PR |
| CG 7 | SPRINGFIELD | Bethlehem Steel Co (Quincy) | 13 Feb 1943 | 9 Mar 1944 | 9 Sep 1944 | 2 July 1960 | AR |

| | |
|---|---|
| Displacement: | 10,670 tons standard |
| | 14,600 tons full load |
| Length: | 600 feet (182.9 m) wl |
| | 610$^{1}/_{12}$ feet (185.9 m) oa |
| Beam: | 66⅓ feet (20.2 m) |
| Draft: | 25 feet (7.6 m) |
| Propulsion: | steam turbines (GE); 100,000 shp; 4 shafts |
| Boilers: | 4 565-psi (Babcock & Wilcox) |
| Speed: | 31.6 knots |
| Complement: | ~1,200 |
| Flag: | 216 (50 O + 166 EM) in CG 5 |
| | |
| Helicopters: | utility helicopter embarked (no hangar) |
| Missiles: | 1 twin Mk 7 Mod 0 launcher for Talos SAM in CG 5 (46) |
| | 1 twin Mk 9 Mod 1 launcher for Terrier SAM in CG 6–7 (60) |
| Guns: | 3 6-inch (152-mm) 47 cal Mk 16 (1 × 3) |
| | 2 5-inch (127-mm) 38 cal Mk 32 (1 × 2) |
| ASW weapons: | none |
| Radars: | SPS-10C surface search |
| | SPS-30 height-finding |
| | SPS-43A air search except SPS-37 in CG 6 |
| | SPS-52 3-D search in CG 6–7 |
| Fire control: | Talos ship (CG 5) |
| | 1 Mk 2 Mod 1 weapon FCS |
| | 1 Mk 34 Mod 10 gun director |
| | 1 Mk 37 Mod 30 gun FCS |
| | 1 Mk 77 Mod 0 missile FCS |
| | 2 SPG-49A radar |
| | 2 SPW-2A radar |
| | Terrier ships (CG 6–7) |
| | 1 Mk 3 Mod 1 weapon FCS |
| | 1 Mk 34 Mod 18' gun director in CG 6; Mod 10 in CG 7 |
| | 1 Mk 37 Mod 50 gun FCS |
| | 1 Mk 73 Mod 1 missile FCS |
| | 2 SPQ-5A radar |

These ships were partially converted from CLEVELAND-class light cruisers to "single-end" missile and fleet flagships; originally three ships were converted to Talos missiles (CLG 3–5) and three to Terriers (CLG 6–8), with two of each type converted to fleet flagships.

The PROVIDENCE was decommissioned on 31 August 1973, the SPRINGFIELD on 15 June 1974; both are in reserve.

Class: The GALVESTON (CLG 3, ex-CL 93) stricken on 21 December 1973; the LITTLE ROCK (CLG 4, ex-CL 92), stricken on 22 November 1976; the TOPEKA (CLG 8, ex-CL 67) stricken on 1 December 1973.

Classification: These ships were classified as guided missile light cruisers (CLG) after being equipped with missiles. The four surviving ships became guided missile cruisers (CG) on 30 June 1975.

Conversion: These ships are partial conversions; unlike the ALBANY class, they retained much of their original superstructure and twin funnel arrangement; their after 6-inch gun turrets were replaced by a missile launcher; their forward superstructure was enlarged for flag accommodations, and only one forward 6-inch gun turret with one 5-inch gun mount was installed, in place of a second 6-inch turret. The original armament was: 12 6-inch guns, 12 5-inch guns, 28 40-mm guns, plus 20-mm AA guns. Original pole masts were replaced by elaborate lattice masts and platforms for radar, TACAN, and EW antennas. The Talos conversions were SCB-140; Terrier conversions were SCB-146A.

SPRINGFIELD (1972, U.S. Navy)

The PROVIDENCE is one of three survivors of six CLEVELAND-class (CL 55) 6-inch gun cruisers partially converted to a missile configuration. Four ships were fitted as fleet flagships and retained only one 6-inch triple gun turret; two others, now stricken, had two 6-inch turrets forward. Note that the antenna arrangements on all three remaining ships differ; the OKLAHOMA CITY and SPRINGFIELD have the large SPS-43A antenna on the forward lattice mast. (U.S. Navy)

OKLAHOMA CITY with SH-3 Sea King (1976, Giorgio Arra)

**3 HEAVY CRUISERS: "DES MOINES" CLASS**

| Number | Name | Builder | Laid down | Launched | Commissioned | Status |
|--------|------|---------|-----------|----------|--------------|--------|
| CA 134 | DES MOINES | Bethlehem Steel Co (Quincy) | 28 May 1945 | 27 Sep 1946 | 16 Nov 1948 | AR |
| CA 139 | SALEM | Bethlehem Steel Co (Quincy) | 4 June 1945 | 25 Mar 1947 | 14 May 1949 | AR |
| CA 148 | NEWPORT NEWS | Newport News | 1 Oct 1945 | 6 Mar 1947 | 29 Jan 1949 | AR |

| | |
|---|---|
| Displacement: | 17,000 tons standard |
| | 21,500 tons full load |
| Length: | 700 feet (213.4 m) wl |
| | 716½ feet (218.4 m) oa |
| Beam: | 76⅓ feet (23.3 m) |
| Draft: | 26 feet (7.9 m) |
| Propulsion: | steam turbines (GE); 120,000 shp; 4 shafts |
| Boilers: | 4 565-psi (Babcock & Wilcox) |
| Speed: | 33 knots |
| Complement: | ~1,300 in CA 148 |
| Flag: | 267 (65 O + 206 EM) in CA 148 |
| | |
| Helicopters: | utility helicopter embarked (no hangar) |
| Guns: | 9 8-inch (203-mm) 55 cal Mk 16 (3 × 3) except 8 guns in CA 148 |
| | 12 5-inch (127-mm) 38 cal DP Mk 32 (6 × 2) |
| | 16 3-inch (76-mm) 50 cal AA Mk 32 (8 × 2) except removed from CA 148 |
| ASW weapons: | none |

| Radars: | CA 134 | CA 139 | CA 148 |
|---------|--------|--------|--------|
| | SG-6 | SG-6 | SPS-6 |
| | SPS-8A | SPS-8A | SPS-8A |
| | | SPS-12 | SPS-10 |
| | | | SPS-29 |

Fire control:
CA 134
4 Mk 37/Mod 50/51/96 gun FCS
2 Mk 54 Mod 1/10 gun director
4 Mk 56 Mod 15 gun FCS
2 Mk 63 Mod 23 gun FCS
2 SPG-50 radar
CA 148
4 Mk 37 Mod 79/80/96 gun FCS
2 Mk 54 Mod 0/1 gun director
4 Mk 56 Mod 15 gun FCS

CA 139
4 Mk 37/Mod 39/84/96 gun FCS
2 Mk 54 Mod 0/1 gun director
4 Mk 56 Mod 15 gun FCS
2 Mk 63 Mod 11 gun FCS

The DES MOINES class represents the final heavy cruiser (8-inch gun) design; these are the largest conventional cruisers constructed by any navy. They were completed too late for service in World War II, but were employed extensively as fleet flagships during their active careers.

The SALEM was decommissioned on 30 January 1959, the DES MOINES on 14 July 1961, and the NEWPORT NEWS on 27 June 1975; all are in reserve.

Aircraft: The DES MOINES was completed with two stern catapults and embarked four floatplanes; the catapults were subsequently removed. All ships operated utility helicopters.

Class: Twelve ships of this class were planned: CA 134, 139–143, 148–153; nine ships were cancelled 1945–1946.

Design: The class was designed specifically to carry the 8-inch gun Mk 16; they thus needed a larger hull than previous heavy cruisers. The design is an improved version of the previous OREGON CITY (CA 122) class which, in turn, was a modification of the BALTIMORE (CA 68) class.

Guns: The principal innovation of this class was the rapid-firing 8-inch gun Mk 16, which used metal cartridge cases in place of the bagged powder charges used in all other 8-inch-gun cruisers.

As built, these ships had a secondary battery of 12 5-inch DP guns, as many as 24 3-inch AA guns, and 12 20-mm AA guns. The 20-mm weapons were quickly removed and the 3-inch guns reduced, with the SALEM and DES MOINES being mothballed with only 16 3-inch guns installed. All 3-inch guns were removed from the NEWPORT NEWS prior to her decommissioning, the last two mounts in 1973.

The NEWPORT NEWS suffered an explosion in her No. 2 main gun turret on 1 October 1972; the turret was not repaired and is inoperable (the center barrel has been removed).

Modernization: The NEWPORT NEWS has been extensively modified to serve as a fleet flagship. Major modifications were made in 1962, including installation of box-like deckhouses amidships to provide additional office and communications spaces.

NEWPORT NEWS (1967, U.S. Navy)

The NEWPORT NEWS was the U.S. Navy's last active all-gun cruiser. This was her final configuration, with her second 8-inch gun turret "frozen" and the center barrel removed. Ships of the DES MOINES class can be easily distinguished from earlier cruisers by their greater size and tall fire control towers. (Wright & Logan)

The DES MOINES as photographed during the 1960s with several 3-inch twin gun mounts still installed (note "tubs" overhaping stern), and HUP "hupmobile" helicopters and ship's boats on her fantail. The DES MOINES has a large, "bee-hive" TACAN pod on her forward mast; the 1973 view of the NEWPORT NEWS shows an improved, smaller TACAN. (U.S. Navy)

## 1 HEAVY CRUISER: "BALTIMORE" CLASS

| Number | Name | Builder | Laid down | Launched | Commissioned | Status |
|---|---|---|---|---|---|---|
| CA 73 | SAINT PAUL | Bethlehem Steel Co (Quincy) | 3 Feb 1943 | 16 Sep 1944 | 17 Feb 1945 | PR |

Displacement: 13,600 tons standard
17,200 tons full load
Length: 664 feet (204.4 m) wl
673½ feet (205.3 m) oa
Beam: 70⅚ feet (21.6 m)
Draft: 26 feet (7.9 m)
Propulsion: steam turbines (GE); 120,000 shp; 4 shafts
Boilers: 4 565-psi (Babcock & Wilcox)
Speed: 33 knots
Complement: 1,146 (61 O + 1,085 EM); designed wartime 1,969
Flag: 217 (37 O + 180 EM)

Guns: 9 8-inch (203-mm) 55 cal Mk 15 (3 × 3)
10 5-inch (127-mm) 38 cal DP Mk 32 (5 × 2)
12 3-inch (76-mm) 50 cal AA Mk 33 (6 × 2)
ASW weapons: none
Radars: SPS-8A height-finding
SPS-10 surface search
SPS-37 air search
Fire control: 2 Mk 34 Mod 16/17 gun director
2 Mk 37 Mod 16/17 gun FCS
4 Mk 56 Mod 15 gun FCS

The SAINT PAUL is the only cruiser of the 14-ship BALTIMORE class still having an all-gun configuration. The CANBERRA (page 82) and two of the ALBANY-class missile cruisers originally were of this class.

The SAINT PAUL was decommissioned on 30 April 1971 and placed in reserve.

Aircraft: As built, ships of this class had two stern catapults and embarked four floatplanes; their catapults were subsequently removed. Utility helicopters were embarked in post-war operations.

Class: The BALTIMORE class originally comprised hull numbers CA 68–75, 130–133, and 135–136.

Guns: As built, ships of this class had a secondary battery of 12 5-inch DP guns, 48 40-mm AA guns, and 23 20-mm AA guns. After World War II, 20 3-inch AA guns were installed in place of the lighter weapons. Later the 3-inch gun battery was reduced and the 5-inch twin mount forward of the bridge was removed.

Modernization: The SAINT PAUL has been modified with additional communications equipment and accommodations to serve as a fleet flagship.

Names: She was renamed during construction; originally she was the ROCHESTER.

SAINT PAUL (1967, U.S. Navy)

## 1 HEAVY CRUISER: "CANBERRA"

| Number | Name | Builder | Laid down | Launched | CA Comm. | CAG Comm. | Status |
|--------|------|---------|-----------|----------|----------|-----------|--------|
| CA 70 | CANBERRA | Bethlehem Steel Co (Quincy) | 3 Sep 1941 | 19 Apr 1943 | 14 Oct 1943 | 15 June 1956 | PR |

Displacement: 13,300 tons standard
17,500 tons full load
Length: 664 feet (204.4 m) wl
673½ feet (205.3 m) oa
Beam: 70⅚ feet (21.6 m)
Draft: 26 feet (7.9 m)
Propulsion: steam turbines (GE); 120,000 shp; 4 shafts
Boilers: 4 565-psi (Babcock & Wilcox)
Speed: 33 knots
Complement: 1,273 (73 O + ~1,200 EM)
Flag: 72 (10 O + 62 EM)

Guns: 6 8-inch (203-mm) 55 cal Mk 15 (2 × 3)
10 5-inch (127-mm) 38 cal DP Mk 32 (5 × 2)
8 3-inch (76-mm) 50 cal AA Mk 33 (4 × 2)
ASW weapons: none
Radars: SPS-10 surface search
SPS-30 height-finding
SPS-43A air search
Fire control: 1 Mk 1 Mod 0 weapons direction system
1 Mk 34 Mod 16 gun FCS
1 Mk 37 Mod 91 gun FCS
4 Mk 56 Mod 15 gun FCS

The CANBERRA is a former BALTIMORE-class heavy cruiser converted to a "single end" guided missile ship. (See the SAINT PAUL listing above for additional class details.) After more than two decades of service as a missile ship the CANBERRA was no longer considered suitable for service in the AAW role, even with additional modifications; she was returned to her heavy cruiser classification for a brief period before being decommissioned in 16 February 1970 and placed in reserve.

Class: The BOSTON (CA 69/CAG 1) underwent a similar conversion; she was stricken on 4 January 1974.

Classification: The CANBERRA was completed as CA 70, reclassified CAG 2 on 4 January 1952 during missile conversion, and was returned to CA 70 on 1 May 1968.

Conversion: The CANBERRA was partially converted to a missile cruiser from 1952–1956; the after 8-inch triple gun turret was removed and two twin launchers for Terrier SAMs and associated magazines were installed. (144 missiles were carried.) Her superstructure was modified with twin funnels replaced by a single stack as in later CA classes. She was fitted with related radars and fire control systems. Unlike the later CLEVELAND-class partial conversions, the CANBERRA retained 10 5-inch guns and 12 3-inch guns (the latter were later reduced). Her conversion was SCB-48.

Missiles: The Terrier missile launchers and associated fire control systems have been removed.

The CANBERRA, a "single-end" missile cruiser carrying her original heavy cruiser hull number. The decision not to update the CANBERRA and her sister ship the BOSTON (CAG 1/CA 69) led to their being briefly redesignated as CAs. The CANBERRA is named for a foreign capital to honor an Australian cruiser of that name which was sunk with several U.S. ships in the 1942 debacle off Savo Island in the Solomons campaign. (1968, U.S. Navy)

## POST-WORLD WAR II CRUISER PROGRAMS

U.S. World War II cruiser programs reached hull number CL 159 (with hulls CL 154–159 being cancelled in 1945). All heavy (CA), light (CL), and anti-aircraft (CLAA) cruisers were numbered in the same series. Only one ship was added to the cruiser list in the post-war period: the nuclear-propelled LONG BEACH, ordered as CLGN 160, changed to CGN 160, and completed as CGN 9.

### HUNTER-KILLER CRUISERS

| | | |
|---|---|---|
| CLK 1 | NORFOLK | completed as DL 1 |
| CLK 2 | NEW HAVEN | deferred 1949; cancelled 1951 |

After World War II the U.S. Navy established the classification of hunter-killer cruiser (CLK) for a planned series of small cruisers designed for ASW operations against high-speed submarines. Only one ship, the NORFOLK, was completed; classified as a frigate (DL), she was employed mainly in ASW test and evaluation (e.g., as an ASROC test ship).

## FRIGATE PROGRAMS

The frigate classifications (DL/DLG/DLGN) were established after 1951 for large destroyers which were designed to operate with fast carrier forces. In general, emphasis has been on AAW systems although some ships also had the most capable ASW systems available (i.e., large sonar, helicopter, ASROC). The hunter-killer cruiser NORFOLK was completed as the DL 1, while four MITSCHER-class ships ordered as destroyers were completed as DL 2–5.

This frigate classification was abolished on 30 June 1975, and frigate (FF/FFG) was established to indicate smaller ocean escort ships (formerly DE/DEG).

### GUIDED MISSILE CRUISERS

| | |
|---|---|
| CAG 1 | BOSTON (ex-CA 69) reverted to CA; stricken 1973 |
| CAG 2 | CANBERRA (ex-CA 70) reverted to CA |
| CLG 3–8 | Converted CLEVELAND class (CL) |
| CGN 9 | LONG BEACH (ex-CLGN/CGN 160) |
| CG 10 | ALBANY (ex-CA 123) |
| CG 11 | CHICAGO (ex-CA 135) |
| CG 12 | COLUMBUS (ex-CA 74) |
| CG 13 | BALTIMORE class; conversion cancelled |
| CG 14 | BALTIMORE class; conversion cancelled |
| CG 15 | Not used |
| CG 16–24 | LEAHY class (ex-DLG 16–24) |
| CGN 25 | BAINBRIDGE (ex-DLGN 25) |
| CG 26–34 | BELKNAP (ex-DLG 26–34) |
| CGN 35 | TRUXTUN (ex-DLGN 35) |
| CGN 36–37 | CALIFORNIA class (ex-DLGN 36–37) |
| CGN 38–40 | VIRGINIA class (ex-DLGN 38–40) |

The guided missile cruiser classifications were established in 1952 to reflect the specialized weapons and AAW role of these ships.

| | | |
|---|---|---|
| DL 1 | NORFOLK (ex-CLK 1) | commissioned 1953; stricken 1973 |
| DL 2 | MITSCHER (ex-DD 927) | converted to DDG 35 |
| DL 3 | JOHN S. MCCAIN (ex-DD 928) | converted to DDG 36 |
| DL 4 | WILLIS A. LEE (ex-DD 929) | commissioned 1954; stricken 1972 |
| DL 5 | WILKINSON (ex-DD 930) | commissioned 1954; stricken 1974 |
| DLG 6–15 | COONTZ class | to DDG 37–46 |
| DLG 16–24 | LEAHY class | to CG 16–24 |
| DLGN 25 | BAINBRIDGE | to CGN 25 |
| DLG 26–34 | BELKNAP class | to CG 26–34 |
| DLGN 35 | TRUXTUN | to CGN 35 |
| DLGN 36–37 | CALIFORNIA class | to CGN 36–37 |
| DLGN 38–40 | VIRGINIA class | to CGN 38–40 |

ALBANY (1972, Giorgio Arra)

# 11 Destroyers

The U.S. Navy destroyer force contains three basic categories of ships: (1) ships with AAW missiles and advanced ASW sensors and weapons, (2) gun-armed ships with advanced ASW systems, and (3) older all-gun ships.

In 1978 the Navy has about 65 destroyers (DD/DDG) in active service and 28 assigned to the Naval Reserve Force (NRF), the latter ships manned by composite active-reserve crews. Numerically the destroyer force, even including the NRF ships, is smaller than at any time since before World War I. Although modern frigates (FF/FFG) are larger than many destroyers, they are not as fast or as fully equipped and armed as most destroyers.

In the following table AAW indicates Terrier/Standard-ER or Tartar/Standard-MR surface-to-air missile system; ASW indicates ASROC and SQS-23/26/53 sonar; Hel. indicates helicopter facilities; and Guns indicates the largest caliber fitted in the ships.

**DESTROYERS**

| Type | Class/Ship | Active | NRF | Bldg. | Comm. | AAW | ASW | Hel. | Guns |
|------|-----------|--------|-----|-------|-------|-----|-----|------|------|
| DDG 37 | COONTZ | 10 | — | — | 1960–1961 | √ | √ | — | 5-inch |
| DDG 35 | Conv. MITSCHER | 2 | — | — | 1953 | √ | √ | — | 5-inch |
| DDG 31 | Conv. SHERMAN | 4 | — | — | 1956–1959 | √ | √ | — | 5-inch |
| DDG 2 | ADAMS | 23 | — | — | 1960–1964 | √ | √ | — | 5-inch |
| DD 963 | SPRUANCE | 10 | — | 20 | 1975–1980 | √ | √ | √ | 5-inch |
| DD 931 | Mod. SHERMAN | 8 | — | — | 1956–1959 | — | √ | — | 5-inch |
| DD 931 | SHERMAN | 5 | 1 | — | 1955–1959 | — | — | — | 5-inch |
| DD 710 | GEARING | 1 | 25 | — | 1945–1946 | — | √ | — | 5-inch |
| DD 825 | CARPENTER | — | 2 | — | 1949 | — | √ | — | 5-inch |

Note: One SHERMAN-class ship is fitted with the prototype 8-inch MCLWG for operational evaluation; the ship retains a two-gun 5-inch battery.

Names: U.S. destroyers are named for officers and enlisted personnel of the Navy and Marine Corps, secretaries of the Navy, members of Congress who have influenced naval affairs, and inventors.

### (1+) AIR-CAPABLE GUIDED MISSILE DESTROYERS

The FY 1978 budget approved by the Congress provides $310 million for the construction of a SPRUANCE-class destroyer with improved air capability, i.e., facilities for more than the two LAMPS which can be embarked in the DDG 47/DD 963 designs. It will probably be designed to operate the planned 45,000-pound Type A VSTOL aircraft. Both a partial flight-deck design (with gun/missile armament forward) and a "through-deck" design are being considered. However, even in the latter arrangement the gas-turbine exhaust stacks could not be moved; thus internal modifications would be minimal. Preliminary analysis indicates that a partial flight deck (with lower hangar connected by an elevator) could accommodate up to four Type A VSTOL aircraft, or eight LAMPS, or a combination of the two. The classifications DD 963 (AC) and DD 963(H) have been applied to this concept in planning documents.

## (16) AEGIS GUIDED MISSILE DESTROYERS

| Number | Name | FY | Commission | Status |
|--------|------|----|-----------|--------|
| DDG 47 | ........ | 78 | 1982 est. | Authorized |
| DDG 48 | ........ | 80 | | Planned |
| DDG 49 | ........ | 80 | | Planned |
| DDG 50 | ........ | 81 | | Planned |
| DDG 51 | ........ | 81 | | Planned |
| DDG 52 | ........ | 81 | | Planned |
| DDG 53 | ........ | 82 | | Planned |
| DDG 54 | ........ | 82 | | Planned |
| DDG 55 | ........ | 82 | | Planned |
| DDG 56–62 | ........ | 83–85 | | Planned |

| | |
|---|---|
| Displacement: | 8,910 tons full load |
| Length: | 563⅓ feet (171.1 m) oa |
| Beam: | 55 feet (17.6 m) |
| Draft: | |
| Propulsion: | gas turbines (General Electric); 80,000 shp; 2 shafts |
| Speed: | 30+ knots |
| Complement: | 316 (27 O + 289 EM) |
| | |
| Helicopters: | 2 LAMPS |
| Missiles: | 2 twin Mk 26 Mod 1 launchers for Standard-ER SAM (88) |
| | 8 Harpoon SSM cannisters (2 × 4) |

| | |
|---|---|
| Guns: | 2 5-inch (127-mm) 54 cal DP Mk 45 (2 × 1) |
| | 2 20-mm Phalanx CIWS Mk 15 (2 × 1) |
| ASW weapons: | ASROC fired from forward Mk 26 launcher |
| | 6 12.75-inch (324-mm) torpedo tubes Mk 32 (2 × 3) |
| Radars: | SPS-49 air search |
| | SPS-55 surface search |
| | (4) SPY-1A phased-array |
| Sonars: | SQS-53 bow-mounted |
| | TACTAS |
| Fire control: | 1 Mk 86 gun FCS |
| | 4 Mk 99 missile FCS |
| | 1 Mk 116 Mod 0 ASW FCS |
| | 1 SPQ-9A radar |

This destroyer class is intended to provide AAW and anti-ship-missile defense for aircraft carriers. Employing the SPRUANCE-class hull design, machinery, guns, and ASW systems, the DDG 47 design also has the Aegis radar/fire control system and two Mk 26 missile launchers. It will be the first combat ship to have the Aegis system.

Planning for advanced destroyers in the early 1960s had envisioned a destroyer design with a specialized ASW system (DX), and one with a AAW/ASW combination (DXG). The DX evolved into the SPRUANCE class; the DXG, which was to have had a pre-Aegis missile system, was not produced. In 1971–1972, however, the Navy developed a design for gas-turbine Aegis destroyers (DG), with funding for the lead ship planned in FY 1977. The current Aegis destroyer program proposes the funding of 16 ships through FY 1982.

Cost: The lead ship of this class is estimated to cost $930 million, and the following ships about $600 million each.

This is an artist's concept of the Aegis-configured DDG 47. Employing the SPRUANCE-class hull and machinery, the DDG 47 will carry essentially all of the weapons and sensors proposed for the strike cruiser (CSGN), which would have been about twice the size of the DDG 47. The CSGN, of course, would have been nuclear propelled, providing an essentially unlimited endurance at high speeds. The DDG 47 design provides for two 5-inch guns compared to a single 8-inch MCLWG in the CSGN design. (U.S. Navy)

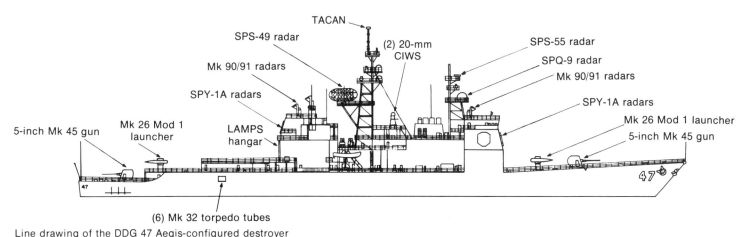

Line drawing of the DDG 47 Aegis-configured destroyer

## 10 GUIDED MISSILE DESTROYERS: "COONTZ" CLASS

| Number | Name | FY/SCB | Builder | Laid down | Launched | Commissioned | Status |
|---|---|---|---|---|---|---|---|
| DDG 37 | FARRAGUT | 56/142 | Bethlehem Steel Co (Quincy) | 3 June 1957 | 18 July 1958 | 10 Dec 1960 | **AA** |
| DDG 38 | LUCE | 56/142 | Bethlehem Steel Co (Quincy) | 1 Oct 1957 | 11 Dec 1958 | 20 May 1961 | **AA** |
| DDG 39 | MACDONOUGH | 56/142 | Bethlehem Steel Co (Quincy) | 15 Apr 1958 | 9 July 1959 | 4 Nov 1961 | **AA** |
| DDG 40 | COONTZ | 56/142 | Puget Sound Naval Shipyard | 1 Mar 1957 | 6 Dec 1958 | 15 July 1960 | **AA** |
| DDG 41 | KING | 56/142 | Puget Sound Naval Shipyard | 1 Mar 1957 | 6 Dec 1958 | 17 Nov 1960 | **AA** |
| DDG 42 | MAHAN | 56/142 | San Francisco Naval Shipyard | 31 July 1957 | 7 Oct 1959 | 25 Aug 1960 | **AA** |
| DDG 43 | DAHLGREN | 57/142 | Philadelphia Naval Shipyard | 1 Mar 1958 | 16 Mar 1960 | 8 Apr 1961 | **AA** |
| DDG 44 | WM V. PRATT | 57/142 | Philadelphia Naval Shipyard | 1 Mar 1958 | 16 Mar 1960 | 4 Nov 1961 | **AA** |
| DDG 45 | DEWEY | 57/142 | Bath Iron Works | 10 Aug 1957 | 30 Nov 1958 | 7 Dec 1959 | **AA** |
| DDG 46 | PREBLE | 57/142 | Bath Iron Works | 16 Dec 1957 | 23 May 1959 | 9 May 1960 | **PA** |

| | |
|---|---|
| Displacement: | 4,700 tons standard |
| | 5,800 tons full load |
| Length: | 512½ feet (156.2 m) oa |
| Beam: | 52½ feet (15.9 m) |
| Draft: | 25 feet (7.6 m) |
| Propulsion: | steam turbines (De Laval in DDG 37–39, 45–46; Allis-Chalmers in DDG 40–44); 85,000 shp; 2 shafts |
| Boilers: | 4 1,200-psi (Foster Wheeler in DDG 37–39; Babcock & Wilcox in DDG 40–46) |
| Speed: | 34 knots |
| Range: | 4,000+ n. miles at 20 knots |
| Complement: | 377 (21 O + 356 EM) |
| Flag: | 19 (7 O + 12 EM) |
| Missiles: | 1 twin Mk 10 Mod 0 launcher for Terrier/Standard-ER SAM (40) |
| Guns: | 1 5-inch (127-mm) 54 cal DP Mk 42 (1 × 1) |
| ASW weapons: | 1 8-tube ASROC launcher Mk 16 |
| | 6 12.75-inch (324-mm) torpedo tubes Mk 32 (2 × 3) |
| Radars: | SPS-10B surface search |
| | SPS-29 or SPS-37 air search |
| | SPS-48 3-D search |
| Sonars: | SQS-23 |
| Fire control: | 1 Mk 11 Mod 4 weapons FCS except Mk 3 Mod 3 in DDG 41 |
| | 1 Mk 68 Mod 6 gun FCS |
| | 2 Mk 76 Mod 3/7 missile FCS |
| | 1 Mk 111 Mod 8 ASW FCS |
| | 1 SPG-53A radar |
| | 2 SPG-55B radar |

These ships originally were classified as "frigates"; although they are now considered destroyers, they have the Terrier/Standard-ER missile launcher and Naval Tactical Data System (NTDS) of U.S. cruiser classes.

Classification: The first three ships of this class were ordered on 27 January 1956 as all-gun frigates (DL 6–8); they were changed to guided missile frigates (DLG 6–8) on 14 November 1956. These ships were classified as DLG 6–15 from the time of their completion until 30 June 1975 when they were changed to guided missile destroyers.

Guns: As built, these ships each had two 3-inch Mk 33 twin gun mounts in "tubs" aft of their second funnel; these were removed during AAW modernization. The KING was fitted with the Phalanx 20-mm Close-In Weapon System (CIWS) from August 1973 until March 1974 for at-sea evaluation. The CIWS was installed on her fantail.

Modernization: All ships underwent AAW modernization between 1968 and 1977 (SCB-243). Radars and fire control systems were updated; NTDS installed (updated in the KING and MAHAN); and 3-inch guns removed.

Names: The LUCE was to have been named the DEWEY; the name was changed in 1957.

The guided missile destroyer FARRAGUT at sea. The ten ships of this class were completed as "frigates" (DLG 6–15); they are the only ships to have had their hull numbers changed in the 1975 reclassification of DLG/DLGN-type ships. The FARRAGUT has an ASROC reload structure forward of the bridge; not provided in the other ships. (1975, U.S. Navy, PH3 John Barber)

COONTZ (U.S. Navy)

## 2 GUIDED MISSILE DESTROYERS: CONVERTED "MITSCHER" CLASS

| Number | Name | FY/SCB | Builder | Laid down | Launched | DL Comm. | DDG Comm. | Status |
|--------|------|--------|---------|-----------|----------|----------|-----------|--------|
| DDG 35 | MITSCHER | 48/5 | Bath Iron Works | 3 Oct 1949 | 26 Jan 1952 | 15 May 1953 | 29 June 1968 | **AA** |
| DDG 36 | ●JOHN S. McCAIN | 48/5 | Bath Iron Works | 24 Oct 1949 | 12 July 1952 | 12 Oct 1953 | 6 Sep 1969 | **PA** |

| | |
|---|---|
| Displacement: | 5,200 tons full load |
| Length: | 476 feet (145. 1m) w |
| | 493 feet (150.3 m) oa |
| Beam: | 50 feet (15.2 m) |
| Draft: | 21 feet (6.7 m) |
| Propulsion: | steam turbines (General Electric); 80,000 shp; 2 shafts |
| Boilers: | 4 600-psi (Combustion Engineering) |
| Speed: | 33 knots |
| Range: | 4,000+ n. miles at 20 knots |
| Complement: | 377 (28 O + 349 EM) |
| | |
| Missiles: | 1 single Mk 13 Mod 2 launcher for Tartar/Standard-MR SAM (40) |
| Guns: | 2 5-inch (127-mm) 54 cal DP Mk 42 (2 × 1) |
| ASW weapons: | 1 8-tube ASROC launcher Mk 16 |
| | 6 12.75-inch (324-mm) torpedo tubes Mk 32 (2 × 3) |
| Radars: | SPS-10C surface search |
| | SPS-37 air search |
| | SPS-48 3-D search |
| Sonars: | SQS-23 |
| Fire control: | 1 Mk 4 Mod 4 weapons FCS |
| | 1 Mk 67 Mod 1 gun FCS |
| | 2 Mk 74 Mod 2 missile FCS |
| | 1 Mk 114 Mod 5 ASW FCS |
| | 2 SPG-51C radars |

These ships originally were all-gun frigates; when converted to guided missile destroyers, they retained essentially their full gun armament, and had their ASW capability increased.

Class: Two additional ships of this class were not converted to missile destroyers and were stricken; see notes at the end of the previous chapter.

Classification: Both ships were ordered with destroyer hull numbers (DD), changed to destroyer leaders (DL) on 9 February 1951 while under construction, and to frigates (with same symbol) on 1 January 1955. They were again changed to DDG on 15 March 1967 during their conversion to missile ships (MITSCHER ex-DD 927, ex-DL 2; JOHN S. McCAIN ex-DD 928, ex-DL 3).

Conversion: Their conversion to Tartar system began in 1966. The basic DL configuration remained, except for replacement of original pole mast with lattice mast, installation of second lattice mast, buildup of superstructure aft of second funnel, and mounting of a Tartar launcher above the missile "drum" magazine. Conversions were SCB-241.

JOHN S. McCAIN (1976, U.S. Navy, PHAN B. R. Tronbecky)

The MITSCHER at sea with guns and ASROC launcher trained to port. ASROC reloads are in the structure between the forward gun mount and the launcher. The platform on the 02 level, between the missile directors and launcher, and the fantail are marked for vertical replenishment by helicopters, not for helicopter landings. (1973, Giorgio Arra)

## 4 GUIDED MISSILE DESTROYERS: CONVERTED "SHERMAN" CLASS

| Number | Name | FY/SCB | Builder | Laid down | Launched | DL Comm. | DDG Comm. | Status |
|--------|------|--------|---------|-----------|----------|----------|-----------|--------|
| DDG 31 | DECATUR | 54/85 | Bethlehem Steel Co (Quincy) | 13 Sep 1954 | 15 Dec 1955 | 7 Dec 1956 | 29 Apr 1967 | **PA** |
| DDG 32 | JOHN PAUL JONES | 53/85 | Bath Iron Works | 18 Jan 1954 | 7 May 1955 | 5 Apr 1956 | 23 Sep 1967 | **PA** |
| DDG 33 | PARSONS | 56/85A | Ingalls SB Corp | 17 June 1957 | 19 Aug 1958 | 29 Oct 1959 | 3 Nov 1967 | **PA** |
| DDG 34 | SOMERS | 56/85A | Bath Iron Works | 4 Mar 1957 | 30 May 1958 | 3 Apr 1959 | 10 Feb 1968 | **PA** |

| | |
|---|---|
| Displacement: | 4,150 tons full load |
| Length: | 407 feet (124 m) wl |
| | DDG 31–32 418⁵/₁₂ feet (127.5 m) oa |
| | DDG 33–34 418 feet (127.4 m) oa |
| Beam: | DDG 31–32 45¹/₆ feet (13.8 m) |
| | DDG 33–34 45 feet (13.7 m) |
| Draft: | 20 feet (6.1 m) |
| Propulsion: | steam turbines (General Electric, except Westinghouse in DDG 32); 70,000 shp; 2 shafts |
| Boilers: | 4 1,200-psi (Foster Wheeler in DDG 31, 33; Babcock & Wilcox in DDG 32, 34) |
| Speed: | 32.5 knots |
| Range: | 3,800+ n. miles at 20 knots |
| Complement: | 335 (22 O + 313 EM) |
| | |
| Missiles: | 1 single Mk 13 Mod 1 launcher for Tartar/Standard-MR SAM (40) |
| Guns: | 1 5-inch (127-mm) 54 cal DP Mk 42 (1 × 1) |
| ASW weapons: | 1 8-tube ASROC launcher Mk 16 |
| | 6 12.75-inch (324-mm) torpedo tubes Mk 32 (2 × 3) |
| Radars: | SPS-10 surface search |
| | SPS-29E air search except SPS-40 in DDG 34 |
| | SPS-48 3-D search |
| Sonars: | SQS-23 |
| Fire control: | 1 Mk 4 Mod 5 weapons FCS |
| | 1 Mk 68 Mod 9/10 gun FCS |
| | 1 Mk 74 Mod 2 missile FCS |
| | 1 Mk 114 Mod 17 ASW FCS |
| | 1 SPG-51C radar |
| | 1 SPG-53B radar |

These ships were converted from FORREST SHERMAN-class destroyers to guided missile ships. They have a credible ASW capability, but retain only one 5-inch gun; along with the larger COONTZ-class ships they are the U.S. Navy's only one-gun destroyers.

Class: Fourteen other SHERMAN-class destroyers remain in service, with the DD classification.

Classification: The DECATUR (ex-DD 936) was changed to DDG 31 on 15 September 1966; the JOHN PAUL JONES (ex-DD 932), PARSONS (ex-DD 949), and SOMERS (ex-DD 947) were changed to DDG 32–34, respectively, on 15 March 1967.

Conversion: Converted to Tartar configuration beginning in 1965–1966. The original tripod masts were replaced with lattice masts to support additional radars; ASROC and deckhouse were added aft of second funnel, two after 5-inch gun mounts were removed and a single-arm missile launcher was installed. The original DDG conversion plan provided for a Drone Antisubmarine Helicopter (DASH) facility; however, this was deleted in favor of ASROC.

Missiles: These ships have been fitted with the Mk 13 lightweight launcher, which is capable of an extremely high rate of fire (8 rounds per minute). They are limited in their firepower, however, by having only one director and associated radars, compared with the two directors found on the ADAMS class and on other U.S. missile destroyers.

The DECATUR is one of four FORREST SHERMAN-class destroyers converted to a DDG configuration. These ships are readily identified by their two large lattice masts supporting radar antennas. The ADAMS-class missile destroyers which evolved from the SHERMAN design have two 5-inch guns compared to only one gun retained in the conversions. (1972, U.S. Navy, PH3 D. L. Pierce)

PARSONS (1976, Giorgio Arra)

## 23 GUIDED MISSILE DESTROYERS: "CHARLES F. ADAMS" CLASS

| Number | Name | FY/SCB | Builder | Laid down | Launched | Commissioned | Status |
|--------|------|--------|---------|-----------|----------|--------------|--------|
| DDG 2 | CHARLES F. ADAMS | 57/155 | Bath Iron Works | 16 June 1958 | 8 Sep 1959 | 10 Sep 1960 | **AA** |
| DDG 3 | JOHN KING | 57/155 | Bath Iron Works | 25 Aug 1958 | 30 Jan 1960 | 4 Feb 1961 | **AA** |
| DDG 4 | LAWRENCE | 57/155 | New York SB Corp | 27 Oct 1958 | 27 Feb 1960 | 6 Jan 1962 | **AA** |
| DDG 5 | CLAUDE V. RICKETTS | 57/155 | New York SB Corp | 18 May 1959 | 4 June 1960 | 5 May 1962 | **AA** |
| DDG 6 | BARNEY | 57/155 | New York SB Corp | 18 May 1959 | 10 Dec 1960 | 11 Aug 1962 | **AA** |
| DDG 7 | HENRY B. WILSON | 57/155 | Defoe SB Co | 28 Feb 1958 | 23 Apr 1959 | 17 Dec 1960 | **PA** |
| DDG 8 | LYNDE McCORMICK | 57/155 | Defoe SB Co | 4 Apr 1958 | 9 Sep 1960 | 3 June 1961 | **PA** |
| DDG 9 | TOWERS | 57/155 | Todd Shipyards (Seattle) | 1 Apr 1958 | 23 Apr 1959 | 6 June 1961 | **PA** |
| DDG 10 | SAMPSON | 58/155 | Bath Iron Works | 2 Mar 1959 | 9 Sep 1960 | 24 June 1961 | **AA** |
| DDG 11 | SELLERS | 58/155 | Bath Iron Works | 3 Aug 1959 | 9 Sep 1960 | 28 Oct 1961 | **AA** |
| DDG 12 | ROBISON | 58/155 | Defoe SB Co | 23 Apr 1959 | 27 Apr 1960 | 9 Dec 1961 | **PA** |
| DDG 13 | HOEL | 58/155 | Defoe SB Co | 1 June 1960 | 4 Aug 1960 | 16 June 1962 | **PA** |
| DDG 14 | BUCHANAN | 58/155 | Todd Shipyards (Seattle) | 23 Apr 1959 | 11 May 1960 | 7 Feb 1962 | **PA** |
| DDG 15 | BERKELEY | 59/155 | New York SB Corp | 1 June 1960 | 29 July 1961 | 15 Dec 1962 | **PA** |
| DDG 16 | JOSEPH STRAUSS | 59/155 | New York SB Corp | 27 Dec 1960 | 9 Dec 1961 | 20 Apr 1963 | **PA** |
| DDG 17 | CONYNGHAM | 59/155 | New York SB Corp | 1 May 1961 | 19 May 1962 | 13 July 1963 | **AA** |
| DDG 18 | SEMMES | 59/155 | Avondale Marine Ways | 18 Aug 1960 | 20 May 1961 | 10 Dec 1962 | **AA** |
| DDG 19 | TATTNALL | 59/155 | Avondale Marine Ways | 14 Nov 1960 | 26 Aug 1961 | 13 Apr 1963 | **AA** |
| DDG 20 | GOLDSBOROUGH | 60/155 | Puget Sound Bridge & Dry Dock Co | 3 Jan 1961 | 15 Dec 1961 | 9 Nov 1963 | **PA** |
| DDG 21 | COCHRANE | 60/155 | Puget Sound Bridge & Dry Dock Co | 31 July 1961 | 18 July 1962 | 21 Mar 1964 | **PA** |
| DDG 22 | BENJAMIN STODDERT | 60/155 | Puget Sound Bridge & Dry Dock Co | 11 June 1962 | 8 Jan 1963 | 12 Sep 1964 | **PA** |
| DDG 23 | RICHARD E. BYRD | 61/155 | Todd Shipyards (Seattle) | 12 Apr 1961 | 6 Feb 1962 | 7 Mar 1964 | **AA** |
| DDG 24 | WADDELL | 61/155 | Todd Shipyards (Seattle) | 6 Feb 1962 | 26 Feb 1963 | 28 Aug 1964 | **PA** |

| | |
|---|---|
| Displacement: | 3,370 tons standard |
| | 4,500 tons full load |
| Length: | 420 feet (128 m) wl |
| | 437 feet (133.2 m) oa |
| Beam: | 47 feet (14.3 m) |
| Draft: | 20 feet (6.1 m) |
| Propulsion: | steam turbines (General Electric in DDG 2–3, 7–8, 10–13, 15–22; Westinghouse in DDG 4–6, 9, 14, 23–24); 70,000 shp; 2 shafts |
| Boilers: | 4 1,200–psi (Babcock & Wilcox in DDG 2–3, 7–8, 10–13, 20–22; Foster Wheeler in DDG 4–6, 9, 14; Combustion Engineering in DDG 15–19) |
| Speed: | 31.5 knots |
| Range: | 4,500 n. miles at 20 knots |
| Complement: | 354 (24 O + 330 EM) |
| | |
| Missiles: | 1 twin Mk 11 Mod 0 launcher for Tartar/Standard-MR SAM (42) in DDG 2–14; 1 single Mk 13 Mod 0 launcher for Tartar/Standard-MR SAM (40) in DDG 15–24 |
| Guns: | 2 5-inch (127-mm) 54 cal DP Mk 42 (2 × 1) |
| ASW weapons: | 1 8-tube ASROC launcher Mk 16 |
| | 6 12.75-inch (324-mm) torpedo tubes Mk 32 (2 × 3) |
| Radars: | SPS-10C D surface search |
| | SPS-29 or SPS-37 air search in DDG 2–14; SPS-40 in DDG 15–24 |
| | SPS-39 3-D search |
| Sonars: | SQS-23 (bow-mounted in DDG 20–24) |
| Fire control: | 1 Mk 4 Mod 0/1 weapons FCS |
| | 1 Mk 68 Mod 4 gun FCS |
| | 2 Mk 74 Mod 0/6/7 missile FCS |
| | 1 Mk 111 Mod 2 ASW FCS in DDG 2–15; Mk 114 Mod 1 in DDG 16–24 |
| | 2 SPG-51C radar |
| | 1 SPG-53A/E/F radar |

This is the largest class of missile-armed surface combatants to be built for the U.S. Navy; the ADAMS class comprises just over one-third of AAW-capable screening ships available for carrier forces.

Class: Three ships of this class were built for Australia (DDG 25–27) and three for West Germany (DDG 28–30).

Classification: The first eight ships of this class were authorized as all-gun/ASW destroyers (DD 952–959), then changed to guided missile ships and reclassified DDG 952–959 on 16 August 1956; they were changed to DDG 2–9 on 26 June 1957.

Design: The ADAMS design is an improved FORREST SHERMAN-class ship with a Tartar missile-launching system in place of the SHERMAN's aftermost 5-inch gun mount.

Modernization: The entire class is scheduled to undergo mid-life modernization; 6 ships are to be funded in FY 1980, 6 in FY 1981, 6 in FY 1982, and 5 in FY 1983. General condition of ships will be updated; existing radars will be replaced by SPS-40C/D air search, SPS-52B 3-D search, and SPS-65; Mk 86 gun FCS will be fitted, which also can serve as a missile illuminator; Mk 74 missile FCS will be upgraded to Mod 8; SPG-9 and SPG-60 fire control radars will be provided as will the Mk 13 weapons direction system; the existing sonar will be reconfigured as SQQ-23 PAIR; and the Harpoon SSM will be carried. With modernization the ships are expected to be capable of 15–20 additional years of operation.

Names : DDG 5 was originally named the BIDDLE; renamed the CLAUDE V. RICKETTS on 28 July 1964 (with DLG/CG 34 subsequently named the BIDDLE).

WADDELL (1976, Giorgio Arra)

HENRY B. WILSON (1977, Giorgio Arra)

The HENRY B. WILSON is one of the early ADAMS-class ships with an SPS-29C air search radar antenna atop the tripod mast and a twin-arm Mk 11 missile launcher aft. Note the SPS-40 antenna and single-arm Mk 13 launcher in the RICHARD E. BYRD. These ships are scheduled to be modernized to extend their useful service life to about 35 years. (1977, Giorgio Arra)

Richard E. Byrd (1973, Giorgio Arra)

Claude V. Ricketts (1973, Giorgio Arra)

**10 + 20 DESTROYERS: "SPRUANCE" CLASS**

| Number | Name | FY/SCB | Builder | Laid down | Launched | Commissioned | Status |
|--------|------|--------|---------|-----------|----------|--------------|--------|
| DD 963 | SPRUANCE | 70/224 | Litton/Ingalls (Pascagoula) | 17 Nov 1972 | 10 Nov 1973 | 20 Sep 1975 | **AA** |
| DD 964 | PAUL F. FOSTER | 70/224 | Litton/Ingalls (Pascagoula) | 6 Feb 1973 | 23 Feb 1974 | 21 Feb 1976 | **PA** |
| DD 965 | KINKAID | 70/224 | Litton/Ingalls (Pascagoula) | 19 Apr 1973 | 25 May 1974 | 10 July 1976 | **PA** |
| DD 966 | HEWITT | 71/224 | Litton/Ingalls (Pascagoula) | 23 July 1973 | 24 Aug 1974 | 25 Sep 1976 | **PA** |
| DD 967 | ELLIOTT | 71/224 | Litton/Ingalls (Pascagoula) | 15 Oct 1973 | 19 Dec 1974 | 22 Jan 1977 | **PA** |
| DD 968 | ARTHUR W. RADFORD | 71/224 | Litton/Ingalls (Pascagoula) | 14 Jan 1974 | 1 Mar 1975 | 9 Apr 1977 | **AA** |
| DD 969 | PETERSON | 71/224 | Litton/Ingalls (Pascagoula) | 29 Apr 1974 | 21 June 1975 | 9 July 1977 | **AA** |
| DD 970 | CARON | 71/224 | Litton/Ingalls (Pascagoula) | 1 July 1974 | 24 June 1975 | 1 Oct 1977 | **AA** |
| DD 971 | DAVID R. RAY | 71/224 | Litton/Ingalls (Pascagoula) | 23 Sep 1974 | 23 Aug 1975 | 19 Nov 1977 | **PA** |
| DD 972 | OLDENDORF | 72/224 | Litton/Ingalls (Pascagoula) | 27 Dec 1974 | 21 Oct 1975 | 1978 | **PA** |
| DD 973 | JOHN YOUNG | 72/224 | Litton/Ingalls (Pascagoula) | 17 Feb 1975 | 7 Feb 1976 | 1978 | Bldg. |
| DD 974 | COMTE DE GRASSE | 72/224 | Litton/Ingalls (Pascagoula) | 4 Apr 1975 | 26 Mar 1976 | 1978 | Bldg. |
| DD 975 | O'BRIEN | 72/224 | Litton/Ingalls (Pascagoula) | 9 May 1975 | 8 July 1976 | 1978 | Bldg. |
| DD 976 | MERRILL | 72/224 | Litton/Ingalls (Pascagoula) | 16 June 1975 | 1 Sep 1976 | 1978 | Bldg. |
| DD 977 | BRISCOE | 72/224 | Litton/Ingalls (Pascagoula) | 21 July 1975 | 8 Jan 1977 | 1978 | Bldg. |
| DD 978 | STUMP | 72/224 | Litton/Ingalls (Pascagoula) | 22 Aug 1975 | 30 Apr 1977 | 1978 | Bldg. |
| DD 979 | CONOLLY | 74/224 | Litton/Ingalls (Pascagoula) | 29 Sep 1975 | 25 June 1977 | 1978 | Bldg. |
| DD 980 | MOOSBRUGGER | 74/224 | Litton/Ingalls (Pascagoula) | 3 Nov 1975 | 20 Aug 1977 | 1978 | Bldg. |
| DD 981 | JOHN HANCOCK | 74/224 | Litton/Ingalls (Pascagoula) | 16 Jan 1976 | 29 Oct 1977 | 1979 | Bldg. |
| DD 982 | NICHOLSON | 74/224 | Litton/Ingalls (Pascagoula) | 20 Feb 1976 | 1977 | 1979 | Bldg. |
| DD 983 | JOHN RODGERS | 74/224 | Litton/Ingalls (Pascagoula) | 12 Aug 1976 | 1978 | 1979 | Bldg. |
| DD 984 | LEFTWICH | 74/224 | Litton/Ingalls (Pascagoula) | 12 Nov 1976 | 1978 | 1979 | Bldg. |
| DD 985 | CUSHING | 74/224 | Litton/Ingalls (Pascagoula) | 1977 | 1978 | 1979 | Bldg. |
| DD 986 | HARRY W. HILL | 75/224 | Litton/Ingalls (Pascagoula) | 1977 | 1978 | 1979 | Bldg. |
| DD 987 | O'BANNON | 75/224 | Litton/Ingalls (Pascagoula) | 1977 | 1978 | 1979 | Bldg. |
| DD 988 | THORN | 75/224 | Litton/Ingalls (Pascagoula) | 1977 | 1978 | 1979 | Bldg. |
| DD 989 | DEYO | 75/224 | Litton/Ingalls (Pascagoula) | 1977 | 1978 | 1980 | Bldg. |
| DD 990 | INGERSOLL | 75/224 | Litton/Ingalls (Pascagoula) | 1978 | 1978 | 1980 | Bldg. |
| DD 991 | FIFE | 75/224 | Litton/Ingalls (Pascagoula) | 1978 | 1978 | 1980 | Bldg. |
| DD 992 | FLETCHER | 75/224 | Litton/Ingalls (Pascagoula) | 1978 | 1979 | 1980 | Bldg. |

| | |
|---|---|
| Displacement: | 7,800 tons full load |
| Length: | 529 feet (161.2 m) wl |
| | 563⅓ feet (171.1 m) oa |
| Beam: | 55 foot (17.6 m) |
| Draft: | 29 feet (8.8 m) |
| Propulsion: | 4 gas turbines (General Electric); 80,000 shp; 2 shafts (controllable-pitch propellers) |
| Speed: | ~33 knots |
| Range: | 6,000 n. miles at 20 knots |
| Complement: | 261 (18 O +243 EM) |
| Helicopters: | 2 LAMPS or 1 SH-3 Sea King |
| Missiles: | 1 8-tube NATO Sea Sparrow launcher Mk 29 IPDMS |
| Guns: | 2 5-inch (127-mm) 54 cal DP Mk 45 (2 ×1) |
| ASW weapons: | 1 8-tube ASROC launcher Mk 16 |
| | 6 12.75-inch (324-mm) torpedo tubes Mk 32 (2 × 3) |
| Radars: | SPS-40 air search |
| | SPS-55 surface search |
| Sonars: | SQS-53 bow-mounted |
| Fire control: | 1 Mk 86 Mod 3 gun FCS |
| | 1 Mk 116 Mod 0 ASW FCS |
| | 1 SPG-60 radar |
| | 1 SPQ-9A radar |

The SPRUANCE-class destroyers were intended as general-purpose ships to replace the large number of World War II-era destroyers which reached the end of their service lives in the mid-1970s. They are specialized ASW ships, with only point defense capabilities against air and missile attack. However they are designed for eventual conversion to an AAW-missile configuration. Four SPRUANCE-class ships being built for the Iranian Navy and the DDG 47-class ships for the U.S. Navy each have two Mk 26 Standard-ER missile launchers and related 3-D radar and fire control systems, while retaining the gun and ASW capabilities of the basic SPRUANCE design.

This is the largest class of surface combatants built for the U.S. Navy since World War II, except for the KNOX class of frigates (FF 1052).

Builders: The entire SPRUANCE class was contracted with a single shipyard to allow for mass production. A contract for the development and production of the 30 ships was awarded on 23 June 1970 to a new yard established by the Ingalls Shipbuilding Division of Litton Industries at Pascagoula, Mississippi. Labor and technical problems delayed the construction of these ships considerably.

Class: Two additional ships of this class with a Standard-ER AAW system were ordered by the Iranian Navy on 15 December 1973, and four additional ships were ordered on 27 August 1974; however, two ships were cancelled on 3 February 1976. The first Iranian ship will be delivered in 1980. U.S. Navy hull numbers DD 993–998 were assigned to the Iranian ships.

Classification: During the proposal stage these ships were assigned the project designation DX, pending completion of their design; a proposed SAM-armed variation (pre-Aegis) was designated DXG.

Design: The basic SPRUANCE design provides for subsequent installation of advanced sensors and weapon systems. The forward 5-inch gun mount is designed for modular replacement by the 8-inch MCLWG, and the ASROC launcher and magazine (forward) and Sea Sparrow system (aft) can be replaced with twin Mk 26 Standard-ER missile launchers (as in the Iranian ships).

Engineering: These are the first U.S. Navy surface combatants to have gas-turbine propulsion. Previously gas turbines were installed in several Navy patrol combatants and in HAMILTON-class (WHEC 715) and some RELIANCE-class (WMEC 615) cutters.

The SPRUANCE-class ships have four LM2500 gas turbines which are modified TF39 aircraft turbofan engines. One engine can propel the ships at about 19 knots, two engines at about 27 knots, and three and four engines can provide speeds in excess of 30 knots. Their range is approximately 6,000 miles at 20 knots.

Guns: Space and weight are provided in the superstructure for later installation of two 20-mm Phalanx CIWS.

Sonar: Original plans provided for these ships to have the SQS-35 Independent Variable Depth Sonar (IVDS) in addition to their bow-mounted SQS-53. The IVDS was deleted because of the effectiveness of the SQS-53.

The HEWITT at high speed. The 30 destroyers of the SPRUANCE class will provide ASW defense for the Fleet. Although they are the largest "destroyers" ever constructed by the U.S.Navy, they lack the surface-to-air missile systems of contemporary foreign ships and the previous U.S. destroyer class. (1976, Ingalls/Litton)

The SPRUANCE is the lead ship for 30 ASW destroyers being built for the U.S. Navy. Although the SPRUANCE has been criticized for being under-armed in comparison with foreign warships of this size, the ship forms the basis for the more capable DDG 47 class as well as the proposed "air capable" DD 963 and cruise missile destroyer (DDM). (1975, U.S. Navy, PH1 Lonnie McKay)

Two SPRUANCE-class destroyers at sea, the PAUL F. FOSTER AND KINKAID. The 30 destroyers of the SPRUANCE class will provide ASW defense to the Fleet. Although they are the largest "destroyers" constructed by the U.S. Navy, they lack the surface-to-air missile systems of contemporary foreign ships and the previous U.S. destroyer class. (1976, Ingalls/Litton)

The PAUL F. FOSTER at sea with an SH-2F LAMPS helicopter from Light Helicopter Antisubmarine Squadron 39 on her deck. Note the ship's box-like superstructure, forward stack offset to port and after stack to starboard, and small 5-inch Mk 45 gun mounts with long-barrel, 54-caliber guns. A NATO Sea Sparrow IPDMS launcher has since been fitted between the helicopter deck and after 5-inch gun mount. (1976, U.S. Navy, PHCS Robert Lawson)

Seven SPRUANCE-class destroyers are shown being assembled at the "west bank" ship assembly facility of the Litton/Ingalls shipyard in Pascagoula, Mississippi. The ships are assembled in three major modules, then joined to form complete hulls, transferred to an outfitting dock, and "launched" by submerging the dock. The TARAWA-class (LHA 1) helicopter ships also were built at the west bank yard. Other Litton/Ingalls ships are constructed at the east bank yard, formerly the Ingalls Shipbuilding Corp. (1976, Litton/Ingalls)

Three of a kind: PAUL F. FOSTER, ELLIOTT, and HEWITT of the SPRUANCE class at San Diego. (1977, U.S. Navy, PHCS Herman Schroeder)

## 14 DESTROYERS: "FORREST SHERMAN" CLASS

| Number | Name | FY/SCB | Builder | Laid down | Launched | Commissioned | Status |
|--------|------|--------|---------|-----------|----------|--------------|--------|
| DD 931 | Forrest Sherman | 53/85 | Bath Iron Works | 27 Oct 1953 | 5 Feb 1955 | 9 Nov 1955 | **AA** |
| *DD 933 | Barry | 53/85 | Bath Iron Works | 15 Mar 1954 | 1 Oct 1955 | 31 Aug 1956 | **AA** |
| *DD 937 | Davis | 54/85 | Bethlehem Steel Co (Quincy) | 1 Feb 1955 | 28 Mar 1956 | 28 Feb 1957 | **AA** |
| *DD 938 | Jonas Ingram | 54/85 | Bethlehem Steel Co (Quincy) | 15 June 1955 | 8 July 1956 | 19 July 1957 | **AA** |
| *DD 940 | Manley | 55/85 | Bath Iron Works | 10 Feb 1955 | 12 Apr 1956 | 1 Feb 1957 | **AA** |
| *DD 941 | Du Pont | 55/85 | Bath Iron Works | 11 May 1955 | 8 Sep 1956 | 1 July 1957 | **AA** |
| DD 942 | Bigelow | 55/85 | Bath Iron Works | 6 July 1955 | 2 Feb 1957 | 8 Nov 1957 | **AA** |
| *DD 943 | Blandy | 55/85 | Bethlehem Steel Co (Quincy) | 29 Dec 1955 | 19 Dec 1956 | 26 Nov 1957 | **AA** |
| DD 944 | Mullinnix | 55/85 | Bethlehem Steel Co (Quincy) | 5 Apr 1956 | 18 Mar 1957 | 7 Mar 1958 | **AA** |
| DD 945 | Hull | 56/85A | Bath Iron Works | 12 Sep 1956 | 10 Aug 1957 | 3 July 1958 | **PA** |
| DD 946 | Edson | 56/85A | Bath Iron Works | 3 Dec 1956 | 1 Jan 1958 | 7 Nov 1958 | **NRF-A** |
| *DD 948 | Morton | 56/85A | Ingalls Shipbuilding Corp | 4 Mar 1957 | 23 May 1958 | 26 May 1959 | **PA** |
| *DD 950 | Richard S. Edwards | 56/85A | Puget Sound Bridge & D.D. Co | 20 Dec 1956 | 24 Sep 1957 | 5 Feb 1959 | **PA** |
| DD 951 | Turner Joy | 56/85A | Puget Sound Bridge & D.D. Co | 30 Sep 1957 | 5 May 1958 | 3 Aug 1959 | **PA** |

* ASW–modified ships

| | |
|---|---|
| Displacement: | ~2,800 tons standard |
| | ~4,050 tons full load |
| Length: | 407 feet (124 m) wl |
| | DD 931–944, 418 feet (127.4 m) oa, except DD 933, 425 feet (125.9 m) |
| | DD 945–951, 418⁵/₁₂ feet (127.5 m) oa |

| | |
|---|---|
| Beam: | DD 931–944, 45 feet (13.7 m) |
| | DD 945–951, 45¹/₁₂ feet (13.8 m) |
| Draft: | 22 feet (6.7 m) |
| Propulsion: | steam turbines (General Electric, except Westinghouse in DD 931, 933); 70,000 shp; 2 shafts |
| Boilers: | 4 1,200-psi (Foster Wheeler, except Babcock & Wilcox in DD 937–938, 943–944, 948) |
| Speed: | 32.5 knots |
| Range: | 4,000+ n. miles at 20 knots |
| Complement: | 292 (17 O + 275 EM), except 304 (17 O + 287 EM) in ASW-modified ships (*) |
| Guns: | 3 5-inch (127-mm) 54 cal DP Mk 42 guns (3 × 1) except 2 guns in ASW modified ships (*) and DD 944 |
| | 1 8-inch (203-mm) 55 cal Mk 71 gun (1 × 1) in DD 945 |
| | 2 3-inch (76-mm) 50 cal AA Mk 33 guns (1 × 2) in DD 944, 946, 951 |
| | 1 20-mm Phalanx Mk 15 CIWS in DD 942 (1 × 1) |
| ASW weapons: | 1 8-tube ASROC launcher Mk 16 in ASW-modified ships (*) |
| | 6 12.75-inch (324-mm) torpedo tubes Mk 32 (2 × 3) |
| Radars: | SPS-10 surface search |
| | SPS-37 air search except SPS-40 in DD 931, 938, 941, 943–945, 948, 950 |
| Sonars: | SQS-23 (bow-mounted in DD 933) |
| | SQS-35 VDS in ASW-modified ships (*) |
| Fire control: | 1 Mk 56 Mod 16/45/48 gun FCS |
| | 1 Mk 68 Mod 0/1/3/5 gun FCS |
| | 1 Mk 105 Mod 16/20 ASW FCS except Mk 114 Mod 18/19 in ASW-modified ships |
| | 1 SPG-53/53A radar |

The 18 Forrest Sherman-class ships were the first U.S. destroyers designed and constructed after World War II, following the large DL 2–5 (DD 927–930). Four have been converted to guided-missile ships and are listed separately (DDG 31–34); eight others have undergone an ASW modification (indicated by asterisks), with six ships retaining essentially their original configuration.

Richard S. Edwards (1977, Giorgio Arra)

The EDSON was assigned to the Naval Reserve Force on 1 April 1977; she also provides training for students at the Surface Warfare Officers School in Newport, Rhode Island. The assignment of other unmodified SHERMANS to the NRF is expected in the near future.

Design: These were the first major U.S. combatants with more firepower aft than forward. The DECATUR and later ships have higher bows; the HULL and later ships have slightly different bow designs. These were the first U.S. destroyers not to have anti-ship torpedo tubes (built with four fixed 21-inch "long" ASW torpedo tubes Mk 25 plus depth-charge racks and hedgehogs).

Guns: As built, these ships each had three 5-inch Mk 42 guns and four 3-inch Mk 33 guns. One 5-inch mount and the 3-inch guns were removed from the ASW-modified ships; the 3-inch guns were removed from most "straight" SHERMANS, with a couple of ships retaining their after 3-inch twin mount. A prototype 8-inch MCLWG Mk 71 gun was fitted to the HULL for at-sea evaluation, in place of the forward 5-inch mount, during 1975.

Modernization: Eight SHERMANS were modernized to improve their ASW capabilities; their guns were reduced and ASROC was installed in conjunction with general updating; the BARRY was fitted with bow-mounted SQS-23; all were provided with variable-depth sonar. The BARRY modernization was SCB-251; the other seven were SCB-221. Plans to modernize six other ships were dropped because of increasing costs.

The MANLEY is one of eight FORREST SHERMAN-class destroyers modernized to an ASW configuration. The ship has lost the No. 2 5-inch gun mount to provide space for an ASROC launcher; VDS has been fitted at the stern. Plans to similarly modify the six other ships were dropped because of fiscal constraints. Four other SHERMANS have been converted to guided missile ships (DDG 31–34). (1973, Giorgio Arra)

The MULLINNIX retains the original three 5-inch Mk 42 guns of the SHERMAN class. The forward 3-inch twin mount has been removed, but the MULLINNIX and a few other ships do have a twin 3-inch mount just forward of the No. 3 5-inch gun. Arrangement of the Mk 56 and Mk 68 GFCS directors differ in the MANLEY and MULLINNIX. (1976, Giorgio Arra)

**28 DESTROYERS: "GEARING" AND "CARPENTER" CLASSES**

| Number | Name | Builder | Laid down | Launched | Commissioned | Status |
|--------|------|---------|-----------|----------|--------------|--------|
| ●DD 714 | WILLIAM R. RUSH | Federal SB & DD Co | 19 Oct 1944 | 8 July 1945 | 21 Sep 1945 | Str. FY 78 |
| DD 718 | HAMNER | Federal SB & DD Co | 23 Apr 1945 | 24 Nov 1945 | 11 July 1946 | **NRF-P** |
| DD 743 | SOUTHERLAND | Bath Iron Works | 27 May 1944 | 5 Oct 1944 | 22 Dec 1944 | **NRF-P** |
| DD 763 | WILLIAM C. LAWE | Bethlehem Steel (San Francisco) | 12 Mar 1944 | 21 May 1945 | 18 Dec 1946 | **NRF-A** |
| DD 784 | McKEAN | Todd-Pacific Shipyards (Seattle) | 15 Sep 1944 | 31 Mar 1945 | 9 June 1945 | **NRF-P** |
| DD 785 | HENDERSON | Todd-Pacific Shipyards (Seattle) | 27 Oct 1944 | 28 May 1945 | 4 Aug 1945 | **NRF-P** |
| DD 788 | HOLLISTER | Todd-Pacific Shipyards (Seattle) | 27 Dec 1944 | 9 Oct 1945 | 26 Mar 1946 | **NRF-P** |
| DD 806 | HIGBEE | Bath Iron Works | 26 June 1944 | 12 Nov 1944 | 27 Jan 1945 | **NRF-P** |
| DD 817 | CORRY | Consolidated Steel Corp | 5 Apr 1945 | 28 July 1945 | 26 Feb 1946 | **NRF-A** |
| DD 820 | RICH | Consolidated Steel Corp | 16 May 1945 | 5 Oct 1945 | 4 July 1946 | **NRF-A** |
| DD 821 | JOHNSTON | Consolidated Steel Corp | 26 Mar 1945 | 19 Oct 1945 | 23 Aug 1946 | **NRF-A** |
| DD 822 | ROBERT H. McCARD | Consolidated Steel Corp | 20 June 1945 | 9 Nov 1945 | 26 Oct 1946 | **NRF-A** |
| ●DD 824 | BASILONE | Consolidated Steel Corp | 7 July 1945 | 21 Dec 1945 | 26 July 1949 | Str. FY 78 |
| DD 825 | CARPENTER | Consolidated Steel Corp | 30 July 1945 | 30 Dec 1945 | 15 Dec 1949 | **NRF-P** |
| DD 826 | AGERHOLM | Bath Iron Works | 10 Sep 1945 | 30 Mar 1946 | 20 June 1946 | **PA** |
| DD 827 | ROBERT A. OWENS | Bath Iron Works | 29 Oct 1945 | 15 July 1946 | 5 Nov 1949 | **NRF-A** |
| DD 829 | MYLES C. FOX | Bath Iron Works | 14 Aug 1944 | 13 Jan 1945 | 20 Mar 1945 | **NRF-A** |
| DD 835 | CHARLES P. CECIL | Bath Iron Works | 2 Dec 1944 | 22 Apr 1945 | 29 June 1945 | **NRF-A** |
| DD 842 | FISKE | Bath Iron Works | 9 Apr 1945 | 8 Sep 1945 | 28 Nov 1945 | **NRF-A** |
| ●DD 845 | BAUSELL | Bath Iron Works | 28 May 1945 | 19 Nov 1945 | 7 Feb 1947 | Str. FY 78 |
| DD 862 | VOGELGESANG | Bethlehem Steel (Staten Island) | 3 Aug 1944 | 15 Jan 1945 | 28 Apr 1945 | **NRF-A** |
| DD 863 | STEINAKER | Bethlehem Steel (Staten Island) | 1 Sep 1944 | 13 Feb 1945 | 26 May 1945 | **NRF-A** |
| DD 864 | HAROLD J. ELLISON | Bethlehem Steel (Staten Island) | 3 Oct 1944 | 14 Mar 1945 | 23 June 1945 | **NRF-A** |
| DD 866 | CONE | Bethlehem Steel (Staten Island) | 30 Nov 1944 | 10 May 1945 | 18 Aug 1945 | **NRF-A** |
| DD 871 | DAMATO | Bethlehem Steel (Staten Island) | 10 May 1945 | 21 Nov 1945 | 27 Apr 1946 | **NRF-A** |
| ●DD 873 | HAWKINS | Consolidated Steel Corp | 14 May 1944 | 7 Oct 1944 | 10 Feb 1945 | Str. FY 78 |
| DD 876 | ROGERS | Consolidated Steel Corp | 3 June 1944 | 20 Nov 1944 | 26 Mar 1945 | **NRF-P** |
| DD 880 | DYESS | Consolidated Steel Corp | 17 Aug 1944 | 26 Jan 1945 | 21 May 1945 | **NRF-A** |
| DD 883 | NEWMAN K. PERRY | Consolidated Steel Corp | 10 Oct 1944 | 17 Mar 1945 | 20 July 1945 | **NRF-A** |
| DD 885 | JOHN R. CRAIG | Consolidated Steel Corp | 17 Nov 1944 | 14 Apr 1945 | 20 Aug 1945 | **NRF-P** |
| DD 886 | ORLECK | Consolidated Steel Corp | 28 Nov 1944 | 12 May 1945 | 15 Sep 1945 | **NRF-P** |
| DD 890 | MEREDITH | Consolidated Steel Corp | 27 Jan 1945 | 28 June 1945 | 31 Dec 1945 | **NRF-A** |

| | |
|---|---|
| Displacement: | 2,425 tons standard |
| | 3,410 to 3,520 tons full load |
| Length: | 383 feet (116.6 m) wl |
| | 390½ feet (119 m) oa |
| Beam: | 40⅚ feet (12.4 m) |
| Draft: | 19 feet (5.8 m) |
| Propulsion: | steam turbines (General Electric or Westinghouse); 60,000 shp; 2 shafts |
| Boilers: | 4 565-psi (Babcock & Wilcox, or Babcock & Wilcox and Westinghouse in combination) |
| Speed: | 34 knots |
| Range: | 4,000+ n. miles at 20 knots |
| Complement: | 307 as NRF ships (12 O + 176 EM active; 7 O + 112 EM reserve); 281 in DD 826 (15 O + 281 EM) |
| Guns: | 4 5-inch (127-mm) 38 cal DP Mk 38 (2 × 2) except 2 guns in DD 825, 827 |
| ASW weapons: | 1 8-tube ASROC launcher Mk 16 |
| | 6 12.75-inch (324-mm) torpedo tubes Mk 32 (2 × 3) |
| Radars: | SPS-10 surface search |
| | SPS-29 or SPS-37 or SPS-40 air search |
| Sonars: | SQS-23, except SQS-56 in DD 821 |
| Fire control: | 1 Mk 37 Mod 49/53/109/110 gun FCS except 1 Mk 56 Mod 43 in DD 825, 827 |
| | 1 Mk 114 Mod 2/3/4 ASW FCS |

These ships are the only U.S. warships constructed during World War II to remain in active service, except for two MIDWAY-class carriers (CV 41, 43). Only the AGERHOLM is in full commission; the 27 other ships are assigned to the Naval Reserve Force, manned by composite active and reserve crews. The CARPENTER and ROBERT A. OWENS were built with a specialized ASW configuration; later they were modernized to conform to the other ships, except that they have only one 5-inch gun mount, and were equipped with a later GFCS, and tripod mast aft.

Builders: The CARPENTER and ROBERT A. OWENS, suspended from the end of World War II until 1947, were towed to the Newport News SB & DD Co for completion as specialized ASW ships.

Class: The GEARING class was the final U.S. destroyer design to be constructed during World War II. The class consisted of hulls DD 710–721, 742–743, 763–769, 782–791, and 805–926; 98 ships were completed through 1952, the last being the TIMMERMAN (DD 828/AG 152) with an experimental light-weight propulsion plant. Forty-nine ships were cancelled in 1945, and four unfinished ships were scrapped in the 1950s.

Ships of this class and several earlier U.S. destroyer classes, continue to serve in several foreign navies.

Disposals since Tenth Edition:

| DD 715 | WILLIAM M. WOOD | stricken 1 Dec 1976 |
|--------|-----------------|---------------------|
| DD 716 | WILTSIE | stricken 23 Jan 1976; to Pakistan |
| DD 717 | THEODORE E. CHANDLER | stricken 1 Apr 1975 |
| DD 719 | EPPERSON | stricken 1 Dec 1975 |
| DD 782 | ROWAN | stricken 18 Dec 1975; to Pakistan |
| DD 783 | GURKE | stricken 20 Jan 1976 |
| DD 786 | RICHARD B. ANDERSON | stricken 20 Dec 1975 |
| DD 818 | NEW | stricken 1 July 1976; to South Korea |
| DD 819 | HOLDER | stricken 1 Oct 1976 |
| DD 836 | GEORGE K. MACKENZIE | stricken 1 Oct 1976 |
| DD 837 | SARSFIELD | stricken 1 Oct 1976, to Korea |
| DD 839 | POWER | stricken 1 Oct 1977; to Taiwan |
| DD 840 | GLENNON | stricken 1 Oct 1976 |
| DD 846 | OZBOURN | stricken 1 June 1975 |
| DD 849 | RICHARD E. KRAUS | stricken 1 July 1976; to South Korea |
| DD 852 | LEONARD F. MASON | stricken 2 Nov 1976 |
| DD 867 | STRIBLING | stricken 1 July 1976 |
| DD 868 | BROWNSON | stricken 30 Sep 1976 |
| DD 878 | VESOLE | stricken 1 Dec 1976 |
| DD 881 | BORDELON | stricken 1 Feb 1977 |

Classification: Seven of the surviving ships were classified as radar picket destroyers from the late 1940s until the FRAM (Fleet Rehabilitation and Modernization) program (DDR 743, 806, 829, 835, 876, 880, 883); the CARPENTER and ROBERT A. OWENS were completed as "hunter-killer" destroyers (DDK), and later changed to escort destroyers (DDE) on 4 March 1950. Upon FRAM conversion they were changed to "straight" DDs on 30 June 1962.

Design: The GEARING-class ships were identical to the previous ALLEN M. SUMNER (DD 692) class, except for the addition of 14 feet to their length to provide additional fuel capacity.

Guns: As built, the GEARINGS had six 5-inch guns, 12 40-mm AA guns, and 11 20-mm AA guns (plus 10 21-inch torpedo tubes and depth charges). After World War II the after bank of tubes was replaced by an additional quad 40-mm gun mount; those ships modified as radar pickets lost the other five-tube bank in favor of a tripod radar mast. Subsequently, all 20-mm guns were removed and 40-mm weapons replaced by up to six 3-inch guns. During FRAM modernization in the 1960s, gun armament was reduced to four 5-inch guns, and ASROC and Mk 32 tubes were installed. The DD 826, 845, and 890 have their guns forward (A and B positions); the other ships have a "balanced" gun arrangement (A and Y positions).

The CARPENTER and ROBERT A. OWENS were completed with four 3-inch 50-cal AA guns in enclosed mounts (plus two Weapon Able ASW weapons); they were rearmed with four 3-inch 70-cal rapid-fire guns in 1957. A single 5-inch gun mount was fitted forward during FRAM modernization.

Modernization: All of the surviving ships of this class were modernized in the 1960s under the FRAM I program. Machinery and electrical systems were updated, new electronic equipment installed, gun armament reduced, ASROC and Mk 32 tubes installed, and facilities provided for the DASH (Drone Antisubmarine Helicopter), although that program was cancelled before being provided to all modified destroyers.

Sonar: The JOHNSTON was fitted with an SQS-56 sonar in 1977 for at-sea evaluation of the PERRY-class (FFG 7) installation.

HAMNER (1976, U.S. Navy, PH1 Carl Begy)

The CHARLES P. CECIL is shown in a typical FRAM II configuration with a twin 5-inch gun mount forward and aft, and triple Mk 32 torpedo tubes in place of the No. 2 gun mount. The few ships with four guns forward have their Mk 32 tubes abaft their second stack. The CECIL has an SPS-37 radar antenna on the tripod mast; the HAMNER and CARPENTER have SPS-40 antennas. The CARPENTER and OWENS have small tripod masts aft; the other ships have lattice "stacks" to hold EW pods. (1971, U.S. Navy, PHC Frederick Gotauco)

The ALGERHOLM barely underway off the California coast during an exercise. The ship is the last World War II-era destroyer in active U.S. Navy commission. Note the all-gun-forward arrangement, EW antenna extending above radar mast, EW van on DASH helicopter deck, and funnel caps. (1976, U.S. Navy, PH3 C. M. Phelps)

CARPENTER (1976, U.S. Navy)

## POST WORLD WAR II DESTROYER PROGRAMS

U.S. World War II destroyer programs reached hull number DD 926 (with hulls DD 891–926 being cancelled in 1945). Many ships built during the war were subsequently reclassified as escort destroyers (DDE), hunter-killer destroyers (DDK), radar picket destroyers (DDR), and experimental destroyers (EDD), keeping the same hull numbers; all survivors reverted to the "straight" DD classification. As noted below, several war prizes and foreign-built ships (offshore procurement) had DD-series hull numbers, as did one British destroyer acquired for transfer to Pakistan. Four SPRUANCE-class ships for Iran are being built in the United States.

| | | |
|---|---|---|
| DD 927–930 | MITSCHER class | completed as DL 2–5 |
| DD 931–933 | FORREST SHERMAN class | |
| DD 934 | ex-Japanese HANAZUKI | |
| DD 935 | ex-German T-35 | |
| DD 936–938 | FORREST SHERMAN class | |
| DD 939 | ex-German Z-39 | |
| DD 940–951 | FORREST SHERMAN class | |
| DD 952–959 | CHARLES F. ADAMS class | completed as DDG 2–9 |
| DD 960 | (AKIZUKI) | Japan OSP 1960 |
| DD 961 | (TERUZUKI) | Japan OSP 1960 |
| DD 962 | (ex-British CHARITY) | to Pakistan 1958 (SHAH JAHAN) |
| DD 963–992 | SPRUANCE class | |
| DD 993 | (Iranian KOUROSH) | |
| DD 994 | (Iranian DARYUSN) | |
| DD 995 | (Iranian ARDESHIR) | |
| DD 996 | (Iranian NADER) | |
| DD 997 | (Iranian SHAPOUR) | cancelled 1976 |
| DD 998 | (Iranian ANOUSHIRVAN) | cancelled 1976 |

### GUIDED MISSILE DESTROYERS

| | | |
|---|---|---|
| DDG 1 | GYATT (ex-DD 712) | Comm. 1956; stricken (as DD 712) |
| DDG 2–24 | CHARLES F. ADAMS class | |
| DDG 25 | (Australian PERTH) | Comm. 1965 |
| DDG 26 | (Australian HOBART) | Comm. 1965 |
| DDG 27 | (Australian BRISBANE) | Comm. 1967 |
| DDG 28 | (German LÜTJENS) | Comm. 1969 |
| DDG 29 | (German MÖLDERS) | Comm. 1969 |
| DDG 30 | (German ROMMEL) | Comm. 1970 |
| DDG 31–34 | Conv. FORREST SHERMAN class (ex-DD 936, 932, 949, 947) | |
| DDG 35–36 | Conv. MITSCHER class (ex-DL 2, 3) | |
| DDG 37–46 | COONTZ class (ex-DLG 6–15) | |

The guided missile destroyer (DDG) classification was established in 1956. The first DDG was the GEARING-class destroyer GYATT (DD 712), fitted with a twin Terrier SAM launcher aft, replacing the after 5-inch twin gun mount. The GYATT became DDG 712 on 3 December 1956 and DDG 1 on 23 April 1957. Subsequent DDGs had the smaller Tartar (later Standard-MR) missile, until the COONTZ-class frigates were reclassified as destroyers in 1975. Note that the missile-armed ships of the SPRUANCE class being built for Iran have U.S. hull numbers in the DD series because they are modifications of the U.S. non-missile design, and are not a new class. Six ADAMS-class DDGs for Germany and Australia were built in the United States.

# 12 Frigates

The U.S. Navy's frigate force is the only category of ships that has increased in number since the end of the Vietnam War and the subsequent decline in Navy force levels. A frigate-building program was initiated in the early 1970s to provide large numbers of ships, albeit ones with limited capabilities and limited growth potential.

In 1978 the Navy has 65 frigates (FF/FFG) in active service, including the OLIVER HAZARD PERRY, the first of a class planned for construction through the mid-1980s. Also in service is the frigate research ship GLOVER (AGFF 1). The GLOVER officially is listed as an auxiliary ship, but is included in this section because she has the same weapons and sensors found in contemporary frigates.

Frigates are intended to provide ocean escort for merchant convoys, underway replenishment groups, and amphibious forces. Operating with antisubmarine aircraft carriers, flying conventional or VSTOL aircraft, or helicopters, frigates could form ASW hunter-killer groups. Frigates traditionally have not operated with attack or fleet aircraft carriers and other main striking forces because they cannot steam at high speeds (greater than 30 knots) and they lack redundancy in weapons and sensors.

However, the U.S. Navy's shortage of destroyers during the past few years has led to the use of frigates in carrier task groups. In effect, frigates are replacing the large number of World War II-era destroyers which have been discarded during the past few years.

All frigates now in service have been completed during the past 15 years. None of the over 600 destroyer escorts/frigates of the World War II programs remain in Navy service, nor do any of the 17 post-war escorts completed for the Navy between 1954–1960. No destroyer escorts/frigates are assigned to the Naval Reserve Force.

In the following table AAW indicates Tartar/Standard-MR surface-to-air missile systems; ASW indicates ASROC and SQS-26/56 sonar; Hel. indicates helicopter hangar; and Guns indicates the largest caliber fitted in the ships.

**FRIGATES**

| Type | Class/Ship | Active | Bldg. | Comm. | AAW | ASW | Hel. | Guns |
|------|-----------|--------|-------|-------|-----|-----|------|------|
| FFG 7 | PERRY | 1 | 17 | 1977– | √ | — | √ | 3-inch |
| FFG 1 | BROOKE | 6 | — | 1966–1968 | √ | √ | √ | 5-inch |
| FF 1052 | KNOX | 46 | — | 1969–1974 | — | √ | √ | 5-inch |
| FF 1040 | GARCIA | 10 | — | 1964–1968 | — | √ | √ | 5-inch |
| FF 1037 | BRONSTEIN | 2 | — | 1963 | — | √ | — | 3-inch |
| AGFF 1 | GLOVER | 1 | — | 1965 | — | √ | √ | 5-inch |

Classification: This type of warship was classified as destroyer escort (DE) from its inception in the U.S. Navy in 1941 until the early 1950s when DE was changed to "ocean escort." Subsequently, guided missile ships were designated DEG and the research ship GLOVER became an AGDE. On 30 June 1975 all such ships were changed to "frigates" (FF/FFG/AGFF).

Names: Most frigates bear the names of deceased Navy, Marine Corps, and Coast Guard personnel.

**PROTOTYPE FRIGATE: 3,000-ton SURFACE EFFECT SHIP**

| Number | Name | Builder | Launch | Commission | Status |
|--------|------|---------|--------|------------|--------|
| — | ...... | Rohr Marine Inc., San Diego | 1981 | 1982 | Planned |

| | |
|---|---|
| Displacement: | 3,000 tons full load |
| Length: | 270 feet (82.30 m) oa |
| Beam: | 108 feet (32.92 m) |
| Draft: | 31 feet (9.45 m) hullborne |
| | 14 feet (4.27 m) on air cushion |
| Propulsion: | 4 gas turbines; 4 waterjets |
| Lift: | 2 gas turbines |
| Speed: | 80+ knots |
| Complement: | 125 |
| Aircraft: | (see notes) |
| Armament: | (see notes) |
| Radars: | air search |
| | surface search |
| Sonars: | towed array |

The Department of Defense has delayed the Navy program to construct a large, oceangoing surface effect ship to evaluate the feasibility of this type of ship in the ocean escort role. If successful, the ship could be the prototype for the advanced frigates planned for construction in the early 1980s (now designated FFGX). Detailed design is now underway with actual construction previously scheduled to begin in 1979. The program is now being reevaluated; see Addenda.

Classification: The Navy used the classification DSX during the early 1970s to indicate a large SES employed in the destroyer or frigate role. However, the classification FFSG is now used to designate the ASW-mission SES.

Cost: The estimated cost of the "weaponized" 3,000-ton SES in the FY 1977–1985 budgets is $550.9 million. That cost includes detailed design and contract design, test and evaluation, and retrofitting more advanced engines when available, as well as the basic construction costs. The ship is funded with Research, Development, Test & Evaluation, Navy (RDT&E,N) authorizations and not Ship Construction, Navy (SCN), as are most new-construction ships.

Design: The SES has rigid sidewalls for stability and support, with lift-fan-generated air being trapped between the sidewalls and flexible seals or "skirts" forward and aft. This concept permits high-speed operation, because there is less hull area in the water to create drag. This design differs from the Air Cushion Vehicle (ACV) which contains the lift air entirely with a flexible skirt.

Artist's concept of 3,000-ton Surface Effect Ship Frigate Prototype (Rohr Marine Inc)

Artist's concept of 3,000-ton Surface Effect Ship Frigate Prototype (Rohr Marine Inc)

Artist's concept of 3,000-ton Surface Effect Ship Frigate Prototype (Rohr Marine Inc)

**1 + 57 GUIDED MISSILE FRIGATES: "OLIVER HAZARD PERRY" CLASS**

| Number | Name | FY/SCB | Builder | Laid down | Launched | Commissioned | Status |
|--------|------|--------|---------|-----------|----------|--------------|--------|
| FFG 7 | OLIVER HAZARD PERRY | 73/261 | Bath Iron Works | 12 June 1975 | 25 Sep 1976 | Dec 1977 | **AA** |
| FFG 8 | MCINERNY | 75/261 | Bath Iron Works | 1977 | 1979 | 1980 | Bldg. |
| FFG 9 | WADSWORTH | 75/261 | Todd Shipyards (San Pedro) | 13 July 1977 | 1978 | 1980 | Bldg. |
| FFG 10 | DUNCAN | 75/261 | Todd Shipyards (Seattle) | 29 Apr 1977 | 1978 | 1980 | Bldg. |
| FFG 11 | ........ | 76/261 | Bath Iron Works | 1978 | 1979 | 1980 | Bldg. |
| FFG 12 | ........ | 76/261 | Todd Shipyards (San Pedro) | 1978 | 1979 | 1980 | Bldg. |
| FFG 13 | ........ | 76/261 | Bath Iron Works | 1978 | 1979 | 1980 | Bldg. |
| FFG 14 | ........ | 76/261 | Todd Shipyards (San Pedro) | 1978 | 1979 | 1980 | Bldg. |
| FFG 15 | ........ | 76/261 | Bath Iron Works | 1979 | 1980 | 1981 | Bldg. |
| FFG 16 | ........ | 76/261 | Bath Iron Works | 1979 | 1980 | 1981 | Bldg. |
| FFG 19 | ........ | 77/261 | Todd Shipyards (San Pedro) | | | 1982 | Bldg. |
| FFG 20 | ........ | 77/261 | Todd Shipyards (Seattle) | | | 1982 | Bldg. |
| FFG 21 | ........ | 77/261 | Bath Iron Works | | | 1982 | Bldg. |
| FFG 22 | ........ | 77/261 | Todd Shipyards (Seattle) | | | 1982 | Bldg. |
| FFG 23 | ........ | 77/261 | Todd Shipyards (San Pedro) | | | 1982 | Bldg. |
| FFG 24 | ........ | 77/261 | Bath Iron Works | | | 1982 | Bldg. |
| FFG 25 | ........ | 77/261 | Todd Shipyards (San Pedro) | | | 1982 | Bldg. |
| FFG 26 | ........ | 77/261 | Bath Iron Works | | | 1982 | Bldg. |
| 8 FFGs | | 78 | | | | | Bldg. |
| 8 FFGs | | 79 | | | | | Planned |
| 8 FFGs | | 80 | | | | | Planned |
| 8 FFGs | | 81 | | | | | Planned |
| 8 FFGs | | 82 | | | | | Planned |

| | |
|---|---|
| Displacement: | 3,605 tons full load |
| Length: | 445 feet (135.6 m) oa |
| Beam: | 45 feet (13.7 m) |
| Draft: | 24½ feet (7.5 m) |
| Propulsion: | 2 gas turbines (General Electric); 40,000 shp; 1 shaft (controllable-pitch propeller) |
| Speed: | 28 knots (sustained) |
| Range: | ~4,500 n. miles at 20 knots |
| Complement: | 176 (14 O + 162 EM) |
| Helicopters: | 2 LAMPS |
| Missiles: | 1 single Mk 13 Mod 4 launcher for Standard-MR SAM and Harpoon SSM (40) |
| Guns: | 1 76-mm 62 cal AA Mk 75 (1 × 1) |
| | 1 20-mm Phalanx CIWS Mk 15 (1 × 1) (see notes) |
| ASW weapons: | 6 12.75-inch (324-mm) torpedo tubes Mk 32 (2 × 3) |
| Radars: | SPS-49 air search |
| | SPS-55 surface search |
| Sonars: | SQS-56 |
| | SQR-19 TACTAS (see notes) |
| Fire control: | Mk 92 Mod 2 weapons FCS |
| | SPG-60 radar |

The PERRY-class frigates are intended to provide open-ocean defense for merchant convoys, underway replenishment groups, and amphibious forces. They have less ASW capability than the previous KNOX-class ships (no ASROC and smaller sonar), but they have greater AAW capability with the Standard-MR launcher system. The PERRY's gun, fire control, and sonar systems were evaluated at sea in the frigate TALBOT.

Class: Two ships of this class are being built for the Australian Navy at the Todd yard in Seattle (FFG 17–18); both ships were ordered on 27 February 1976. Reportedly, other navies have expressed interest in ships of this class.

Classification: When conceived, these ships were classified as "patrol frigates" (PF), a term previously applied to a series of World War II-era escorts (PF 1–102) and post-war coastal escorts which were constructed specifically for foreign transfer (PF 103–108). The PERRY was assigned the hull number PF 109 until changed to "frigate" FFG 7 on 30 June 1975.

Design: These ships are designed specifically for modular assembly and mass production. All major components were tested at sea or on land before the completion of the lead ship. Space and weight are reserved for fin stabilizers.

Cost: Estimated cost of the ships in the FY 1978 program is $147 million per ship.

Electronics: The frigates in the FY 1979 or 1980 program will be the first to have TACTAS and LAMPS III helicopters provided; these will be backfitted in the earlier ships.

Engineering: These ships have LM2500 gas-turbine engines (also installed in SPRUANCE-class destroyers and the PEGASUS hydrofoil missile craft). They can attain 25 knots on one engine. Two auxiliary propulsion pods are fitted in the hull, aft of the sonar dome; these are 325-hp auxiliary engines which can propel the ship up to 6 knots in the event of a casualty to the main propulsion plant.

Guns: The FY 1978 ships will be the first to be fitted with the Phalanx CIWS; it will be backfitted in the earlier ships.

The OLIVER HAZARD PERRY on sea trials. The PERRY is the lead ship of a planned frigate class which probably will be the largest oceangoing warship class built since World War II. The ship has helicopter and limited SAM/SSM capabilities, but limited gun firepower. (1977, Bath Iron Works)

OLIVER HAZARD PERRY (1977, Bath Iron Works)

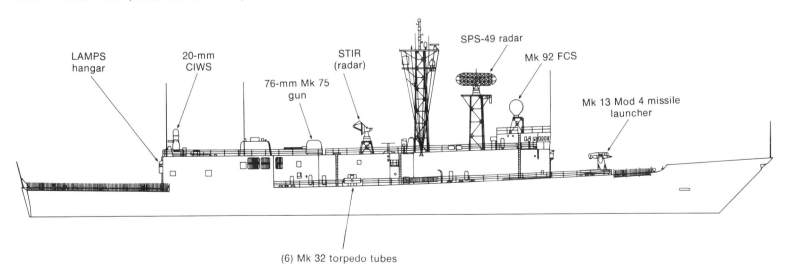

LAMPS hangar

20-mm CIWS

76-mm Mk 75 gun

STIR (radar)

SPS-49 radar

Mk 92 FCS

Mk 13 Mod 4 missile launcher

(6) Mk 32 torpedo tubes

Line drawing of the OLIVER HAZARD PERRY-class frigate

## 6 GUIDED MISSILE FRIGATES: "BROOKE" CLASS

| Number | Name | FY/SCB | Builder | Laid down | Launched | Commissioned | Status |
|--------|------|--------|---------|-----------|----------|--------------|--------|
| FFG 1 | BROOKE | 62/199B | Lockheed SB & Constn Co. | 10 Dec 1962 | 19 July 1963 | 12 Mar 1966 | **PA** |
| FFG 2 | RAMSEY | 62/199B | Lockheed SB & Constn Co. | 4 Feb 1963 | 15 Oct 1963 | 3 June 1967 | **PA** |
| FFG 3 | SCHOFIELD | 62/199B | Lockheed SB & Constn Co. | 15 Apr 1963 | 7 Dec 1963 | 11 May 1968 | **PA** |
| FFG 4 | TALBOT | 63/199B | Bath Iron Works Corp | 4 May 1964 | 6 Jan 1966 | 22 Apr 1967 | **AA** |
| FFG 5 | RICHARD L. PAGE | 63/199B | Bath Iron Works Corp | 4 Jan 1965 | 4 Apr 1966 | 5 Aug 1967 | **AA** |
| FFG 6 | JULIUS A. FURER | 63/199B | Bath Iron Works Corp | 12 July 1965 | 22 July 1966 | 11 Nov 1967 | **AA** |

| | |
|---|---|
| Displacement: | 2,640 tons standard |
| | 3,245 tons full load |
| Length: | 390 feet (118.9 m) wl |
| | 414½ feet (126.3 m) oa |
| Beam: | 44⅛ feet (13.5 m) |
| Draft: | 24 feet (7.3 m) |
| Propulsion: | steam turbine (Westinghouse); 35,000 shp; 1 shaft |
| Boilers: | 2 1,200-psi (Foster Wheeler) |
| Speed: | 27 knots |
| Range: | 4,000 n. miles at 20 knots |
| Complement: | 236 (17 O + 219 EM) |
| | |
| Helicopters: | 1 SH-2 LAMPS |
| Missiles: | 1 single Mk 22 Mod 0 launcher for Tartar/Standard-MR SAM (16) |
| Guns: | 1 5-inch (127-mm) 38 cal DP Mk 30 (1 × 1) |
| ASW weapons: | 1 8-tube ASROC launcher Mk 16 |
| | 6 12.75-inch (324 mm) torpedo tubes Mk 32 (2 × 3) |
| Radars: | SPS-10F surface search |
| | SPS-52 3-D search |
| Sonars: | SQS-26AX bow-mounted |

| | |
|---|---|
| Fire control: | 1 Mk 56 Mod 43 gun FCS |
| | 1 Mk 74 Mod 2/6 missile FCS |
| | 1 Mk 114 Mod 10/13 ASW FCS |
| | 1 SPG-51C radar |

These ships are similar to the GARCIA-class frigates but with a SAM launcher in place of the second 5-inch-gun mount and the related radar/fire control systems.

Aircraft: These ships were designed to carry the Drone Anti-submarine Helicopter (DASH); that program was cancelled before these ships were completed. They subsequently were modified to operate the SH-2 LAMPS.

Classification: These ships originally were classified as escort ships (DEG 1–6, respectively); they were changed to FFGs on 30 June 1975.

Torpedoes: These ships were built with two Mk 25 torpedo tubes in their stern for ASW torpedoes; they were subsequently removed.

RICHARD L. PAGE (1976, U.S. Navy, PH3 John Barber)

RAMSEY (1977, Giorgio Arra)

The TALBOT is shown at sea as refitted to evaluate various systems planned for installation in the PERRY-class frigates. Forward the TALBOT has a 75-mm Mk 75 OTO Melara gun, atop the after deck house is a Mk 92 weapons control radar, and on the fantail is the STIR radar; the SQS-56 sonar was also installed. The TALBOT has since been refitted as a "straight" DEG/FFG. (1974, U.S. Navy)

RonCalhoon
USNA 1963.

## 46 FRIGATES: "KNOX" CLASS

| Number | Name | FY/SCB | Builder | Laid down | Launched | Commissioned | Status |
|---|---|---|---|---|---|---|---|
| FF 1052 | KNOX | 64/199C | Todd Shipyards (Seattle) | 5 Oct 1965 | 19 Nov 1966 | 12 Apr 1969 | **PA** |
| FF 1053 | ROARK | 64/199C | Todd Shipyards (Seattle) | 2 Feb 1966 | 24 Apr 1967 | 22 Nov 1969 | **PA** |
| FF 1054 | GRAY | 64/199C | Todd Shipyards (Seattle) | 19 Nov 1966 | 3 Nov 1967 | 4 Apr 1970 | **PA** |
| FF 1055 | HEPBURN | 64/199C | Todd Shipyards (San Pedro) | 1 June 1966 | 25 Mar 1967 | 3 July 1969 | **PA** |
| FF 1056 | CONNOLE | 64/199C | Avondale Shipyards | 23 Mar 1967 | 20 July 1968 | 30 Aug 1969 | **AA** |
| FF 1057 | RATHBURNE | 64/199C | Lockheed SB & Constn Co | 8 Jan 1968 | 2 May 1969 | 16 May 1970 | **PA** |
| FF 1058 | MEYERKORD | 64/199C | Todd Shipyards (San Pedro) | 1 Sep 1966 | 15 July 1967 | 28 Nov 1969 | **PA** |
| FF 1059 | W. S. SIMS | 64/199C | Avondale Shipyards | 10 Apr 1967 | 4 Jan 1969 | 3 Jan 1970 | **AA** |
| FF 1060 | LANG | 64/199C | Todd Shipyards (San Pedro) | 25 Mar 1967 | 17 Feb 1968 | 28 Mar 1970 | **PA** |
| FF 1061 | PATTERSON | 64/199C | Avondale Shipyards | 12 Oct 1967 | 3 May 1969 | 14 Mar 1970 | **AA** |
| FF 1062 | WHIPPLE | 65/200 | Todd Shipyards (Seattle) | 24 Apr 1967 | 12 Apr 1968 | 22 Aug 1970 | **PA** |
| FF 1063 | REASONER | 65/200 | Lockheed SB & Constn Co | 6 Jan 1969 | 1 Aug 1970 | 31 July 1971 | **PA** |
| FF 1064 | LOCKWOOD | 65/200 | Todd Shipyards (Seattle) | 3 Nov 1967 | 5 Sep 1964 | 5 Dec 1970 | **PA** |
| FF 1065 | STEIN | 65/200 | Lockheed SB & Constn Co | 1 June 1970 | 19 Dec 1970 | 8 Jan 1972 | **PA** |
| FF 1066 | MARVIN SHIELDS | 65/200 | Todd Shipyards (Seattle) | 12 Apr 1968 | 23 Oct 1969 | 10 Apr 1971 | **PA** |
| FF 1067 | FRANCIS HAMMOND | 65/200 | Todd Shipyards (San Pedro) | 15 July 1967 | 11 May 1968 | 25 July 1970 | **PA** |
| FF 1068 | VREELAND | 65/200 | Avondale Shipyards | 20 Mar 1968 | 14 June 1969 | 13 June 1970 | **AA** |
| FF 1069 | BAGLEY | 65/200 | Lockheed SB & Constn Co | 22 Sep 1970 | 24 Apr 1971 | 9 May 1972 | **PA** |
| FF 1070 | DOWNES | 65/200 | Todd Shipyards (Seattle) | 5 Sep 1968 | 13 Dec 1969 | 28 Aug 1971 | **PA** |
| FF 1071 | BADGER | 65/200 | Todd Shipyards (Seattle) | 17 Feb 1968 | 7 Dec 1968 | 1 Dec 1970 | **PA** |
| FF 1072 | BLAKELY | 65/200 | Avondale Shipyards | 3 June 1968 | 23 Aug 1969 | 18 July 1970 | **AA** |
| FF 1073 | ROBERT E. PEARY | 65/200 | Lockheed SB & Constn Co | 20 Dec 1970 | 23 June 1971 | 23 Sep 1972 | **PA** |
| FF 1074 | HAROLD E. HOLT | 65/200 | Todd Shipyards (San Pedro) | 11 May 1968 | 3 May 1969 | 26 Mar 1971 | **PA** |
| FF 1075 | TRIPPE | 65/200 | Avondale Shipyards | 29 July 1968 | 1 Nov 1969 | 19 Sep 1970 | **AA** |
| FF 1076 | FANNING | 65/200 | Todd Shipyards (San Pedro) | 7 Dec 1968 | 24 Jan 1970 | 23 July 1971 | **PA** |
| FF 1077 | QUELLET | 65/200 | Avondale Shipyards | 15 Jan 1969 | 17 Jan 1970 | 12 Dec 1970 | **PA** |
| FF 1078 | JOSEPH HEWES | 66/200 | Avondale Shipyards | 15 May 1969 | 7 Mar 1970 | 27 Feb 1971 | **AA** |
| FF 1079 | BOWEN | 66/200 | Avondale Shipyards | 11 July 1969 | 2 May 1970 | 22 May 1971 | **AA** |
| FF 1080 | PAUL | 66/200 | Avondale Shipyards | 12 Sep 1969 | 20 June 1970 | 14 Aug 1971 | **AA** |
| FF 1081 | AYLWIN | 66/200 | Avondale Shipyards | 13 Nov 1969 | 29 Aug 1970 | 18 Sep 1971 | **AA** |
| FF 1082 | ELMER MONTGOMERY | 66/200 | Avondale Shipyards | 23 Jan 1970 | 21 Nov 1970 | 30 Oct 1971 | **AA** |
| FF 1083 | COOK | 66/200 | Avondale Shipyards | 20 Mar 1970 | 23 Jan 1971 | 18 Dec 1971 | **PA** |
| FF 1084 | McCANDLESS | 66/200 | Avondale Shipyards | 4 June 1970 | 20 Mar 1971 | 18 Mar 1972 | **AA** |
| FF 1085 | DONALD B. BEARY | 66/200 | Avondale Shipyards | 24 July 1970 | 22 May 1971 | 22 July 1972 | **AA** |
| FF 1086 | BREWTON | 66/200 | Avondale Shipyards | 2 Oct 1970 | 24 July 1971 | 8 July 1972 | **PA** |
| FF 1087 | KIRK | 66/200 | Avondale Shipyards | 4 Dec 1970 | 25 Sep 1971 | 9 Sep 1972 | **PA** |
| FF 1088 | BARBEY | 67/200 | Avondale Shipyards | 5 Feb 1971 | 4 Dec 1971 | 11 Nov 1972 | **PA** |
| FF 1089 | JESSE L. BROWN | 67/200 | Avondale Shipyards | 8 Apr 1971 | 18 Mar 1972 | 17 Feb 1973 | **AA** |
| FF 1090 | AINSWORTH | 67/200 | Avondale Shipyards | 11 June 1971 | 15 Apr 1972 | 31 Mar 1973 | **AA** |
| FF 1091 | MILLER | 67/200 | Avondale Shipyards | 6 Aug 1971 | 3 June 1972 | 30 June 1973 | **AA** |
| FF 1092 | THOMAS C. HART | 67/200 | Avondale Shipyards | 8 Oct 1971 | 12 Aug 1972 | 28 July 1973 | **AA** |
| FF 1093 | CAPODANNO | 67/200 | Avondale Shipyards | 12 Oct 1971 | 21 Oct 1972 | 17 Nov 1973 | **AA** |
| FF 1094 | PHARRIS | 67/200 | Avondale Shipyards | 11 Feb 1972 | 16 Dec 1972 | 26 Jan 1974 | **AA** |
| FF 1095 | TRUETT | 67/200 | Avondale Shipyards | 27 Apr 1972 | 3 Feb 1973 | 1 June 1974 | **AA** |
| FF 1096 | VALDEZ | 67/200 | Avondale Shipyards | 30 June 1972 | 24 Mar 1973 | 27 July 1974 | **AA** |
| FF 1097 | MOINESTER | 67/200 | Avondale Shipyards | 25 Aug 1972 | 12 May 1973 | 2 Nov 1974 | **AA** |

| | | | |
|---|---|---|---|
| Displacement: | 3,011 tons standard | Missiles: | 1 8-tube Sea Sparrow launcher Mk 25 BPDMS in FF 1052–1069 and |
| | 4,100 tons full load | | 1071–1083; 1 8-tube NATO Sea Sparrow launcher Mk 29 IPDMS |
| Length: * | 415 feet (126.5 m) wl | | in FF 1070 |
| | 438 feet (133.5 m) oa | | Harpoon missile can be fired from ASROC launcher after |
| Beam: | 46¾ feet (14.25 m) | | modification |
| Draft: | 24¾ feet (7.6 m) | Guns: | 1 5-inch (127-mm) 54 cal DP Mk 42 (1 × 1) |
| Propulsion: | steam turbine (Westinghouse); 35,000 shp; 1 shaft | ASW weapons: | 1 8-tube ASROC launcher Mk 16 |
| Boilers: | 2 1,200 psi (Combustion Engineering) | | 4 12.75-inch (324-mm) torpedo tubes Mk 32 (4 × 1 fixed) |
| Speed: | 27+ knots (sustained) | Radars: | SPS-10 surface search |
| Range: | ~4,500 n. miles at 20 knots | | SPS-40 air search |
| Complement: | 217 (16 O + 201 EM) | | SPS-58 threat warning in some ships |
| | | Sonars: | SQS-26CX bow-mounted |
| Helicopters: | 1 SH-2 LAMPS | | SQS-35 IVDS in FF 1052, 1056, 1063–1071, 1073–1076, 1078–1097 |

**Fire control:**
- 1 Mk 68 Mod 11/13/14 gun FCS
- 1 Mk 114 Mod 14/16 ASW FCA
- 1 Mk 115 Mod 0 missile FCS in FF 1052–1083 except 1 Mk 91 Mod 1 missile FCS in FF 1070
- 1 SPG-53A/D/F radar

This is the largest class of surface combatants constructed in the West since World War II; the Soviet SKORYY class of destroyers was larger, and the Navy plans to construct a greater number of PERRY-class frigates.

Aircraft: These ships were built to operate the DASH (Drone Anti-submarine Helicopter; that program was cancelled, however, before these ships were completed. They were later modified to operate the SH-2 LAMPS helicopter.

Class: Ten additional ships were authorized in the FY 1968 program (DE 1098–1107); the construction of six ships (DE 1102–1107) was deferred in 1968 in favor of more capable destroyer-type ships; three ships were deferred later that year (DE 1099–1101) to finance cost overruns of nuclear-propelled submarines; and one ship (DE 1098) was deferred in 1969.

Classification: These ships were built as ocean escorts (DE); they were changed to frigates (FF) on 30 June 1975.

Design: These ships are significantly larger than the BROOKE and GARCIA classes because of the use of non-pressure-fired boilers. The superstructure is topped by a distinctive cylindrical "mack," which combines mast and stacks. A port-side anchor is fitted at the bow and a second larger anchor retracts into the after end of the bow sonar dome.

Missiles: The DOWNES was an evaluation ship for the NATO Sea Sparrow. The KNOX-class ships are being fitted to fire the Harpoon anti-ship missile from their ASROC launchers.

Torpedoes: The Mk 32 torpedo tubes are fixed in the superstructure.

The RATHBURNE, a KNOX-class frigate with an SH-2 LAMPS helicopter on board. These ships are under-armed by foreign standards, but are effective ASW platforms with their large, SQS-26 sonar, VDS in some ships, and LAMPS helicopter. The HAROLD E. HOLT is one of the few U.S. ships named for a foreigner; as prime minister of Australia he supported American policies in the Vietnam War. (1977, Giorgio Arra)

BREWTON (1977, Giorgio Arra)

HAROLD E. HOLT (1972, U.S. Navy, PHC Bernard Norman)

CONNOLE (1972, Giorgio Arra)

An SH-3D Sea King refuels from the ELMER MONTGOMERY while hovering over the frigate's stern. When this photo was taken the ship had not been modified to take aboard the LAMPS or heavier SH-3 helicopters. Note the Sea Sparrow BPDMS launcher and the stern opening for VDS. (1975, U.S. Navy, JOCS Richard Benjamin)

Cook (1976, Giorgio Arra)

The Downes was the test ship for the NATO Sea Sparrow IPDMS. Two Mk 91 FCS directors are on a lattice mast atop the bridge and atop the helicopter hangar; the SPS-40A antenna has been mounted on a second lattice mast, with its place on the "mack" taken by a Mk 23 Target Acquisition System (TAS) antenna; and the NATO Sea Sparrow launcher is on the fantail. (1972, U.S. Navy)

**10 FRIGATES: "GARCIA" CLASS**

| Number | Name | FY/SCB | Builder | Laid down | Launched | Commissioned | Status |
|--------|------|--------|---------|-----------|----------|--------------|--------|
| FF 1040 | GARCIA | 61/199A | Bethlehem Steel (San Francisco) | 16 Oct 1962 | 31 Oct 1963 | 21 Dec 1964 | **AA** |
| FF 1041 | BRADLEY | 61/199A | Bethlehem Steel (San Francisco) | 17 Jan 1963 | 26 Mar 1964 | 15 May 1965 | **PA** |
| FF 1043 | EDWARD MCDONNELL | 62/199A | Avondale Shipyards | 1 Apr 1963 | 15 Feb 1964 | 15 Feb 1965 | **AA** |
| FF 1044 | BRUMBY | 62/199A | Avondale Shipyards | 1 Aug 1963 | 6 June 1964 | 5 Aug 1965 | **AA** |
| FF 1045 | DAVIDSON | 62/199A | Avondale Shipyards | 20 Sep 1963 | 2 Oct 1964 | 7 Dec 1965 | **PA** |
| FF 1047 | VOGE | 63/199A | Defoe Shipbuilding Co | 21 Nov 1963 | 4 Feb 1965 | 25 Nov 1966 | **AA** |
| FF 1048 | SAMPLE | 63/199A | Lockheed SB & Constn Co | 19 July 1963 | 28 Apr 1964 | 23 Mar 1968 | **PA** |
| FF 1049 | KOELSCH | 63/199A | Defoe Shipbuilding Co | 19 Feb 1964 | 8 June 1965 | 10 June 1967 | **AA** |
| FF 1050 | ALBERT DAVID | 63/199A | Lockheed SB & Constn Co | 29 Apr 1964 | 19 Dec 1964 | 19 Oct 1968 | **PA** |
| FF 1051 | O'CALLAHAN | 63/199A | Defoe Shipbuilding Co | 19 Feb 1964 | 20 Oct 1965 | 13 July 1968 | **PA** |

| | |
|---|---|
| Displacement: | 2,620 tons standard, 3,400 tons full load |
| Length: | 390 feet (118.9 m) w |
| | 414½ feet (126.3 m) oa |
| Beam: | 44⅙ feet (13.5 m) |
| Draft: | 24 feet (7.3 m) |
| Propulsion: | steam turbine (Westinghouse); 35,000 shp; 1 shaft |
| Boilers: | 2 1,200-psi (Foster Wheeler) |
| Speed: | 27 knots |
| Range: | 4,000 n. miles at 20 knots |
| Complement: | 247 |
| Helicopters: | 1 SH-2 LAMPS |
| Guns: | 2 5-inch (127-mm) 38 cal DP Mk 30 (2 × 1) |
| ASW weapons: | 1 8-tube ASROC launcher Mk 16 |
| | 6 12.75-inch (324-mm) torpedo tubes Mk 32 (2 × 3) |
| Radars: | SPS-10 surface search |
| | SPS-40 air search |
| Sonars: | SQS-26AXR in FF 1040–1045; SQS-26BX in FF 1046–1051 bow-mounted |
| Fire control: | 1 Mk 56 Mod 43 gun FCS |
| | 1 Mk 114 Mod 8/11 ASW FCS |

These ships are similar to the contemporary BROOKE-class frigates, but with a second 5-inch gun in place of the latter's Tartar missile launcher.

Aircraft: DASH facilities originally provided; modified to operate LAMPS during the 1970s.

Classification: As built, these ships were classified as ocean escorts (DE); they were changed to frigates (FF) on 30 June 1975.

Missiles: The BRADLEY evaluated the Sea Sparrow BPDMS in 1967–1968, with the launcher being fitted between the funnel and after 5-inch gun mount.

Torpedoes: As built, several ships had two Mk 25 torpedo tubes for ASW torpedoes built into their transom; these have been removed from the earlier ships and were not fitted in the later ships.

The GARCIA was the first of 16 similar frigates (FF/FFG) built with pressure-fired boilers. Maintenance problems led to a return to conventional boilers in the subsequent KNOX class, accounting in part for the later ships' larger size. The two classes have similar sensors with the GARCIA/BROOKE design having a second 5-inch gun or a Mk 22 Tartar/Standard missile launcher. (1973, Giorgio Arra)

## 1 FRIGATE RESEARCH SHIP: "GLOVER"

| Number | Name | FY/SCB | Builder | Laid down | Launched | Commissioned | Status |
|--------|------|--------|---------|-----------|----------|--------------|--------|
| AGFF 1 | GLOVER | 61/198 | Bath Iron Works | 29 July 1963 | 17 Apr 1965 | 13 Nov 1965 | **AA** |

| | |
|---|---|
| Displacement: | 2,643 tons standard |
| | 3,426 tons full load |
| Length: | 414½ feet (126.3 m) oa |
| Beam: | 44⅙ feet (13.5 m) |
| Draft: | 14½ feet (4.3 m) |
| Propulsion: | steam turbine (Westinghouse); 35,000 shp; 1 shaft |
| Boilers: | 2 1,250 psi (Foster Wheeler) |
| Speed: | 27 knots |
| Complement: | 236 + 38 civilian technicians |
| | |
| Guns: | 1 5-inch (127-mm) 38 cal DP Mk 30 (1 × 1) |
| ASW weapons: | 1 8-tube ASROC launcher Mk 16 |
| | 6 12.75-inch (324-mm) torpedo tubes Mk 32 (2 × 3) |
| Radars: | SPS-10 surface search |
| | SPS-40 air search |
| Sonars: | SQR-13 PADLOC |
| | SQS-26AXR bow-mounted |
| | SQS-35 IVDS |

| | |
|---|---|
| Fire control: | 1 Mk 56 Mod 43 gun FCS |
| | 1 Mk 114 Mod 15 ASW FCS |

The GLOVER is an experimental frigate with a modified hull and research facilities. The ship originally was authorized in the FY 1960 program but was postponed until FY 1961.

Aircraft: Provided with facilities for DASH; not refitted to operate LAMPS.

Classification: The GLOVER was authorized as a miscellaneous auxiliary (AG 163); completed as an escort research ship (AGDE 1) and changed to frigate research ship (AGFF) on 30 June 1975.

Torpedoes: As built, the GLOVER had two Mk 24 tubes for ASW torpedoes; these were subsequently removed.

GLOVER (1975, Giorgio Arra)

## 2 FRIGATES: "BRONSTEIN" CLASS

| Number | Name | FY/SCB | Builder | Laid down | Launched | Commissioned | Status |
|--------|------|--------|---------|-----------|----------|--------------|--------|
| FF 1037 | BRONSTEIN | 60/199 | Avondale Shipyards | 16 May 1961 | 31 Mar 1962 | 15 June 1963 | **PA** |
| FF 1038 | McCLOY | 60/199 | Avondale Shipyards | 15 Sep 1961 | 9 June 1962 | 21 Oct 1963 | **AA** |

| | |
|---|---|
| Displacement: | 2,360 tons standard |
| | 2,650 tons full load |
| Length: | 350 feet (106.7 m) wl |
| | 371½ feet (113.2 m) oa |
| Beam: | 40½ feet (12.3 m) |
| Draft: | 23 feet (7 m) |
| Propulsion: | steam turbine (De Laval); 20,000 shp; 1 shaft |
| Boilers: | 2 600–psi (Foster Wheeler) |
| Speed: | 24 knots |
| Range: | 3,000+ n. miles at 20 knots |
| Complement: | 199 (16 O + 183 EM) |
| | |
| Guns: | 2 3-inch (76-mm) 50 cal AA Mk 33 (1 × 2) |
| ASW weapons: | 1 8-tube ASROC launcher Mk 16 |
| | 6 12.75-inch (324-mm) torpedo tubes Mk 32 (2 × 3) |
| Radars: | SPS-10 surface search |
| | SPS-40 air search |
| Sonars: | SQS-26 bow-mounted |
| | TASS |
| Fire control: | 1 Mk 56 Mod 39 gun FCS |
| | 1 Mk 114 Mod 7 ASW FCS |

These were the lead ships for a new generation of ASW ocean escorts, introducing the large SQS-26 bow-mounted sonar and ASROC. However, they lack the 5-inch guns and helicopter facilities of the later BROOKE, GARCIA, and KNOX classes.

Classification: These ships were built as ocean escorts (DE) and changed to frigates (FF) on 30 June 1975.

Electronics: A Towed Array Surveillance System (TASS) was fitted to each of these ships in the mid-1970s.

Guns: As built, each ship also had a single 3-inch gun aft; these were subsequently removed. The next 63 frigates built by the U.S. Navy had 5-inch guns; the 76-mm gun was revived in the PERRY-class design.

McCLOY (1975, U.S. Navy, Ed Dowling)

McCLOY (1976, U.S. Navy, PH2 D. L. Thompson)

## POST-WORLD WAR II ESCORT/FRIGATE PROGRAMS

U.S. World War II destroyer escort programs reached hull number DE 1005 (with DE 801–1005 being cancelled). After the war several ships were converted to radar picket escorts (DER), a few for the tactical fleet role, but most for strategic early warning. A few also were modified to a control escort (DEC) configuration, to support amphibious landings. With the start of post-war construction these ships were reclassified as ocean escorts (DE), partly so that they would not be confused with escort destroyers (DDE). U.S. hull numbers were assigned to 17 ships built in Europe with American funds (Offshore Procurement or OSP). Thirteen U.S. ships were completed between 1954 and 1957, built to the similar DEALEY and COURTNEY designs, and four ships to the CLAUD JONES design.

| | | |
|---|---|---|
| DE 1006 | DEALEY | Comm. 1954; to Uruguay 1972 |
| DE 1007 | (French LE NORMAND) | OSP 1956 |
| DE 1008 | (French LE LORRAIN) | OSP 1956 |
| DE 1009 | (French LE PICARD) | OSP 1956 |
| DE 1010 | (French LE GASCON) | OSP 1957 |
| DE 1011 | (French LE CHAMPENOIS) | OSP 1957 |
| DE 1012 | (French LE SAVOYARD) | OSP 1957 |
| DE 1013 | (French LE BOURGUIGNON) | OSP 1957 |
| DE 1014 | CROMWELL | Comm. 1954; stricken 1972 |
| DE 1015 | HAMMERBERG | Comm. 1955; stricken 1973 |
| DE 1016 | (French LE CORSE) | OSP 1952 |
| DE 1017 | (French LE BRESTOIS) | OSP 1952 |
| DE 1018 | (French LE BOULONNAIS) | OSP 1953 |
| DE 1019 | (French LE BORDELAIS) | OSP 1953 |
| DE 1020 | (Italian CIGNO) | OSP 1957 |
| DE 1021 | COURTNEY | Comm. 1956; stricken 1973 |
| DE 1022 | LESTER | Comm. 1957; stricken 1973 |
| DE 1023 | EVANS | Comm. 1957; stricken 1973 |
| DE 1024 | BRIDGET | Comm. 1957; stricken 1973 |
| DE 1025 | BAUER | Comm. 1957; stricken 1973 |
| DE 1026 | HOOPER | Comm. 1958; stricken 1973 |
| DE 1027 | JOHN WILLIS | Comm. 1957; stricken 1972 |
| DE 1028 | VAN VOORHIS | Comm. 1957; stricken 1972 |
| DE 1029 | HARTLEY | Comm. 1957; to Colombia 1972 |
| DE 1030 | JOSEPH K. TAUSSIG | Comm. 1957; stricken 1972 |
| DE 1031 | (Italian CASTORE) | OSP 1957 |
| DE 1032 | (Portuguese PERO ESCOBAR) | OSP 1957 |
| DE 1033 | CLAUD JONES | Comm. 1959; to Indonesia 1974 |
| DE 1034 | JOHN R. PERRY | Comm. 1959; to Indonesia 1973 |
| DE 1035 | CHARLES BERRY | Comm. 1959; to Indonesia 1974 |
| DE 1036 | MCMORRISS | Comm. 1960; to Indonesia 1974 |
| DE 1037–1038 | BRONSTEIN class | |
| DE 1039 | (Portuguese ALMIRANTE PEREIRA DA SILVA) | OSP 1966 |
| DE 1040–1041 | GARCIA class | |
| DE 1042 | (Portuguese ALMIRANTE GAGO COUTINHO) | OSP 1967 |
| DE 1043–1045 | GARCIA class | |
| DE 1046 | (Portuguese ALMIRANTE MAGALHAES CORREA) | OSP 1967 |
| DE 1047–1051 | GARCIA class | |
| DE 1052–1107 | KNOX class | |

# 13 Command Ships

In 1978, the Navy has only one active command ship, the LA SALLE, which operates in the Persian Gulf and Indian Ocean, serving as flagship for the Commander U.S. Middle East Force (a rear admiral). The NORTHAMPTON and WRIGHT were configured to serve as National Emergency Command Posts Afloat (NECPA) for the President or other national command authorities. However, the NECPA concept was abandoned in 1970 and both command ships were laid up in reserve. Both were stricken on 1 December 1977.

**1 MISCELLANEOUS FLAGSHIP: CONVERTED "RALEIGH" CLASS**

| Number | Name | FY/SCB | Builder | Laid down | Launched | Commissioned | Status |
|--------|------|--------|---------|-----------|----------|--------------|--------|
| AGF 3 | LA SALLE | 61/187A | New York Naval Shipyard | 2 Apr 1962 | 3 Aug 1963 | 22 Feb 1964 | **A-IO** |

| | |
|---|---|
| Displacement: | 8,040 tons light |
| | 13,900 tons full load |
| Length: | 500 feet (152 m) wl |
| | 521¾ feet (158.4 m) oa |
| Beam: | 84 feet (25.6 m) |
| Draft: | 21 feet (6.4 m) |
| Propulsion: | steam turbines (De Laval); 24,000 shp; 2 shafts |
| Boilers: | 2 600-psi (Babcock & Wilcox) |
| Speed: | 20 knots (sustained; 21.6 knots maximum) |
| Complement: | 387 (18 O + 369 EM) |
| Flag: | 59 (12 O + 47 EM) |
| Helicopters: | utility helicopters |
| Guns: | 8 3-inch (76-mm) 50 cal AA Mk 33 (4 × 2) |
| Radars: | SPS-10 surface search |
| | SPS-40 air search |
| Fire control: | (local control only) |

The LA SALLE was converted from an amphibious transport dock specifically to serve as flagship for the U.S. Middle East Force. She has retained an amphibious assault capability.

Class: The LA SALLE was one of three ships of the RALEIGH-class amphibious transport docks.

Classification: The ship was completed as LPD 3; changed to AGF 3 on 1 July 1972.

Conversion: During 1972 the LA SALLE was fitted with elaborate command and communications facilities, accommodations for an admiral and his staff, a helicopter hangar, and additional air conditioning. The ship was painted white to reflect heat.

The Navy's only white warship, the LA SALLE, steams through the Indian Ocean. The LA SALLE retains most of her LPD assault capability, but has a helicopter structure and covered assembly area on her flight deck. Note that her 3-inch Mk 33 gun mounts have had covers installed (now Mod 13; originally Mod 0). (1975, U.S. Navy, PH1 R. H. Green)

LA SALLE (1972, U.S. Navy)

**1 NATIONAL COMMAND SHIP: CONVERTED LIGHT CARRIER**

| Number | Name | Builder | Laid down | Launched | CVL Comm. | CC Comm. | Status |
|--------|------|---------|-----------|----------|-----------|----------|--------|
| CC 2 | ●WRIGHT | New York SB Corp | 21 Aug 1944 | 1 Sep 1945 | 9 Feb 1947 | 11 May 1963 | Str. 1977 |

| | |
|---|---|
| Displacement: | 14,500 tons standard |
| | 19,600 tons full load |
| Length: | 664 feet (202.4 m) wl |
| | 683½ feet (208.4 m) oa |
| Beam: | 78¾ feet (23.6 m) |
| Draft: | 28 feet (8.5 m) |
| Extreme width: | 109 feet (33.2 m) |
| Propulsion: | steam turbines (General Electric); 120,000 shp; 4 shafts |
| Boilers: | 4 550-psi (Babcock & Wilcox) |
| Speed: | 33 knots |
| Complement: | 1,317 (73 O + 1,244 EM) |
| Flag: | 522 (168 O + 354 EM) |
| | |
| Aircraft: | 5 helicopters |
| Elevators: | 1 centerline |
| Guns: | 8 40-mm AA Mk 1 (4 × 2) |
| Radars: | SPS-6B air search |
| | SPS-10 surface search |
| Fire control: | 4 Mk 51 Mod 3 gun FCS |

The WRIGHT was built as a light aircraft carrier and operated primarily as an experimental and training carrier before being mothballed in 1956. She was converted to the NECPA role in 1962–1963. The WRIGHT was decommissioned on 22 May 1970 and again laid up in reserve.

Aircraft: The ship has flight-deck landing "spots" for two helicopters and sufficient hangar space for three CH-46 Sea Knights plus two UH-43 utility helicopters.

Classification: The WRIGHT was completed as the "small" aircraft carrier CVL 49. While laid up as a carrier she was changed to aircraft transport (AVT 7) on 15 May 1959. The CC 2 classification was assigned on 1 September 1962.

Conversion: The WRIGHT was converted to a command ship at the Puget Sound Naval Shipyard in 1962–1963 (funded under the FY 1962 program). She was fitted with extensive command and communications facilities and special accommodations. A "forest" of antenna masts was fitted on the former flight deck, the tallest being 83 feet high. Her conversion design was SCB-228.

WRIGHT (1963, U.S. Navy)

WRIGHT (1963, U.S. Navy)

NORTHAMPTON laid up (1974, William Whalen, Jr.)

## 1 NATIONAL COMMAND SHIP: CONVERTED HEAVY CRUISER

| Number | Name | Builder | Laid down | Launched | Commissioned | Status |
|---|---|---|---|---|---|---|
| CC 1 | •NORTHAMPTON | Bethlehem Steel Co (Quincy) | 31 Aug 1944 | 27 Jan 1951 | 7 Mar 1953 | Str. 1977 |

| | |
|---|---|
| Displacement: | 14,700 tons standard |
| | 17,200 tons full load |
| Length: | 664 feet (202.4 m) wl |
| | 676 feet (206 m) oa |
| Beam: | 71 feet (21.6 m) |
| Draft: | 29 feet (8.8 m) |
| Propulsion: | steam turbines (General Electric); 120,000 shp; 4 shafts |
| Boilers: | 4 565-psi (Babcock & Wilcox) |
| Speed: | 32.6 knots |
| Complement: | 1,191 (68 O + 1,123 EM) |
| Flag: | 328 (191 O + 137 EM) |
| | |
| Helicopters: | 3 utility helicopters |
| Guns: | 1 5-inch (127-mm) 54 cal DP Mk 42 (1 × 1) |
| Radars: | SPS-8A height-finding |
| | SPS-10 surface search |
| | SPS-29 air search |
| Fire control: | 1 Mk 56 Mod 45 gun FCS |

The NORTHAMPTON was laid down as a heavy cruiser of the OREGON CITY class, but the ship was cancelled on 11 August 1945 when 56.2 percent complete. She was then reordered on 1 July 1948 as a light tactical command ship (CLC 1). After completion in that configuration in 1953 the NORTHAMPTON served as flagship of the U.S. Sixth Fleet in the Mediterranean in 1954–1955, and then as flagship of the U.S. Second Fleet in the Atlantic from 1955 to 1961. At that time she was reconfigured for the NECPA role (CC 1). The ship was decommissioned on 8 April 1970 and placed in reserve.

Aircraft: There is a large helicopter landing area aft and hangar space for three UH-34 utility helicopters.

Classification: The NORTHAMPTON was begun as CA 125. As a fleet command ship she initially was classified as a task force command ship and then tactical command ship (both CLC 1); changed to command ship (CC 1) for NECPA role on 15 April 1961.

Design: As completed the NORTHAMPTON was one deck higher than other U.S. heavy cruisers, with the additional space devoted to offices and communications spaces. Her superstructure was extensively modified with towers installed to support large antenna arrays (from 1953 to 1963 the NORTHAMPTON had a massive SPS-2

air search radar mounted on the forward pylon). The ship's foremast is the tallest unsupported structure afloat (125 feet). The command ship design was SCB-13.

Guns: The ship was built with a gun armament of four 5-inch 54 cal Mk 42 single guns and eight 3-inch 50 cal Mk 33 guns in twin mounts. The original 3-inch guns were later replaced with twin 3-inch 70 cal rapid-fire guns (twin), but the newer weapons were removed in 1962 because of high maintenance requirements. Subsequently, the 5-inch gun battery was reduced to the single after gun on the 01 level. Removal of the guns and their magazines made more space available for offices and storage.

The NORTHAMPTON was the first ship to be configured specifically as a fleet/task force flagship and, subsequently, the first to be configured as a seagoing presidential command post. The photograph above shows the NORTHAMPTON in her ultimate configuration, with only one 5-inch gun installed, aft on the 01 level. Her hull is one deck higher than contemporary war-built heavy cruisers. (U.S. Navy)

# 14 Amphibious Warfare Ships

The U.S. Navy in 1978 operates 64 amphibious warfare ships which have a nominal lift capacity of slightly more than one reinforced Marine division and its supporting ground and air units (approximately 30,000 troops; designated a Marine Assault Force or MAF). The term "nominal" is used because only some 85 percent of the ships normally are operational, with the remainder being in overhaul or undergoing repair. Three additional amphibious ships are operated by the Naval Reserve Force. These ships normally operate in amphibious task forces, which consist of squadrons of amphibious ships with a reinforced Marine battalion (Marine Amphibious Unit) embarked in each PhibRon. There is normally one PhibRon forward deployed in the Mediterranean, and two in the western Pacific.

All active amphibious ships are of post-World War II construction. These ships have a sustained speed of 20 knots, helicopter fa-

cilities, and relatively comfortable troop accommodations (compared to their World War II counterparts). The last feature has been made necessary by the regular six-month forward deployment of amphibious task forces in the Mediterranean and western Pacific.

The more capable amphibious ships initiated during the early 1960s were part of Secretary of Defense Robert McNamara's concept of "flexible response" to world crises. The most impressive of these ships are the new TARAWA-class LHAs. One LHA together with one or two LSTs can transport and put ashore a reinforced Marine battalion, a task that would otherwise require five amphibious ships.

In the following table Hel. indicates helicopter support capabilities (including hangar), Well indicates a docking well for landing craft, and Troops indicates berthing for several hundred troops.

**AMPHIBIOUS WARFARE SHIPS**

| Type | Class/Ship | Active | NRF | Bldg. | Reserve | Comm. | Hel. | Well | Troops |
|---|---|---|---|---|---|---|---|---|---|
| LCC 19 | BLUE RIDGE | 2 | — | — | — | 1970–1971 | — | — | — |
| LHA 1 | TARAWA | 2 | — | 3 | — | 1976– | √ | √ | √ |
| LPH 2 | IWO JIMA | 7 | — | — | — | 1961–1970 | √ | — | √ |
| LKA 113 | CHARLESTON | 5 | — | — | — | 1968–1970 | — | — | — |
| LKA 112 | TULARE | — | 1 | — | — | 1956 | — | — | — |
| LPA 248 | PAUL REVERE | — | 2 | — | — | 1958–1961 | — | — | √ |
| LPD 4 | AUSTIN | 12 | — | — | — | 1965–1971 | √ | √ | √ |
| LPD 1 | RALEIGH | 2 | — | — | — | 1962–1963 | — | √ | √ |
| LSD 36 | ANCHORAGE | 5 | — | — | — | 1969–1972 | — | √ | — |
| LSD 28 | THOMASTON | 8 | — | — | — | 1954–1957 | — | √ | — |
| LST 1179 | NEWPORT | 20 | — | — | — | 1969–1972 | — | — | — |
| LST 1171 | SUFFOLK COUNTY | — | — | — | 3 | 1957–1959 | — | — | — |
| LST 1156 | TERREBONNE PARISH | — | — | — | 2 | 1953–1954 | — | — | — |
| LST 511 | | — | — | — | 2 | 1944–1945 | — | — | — |
| *LPSS 574 | GRAYBACK | 1 | — | — | — | 1958 | — | — | — |

* Note: Transport submarines are listed in Chapter 7.

Guns: The larger amphibious assault ships (LHA) are the only "amphibs" with 5-inch guns. All other active ships have 3-inch guns, with the LCC/LHA/LPH types also having point defense missile systems. Maintenance problems and the limited effective-

ness of the 3-inch guns has led to some mounts being removed. The Navy has long-term plans calling for installation of the 20-mm Phalanx CIWS (two mounts) in all active amphibious ships. "Conventional" 20-mm guns are fitted in the LHAs.

**2 AMPHIBIOUS COMMAND SHIPS: "BLUE RIDGE" CLASS**

| Number | Name | FY/SCB | Builder | Laid down | Launched | Commissioned | Status |
|--------|------|--------|---------|-----------|----------|--------------|--------|
| LCC 19 | BLUE RIDGE | 65/400 | Philadelphia Naval Shipyard | 27 Feb 1967 | 4 Jan 1969 | 14 Nov 1970 | **PA** |
| LCC 20 | MOUNT WHITNEY | 66/400 | Newport News | 8 Jan 1959 | 8 Jan 1970 | 16 Jan 1971 | **AA** |

| | |
|---|---|
| Displacement: | 19,290 tons full load |
| Length: | 620 feet (188.5 m) oa |
| Beam: | 82 feet (25.3 m) |
| Extreme width: | 108 feet (33 m) |
| Draft: | 27 feet (8.2 m) |
| Propulsion: | steam turbine (General Electric); 22,000 shp; 1 shaft |
| Boilers: | 2 600-psi (Foster Wheeler) |
| Speed: | 20 knots (sustained) |
| Complement: | 720 (40 O + 680 EM) |
| Flag: | 700 (200 O + 500 EM) |
| Missiles: | 2 8-tube Sea Sparrow launchers Mk 25 BPDMS |
| Guns: | 4 3-inch (76-mm) 50 cal AA Mk 33 (2 × 2) |
| Radars: | SPS-10 surface search |
| | SPS-40 air search |
| | SPS-48 3-D search |
| Fire control: | 2 Mk 56 Mod 39A gun FCS |
| | 2 Mk 115 Mod 0 missile FCS |

These are large amphibious command ships, the first and only ones to be constructed specifically for that role. They have large, open decks which allow room for antenna placement. Flag accommodations and facilities provide for a Navy amphibious task-force commander, the Marine assault-force commander, and their staffs.

Classification: These ships were originally classified as amphibious force flagships (AGC); they were changed to amphibious command ships (LCC) on 1 January 1969.

Design: The hull and machinery arrangements of these ships are similar to the IWO JIMA-class helicopter carriers. A small vehicle hangar is fitted with a cargo elevator connecting it with the flight deck; no helicopter hangar is provided.

Guns: Early designs for this class provided two additional 3-inch twin mounts on the forecastle; they were not installed, however. Fire arcs are severely restricted by the antennas.

Missiles: The Sea Sparrow BPDMS launchers were fitted in 1974.

BLUE RIDGE superstructure (1977, Giorgio Arra)

The BLUE RIDGE's numerous antennas predominate in this view of the Pacific Fleet's LCC. The MOUNT WHITNEY, in the Atlantic, is almost identical (e.g., the MOUNT WHITNEY has only one satellite disc antenna atop the after antenna pyramid while the BLUE RIDGE has two). (1977, Giorgio Arra)

The BLUE RIDGE is one of two built-for-the-purpose amphibious command ships. They are intended to control amphibious task forces and complex landing operations. Ships of this type are named for mountain ranges. (1977, Giorgio Arra)

The TARAWA is the first of a series of multi-capability amphibious assault ships which are the size of ESSEX/HANCOCK-class aircraft carriers. Note the box-like superstructure and two squat stacks. Amphibious assault ships are named for battles in which Marines participated. (1976, U.S. Navy, PH2 P. Arciniega)

## 5 AMPHIBIOUS ASSAULT SHIPS: "TARAWA" CLASS

| Number | Name | FY/SCB | Builder | Laid down | Launched | Commissioned | Status |
|--------|------|--------|---------|-----------|----------|--------------|--------|
| LHA 1 | TARAWA | 69/410 | Litton/Ingalls (Pascagoula) | 15 Nov 1971 | 1 Dec 1973 | 29 May 1976 | **PA** |
| LHA 2 | SAIPAN | 70/410 | Litton/Ingalls (Pascagoula) | 21 July 1972 | 18 July 1974 | 15 Oct 1977 | **AA** |
| LHA 3 | BELLEAU WOOD | 70/410 | Litton/Ingalls (Pascagoula) | 5 Mar 1973 | 11 Apr 1977 | late 1978 | Bldg. |
| LHA 4 | NASSAU | 71/410 | Litton/Ingalls (Pascagoula) | 13 Aug 1973 | early 1978 | mid 1979 | Bldg. |
| LHA 5 | DA NANG | 71/410 | Litton/Ingalls (Pascagoula) | 12 Nov 1976 | mid 1978 | early 1980 | Bldg. |

| | |
|---|---|
| Displacement: | 39,300 tons full load |
| Length: | 778 feet (237.8 m) wl |
| | 820 feet (250 m) oa |
| Beam: | 106⅔ feet (32.5 m) |
| Draft: | 27½ feet (8.5 m) |
| Propulsion: | steam turbines (Westinghouse); 70,000 shp; 2 shafts |
| Boilers: | 2 600-psi (Combustion Engineering) |
| Complement: | 731 (48 O + 678 EM Navy; 2 O + 3 EM Marine Corps) |

| | |
|---|---|
| Troops: | ~1,900 |
| Helicopters: | ~30 |
| Elevators: | 1 deck edge + 1 stern |
| Missiles: | 2 8-tube Sea Sparrow launchers Mk 25 BPDMS |
| Guns: | 3 5-inch (127-mm) 54 cal DP Mk 45 (3 × 1) |
| | 6 20-mm AA Mk 67 (6 × 1) |
| Radars: | SPS-10F surface search |
| | SPS-40B air search |
| | SPS-52B 3-D search |
| Fire control: | 1 Mk 86 Mod 4 gun FCS |
| | 2 Mk 115 Mod 0 missile FCS |
| | 1 SPG-60 radar |
| | 1 SPQ-9A radar |

Engineering: These ships have a 900-hp through thruster in the forward hull to assist in maneuvering while launching landing craft. The boilers are the largest ever manufactured in the United States.

Medical: Extensive medical facilities are provided, with permanent intensive-care space for 300 patients.

TARAWA (1975, Litton/Ingalls)

These are large helicopter carriers, combining the features of several previous amphibious ships into one hull. In addition to a full-length flight deck and large helicopter hangar, they have accommodations for a reinforced Marine battalion, a large combat-vehicle capacity, and a docking well for landing craft and amphibious tractors.

Aircraft: These ships have flight-deck "spots" for 12 CH-46 Sea Knights or 9 CH-53 Sea Stallions; the hangar deck can accommodate 30 Sea Knights or 19 Sea Stallions, or various combinations of helicopters or VSTOL aircraft.

Class: Nine ships of this class were originally planned. The Navy announced on 20 January 1971 that LHA 6–9 would not be constructed.

Cost: The estimated average cost per ship is over $230 million.

Design: Special features of this class include an 18-foot tilting mast to permit passage under bridges, a 5,000-square-foot training and acclimatization room to permit troops to exercise in a controlled environment, 30,000 square feet of vehicle storage decks, and five cargo elevators to move equipment from holds to flight deck. The stern docking well is 78 feet wide and 268 feet in length, and can accommodate 4 LCU-1610 landing craft, or 2 LCUs and 3 LCM-8s, or 17 LCM-6s. (In addition, 40 LVTs can be carried on the vehicle decks.)

The TARAWA at sea with her stern elevator lowered to the hangar deck level. A 5-inch Mk 45 light-weight gun and a Sea Sparrow "box" launcher are notched into the stern. LCMs and other small craft are stowed aft of the island structure; ramps from the hangar and garage levels exit from the front end of the island. (1976, Litton/Ingalls)

Amphibious tractors (LVTs) float out of the open stern well of the TARAWA. Note the opening in the stern counter when the stern elevator is at the flight deck level. (1977, U.S. Navy, PH3 Tilman)

The seven IWO JIMA-class LPHs have been the backbone of the Navy's amphibious forces for almost two decades. Their successors of the TARAWA class, at double the displacement, add landing craft and vehicle stowage to the troop and helicopter capabilities of the IWO JIMA class. (1975, U.S. Navy)

## 7 AMPHIBIOUS ASSAULT SHIPS: "IWO JIMA" CLASS

| Number | Name | FY/SCB | Builder | Laid down | Launched | Commissioned | Status |
|--------|------|--------|---------|-----------|----------|--------------|--------|
| LPH 2 | IWO JIMA | 58/157 | Puget Sound Naval Shipyard | 2 Apr 1959 | 17 Sep 1960 | 26 Aug 1961 | **AA** |
| LPH 3 | OKINAWA | 59/157 | Philadelphia Naval Shipyard | 1 Apr 1960 | 14 Aug 1961 | 14 Apr 1962 | **PA** |
| LPH 7 | GUADALCANAL | 60/157 | Philadelphia Naval Shipyard | 1 Sep 1961 | 16 Mar 1963 | 20 July 1963 | **AA** |
| LPH 9 | GUAM | 62/157 | Philadelphia Naval Shipyard | 15 Nov 1962 | 22 Aug 1964 | 16 Jan 1965 | **AA** |
| LPH 10 | TRIPOLI | 63/157 | Ingalls SB Corp | 15 June 1964 | 31 July 1965 | 6 Aug 1966 | **PA** |
| LPH 11 | NEW ORLEANS | 65/157 | Philadelphia Naval Shipyard | 1 Mar 1966 | 3 Feb 1968 | 16 Nov 1968 | **PA** |
| LPH 12 | INCHON | 66/157 | Ingalls SB Corp | 8 Apr 1968 | 24 May 1969 | 20 June 1970 | **AA** |

| | |
|--|--|
| Displacement: | 17,000 tons light |
| | 18,300 tons full load |
| Length: | 592 feet (180 m) oa |
| Beam: | 84 feet (25.6 m) |
| Extreme width: | 104 feet (31.9 m) |
| Draft: | 26 feet (7.9 m) |
| Propulsion: | steam turbine (Westinghouse); 22,000 shp; 1 shaft |
| Boilers: | 2 (Combustion Engineering or Babcock & Wilcox) |
| Speed: | 20 knots (sustained) |
| Complement: | 528 (48 O + 480 EM) |
| | |
| Troops: | 2,090 (190 O + 1,900 EM) |
| Helicopters: | 20–24 |
| Elevators: | 2 deck edge |
| Missiles: | 2 8-tube Sea Sparrow launchers Mk 25 BPDMS |
| Guns: | 4 3-inch (76-mm) 50 cal AA Mk 33 (2 × 2) |
| Radars: | SPS-10 surface search |
| | SPS-40 air search |
| Fire control: | 2 Mk 63 Mod 23/28/29 guns FCS |
| |    except 2 Mk 70 Mod 5 in LPH 2 |
| | 2 Mk 115 Mod 0 missile FCS |
| | 1 SPG-52A radar in LPH 2 |
| | 2 SPG-50 radar in LPH 3, 10, 12 |

These ships were the world's first designed specifically to operate helicopters. Unlike the Royal Navy's commando ships and the later TARAWA class, the ships do not carry landing craft and are thus limited in the size of vehicles that they can carry (except for LCVP davits in the INCHON).

The GUAM of this class operated from 1972 to 1974 as an interim sea-control ship to evaluate the concept of flying VSTOL fighters and ASW helicopters from a ship of this size in the convoy defense role; she subsequently reverted to an amphibious-assault role. These ships also have been used to support minesweeping helicopters.

Aircraft: These ships have flight-deck "spots" for seven CH-46 Sea Knight or four CH-53 Sea Stallion helicopters; the hangar deck can accommodate 19 Sea Knights or 11 Sea Stallions, or various combinations of helicopters.

Design: These ships represent an improved World War II-type escort carrier design with accommodations for a Marine battalion. The INCHON has davits aft for two LCVPs. No catapults or arresting gear are fitted.

Guns: As built, these ships had four 3-inch twin gun mounts. Between 1970 and 1974 all ships had two mounts replaced by the Sea Sparrow launchers (one on the flight deck forward of the island structure, and one on the port quarter).

Medical: These ships have extensive medical facilities.

The INCHON enters port after Operation Endsweep, the sweeping of U.S.-laid mines from the coast and harbor entrances of North Vietnam. Her deck is crowded with the large, CH-53 Sea Stallion helicopters used to two mine countermeasure "sleds." (1973, U.S. Navy)

GUADALCANAL (1977, U.S. Navy)

OKINAWA (1976, Giorgio Arra)

OKINAWA superstructure (1976, Giorgio Arra)

## AMPHIBIOUS ASSAULT SHIP PROGRAMS

The LPH classification was established in 1955. The World War II-era escort carrier BLOCK ISLAND was to have been LPH 1, but her conversion was cancelled. Three ESSEX-class carriers were subsequently modified to LPHs, as was the escort carrier THETIS BAY. The smaller ship had been designated a helicopter assault carrier (CVHA 1) upon her conversion in 1955–1956. She was changed to LPH to avoid confusion with CV-type aircraft carriers.

| | | |
|---|---|---|
| LPH 1 | BLOCK ISLAND (ex-CVE 106) | conversion cancelled |
| LPH 2–3 | IWO JIMA class | |
| LPH 4 | BOXER (ex-CVA/CVS 21) | to LPH 1959; stricken 1969 |
| LPH 5 | PRINCETON (ex-CVA/CVS 37) | to LPH 1959; stricken 1970 |
| LPH 6 | THETIS BAY (ex-CVE 90) | to CVHA 1/LPH 1956; stricken 1966 |
| LPH 7 | IWO JIMA class | |
| LPH 8 | VALLEY FORGE (ex-CVA/CVS 45) | to LPH 1961; stricken 1970 |
| LPH 9–12 | IWO JIMA class | |

### 5 AMPHIBIOUS CARGO SHIPS: "CHARLESTON" CLASS

| Number | Name | FY/SCB | Builder | Laid down | Launched | Commissioned | Status |
|---|---|---|---|---|---|---|---|
| LKA 113 | CHARLESTON | 65/403 | Newport News | 5 Dec 1966 | 2 Dec 1967 | 14 Dec 1968 | **AA** |
| LKA 114 | DURHAM | 65/403 | Newport News | 10 July 1967 | 29 Mar 1968 | 24 May 1969 | **PA** |
| LKA 115 | MOBILE | 65/403 | Newport News | 15 Jan 1968 | 19 Oct 1968 | 20 Sep 1969 | **PA** |
| LKA 116 | ST. LOUIS | 65/403 | Newport News | 3 Apr 1968 | 4 Jan 1969 | 22 Nov 1969 | **PA** |
| LKA 117 | EL PASO | 66/403 | Newport News | 22 Oct 1968 | 17 May 1969 | 17 Jan 1970 | **AA** |

| | |
|---|---|
| Displacement: | 20,700 tons full load |
| Length: | 575½ feet (175.4 m) oa |
| Beam: | 82 feet (25 m) |
| Draft: | 25½ feet (7.7 m) |
| Propulsion: | steam turbine (Westinghouse); 22,000 shp; 1 shaft |
| Boilers: | 2 600-psi (Combustion Engineering) |
| Speed: | 20+ knots (sustained) |
| Complement: | 334 (24 O + 310 EM) |
| | |
| Troops: | 226 (15 O + 211 EM) |
| Guns: | 6 3-inch (127-mm) 50 cal AA Mk 33 (3 × 2) |
| Radars: | SPS-10 surface search |
| Fire control: | (local control only) |

These ships carry heavy equipment and supplies for amphibious assaults. They are the first ships to be designed and constructed specifically for the amphibious role; previous ships of this type were converted or built to merchant designs.

Classification: As ordered, these ships were classified as attack cargo ships (AKA); the CHARLESTON was changed to an amphibious cargo ship (LKA) on 14 December 1968; others were changed to LKA on 1 January 1969.

Design: These ships each carry nine LCMs as deck cargo. There are two 78-ton capacity cranes, two 40-ton capacity booms, and eight 15-ton capacity booms. A helicopter deck is fitted aft.

Guns: As built, four 3-inch twin mounts were provided; one mount is being removed with the Mk 56 GFCS.

An LCM maneuvers alongside the attack cargo ship DURHAM. Note the heavy-lift booms for handling large landing craft, vehicles, and other cargo. A CH-46 Sea Knight is on the ship's stern helicopter deck. Attack cargo ships are named for counties. (1975, U.S. Navy, PH3 Harold Brown)

**1 AMPHIBIOUS CARGO SHIP: "MARINER" CLASS**

| Number | Name | Builder | Laid down | Launched | Commissioned | Status |
|---|---|---|---|---|---|---|
| LKA 112 | TULARE | Bethlehem Steel Co (San Francisco) | 16 Feb 1953 | 22 Dec 1953 | 12 Jan 1956 | **NRF-P** |

| | |
|---|---|
| Displacement: | 12,000 tons light |
| | 16,800 tons full load |
| Length: | 564 feet (171.9 m) oa |
| Beam: | 76 feet (23.2 m) |
| Draft: | 26 feet (7.9 m) |
| Propulsion: | steam turbine (De Laval); 22,000 shp; 1 shaft |
| Boilers: | 2 (Combustion Engineering) |
| Speed: | 22 knots |
| Complement: | 393 (10 O + 154 EM active; 21 O + 208 EM reserve) |
| | |
| Troops: | 319 (18 O + 301 EM) |
| Guns: | 6 3-inch (76-mm) 50 cal AA Mk 33 (3 × 2) |
| Radars: | SPS-10 surface search |
| | SPS-12 air search |
| Fire control: | (local control only) |

The TULARE was acquired by the Navy while under construction as a "Mariner"-class merchant ship; she was converted to an amphibious ship, and assigned to the Naval Reserve Force on 1 July 1975.

Class: Thirty-five "Mariner"-class merchant ships were built during the early 1950s; five of them being acquired by the Navy: two ships were converted to attack transports (APA/LPA) and two to experimental ships used for the fleet ballistic-missile programs (AG), plus the TULARE.

Classification: The TULARE originally was classified as an attack cargo ship (AKA); she was changed to amphibious cargo ship (LKA) on 1 January 1969.

Design: The TULARE has 60-ton-capacity booms, a helicopter deck aft, and can carry 9 LCM-6s and 11 LCVPs as deck cargo. The construction design was Maritime Administration C4-S-1A and the amphibious conversion was SCB-77.

Guns: As built, the TULARE was armed with 12 3-inch guns; the number of guns was reduced in the mid-1970s because of maintenance problems and limited effectiveness. Her Mk 63 GFCS was also removed.

Names: Ex-EVERGREEN MARINER.

TULARE (1969, U.S. Navy)

## Amphibious Cargo Ship Disposals

All surviving World War II-era amphibious cargo ships have been stricken (all LKA, formerly AKA). Of the TOLLAND class (C2-S-AJ3), the SEMINOLE (LKA 104), UNION (LKA 106), and WASHBURN (LKA 108) were stricken on 1 September 1976; the RANKIN (LKA 103) and VERMILLION (LKA 107) were stricken on 1 September 1977.

Of the ANDROMEDA class (C2-S-B1), the WINSTON (LKA 94) and MERRICK (LKA 97) were stricken on 1 September 1976; the THUBAN (LKA 19), ALGOL (LKA 54), CAPRICORNUS (LKA 57), MULIPHEN (LKA 61), and YANCEY (LKA 93) were stricken on 1 September 1977.

### 2 AMPHIBIOUS TRANSPORTS: "MARINER" CLASS

| Number | Name | Builder | Laid down | Launched | Commissioned | Status |
|--------|------|---------|-----------|----------|--------------|--------|
| LPA 248 | PAUL REVERE | New York SB Corp | 15 May 1952 | 11 Apr 1953 | 3 Sep 1958 | **NRF-P** |
| LPA 249 | FRANCIS MARION | New York SB Corp | 30 Mar 1953 | 12 Feb 1954 | 6 July 1961 | **NRF-A** |

| | |
|---|---|
| Displacement: | 10,709 tons light |
| | 16,838 tons full load |
| Length: | 563½ feet (171.8 m) oa |
| Beam: | 76 feet (23.2 m) |
| Draft: | 27 feet (8.2 m) |
| Propulsion: | steam turbine (General Electric); 22,000 shp; 1 shaft |
| Boilers: | 2 (Foster Wheeler) |
| Speed: | 22 knots |
| Complement: | 307 (13 O + 187 EM active; 15 O + 237 EM reserve) |
| | |
| Troops: | 1,657 (96 O + 1,561 EM) |
| Guns: | 8 3-inch (76-mm) 50 cal AA Mk 33 (4 × 2) |
| Radars: | SPS-10 surface search |
| | SPS-40 air search |
| Fire control: | 4 Mk 63 Mod 23 gun FCS |
| | 4 SPG-50 radar |

These ships were acquired by the Navy in 1953 and 1954, respectively, for conversion from "Mariner"-class merchant ships to amphibious ships. The PAUL REVERE was assigned to the Naval Reserve on 1 July 1975 and the FRANCIS MARION on 1 August 1975.

Classification: These ships originally were classified as attack transports (APA); they were changed to amphibious transports (LPA) on 1 January 1969.

Design: A helicopter deck is fitted aft; the ships can carry 7 LCM-6s and 16 LCVPs as deck cargo. They are Maritime Administration C4-S-1A type; their amphibious conversion was SCB-78. Each is fitted to serve as an amphibious force flagship.

Guns: As built, four 3-inch twin mounts were provided; all are scheduled to be retained although the GFCS will be removed.

Names: Merchant names were DIAMOND MARINER and PRAIRIE MARINER, respectively.

FRANCIS MARION (1975, Giorgio Arra)

Amphibious transports were built to carry troops to the assault area and unload them into landing craft. While the two post-World War II APA/LPA conversions of the "Mariner" type were named for Revolutionary War heroes, most of their predecessors carried county and parish names. Note the large SPS-40 air search radar atop the FRANCIS MARION's after boom structure. (1975, Giorgio Arra)

## Amphibious Transport Disposals

All surviving World War II-era amphibious transports have been stricken (all LPA, formerly APA). Of the HASKELL class (VC2-S-AP5), the SANDOVAL (LPA 194), MAGOFFON (LPA 199), TALLADEGA (LPA 208), MOUNTRAIL (LPA 213), NAVARRO (LPA 215), PICKAWAY (LPA 222), and BEXAR (LPA 237) were stricken on 1 December 1976.

**12 AMPHIBIOUS TRANSPORT DOCKS: "AUSTIN" CLASS**

| Number | Name | FY/SCB | Builder | Laid down | Launched | Commissioned | Status |
|--------|------|--------|---------|-----------|----------|--------------|--------|
| LPD 4 | AUSTIN | 62/187B | New York Naval Shipyard | 4 Feb 1963 | 27 June 1964 | 6 Feb 1965 | **AA** |
| LPD 5 | OGDEN | 62/187B | New York Naval Shipyard | 4 Feb 1963 | 27 June 1964 | 19 June 1965 | **PA** |
| LPD 6 | DULUTH | 62/187B | New York Naval Shipyard | 18 Dec 1963 | 14 Aug 1965 | 18 Dec 1965 | **PA** |
| LPD 7 | CLEVELAND | 63/187B | Ingalls SB Corp | 30 Nov 1964 | 7 May 1966 | 21 Apr 1967 | **PA** |
| LPD 8 | DUBUQUE | 63/187B | Ingalls SB Corp | 25 Jan 1965 | 6 Aug 1966 | 1 Sep 1967 | **PA** |
| LPD 9 | DENVER | 63/187B | Lockheed SB & Constn Co | 7 Feb 1964 | 23 Jan 1965 | 26 Oct 1968 | **PA** |
| LPD 10 | JUNEAU | 63/187B | Lockheed SB & Constn Co | 23 Jan 1965 | 12 Feb 1966 | 12 July 1969 | **PA** |
| LPD 11 | CORONADO | 64/187C | Lockheed SB & Constn Co | 3 May 1965 | 30 July 1966 | 23 May 1970 | **AA** |
| LPD 12 | SHREVEPORT | 64/187C | Lockheed SB & Constn Co | 27 Dec 1965 | 25 Oct 1966 | 12 Dec 1970 | **AA** |
| LPD 13 | NASHVILLE | 64/187C | Lockheed SB & Constn Co | 14 Mar 1966 | 7 Oct 1967 | 14 Feb 1970 | **AA** |
| LPD 14 | TRENTON | 65/402 | Lockheed SB & Constn Co | 8 Aug 1966 | 3 Aug 1968 | 6 Mar 1971 | **AA** |
| LPD 15 | PONCE | 65/402 | Lockheed SB & Constn Co | 31 Oct 1966 | 30 May 1970 | 10 July 1971 | **AA** |

| | |
|---|---|
| Displacement: | 10,000 tons light |
| | 16,900 tons full load |
| Length: | 570 feet (173.3) oa |
| Beam: | 84 feet (25.6 m) |
| Draft: | 23 feet (7 m) |
| Propulsion: | steam turbines (De Laval); 24,000 shp; 2 shafts |
| Boilers: | 2 580-psi (Babcock & Wilcox) |
| Speed: | 20 knots (sustained) |
| Complement: | 490 (30 O + 460 EM) |
| Flag: | 90 in LPD 7–13 |
| Troops: | 930 in LPD 4–6 and 14–16; 840 in LPD 7–13 |
| Helicopters: | up to 6 CH-46 Sea Knights |
| Guns: | 4 3-inch (76-mm) 50 cal AA Mk 33 (2 × 2) |
| Radars: | SPS-10 surface search |
| | SPS-40 air search |
| Fire control: | (local control only) |

These ships are enlarged versions of the previous RALEIGH-class LPDs; the general configuration of both classes is similar.

Aircraft: These ships have been fitted with a telescoping hangar aft of their superstructure to service helicopters. The hangar extends from 25 feet to 62 feet.

Builders: The DULUTH was completed at the Philadelphia Naval Shipyard after the closing of the New York yard; she was reassigned on 24 November 1965.

Class: An additional ship (LPD 16) was provided in FY 1966, but construction of the ship was deferred in favor of the LHA program and officially cancelled in February 1969.

Design: The LPD 7–13 are configured as amphibious squadron flagships. All ships have a docking well 168 feet long and 50 feet wide; see RALEIGH-class listing for well capacity. These ships have a fixed flight deck above the docking well. Vehicle deck space is increased over that of the RALEIGH class.

Guns: As completed, these ships had eight 3-inch guns; these were reduced in the mid-1970s because of maintenance problems and limited effectiveness. Their FCS are also being removed.

NASHVILLE (1973, Giorgio Arra)

The TRENTON, one of the last LPDs, at sea off Norfolk, Va. These ships are the successors to the APA/LPA transports, but have improved landing craft, vehicle, and helicopter capabilities. The TRENTON has a small lattice mast aft of her mainmast to support a satellite communications antenna. These ships are named for American cities that honor explorers and pioneers. (1976, Giorgio Arra)

The SHREVEPORT at anchor with the stern gate to her docking well open. The LPD sidewalls join directly to the helicopter deck; in LSDs they are above the sidewalls. "KA 113-7" indicates the seventh landing craft of the CHARLESTON (LKA 113); the letters "CH" are painted on the craft's bow ramp. (1973, Giorgio Arra)

DUBUQUE (1977, Giorgio Arra)

## 2 AMPHIBIOUS TRANSPORT DOCKS: "RALEIGH" CLASS

| Number | Name | FY/SCB | Builder | Laid down | Launched | Commissioned | Status |
|--------|------|--------|---------|-----------|----------|--------------|--------|
| LPD 1 | RALEIGH | 59/187 | New York Naval Shipyard | 23 June 1960 | 17 Mar 1962 | 8 Sep 1962 | **AA** |
| LPD 2 | VANCOUVER | 60/187 | New York Naval Shipyard | 19 Nov 1960 | 15 Sep 1962 | 11 May 1963 | **PA** |

Displacement: 8,040 tons light
13,900 tons full load
Length: 521¾ feet (158.4 m) oa
Beam: 84 feet (25.6 m)
Draft: 21 feet (6.4 m)
Propulsion: steam turbines (De Laval); 24,000 shp; 2 shafts
Boilers: 2 580-psi (Babcock & Wilcox)
Speed: 20 knots (sustained)
Complement: 490 (30 O + 460 EM)

Troops: 930
Guns: 6 3-inch (76-mm) 50 cal AA Mk 33 (3 × 2)
Radars: SPS-10 surface search
SPS-40 air search
Fire control: 1 Mk 56 Mod 39 gun FCS
2 Mk 51 Mod 3 gun FCS
1 Mk 35 Mod 2 radar in LPD 1

Guns: As built, these ships were armed with eight 3-inch guns; that number was reduced in the mid-1970s.

VANCOUVER (1976, Giorgio Arra)

The LPD is a development of the dock landing ship, incorporating additional troop capacity and cargo capacity, especially for wheeled and tracked vehicles. Thus, the LPD combines many of the features of the LSD/LPA/LKA-type ships in a single hull.

Aircraft: These ships have not been fitted with the telescoping helicopter hangars fitted in the later AUSTIN-class ships. (These ships can fuel helicopters and provide certain other services.

Class: The third ship of this class, the LA SALLE (LPD 3), has been reclassified as a miscellaneous flagship (AGF 3) and is listed in Chapter 13 of this edition.

Design: There is a permanent helicopter deck fitted over the docking well in these ships. They have a well 168 feet long and 50 feet wide which can accommodate one LCU and three LCM-6s, or four LCM-8s, or 20 LVTs (amphibious tractors). In addition, two LCM-6s or four LCPLs are normally carried on the helicopter deck.

VANCOUVER—no hangar (1976, Giorgio Arra)

## 5 DOCK LANDING SHIPS: "ANCHORAGE" CLASS

| Number | Name | FY/SCB | Builder | Laid down | Launched | Commissioned | Status |
|---|---|---|---|---|---|---|---|
| LSD 36 | ANCHORAGE | 65/404 | Ingalls SB Corp | 13 Mar 1967 | 5 May 1968 | 15 Mar 1969 | **PA** |
| LSD 37 | PORTLAND | 66/404 | General Dynamics (Quincy) | 21 Sep 1967 | 20 Dec 1969 | 3 Oct 1970 | **AA** |
| LSD 38 | PENSACOLA | 66/404 | General Dynamics (Quincy) | 12 Mar 1969 | 11 July 1970 | 27 Mar 1971 | **AA** |
| LSD 39 | MOUNT VERNON | 66/404 | General Dynamics (Quincy) | 29 Jan 1970 | 17 Apr 1971 | 13 May 1972 | **PA** |
| LSD 40 | FORT FISHER | 67/404 | General Dynamics (Quincy) | 15 July 1970 | 22 Apr 1972 | 9 Dec 1972 | **PA** |

| | |
|---|---|
| Displacement: | 8,600 tons light |
| | 13,700 tons full load |
| Length: | 553⅓ feet (168.6 m) oa |
| Beam: | 84 feet (25.6 m) |
| Draft: | 18½ feet (5.6 m) |
| Propulsion: | steam turbines (De Laval); 24,000 shp; 2 shafts |
| Boilers: | 2 585-psi (Foster Wheeler, except Combustion Engineering in LSD 36) |
| Speed: | 20 knots (sustained) |
| Complement: | 397 (21 O + 376 EM) |
| | |
| Troops: | 376 (28 O + 348 EM) |
| Guns: | 6 3-inch (76-mm) 50 cal AA Mk 33 (3 × 2) |

| | |
|---|---|
| Radars: | SPS-10 surface search |
| | SPS-40 air search |
| Fire control: | (local control only) |

Aircraft: These ships have a removable helicopter deck above their docking well; no hangar is provided.

Design: Two 50-ton-capacity cranes are provided. The docking well is 430 feet long and 50 feet wide, and can accommodate 3 LCUs, or 9 LCM-8s, or approximately 50 LVTs.

Guns: These ships originally were armed with eight 3-inch guns; their number was reduced during the 1970s.

The PORTLAND is one of five LSDs constructed during the emphasis on amphibious force modernization during the early 1960s. These ships principally carry cargo and landing craft. The ANCHORAGE-class ships are similar in design to the previous THOMASTON class. LSDs are named for historic sites, with the first three ships of this class honoring historic cities. (1973, Giorgio Arra)

PENSACOLA (1975, Giorgio Arra)

FORT FISHER (1974, J. Mortimer)

## 8 DOCK LANDING SHIPS: "THOMASTON" CLASS

| Number | Name | FY/SCB | Builder | Laid down | Launched | Commissioned | Status |
|--------|------|--------|---------|-----------|----------|--------------|--------|
| LSD 28 | THOMASTON | 52/75 | Ingalls SB Corp | 3 Mar 1953 | 9 Feb 1954 | 17 Sep 1954 | **PA** |
| LSD 29 | PLYMOUTH ROCK | 52/75 | Ingalls SB Corp | 5 May 1953 | 7 May 1954 | 29 Nov 1954 | **AA** |
| LSD 30 | FORT SNELLING | 52/75 | Ingalls SB Corp | 17 Aug 1953 | 16 July 1954 | 24 Jan 1955 | **AA** |
| LSD 31 | POINT DEFIANCE | 52/75 | Ingalls SB Corp | 23 Nov 1953 | 28 Sep 1954 | 31 Mar 1955 | **PA** |
| LSD 32 | SPIEGEL GROVE | 54/75 | Ingalls SB Corp | 7 Sep 1954 | 10 Nov 1955 | 8 June 1956 | **AA** |
| LSD 33 | ALAMO | 54/75 | Ingalls SB Corp | 11 Oct 1954 | 20 Jan 1956 | 24 Aug 1956 | **PA** |
| LSD 34 | HERMITAGE | 55/75 | Ingalls SB Corp | 11 Apr 1955 | 12 June 1956 | 14 Dec 1956 | **AA** |
| LSD 35 | MONTICELLO | 55/75 | Ingalls SB Corp | 6 June 1955 | 10 Aug 1956 | 29 Mar 1957 | **PA** |

| | |
|---|---|
| Displacement: | 6,880 tons light |
| | 11,270 tons full load; except LSD 32–34, 12,150 tons |
| Length: | 510 feet (155.5 m) oa |
| Beam: | 84 feet (25.6 m) |
| Draft: | 19 feet (5.8 m) |
| Propulsion: | steam turbines (General Electric); 24,000 shp; 2 shafts |
| Boilers: | 2 (Babcock & Wilcox) |
| Speed: | 22.5 knots |
| Complement: | 404 (21 O + 383 EM) |
| | |
| Troops: | 341 (29 O + 312 EM) |
| Guns: | 6 3-inch (76-mm) 50 cal AA Mk 33 (3 × 2) |
| Radars: | SPS-6 air search |
| | SPS-10 surface search |
| Fire control: | (local control only) |

MONTICELLO (1967, U.S. Navy)

Aircraft: A removable helicopter deck is fitted above the docking well, no hangar is provided.

Design: These ships have two 5-ton-capacity cranes. The docking well is 391 feet long and 48 feet wide; it can accommodate 3 LCUs, or 9 LCM-8s, or about 50 LVTs.

Guns: As built, these ships were armed with 16 3-inch guns and 12 20-mm AA guns; their armament was reduced to 12 3-inch guns during the 1960s and to 6 3-inch guns during the mid-1970s (with fire control directors also removed).

POINT DEFIANCE (1976, Giorgio Arra)

POINT DEFIANCE (1976, Giorgio Arra)

ALAMO (1974, J. Mortimer)

## Dock Landing Ship Disposals

All dock landing ships of the CASA GRANDE class have been stricken from the Naval Register. The class, completed 1943–1945, originally included hulls LSD 9–27. LSD 9–12 were transferred to Great Britain upon completion and LSD 23 and 24 were cancelled; the latter was completed for commercial use but subsequently reacquired by the Navy (renamed the TARUS and successively reclassified AK 273, LSV 8, and AKR 8; stricken in 1969). Thirteen ships were operated by the U.S. Navy:

| LSD 13 | CASA GRANDE | stricken 1 Nov 1976 |
|---|---|---|
| LSD 14 | RUSHMORE | stricken 1 Nov 1976 |
| LSD 15 | SHADWELL | stricken 1 Nov 1976; to Energy Research and Development Administration |
| LSD 16 | CABILDO | stricken 1977 |
| LSD 17 | CATAMOUNT | stricken 31 Oct 1974 |
| LSD 18 | COLONIAL | stricken 15 Oct 1976 |
| LSD 19 | COMSTOCK | to Taiwan China 1976 |
| LSD 20 | DONNER | stricken 1 Nov 1976; to Energy Research and Development Administration |
| LSD 21 | FORT MANDAN | to Greece 1971 |
| LSD 22 | FORT MARION | to South Korea 1976 |
| LSD 25 | SAN MARCOS | to Spain 1971 |
| LSD 26 | TORTUGA | stricken 15 Oct 1976 |
| LSD 27 | WHETSTONE | to Peru 1976 |

A Marine Corps M48 medium gun tank coming aboard an Australian landing craft, from the USS POINT DEFIANCE (LSD 31), during preparations for a beach assault in Operation Kangaroo II.

Casa Grande (1968, U.S. Navy)

The Fairfax County (LST 1193) and the Inchon (LPH 12), cruising in the Mediterranean.

## 20 TANK LANDING SHIPS: "NEWPORT" CLASS

| Number | Name | FY/SCB | Builder | Laid down | Launched | Commissioned | Status |
|--------|------|--------|---------|-----------|----------|--------------|--------|
| LST 1179 | NEWPORT | 65/405 | Philadelphia Naval Shipyard | 1 Nov 1966 | 3 Feb 1968 | 7 June 1969 | **AA** |
| LST 1180 | MANITOWOC | 66/405 | Philadelphia Naval Shipyard | 1 Feb 1967 | 4 June 1969 | 24 Jan 1970 | **AA** |
| LST 1181 | SUMTER | 66/405 | Philadelphia Naval Shipyard | 14 Nov 1967 | 13 Dec 1969 | 20 June 1970 | **AA** |
| LST 1182 | FRESNO | 66/405 | National Steel & SB Co | 16 Dec 1967 | 20 Sep 1968 | 22 Nov 1969 | **PA** |
| LST 1183 | PEORIA | 66/405 | National Steel & SB Co | 22 Feb 1968 | 23 Nov 1968 | 21 Feb 1970 | **PA** |
| LST 1184 | FREDERICK | 66/405 | National Steel & SB Co | 13 Apr 1968 | 8 Mar 1969 | 11 Apr 1970 | **PA** |
| LST 1185 | SCHENECTADY | 66/405 | National Steel & SB Co | 2 Aug 1968 | 24 May 1969 | 13 June 1970 | **PA** |
| LST 1186 | CAYUGA | 66/405 | National Steel & SB Co | 28 Sep 1968 | 12 July 1969 | 8 Aug 1970 | **PA** |
| LST 1187 | TUSCALOOSA | 66/405 | National Steel & SB Co | 23 Nov 1968 | 6 Sep 1969 | 24 Oct 1970 | **PA** |
| LST 1188 | SAGINAW | 67/405 | National Steel & SB Co | 24 May 1969 | 7 Feb 1970 | 23 Jan 1971 | **AA** |
| LST 1189 | SAN BERNARDINO | 67/405 | National Steel & SB Co | 12 July 1969 | 28 Mar 1970 | 27 Mar 1971 | **PA** |
| LST 1190 | BOULDER | 67/405 | National Steel & SB Co | 6 Sep 1969 | 22 May 1970 | 4 June 1971 | **AA** |
| LST 1191 | RACINE | 67/405 | National Steel & SB Co | 13 Dec 1969 | 15 Aug 1970 | 9 July 1971 | **PA** |
| LST 1192 | SPARTANBURG COUNTY | 67/405 | National Steel & SB Co | 7 Feb 1970 | 11 Nov 1970 | 1 Sep 1971 | **AA** |
| LST 1193 | FAIRFAX COUNTY | 67/405 | National Steel & SB Co | 28 Mar 1970 | 19 Dec 1970 | 16 Oct 1971 | **AA** |
| LST 1194 | LA MOURE COUNTY | 67/405 | National Steel & SB Co | 22 May 1970 | 13 Feb 1971 | 18 Dec 1971 | **AA** |
| LST 1195 | BARBOUR COUNTY | 67/405 | National Steel & SB Co | 15 Aug 1970 | 15 May 1971 | 12 Feb 1972 | **PA** |
| LST 1196 | HARLAN COUNTY | 67/405 | National Steel & SB Co | 7 Nov 1970 | 24 July 1971 | 8 Apr 1972 | **AA** |
| LST 1197 | BARNSTABLE COUNTY | 67/405 | National Steel & SB Co | 19 Dec 1970 | 2 Oct 1971 | 27 May 1972 | **AA** |
| LST 1198 | BRISTOL COUNTY | 67/405 | National Steel & SB Co | 13 Feb 1971 | 4 Dec 1971 | 5 Aug 1972 | **PA** |

| | |
|--|--|
| Displacement: | 8,342 tons full load |
| Length: | 522⅓ feet (159.2 m) hull oa; 562 feet (171.3 m) over derrick arms |
| Beam: | 69½ feet (21.2 m) |
| Draft: | 17½ feet (5.3 m) |
| Propulsion: | diesels (Alco); 16,500 bhp; 2 shafts |
| Speed: | 20 knots (sustained) |
| Complement: | 223 (12 O + 211 EM) |
| | |
| Troops: | 386 (20 O + 366 EM) |
| Guns: | 4 3-inch (76-mm) 50 cal AA Mk 33 (2 × 2) |
| Radars: | SPS-10 surface search |
| Fire control: | 3 Mk 63 Mod 29 gun FCS |
| | 3 SPG-50 radar |

These ships represent the "ultimate" design in landing ships that can be "beached." They depart from the traditional LST bow-door design by using a pointed bow; this allows them to sustain a speed of 20 knots.

Design: This design has bow and stern ramps for unloading tanks and other vehicles. The bow ramp is 112 feet long and is handled over the bow by twin fixed derrick arms. Vehicles can be driven to the lower deck via a ramp, or through a passage in superstructure which leads to the helicopter deck aft. The stern ramp permits unloading of amphibious vehicles into water, or "mating" to landing craft or a pier. These ships' cargo capacity is 500 tons of vehicles, on 19,000 square feet of parking area (not including the helicopter deck). The draft listed above is maximum aft; the full-load draft forward is 11½ feet.

Engineering: They are fitted with six diesel engines. A through-hull bow thruster is provided to maintain the ship's position while unloading amphibious vehicles.

Guns: The twin 3-inch gun mounts, installed atop the superstructure, will be replaced by two 20-mm CIWS when the latter become available.

The SAGINAW with bow ramp lowered through open bows and bulwarks. The angle of the bow ramp onto a becah would be steeper. The aluminum ramp weighs 35 tons. (1974, U.S. Navy, PH3 A. M. Page)

The BARNSTABLE COUNTY, the penultimate NEWPORT-class LST, transiting the Suez Canal. She has an unusual LST configuration: Note bow ramp on main deck behind protruding derrick arms, twin 3-inch gun mounts atop cluttered superstructure, two stacks of different shape aft of boat davits, and open helicopter-vehicle parking area aft. (1974, U.S. Navy)

CAYUGA (1976, U.S. Navy, PH1 J. R. Sheppard)

**3 TANK LANDING SHIPS: "SUFFOLK COUNTY" CLASS**

| Number | Name | FY/SCB | Builder | Laid down | Launched | Commissioned | Status |
|--------|------|--------|---------|-----------|----------|--------------|--------|
| LST 1173 | SUFFOLK COUNTY | 55/199 | Boston Navy Yard | 17 July 1956 | 5 Sep 1956 | 15 Aug 1957 | AR |
| LST 1177 | LORAIN COUNTY | 55/119 | American SB Co | 9 Aug 1956 | 22 June 1957 | 3 Oct 1958 | MR |
| LST 1178 | WOOD COUNTY | 55/119 | American SB Co | 1 Oct 1956 | 14 Dec 1957 | 5 Aug 1959 | MR |

| | |
|---|---|
| Displacement: | 4,164 tons light |
| | 8,000 tons full load |
| Length: | 445 feet (138.7 m) oa |
| Beam: | 62 feet (18.9 m) |
| Draft: | 16½ feet (5 m) |
| Propulsion: | diesels; 14,440 bhp; 2 shafts (controllable-pitch propellers) |
| Speed: | 17.5 knots |
| Complement: | 184 (10 O + 174 EM) |

| | |
|---|---|
| Troops: | ~575 |
| Guns: | 6 3-inch (76-mm) 50 cal AA Mk 33 (3 × 2) |
| Radars: | SPS-10 surface search |
| Fire control: | 2 Mk 63 Mod 14 gun FCS |
| | 2 SPG-34 radar |

These were the last U.S. Navy LSTs with the traditional bow doors and ramp.

Builders: The LORAIN COUNTY was transferred to Todd-Pacific Shipyards for trials and completion.

Class: This class originally included seven ships (LST 1171, 1173–1178) completed 1957–1959. The unnamed LST 1172 was cancelled in 1955. The GRAHAM COUNTY (LST 1176) was converted to a gunboat support ship (AGP 1176); see p. 188. Three other ships were transferred to Brazil and Italy in 1972–1973.

Conversion: The WOOD COUNTY was scheduled for conversion to support the PEGASUS-class (PHM 1) patrol hydrofoil combatants (to be designated AGHS). That conversion was deferred in 1977 (see AGHS listing in Chapter 18).

Design: These ships are more habitable than earlier LSTs, with air-conditioned crew and troop spaces. Up to 20 amphibious tractors, 23 medium tanks, or vehicles up to 75 tons can be carried on the 288-foot tank deck. Four LCVPs are carried in davits.

Engineering: All were built with six Nordburg diesel engines; the SUFFOLK COUNTY was refitted with Fairbanks Morse diesels, and the two other surviving ships with Cooper Bessemer diesels.

The LORAIN COUNTY, one of the last "conventional" LSTs. The LSTs were assigned county and parish names in 1955, all with the suffix "County" or "Parish." The NEWPORT of 1969 changed this practice, with many ships of that class having city names as well. (1969, U.S. Navy)

**2 TANK LANDING SHIPS: "TERREBONNE PARISH" CLASS**

| Number | Name | FY/SCB | Builder | Laid down | Launched | Commissioned | Status |
|--------|------|--------|---------|-----------|----------|--------------|--------|
| LST 1157 | TERRELL COUNTY | 52/9 | Bath Iron Works | 3 Mar 1952 | 6 Dec 1952 | 14 Mar 1953 | PR |
| LST 1169 | WHITFIELD COUNTY | 52/9 | Christy Corp | 26 Nov 1952 | 22 Aug 1953 | 14 Sep 1954 | PR |

| | |
|---|---|
| Displacement: | 2,580 tons light |
| | 5,800 tons full load |
| Length: | 384 feet (117 m) oa |
| Beam: | 55 feet (16.8 m) |
| Draft: | 17 feet (5.2 m) |
| Propulsion: | diesels (General Motors); 6,000 bhp; 2 shafts (controllable-pitch propellers) |
| Speed: | 15 knots |
| Complement: | 157 (10 O + 147 EM) |
| | |
| Troops: | 392 (15 O + 377 EM) |
| Guns: | 6 3-inch (76-mm) 50 cal AA Mk 33 (3 × 2) |
| Radars: | SPS-10 |
| Fire control: | 2 Mk 63 Mod 14 gun FCS |
| | 2 SPG-34 radar |

Fifteen ships of this class were authorized in the FY 1952 shipbuilding program in response to the renewed interest in amphibious warfare during the Korean War. They saw service in the Vietnam War, after which six ships were transferred to the Military Sealift Command (1972) but were stricken shortly afterward, and transferred to Maritime Administration in 1973–1974 for disposal.

Class: Originally LST 1156–1170. The WASHTENAW COUNTY (LST 1166) was reclassified as a minesweeper support ship (MSS 2), and subsequently stricken. Six ships were transferred to Spain, Turkey, and Venezuela in 1971–1974, and six ships operated by MSC were stricken in 1973–1974.

Design: These ships are similar to the previous TALBOT COUNTY class (LST 1153) except the later ships have diesel rather than steam propulsion. Up to 17 amphibious tanks (LVT) can be carried on the tank deck. Four LCVPs are carried in davits.

The TERRELL COUNTY rides at anchor in the South China Sea with a UH-1 "Huey" helicopter on deck. LSTs operated helicopters as early as the Korean War for mine spotting. All post-World War II ships had 3-inch guns except the two TALBOTS COUNTY-class ships (LST 1153-1154), which had two 5-inch single mounts. LSTs have stern anchors for retracting off beaches. (1969, U.S. Navy)

## 2 TANK LANDING SHIPS: LST 1–1152 CLASS

| Number | Name | Builder | Laid down | Launched | Commissioned | Status |
|---|---|---|---|---|---|---|
| LST 758 | DUVAL COUNTY | American Bridge Co | 5 June 1944 | 25 July 1944 | 19 Aug 1944 | AR |
| LST 1148 | SUMNER COUNTY | Chicago Bridge & Iron Co | 15 Feb 1945 | 23 May 1945 | 9 June 1945 | PR |

| | |
|---|---|
| Displacement: | 1,653 tons standard |
| | 2,080 tons full load |
| Length: | 328 feet (110 m) oa |
| Beam: | 50 feet (15.2 m) |
| Draft: | 14 feet (4.3 m) |
| Propulsion: | diesels (General Motors); 1,700 bhp; 2 shafts |
| Speed: | 11.6 knots |
| Complement: | 115 (9 O + 106 EM) |
| | |
| Troops: | 137 (10 O + 127 EM) |
| Guns: | 8 40-mm AA (2 × 2 Mk 1, 4 × 1 Mk 3) |
| Radars: | SPS-10 surface search |
| Fire control: | 2 Mk 51 Mod 2 gun directors |

These ships are the survivors of the 1,052 tank landing ships built by the U.S. Navy during World War II. Many have been transferred to other navies, while others have been converted to auxiliary configurations (AG, AGP, ARB, ARL, ARVA, ARVE, AVB, IX); and one ship (LST 735) was transferred to Taiwan and modified to an amphibious command ship (AGC).

Class: Originally LST 1–1152, with 100 units cancelled.

Design: Maritime Administration S3-M2-K2 design. Cargo capacity is 2,100 tons or 14 amphibious tractors (LVT). Two LCVPs are carried in davits.

Names: LST numbers were assigned until 1 July 1955, when county and parish names were assigned to 158 Navy LSTs (36 Japanese-manned T-LSTs were not named).

## POST-WORLD WAR II TANK LANDING SHIP PROGRAMS

Through June 1945 a total of 1,052 LSTs were completed (numbered LST 1–1152, with 100 ships cancelled); the latter 611 ships (LST 542 onward) had minor improvements over the earlier series. Three ships of a larger improved design (steam-turbine propulsion) were ordered during the war, with two (LST 1153–1154) completed in 1947. (All other U.S. LSTs have been diesel-propelled.)

| | | |
|---|---|---|
| LST 1153 | TALBOT COUNTY | Comm. 1947; stricken 1973 |
| LST 1154 | TALLAHATCHEE COUNTY | Comm. 1949; conv. to AVB 2 |
| LST 1155 | cancelled 1946 | |
| LST 1156–1170 | TERREBONNE PARISH class | |
| LST 1171–1178 | SUFFOLK COUNTY class | |
| LST 1179–1198 | NEWPORT class | |

The DUVALL COUNTY, the oldest LST retained by the U.S. Navy. She was built with a pole mast; replaced by a tripod to support surface radar and minimal EW equipment. She has empty "tubs" forward for single 40-mm AA guns in this photograph taken shortly before her decommissioning. A mobile cargo crane is aft of the helicopter "spot." (1968, U.S. Navy)

## FIRE SUPPORT SHIP PROGRAMS

In World War II numerous production landing ships were modified during construction or converted to the fire-support role for amphibious landings (LCIG, LCIM, LCIR, LSMR) and the LCSL was constructed specifically for that role. The CARRONADE was an improved LSMR with a single 5-inch gun and rapid-fire rocket launchers (designation changed from IFS to LFR 1 on 1 January 1969, along with surviving LSMRs).

| | | |
|---|---|---|
| IFS 1 | CARRONADE | Comm. 1955; stricken 1973 (LFR 1) |

# 15 Landing Craft

The U.S. Navy has several hundred landing craft. The principal types, as well as two prototype air cushion vehicles, are listed here. There are also a few Navy-operated amphibious wheeled and tracked vehicles in use, while the Marine Corps has several hundred amphibious tractors ("amtracs") of the LVTP-7 series (Landing Vehicle, Tracked, Personnel, Model 7). Some of these are configured as command vehicles (LVTC-7), recovery vehicles (LVTR-7), and mine clearing (engineer) vehicles (LVTE-7).

## 1 AMPHIBIOUS ASSAULT LANDING CRAFT: "JEFF-A"

| Number | Name | Status |
|--------|------|--------|
| (AALC) | JEFF-A | **Test** |

| | |
|---|---|
| Weight: | 85.8 tons empty |
| | 166.4 tons gross |
| Length: | 97 feet (29.6 m) hullborne |
| | 96⅙ feet (29.3 m) on air cushion |
| Beam: | 44 feet (13.4 m) hullborne |
| | 48 feet (14.6 m) on air cushion |
| Propulsion: | 4 gas turbines (Avco-Lycoming); 11,200 shp; 4 aircraft-type propellers in shrouds |
| Lift: | 2 gas turbines (Avco-Lycoming); 5,600 shp; 8 horizontal fans |
| Speed: | ~50 knots |
| Complement: | 6 |
| Armament: | none |

The JEFF-A is one of two competitive prototypes of Amphibious Assault Landing Craft (AALC) constructed for Navy–Marine Corps evaluation. The JEFF-A design was developed by the Aerojet-General Corporation, built by Todd Shipyards, Seattle (Washington), and delivered in 1977.

Design: The all-aluminum craft has bow and stern ramps, 2,100 square feet of open cargo area, and can carry 120,000 pounds of cargo or vehicles. No SCB number is assigned.

## 1 AMPHIBIOUS ASSAULT LANDING CRAFT: "JEFF-B"

| Number | Name | Status |
|--------|------|--------|
| (AALC) | JEFF-B | **Test** |

| | |
|---|---|
| Weight: | 162.5 tons gross |
| Length: | 80 feet (24.4 m) hullborne |
| | 86¾ feet (26.4 m) on air cushion |
| Beam: | 43 feet (13.1 m) hullborne |
| | 47 feet (14.3 m) on air cushion |
| Propulsion: | 6 gas turbines (Avco-Lycoming); 16,800 shp; 2 aircraft-type propellers in shrouds |
| Lift: | 4 horizontal fans (interconnected to propulsion engines) |
| Speed: | ~50 knots |
| Complement: | 6 |
| Armament: | none |

The JEFF-B is a competitive prototype with the JEFF-A landing craft. This craft was developed and built by Bell Aerosystems at the National Aeronautics and Space Administration's former facility in Michoud, Louisiana, and delivered in 1977.

Design: The craft has bow and stern ramps, 1,738 square feet of open cargo area, and a cargo capacity of about 120,000 pounds. The JEFF-B is all-aluminum construction. Unlike the JEFF-A, this craft does not have separate lift engines. No SCB number is assigned to this craft.

JEFF-A (Aerojet-General)

JEFF-B (Bell Aerospace Textron)

## 54 UTILITY LANDING CRAFT: "LCU 1610" CLASS

| Number | Number | Number | Number |
|---|---|---|---|
| LCU 1613 | LCU 1632 | LCU 1655 | LCU 1669 |
| LCU 1614 | LCU 1633 | LCU 1656 | LCU 1670 |
| LCU 1616 | LCU 1634 | LCU 1657 | LCU 1671 |
| LCU 1617 | LCU 1641 | LCU 1658 | LCU 1672 |
| LCU 1618 | LCU 1644 | LCU 1659 | LCU 1673 |
| LCU 1619 | LCU 1645 | LCU 1660 | LCU 1674 |
| LCU 1621 | LCU 1646 | LCU 1661 | LCU 1675 |
| LCU 1623 | LCU 1647 | LCU 1662 | LCU 1676 |
| LCU 1624 | LCU 1648 | LCU 1663 | LCU 1677 |
| LCU 1627 | LCU 1649 | LCU 1664 | LCU 1678 |
| LCU 1628 | LCU 1650 | LCU 1665 | LCU 1679 |
| LCU 1629 | LCU 1651 | LCU 1666 | LCU 1680 |
| LCU 1630 | LCU 1653 | LCU 1667 | |
| LCU 1631 | LCU 1654 | LCU 1668 | |

| | |
|---|---|
| Displacement: | 170 tons light |
| | 390 tons full load |
| Length: | 134¾ feet (41 m) oa |
| Beam: | 29¾ feet (9 m) |
| Draft: | 6 feet (1.8 m) |
| Propulsion: | geared diesels (Detroit); 2,000 bhp; 2 shafts (see Engineering notes) |
| Speed: | 11 knots |
| Range: | 1,200 n. miles at 11 knots (loaded) |
| Complement: | 6 (EM) |
| Troops: | 8 |
| Guns: | 2 20-mm AA or 2 .50-cal MG (2 × 1) |

These are improved LCUs with 15 units (LCU 1610–1624) completed in 1960, and the remainder from 1967 to 1976. Several small shipyards constructed these craft.

Class: This class originally consisted of hull numbers LCU 1610–1624 and 1627–1680. Several units have been transferred to other navies, stricken, or reclassified as ferry boats (YFB) or harbor utility craft (YFU). The latter are listed with Service Craft (Chapter 19).

Design: These LCUs have a "drive-through" configuration with bow and stern ramps, and a small, starboard-side island structure, housing controls and accommodations. They are welded-steel construction. The mast folds down for entering well decks in amphibious ships. Cargo capacity is three M-48 or M-103 tanks or up to about 150 tons. The LCU 1610–1624 were SCB-149 and the LCU 1627 and later units were SCB-149B (later SCB-406).

Engineering: The LCU 1621 has vertical shafts fitted with vertical axis, cycloidal six-bladed propellers. All other units have Kort-nozzle propellers.

Guns: Weapons are not normally carried in these craft.

## 1 UTILITY LANDING CRAFT: "LCU 1637"

| Number |
|---|
| LCU 1637 |

| | |
|---|---|
| Displacement: | 135 tons light |
| | 357 tons full load |
| Length: | 134¾ feet (41 m) oa |
| Beam: | 29¾ feet (9 m) |
| Draft: | 6 feet (1.8 m) |
| Propulsion: | geared diesels (Detroit); 2,000 bhp; 2 shafts |
| Speed: | 12 knots |
| Complement: | 6 (EM) |
| Troops: | 8 |
| Guns: | 2 20-mm AA (2 × 1) |

The LCU 1637 was a prototype craft of all-aluminum construction which is otherwise identical to the LCU 1610 class. The LCU 1637 is slightly faster than a steel LCU. The mast folds down, as in other LCUs, for transport in amphibious docking wells. No additional units of this type have been constructed.

LCU 1653 with mast lowered (1975, Giorgio Arra)

LCU 1662 (1971, Defoe Shipbuilding)

LCU 1627 (U.S. Navy)

LCU 1661 (1975, Giorgio Arra)

## 25 UTILITY LANDING CRAFT: "LCU 1466" CLASS

| Number | Number | Number | Number |
|---|---|---|---|
| LCU 1466 | LCU 1477 | LCU 1489 | LCU 1539 |
| LCU 1467 | LCU 1482 | LCU 1490 | LCU 1547 |
| LCU 1468 | LCU 1484 | LCU 1492 | LCU 1548 |
| LCU 1469 | LCU 1485 | LCU 1525 | LCU 1559 |
| LCU 1470 | LCU 1486 | LCU 1535 | |
| LCU 1472 | LCU 1487 | LCU 1536 | |
| LCU 1473 | LCU 1488 | LCU 1537 | |

| | |
|---|---|
| Displacement: | 180 tons light |
| | 360 tons full load |
| Length: | 119 feet (39 m) oa |
| Beam: | 34 feet (10.4 m) |
| Draft: | 6 feet (1.8 m) |
| Propulsion: | geared diesels (Gray Marine); 675 bhp; 3 shafts |
| Speed: | 8 knots |
| Complement: | 6 (EM) |
| Troops: | 8 |
| Guns: | 2 20-mm AA (2 × 1) |

These LCUs are similar to their World War II-era predecessors. The units delivered to the U.S. Navy were completed between 1954 and 1957. The LCU 1473, which had been laid up in reserve, was reactivated in 1973 and assigned to the Naval Reserve Force (Reserve Assault Craft Unit 2).

Class: This class covered hull numbers LCU 1466–1609, with 14 units constructed in Japan under offshore procurement for foreign service (LCU 1594–1601 completed for Taiwan and LCU 1602–1607 completed for Japan, all in 1955); others were built for U.S. Army service.

Several U.S. units have been transferred to other navies and others have been scrapped. Some became harbor utility craft (YFU); one of these, the LCU 1488 (ex-YFU 94) reverted to LCU status on 1 February 1972.

Classification: The LCU 1466–1503 were ordered as utility landing ships (LSU 1466–1503) on 31 October 1951; they were reclassified as LCUs on 15 April 1952.

Design: These craft have a bow ramp and stern superstructure. They are welded-steel construction. Design was SCB-25.

LCU 1469, with mast lowered, unloading mobile crane (U.S. Navy)

LCU 1488 (U.S. Navy)

LCU 1491 carrying three Marine medium tanks (U.S. Navy)

## 23 UTILITY LANDING CRAFT: "LCU 501" CLASS

| Number | Number | Number | Number |
| --- | --- | --- | --- |
| LCU 539 | LCU 666 | LCU 871 | LCU 1387 |
| LCU 588 | LCU 667 | LCU 893 | LCU 1430 |
| LCU 599 | LCU 674 | LCU 1045 | LCU 1451 |
| LCU 608 | LCU 742 | LCU 1124 | LCU 1462 |
| LCU 654 | LCU 768 | LCU 1241 | |
| LCU 660 | LCU 803 | LCU 1348 | |

Displacement: 143–160 tons light
    309–320 tons full load
Length: $119^{1}/_{12}$ feet (39 m) oa
Beam: $32^{2}/_{3}$ feet (10 m)
Draft: $3^{3}/_{4}$ feet (1.1 m)
Propulsion: diesels (Gray Marine); 675 bhp; 3 shafts
Speed: 10 knots
Complement: } 12–13 (EM)
Troops:
Guns: 2 20-mm AA (2 × 1)

These craft were completed in 1943–1944.

Class: This class originally consisted of hull numbers 501–1465. Numerous units were transferred to other navies, scrapped, or lost; several employed as harbor utility craft (YFU) or salvage lifting craft (YLLC), with the LCU 666 (ex-YFU 9) reverting to LCU status on 1 January 1962.

Classification: These craft were built as tank landing craft (LCT(6) 501–1465). The surviving units were reclassified as utility landing ships (LSU) in 1949 and were changed again to LCUs on 15 April 1952.

The subsequent LCT(7) 1501–1830 were completed with the designation LSM for medium landing ship, with hull numbers beginning with LSM 1.

Design: These craft have a bow ramp and superstructure aft. They were built in three sections for transport as deck cargo and welded together at forward bases. Cargo capacity is almost 200 tons.

## MECHANIZED LANDING CRAFT: LCM(8) Mod 2 DESIGN

Displacement: 36.5 tons light
    106.75 tons full load
Length: $74^{1}/_{2}$ feet (22.7 m) oa
Beam: $21^{1}/_{12}$ feet (6.4 m)
Draft: $4^{1}/_{2}$ feet (1.4 m)
Propulsion: diesels (Detroit); 1,300 bhp; 2 shafts
Speed: 12 knots
Complement: 5 (EM)
Armament: none

The LCM(8) Mod 2 is an aluminum version of the steel LCM(8) which was developed for use with the CHARLESTON-class (LKA 113) attack cargo ships.

Design: These craft are constructed of welded aluminum. Cargo capacity is one M-60 tank or 65 tons.

Engineering: Some units have been refitted with Kort nozzles.

## MECHANIZED LANDING CRAFT: LCM(8) Mod 1 DESIGN

Displacement: 62.65 tons light
    130.25 tons full load
Length: $73^{7}/_{12}$ feet (22.4 m) oa
Beam: $21^{1}/_{12}$ feet (6.4 m)
Draft: $5^{1}/_{6}$ feet (1.6 m)
Propulsion: diesels (Detroit); 1,300 bhp; 2 shafts
Speed: 9 knots
Complement: 5 (EM)
Armament: none

Design: These are welded-steel landing craft with a cargo capacity of one M-60 tank or 65 tons.

Engineering: Some units have been refitted with Kort nozzles.

LCM(8) landing craft carrying Marine medium tanks are unloaded from the dock landing ship FORT FISHER (LSD 40) during multi-national amphibious exercises at Queensland, Australia. These conventional landing craft are carried to the assault area by LSD, LPD, LHA, and LKA-type ships. (1974, U.S. Navy, PH1 John R. Sheppard)

LCM(8) with Marine medium tank and troops (1970, U.S. Navy, PH1 Robert E. Woods)

## MECHANIZED LANDING CRAFT: LCM(6) Mod 2 DESIGN

| | |
|---|---|
| Displacement: | 26.7 tons light |
| | 62.35 tons full load |
| Length: | 56 feet (17 m) oa |
| Beam: | 14⅓ feet (4.4 m) |
| Draft: | 3⅚ feet (1.2 m) |
| Propulsion: | diesels (Gray Marine); 450 bhp; 2 shafts |
| Speed: | 10 knots |
| Complement: | 5 (EM) |
| Armament: | none |

Many of these craft have been converted to riverine combat craft.

Design: These craft are constructed of welded steel. Their cargo capacity is 34 tons or 80 troops.

LCM(6)s in TARAWA (LHA 1) (1976, U.S. Navy, PH3 D. A. Fort)

LCM(6)s in TORTUGA (LSD 26) (U.S. Navy)

## LANDING CRAFT VEHICLE AND PERSONNEL (LCVP)

| | |
|---|---|
| Displacement: | 13.5 tons full load |
| Length: | 35¾ feet (11.7 m) oa |
| Beam: | 10½ feet (3.4 m) |
| Draft: | 3½ feet (1.1 m) |
| Propulsion: | diesel; 325 bhp; 1 shaft |
| Speed: | 9 knots |
| Armament: | fitted with MG in combat areas |

Design: These craft are built of wood or fiberglass-reinforced plastic. They can carry light vehicles or four tons of cargo.

LCVP from MOUNT WHITNEY (LCC 20) (1973, Giorgio Arra)

LCVPs loading troops from BEXAR (LPA 237) (U.S. Navy)

LCVP from BLUE RIDGE (LCC 19)(U.S. Navy)

# 16 Patrol Ships and Craft

The U.S. Navy operates several patrol ships and small craft, most of them in the test and evaluation role. After several delays and program reductions, in August 1977 the Navy received approval to proceed with the construction of five additional hydrofoil missile combatants (PHM) to join a prototype ship commissioned a few weeks earlier. In addition, several small craft are operated by the Naval Reserve Force.

A number of patrol ships and craft for foreign navies are under construction in U.S. shipyards. It is unlikely that any units of these designs will be acquired by the U.S. Navy. However, by producing these ships and craft, the United States maintains a limited design and construction base for small combatants. The largest units now under construction are nine 400-ton patrol gunboats—missile (F-PGG 1-9) being built by Peterson Builders for delivery to Saudi Arabia in 1980–1982.

Recent foreign transfers include three 165-foot, modified Asheville-class patrol missile ships and the prototype 100-foot coastal patrol and interdiction craft to South Korea in 1975–1976. No U.S. hull numbers were assigned to these craft, all of which were built by the Tacoma Boatbuilding Company in Tacoma, Washington. Additional units of both designs are being constructed in Korean shipyards. Numerous smaller, PB-type gunboats recently constructed in U.S. yards have been transferred to Guatemala, Iran, and the Philippines.

## 1 + 5 PATROL COMBATANTS—MISSILE (HYDROFOIL): "PEGASUS" CLASS

| Number | Name | FY/SCB | Builder | Laid down | Launched | Commissioned | Status |
|--------|------|--------|---------|-----------|----------|--------------|--------|
| PHM 1 | Pegasus | 73/602 | Boeing Co, Seattle | 10 May 1973 | 9 Nov 1974 | 9 July 1977 | **PA** |
| PHM 2 | Hercules | 73/602 | Boeing Co, Seattle | 30 May 1974 | | | Bldg. |
| PHM 3 | ...... | 74/602 | Boeing Co, Seattle | | | | Auth. |
| PHM 4 | ...... | 74/602 | Boeing Co, Seattle | | | | Auth. |
| PHM 5 | ...... | 74/602 | Boeing Co, Seattle | | | | Auth. |
| PHM 6 | ...... | 74/602 | Boeing Co, Seattle | | | | Auth. |

| | |
|---|---|
| Displacement: | 231 tons full load |
| Length: | 147½ feet (45 m) oa foils retracted |
| | 131½ feet (40 m) oa foils extended |
| Beam: | 28⅙ feet (8.6 m) |
| Draft: | 6⅙ feet (1.9 m) foils retracted |
| | 23⅙ feet (7.1 m) foils extended |
| Propulsion: | 2 diesels (Mercedes-Benz); 1,600 bhp; 2 waterjets hullborne |
| | 1 gas turbine (General Electric); 18,000 shp; 2 waterjets on foils |
| Speed: | 12 knots hullborne |
| | 40+ knots on foils |
| Complement: | 21 (4 0 + 17 EM) |
| Missiles: | 8 Harpoon SSMs in cannisters Mk 140 (2 × 4) except PHM 2 |
| Guns: | 1 76-mm 62 cal AA Mk 75 (1 × 1) except PHM 2 |
| Radars: | (see Fire Control) |
| Fire control: | 1 Mk 94 Mod 1 weapons FCS in PHM 1; Mk 92 Mod 1 in PHM 3–6 |

The Pegasus is the lead ship of 30 hydrofoil missile combatants originally planned for the FY 1973–1977 shipbuilding programs. Two ships were authorized with FY 1973 research and development funds. Construction of the second ship (PHM 2) was suspended in 1976 when she was about 20 percent complete, to provide funds for completion of the Pegasus. Four additional ships were funded in FY 1974.

The original 30-PHM program was reduced to the six funded ships in February 1976, principally because of cost increases. Subsequently, Secretary of Defense Harold Brown on 6 April 1977 announced his decision to cancel the entire PHM program except for the lead ship. He cited the program's high costs and limited operational effectiveness. However, the Congress refused to rescind the authorization and funding of the PHM 2-6, and in August

1977 the Department of Defense approved construction of the five additional ships. However, because of structural problems encountered in construction, the HERCULES will not be armed, but will be used in testing and evaluation.

Classification: When originally established, the designation PHM meant Patrol Hydrofoil—Missile. On 30 June 1975, however, the name of this type was changed to Patrol Combatant-Missile (Hydrofoil), with its designation remaining PHM.

Design: The PHM design evolved from a NATO requirement. The Italian and West German governments participated in the development of the design, with the latter navy planning to build up to 12 ships of this design in German shipyards. When riding on foils the ship's draft is 8¾ feet.

Engineering: Fitted with two separate diesel engines and one LM2500 gas turbine. A through-bow thruster is provided for low-speed maneuvering. Endurance is 32 hours at 38.28 knots (1,225 n. miles).

Fire control: Mk 94 is the U.S. designation for the Netherlands Hollandse Signaalapparaten WM-28 fire control system. The PHM 3-6 are to be fitted with the Mk 92 Mod 1, a modified WM-28 manufactured by the Sperry Company (also used in the PERRY-class (FFG 7) frigates).

Guns: No secondary gun battery is provided in the U.S. ships; the PHM design provides for two 20-mm Mk 20 single gun mounts to be fitted abaft the mast.

Missiles: The original PHM design provided four single Harpoon SSM tubes; the design was revised to permit carrying two quad launchers on the fantail.

Names: The PHM 1 originally was named the DELPHINUS. She was renamed the PEGASUS on 26 April 1974.

PEGASUS (1975, Boeing Aerospace)

PEGASUS (1975, Boeing Aerospace)

PEGASUS (1975, U.S. Navy, JOC Warren Grass)

PEGASUS with foils raised (1974, U.S. Navy, PH2 Paul S. Burns)

PEGASUS with foils raised (1974, U.S. Navy, PH2 Paul S. Burns)

## 2 PATROL COMBATANTS: "ASHEVILLE" CLASS

| Number | Name | FY/SCB | Builder | Laid down | Launched | Commissioned | Status |
|--------|------|--------|---------|-----------|----------|--------------|--------|
| PG 92 | TACOMA | 66/600 | Tacoma Boatbuilding | 24 July 1967 | 13 April 1968 | 14 July 1969 | **AA** |
| PG 93 | WELCH | 66/600 | Peterson Builders | 8 Aug 1967 | 25 July 1968 | 8 Sep 1969 | **AA** |

Displacement: 225 tons standard
      245 tons full load
Length: 164½ feet (50.1 m) oa
Beam: 23¹¹/₁₂ feet (7.3 m)
Draft: 9½ feet (2.9 m)
Propulsion: 2 diesels (Cummins), 1,750 bhp; 1 gas turbine (General Electric), 14,000 shp; 2 shafts (controllable-pitch propellers)
Speed: 16 knots on diesels; 40+ knots on gas turbine
Complement: 25–29 (4 0 + 21–25 EM)
Guns: 1 3-inch (76-mm) 50 cal AA Mk 34 (1 × 1)
      1 40-mm AA Mk 3 (1 × 1)
      4 .50-cal MG (2 × 2)
Radars: Raytheon Pathfinder surface search
Fire control: 1 Mk 63 Mod 29 gun FCS
      1 SPG-50 radar

Seventeen ASHEVILLE-class patrol gunboats were completed 1966–1971 for coastal patrol and blockade missions. They were developed in response to the Cuban situation of the early 1960s; subsequently they were used extensively in the Vietnam War, and in the 1970s four of them operated in the Mediterranean carrying Standard-ARM 33Ms.

The two surviving units are used at Norfolk, Virginia, to train Saudi Arabian naval personnel.

Class: This class originally consisted of PGM/PG 84–90 and 92–101. (The hull numbers PGM 33–83, 91, and 102–121 were assigned to gunboats built from 1955 onward for transfer to foreign navies; the PGG 1–9 are under construction for Saudi Arabia, to be delivered in 1980–1982.)

The CHEHALIS (PG 94) and GRAND RAPIDS (PG 98) have been stripped of armament and are employed as research craft (the CHEHALIS was renamed the ATHENA; see Chapter 19).

Disposals since Tenth Edition:

| PG 84 | ASHEVILLE (NRF) | stricken 31 Jan 1977 |
|-------|-----------------|----------------------|
| PG 85 | GALLUP (NRF) | stricken 31 Jan 1977 |
| PG 86 | ANTELOPE | stricken 1 Oct 1977 |
| PG 87 | READY | stricken 1 Oct 1977 |
| PG 88 | CROCKETT (NRF) | stricken 31 Jan 1977 |
| PG 89 | MARATHON (NRF) | stricken 31 Jan 1977 |
| PG 90 | CANON (NRF) | stricken 31 Jan 1977 |
| PG 95 | DEFIANCE | to Turkey 11 June 1973 |
| PG 96 | BENICIA | to South Korea 2 Oct 1971 |
| PG 97 | SURPRISE | to Turkey 28 Feb 1973 |
| PG 99 | BEACON | to Greece 1977 |
| PG 100 | DOUGLAS | stricken 1 Oct 1977 |
| PG 101 | GREEN BAY | to Greece 1977 |

Classification: As built, these ships were classified as motor gunboats (PGM). They were reclassified as patrol gunboats (PG)

on 1 April 1967. The designation of the fourteen surviving units was eventually changed to patrol combatants (PG) on 30 June 1975.

Design: These ships have aluminum hulls and aluminum-fiberglass superstructures.

Engineering: CODOG (Combination Diesel or Gas-turbine) propulsion is provided, with two diesels for cruising and a single, LM1500 gas turbine for high-speed operations. The ships can transfer from diesel to gas turbine (or back) without loss of power; they also can accelerate from a full stop to 40 knots in one minute.

Missiles: The BENICIA was fitted with a single "box" launcher for the Standard-ARM SSM in 1971. When successful test firings were made, this led to two launchers being installed in the PG 86, 87, 98, and 100.

WELCH (1976, Stefan Terzibaschitsch)

TACOMA (1975, Giorgio Arra)

**1 HYDROFOIL SUBMARINE CHASER: "HIGH POINT"**

| Number | Name | FY/SCB | Builder | Laid down | Launched | In Service | Status |
|--------|------|--------|---------|-----------|----------|------------|--------|
| PCH 1 | HIGH POINT | 60/202 | J. M. Martinac | 27 Feb 1961 | 17 Aug 1962 | 15 Aug 1963 | **PA** |

Displacement: 100 tons full load
Length: 115 feet (35 m) oa
Beam: 31 feet (9.4 m)
Draft: 6 feet (1.8 m) foils retracted
17 feet (5.2 m) foils extended
Propulsion: 1 diesel (Curtis Wright); 600 bhp; retractable outdrive hullborne
2 gas turbines (Bristol Siddeley Marine Proteus); 6,200 shp; 2 paired counter-rotating propellers on foils
Speed: 12 knots hullborne
48 knots on foils
Complement: 13 (1 O + 12 EM)
Guns: removed
ASW weapons: removed
Radars:

The HIGH POINT was the U.S. Navy's first operational hydrofoil. She was built to evaluate structural and hydrodynamic features of hydrofoils, as well as develop ASW concepts for the use of this type of craft. The craft was transferred to the Coast Guard for evaluation during 1975; she was subsequently returned to Navy use.

Builders: The HIGH POINT was designed and built by the Grumman Aircraft Corporation at the Martinac boatyard in Tacoma, Washington.

Design: The craft has an all-welded aluminum hull and superstructure. She was the first large craft to have fully submerged foils. The canard foil arrangement provides for most of the ship's weight to be carried by the large after foil, which is supported by two $18^5/_6$-foot struts that can partially retract into the after deck housings. An autopilot activated by an electronic wave height sensor controls the roll and pitch.

Guns: Machine guns were originally installed.

Missiles: During 1973–1974 the HIGH POINT was employed in tests of the Harpoon SSM in support of the PHM program.

Sonar: The Variable Depth Sonar (VDS) was extensively tested in this ship.

Torpedoes: As built, four 12.75-inch ASW torpedo tubes were installed (2 × 2).

HIGH POINT during Coast Guard evaluation (1975, U.S. Navy, JOC Warren Grass)

HIGH POINT during Harpoon test firings (1974, U.S. Navy)

## Hydrofoil Gunboat Disposals

Two competitive prototype hydrofoil gunboats were constructed during the 1960s: The FLAGSTAFF (PGH 1) was transferred to the Coast Guard in 1976; the TUCUMCARI (PGH 2) was wrecked in a grounding on 16 November 1972, and scrapped in October 1973.

### 4 FAST PATROL BOATS: "OSPREY" CLASS

| Number | FY | In Service | Status |
|--------|-----|-------------|--------|
| PTF 23 | 67 | 13 Mar 1968 | **NRF** |
| PTF 24 | 67 | 13 Mar 1968 | **NRF** |
| PTF 25 | 67 | 8 Apr 1968 | **NRF** |
| PTF 26 | 67 | 8 Apr 1968 | **NRF** |

| | |
|---|---|
| Builders: | Sewart Seacraft, Berwick, Louisiana |
| Displacement: | 80 tons light |
| | 105 tons full load |
| Length: | 94¾ feet (28.8 m) oa |
| Beam: | 23¹/₆ feet (7 m) |
| Draft: | 7 feet (2.1 m) |
| Propulsion: | diesels (Napier-Deltic); 6,200 bhp; 2 shafts |
| Speed: | ~40 knots |
| Complement: | 19 (1 O + 18 EM) |
| Guns: | 1 40-mm AA Mk 3 (1 × 1) |
| | 2 20-mm AA Mk 67 (2 × 1) |
| | 1 81-mm mortar Mk 2/1 .50-cal MG M2 (1 × 1/1) |
| Radars: | commercial surface search |

These are improvements of the "Nasty" PTF design. They have aluminum hulls and better habitability than their predecessors. They can be configured as torpedo boats, minelayers, or submarine chasers. "Osprey" is the commercial name of this design.

PTF 23 (1975, Giorgio Arra)

"OSPREY"-class PTF (U.S. Navy)

PTF 6 (left) and PTF 25 at Little Creek, the Navy's amphibious and small craft base at Norfolk, Va. Note the 20-mm gun shields and camouflage paint scheme of the PTF 25. The "Osprey" and "Nasty" classes can be distinguished by their search/navigation radar antenna mounts. These PTFs, like most other U.S. small combatants, are operated by the Naval Reserve. (1975, Giorgio Arra)

## 13 FAST PATROL BOATS: "NASTY" CLASS

| Number | FY | In Service | Status |
|--------|-----|-----------|--------|
| PTF 3 | — | 1 Jan 1963 | **NRF** |
| PTF 5 | — | 1 Mar 1964 | **NRF** |
| PTF 6 | — | 1 Mar 1964 | **NRF** |
| PTF 7 | — | 1 Mar 1964 | **NRF** |
| PTF 10 | 64 | 22 Apr 1965 | **NRF** |
| PTF 11 | 64 | 7 July 1965 | **NRF** |
| PTF 12 | 64 | 7 July 1965 | **NRF** |
| PTF 17 | 67 | 1 July 1968 | **NRF** |
| PTF 18 | 67 | 1 July 1968 | **NRF** |
| PTF 19 | 67 | 5 Oct 1968 | **NRF** |
| PTF 20 | 67 | 5 Oct 1968 | **NRF** |
| PTF 21 | 67 | 23 Sep 1970 | **NRF** |
| PTF 22 | 67 | 23 Sep 1970 | **NRF** |

| | |
|---|---|
| Builders: | PTF 3, 5–7, 10–13 Boatservice, Oslo, Norway |
| | PTF 17–22 John Trumpy & Sons, Annapolis |
| Displacement: | 85 tons full load |
| Length: | 80⅓ feet (24.5 m) oa |
| Beam: | 24½ feet (7.5 m) |
| Draft: | 6¾ feet (2.1 m) |
| Propulsion: | diesels (Napier-Deltic); 6,200 bhp; 2 shafts |
| Speed: | ~45 knots |
| Complement: | 19 (3 O + 16 EM) |
| Guns: | 1 40-mm AA Mk 3 (1 × 1) (see notes) |
| | 2 20-mm AA Mk 67 (2 × 1) |
| | 1 81-mm mortar Mk 2/1 .50-cal MG M2 (1 × 1/1) |
| Radars: | commercial surface search |

These boats were acquired for use in the Vietnam War, primarily to land and support raiders and agents behind enemy lines. Fourteen units (PTF 3–16) were purchased from their Norwegian builder, with six duplicates (PTF 17–22) being built in the United States with some Norwegian-produced components. The NASTY was the lead unit of this class, constructed for the Norwegian Navy.

Class: The PTF 4 was sunk off Vietnam on 4 November 1965; PTF 8–9 and 14–16 were stricken in 1966; and PTF 13 was stricken in 1972.

Design: These boats have double-layer mahogany hulls, sandwiching a layer of fiberglass.

Guns: As built, these ships had two 40-mm guns and two 20-mm guns. The PTF 18 and possibly some other units currently have two 40-mm guns.

Names: The PTF 3 was named the SKREI prior to transfer to the U.S. Navy.

Torpedoes: These boats were designed to mount four 21-inch torpedo tubes; the tubes were not installed in U.S. service.

PTF 18 with two 40-mm guns (1976, Giorgio Arra)

PTF 10 (1976, Giorgio Arra)

PTF 6 (1973, U.S. Navy, AN T. Ackerman)

"Nasty"-class PTF (1972, courtesy *Ships of the World*)

## Motor Torpedo Boat Disposals

The U.S. Navy built four motor torpedo boats after World War II, the PT 809–812, all completed in 1950–1951, to slightly different designs. They were reclassified as service craft (PT 809–812) in 1951. After several years of evaluation all were laid up in reserve.

The PT 812 (renamed the GUARDIAN) was reactivated and employed by the Secret Service to escort the presidential yacht on the Potomac River until 1974. She was reclassified as a drone recovery craft (DR-1) in 1975 (see Chapter 19).

The PT 810 and 811 were reactivated in 1962 and reclassified as fast patrol boats, PTF 1 and 2, respectively. Both were stricken on 1 August 1965 and expended as targets.

### 10 + 4 PATROL BOATS: PB Mk III DESIGN

| | |
|---|---|
| Displacement: | 31.5 tons light |
| | 41.25 tons full load |
| Length: | 64$^{11}/_{12}$ ft (19.8 m) oa |
| Beam: | 18$^{1}/_{12}$ ft (5.5 m) |
| Draft: | 5$^{5}/_{6}$ ft (1.8 m) |
| Propulsion: | diesels (GM); 1,950 bhp; 3 shafts |
| Speed: | 26 knots |
| Range: | 450 nautical miles at full power |
| | 2,000 nautical miles at slow speeds |
| Complement: | 5 (1 O + 4 EM, minimum) |
| Guns: | (see notes) |

The PB Mk III was developed as a multi-mission inshore warfare craft for U.S. and foreign naval service. Ten units are being acquired by the U.S. Navy for assignment to reserve Coastal River Division 12, with four additional units funded in FY 1978. They are built by Peterson Builders (Sturgeon Bay, Wisconsin).

Design: The Mk III design is modified from a commercial craft used to support offshore drilling rigs in the Gulf of Mexico. The craft are of all-aluminum construction with their pilot house offset to starboard to provide maximum deck space for weapons and equipment. The craft has a low radar cross-section and quiet engines for clandestine operations.

Guns: These ships are designed for a nominal armament of four .50-cal single machine guns (one on each quarter). The main deck is reinforced for carrying heavier weapons, including guns, mines, and torpedoes, as well as minesweeping gear.

PB Mk III (1975, Giorgio Arra)

### 2 PATROL BOATS: PB Mk I DESIGN

| | |
|---|---|
| Displacement: | 26.9 tons light |
| | 36.3 tons full load |
| Length: | 65 feet (19.8 m) oa |
| Beam: | 16 feet (4.9 m) |
| Draft: | 4$^{5}/_{6}$ feet (1.5 m) |
| Propulsion: | diesels (Detroit); 1,635 bhp; 3 shafts |
| Speed: | 26 knots |
| Complement: | |
| Guns: | 6 20-mm or .50-cal MG (1 × 2, 4 × 1) |

These are prototype patrol boats developed as replacements for the "Swift" PCFs. Both were built by Sewart Seacraft of Berwick, Louisiana; they were completed in 1972 and delivered to the Navy in 1973 for evaluation. Subsequently they were transferred to the Naval Reserve Force.

PB Mk I (1976, Giorgio Arra)

### 5 INSHORE PATROL CRAFT: PCF Mk I DESIGN

| | |
|---|---|
| Displacement: | 22.5 tons full load |
| Length: | 50$^{1}/_{12}$ feet (15.3 m) oa |
| Beam: | 13 feet (4 m) |
| Draft: | 3½ feet (1.1 m) |
| Propulsion: | diesels (General Motors), 960 bhp, 2 shafts |
| Speed: | 28 knots |
| Complement: | 6 (1 O + 5 EM) |
| Guns: | 2 .50-cal MG (1 × 2) |
| | 1 81-mm mortar Mk 2/1 .50-cal MG M2 (1 × 1/1) |

These are all-metal inshore patrol craft, generally referred to as "Swift" boats. All are assigned to the Naval Reserve Force.

Class: Approximately 125 units have been built since 1965. Most were used by the U.S. Navy in Vietnam, with 104 being transferred to the South Vietnamese government in 1968–1970. Others have been built for South Korea, the Philippines, and Thailand.

Classsification: PCF originally stood for fast patrol craft; changed to inshore patrol craft on 14 August 1968.

Design: This design is adapted from a commercial "crew boat" employed in support of offshore oil rigs in the Gulf of Mexico.

PCF Mk I (1969, U.S. Navy)

PBR Mk II (1968, U.S. Navy)

### 29 RIVER PATROL BOATS: PBR Mk II DESIGN

| | |
|---|---|
| Displacement: | 7.5 tons light |
| | 8.9 tons full load |
| Length: | 32 feet (9.8 m) oa |
| Beam: | 11⅔ feet (3.5 m) |
| Draft: | 2⁷/₁₂ feet (0.8 m) |
| Propulsion: | geared diesels (General Motors); 420 bhp; waterjets |
| Speed: | 25+ knots |
| Complement: | 4–5 (EM) |
| Guns: | 3 .50-cal MG (1 × 2, 1 × 1) |
| | 1 40-mm grenade launcher Mk 19 (1 × 1) |
| | 1 60-mm mortar Mk 4 in some units |

These craft were developed for riverine combat in the Vietnam War. They have fiberglass-reinforced plastic hulls and ceramic armor. The surviving U.S. units are operated by the Naval Reserve Force.

Class: More than 500 PBRs were built in 1967–1973, with most transferred to South Vietnam.

### 2 ASSAULT SUPPORT PATROL BOATS: ASPB Mk I DESIGN

| | |
|---|---|
| Displacement: | 33.25 tons light |
| | 39.35 tons full load |
| Length: | 50¹/₆ feet (15.3 m) oa |
| Beam: | 17⁵/₁₂ feet (5.3 m) |
| Draft: | 3¾ feet (1.1 m) |
| Propulsion: | diesels (General Motors); 850 bhp; 2 shafts |
| Speed: | 14 knots (sustained) |
| Crew: | 5–6 (EM) |
| Guns: | 1 or 2 20-mm (1–2 × 2) |
| | 2 .50-cal MG in boats with 1 20-mm gun (1 × 2) |
| | 2 .30-cal MG (2 × 1) |
| | 2 40-mm grenade launchers (2 × 1) |

These riverine "battleships" were developed to provide fire support for other craft, counter shallow-water mines, and interdict enemy river traffic. They have welded-steel hulls and aluminum superstructures.

Both units are operated by the Naval Reserve Force.

Guns: In some units the forward "turret" had two machine guns in lieu of the single 20-mm gun. Some units also had an 81-mm mortar/.50-cal MG mount aft.

PBR Mk II (1968, U.S. Navy)

ASPB with 81-mm mortar aft (U.S. Navy)

**14 ARMORED TROOP CARRIERS: "MINI" ATC DESIGN**

| | |
|---|---|
| Displacement: | 11 tons light |
| | 14.75 tons full load |
| Length: | 36 feet (11 m) oa |
| Beam: | 12¾ feet (3.9 m) |
| Draft: | 3½ feet (1.1 m) |
| Propulsion: | diesels (General Motors); 560 bhp; waterjets |
| Speed: | 28 knots |
| Complement: | 2 (EM) |
| Troops: | 15 |
| Guns: | (see notes) |

These craft were developed from lessons of the Vietnam War and are intended for clandestine operations. They are difficult to detect by radar and have quiet engines. They feature aluminum hulls and ceramic armor. At high speeds they have a one-foot draft.

All are operated by the Naval Reserve Force.

Guns: A maximum of seven pintel-mounted weapons can be fitted (machine guns, grenade launchers, mortars).

**1 COMMAND AND CONTROL BOAT: CCB Mk I DESIGN**

| | |
|---|---|
| Displacement: | 67 tons light |
| | 83.5 tons full load |
| Length: | 60 feet (18.3 m) oa |
| Beam: | 17½ feet (5.3 m) |
| Draft: | 3⅓ feet (1 m) |
| Propulsion: | diesels (Gray Marine); 450 bhp; 2 shafts |
| Speed: | 8.5 knots (6 knots sustained) |
| Complement: | 11 |
| Guns: | 1 40-mm/1 20-mm (1 × 1/1) |
| | several 20-mm AA (? × 1) |
| | several .30-cal MG (? × 1) |

The CCB was developed as a command post for riverine operations. A command "module" is fitted between the after "superstructure" and forward gun "turret." The craft was converted from an LCM; it is similar to the now-discarded riverine monitors (MON) which had an 81-mm mortar in place of the command module. Several command radios are fitted.

"MINI" ATC (1974, U.S. Navy, PH2 Terry C. Mitchell)

CCB (U.S. Navy)

# 17 Mine Warfare Ships and Craft

The U.S. Navy retains three ocean minesweepers (MSO) in active commission to support mine research and development activities at the Naval Coastal Systems Laboratory in Panama City, Florida. Another 22 MSOs are assigned to the Naval Reserve Force and are manned by composite active–reserve crews.

The Navy's principal mine countermeasures capability consists of one helicopter squadron (HM-12), flying RH-53D Sea Stallions. While effective in countering shallow-water mines, the Navy has only 23 of these helicopters and their deployment aboard amphibious ships (LHA/LPH/LPD) displaces troop-carrying helicopters and Marines. (The helicopters are described in Chapter 23, page 289.)

The Navy has belatedly initiated development of a new class of ocean-going minesweepers, designated Mine Countermeasure Ships (MCM), to counter advanced Soviet deep-ocean mines. Several smaller coastal minesweepers are under construction for transfer to foreign navies.

All coastal minesweepers (MSC) have been discarded, while the surviving minesweeping boats (MSB) and minesweeping launches (MSL) have been stripped of their specialized equipment and are employed as utility craft. The two surviving minesweepers of the ABILITY class (MSO 520–521) were reclassified as auxiliary ships (AG 520–521) and subsequently stricken; see Chapter 18.

Names: Ocean minesweepers have "action word" names.

## 2 OCEAN MINESWEEPERS: "ACME" CLASS

| Number | Name | FY/SCB | Builder | Laid down | Launched | Commissioned | Status |
|--------|------|--------|---------|-----------|----------|--------------|--------|
| MSO 509 | ADROIT | 54/45A | Frank L. Sample Jr. | 18 Nov. 1954 | 20 Aug 1955 | 4 Mar 1957 | **NRF-A** |
| MSO 511 | AFFRAY | 54/45A | Frank L. Sample Jr. | 24 Aug 1955 | 18 Dec 1956 | 8 Dec 1958 | **NRF-A** |

| | |
|---|---|
| Displacement: | 720 tons light |
| | 780 tons full load |
| Length: | 173 feet (52.7 m) oa |
| Beam: | 36 feet (11 m) |
| Draft: | 14 feet (4.3 m) |
| Propulsion: | diesels (Packard); 2,800 bhp; 2 shafts (controllable-pitch propellers) |
| Speed: | 14 knots |
| Complement: | 86 (3 O + 36 EM active; 3 O + 44 EM reserve) |
| Guns: | 1 20-mm AA Mk 24 (1 × 1) |

| | |
|---|---|
| Radars: | SPS-53L in MSO 509; SPS-53E in MSO 511 |
| Sonars: | SQQ-14 mine detection |

These ships are improved versions of the AGILE and AGGRESSIVE classes. They are fitted as mine division flagships. The notes for the AGILE and AGGRESSIVE classes apply to these ships.

Class: Originally four ships were in this class; the ACME (MSO 508) and ADVANCE (MSO 510) were stricken on 15 May 1976.

The AFFRAY is one of four "sweeps" built to an improved AGILE/AGGRESSIVE design. The forward 40-mm gun has since been removed, primarily to provide space for the SQQ-14 sonar. Note the reels for cable stowage aft of the funnel, and the floats or "pigs" for streaming mine gear on the fantail. (1969, U.S. Navy)

Three ocean minesweepers, all now assigned to the Naval Reserve Force, steam through a placid Pacific. The GALLANT (foreground), PLUCK, and EXCEL are typical of the 65 ocean minesweepers built for the U.S. Navy in the 1950s. The survivors are too slow and limited for potential U.S. Navy mine countermeasure requirements. (U.S. Navy)

ENHANCE (1973, U.S. Navy, RP1 E. L. Goligoski)

ILLUSIVE alongside WESTCHESTER COUNTY (LST 1167) (1973, U.S. Navy, JOC John J. Gravat)

**25 OCEAN MINESWEEPERS: "AGILE" AND "AGGRESSIVE" CLASSES**

| Number | Name | FY/SCB | Builder | Laid down | Launched | Commissioned | Status |
|---|---|---|---|---|---|---|---|
| MSO 427 | CONSTANT | 51/45A | Fulton Shipyard Co | 16 Aug 1951 | 14 Feb 1953 | 8 Sep 1954 | **NRF-P** |
| MSO 428 | DASH | 51/45A | Astoria Marine Constn Co | 2 July 1951 | 20 Sep 1952 | 14 Aug 1953 | **NRF-A** |
| MSO 429 | DETECTOR | 51/45A | Astoria Marine Constn Co | 1 Oct 1951 | 5 Dec 1952 | 26 Jan 1954 | **NRF-A** |
| MSO 430 | DIRECT | 51/45A | C. Hiltebrant DD Co | 2 Feb 1952 | 27 May 1953 | 9 July 1954 | **NRF-A** |
| MSO 431 | DOMINANT | 51/45A | C. Hiltebrant DD Co | 23 Apr 1952 | 5 Nov 1953 | 8 Nov 1954 | **NRF-A** |
| MSO 433 | ENGAGE | 51/45A | Colberg Boat Works | 7 Nov 1951 | 18 June 1953 | 29 June 1954 | **NRF-A** |
| MSO 437 | ENHANCE | 51/45A | Martinolich SB Co | 12 July 1952 | 11 Oct 1952 | 16 Apr 1955 | **NRF-P** |
| MSO 438 | ESTEEM | 51/45A | Martinolich SB Co | 1 Sep 1952 | 20 Dec 1952 | 10 Sep 1955 | **NRF-P** |
| MSO 439 | EXCEL | 51/45A | Higgins Inc | 9 Feb 1953 | 25 Sep 1953 | 24 Feb 1955 | **NRF-P** |
| MSO 440 | EXPLOIT | 51/45A | Higgins Inc | 28 Dec 1951 | 10 Apr 1953 | 31 Mar 1954 | **NRF-A** |
| MSO 441 | EXULTANT | 51/45A | Higgins Inc | 22 May 1952 | 6 June 1953 | 22 June 1954 | **NRF-A** |
| MSO 442 | FEARLESS | 51/45A | Higgins Inc | 23 July 1952 | 17 July 1953 | 22 Sep 1954 | **NRF-A** |
| MSO 443 | FIDELITY | 51/45A | Higgins Inc | 15 Dec 1952 | 21 Aug 1953 | 19 Jan 1955 | **AA** |
| MSO 446 | FORTIFY | 51/45A | Seattle SB & DD Co | 30 Nov 1951 | 14 Feb 1953 | 16 July 1954 | **NRF-A** |
| MSO 448 | ILLUSIVE | 51/45A | Martinolich SB Co | 23 Oct 1951 | 12 July 1952 | 14 Nov 1953 | **AA** |
| MSO 449 | IMPERVIOUS | 51/45A | Martinolich SB Co | 18 Nov 1951 | 29 Aug 1952 | 15 July 1954 | **NRF-A** |
| MSO 455 | IMPLICIT | 52/45A | Wilmington Boat Works Inc | 29 Oct 1951 | 1 Aug 1953 | 10 Mar 1954 | **NRF-P** |
| MSO 456 | INFLICT | 52/45A | Wilmington Boat Works Inc | 29 Oct 1951 | 6 Oct 1953 | 11 May 1954 | **NRF-A** |
| MSO 458 | LUCID | 52/45A | Higgins Inc | 16 Mar 1953 | 14 Nov 1953 | 4 May 1955 | PR |
| MSO 459 | NIMBLE | 52/45A | Higgins Inc | 27 Apr 1953 | 6 Aug 1954 | 11 May 1955 | AR |
| MSO 464 | PLUCK | 52/45A | Wilmington Boat Works Inc | 31 Mar 1952 | 6 Feb 1954 | 11 Aug 1954 | **NRF-P** |
| MSO 488 | CONQUEST | 53/45A | J. M. Martinac SB Corp | 26 Mar 1953 | 20 May 1954 | 20 July 1955 | **NRF-P** |
| MSO 489 | GALLANT | 53/45A | J. M. Martinac SB Corp | 21 May 1953 | 4 June 1954 | 14 Sep 1955 | **NRF-P** |
| MSO 490 | LEADER | 53/45A | J. M. Martinac SB Corp | 22 Sep 1953 | 15 Sep 1954 | 16 Nov 1955 | **AA** |
| MSO 492 | PLEDGE | 53/45A | J. M. Martinac SB Corp | 24 June 1954 | 20 July 1955 | 20 Apr 1956 | **NRF-P** |

| | |
|---|---|
| Displacement: | 665 tons light |
| | 750 tons full load |
| Length: | 172 feet (52.4 m) oa |
| Beam: | 35 feet (10.7 m) |
| Draft: | 14 feet (4.3 m) |
| Propulsion: | diesels (Packard except General Motors in MSO 428–431, Waukesha in MSO 433, 437–438, 441–443, 446, 448–449, 456, 488, 490); 2,280 bhp except 1,520 bhp in ships with GM diesels; 2 shafts (control-lable-pitch propellers) |
| Speed: | 15.5 knots except 15 knots in ships with GM diesels |
| Complement: | 78 (8 O + 70 EM) in active ships (designed) |
| | 86 (3 O +36 EM active; 3 O + 44 EM reserve) in NRF ships |
| Guns: | 1 40-mm AA M3 (1 × 1) or |
| | 1 20-mm AA Mk 68 (1 × 1) |
| Radars: | SPS-5C or SPS-53E/L surface search |
| Sonars: | UQS-1 or SQQ-14 mine detection |

The large ocean minesweeper construction program of the 1950s was initiated in response to the extensive use of Soviet-provided mines in the Korean War (1950–1953). Large numbers of these ships were built for the U.S. Navy and several NATO navies (see Class notes). Of the surviving ships, 3 are in active Navy service, 20 are NRF ships, and 2 are laid up in reserve.

Builders: Most of the MSOs were constructed at small boatyards.

Class: Fifty-eight ships of these classes were built for the U.S. Navy plus seven ships of the similar ACME and ABILITY classes, which are listed separately. Another 3 MSOs of these classes were built specifically for other NATO navies (plus the cancelled MSO 497). The total MSO program covered hull numbers 421–522. Sixteen additional MSOs funded in FY 1966–1968 were not built.

Twenty-five ships of the AGILE and AGGRESSIVE classes have been lost, stricken, or transferred to other navies through 1976 (see previous editions). Eight additional ships which were laid up in reserve were stricken on 1 September 1977:

| | | | |
|---|---|---|---|
| MSO 421 | AGILE | MSO 474 | VITAL |
| MSO 461 | OBSERVER | MSO 494 | STURDY |
| MSO 462 | PINNACLE | MSO 495 | SWERVE |
| MSO 471 | SKILL | MSO 496 | VENTURE |

Classification: All MSOs originally were classified as mine-sweepers (AM); they were changed to MSOs on 7 February 1955.

Design: These ships are of lightweight wooden construction with laminated timbers; the fittings and machinery are of bronze and stainless steel. Magnetic items have been reduced to a minimum. They were fitted for sweeping contact, magnetic, and acoustic mines.

Guns: As built, these ships had one 40-mm gun and two .50-cal MG. Most have been rearmed with provisions for a 20-mm mount forward, originally a twin-barrel Mk 24 and subsequently a single-barrel Mk 68 gun. Originally the 20-mm mount was required in modernized ships to permit installation of the larger, retractable SQQ-14 sonar in the forward hull.

Modernization: In FY 1968 a program was begun to modernize the existing MSOs (SCB-502). New engines, communications, and sonar (SQQ-14) were to be installed, habitability improved, and advanced sweep gear provided. However, increasing costs and conversion delays caused the program to be halted after only 13 ships had been fully modernized (MSO 433, 437–438, 441–443, 445–446, 448–449, 456, 488, and 490). Subsequently, some features, especially the improved sonar, were fitted to several additional ships.

Sonars: These ships originally had UQS-1 mine-detecting sonar; most have been refitted with SQQ-14, which has additional mine classification capabilities.

DIRECT (1976, Giorgio Arra)

### Coastal Minesweeper Disposals

All U.S. Navy coastal minesweepers of the similar FALCON (MSC 190–199) and REDWING (MSC 200–209) classes have been discarded. Most of these 145-foot craft were operated by the NRF during their last years of U.S. service.

| | | |
|---|---|---|
| MSC 198 | PEACOCK | stricken 1 July 1975 |
| MSC 199 | PHOEBE | stricken 1 July 1975 |
| MSC 201 | SHRIKE | stricken 1 July 1975 |
| MSC 203 | THRASHER | to Singapore 5 Dec 1975 |
| MSC 204 | THRUSH | leased to Virginia Institute of Marine Sciences 1 July 1975 |
| MSC 205 | VIREO | to Fiji 14 Oct 1975 |
| MSC 206 | WARBLER | to Fiji 14 Oct 1975 |
| MSC 207 | WHIPPOORWILL | to Singapore 5 Dec 1975 |
| MSC 209 | WOODPECKER | to Fiji 1976 |

DOMINANT (1975, U.S. Navy, PHAN J. Giesel)

# 18 Auxiliary Ships

Auxiliary ships are non-combatant ships which provide support for the "fighting fleet." This category is made up of a variety of types and classes, most of which are highly specialized. All of these ships are government-owned (some acquired through long-term government financing); however, many of the Underway Replenishment (UNREP) ships, tugs, logistic ships, and research ships are operated by the Navy's Military Sealift Command (MSC) with civilian crews—either Civil Service or merchant seamen under commercial operating contracts. Several research ships are operated by scientific and educational institutions. In addition, since 1977 several tug-type ships have been assigned to the Naval Reserve Force (NRF) with composite active-reserve crews.

Those ships operated by MSC have the prefix USNS for United States Naval Ship, and their hull designations are prefixed with the letter "T."

Most U.S. Navy tabulations of auxiliary ships, and hence those generally quoted in the press and reference works, do not include those ships operated by MSC, NRF, or institutions. Thus, the U.S. Navy's official listing of some 100 auxiliary ships should be almost doubled to give an accurate idea of the number of ships in this category.

Several ships officially classified as auxiliaries are listed elsewhere in this volume and are not included in the following table. Those ships are the miscellaneous command ship (AGF), frigate research ship (AGFF), auxiliary submarines (AGSS), and training aircraft carrier (CVT).

**AUXILIARY SHIPS**

| Type | | Active | | | | | Bldg. | Res. |
|------|--|-------|-----|-----|----------|------|-------|------|
| | | Total | Navy | MSC | NRF | Academic | Bldg. | Res. |
| AD | Destroyer Tenders | 9 | 9 | | | | 2 | 1 |
| AE | Ammunition Ships | 13 | 13 | | | | | |
| AF | Store Ships | 2 | 1 | 1 | | | | |
| AFS | Combat Store Ships | 7 | 7 | | | | | |
| AG | Miscellaneous Auxiliaries | 2 | 1 | 1 | | | | 1 |
| AGDS | Deep Submergence Support Ships | 1 | 1 | | | | | |
| AGEH | Hydrofoil Research Ships | 1 | 1 | | | | | |
| AGM | Missile Range Instrumentation Ships | 6 | | 6 | | | | |
| AGOR | Oceanographic Research Ships | 14 | | 5 | | 9 | | |
| AGS | Surveying Ships | 9 | | 9 | | | | |
| AH | Hospital Ships | | | | | | | 1 |
| AK | Cargo Ships | 8 | | 8 | | | | 1 |
| AKR | Vehicle Cargo Ships | 3 | | 3 | | | | |
| AO | Oilers | 16 | 8 | 8 | | | 3 | 2 |
| AO | Tankers | 18 | | 18 | | | | 5 |
| AOE | Fast Combat-Support Ships | 4 | 4 | | | | | |
| AOG | Gasoline Tankers | 3 | | 3 | | | | |
| AOR | Replenishment Oilers | 7 | 7 | | | | | |

**AUXILIARY SHIPS** (continued)

| Type | | Active | | | | | Bldg. | Res. |
|------|--|--------|--|--|--|--|-------|------|
| | | Total | Navy | MSC | NRF | Academic | | |
| AR | Repair Ships | 5 | 5 | | | | | |
| ARC | Cable Repairing Ships | 3 | | 3 | | | | |
| ARL | Landing Craft Repair Ships | | | | | | | 4 |
| ARS | Salvage Ships | 9 | 9 | | | | | |
| AS | Submarine Tenders | 11 | 11 | | | | 3 | 2 |
| ASR | Submarine Rescue Ships | 6 | 6 | | | | | |
| ATA | Auxiliary Ocean Tugs | | | | | | | 4 |
| ATF | Fleet Ocean Tugs | 10 | 2 | 4 | 4 | | 4 | 1 |
| ATS | Salvage and Rescue Ships | 3 | 3 | | | | | |
| AVM | Guided Missile Ships | 1 | 1 | | | | | |
| IX | Unclassified Miscellaneous Ships* | 7 | 7 | | | | | |
| MSI | Inshore Minesweepers | 2 | | | | 2 | | |
| SES | Surface Effect Ships | 2 | 2 | | | | | |

*These ships officially are classified as Service Craft.

## UNDERWAY REPLENISHMENT SHIPS

AE, AF, AFS, AO (oiler), AOE, and AOR ships provide provisions, munitions, and fuels to forward-deployed naval forces. These ships can transfer material to warships while underway, steaming on parallel courses a few hundred feet apart. Helicopters can transfer all material except fuels to ships alongside or miles apart.

Names: Ammunition ships traditionally have been named for explosives (the NITRO for nitroglycerine) or volcanoes (the SURIBACHI); store ships for stars or constellations (the VEGA); and oilers for rivers with Indian names (the NEOSHO). The new types of underway replenishment ships which began entering service in the 1960s, the combat store ships, fast combat-support ships, and replenishment oilers, are named for American cities. That name source previously had been used for U.S. Navy cruisers and since 1971 has been used for attack submarines, demonstrating the considerable confusion in U.S. ship nomenclature.

The following groupings have been developed by the author, based on types of functions; they are not official groupings.

## SUPPORT SHIPS

AD, AGDS, AGP, APB, AR, ARC, ARL, and AS ships provide maintenance, repairs, and other support to the Fleet. The destroyer and submarine tenders provide a wide range of services to their "broods," both at U.S. ports and overseas. The submarine tenders supply electrical power for "hotel" services to nuclear submarines whose reactor plants are closed down; the SSBN tenders also have Polaris or Poseidon missile reloads. The cable ships lay and maintain seafloor acoustic sensors. The only seaplane tender (AV) remaining in Navy service is the NORTON SOUND, which has long been employed as a guided-missile and gunnery test ship (designated AVM 1).

Names: Destroyer tenders generally are named for geographic areas (DIXIE), except for the SAMUEL GOMPERS, which honors an American labor leader. The lone deep submergence support ship, the POINT LOMA, is named for the section of San Diego which serves as base for the Navy's deep submergence activities. Repair ships are named for mythological characters (the VULCAN), and submarine tenders for mythological characters (the ORION) or pioneers in submarine development or submarine heroes (the L. Y. SPEAR and HOWARD W. GILMORE, respectively).

## TUG-TYPE SHIPS

ARS, ASR, ATA, ATF, and ATS ships provide towing, salvage, target, submarine rescue, and other services to the Fleet. The salvage ships, submarine rescue ships, and ATS tugs are fitted for heavy salvage work. The ASRs are the Navy's principal deep-ocean diver support ships, and have the McCann submarine rescue chamber and, in the newer ships, Deep-Submergence Rescue Vehicles (DSRV) to save crewmen trapped in submarines disabled on the ocean floor at depths above their hull-collapse depth.

Names: Salvage ships are named for terms related to salvage activity (CLAMP); submarine rescue ships have bird names (the PIGEON), a scheme begun when the first ASRs were converted from World War I "Bird"-class minesweepers; and Navy tugs traditionally have had Indian names (the SHAKORI, SAMOSET, and KOKA). The large EDENTON-class tugs have been named for American towns with English namesakes; a reasonable scheme for these ships, which were constructed in England.

## SEALIFT SHIPS

AK, AKR, AO (tanker), and AOG ships carry cargo from point to point and do not undertake underway replenishment or amphibious operations. Four modified "Victory" cargo ships are employed exclusively in supplying the Polaris/Poseidon submarine tenders forward deployed at Holy Loch, Scotland; Rota, Spain; and Apra Harbor, Guam. All other sealift ships carry cargo for all Department of Defense agencies. (These ships all are civilian-manned under MSC control with the Polaris/Poseidon resupply ships having small Navy detachments for missile warhead security and communications.)

Names: Most MSC-operated cargo ships are named for U.S. Army heroes of World War II (the PVT. LEONARD C. BROSTROM), with the ADMIRAL WILLIAM M. CALLAGHAN honoring the first commander of the Military Sea Transportation Service (the previous name of MSC from 1949 to 1970); tankers have Indian river names (the POTOMAC), and the new "Sealift" class has geographic area names (the SEALIFT PACIFIC). Ships named for persons are generally referred to by last names only.

## EXPERIMENTAL, RESEARCH, SURVEYING SHIPS

AG, AGEH, AGM, AGMR, AGOR, AGOS, AGS, AVM, and certain IX ships in this grouping perform a variety of services in support of Navy programs and national ocean and space activities. Most of these ships are manned by civilians under MSC control or are operated by institutions. Details of their employment and operation are found under the individual ship listings.

Names: Name sources for these ships vary; most ocean research and surveying ships are named for oceanographers and other ocean-science pioneers (the LYNCH and HAYES, respectively; the latter honors the "father of sonar" in the U.S. Navy).

### 2 + 5 DESTROYER TENDERS: "GOMPERS" CLASS

| Number | Name | FY/SCB | Launched | Commissioned | Status |
|--------|------|--------|----------|--------------|--------|
| AD 37 | SAMUEL GOMPERS | 64/244 | 14 May 1966 | 1 July 1967 | **PA** |
| AD 38 | PUGET SOUND | 65/700 | 16 Sep 1966 | 27 Apr 1968 | **AA** |
| AD 41 | YELLOWSTONE | 75/700 | 1978 | 1980 | Bldg. |
| AD 42 | ACADIA | 76/700 | 1979 | 1980 | Bldg. |
| AD 43 | ........ | 77/700 | | | Auth. |
| AD 44 | ........ | 79/700 | | | Planned |
| AD 45 | ........ | 80/700 | | | Planned |

| | |
|---|---|
| Builders: | AD 37–38 Puget Sound Naval Shipyard |
| | AD 41–43 National Steel & Shipbuilding Co, San Diego |
| Displacement: | 22,260 tons full load |
| Length: | 643 feet (196 m) oa |
| Beam: | 85 feet (25.9 m) |
| Draft: | 22½ feet (6.9 m) |
| Propulsion: | steam turbine (De Laval); 20,000 shp; 1 shaft |
| Boilers: | 2 (Combustion Engineering) |
| Speed: | 20 knots |
| Complement: | 1,806 (135 O + 1,671 EM) |

| | |
|---|---|
| Guns: | 1 5-inch (127-mm) 38 cal DP Mk 30 in AD 38 (1 × 1) |
| | 2 40-mm AA Mk 64 in AD 41 and later ships (2 × 1) |
| | 4 20-mm AA Mk 67 in AD 37–38 (4 × 1); 2 guns in later ships (2 × 1) |

These ships are intended to provide complete support to modern destroyers and frigates; they can support ships with either gas-turbine or nuclear propulsion, and modern weapon systems.

Class: The AD 39 was authorized in the FY 1969 program but cancelled prior to the start of construction due to cost overruns in other new-ship programs; the AD 40 was authorized in FY 1973 but was not built.

Cost: Estimated cost of the AD 44 is $318 million.

Design: These ships are similar to the L. Y. SPEAR (AS 36) class. The destroyer tenders have a helicopter hangar and landing area to maintain LAMPS; two 7,000-pound capacity cranes are provided.

Guns: As built, the AD 37–38 both had a single 5-inch gun mount and one Mk 56 Mod 43 gun FCS; the gun was removed from the GOMPERS and the FCS was removed from both ships. Earlier plans to install NATO Sea Sparrow have been dropped.

The SAMUEL GOMPERS is lead ship of the Navy's post-war destroyer tender program. She is similar in design to the L. Y. SPEAR-class submarine tenders. The 5-inch gun originally mounted forward of the bridge has been removed. Note servicing boats under cranes. These ships have a large stern anchor as well as two bow anchors. (1977, Giorgio Arra)

## 3 DESTROYER TENDERS: "KLONDIKE" CLASS

| Number | Name | Launched | Commissioned | Status |
|--------|------|----------|--------------|--------|
| AD 24 | EVERGLADES | 28 Jan 1945 | 25 May 1951 | MR |
| AD 26 | SHENANDOAH | 29 Mar 1945 | 13 Aug 1945 | **AA** |
| AD 36 | BRYCE CANYON | 7 Mar 1946 | 15 Sep 1950 | **PA** |

Builders:     AD 24 Los Angeles Shipbuilding & DD Co
           AD 26 Todd-Pacific Shipyards, Tacoma
           AD 36 Charleston Navy Yard
Displacement:   8,165 tons standard
           16,635 to 16,900 tons full load
Length:        492 feet (150 m) oa
Beam:         69½ feet (21.2 m)
Draft:         27⅛ feet (8.3 m)
Propulsion:     steam turbine (General Electric in AD 24; Westinghouse in others);
           8,500 shp; 1 shaft
Boilers:       2 (General Electric in AD 24; Foster Wheeler in others)
Speed:        18.4 knots
Complement:   778 to 918
Guns:         1 5-inch (127-mm) 38 cal DP Mk 37 in AD 36 (1 × 1)
           2 3-inch (76-mm) 50 cal AA Mk in AD 24 (2 × 1)
           4 20-mm AA Mk 68 in AD 26 (4 × 1)

These ships were built to a merchant design specifically as tenders. Completion of the EVERGLADES and BRYCE CANYON was delayed after World War II.

Class: Thirteen destroyer tenders were built to this configuration: the KLONDIKE class (AD 22–25) and the SHENANDOAH class (AD 26–29, 31, 36). Three additional ships were cancelled (AD 30, 33, 35). The AD 16 and 20–21 were similar to these ships. The KLONDIKE (AD 22) and GRAND CANYON (AD 28) were reclassified as repair ships (changed to AR with same hull numbers) in 1960 and 1971, respectively. The ISLE ROYAL (AD 29) was stricken on 15 September 1976. See previous editions for earlier disposals.

Classification: The BRYCE CANYON originally was ordered as a seaplane tender (AV 20).

Design: Maritime Administration C3 design, modified for the AD role.

Guns: The original armament for the KLONDIKE class was 1 5-inch gun, 4 3-inch guns, and 4 40-mm guns; for the SHENANDOAH class, 2 5-inch guns and 8 40-mm guns.

Modernization: These ships have been extensively modernized to permit them to support modern destroyers and frigates; the helicopter platform and hangar are provided to support the Drone Antisubmarine Helicopter (DASH) program and cannot land manned helicopters.

BRYCE CANYON (U.S. Navy)

SHENANDOAH (1976, Giorgio Arra)

## 5 DESTROYER TENDERS: "DIXIE" CLASS

| Number | Name | Launched | Commissioned | Status |
|--------|------|----------|--------------|--------|
| AD 14 | DIXIE | 27 May 1939 | 25 Apr 1940 | **PA** |
| AD 15 | PRAIRIE | 9 Dec 1939 | 5 Aug 1940 | **PA** |
| AD 17 | PIEDMONT | 7 Dec 1942 | 5 Jan 1944 | **AA** |
| AD 18 | SIERRA | 23 Feb 1943 | 20 Mar 1944 | **AA** |
| AD 19 | YOSEMITE | 16 May 1943 | 25 May 1944 | **AA** |

| | |
|--|--|
| Builders: | AD 14–15 New York Shipbuilding Corp, Camden |
| | AD 17–19 Tampa Shipbuilding Co |
| Displacement: | 9,450 tons standard |
| | 17,176 tons full load |
| Length: | 530½ feet (161.7 m) oa |
| Beam: | 73⅓ feet (22.3 m) |
| Draft: | 25½ feet (7.8 m) |
| Propulsion: | steam turbine (Parsons in AD 14–15, Allis Chalmers in AD 17–19); |
| | 11,000 shp; 2 shafts |
| Boilers: | 4 (Babcock & Wilcox) |
| Speed: | 19.6 knots |

| | |
|--|--|
| Complement: | ~1,070 |
| Guns: | 4 20-mm AA Mk 67 in AD 14–15, 17; 4 20-mm AA Mk 68 in AD 18–19 |
| | (4 × 1) |

These are the oldest ships in U.S. Navy commission except for the sail frigate CONSTITUTION, which is retained as a relic. They have been modernized to service ships with ASROC, improved electronics, etc.

Class: Five ships were built to this design (AD 14–15, 17–19); the later NEW ENGLAND (AD 32, ex-AS 28), cancelled in 1945, was to have been similar.

Guns: As completed, these ships had four 5-inch DP guns and eight 40-mm AA guns; these were reduced into the mid-1970s when minimal 20-mm armament was provided.

Modernization: Modernization programs provided helicopter hangar and flight deck to support DASH helicopters. Manned helicopters cannot operate from these ships.

The PIEDMONT, one of the Navy's pre-war tender designs with almost yacht-like lines. The VULCAN-class repair ships and FULTON-class submarine tenders are similar. The ship's gun battery—originally comparable to that of a contemporary destroyer—has been removed. The small helicopter deck and hangar aft cannot handle manned helicopters. (1976, Giorgio Arra)

DIXIE (1976, U.S. Navy)

## Destroyer Tender Disposals

Disposals since Tenth Edition: the CASCADE (AD 16), a merchant conversion, was stricken on 23 November 1974.

### 8 AMMUNITION SHIPS: "KILAUEA" CLASS

| Number | Name | FY/SCB | Launched | Commissioned | Status |
|--------|------|--------|----------|--------------|--------|
| AE 26 | KILAUEA | 65/703 | 9 Aug 1967 | 10 Aug 1968 | **PA** |
| AE 27 | BUTTE | 65/703 | 9 Aug 1967 | 29 Nov 1968 | **AA** |
| AE 28 | SANTA BARBARA | 66/703 | 23 Jan 1968 | 11 July 1970 | **AA** |
| AE 29 | MOUNT HOOD | 66/703 | 17 July 1968 | 1 May 1971 | **PA** |
| AE 32 | FLINT | 67/703 | 9 Nov 1970 | 20 Nov 1971 | **PA** |
| AE 33 | SHASTA | 67/703 | 3 Apr 1971 | 26 Feb 1972 | **PA** |
| AE 34 | MOUNT BAKER | 68/703 | 23 Oct 1971 | 22 July 1972 | **AA** |
| AE 35 | KISKA | 68/703 | 11 Mar 1972 | 16 Dec 1972 | **PA** |

FLINT (1976, Giorgio Arra)

| | |
|---|---|
| Builders: | AE 26–27 General Dynamics Corp, Quincy |
| | AE 28–29 Bethlehem Steel Corp, Sparrows Point |
| | AE 30–35 Ingalls Shipbuilding Corp, Pascagoula |
| Displacement: | 20,500 tons full load |
| Length: | 564 feet (171.9 m) oa |
| Beam: | 81 feet (24.7 m) |
| Draft: | 25¾ feet (7.8 m) |
| Propulsion: | steam turbine (General Electric); 22,000 shp; 1 shaft |
| Boilers: | 3 (Foster Wheeler) |
| Speed: | 20 knots (sustained) |
| Complement: | 401 (28 O + 373 EM) |
| Helicopters: | 2 CH-46 Sea Knight |
| Guns: | 4 3-inch (76-mm) 50 cal AA Mk 33 (2 × 2) |

These are high-capability underway replenishment ships, fitted for rapid transfer of missiles and other munitions.

Design: Fitted with helicopter landing area aft and hangar. They have a cargo capacity of 6,500 deadweight tons.

Guns: As built, these ships had eight 3-inch guns (with two Mk 56 Mod 39/39A gun FCS); these were reduced during the late 1970s. Two 20-mm CIWS are planned for installation when available.

SHASTA (1977, Giorgio Arra)

The BUTTE with a CH-46 Sea King on her helicopter deck. Her superstructure is aft of amidships; refrigerated munitions holds are forward. Two enclosed 3-inch gun mounts are forward and two at after end of superstructure; the battery has since been halved because of maintenance and manning problems with the 3-inch guns and their limited effectiveness. (1968, U.S. Navy)

## 5 AMMUNITION SHIPS: "SURIBACHI" CLASS

| Number | Name | FY/SCB | Launched | Commissioned | Status |
|--------|------|--------|----------|--------------|--------|
| AE 21 | SURIBACHI | 54/114A | 2 Nov 1955 | 17 Nov 1956 | **AA** |
| AE 22 | MAUNA KEA | 54/114A | 3 May 1956 | 30 Mar 1957 | **PA** |
| AE 23 | NITRO | 56/114A | 25 June 1958 | 1 May 1959 | **AA** |
| AE 24 | PYRO | 56/114A | 5 Nov 1958 | 24 July 1959 | **PA** |
| AE 25 | HALEAKALA | 57/114A | 17 Feb 1959 | 3 Nov 1959 | **PA** |

| | |
|---|---|
| Builders: | Bethlehem Steel Corp, Sparrows Point |
| Displacement: | 10,000 tons standard |
| | 17,500 tons full load |
| Length: | 512 feet (156.1 m) oa |
| Beam: | 72 feet (21.9 m) |
| Draft: | 29 feet (8.8 m) |
| Propulsion: | steam turbine (Bethlehem); 16,000 shp; 1 shaft |
| Boilers: | 2 (Combustion Engineering) |

| | |
|---|---|
| Speed: | 20.6 knots |
| Complement: | 316 (18 O + 298 EM) |
| Guns: | 4 3-inch (76 mm) 50 cal AA Mk 33 (2 × 2) |

These ships were designed and constructed specifically for munitions underway replenishment.

Class: A sixth ship proposed for the FY 1959 shipbuilding program was cancelled.

Design: Cargo capacity is 7,500 deadweight tons.

Guns: As built, these ships carried eight 3-inch guns (see Modernization). The arrangement of forward guns vary; some have 3-inch mounts in tandem and others side-by-side.

Modernization: All five ships were extensively modernized during the 1960s (SCB-232); they were fitted to carry and transfer guided missiles; thereafter, 3-inch gun mounts were removed and a helicopter deck was installed (but no hangar provided).

The ammunition ship NITRO at anchor in Norfolk. She has a CH-46 Sea Knight on her fantail flight deck. As built, ships of this class had an SPS-6 air search radar atop their pole mast in addition to the smaller, SPS-10 navigation radar visible here. The RIGEL-class store ships are similar in appearance. (1975, Giorgio Arra)

MAUNA KEA (1977, Giorgio Arra)

## Ammunition Ship Disposals

The last ships of the MOUNT HOOD class (AE 11–12, 14–19) and the similar LASSEN class (AE 3–6, 8–10, 13) in U.S. Navy service have been stricken; the FIREDRAKE (AE 14) on 15 July 1976, and the MAUNA LOA (AE 8) and WRANGELL (AE 12) on 1 October 1976.

### 2 STORE SHIPS: "RIGEL" CLASS

| Number | Name | FY/SCB | Launched | Commissioned | Status |
|--------|------|--------|----------|--------------|--------|
| T-AF 58 | RIGEL | 53/97 | 15 Mar 1955 | 2 Sep 1955 | **MSC-A** |
| AF 59 | VEGA | 53/97 | 26 Apr 1955 | 10 Nov 1955 | **PA** |

| | |
|---|---|
| Builders: | Ingalls Shipbuilding Corp, Pascagoula |
| Displacement: | 7,950 tons light |
| | 15,540 tons full load |
| Length: | 502 feet (153 m) oa |
| Beam: | 72 feet (22 m) |
| Draft: | 29 feet (8.8 m) |
| Propulsion: | steam turbine (General Electric); 16,000 shp; 1 shaft |
| Boilers: | 2 (Combustion Engineering) |
| Speed: | 20 knots |

| | |
|---|---|
| Complement: | 350 in AE 59; 115 in T-AF 58 |
| Guns: | 4 3-inch (76-mm) 50 cal AA Mk 33 in AF 59 (2 × 2); removed from T-AF 58 |

These are the U.S. Navy's only built-for-the-purpose store ships (AF). The RIGEL was assigned to the Military Sealift Command on 23 June 1975; she is manned by civilians.

Design: Modified Maritime Administration R3-S-A4 design. They have a cargo capacity of 4,650 deadweight tons.

Guns: These ships were completed with four 3-inch twin gun mounts; the two after mounts were subsequently removed for the installation of a helicopter platform. The remaining guns were removed from the RIGEL when she was assigned to MSC.

VEGA (1974, U.S. Navy, PH2 John Kristoffersen)

RIGEL (1977, Giorgio Arra)

## Store Ship Disposals

Disposals since Tenth Edition: The ZELIMA (AF 49), PICTOR (AF 54), ALUDRA (AF 55), and PROCTON (AF 61), all R2-S-BV1 design, were stricken on 1 June 1976. The DENEBOLA (AF 56), VC2-S-AP3 design, was transferred to Spain in April 1976. The HYADES (AF 28), C2-S-1E design, and the ARCTURUS (AF 52), C2-S-B1 design, were both stricken on 1 October 1976.

### 7 COMBAT STORE SHIPS: "MARS" CLASS

| Number | Name | FY/SCB | Launched | Commissioned | Status |
|--------|------|--------|----------|--------------|--------|
| AFS 1 | MARS | 61/208 | 15 June 1963 | 21 Dec 1963 | **PA** |
| AFS 2 | SYLVANIA | 62/208 | 15 Aug 1963 | 11 July 1964 | **AA** |
| AFS 3 | NIAGARA FALLS | 64/208 | 26 Mar 1966 | 29 Apr 1967 | **PA** |
| AFS 4 | WHITE PLAINS | 65/705 | 23 July 1966 | 23 Nov 1968 | **PA** |
| AFS 5 | CONCORD | 65/705 | 17 Dec 1966 | 27 Nov 1968 | **AA** |
| AFS 6 | SAN DIEGO | 66/705 | 13 Apr 1968 | 24 May 1969 | **AA** |
| AFS 7 | SAN JOSE | 67/705 | 13 Dec 1969 | 23 Oct 1970 | **PA** |

| | |
|--|--|
| Builders: | National Steel & Shipbuilding Co, San Diego |
| Displacement: | 16,500 tons full load |
| Length: | 581 feet (177.1 m) oa |
| Beam: | 79 feet (24.1 m) |
| Draft: | 24 feet (7.3 m) |
| Propulsion: | steam turbine (De Laval in AFS 1–2, 4–5, 7); 22,000 shp; 1 shaft |
| Boilers: | 3 (Babcock & Wilcox) |
| Speed: | 20 knots |
| Complement: | 430 (30 O + 400 EM) |
| Helicopters: | 2 CH-46 Sea Knight |
| Guns: | 4 3-inch (76-mm) 50 cal AA Mk 33 (2 × 2) |

These are large, built-for-the-purpose underway replenishment ships combining the capabilities of store ships (AF), stores-issue ships (AKS), and aviation store ships (AVS).

Class: Three additional ships were planned for the FY 1977–1978 shipbuilding programs, but were not requested when the budgets were submitted to Congress.

Design: These ships have advanced cargo-transfer equipment; they are fitted with five cargo holds (one refrigerated), and have a 7,000-ton deadweight capacity. A helicopter hangar and platform are fitted aft.

Engineering: Two boilers are normally used for full-power steaming, with the third shut down for maintenance (all are 570-psi).

Guns: These ships were built with four 3-inch twin gun mounts; two mounts were removed during the late 1970s.

NIAGARA FALLS (1970, U.S. Navy, PH2 G. R. Dahlberg)

WHITE PLAINS (1976, Giorgio Arra)

## 1 HYDROGRAPHIC RESEARCH SHIP: "VICTORY" CLASS

| Number | Name | Launched | In service | Status |
|--------|------|----------|-----------|--------|
| T-AG 164 | KINGSPORT | 29 May 1944 | 1 Mar 1950 | **MSC-A** |

| | |
|---|---|
| Builders: | California Shipbuilding Corp, Los Angeles |
| Displacement: | 7,190 tons light |
| | 10,680 tons full load |
| Length: | 455 feet (138.7 m) oa |
| Beam: | 62 feet (18.9 m) |
| Draft: | 22 feet (6.7 m) |
| Propulsion: | steam turbine; 8,500 shp; 1 shaft |
| Boilers: | 2 |
| Speed: | 15.2 knots |
| Complement: | 54 + 15 technical personnel |
| Armament: | none |

The KINGSPORT was built as a cargo ship and employed in carrying military cargoes until acquired by the Navy on 1 March 1950 and assigned to MSTS (retaining her original name, KINGSPORT VICTORY). She continued in the cargo role as the T-AK 239 until 1961, when she was converted to support the Project Advent defense satellite communications program; in that role she was renamed the KINGSPORT and changed to T-AG 164. The support of Project Advent and other space programs was completed in 1966 and the KINGSPORT was reassigned to hydrographic research activities in support of undersea surveillance programs. Operated by MSC in support of the Naval Electronic Systems Command, she is civilian-manned.

Classification: She was changed from T-AK 239 to T-AG 164 (and renamed) on 14 November 1961.

Conversion: Conversion to a satellite communications ship included provision of extensive communications and satellite tracking equipment, including a 30-foot parabolic communications antenna housed in a 53-foot diameter plastic radome aft of the superstructure. (This was later removed.) The ship was painted white for operations in the tropics. The conversion was SCB-225.

Design: Maritime Administration VC2-S-AP3 design.

KINGSPORT (U.S. Navy)

## 1 MISSILE TEST SHIP: "MARINER" CLASS

| Number | Name | Launched | Commissioned | Status |
|--------|------|----------|--------------|--------|
| AG 154 | OBSERVATION ISLAND | 15 Aug 1953 | 5 Dec 1958 | MR |

| | |
|---|---|
| Builders: | New York Shipbuilding Corp, Camden |
| Displacement: | 17,600 tons full load |
| Length: | 563 feet (171.6 m) oa |
| Beam: | 76 feet (23.2 m) |
| Draft: | 29 feet (8.8 m) |
| Propulsion: | steam turbine (General Electric); 22,000 shp; 1 shaft |
| Boilers: | 2 |
| Speed: | 20 knots |
| Complement: | ~350 |
| Armament: | none |

The OBSERVATION ISLAND was acquired prior to her completion as a merchant ship and completed as a missile test ship for the Polaris SLBM. She subsequently was modified to fire the Poseidon missile. The ship was Navy-manned. She was decommissioned on 25 Sep 1972 and placed in Maritime Administration reserve.

Class: Plans to acquire a third "Mariner"-class ship (i.e., AG 155) to support the Polaris SLBM program were cancelled.

Classification: Originally classified YAG 57, she was changed to AG 154 on 19 June 1956; listed as EAG 154 until 1 April 1968, she was then "reclassified" as AG 154.

Design: Maritime Administration C4-S-1A. She is fitted with two SLBM launch tubes.

Names: Merchant name was the EMPIRE STATE MARINER.

OBSERVATION ISLAND (1971, U.S. Navy)

## 1 EXPERIMENTAL NAVIGATION SHIP: "MARINER" CLASS

| Number | Name | Launched | Commissioned | Status |
|--------|------|----------|--------------|--------|
| AG 153 | COMPASS ISLAND | 24 Oct 1953 | 3 Dec 1956 | **AA** |

| | |
|---|---|
| Builders: | New York Shipbuilding Corp, Camden |
| Displacement: | 16,076 tons full load |
| Length: | 563 feet (171.6 m) oa |
| Beam: | 76 feet (23.2 m) |
| Draft: | 29 feet (8.8 m) |
| Propulsion: | steam turbine (General Electric); 22,000 shp; 1 shaft |
| Boilers: | 2 |
| Speed: | 20 knots |
| Complement: | |
| Armament: | none |

The COMPASS ISLAND was acquired by the Navy while under construction and was completed as a test ship for the inertial navigation systems to be used in the Polaris SSBNs. She remains in service, manned by a Navy crew, supporting the development of advanced navigation equipment.

Classification: Originally classified YAG 56, she was changed to AG 153 on 19 June 1956; she was listed as EAG 153 until 1 April 1968, when she was "reclassified" as AG 153.

Conversion: She is fitted with Ships Inertial Navigation System (SINS), with star trackers mounted in a 67-ton stabilized tower or observatory forward of the bridge. Active-fin roll stabilizers are installed, and she has been fitted with large sonar dome.

Design: Maritime Administration C4-S-1A.

Names: Merchant name was the GARDEN MARINER.

COMPASS ISLAND (U.S. Navy)

### Miscellaneous Auxiliary Disposals

Disposals since Tenth Edition: FLYER (T-AG 178), C2-S-B1 design modified for hydrographic research in support of undersea surveillance, stricken on 17 July 1975; CHEYENNE (T-AG 174), PROVO (T-AG 173), and PHOENIX (T-AG 172), all "Victory"-class cargo and forward depot ships, stricken on 19 June 1973; SEQUOIA (AG 23), long serving as a yacht for the Secretary of the Navy and, since 1968, the President, stricken in 1977. The deep ocean salvage ship GLOMAR EXPLORER, built in 1972–1973 by the Central Intelligence Agency to salvage a sunken Soviet submarine, was placed on the Navy Register as the AG 193 on 30 September 1976; she was subsequently transferred to the Maritime Administration for layup on 17 January 1977. The two former ocean minesweepers used as sonar test ships, the ALACRITY (AG 520, ex-MSO 520) and ASSURANCE (AG 521, ex-MOS 521), listed as auxiliary ships since 1970, were both stricken on 30 September 1977.

## 1 AUXILIARY DEEP SUBMERGENCE SUPPORT SHIP: "POINT LOMA"

| Number | Name | Launched | T-AKD in service | AGDS Comm. | Status |
|--------|------|----------|------------------|------------|--------|
| AGDS 2 | POINT LOMA | 25 May 1957 | 29 May 1958 | 3 July 1976 | **PA** |

| | |
|---|---|
| Builders: | Maryland Shipbuilding & Dry Dock Co, Baltimore |
| Displacement: | 9,415 tons standard |
| | 14,094 tons full load |
| Length: | 492 feet (150 m) oa |
| Beam: | 90 feet (27.4 m) |
| Draft: | 26 feet (7.9 m) |
| Propulsion: | steam turbines; 6,000 shp; 2 shafts |
| Boilers: | 2 |
| Speed: | 15 knots |
| Complement: | 259 (10 O + 249 EM) + 8 scientists |
| Armament: | none |

The POINT LOMA was built as a "wet well" dock cargo ship (originally the POINT BARROW, T-AKD 1) to carry vehicles, supplies, and landing craft to U.S. radar warning installations in the arctic. Assigned to MSTS upon completion and operated in that role until 1965 (during that period she also transported the fixed-array radar antennas for the carrier ENTERPRISE and cruiser LONG BEACH); she was modified in 1965 and then used until 1970 to carry Saturn rockets and other space program equipment from California to Cape Kennedy. She also made some trips to Vietnam carrying landing craft.

The ship was laid up in 1971–1972, then returned to general cargo work under Military Sealift Command; she was converted in 1974–1976 to carry and support the research submersible TRIESTE.

The POINT LOMA is operated by Submarine Development Group One at Point Loma (San Diego), California.

Classification: The classification AGDS was established on 3 January 1974. The previous TRIESTE II support ship, the modified floating dry dock WHITE SANDS (ARD 20), was briefly assigned the hull number AGDS 1.

Conversion: The ship was specifically converted in 1974–1976 for use with the TRIESTE II; she can carry, launch, recover, and service the submersible. Tankage is provided for approximately 100,000 gallons of aviation gasoline which is used for flotation by the TRIESTE II, and the lead shot which is used by the submersible for ballast.

Design: Maritime Administration S2-ST-23A design. The ship is ice-strengthened and winterized for arctic operation.

POINT LOMA (1977, U.S. Navy)

### 1 HYDROFOIL RESEARCH SHIP: "PLAINVIEW"

| Number | Name | FY/SCB | Launched | In service | Status |
|--------|------|--------|----------|-----------|--------|
| AGEH 1 | PLAINVIEW | 62/219 | 28 June 1965 | 3 March 1969 | **PA** |

| | |
|---|---|
| Builders: | Lockheed Shipbuilding & Constn Co, Seattle |
| Displacement: | 320 tons full load |
| Length: | 212 feet (64.6 m) oa |
| Beam: | 40½ feet (12.3 m) |
| Draft: | 10 feet (3 m) hullborne |
| | 26 feet (7.9 m) foilborne |
| Propulsion: | 2 diesels; 1,200 bhp; 2 outboard propeller units |
| | 2 gas turbines (General Electric); 30,000 shp; 2 waterjets |
| Speed: | 12 knots |
| | ~50 knots |
| Complement: | 20 (6 O + 14 EM) |
| Guns: | none |
| ASW weapons: | 6 12.75-inch (324-mm) torpedo tubes Mk 32 (2 × 3) |

The PLAINVIEW was developed for the evaluation of a large hydrofoil ship. She is the largest military hydrofoil constructed by any nation. Engineering difficulties delayed her completion (five years from keel-laying to acceptance).

Design: The ship has an aluminum hull, and is fitted with three fully submerged, retractable foils, one each on her port and starboard sides, and one at her stern; most of the ship's weight is supported by the large forward foils.

Engineering: The gas turbines are modified J79 aircraft engines. Speeds of about 80 knots are believed possible after certain modifications to the ship are made.

PLAINVIEW at high speed with CH-46A Sea Knight (1972, U.S. Navy, PH2 E. E. Murphy)

## Hydrofoil Patrol Combatant Support Ships

The WOOD COUNTY (LST 1178), was scheduled for conversion to a hydrofoil patrol combatant support ship (AGHS); that conversion was cancelled early in 1977 when Secretary of Defense Brown

decided to terminate the PHM program with only one ship being completed. The subsequent refusal by Congress to allow the program to be halted has reopened the possibility that the WOOD COUNTY may be converted at a later date.

### 2 MISSILE RANGE INSTRUMENTATION SHIPS: "VICTORY" CLASS

| Number | Name | Launched | APA Comm. | T-AGM in service | Status |
|--------|------|----------|-----------|-----------------|--------|
| T-AGM 8 | WHEELING | 22 May 1945 | — | 28 May 1964 | **MSC-P** |
| T-AGM 22 | RANGE SENTINEL | 10 July 1944 | 20 Sep 1944 | 14 Oct 1971 | **MSC-A** |

| | |
|---|---|
| Builders: | T-AGM 8 Oregon Shipbuilding Corp, Portland |
| | T-AGM 22 Permanente Metals Corp., Richmond, Calif. |
| Displacement: | 10,680 tons full load T-AGM 8 |
| | 11,860 tons full load T-AGM 22 |
| Length: | 455 feet (138.7 m) oa |
| Beam: | 62 feet (18.9 m) |
| Draft: | |
| Propulsion: | steam turbine (Westinghouse); 8,500 shp; 1 shaft |
| Boilers: | 2 |
| Speed: | 17.7 knots |
| Complement: | 58 + 48 technicians in T-AGM 8 |
| | 68 + 27 technicians in T-AGM 22 |
| Armament: | none |

These ships are a former merchant ship and Navy attack transport (APA 205), respectively, converted to missile range instrumentation ships. The WHEELING is the survivor of several "Victory"-class ships which were converted to the AGM role during the intensive U.S. space and strategic weapon programs of the 1960s (AGM 1, 3–8).

The RANGE SENTINEL served as an APA during World War II; she was subsequently laid up and stricken on 1 October 1958. She was reacquired from the Maritime Administration on 22 October 1969 for conversion to an AGM, and reclassified as AGM 22 on 26 April 1971.

Both ships are civilian-manned.

Design: Maritime Administration VC2-S-AP3 and VC2-S-AP5 designs, respectively.

Names: The RANGE SENTINEL was formerly the SHERBURNE (APA 205).

The Navy's four missile range instrumentation ships in the Atlantic, all operated by the Military Sealift Command, are seen here in Port Canaveral, Florida. From left are the VANGUARD, GENERAL HOYT S. VANDENBERG, REDSTONE, and RANGE SENTINEL. (1977, U.S. Navy, CDR Charles M. Rowland)

WHEELING (U.S. Navy)

RANGE SENTINEL (1973, U.S. Navy)

## 2 MISSILE RANGE INSTRUMENTATION SHIPS: CONVERTED OILERS

| Number | Name | Launched | AO Comm. | T-AGM in service | Status |
|---|---|---|---|---|---|
| T-AGM 19 | VANGUARD | 25 Nov 1943 | 21 Oct 1947 | 28 Feb 1966 | **MSC-A** |
| T-AGM 20 | REDSTONE | 28 Feb 1944 | 22 Oct 1947 | 30 June 1966 | **MSC-A** |

| | |
|---|---|
| Builders: | Marine Ship Corp, Sausalito, California |
| Displacement: | 21,626 tons full load |
| Length: | 595 feet (181.4 m) oa |
| Beam: | 75 feet (22.9 m) |
| Draft: | 25 feet (7.6 m) |
| Propulsion: | turbo-electric drive (General Electric); 10,000 shp; 1 shaft |
| Boilers: | 2 (Babcock & Wilcox) |
| Speed: | 16 knots |
| Complement: | 86 + 108 technicians in T-AGM 19 |
| | 76 + 120 technicians in T-AGM 20 |
| Armament: | none |

These ships are former "Mission"-class tankers extensively converted for the AGM role. Both ships were commissioned in naval service and transferred to MSTS on 1 October 1949 when that service was created. The VANGUARD, as AO 122, was stricken on 4 September 1957 and reacquired by the Navy on 28 September 1964 for conversion to AGM 19; the REDSTONE, as AO 114, was stricken on 13 March 1958 and reacquired on 19 September 1964 to become AGM 20.

Both ships are civilian-manned.

Class: A third ship of this type, the MERCURY (T-AGM 21), has been stricken.

Conversion: Both ships were extensively converted at the General Dynamics yard at Quincy, Massachusetts; a 72-foot midships section was installed, increasing the ships' length and beam. Fitted with missile/space tracking and communications systems, and accommodations for a large technical staff. Configurations as T-AGMs differ.

Design: Original Maritime Administration T2-SE-A2 design.

Names: The T-AO 122 was the MISSION SAN FERNANDO; renamed the MUSCLE SHOALS on 8 April 1965 and then the VANGUARD on 1 September 1965; the T-AO 114 was the MISSION DE PALA; renamed the JOHNSTOWN on 8 April 1965 and then the REDSTONE on 1 September 1965.

REDSTONE (1970, U.S. Air Force)

VANGUARD (U.S. Navy)

## 2 MISSILE RANGE INSTRUMENTATION SHIPS: CONVERTED TRANSPORTS

| Number | Name | Launched | AP Comm. | T-AGM in service | Status |
|--------|------|----------|----------|------------------|--------|
| T-AGM 9 | GENERAL H. H. ARNOLD | 23 May 1944 | 17 Aug 1944 | 1 July 1964 | **MSC-P** |
| T-AGM 10 | GENERAL HOYT S. VANDENBERG | 10 October 1943 | 1 Apr 1944 | 13 July 1964 | **MSC-A** |

| | |
|---|---|
| Builders: | Kaiser Co, Richmond, Calif. |
| Displacement: | 16,600 tons full load |
| Length: | 522⅚ feet (159.4 m) oa |
| Beam: | 71½ feet (21.8 m) |
| Draft: | 26⅓ feet (8 m) |
| Propulsion: | steam turbine (Westinghouse); 9,000 shp; 1 shaft |
| Boilers: | 2 (Babcock & Wilcox) |
| Speed: | 16.5 knots |
| Complement: | 90 + 113 technicians |
| Armament: | none |

These ships were converted from "General"-class transports (T-AP 139 and T-AP 145, respectively) into missile range ships to support Air Force ICBM tests. Upon conversion both ships were placed in Air Force service in 1963 with civilian contract crews. They were subsequently designated T-AGMs and assigned to MSTS in 1964.

Both ships are civilian-manned.

Design: Maritime Administration C4-S-A1 design. As transports, these ships carried approximately 3,300 troops.

Names: T-AGM 9 originally was named the GENERAL R. E. CALLAN and the T-AGM 10 was the GENERAL HARRY TAYLOR.

GENERAL H. H. ARNOLD (U.S. Navy)

GENERAL H. H. ARNOLD (1977, Giorgio Arra)

GENERAL HOYT S. VANDENBERG (U.S. Navy)

## Major Communications Relay Ship Disposals

The ARLINGTON (AGMR 2; the former light carrier SAIPAN; ex-CC 3, ex-AVT 6, ex-CVL 48), was stricken on 15 August 1975. The ANNAPOLIS (AGMR 1; the former escort carrier GILBERT ISLANDS; ex-AKV 39, ex-CVE 107), was stricken on 15 October 1976.

### 2 OCEANOGRAPHIC RESEARCH SHIPS: "GYRE" CLASS

| Number | Name | FY/SCB | Launched | Delivered | Status |
|---|---|---|---|---|---|
| (AGOR 21) | GYRE | 71/734 | 25 May 1973 | 14 Nov 1973 | **Academic** |
| (AGOR 22) | MOANA WAVE | 71/734 | 18 June 1973 | 16 Jan 1974 | **Academic** |

| | |
|---|---|
| Builders: | Halter Marine Service, New Orleans |
| Displacement: | 950 tons full load |
| Length: | 176 feet (53.6 m) oa |
| Beam: | 36 feet (11 m) |
| Draft: | 14½ feet (4.4 m) |
| Propulsion: | turbo-charged diesels (Caterpillar); 1,700 bhp; 2 shafts (controllable-pitch propellers) |
| Speed: | 13 knots |
| Complement: | 10 + 11 scientists |
| Armament: | none |

These are small, "utility" research ships designed specifically for operation by research institutions. They are operated for the Oceanographer of the Navy by Texas A&M University and the University of Hawaii, respectively.

Design: These ships are based on a commercial design. The open deck aft provides space for special-purpose vans and research equipment.

Engineering: A small, 50-hp retractable propeller pod is fitted for low-speed maneuvering or station-keeping during research operations, thus permitting main engines to be shut down to reduce noise and vibration.

### 1 OCEANOGRAPHIC RESEARCH SHIP: CONVERTED SALVAGE SHIP

| Number | Name | Launched | ARS Comm. | AGOR in service | Status |
|---|---|---|---|---|---|
| (AGOR 17) | CHAIN | 3 June 1943 | 31 Mar 1944 | 1957 | **Academic** |

| | |
|---|---|
| Builders: | Basalt Rock Co, Napa, California |
| Displacement: | 2,100 tons full load |
| Length: | 213½ feet (65.1 m) oa |
| Beam: | 39 feet (11.9 m) |
| Draft: | 15 feet (4.6 m) |
| Propulsion: | diesel-electric (Cooper Bessemer diesels); ~3,000 bhp; 2 shafts |
| Speed: | 12 knots |
| Complement: | 31 + 26 scientists |
| Armament: | none |

The CHAIN is a former Navy salvage ship (ARS 20) converted to an AGOR in 1958. She is operated by the Woods Hole Oceanographic Institution for the Office of Naval Research, under the technical direction of the Oceanographer of the Navy. She is civilian manned.

Class: A second ship of this class, the SNATCH (ARS 27), was similarly converted to the AGOR 18 and renamed the ARGO; she was subsequently stricken.

Classification: Changed from ARS to AGOR on 1 April 1957.

Conversion: Extensively modified and fitted with laboratories and equipment for ocean research. Also fitted with 250 bhp outboard propulsion unit for maneuvering at speeds up to 4.5 knots.

GYRE (Halter Marine Service)

CHAIN (Woods Hole Oceanographic Institute)

## 1 OCEANOGRAPHIC RESEARCH SHIP: "HAYES"

| Number | Name | FY/SCB | Launched | In service | Status |
|--------|------|--------|----------|-----------|--------|
| T-AGOR 16 | HAYES | 67/726 | 2 July 1970 | 21 July 1971 | **MSC-A** |

| | |
|---|---|
| Builders: | Todd Shipyards, Seattle |
| Displacement: | 3,080 tons full load |
| Length: | $246^{5}/_{12}$ feet (75.1 m) oa |
| Beam: | 75 feet (22.9 m) |
| Draft: | $18\frac{1}{2}$ feet (5.6 m) |
| Propulsion: | geared diesels (General Motors); 5,400 bhp; 2 shafts (controllable-pitch propellers) |
| Speed: | 15 knots (sustained) |
| Complement: | 44 + 30 scientists |
| Armament: | none |

The HAYES is the Navy's largest built-for-the-purpose oceanographic research ship. The catamaran design provides a stable work platform with a large open deck area; also, a center-line well makes it possible to lower research equipment into sheltered water between the two hulls. However, some seakeeping problems were encountered in this design, and it has not been repeated.

The HAYES is operated by MSC for the Office of Naval Research under the technical control of the Oceanographer of the Navy, with a civilian crew.

Design: The HAYES has two hulls, each with a 24-foot beam, spaced 27 feet apart for an overall ship beam of 75 feet. Berthing

and messing spaces are located in the forward superstructure "block" while the laboratories are located aft.

Engineering: An auxiliary, 165 bhp diesel engine is provided in each hull to permit a "creeping" speed of 2–4 knots.

HAYES (1975, U.S. Navy, CAPT A. J. Cotterell)

HAYES (1971, Todd Shipyards)

## 2 OCEANOGRAPHIC RESEARCH SHIPS: "MELVILLE" CLASS

| Number | Name | FY/SCB | Launched | Commissioned | Status |
|--------|------|--------|----------|--------------|--------|
| (AGOR 14) | MELVILLE | 66/710 | 10 July 1968 | 27 Aug 1969 | **Academic** |
| (AGOR 15) | KNORR | 66/710 | 21 Aug 1968 | 14 Jan 1970 | **Academic** |

| | |
|---|---|
| Builders: | Defoe Shipbuilding Co, Bay City, Mich. |
| Displacement: | 1,915 tons standard |
| | 2,080 tons full load |
| Length: | 244⁵/₆ feet (74.6 m) oa |
| Beam: | 46⅓ feet (14.1 m) |
| Draft: | 15 feet (4.6 m) |
| Propulsion: | diesel (Enterprise); 2,500 bhp; 2 cycloidal propellers |
| Speed: | 12.5 knots (sustained) |
| Complement: | 25 + 25 scientists |
| Armament: | none |

These ships are the U.S. Navy's first oceangoing ships with cycloidal propellers (see Engineering notes). These ships have essentially the same capabilities as the previous CONRAD class.

The MELVILLE is operated by the Scripps Institution of Oceanography and the KNORR by the Woods Hole Oceanographic Institution, both for the Office of Naval Research under the technical control of the Oceanographer of the Navy. They are civilian-manned.

Class: AGOR 19–20 were in the FY 1968 program, but their construction was cancelled.

Design: These ships are radically different in design from the CONRAD class, although both classes share a common SCB number. There is a bow observation dome.

Engineering: These ships have a single diesel engine, driving two cycloidal (vertical) propellers; the forward propeller is just aft of the bow observation dome and the after propeller is forward of the rudder. Cycloidal propulsion—controlled by a "joystick"—allows the ships to be propelled in any direction and to turn up to 360° in their own length. This type of propulsion also allows precise station-keeping and slow speeds, without the use of auxiliary propulsion units. The ships have experienced some transmission system difficulties.

MELVILLE (U.S. Navy)

KNORR (U.S. Navy)

## 7 OCEANOGRAPHIC RESEARCH SHIPS: "CONRAD" CLASS

| Number | Name | FY/SCB | Launched | Delivered | Status |
|--------|------|--------|----------|-----------|--------|
| (AGOR 3) | Robert D. Conrad | 60/185 | 26 May 1962 | 29 Nov 1962 | **Academic** |
| (AGOR 4) | James M. Gilliss | 60/185 | 19 May 1962 | 5 Nov 1962 | **Academic** |
| T-AGOR 7 | Lynch | 62/185 | 17 Mar 1964 | 22 Oct 1965 | **MSC-A** |
| (AGOR 9) | Thomas G. Thompson | 63/185 | 18 July 1964 | 4 Sep 1965 | **Academic** |
| (AGOR 10) | Thomas Washington | 63/185 | 1 Aug 1964 | 17 Sep 1965 | **Academic** |
| T-AGOR 12 | De Steiguer | 65/710 | 21 Mar 1966 | 28 Feb 1969 | **MSC-P** |
| T-AGOR 13 | Bartlett | 65/710 | 24 May 1966 | 15 Apr 1969 | **MSC-A** |

| | | |
|---|---|---|
| Builders: | AGOR 3 | Gibbs Corp, Jacksonville |
| | AGOR 4 | Christy Corp, Sturgeon Bay |
| | AGOR 7 | Marietta Manufacturing Co, Point Pleasant, West Va. |
| | AGOR 9–10 | Marinette Marine Corp, Marinette, Wisc. |
| | AGOR 12–13 | Northwest Marine Iron Works, Portland |
| Displacement: | (varies) ~1,200 tons standard | |
| | ~1,380 tons full load | |
| Length: | 208$^{5}$/$_{6}$ feet (63.7 m) oa | |
| Beam: | 37$^{5}$/$_{12}$ feet (11.4 m) | |
| Draft: | ~15$^{1}$/$_{3}$ feet (4.7 m) | |
| Propulsion: | diesel-electric (Caterpillar Tractor diesels); 10,000 bhp; 1 shaft | |
| Speed: | 13.5 knots | |
| Complement: | 26 + 15 scientists | |
| Armament: | none | |

These were the U.S. Navy's first built-for-the-purpose oceanographic research ships. Three ships are operated by MSC; the Conrad is operated by the Lamont Geological Observatory of Columbia University, the Gilliss by the University of Miami (Florida), the Thompson by the University of Washington (state), and the Washington by the Scripps Institution of Oceanography; all are under the technical control of the Oceanographer of the Navy, and all have civilian crews.

Class: Two ships have been transferred to other nations: the Charles H. Davis (AGOR 5) to New Zealand in 1970, and the Sands (AGOR 6) to Brazil in 1974.

Design: These ships vary in detail, each with different bridge, amidships side structure, mast, and laboratory arrangements. The last two ships have SCB numbers in the new scheme (i.e., SCB-185 and -710 are the same design).

Engineering: The large stacks contain a small diesel exhaust funnel and provide space for the small 620 shp gas-turbine engine used to provide "quiet" power during experiments in which the noise generated by the main propulsion diesel would be unacceptable. The gas turbine can be linked to the propeller shaft for speeds of up to 6.5 knots. There is also a bow propeller pod which allows precise maneuvering and can propel the ship at speeds up to 4.5 knots.

Lynch (1973, Giorgio Arra)

Thomas Washington (U.S. Navy)

**1 OCEANOGRAPHIC RESEARCH SHIP: CONVERTED CARGO SHIP**

| Number | Name | Launched | AK in service | AGOR in service | Status |
|--------|------|----------|---------------|-----------------|--------|
| T-AGOR 11 | MIZAR | 7 Oct 1957 | 7 Mar 1958 | 1965 | **MSC-P** |

| | |
|---|---|
| Builders: | Avondale Marine Ways |
| Displacement: | 2,036 tons light |
| | 4,942 tons full load |
| Length: | 262⅙ feet (79.9 m) oa |
| Beam: | 51½ feet (15.7 m) |
| Draft: | 22¾ feet (7 m) |
| Propulsion: | diesel-electric (Alco diesels; Westinghouse electric motors); 3,200 bhp; 2 shafts |
| Speed: | 12 knots |
| Complement: | 46 + 15 scientists |
| Armament: | none |

The MIZAR was converted from an ice-strengthened cargo ship (T-AK 272) to a deep-ocean research ship. The ship was operated in the cargo role by MSC from 1958 to 1963, primarily in supplying U.S. bases in the Arctic. The MIZAR is operated by MSC for the Naval Research Laboratory; she is, however, under the technical control of the Oceanographer of the Navy. She is civilian-manned.

Class: A sister ship, the ELTANIN (T-AGOR 8), was transferred to Argentina in 1973.

Classification: Changed from AK 272 to AGOR 11 on 15 April 1964.

Conversion: The MIZAR was converted to an AGOR in 1964–1965, being fitted with a center well for lowering towed sensors and instruments; laboratories; and photographic facilities. She has an elaborate computer-controlled hydrophone system which makes precise sea-floor navigation possible, and assists in locating underwater objects. The center well is 23 feet long and 10 feet wide.

After her partial conversion in 1964, the MIZAR participated in the search for the sunken submarine THRESHER (SSN 593). At the conclusion of that operation, the MIZAR's conversion to an AGOR was completed.

Design: Originally Maritime Administration C1-ME2-13a.

MIZAR (U.S. Navy, Bill Connick)

## Gunboat Support Ship Disposals

The GRAHAM COUNTY (AGP 1176, ex-LST 1176) was converted to support missile-armed ASHEVILLE-class (PG 84) patrol gunboats in the Mediterranean; she was stricken on 1 March 1977.

### 1 SURVEYING SHIP: "H. H. HESS"

| Number | Name | Launched | In service | Status |
|--------|------|----------|------------|--------|
| T-AGS 38 | H. H. HESS | 30 May 1964 | Nov 1977 | **MSC-P** |

| | |
|--------------|--------------------------------------------|
| Builders: | National Steel and Shipbuilding Co, San Diego |
| Displacement: | 3,127 tons light |
| | 17,874 tons full load |
| Length: | 564 feet (171.9 m) oa |
| Beam: | 76 feet (23.2 m) |
| Draft: | 32¾ feet (10 m) |
| Propulsion: | steam turbine; 19,250 shp; 1 shaft |
| Boilers: | 2 |
| Speed: | 20 knots |
| Complement: | 48 |
| Armament: | none |

This ship is the former merchant ship CANADA MAIL acquired by the Navy in 1975 for conversion to an AGS to replace the MICHELSON. She is operated by MSC for the Oceanographer of the Navy, with a civilian crew.

Classification: Classified as an AGS and renamed on 1 November 1976.

Conversion: Converted to an AGS in 1975–1977.

H. H. HESS (1977, Giorgio Arra)

H. H. HESS with floating crane YD 116 (1977, U.S. Navy)

## Surveying Ship Disposals

The surveying ship COASTAL CRUSADER (T-AGS 36, ex-T-AGM 16), which had been laid up in reserve in a missile-range-ship configuration, was stricken on 30 April 1976. She was a former coastal merchant ship. The missile range ship TWIN FALLS (T-AGM 11), stricken on 28 April 1970, was reacquired by the Navy for conversion to a surveying ship (T-AGS 37). However, the conversion was not undertaken and the TWIN FALLS was again stricken on 1 September 1972.

### 4 SURVEYING SHIPS: "SILAS BENT" CLASS

| Number | Name | FY/SCB | Launched | Delivered | Status |
|---|---|---|---|---|---|
| T-AGS 26 | SILAS BENT | 63/226 | 16 May 1964 | 23 July 1965 | **MSC-P** |
| T-AGS 27 | KANE | 64/226 | 20 Nov 1965 | 19 May 1967 | **MSC-A** |
| T-AGS 33 | WILKES | 67/725 | 31 July 1969 | 28 June 1971 | **MSC-A** |
| T-AGS 34 | WYMAN | 67/728 | 30 Oct 1969 | 3 Nov 1971 | **MSC-A** |

Builders:     AGS 26      American Shipbuilding Co, Lorain
              AGS 27      Christy Corp, Sturgeon Bay
              AGS 33–34 Defoe Shipbuilding Co, Bay City
Displacement: 1,935 tons standard
              AGS 26–27 2,558 tons full load, AGS 33 2,540 tons, AGS 34 2,420 tons
Length:       285⅓ feet (87 m) oa
Beam:         48 feet (14.6 m)
Draft:        15 feet (4.6 m)
Propulsion:   diesel-electric (Westinghouse diesels); 3,600 bhp; 1 shaft
Speed:        14 knots
Complement:   44–49 + 30 scientists
Armament:     none

These ships were designed specifically for surveying operations. They differ in detail. All four ships are operated by MSC for the Oceanographer of the Navy, with civilian crews.

Design: Two ships have old-system SCB numbers and two have new-system numbers.

Engineering: These ships have bow propulsion units for precise maneuvering and station-keeping.

WYMAN (1971, U.S. Navy)

WILKES (1971, U.S. Navy)

## 2 SURVEYING SHIPS: "CHAUVENET" CLASS

| Number | Name | FY/SCB | Launched | Delivered | Status |
|--------|------|--------|----------|-----------|--------|
| T-AGS 29 | CHAUVENET | 65/723 | 13 May 1968 | 13 Nov 1970 | **MSC-P** |
| T-AGS 32 | HARKNESS | 66/723 | 12 June 1968 | 29 Jan 1971 | **MSC-A** |

| | |
|--|--|
| Builders: | Upper Clyde Shipbuilders, Glasgow |
| Displacement: | 4,200 tons full load |
| Length: | 393⅙ feet (119.8 m) oa |
| Beam: | 54 feet (16.5 m) |
| Draft: | 16 feet (4.9 m) |
| Propulsion: | diesel (Westinghouse); 3,600 bhp; 1 shaft |
| Speed: | 15 knots |
| Complement: | ~165 + 12 scientists |
| Armament: | none |
| Helicopters: | 2 utility |

These are British-built ocean surveying ships capable of extensive hydrographic and oceanographic surveys. Both ships are operated by MSC for the Oceanographer of the Navy. Their complements consist of 69 civilians and up to 100 naval personnel.

Builders: These are the first ships since World War II to be built in Britain for U.S. naval service. Also see the EDENTON-class (ATS 1–3) salvage and rescue ships.

## 2 SURVEYING SHIPS: "VICTORY" CLASS

| Number | Name | Launched | In service | Status |
|--------|------|----------|-----------|--------|
| T-AGS 21 | BOWDITCH | 30 June 1945 | 8 Oct 1958 | **MSC-A** |
| T-AGS 22 | DUTTON | 8 May 1945 | 1 Nov 1958 | **MSC-P** |

| | |
|--|--|
| Builders: | Oregon Shipbuilding Co, Portland |
| Displacement: | 13,050 tons full load |
| Length: | 455⅙ feet (138.7 m) oa |
| Beam: | 62⅙ feet (19 m) |
| Draft: | 25 feet (7.6 m) |
| Propulsion: | steam turbine; 8,500 shp; 1 shaft |
| Boilers: | 2 |
| Speed: | 15 knots |
| Complement: | ~60 + ~40 technical personnel |
| Armament: | none |

These are converted "Victory"-class merchant ships, which were acquired by the Navy in 1957 for sea-floor charting and magnetic surveys to support the fleet ballistic missile program. They are operated by MSC for the Oceanographer of the Navy, with civilian crews.

Class: A third ship of this configuration, the MICHELSON (T-AGS 23), was stricken on 15 April 1975.

Conversion: Both ships were converted in 1957–1958; the conversion was SCB-179.

Design: These ships are Maritime Administration VC2-S-AP3 design.

Names: Their merchant names were the SOUTH BEND VICTORY and TUSKEGEE VICTORY, respectively.

The CHAUVENET (above) and HARKNESS are the largest ships to be constructed specifically for research by the U.S. Navy. They were among the few post-World War II ships to be built in foreign yards. Note the davits for surveying boats and the twin helicopter hangars aft. (U.S. Navy)

DUTTON (1976, U.S. Navy)

## 1 DEPENDENT SUPPORT SHIP: "HAVEN" CLASS

| Number | Name | Launched | Commissioned | Status |
|--------|------|----------|--------------|--------|
| AH 17 | SANCTUARY | 15 Aug 1944 | 20 June 1945 | MR |

| | |
|---|---|
| Builders: | Sun SB & DD Co, Chester, Pa. |
| Displacement: | 11,141 tons standard |
| | 15,400 tons full load |
| Length: | 529 feet (161.2 m) oa |
| Beam: | 71½ feet (21.8 m) |
| Draft: | 24 feet (7.3 m) |
| Propulsion: | steam turbine (General Electric); 9,000 shp; 1 shaft |
| Boilers: | 2 (Babcock & Wilcox) |
| Speed: | 18.3 knots |
| Complement: | 530 (70 O + 460 EM) |

The SANCTUARY was converted while under construction to serve as a naval hospital ship. She was decommissioned from 1946 until stricken from the Navy list on 1 September 1961 and transferred to the Maritime Administration. The ship was reacquired by the Navy on 1 March 1966 and, after modernization, served extensively in the Vietnam area. She was converted in 1971–1973 to serve as a dependent support ship in conjunction with plans to base an aircraft carrier at Piraeus, Greece. She was assigned the first mixed male–female crew in the history of the U.S. Navy (excluding female medical personnel). The ship was again decommissioned on 28 March 1974 and laid up in reserve.

Class: Six ships of this class were completed as hospital ships, AH 12–17.

Conversion: As a dependent support ship the SANCTUARY was fitted with special facilities for obstetrics, gynecology, maternity, and nursery services, and was fitted with a 74-bed hospital that could be expanded to 300 beds in 72 hours; she also had a commissary.

Design: Maritime Administration C4-S-B2 design.

Names: Merchant name was to have been the MARINE OWL.

SANCTUARY (1973, U.S. Navy)

SANCTUARY (1974, U.S. Navy)

## 1 CARGO SHIP: Ex-ATTACK CARGO SHiP

| Number | Name | Launched | Commissioned | Status |
|---|---|---|---|---|
| T-AK 283 | WYANDOT | 28 June 1944 | 30 Sep 1944 | MR |

| | |
|---|---|
| Builders: | Moore Dry Dock Co, Oakland |
| Displacement: | 7,430 tons light |
| | 14,000 tons full load |
| Length: | 459⅙ feet (140 m) oa |
| Beam: | 63 feet (19.2 m) |
| Draft: | 24 feet (7.3 m) |
| Propulsion: | steam turbine (General Electric); 6,000 shp; 1 shaft |
| Boilers: | 2 (Combustion Engineering) |
| Speed: | 16.5 knots |
| Complement: | |
| Guns: | removed |

The WYANDOT was completed as an attack cargo ship (AKA 92) of the ANDROMEDA class (AKA 15). She was stricken after the Korean War but reacquired in 1961 and assigned to the Military Sea Transportation Service in 1963 as a cargo ship (T-AKA 92). She is laid up in Maritime Administration reserve.

Classification: Changed from AKA 92 to AK 283 on 1 January 1969.

Design: Maritime Administration C2-S-B1 design.

WYANDOT (U.S. Navy)

## 4 FLEET BALLISTIC MISSILE CARGO SHIPS: "VICTORY" CLASS

| Number | Name | Launched | In service | Status |
|---|---|---|---|---|
| T-AK 279 | NORWALK | 10 July 1945 | 30 Dec 1963 | **MSC-A** |
| T-AK 280 | FURMAN | 6 May 1945 | 18 Sep 1963 | **MSC-P** |
| T-AK 281 | VICTORIA | 28 April 1944 | 11 Oct 1965 | **MSC-A** |
| T-AK 282 | MARSHFIELD | 15 May 1944 | 28 May 1970 | **MSC-A** |

| | |
|---|---|
| Builders: | Oregon Shipbuilding Corp, Portland, except T-AK 281 Permanente Metals Corp, Richmond, Calif. |
| Displacement: | 6,700 tons light |
| | 11,150 tons full load |
| Length: | 455¼ feet (138.8 m) oa |
| Beam: | 62 feet (18.9 m) |
| Draft: | 24 feet (7.3 m) |
| Propulsion: | steam turbine; 8,500 shp; 1 shaft |
| Boilers: | 2 |
| Speed: | 17 knots |
| Complement: | 66–69 + Navy security detachment |
| Armament: | none |

MARSHFIELD (1970, U.S. Navy)

These are former merchant ships taken over by the Navy specifically for conversion into supply ships to support SSBN tenders. (See Conversion notes for special features.) All four ships are operated by MSC with civilian crews; Navy security personnel are assigned to safeguard the missiles and their nuclear warheads.

Class: Two earlier Polaris supply ships have been stricken, the "Victory"-class ALCOR (AK 259) and BETELGEUSE (AK 260), stricken on 31 December 1968 and 1 February 1974, respectively. Those ships were Navy-manned.

Conversion: As SSBN tender supply ships, these four ships were refitted to carry black oil, bottled gases, diesel fuel, dry and frozen provisions, packaged petroleum products, spare parts, and torpedoes. The No. 3 hold was configured to carry 16 missiles—initially the Polaris, but the three Atlantic ships can now carry the Poseidon missile. Cargo tanks were installed for 355,000 gallons of diesel oil, plus 430,000 gallons of fuel oil for submarine tenders (in addition to ship bunkers). Conversion number for these ships was SCB-234.

Design: Maritime Administration VC2-S-AP3 design.

Names: Merchant names for these ships were: the NORWALK VICTORY (T-AK 279), FURMAN VICTORY (T-AK 280), ETHIOPIA VICTORY (T-AK 281), and MARSHFIELD VICTORY (T-AK 282).

**1 CARGO SHIP: "SCHUYLER OTIS BLAND"**

| Number | Name | Launched | In service | Status |
|--------|------|----------|------------|--------|
| T-AK 277 | SCHUYLER OTIS BLAND | 30 Jan 1951 | 28 Aug 1961 | **MSC-P** |

| | |
|---|---|
| Builders: | Ingalls Shipbuilding Corp |
| Displacement: | 15,910 tons full load |
| Length: | 478 feet (145.7 m) oa |
| Beam: | 66 feet (20.1 m) |
| Draft: | 30 feet (9.1 m) |
| Propulsion: | steam turbines; 13,750 shp; 1 shaft |
| Boilers: | 2 |
| Speed: | 18.5 knots |
| Complement: | |
| Armament: | none |

The BLAND was a prototype advanced cargo ship developed by the Maritime Administration. Many of her features were provided in the subsequent "Mariner"-class merchant ships, five of which were acquired for Navy service.

The BLAND operated in commercial service for only one year after completion in 1951, and was laid up in MarAd reserve in 1952. After returning to commercial service from 1957 to 1959, the BLAND was again laid up, because she was not economically competitive. The ship was acquired by the Navy on 4 August 1961.

The BLAND is operated by MSC with a civilian crew. The ship currently is in reduced operational status (ready reserve).

Design: Maritime Administration C3-S-DX1. The BLAND has highly automated cargo handling equipment.

SCHUYLER OTIS BLAND (U.S. Navy)

**1 CARGO SHIP: "ELTANIN" CLASS**

| Number | Name | Launched | In service | Status |
|--------|------|----------|------------|--------|
| T-AK 271 | MIRFAK | 5 Aug 1957 | 30 Dec 1957 | **MSC-A** |

| | |
|---|---|
| Builders: | Avondale Marine Ways |
| Displacement: | 2,036 tons light |
| | 4,942 tons full load |
| Length: | 262⅙ feet (79.9 m) oa |
| Beam: | 51½ feet (15.7 m) |
| Draft: | 18¾ feet (5.7 m) |
| Propulsion: | diesel-electric (Alco diesels, Westinghouse electric motors); 3,200 bhp; 2 shafts |
| Speed: | 13 knots |
| Complement: | 36 |
| Armament: | none |

The MIRFAK was one of three small, ice-strengthened cargo ships built especially for the Military Sea Transportation Service to operate in support of U.S. military activities in the Arctic. She now supports U.S. research activities in the Antarctic. The MIRFAK is operated by MSC with a civilian crew.

Class: The ELTANIN (T-AK 270) and MIZAR (T-AK 272) were converted to oceanographic research ships, T-AGOR 8 and T-AGOR 11, respectively.

Design: Maritime Administration C1-ME2-13a type. The ship has an ice-breaking prow, enclosed observation tower, and other features necessary for Arctic operation.

MIRFAK (U.S. Navy)

## 1 HEAVY LIFT CARGO SHIP: "PVT. LEONARD C. BROSTROM"

| Number | Name | Launched | In service | Status |
|---|---|---|---|---|
| T-AK 255 | PVT. LEONARD C. BROSTROM | 10 May 1943 | 30 Aug 1950 | **MSC-P** |

| | |
|---|---|
| Builders: | Sun Shipbuilding and DD Co, Chester, Pa. |
| Displacement: | 22,056 tons full load |
| Length: | 520 feet (158.5 m) oa |
| Beam: | 71½ feet (21.8 m) |
| Draft: | 33 feet (10.1 m) |
| Propulsion: | steam turbine; 9,000 shp; 1 shaft |
| Boilers: | 2 |
| Speed: | 15.8 knots |
| Complement: | 52 |
| Armament: | none |

The BROSTROM was completed as a merchant ship and initially employed in carrying tanks. The ship was acquired by the Army Transportation Service in 1948 and subsequently transferred to the Navy on 9 August 1950. In 1953–1954 the ship was converted to a heavy lift configuration to carry locomotives, large mooring buoys, etc. The ship is operated by MSC with a civilian crew.

Design: Originally Maritime Administration C4-S-B1 type. The ship is fitted with 150-ton capacity booms, the largest in any U.S. ship.

Names: The ship's original merchant name was the MARINE EAGLE (renamed in 1948).

PVT. LEONARD C. BROSTROM (U.S. Navy)

## 1 CARGO SHIP: "VICTORY" CLASS

| Number | Name | Launched | In service | Status |
|---|---|---|---|---|
| T-AK 240 | PVT. JOHN R. TOWLE | 19 Jan 1945 | 1 Mar 1950 | **MSC-A** |

| | |
|---|---|
| Builders: | Oregon Shipbuilding Corp, Portland |
| Displacement: | 6,700 tons light |
| | 12,450 tons full load |
| Length: | 455½ feet (138.9 m) oa |
| Beam: | 62 feet (18.9 m) |
| Draft: | 28½ feet (8.9 m) |
| Propulsion: | steam turbine; 8,500 shp, 1 shaft |
| Boilers: | 2 |
| Speed: | 17 knots |
| Complement: | 49 |
| Armament: | none |

The TOWLE is the last of a large number of "Victory" class ships operated by MSTS/MSC in the conventional cargo role. The TOWLE was completed for merchant service, acquired by the Army Transportation Service in 1946, and subsequently acquired by the Navy in March 1950. The ship was modified for Arctic operation and is now employed by MSC with a civilian crew.

Design: Maritime Administration VC2-S-AP3 type.

Names: The TOWLE's merchant name was the APPLETON VICTORY (renamed in 1947 after initial Army operation with merchant name).

PVT. JOHN R. TOWLE (U.S. Navy)

**1 VEHICLE CARGO SHIP: "ADM. WM. M. CALLAGHAN"**

| Number | Name | Launched | In service | Status |
|--------|------|----------|-----------|--------|
| — | ADM. WM. M. CALLAGHAN | 17 Oct 1967 | 19 Dec 1967 | **MSC-A** |

| | |
|---|---|
| Builders: | Sun Shipbuilding and DD Co, Chester Pa. |
| Displacement: | 24,500 tons full load |
| Length: | 694 feet (211.5 m) oa |
| Beam: | 92 feet (28 m) |
| Draft: | 29 feet (8.8 m) |
| Propulsion: | 2 gas turbines (General Electric); 50,000 shp; 2 shafts |
| Speed: | 26 knots |
| Complement: | 33 |
| Armament: | none |

The CALLAGHAN is technically a chartered ship rather than a Navy-owned ship of the MSC "nucleus" fleet. However, the ship was designed and constructed specifically for Navy charter, and as such is fully committed to MSC. The ship is manned by a civilian crew, and has no Navy hull number.

Design: The ship has internal parking decks and ramps for carrying some 750 vehicles on 167,537 square feet of deck. They can be loaded or unloaded via four side ramps and a stern ramp. The ship can offload and reload a full cargo of vehicles in 27 hours.

Engineering: The CALLAGHAN was the first all-gas-turbine ship constructed for the U.S. Navy. The engines are LM2500s of the type used in subsequent warship classes.

ADMIRAL WM. M. CALLAGHAN (U.S. Navy)

ADMIRAL WM. M. CALLAGHAN (U.S. Navy)

## 1 VEHICLE CARGO SHIP: "METEOR"

| Number | Name | FY/SCB | Launched | In service | Status |
|--------|------|--------|----------|------------|--------|
| T-AKR 9 | METEOR | 63/236 | 18 Apr 1965 | 19 May 1967 | **MSC-P** |

| | |
|---|---|
| Builders: | Lockheed Shipbuilding & Construction Co, Seattle |
| Displacement: | 11,130 tons standard |
| | 16,940 tons standard |
| | 21,700 tons full load |
| Length: | 540 feet (164.6 m) oa |
| Beam: | 83 feet (25.3 m) |
| Draft: | 29 feet (8.8 m) |
| Propulsion: | steam turbines; 19,400 shp; 2 shafts |
| Boilers: | 2 |
| Speed: | 20 knots |
| Complement: | 47 |
| Passengers: | 12 |
| Armament: | none |

The METEOR, originally named the SEA LIFT, was built specifically as a roll-on/roll-off ship for Navy service. She is operated by MSC with a civilian crew.

Classification: The ship was authorized as T-AK 278 but placed in service as the vehicle cargo ship T-LSV 9; she was changed to vehicle cargo ship T-AKR 9 on 14 August 1969.

Design: This is one of the few ships to have both an SCB (236) and Maritime Administration design (C4-ST-67a).

Names: Originally named SEA LIFT; her name was changed on 12 September 1975 to avoid confusion with the "Sealift"-class tankers.

METEOR (Lockheed Shipbuilding & Construction Co)

## 1 VEHICLE CARGO SHIP: "COMET"

| Number | Name | Launched | In service | Status |
|--------|------|----------|------------|--------|
| T-AKR 7 | COMET | 31 July 1957 | 27 Jan 1958 | **MSC-A** |

| | |
|---|---|
| Builders: | Sun Shipbuilding and DD Co, Chester, Pa. |
| Displacement: | 7,605 tons light |
| | 18,150 tons full load |
| Length: | 499 feet (152.1 m) oa |
| Beam: | 78 feet (23.8 m) |
| Draft: | 28¾ feet (8.8 m) |
| Propulsion: | steam turbines (General Electric); 13,200 shp; 2 shafts |
| Boilers: | 2 (Babcock & Wilcox) |
| Speed: | 18 knots |
| Complement: | 56 |
| Armament: | none |

The COMET was built specifically for the Navy. She is operated by MSC with a civilian crew. Currently the ship is in reduced operational status.

Classification: The COMET originally was classified T-AK 269. She was changed to vehicle cargo ship T-LSV 7 on 1 June 1963, and again to T-AKR 7 on 1 January 1969.

Design: Maritime Administration C3-ST-14a design. She can accommodate 700 vehicles in her two after holds, with the two forward holds intended for general cargo.

COMET (U.S. Navy)

## (5+) OILERS: NEW CONSTRUCTION

| Number | Name | FY/SCB | Launched | Commissioned | Status |
|--------|------|--------|----------|--------------|--------|
| AO 177 | ...... | 76/739 | 1979 | 1980 | Bldg. |
| AO 178 | ...... | 76/739 | 1980 | 1980 | Bldg. |
| AO 179 | ...... | 77/739 | 1980 | 1980 | Bldg. |
| AO 180 | ...... | 78/739 | | | Auth. |
| AO 186 | ...... | 78/739 | | | Auth. |
| ? | ...... | 79/739 | | | |
| ? | ...... | 80/739 | | | |
| ? | ...... | 81/739 | | | |
| ? | ...... | 82/739 | | | |

| | |
|--|--|
| Builders: | AO 177–179 Avondale Shipyards, La. |
| Displacement: | 27,500 tons full load |
| Length: | 586½ feet (178.8 m) oa |
| Beam: | 88 feet (26.8 m) |
| Draft: | 33½ feet (10.2 m) |
| Propulsion: | steam turbine; 24,000 shp; 1 shaft |
| Boilers: | 2 |
| Speed: | 20 knots (sustained) |
| Complement: | ~135 |
| Guns: | space provided for 2 20-mm Phalanx Mk 15 CIWS (2 × 1) |

This class of fleet oilers is designed to provide two complete fuelings for a conventional aircraft carrier and six to eight accompanying destroyers. As indicated above, a large number of these ships is planned; however, consideration is being given to increasing the use of commercial tankers in UNREP. Also, although designed for Navy manning, these ships may be assigned to MSC for operation.

Design: These ships will carry approximately 120,000 barrels of petroleum products. A helicopter landing area will be provided aft. These ships are SCB-739.

## 4 TANKERS: "FALCON" CLASS

| Number | Name | Launched | In service | Status |
|--------|------|----------|------------|--------|
| T-AO 182 | COLUMBIA | 12 Sep 1970 | 1976 | **MSC** |
| T-AO 183 | NECHES | 30 Jan 1971 | 1976 | **MSC** |
| T-AO 184 | HUDSON | 8 Jan 1972 | 1976 | **MSC** |
| T-AO 185 | SUSQUEHANNA | 2 Oct 1971 | 1976 | **MSC** |

| | |
|--|--|
| Builders: | Ingalls Shipbuilding Corp, Pascagoula, Miss. |
| Displacement: | 8,601 tons light |
| | 45,877 tons full load |
| Length: | 672 feet (204.8 m) oa |
| Beam: | 89 feet (27.1 m) |
| Draft: | 36 feet (11 m) |
| Propulsion: | steam turbine; 1 shaft |
| Boilers: | 2 |
| Speed: | 16.5 knots |
| Complement: | |
| Armament: | none |

These ships were operated briefly under charter to MSC from their completion until acquired by MSC early in 1976. They are contract-operated for MSC with civilian crews.

Design: Cargo capacity is 310,000 barrels.

Names: The merchant names for these ships were the FALCON LADY (T-AO 182), FALCON DUCHESS (T-AO 183), FALCON PRINCESS (T-AO 184), FALCON COUNTESS (T-AO 185).

HUDSON (U.S. Navy)

SUSQUEHANNA ballasted down aft (1977, Giorgio Arra)

## 1 TANKER: "POTOMAC"

| Number | Name | Launched | In service | Status |
|---|---|---|---|---|
| T-AO 181 | POTOMAC | 8 Oct 1956 | 12 Jan 1976 | **MSC** |

| | |
|---|---|
| Builders: | Sun Shipbuilding and DD Co, Chester, Pa. |
| Displacement: | 7,333 tons light |
| | 34,800 tons full load |
| Length: | 620 feet (189 m) oa |
| Beam: | 83½ feet (25.5 m) |
| Draft: | 34 feet (10.4 m) |
| Propulsion: | steam turbine; 20,460 shp; 1 shaft |
| Boilers: | 2 |
| Speed: | 18 knots |
| Complement: | |
| Armament: | none |

The POTOMAC was constructed from the stern of an earlier naval tanker, with mid-body and bow sections built to mate with that stern section. The "new" tanker, named the SHENANDOAH, was operated under commercial charter to MSC for several years until she was formally acquired in 1976. The ship's current MSC name is the same as the original naval tanker (T-AO 150) from which the stern section was salvaged. (The earlier POTOMAC was partially destroyed by fire on 26 September 1961, but the stern section and machinery were relatively intact. The POTOMAC's original design was T5-S-12a.)

The POTOMAC is contractor-operated for MSC with a civilian crew.

Design: Cargo capacity is 200,000 barrels.

## 9 TANKERS: "SEALIFT" CLASS

| Number | Name | Launched | In service | Status |
|---|---|---|---|---|
| T-AO 168 | SEALIFT PACIFIC | 13 Oct 1973 | 14 Aug 1974 | **MSC** |
| T-AO 169 | SEALIFT ARABIAN SEA | 26 Jan 1974 | 6 Feb 1975 | **MSC** |
| T-AO 170 | SEALIFT CHINA SEA | 20 Apr 1974 | 19 May 1975 | **MSC** |
| T-AO 171 | SEALIFT INDIAN OCEAN | 27 July 1974 | 29 Aug 1975 | **MSC** |
| T-AO 172 | SEALIFT ATLANTIC | 26 Jan 1974 | 26 Aug 1974 | **MSC** |
| T-AO 173 | SEALIFT MEDITERRANEAN | 9 Mar 1974 | 6 Nov 1974 | **MSC** |
| T-AO 174 | SEALIFT CARIBBEAN | 8 June 1974 | 10 Feb 1975 | **MSC** |
| T-AO 175 | SEALIFT ARCTIC | 31 Aug 1974 | 22 May 1975 | **MSC** |
| T-AO 176 | SEALIFT ANTARCTIC | 26 Oct 1974 | 1 Aug 1975 | **MSC** |

| | |
|---|---|
| Builders: | T-AO 168–171 Todd Shipyards, Los Angeles |
| | T-AO 172–176 Bath Iron Works |
| Displacement: | 32,000 tons full load |
| Length: | 587 feet (178.9 m) oa |
| Beam: | 84 feet (25.6 m) |
| Draft: | 34⅓ feet (10.5 m) |
| Propulsion: | turbo-charged diesels; 14,000 bhp; 1 shaft (controllable-pitch propellers) |
| Speed: | 16 knots |
| Complement: | 30 + 2 Maritime Academy cadets |
| Armament: | none |

These ships were built specifically for MSC to replace World War II-era tankers of the T2 series. The ships are contractor-operated for MSC with civilian crews.

Design: These ships have a cargo capacity of 220,000 barrels.

Engineering: A bow thruster is provided to assist in docking the ships.

SEALIFT PACIFIC (U.S. Navy)

SEALIFT ANTARCTIC (1975, U.S. Navy)

## 1 TANKER: "AMERICAN EXPLORER"

| Number | Name | Launched | In service | Status |
|--------|------|----------|------------|--------|
| T-AO 165 | AMERICAN EXPLORER | 11 Apr 1958 | 27 Oct 1959 | **MSC** |

| | |
|---|---|
| Builders: | Ingalls Shipbuilding Corp |
| Displacement: | 31,300 tons full load |
| Length: | 615 feet (187.5 m) oa |
| Beam: | 80 feet (24.4 m) |
| Draft: | 32 feet (9.8 m) |
| Propulsion: | steam turbine; 22,000 shp; 1 shaft |
| Boilers: | 2 |

| | |
|---|---|
| Speed: | 20 knots |
| Complement: | |
| Armament: | none |

The AMERICAN EXPLORER was built for merchant use. Upon her completion, however, she was acquired for use in naval service. She is similar in design to the MAUMEE-class tankers. The AMERICAN EXPLORER is contractor-operated for MSC with a civilian crew.

Design: Maritime Administration T5-S-RM2a design. Cargo capacity is 190,300 barrels.

AMERICAN EXPLORER (U.S. Navy)

## 3 TANKERS: "MAUMEE" CLASS

| Number | Name | Launched | In service | Status |
|--------|------|----------|-----------|--------|
| T-AO 149 | Maumee | 16 Feb 1956 | Dec 1956 | **MSC** |
| T-AO 151 | Shoshone | 17 Jan 1957 | Apr 1957 | **MSC** |
| T-AO 152 | Yukon | 16 Mar 1956 | May 1957 | **MSC** |

| | |
|--|--|
| Builders: | T-AO 149, 152  Ingalls Shipbuilding Corp |
| | T-AO 151        Sun Shipbuilding and DD Co, Chester, Pa. |
| Displacement: | 32,953 tons full load |
| Length: | 620 feet (189 m) oa |
| Beam: | 83½ feet (25.5 m) |
| Draft: | 32 feet (9.8 m) |
| Propulsion: | steam turbine; 20,460 shp; 1 shaft |
| Boilers: | 2 |
| Speed: | 18 knots |
| Complement: | |
| Armament: | none |

These ships were built for naval service. All are contractor-operated for MSC with civilian crews.

Class: The Potomac (T-AO 150) of this class was partially destroyed by fire in 1961; she was rebuilt in 1963–1964 and is listed separately as the T-AO 181. Hull numbers AO 166–167 were reserved for planned "Mission"-class (T2-SE-A2) tanker "jumbo" conversions (to have been SCB-713); the T-AO 153–164 were T2-SE-A1 tankers acquired during the 1950 Suez crisis and stricken 1957–1958.

Design: Maritime Administration T5-S-12a type. Cargo capacity is 203,200 barrels. The Maumee was modified in 1969–1970, being fitted with a strengthened prow and other features enabling her to transport petroleum to U.S. arctic research sites.

Maumee (1970, U.S. Navy)

Maumee (1970, U.S. Navy)

## 6 OILERS: "NEOSHO" CLASS

| Number | Name | FY/SCB | Launched | Commissioned | Status |
|--------|------|--------|----------|--------------|--------|
| AO 143 | NEOSHO | 52/82 | 10 Nov 1953 | 24 Sep 1954 | **AA** |
| T-AO 144 | MISSISSINEWA | 52/82 | 12 June 1954 | 18 Jan 1955 | **MSC-A** |
| AO 145 | HASSAYAMPA | 52/82 | 12 Sep 1954 | 19 Apr 1955 | **PA** |
| AO 146 | KAWISHIWI | 52/82 | 11 Dec 1954 | 6 July 1955 | **PA** |
| AO 147 | TRUCKEE | 52/82 | 10 Mar 1955 | 23 Nov 1955 | **AA** |
| AO 148 | PONCHATOULA | 52/82 | 9 July 1955 | 12 Jan 1956 | **PA** |

| | | |
|---|---|---|
| Builders: | AO 143 | Bethlehem Steel Co, Quincy |
| | AO 144–148 | New York Shipbuilding Corp, Camden, N.J. |
| Displacement: | 11,600 tons light | |
| | 38,000–40,000 tons full load | |
| Length: | 655 feet (199.6 m) oa | |
| Beam: | 86 feet (26.2 m) | |
| Draft: | 35 feet (10.7 m) | |
| Propulsion: | steam turbines (General Electric); 28,000 shp; 2 shafts | |
| Boilers: | 2 (Babcock & Wilcox) | |
| Speed: | 20 knots | |
| Complement: | ~360 (30 O + 330 EM) in Navy-manned ships; 105 in T-AO 144 | |
| Flag: | 12 | |
| Guns: | 4 3-inch (76 mm) 50 cal AA Mk 33 (2 × 2) in Navy-manned ships | |

These ships are the largest "straight" oilers constructed by the U.S. Navy for underway replenishment. The NEOSHO, MISSIS- SINEWA, and TRUCKEE have been fitted with a helicopter landing platform aft, but they have no hangar. Five ships are Navy-operated with the MISSISSINEWA being MSC-operated with a civilian crew; all serve in the UNREP role. The last was assigned to MSC on 2 February 1976.

Design: Cargo capacity approximately 180,000 barrels. These ships were built to a Navy design (SCB-82) and do not have a MarAd designation.

Guns: As built, these ships had two 5-inch DP guns and 12 3-inch AA guns. The former were removed in 1969 and the 3-inch battery was subsequently reduced to two mounts in Navy-manned ships.

TRUCKEE (1972, Giorgio Arra)

TRUCKEE (1972, Giorgio Arra)

NEOSHO (1975, U.S. Navy, PH2 George D. Meade)

PONCHATOULA—no helicopter platform; aftermost 3-inch guns removed (1977, Giorgio Arra)

## 5 OILERS: "MISPILLION" CLASS

| Number | Name | Launched | Commissioned | Status |
|--------|------|----------|--------------|--------|
| T-AO 105 | MISPILLION | 10 Aug 1945 | 29 Dec 1945 | **MSC-P** |
| T-AO 106 | NAVASOTA | 30 Aug 1945 | 27 Feb 1946 | **MSC-P** |
| T-AO 107 | PASSUMPSIC | 31 Oct 1945 | 1 Apr 1946 | **MSC-P** |
| T-AO 108 | PAWCATUCK | 19 Feb 1945 | 10 May 1946 | **MSC-A** |
| T-AO 109 | WACCAMAW | 30 Mar 1946 | 25 June 1946 | **MSC-A** |

| | |
|---|---|
| Builders: | Sun Shipbuilding and DD Co, Chester, Pa. |
| Displacement: | 11,000 tons light |
| | 34,750 tons full load |
| Length: | 646 feet (196.9 m) oa |
| Beam: | 75 feet (22.9 m) |
| Draft: | 35½ feet (10.8 m) |
| Propulsion: | steam turbines (Westinghouse); 13,500 shp; 2 shafts |
| Boilers: | 4 (Babcock & Wilcox) |
| Speed: | 16 knots |
| Complement: | 110 |
| Guns: | removed |

MISPILLION (1976, Giorgio Arra)

These ships were built during World War II as Navy oilers. They were converted under the "jumbo" process in the mid-1960s to increase their cargo capacity, thus forming a new five-ship class. (Three Navy-manned "jumboized" oilers are similar; see next listing.) These five ships were assigned to MSC in 1974–1975; they are civilian-manned and serve in the UNREP role.

Design: These ships originally were Maritime Administration T3-S2-A3 type. They were converted ("jumboized") in the mid-1900s with addition of a 93-foot midsection, thus increasing cargo capacity to approximately 150,000 barrels. A helicopter area is provided *forward*, but it is used primarily for vertical replenishment and not for landings.

Guns: As built, these ships had a designed armament of 1 5-inch DP gun, 4 3-inch AA guns, and 8 40-mm AA guns. These were successively reduced until only four 3-inch single mounts were left when they were transferred to MSC.

NAVASOTA (1977, Giorgio Arra)

WACCAMAW (1975, Giorgio Arra)

## 3 OILERS: "ASHTABULA" CLASS

| Number | Name | Launched | Commissioned | Status |
|--------|------|----------|--------------|--------|
| AO 51 | ASHTABULA | 22 May 1943 | 7 Aug 1943 | **PA** |
| AO 98 | CALOOSAHATCHEE | 2 June 1945 | 10 Oct 1945 | **AA** |
| AO 99 | CANISTEO | 6 July 1945 | 3 Dec 1945 | **AA** |

Builders: Bethlehem Steel Co, Sparrows Point, Md.
Displacement: 34,750 tons full load
Length: 644 feet (196.3 m) oa
Beam: 75 feet (22.9 m)
Draft: 31½ feet (9.6 m)
Propulsion: steam turbines (Bethlehem); 13,500 shp; 2 shafts
Boilers: 4 (Foster Wheeler)
Speed: 18 knots
Complement: 300 (13 O + 287 EM)
Guns: 2 3-inch (76-mm) 50 cal AA Mk 26 (2 × 1)

These oilers were built for Navy use. They were "jumboized" to increase their cargo capacity. All three are Navy-manned.

Design: Originally Maritime Administration T3-S2-A1 type, they were converted in the mid-1960s under the "jumbo" program (SCB-224). They were lengthened 91 feet to increase their cargo capacity to approximately 143,000 barrels, along with a limited capacity for munitions and stores. No helicopter platform was fitted.

Guns: See the MISPILLION class for notes on original armament.

CALOOSHATCHEE (1976, U.S. Navy)

ASHTABULA (1976, Giorgio Arra)

CANISTEO (1973, Giorgio Arra)

**4 OILERS: "CIMARRON" CLASS**

| Number | Name | Launched | Commissioned | Status |
|--------|------|----------|--------------|--------|
| AO 54 | CHIKASKIA | 2 Oct 1943 | 10 Nov 1943 | MR |
| AO 56 | AUCILLA | 20 Nov 1943 | 22 Dec 1943 | MR |
| T-AO 57 | MARIAS | 21 Dec 1943 | 12 Feb 1944 | **MSC-A** |
| T-AO 62 | TALUGA | 10 July 1944 | 25 Aug 1944 | **MSC-P** |

| | |
|---|---|
| Builders: | Bethlehem Steel Co, Sparrows Point, Md. |
| Displacement: | 25,525 tons full load |
| Length: | 553 feet (168.6 m) oa |
| Beam: | 75 feet (22.9 m) |
| Draft: | 31½ feet (9.6 m) |
| Propulsion: | steam turbines (Bethlehem); 13,500 shp; 2 shafts |
| Boilers: | 4 (Foster Wheeler) |
| Speed: | 18 knots |

| | |
|---|---|
| Complement: | 274 (14 O + 260 EM) in Navy-manned ships; 105–107 in T-AOs. |
| Guns: | 4 3-inch (76-mm) 50 cal AA (4 × 1) in Navy-manned ships |

These are the survivors of a large number of twin-screw fleet oilers constructed during World War II. Ships that have been enlarged under the "jumbo" program are listed separately. The TALUGA was transferred to MSC in 1972 and the MARIAS in 1973 for operation in the UNREP role.

Design: Maritime Administration T3-S2-A1 design. Cargo capacity is approximately 115,000 barrels. These ships were designed to carry 145,000 barrels of liquid cargo; however, provision for armament, communications, and increased accommodations reduced the cargo space from what had been provided in the original design.

Guns: See the MISPILLION class for notes on original armament.

MARIAS (1975, Giorgio Arra)

TALUGA (1977, Giorgio Arra)

## 4 + 1 FAST COMBAT SUPPORT SHIPS: "SACRAMENTO" CLASS

| Number | Name | FY/SCB | Launched | Commissioned | Status |
|--------|------|--------|----------|--------------|--------|
| AOE 1 | SACRAMENTO | 61/196 | 14 Sep 1963 | 14 Mar 1964 | **PA** |
| AOE 2 | CAMDEN | 63/196 | 29 May 1965 | 1 Apr 1967 | **PA** |
| AOE 3 | SEATTLE | 65/196 | 2 Mar 1968 | 5 Apr 1969 | **AA** |
| AOE 4 | DETROIT | 66/196 | 21 June 1969 | 28 Mar 1970 | **AA** |
| AOE 5 | ...... | 80/196 | | | Planned |

| | |
|---|---|
| Builders: | AOE 1, 3–4 Puget Sound Naval Shipyard |
| | AOE 2       New York Shipbuilding Corp, Camden, N.J. |
| Displacement: | 19,200 tons light |
| | 53,600 tons full load |
| Length: | 793 feet (241.7 m) oa |
| Beam: | 107 feet (32.6 m) |
| Draft: | 39⅓ feet (12 m) |
| Propulsion: | steam turbines (General Electric); 100,000 shp; 2 shafts |
| Boilers: | 4 (Combustion Engineering) |
| Speed: | 26 knots |
| Complement: | 600 (33 officers + 567 EM) |
| Helicopters: | 2 UH-46 Sea Knights |
| Guns: | 4 or 6 3-inch (76-mm) 50 cal AA Mk 33 (2 or 3 × 2) |

These are the largest auxiliary ships to be built for the U.S. Navy. They operate as "one-stop" UNREP ships with fast carrier task forces, providing fuels, munitions, dry and frozen provisions, and other supplies. The AOE 5 originally was planned for FY 1968, but her construction was deferred and then cancelled in November 1969. A fifth ship is now planned for the FY 1980 shipbuilding pro-program. ·

Design: These ships can carry 177,000 barrels of fuels, 2,150 tons of munitions, 250 tons of dry stores, and 250 tons of refriger-ated stores. They are provided with highly automated cargo-han-dling equipment. They are fitted with a large helicopter landing deck aft and a three-bay hangar.

Engineering: The first two ships have the machinery produced for the cancelled battleship KENTUCKY (BB 66).

Guns: As built, these ships had eight 3-inch guns in twin mounts; these were subsequently reduced in the mid-1970s. They are scheduled to eventually have two 20-mm Phalanx CIWS installed.

Missiles: The installation of one NATO Sea Sparrow Mk 29 launcher is planned.

DETROIT (1972, U.S. Navy, Joseph R. Andrews)

SEATTLE (1970, U.S. Navy)

SEATTLE (1972, Giorgio Arra)

**3 GASOLINE TANKERS: "TONTI" CLASS**

| Number | Name | Launched | In service | Status |
|--------|------|----------|------------|--------|
| T-AOG 77 | RINCON | 5 Jan 1945 | 1 July 1950 | **MSC-P** |
| T-AOG 78 | NODAWAY | 15 May 1945 | 7 Sep 1950 | **MSC-P** |
| T-AOG 79 | PETALUMA | 9 Aug 1945 | 7 Sep 1950 | **MSC-P** |

| | |
|---|---|
| Builders: | Todd Shipyards, Houston |
| Displacement: | 2,060 tons light |
| | 6,000 tons full load |
| Length: | 325⅙ feet (99.1 m) oa |
| Beam: | 48⅙ feet (14.7 m) |
| Draft: | 19 feet (5.8 m) |
| Propulsion: | diesel; 1,400 bhp; 1 shaft |
| Speed: | 10 knots |
| Complement: | 36 |
| Armament: | none |

These are the only survivors in U.S. service of a once-numerous type of small gasoline tanker. Five ships of this design were built as merchant tankers; all were acquired by the Navy in 1950 and assigned to MSTS (Military Sea Transportation Service, the forerunner of the Military Sealift Command) for operation. These ships are operated by MSC with civilian crews, in the point-to-point carrying of petroleum.

Class: T-AOG 76–80 were originally in this class. The AOG 64–75 were similar (BT1 design).

Design: Maritime Administration T1-M-BT2 design. Cargo capacity is 30,000 barrels.

Names: Merchant names were T-AOG 77, ex-TARLAND; T-AOG 78, ex-BELRIDGE; and T-AOG 79, ex-RACCOON BEND, ex-TAVISPAN.

RINCON (U.S. Navy)

## Gasoline Tanker Disposals

The last three Navy-manned gasoline tankers of the PATAPSCO class have been stricken: the CHEWAUCAN (AOG 50) transferred to Colombia on 1 July 1975; the NESPELEN (AOG 55) and NOXUBEE (AOG 56) stricken on 1 July 1975.

## 7 REPLENISHMENT OILERS: "WICHITA" CLASS

| Number | Name | FY/SCB | Launched | Commissioned | Status |
|--------|------|--------|----------|--------------|--------|
| AOR 1 | WICHITA | 65/707 | 18 Mar 1968 | 7 June 1969 | **PA** |
| AOR 2 | MILWAUKEE | 65/707 | 17 Jan 1969 | 1 Nov 1969 | **AA** |
| AOR 3 | KANSAS CITY | 66/707 | 28 June 1969 | 6 June 1970 | **PA** |
| AOR 4 | SAVANNAH | 66/707 | 25 Apr 1970 | 5 Dec 1970 | **AA** |
| AOR 5 | WABASH | 67/707 | 6 Feb 1971 | 20 Nov 1971 | **PA** |
| AOR 6 | KALAMAZOO | 67/707 | 11 Nov 1972 | 11 Aug 1973 | **AA** |
| AOR 7 | ROANOKE | 72/707 | 7 Dec 1974 | 15 Dec 1975 | **PA** |

| | |
|---|---|
| Builders: | AOR 1–6 General Dynamics Corp, Quincy |
| | AOR 7    National Steel and SB Co, San Diego |
| Displacement: | 38,100 tons full load |
| Length: | 659 feet (206.9 m) oa |
| Beam: | 96 feet (29.3 m) |
| Draft: | 33⅓ feet (10.2 m) |
| Propulsion: | steam turbines; 32,000 shp; 2 shafts |
| Boilers: | 3 (Foster Wheeler) |
| Speed: | 20 knots |
| Complement: | 345 (20 O + 325 EM) |
| Helicopters: | 2 UH-46 Sea Knights in modified ships |
| Guns: | 4 3-inch (76-mm) 50 cal AA Mk 33 (2 × 2) except AOR 7; these are being removed from modified ships |
| | 4 20-mm AA Mk 68 (4 × 1) in AOR 7 and modified ships |
| Missile launchers: | 1 8-tube NATO Sea Sparrow SAM Mk 29 in AOR 7 |

These ships carry petroleum and munitions, and have a limited capacity for dry and frozen provisions. As built, AOR 1–6 had large helicopter decks but no hangar; all are being modified to provide two hangars abaft the funnel.

Classification: The German war prize CONECUH, formerly a U-boat tender, was employed as a replenishment fleet tanker (AOR 110) in the 1950s. The WACCAMAW was to be similarly modified (AOR 109), but she remained a "straight" fleet oiler. The classification AOR was established as replenishment oiler in 1964.

Design: These ships can carry 160,000 barrels of liquid cargo, 600 tons of munitions, 200 tons of dry stores, and 100 tons of refrigerated stores. They have highly automated cargo-handling equipment.

Engineering: Ships of this class can steam at 18 knots on two boilers while one is maintained.

The ROANOKE is the seventh and at this time last of the highly successful WICHITA class of replenishment oilers. These are essentially smaller AOEs. Their major shortcoming, a lack of helicopter support capability, is being corrected; note the two open hangars in this view. Note that the 3-inch guns have been removed from the after superstructure of the other ships shown here. (1976, National Steel and Shipbuilding Co)

MILWAUKEE (1972, Giorgio Arra)

MILWAUKEE (1976, U.S. Navy)

## 1 REPAIR SHIP: Ex-DESTROYER TENDER

| Number | Name | Launched | Commissioned | Status |
|--------|------|----------|--------------|--------|
| AR 28 | GRAND CANYON | 27 Apr 1945 | 5 Apr 1946 | **AA** |

| | |
|--|--|
| Builders: | Todd Shipyards Corp, Tacoma, Wash. |
| Displacement: | 8,165 tons standard |
| | 16,635 tons full load |
| Length: | 492 feet (150 m) oa |
| Beam: | 69½ feet (21.2 m) |
| Draft: | 27⅙ feet (8.3 m) |
| Propulsion: | steam turbines (Westinghouse); 8,500 shp; 1 shaft |
| Boilers: | 2 (Foster Wheeler) |
| Speed: | 18.4 knots |
| Complement: | 708 (30 O + 678 EM) |
| Guns: | 4 20-mm AA Mk 68 (4 × 1) |

The GRAND CANYON is a modified C-3 cargo design completed as a destroyer tender shortly after World War II. She subsequently operated in the AD role until 1971 when she was changed to a repair ship. A helicopter deck has been fitted aft. The ship has been scheduled for disposal in FY 1978.

Class: This ship was originally of the KLONDIKE class. The KLONDIKE (AD 22) was similarly changed to a repair ship (AR 22) and stricken on 15 September 1974.

Disposals of other repair ships of C-3 cargo design include the DELTA (AR 9, ex-AK 29) stricken on 1 October 1977; the BRIAREUS (AR 12), stricken on 1 January 1977; and the MARKAB (AR 23, ex-AD 21, ex-AK 31).

Classification: The GRAND CANYON was formerly AD 28; changed to AR 28 on 10 March 1971.

Guns: As built, the GRAND CANYON had 2 5-inch DP guns, 8 40-mm AA guns, and 12 20-mm AA guns. The lighter weapons were successively reduced and the after 5-inch gun replaced by a helicopter deck; the forward 5-inch gun was removed in the mid-1970s and minimal 20-mm armament was provided.

GRAND CANYON (as AD 28) (1971, Anthony & Joseph Pavia)

GRAND CANYON (as AD 28; forward gun since removed) (1971, U.S. Navy)

**4 REPAIR SHIPS: "VULCAN" CLASS**

| Number | Name | Launched | Commissioned | Status |
|--------|------|----------|--------------|--------|
| AR 5 | VULCAN | 14 Dec 1940 | 16 June 1941 | **AA** |
| AR 6 | AJAX | 22 Aug 1942 | 30 Oct 1943 | **PA** |
| AR 7 | HECTOR | 11 Nov 1942 | 7 Feb 1944 | **PA** |
| AR 8 | JASON | 3 Apr 1943 | 19 June 1944 | **PA** |

| | |
|---|---|
| Builders: | AR 5    New York Shipbuilding Corp, Camden, N.J. |
| | AR 6–8 Los Angeles Shipbuilding and DD Corp |
| Displacement: | 9,140 tons standard |
| | 16,200 tons full load |
| Length: | 529½ feet (161.4 m) oa except AR 8 530 feet (161.5 m) |
| Beam: | 73⅓ feet (22.3 m) |
| Draft: | 23⅓ feet (7.1 m) |
| Propulsion: | steam turbines (Allis Chalmers except New York Shipbuilding in AR 5); 11,000 shp; 2 shafts |
| Boilers: | 4 (Babcock & Wilcox) |
| Speed: | 19.2 knots |
| Complement: | 715 (23 O + 692 EM)(~950 designed wartime) |
| Guns: | 4 5-inch (127-mm) 38 cal DP Mk 30 (4 × 1) in AR 5 |
| | 4 20-mm AA Mk 67 (4 × 1) in AR 6–8 |
| | 4 20-mm AA Mk 68 (4 × 1) in AR 5 |

AJAX—5-inch guns since removed (1970, U.S. Navy)

These are large, highly capable repair ships in many respects; however, they lack the capability to support advanced weapon and sensor systems. Their replacement with new-construction ARs is planned for the 1980s.

Classification: The JASON was completed as a heavy hull repair ship (ARH 1); she was reclassified as AR 8 on 9 September 1957.

Design: These ships have 20-ton-capacity booms.

Guns: As built, these ships had 4 5-inch DP guns and 8 40-mm AA guns.

VULCAN (1975, Giorgio Arra)

HECTOR—5-inch guns since removed (1971, U.S. Navy, PH2 Louis D. Adzima)

## 2 CABLE REPAIRING SHIPS: "NEPTUNE" CLASS

| Number | Name | Launched | Commissioned | Status |
|---|---|---|---|---|
| T-ARC 2 | NEPTUNE | | 1 June 1953 | **MSC-A** |
| T-ARC 6 | ALBERT J. MEYER | | (13 May 1963) | **MSC-P** |

| Builders: | |
|---|---|
| Displacement: | 7,400 tons full load |
| Length: | 370 feet (112.8 m) oa |
| Beam: | 47 feet (14.3 m) |
| Draft: | 18 feet (5.5 m) |
| Propulsion: | reciprocating engines (Skinner); 4,800 ihp; 2 shafts |
| Boilers: | 2 (Combustion Engineering) |
| Speed: | 14 knots |
| Complement: | 85 in T-ARC 2; 74 in T-ARC 6 |
| Armament: | none |

These are large cable repair and laying ships employed to support sea-floor surveillance and communication systems. The NEPTUNE was completed as a merchant cable layer; she was acquired by the Navy in 1953 and Navy-manned until transferred to MSC in 1973. The ALBERT J. MEYER was used by the Army Signal Corps until transferred to the Navy in 1963 on loan (permanently in 1966); the ship was placed in service (instead of in commission) with MSTS/MSC in 1963. Both ships are civilian-manned.

Design: These ships are Maritime Administration S3-S2-BP1 design. They have electric cable handling machinery (in place of the original steam equipment) and precise navigation equipment; the NEPTUNE has a helicopter platform aft.

Engineering: These are believed to be the last reciprocating-engine ships in U.S. naval service.

Modernization: These ships are scheduled to be modernized in the near future to extend their useful lives some 10–15 years.

Names: The NEPTUNE was named the WILLIAM H. G. BULLARD while in merchant service.

## 1 CABLE REPAIRING SHIP: "AEOLUS" CLASS

| Number | Name | Launched | AKA Comm. | ARC Comm. | Status |
|---|---|---|---|---|---|
| T-ARC 3 | AEOLUS | 20 May 1945 | 18 June 1945 | 14 May 1955 | **MSC-P** |

| Builders: | Walsh-Kaiser Co, Providence |
|---|---|
| Displacement: | 7,040 tons full load |
| Length: | 438 feet (133.5 m) oa |
| Beam: | 58 feet (17.7 m) |
| Draft: | 19¼ feet (5.9 m) |
| Propulsion: | turbo-electric (Westinghouse turbines); 6,000 shp; 2 shafts |
| Boilers: | 2 (Wickes) |
| Speed: | 16.9 knots |
| Complement: | 86 |
| Armament: | none |

The AEOLUS is a cable repair and laying ship used to support sea-floor surveillance and communication systems. The ship was completed as an attack cargo ship (AKA 47); laid up in reserve from 1946 until converted to a cable ship in 1955. She was provided with bow sheaves, cable-stowage tanks, cable-repair facilities, and a helicopter platform. Precise navigation and bottom-survey equip-

ALBERT J. MEYER in Yokosuka, Japan (1977, Giorgio Arra)

NEPTUNE (1975, Giorgio Arra)

ment is installed. The ship was Navy-manned from 1955 until 1973 when transferred to MSC for operation with a civilian crew.

Class: A sister ship, the THOR (T-ARC 4, formerly AKA 49), is laid up in MarAd reserve pending disposal.

Design: Originally Maritime Administration S4-SE2-BE1 type.

Names: The AEOLUS was named the TURANDOT as AKA 47.

AEOLUS (1970, U.S. Navy)

## 2 LANDING CRAFT REPAIR SHIPS: CONVERTED LSTs

| Number | Name | Launched | Commissioned | Status |
|---|---|---|---|---|
| ARL 8 | EGERIA | 23 Nov 1943 | 18 Dec 1943 | PR |
| ARL 24 | SPHINX | 18 Nov 1944 | 12 Dec 1944 | PR |
| ARL 31 | BELLEROPHON | 7 Mar 1945 | 19 Mar 1945 | PR |
| ARL 37 | INDRA | 21 May 1945 | 28 May 1945 | AR |

Builders: Chicago Bridge and Iron Co, Seneca, Ill. except ARL 24 Bethlehem Steel Co, Higham, Mass.
Displacement: 1,625 tons light
4,100 tons full load
Length: 328 feet (100 m) oa
Beam: 50 feet (15.2 m)
Draft: 11 feet (3.4 m)
Propulsion: diesels (General Motors); 1,800 bhp; 2 shafts
Speed: 11.6 knots
Complement: ~250 (20 O + 130 EM)
Guns: 8 40-mm AA (2 × 4)

These are the last of a large number of LSTs converted to various repair ship configurations. The ARL conversion was intended to provide maintenance for landing craft and small boats. Each ship has been fitted with machine shops, carpenter's shop, brass foundry, welding facilities, and increased distilling capacity; two 10-ton-capacity booms were provided forward, and a 50-ton sheerleg and winch are mounted on top of the deckhouse for lifting small craft or engines.

The EGERIA has been in reserve since 1947; the INDRA was laid up from 1947 to 1968, at which time she made one tour in Vietnam and was again decommissioned in 1970. She was then placed in service in reserve as an accommodation and depot ship for the laid-up ships at Norfolk. The SPHINX was in reserve from 1947–1950, 1956–1967, and since 1971, having seen active service in the Korean and Vietnam wars; the BELLEROPHON has been in reserve since 1948.

Class: This class originally consisted of 39 ships (ARL 1–24, 26–33, 35–41, with ARL 25 and 34 cancelled). The EGERIA is ex-LST 136, the SPHINX ex-LST 963, the BELLEROPHON ex-LST 1132, and the INDRA ex-LST 1147.

Guns: The original ARL armament consisted of 1 3-inch AA gun and 8 20-mm AA guns in addition to the 40-mm weapons.

INDRA (1968, U.S. Navy)

INDRA (1967, U.S. Navy)

## Battle Damage Repair Ship Disposals

The last battle damage repair ships (ARB, converted LST) have been stricken: MIDAS (ARB 5, ex-LST 514) and SARPEDON (ARB 7, ex-LST 956) stricken on 15 April 1976.

### 9 SALVAGE SHIPS: "ESCAPE" AND "BOLSTER" CLASSES

| Number | Name | Launched | Commissioned | Status |
|--------|------|----------|--------------|--------|
| ARS 8 | PRESERVER | 1 Apr 1943 | 11 Jan 1944 | **AA** |
| (ARS 19) | CABLE | 1 Apr 1943 | 6 Mar 1944 | Loan |
| (ARS 21) | CURB | 24 Apr 1943 | 12 May 1944 | Loan |
| ARS 23 | DELIVER | 25 Sep 1943 | 18 July 1944 | **PA** |
| ARS 25 | SAFEGUARD | 20 Nov 1943 | 31 Oct 1944 | **PA** |
| (ARS 33) | CLAMP | 24 Oct 1942 | 23 Aug 1943 | Loan |
| (ARS 34) | GEAR | 24 Oct 1942 | 24 Sep 1943 | Loan |
| ARS 38 | BOLSTER | 23 Dec 1944 | 1 May 1945 | **PA** |
| ARS 39 | CONSERVER | 27 Jan 1945 | 9 June 1945 | **PA** |
| ARS 40 | HOIST | 31 Mar 1945 | 21 July 1945 | **AA** |
| ARS 41 | OPPORTUNE | 31 Mar 1945 | 5 Oct 1945 | **AA** |
| ARS 42 | RECLAIMER | 25 June 1945 | 20 Dec 1945 | **PA** |
| ARS 43 | RECOVERY | 4 Aug 1945 | 15 May 1946 | **AA** |

| | |
|--|--|
| Builders: | Basalt Rock Co, Napa, Calif. |
| Displacement: | 1,530 tons standard |
| | 1,900 tons full load |
| Length: | 213½ feat (65.1 m) oa |
| Beam: | 39 feet (11.9 m) except ARS 38–43 43 feet (13.1 m) |
| Draft: | 13 feet (4 m) |
| Propulsion: | diesel-electric (Cooper Bessemer diesels); 3,000 bhp; 2 shafts |
| Speed: | 14.8 knots, except ARS 38–43 16 knots |
| Complement: | 83 (6 O + 77 EM) (120 designed wartime) |
| Guns: | 2 20-mm AA Mk 68 (2 × 1) |

RECLAIMER and PLUNGER (SSN 595) (1976, Giorgio Arra)

RECLAIMER (1976, Giorgio Arra)

These ships are fitted for salvage and towing. They have compressed-air diving equipment; earlier ships have 8-ton and 10-ton capacity booms while the later ones have 10-ton and 20-ton booms.

The CLAMP was stricken from the Navy list in 1963 but she was reacquired in 1973 and returned to service. The CHAIN (ARS 20) and SNATCH (ARS 27) were converted to oceanographic research ships (AGOR 17 and 18, respectively).

Four ships listed above are on loan to commercial salvage firms; they can support naval requirements in an emergency situation.

Class: These classes originally included 22 ships (ARS 5–9, 19–29, 38–43 plus ARS 44–49 which were cancelled). Disposals since Tenth Edition: the ESCAPE (ARS 6), GRAPPLE (ARS 7), GRASP (ARS 24) were stricken 1977–1978, with the GRAPPLE transferred to Taiwan.

Guns: The original armament for these classes was up to four 20-mm AA guns in twin mounts. During the post-World War II period, most carried a single 40-mm gun atop the superstructure.

## 2 + 3 SUBMARINE TENDERS: "L.Y. SPEAR" CLASS

| Number | Name | FY/SCB | Launched | Commissioned | Status |
|--------|------|--------|----------|--------------|--------|
| AS 36 | L. Y. Spear | 65/702 | 7 Sep 1967 | 28 Feb 1970 | **AA** |
| AS 37 | Dixon | 66/702 | 20 June 1970 | 7 Aug 1971 | **PA** |
| AS 39 | Emory S. Land | 72/737 | 4 May 1977 | 1979 | Bldg. |
| AS 40 | Frank Cable | 73/737 | 14 Jan 1978 | 1979 | Bldg. |
| AS 41 | McKee | 77/737 | | | Bldg. |

| | |
|---|---|
| Builders: | AS 36–37 General Dynamics Corp, Quincy |
| | AS 39–41 Lockheed Shipbuilding and Constn Co, Seattle |
| Displacement: | AS 36–37 12,770 tons light; AS 39–41 13,842 tons light |
| | AS 36–37 22,628 tons full load; AS 39–41 23,000 tons full load |
| Length: | 645⅔ feet (196.8 m) oa |
| Beam: | 85 feet (25.9 m) |
| Draft: | AS 36–37 24⅔ feet (7.5 m); AS 39–41 25 feet (7.6 m) |
| Propulsion: | steam turbines (General Electric); 20,000 shp; 1 shaft |
| Boilers: | 2 (Foster Wheeler) |
| Speed: | 18 knots (sustained) |
| Complement: | AS 36–37 1,072 (42 O + 1,030 EM); AS 39–41 1,158 (50 O + 1,108 EM) |
| Flag: | 69 (25 O + 44 EM) |
| Guns: | 4 20-mm AA Mk 67 (4 × 1) |

These are the U.S. Navy's first submarine tenders designed specifically to support nuclear-propelled attack submarines; the later ships (SCB-737) have special facilities for maintaining Los Angeles-class (SSN 688) submarines. The ships have maintenance shops, weapon and provision stowage, and spare-parts lockers. A helicopter platform is provided, but no hangar. One of those ships can support four SSNs alongside simultaneously.

Class: The AS 38 of this design was provided in the FY 1969 budget, but was not built because of fund shortages in other programs.

Guns: As built, the Spear and Dixon each had two 5-inch DP guns. They have been removed and minimal 20-mm gun armament provided.

Emory S. Land at launching (1977, Lockheed Shipbuilding and Construction Co, Jim Davis)

Submarine tenders at work: Moored off Point Loma peninsula in San Diego, the Dixon (foreground) and Sperry tend the submarines and undersea craft of Submarine Squadron 3 and Submarine Development Group 1. Both tenders have SSNs alongside in this view; the Dixon has her stern to the pier in a "Mediterranean moor." (1975, U.S. Navy, PH3 H. J. Burgess)

UBS HUNLEY
AS-31 16 JUNE
62

## 2 FBM SUBMARINE TENDERS: "SIMON LAKE" CLASS

| Number | Name | FY/SCB | Launched | Commissioned | Status |
|--------|------|--------|----------|--------------|--------|
| AS 33 | SIMON LAKE | 63/238 | 8 Feb 1964 | 7 Nov 1964 | **AA** |
| AS 34 | CANOPUS | 64/238 | 12 Feb 1965 | 4 Nov 1965 | **AA** |

| | |
|---|---|
| Builders: | AS 33 Puget Sound Naval Shipyard |
| | AS 34 Ingalls Shipbuilding Corp |
| Displacement: | 21,500 tons full load |
| Length: | 643¾ feet (196.2 m) oa |
| Beam: | 85 feet (25.9 m) |
| Draft: | 30 feet (9.1 m) |
| Propulsion: | steam turbines; 20,000 shp; 1 shaft |
| Boilers: | 2 (Combustion Engineering) |
| Speed: | 18 knots (sustained) |
| Complement: | 1,075 (55 O + 1,020 EM) |
| Guns: | 4 3-inch (76-mm) 50 cal AA Mk 33 (2 × 2) |

These tenders are designed to support FBM submarines with up to three SSBNs moored alongside simultaneously. The ships have extensive machine shops, weapons and provisions stowage, spare parts lockers, and replacement missiles. They were originally configured to support Polaris missiles; the SIMON LAKE was modified in 1970–1971 and the CANOPUS in 1969–1970 to handle Poseidon missiles.

Class: The AS 35 of this design was authorized in FY 1965 but her construction was deferred and the ship was not built. The ship would have provided one tender for each of five planned SSBN squadrons with a sixth ship in overhaul and transit. However, the Polaris SSBN program was cut from a proposed 45 submarines to 41, and only four squadrons were established.

## 2 FBM SUBMARINE TENDERS: "HUNLEY" CLASS

| Number | Name | FY/SCB | Launched | Commissioned | Status |
|--------|------|--------|----------|--------------|--------|
| AS 31 | HUNLEY | 60/194 | 28 Sep 1961 | 16 June 1962 | **AA** |
| AS 32 | HOLLAND | 62/194 | 19 Jan 1963 | 7 Sep 1963 | **AA** |

| | |
|---|---|
| Builders: | AS 31 Newport News Shipbuilding and DD Co |
| | AS 32 Ingalls Shipbuilding Corp |
| Displacement: | 10,500 tons standard |
| | 18,300 tons full load |
| Length: | 599 feet (182.6 m) oa |
| Beam: | 83 feet (25.3 m) |
| Draft: | 24 feet (7.3 m) |
| Propulsion: | diesel-electric (10 Fairbanks-Morse diesels); 15,000 bhp; 1 shaft |
| Speed: | 19 knots |
| Complement: | 1,081 (58 O + 1,023 EM) |
| Guns: | 4 20-mm AA Mk 67 (4 × 1) |

These ships were the first U.S. submarine tenders constructed to support FBM submarines; three SSBNs can be serviced alongside simultaneously. They have extensive maintenance and stowage facilities, including vertical stowage for replacement missiles. As built, they could handle Polaris missiles; the HUNLEY was modified in 1973–1974 and the HOLLAND in 1974–1975 to support Poseidon-armed submarines.

Design: As built, each of these ships had a 32-ton-capacity hammerhead crane fitted aft. It has been replaced in both ships with amidships cranes, as in the later SIMON LAKE class. As in all post war sub tenders, there is a helicopter deck, but no hangar.

Guns: The original armament in both ships was four 3-inch AA guns.

CANOPUS (U.S. Navy)

HOLLAND with two SSBNs (1970, U.S. Navy)

AS-32

## 1 FBM SUBMARINE TENDER: "PROTEUS"

| Number | Name | Launched | Commissioned | Status |
|--------|------|----------|--------------|--------|
| AS 19 | PROTEUS | 12 Nov 1942 | 31 Jan 1944 | **PA** |

| | |
|---|---|
| Builder: | Moore Shipbuilding and Dry Dock Co, Oakland |
| Displacement: | 10,234 tons standard |
| | 18,500 tons full load |
| Length: | 574½ feet (175.1 m) oa |
| Beam: | 73⅓ feet (22.3 m) |
| Draft: | 25½ feet (7.8 m) |
| Propulsion: | diesel-electric (General Motors diesels); 11,200 shp; 2 shafts |
| Speed: | 15 knots |
| Complement: | 1,121 (51 O + 1,070 EM) |
| Guns: | 4 20-mm AA Mk 68 (4 × 1) |

The PROTEUS originally was a submarine tender of the FULTON class. She was laid up in reserve in 1947; from 1959–1960 she was extensively converted (SCB-190) to support Polaris-armed SSBNs (see Conversion notes). She was recommissioned on 8 July 1960.

Conversion: The PROTEUS was converted at the Charleston Naval Shipyard to the first U.S. Navy FBM submarine tender. A 44-foot amidships section was added to provide space for additional shops and support facilities as well as vertical Polaris-missile stowage. This "insert" was six decks high and weighed about 500 tons. A travelling crane was installed to handle the missiles. Nuclear support capability was added, with the gun battery being reduced to two (forward) 5-inch guns; these guns were removed in the mid-1970s.

PROTEUS before her 5-inch gun was removed (U.S. Navy)

## 6 SUBMARINE TENDERS: "FULTON" CLASS

| Number | Name | Launched | Commissioned | Status |
|--------|------|----------|--------------|--------|
| AS 11 | FULTON | 27 Dec 1940 | 12 Sep 1941 | **AA** |
| AS 12 | SPERRY | 17 Dec 1941 | 1 May 1942 | **PA** |
| AS 15 | BUSHNELL | 14 Sep 1942 | 10 Apr 1943 | MR |
| AS 16 | HOWARD W. GILMORE | 16 Sep 1943 | 24 May 1944 | **PA** |
| AS 17 | NEREUS | 12 Feb 1945 | 27 Oct 1945 | PR |
| AS 18 | ORION | 14 Oct 1942 | 30 Sep 1943 | **PA** |

| | |
|---|---|
| Builders: | AS 11, 15–17 Mare Island Navy Yard |
| | AS 12, 18 Moore Shipbuilding and DD Co, Oakland |
| Displacement: | 9,734 tons standard |
| | 18,000 tons full load |
| Length: | 529½ feet (161.4 m) oa except AS 12, 15 530½ feet (161.7) |
| Beam: | 73⅓ feet (22.3 m) |
| Draft: | 25½ feet (7.8 m) |
| Propulsion: | diesel-electric (General Motors diesels); 11,200 bhp except AS 11 11,500 bhp, AS 12 11,800 bhp; 2 shafts |
| Speed: | 15 knots |
| Complement: | 917 (34 O + 883 EM) |
| Guns: | 2 5-inch (127-mm) 38 cal DP Mk 30 (2 × 1) in AS 15, 17 |
| | 4 20-mm AA Mk 68 (4 × 1) in AS 11–12, 16, 18 |

These ships are similar in design to the contemporary DIXIE-class (AD 14) destroyer tenders. The FULTONS have been modernized to provide a limited capability to support nuclear attack submarines, as well as the Navy's few remaining diesel submarines. Their helicopter decks are suitable only for VERTREP and not for landings. The original 20-ton-capacity cranes have been replaced in the GILMORE.

Class: Originally seven ships were in this class. The PROTEUS has been converted to an FBM submarine tender and is listed separately.

Guns; As built, these ships each had 4 5-inch DP guns and 8 40-mm AA guns.

HOWARD W. GILMORE (1973, Giorgio Arra)

## 2 SUBMARINE RESCUE SHIPS: "PIGEON" CLASS

| Number | Name | FY/SCB | Launched | Commissioned | Status |
|--------|------|--------|----------|--------------|--------|
| ASR 21 | PIGEON | 67/721 | 13 Aug 1969 | 28 Apr 1973 | **PA** |
| ASR 22 | ORTOLAN | 68/721 | 10 Sep 1969 | 14 July 1973 | **AA** |

| | |
|---|---|
| Builders: | Alabama Dry Dock and Shipbuilding Co, Mobile |
| Displacement: | 4,200 tons full load |
| Length: | 251 feet (76.5 m) oa |
| Beam: | 86 feet (26.2 m) |
| Draft: | 21¼ feet (6.5 m) |
| Propulsion: | diesels; 6,000 bhp; 2 shafts |
| Speed: | 15 knots |
| Complement: | 115 (6 O + 109 EM) + 38 technicians (8 O + 30 EM) |
| Guns: | 2 20-mm AA Mk 68 (2 × 1) |

These are the world's first built-for-the-purpose submarine rescue ships. They were constructed specifically to carry Deep Submergence Rescue Vehicles (DSRV) and support deep-ocean diving operations. For the latter role they have the Mk II Deep Diving System (DDS) which can support up to eight divers operating to depths of 1,000 feet in helium–oxygen saturation conditions.

These ships were delayed by problems in design, construction, and fitting out.

Class: The Navy had planned to construct a minimum of three ships of this class to support six DSRVs at three rescue unit home ports. At one point long-range planning called for ten ships as replacements for the older ASR force. However, only two ships were funded. Additional ASRs are planned but they will not be DSRV support ships.

Design: These are the Navy's largest catamaran ships, being larger than the research ship HAYES (T-AGOR 16). Each ASR hull is 26 feet wide with a separation of 34 feet between the two. The open well facilitates the raising and lowering of DSRVs and diving chambers. These ships have a precision three-dimensional sonar tracking system for directing DSRV operations, and a helicopter deck is fitted aft. Accommodations are provided for a salvage staff of 14 and a DSRV operator and maintenance team of 24.

Engineering: Through-bow thrusters are fitted in each hull for maneuvering and station-keeping during diving and salvage operations (the ships are not moored while operating DSRVs).

Guns: As built, the PIGEON had two 3-inch AA guns in "tubs" forward on her hulls. After their removal the large mooring buoys ("spuds") were mounted in their place; previously she had two buoys forward of the bridge and two between the hulls aft.

PIGEON (1974, U.S. Navy)

ORTOLAN (1976, Giorgio Arra)

**4 SUBMARINE RESCUE SHIPS: "CHANTICLEER" CLASS**

| Number | Name | Launched | Commissioned | Status |
|---|---|---|---|---|
| ASR 9 | Florikan | 14 June 1942 | 5 Apr 1943 | **PA** |
| ASR 13 | Kittiwake | 10 July 1945 | 18 July 1946 | **AA** |
| ASR 14 | Petrel | 25 Sep 1945 | 24 Sep 1946 | **AA** |
| ASR 15 | Sunbird | 25 June 1945 | 28 Jan 1947 | **AA** |

| | |
|---|---|
| Builders: | ASR 9    Moore Shipbuilding and Dry Dock Co, Oakland |
| | ASR 13–15 Savannah Machine and Foundry Co |
| Displacement: | 1,635 tons standard |
| | 2,290 tons full load |
| Length: | 251⅓ feet (76.7 m) oa |
| Beam: | 42 feet (12.8 m) |
| Draft: | 14⅚ feet (4.5 m) |
| Propulsion: | diesel-electric (General Motors diesel, except Alco in ASR 9); 3,000 bhp; 1 shaft |
| Speed: | 15 knots |
| Complement: | 85 (102 designed wartime) |
| Guns: | 2 20-mm AA Mk 68 (2 × 1) |

These are large tug-type ships fitted for salvage and helium–oxygen diving operations.

Class: Originally there were eight ships in this class (ASR 7–11, 13–15 plus the cancelled ASR 16–18). Disposals since the Tenth Edition: the Coucal (ASR 8) stricken on 15 September 1977; the Tringa (ASR 16) stricken on 30 September 1977.

**4 AUXILIARY TUGS: "SOTOYOMO" CLASS**

| Number | Name | Launched | Commissioned | Status |
|---|---|---|---|---|
| ATA 181 | Accokeek | 27 July 1944 | 7 Oct 1944 | MR |
| ATA 190 | Samoset | 26 Oct 1944 | 1 Jan 1945 | MR |
| ATA 193 | Stallion | 24 Nov 1944 | 26 Feb 1945 | MR |
| ATA 213 | Keywadin | 9 Apr 1945 | 1 June 1945 | MR |

| | |
|---|---|
| Builders: | Levingston Shipbuilding Co, Orange, Texas, except ATA 213 Gulfport Boiler and Welding Works, Port Arthur, Texas |
| Displacement: | 534 tons standard |
| | 835 tons full load |
| Length: | 143 feet (43.6 m) oa |
| Beam: | 33⅚ feet (10.3 m) |
| Draft: | 14 feet (4.3 m) |
| Propulsion: | diesel-electric (General Motors diesels); 1,500 bhp; 1 shaft |
| Speed: | 13 knots |
| Complement: | 45 (5 O + 40 EM) |
| Guns: | 1 3-inch (76-mm) 50 cal AA (1 × 1) |
| | or 4 20-mm AA Mk 24 (2 × 2); all guns removed from some ships |

These are the survivors of a large class of oceangoing small tugs.

Class: Disposals since Tenth Edition: the Tatnuck (ATA 195) stricken on 1 October 1977.

Classification: These ships originally were classified as rescue tugs (ATR); they were renumbered in the same series as the larger fleet tugs (ATF) on 15 May 1944.

Design: These are steel-hulled ships.

Names: These ships were assigned the names of discarded fleet and yard tugs in 1948.

Kittiwake with submarine rescue chamber on fantail (1976, Stefan Terzibaschitsch)

Sunbird (1975, Giorgio Arra)

Accokeek (1970, U.S. Navy)

## (7+) FLEET TUGS: "POWHATAN" CLASS

| Number | Name | FY/SCB | Launch | In service | Status |
|--------|------|--------|--------|-----------|--------|
| T-ATF 166 | POWHATAN | 75/744 | 1977 | 1978 | Bldg. |
| T-ATF 167 | NARRAGANSETT | 75/744 | 1978 | 1979 | Bldg. |
| T-ATF 168 | CATAWBA | 75/744 | 1978 | 1979 | Bldg. |
| T-ATF 169 | NAVAJO | 75/744 | 1979 | 1980 | Bldg. |
| T-ATF 170 | ...... | 78/744 | | | Auth. |
| T-ATF 171 | ...... | 78/744 | | | Auth. |
| T-ATF 172 | ...... | 78/744 | | | Auth. |

Builders:        T-ATF 166–169 Marinette Marine, Wisc.
Displacement:  2,000 tons full load
Length:           218 feet (66.5 m) oa
Beam:             42 feet (12.8 m)

Draft:              15 feet (4.6 m)
Propulsion:     diesels (General Motors); 4,500 bhp; 2 shafts (controllable-pitch propellers)
Speed:            15 knots
Complement:   16 + 24 technicians
Guns:              space provided for 2 20-mm AA Mk 67 (2 × 1) and 2 .50-cal MG

These tugs are being constructed to a commercial tug design as replacements for the World War II-era ATFs. They will be operated by MSC with civilian crews. Space is provided for 4 Navy communications personnel and 20 diving and salvage personnel.

The cost of the three FY 1978 ships is $52.7 million.

Design: These ships have clear afterdeck areas for diving and salvage equipment. The starboard-side boom has a 10-ton capacity.

Engineering: A 300-hp bow thruster is provided.

## 11 FLEET TUGS: "NAVAJO" CLASS

| Number | Name | Launched | Commissioned | Status |
|--------|------|----------|--------------|--------|
| T-ATF 76 | UTE | 24 June 1942 | 31 Dec 1942 | **MSC-A** |
| T-ATF 85 | LIPAN | 17 Sep 1942 | 29 Apr 1943 | **MSC-P** |
| ATF 91 | SENECA | 2 Feb 1943 | 30 Apr 1943 | MR |
| ATF 105 | MOCTOBI | 25 Mar 1944 | 25 July 1944 | **NRF-P** |
| ATF 110 | QUAPAW | 15 May 1943 | 6 May 1944 | **NRF-P** |
| ATF 113 | TAKELMA | 18 Sep 1943 | 3 Aug 1944 | **PA** |
| T-ATF 149 | ATAKAPA | 11 July 1944 | 8 Dec 1944 | **MSC-A** |
| T-ATF 158 | MOSOPELEA | 7 Mar 1945 | 28 July 1945 | **MSC-A** |
| ATF 159 | PAIUTE | 4 June 1945 | 27 Aug 1945 | **NRF-A** |
| ATF 160 | PAPAGO | 21 June 1945 | 3 Oct 1945 | **NRF-P** |
| ATF 162 | SHAKORI | 9 Aug 1945 | 20 Dec 1945 | **AA** |

Builders:        ATF 76, 85, 110, 113    United Engineering Co, Alameda, Calif.
                     ATF 91                         Cramp Shipbuilding Co, Philadelphia
                     ATF 105, 149, 158–160, 162    Charleston Shipbuilding and DD Co
Displacement:  1,235 tons standard
                     1,675 tons full load
Length:           205 feet (62.5 m) oa
Beam:             38½ feet (11.7 m)
Draft:              15½ feet (4.7 m)
Propulsion:     diesel-electric; 3,000 bhp; 1 shaft
Speed:            15 knots
Complement:   67 (5 O + 62 EM) in active Navy ships; 27–28 + 6 technicians in MSC ships (85 designed wartime)
Guns:              1 3-inch (76-mm) 50 cal AA Mk 22 (1 × 1); removed from MSC ships

These ships are the survivors of a large, highly successful series of ATFs. The SENECA was laid up in Maritime Administration reserve in 1971; the MOSOPELEA was assigned to the Military Sealift Command in 1973 and three others followed in 1974. They are civilian-manned with six Navy communications personnel sometimes embarked. Four ships were transferred to the Naval Reserve Force in 1977; they have composite active–reserve crews.

Class: The ATF 66–76 and 81–118 were built to the same basic configuration. (See Design notes). They generally are known as the CHEROKEE class (ATF 66) after the loss of the NAVAJO (ATF 64) in 1943.

Disposals since Tenth Edition: the TAWASA (ATF 92), stricken on 1 April 1975; the CREE (ATF 84), MATACO (ATF 86), ABNAKI (ATF 96), CHOWANOC (ATF 100), COCOPA (ATF 101), HITCHITI (ATF 103), MOLALA (ATF 106), TAWAKONI (ATF 114), NIPMUC (ATF 157), and SALINAN (ATF 161), stricken 1977–1978.

Design: These are steel-hulled ships. They are fitted with a 10- or 20-ton-capacity boom. Most have compressed-air diving equipment. The ATF 96 and later ships have a smaller funnel than the earlier ships.

Guns: As built, these ships had two 40-mm AA guns in addition to the 3-inch gun. The ships assigned to MSC are unarmed.

PAPAGO—large funnel type (1976, Giorgio Arra)

QUAPAW—small funnel type (1976, Giorgio Arra)

## 3 SALVAGE AND RESCUE SHIPS: "EDENTON" CLASS

| Number | Name | FY/SCB | Launched | Commissioned | Status |
|--------|------|--------|----------|--------------|--------|
| ATS 1 | EDENTON | 66/719 | 15 May 1968 | 23 Jan 1971 | **AA** |
| ATS 2 | BEAUFORT | 67/719 | 20 Dec 1968 | 22 Jan 1972 | **PA** |
| ATS 3 | BRUNSWICK | 67/719 | 14 Oct 1969 | 10 Dec 1972 | **PA** |

| | |
|---|---|
| Builders: | Brooke Marine, Lowestoft, England |
| Displacement: | 3,117 tons full load |
| Length: | 282⅔ feet (86.1 m) oa |
| Beam: | 50 feet (15.2 m) |
| Draft: | 15⅙ feet (4.6 m) |
| Propulsion: | diesels (Paxman); 6,000 bhp; 2 shafts (controllable-pitch propellers) |
| Speed: | 16 knots |
| Complement: | 96 (8 O + 88 EM); designed 102 (9 O + 93 EM) |
| Guns: | 4 20-mm AA Mk 24 (2 × 2) in ATS 1 |
| | 2 20-mm AA Mk 68 (2 × 1) in ATS 2–3 |

These are large ocean tugs with salvage and diving capabilities. They are one of two British-built classes of auxiliary ships constructed in the post-World War II period for the U.S. Navy (see the CHAUVENET class, T-AGS 29). There have been difficulties in maintaining these ships because of their foreign-manufactured components.

Class: The ATS 4 was authorized in FY 1972 and the ATS 5 in FY 1973. Their construction was deferred in 1973 and plans for additional ships of this class were dropped because of the high costs; instead, the commercial-design ATF 166 has been procured.

Classification: The classification ATS was changed from salvage tug to salvage and rescue ship on 16 February 1971.

Design: These ships have large open work spaces forward and aft. They have four mooring buoys, two on each side of the funnel, similar to those carried by submarine rescue ships to facilitate four-point moors. A 10-ton-capacity crane is fitted forward and a 20-ton capacity crane aft. The ships have compressed-air diving equipment, but are designed to accommodate the air-transportable Mk 1 Deep Diving System (DDS) which can support helium–oxygen saturation divers, working at nominal depths of 850 feet for sustained periods.

Engineering: The ships are fitted with through-bow thrusters for precise maneuvering and station-keeping.

EDENTON (1976, Stefan Terzibaschtsch)

BRUNSWICK (1974, U.S. Navy, PHCS Robert Lawson)

## 1 GUIDED MISSILE SHIP: "NORTON SOUND"

| Number | Name | Launched | Commissioned | Status |
|--------|------|----------|--------------|--------|
| AVM 1 | NORTON SOUND | 28 Nov 1943 | 8 Jan 1945 | **PA** |

| | |
|---|---|
| Builders: | Los Angeles Shipbuilding and Dry Dock Co |
| Displacement: | 9,106 tons standard |
| | 15,170 tons full load |
| Length: | 543¼ feet (165.6 m) oa |
| Beam: | 69¼ feet (21.1 m) |
| Draft: | 23½ feet (7.2 m) |
| Propulsion: | steam turbines (Allis Chalmers); 12,000 shp; 2 shafts |
| Boilers: | 4 (Babcock & Wilcox) |
| Speed: | 19 knots |
| Complement: | ~300 |
| Missiles: | 1 twin Mk 26 Mod 0 launcher for Standard-MR SAM |
| Radars: | SPS-10 surface search |
| | SPS-40 air search |
| | SPS-52 3-D search |
| | SPY-1A phased array |

NORTON SOUND (1975, U.S. Navy)

The NORTON SOUND is a test ship for advanced weapons development. She originally was a seaplane tender of the CURRITUCK class (AV 7). From 1948 onward she has been employed in the test and evaluation of missiles, guns, and electronic systems (see Guns and Missiles notes). In 1974 she was modified to serve as the test ship for the Aegis system. One "face" of the four-array SPY-1 radar system was fitted on the ship's starboard side above the bridge (with a dummy face to port). The related Aegis computers and fire control systems have been installed and a twin Mk 26 missile launcher installed aft.

Classification: The NORTON SOUND was reclassified from AV 11 to AVM 1 on 8 August 1951.

Design: A 30-ton-capacity crane is fitted.

Guns: The ship's original armament as AV 11 consisted of 4 5-inch DP guns and 20 40-mm AA guns. All guns have been removed.

In 1968 the 5-inch/54 cal lightweight Mk 45 gun and associated Mk 86 gun FCS were installed for at-sea evaluation; they were subsequently removed.

Missiles: The NORTON SOUND has served as test ship for at-sea launchings of several rockets and missiles, among them the Loon (U.S. version of the German V-1 "buzz bomb"), Aerobee, Lark, Regulus I, Terrier, Tartar, Sea Sparrow, and Standard-ER/MR. In 1958 the ship launched multi-stage missiles carrying low-yield nuclear warheads which were detonated some 300 miles above the earth (Project Argus).

## UNCLASSIFIED MISCELLANEOUS SHIPS

These ships are officially considered to be Service Craft, but are traditionally listed as Auxiliaries.

The hull number IX 505 was assigned to the former medium harbor tug YTM 759; that craft was stricken on 1 December 1977.

The hull number IX 310 is assigned to two test barges linked together and used for research at the Naval Underwater System Center's laboratory at Lake Seneca, N.Y. No name is assigned to this "craft."

## 3 SELF-PROPELLED BARRACKS SHIPS: MODIFIED LST DESIGN

| Number | Name | Launched | Commissioned | Status |
|--------|------|----------|--------------|--------|
| IX 502 | MERCER | 17 Nov 1944 | 19 Sep 1945 | **PA** |
| IX 503 | NUECES | 6 May 1945 | 30 Nov 1945 | **PA** |
| IX 504 | ECHOLS | 30 July 1945 | (1 Jan 1947) | **AA** |

| | |
|---|---|
| Builders: | IX 502–504 Boston Navy Yard |
| | APB 47   Missouri Valley Bridge and Iron Co, Evansville, Ind. |
| Displacement: | 2,190 tons light |
| | 4,080 tons full load |
| Length: | 328 feet (100 m) oa |
| Beam: | 50 feet (15.2 m) |
| Draft: | 11 feet (3.4 m) |
| Propulsion: | diesels (General Motors); 1,600 bhp except APB 47 1,800 bhp; 2 shafts |
| Speed: | 10 knots except APB 47 12 knots |
| Complement: | 193 (13 O + 180 EM) as APB |
| Troops: | 1,226 (26 O + 1,200 EM) as APB |
| Guns: | 16 40-mm AA in APB 47 (1 × 4 Mk 2, 6 × 2 Mk 24) |

These ships were built to provide accommodations and support for small craft and riverine forces. All three ships were built as barracks ships (APL, later APB) to serve at shipyards for crews of ships being built or under repair. They were then given "unclassified" (IX) designations with their APB hull numbers in 1975–1976.

The ECHOLS was placed in service, instead of being commissioned, in 1947. All of these ships were laid up in reserve after World War II. The MERCER and NUECES were recommissioned in 1968 for service in Vietnam. They were rearmed with two 3-inch guns, eight 40-mm guns (2 × 4), and several MGs. As modified to support riverine forces, they had crews of 12 officers and 186 enlisted men, and could accommodate 900 troops and small-boat crewmen. Both ships were again laid up in 1969–1971 until reactivated in 1975; the ECHOLS was reactivated in 1976.

Class: There were originally 14 ships of this class (APB 35–48); the KINGMAN (APB 47) was stricken on 1 October 1977.

Classification: IX 502 ex-APB 39, ex-APL 39; IX 503 ex-APB 40, ex-APL 40; and IX 504 ex-APB 37, ex-APL 37; the MERCER and NUECES were changed to IX on 1 November 1975; the ECHOLS on 1 February 1976.

## 1 TEST RANGE SUPPORT SHIP: "ELK RIVER"

| Number | Name | Launched | Commissioned | Status |
|--------|------|----------|--------------|--------|
| IX 501 | ELK RIVER | 21 Apr 1945 | 27 May 1945 | **PA** |

| | |
|---|---|
| Builders: | Brown Shipbuilding Co, Houston |
| Displacement: | 1,100 tons full load |
| Length: | 230 feet (70.1 m) oa |
| Beam: | 50 feet (15.2 m) |
| Draft: | 9⅚ feet (3 m) |
| Propulsion: | diesels; 1,400 bhp; 2 shafts |
| Speed: | 6 knots |
| Complement: | 71 (20 O + 51 EM) |
| Armament: | none |

The ELK RIVER is a converted rocket landing ship (ex-LSMR 501) employed as a test and training ship for deep-sea diving and salvage. She is operated by the Naval Ocean Systems Center in San Diego.

Class: The ELK RIVER was one of several medium landing ships (LSM) completed as rocket fire support ships. All other ships of this type have been stricken, the last three having been used in the Vietnam War.

Conversion: The ELK RIVER was converted to a test range support ship in 1967–1968 at Avondale Shipyards, Westwego, Louisiana, and the San Francisco Naval Shipyard. The basic 203½-foot LSMR hull was lengthened and eight-foot sponsons were added to both sides to improve the ship's stability and increase working space. A superstructure was added forward and an open center well was provided for lowering and raising equipment. The 65-ton-capacity gantry crane runs on tracks above the opening to handle submersibles and diver-transfer chambers. An active precision maneuvering system is installed for holding position without mooring.

The prototype Mk II Deep Diving System (DDS) has been installed. It can support eight divers operating at depths of 1,000 feet in helium–oxygen saturation conditions. This is the most advanced diving system in use today; the Mk II DDS is also in the PIGEON-class (ASR 21) ships.

ECHOLS in reserve as APB 37 (1976, Giorgio Arra)

ELK RIVER (1968, U.S. Navy)

**1 TORPEDO TEST SHIP: "NEW BEDFORD"**

| Number | Name | Status |
|--------|------|--------|
| IX 308 | NEW BEDFORD | **PA** |

| | |
|---|---|
| Builders: | Wheeler Shipbuilding Co |
| Displacement: | ~700 tons |
| Length: | 176½ feet (53.8 m) oa |
| Beam: | 32¾ feet (10 m) |
| Draft: | 10 feet (3.1 m) |
| Propulsion: | diesel; 1,000 bhp; 1 shaft |
| Speed: | 13 knots |
| Complement: | |
| Armament: | none |

The NEW BEDFORD is a former U.S. Army cargo ship (FS 289). She was acquired by the Navy on 1 March 1950 for cargo work and subsequently converted for torpedo testing. Since 1963 she has been operated by the Naval Torpedo Station, Keyport, Washington.

Classification: As a Navy cargo ship the NEW BEDFORD was operated by the Military Sea Transportation Service and classified T-AKL 17.

NEW BEDFORD (1973, U.S. Navy)

**1 INSTRUMENTATION PLATFORM: "BRIER"**

| Number | Name | Status |
|--------|------|--------|
| IX 307 | BRIER | **AA** |

| | |
|---|---|
| Builders: | |
| Displacement: | 178 tons full load |
| Length: | 100 feet (30.1 m) oa |
| Beam: | 24 feet (7.3 m) |
| Draft: | 4½ feet (1.4 m) |
| Propulsion: | diesel; 300 bhp; 2 shafts |
| Speed: | 8.5 knots |
| Complement: | |
| Armament: | none |

The BRIER is a former Coast Guard buoy tender. She was acquired by the Navy on 10 March 1969 to be used as an instrument platform for testing explosives at the Naval Ordnance Center's facility at Solomons Island, Maryland.

Classification: Formerly classified WLI 299 in Coast Guard service, the BRIER was assigned IX 307 on 29 August 1970.

**1 TORPEDO TEST SHIP: Ex-CARGO SHIP**

| Number | | Status |
|--------|--|--------|
| IX 306 | (unnamed) | **AA** |

| | |
|---|---|
| Builders: | Higgins Industries, New Orleans, La. |
| Displacement: | 906 tons full load |
| Length: | 179 feet (54.6 m) oa |
| Beam: | 33 feet (10.1 m) |
| Draft: | 10 feet (3.1 m) |
| Propulsion: | diesel; 1 shaft |
| Speed: | 12 knots |
| Complement: | |
| Armament: | none |

The IX 306 is a former U.S. Army cargo ship (FS 221). She was acquired from the Army in January 1969 and converted to a torpedo test ship, being placed in service late in 1969. The ship supports research activities of the Naval Underwater Weapons Research and Engineering Station, Newport, Rhode Island, and operates in the Atlantic Underwater Test and Evaluation Center (AUTEC) range in the Caribbean. The ship is manned by Navy and RCA personnel.

IX 306 (1969, U.S. Navy)

## 1 RELIC: "CONSTITUTION"

| Number | Name | Launched | Commissioned | Status |
|--------|------|----------|--------------|--------|
| (IX 21) | CONSTITUTION | 21 Oct 1797 | 1798 | Relic |

| | |
|---|---|
| Builder: | Hartt's Shipyard, Boston |
| Displacement: | ~2,200 tons |
| Length: | 175 feet (53.3 m) wl |
| Beam: | 45 feet (13.7 m) |
| Draft: | 20 feet (6.1 m) |
| Masts: | fore 94 feet (28.7 m) |
| | main 104 feet (31.7 m) |
| | mizzen 81 feet (24.7 m) |
| Speed: | 13 knots (under sail) |
| Complement: | |
| Guns: | several smooth-bore cannon |

The CONSTITUTION is the oldest U.S. ship in Navy commission. Her original commission date is not known; she first put to sea on 22 July 1798. She is moored as a relic at the Boston Naval Shipyard. As a sail frigate the CONSTITUTION fought in the "Quasi-War" with France, against the Barbary pirates, and in the War of 1812 with Britain. She has been rebuilt several times and restored as much as possible to her original configuration.

No sails are fitted. Twice a year she is taken out into Boston harbor under tow and "turned around" so that her masts do not bend from the effects of sun and wind.

Class: The CONSTITUTION was one of six sail frigates built under an Act of Congress of 1794. A sister ship, the CONSTELLATION, was broken up at Norfolk, Virginia in 1852–1853 and much of her material was used in building another sailing ship of that name. That ship, also named the CONSTELLATION, served as IX 20 until transferred in 1954 to a private group in Baltimore, Maryland, where she is maintained.

Classification: The CONSTITUTION was classified as an "unclassified" ship in 1920 (IX, without a hull number). She became the IX 21 on 8 December 1941 and carried that classification until 1 September 1975 when it was withdrawn because, according to Navy officials, the designation "tended to demean and degrade the CONSTITUTION through association with a group of insignificant craft of varied missions and configuration."

Names: From 1917 to 1925 the ship was named OLD IRONSIDES while the name CONSTITUTION was assigned to a battle cruiser (CC 5) which was never completed.

## 2 RESEARCH SHIPS: Ex-MINESWEEPERS

| Number | Name | FY/SCB | Launched | In service | Status |
|--------|------|--------|----------|------------|--------|
| (MSI 1) | COVE | 56/136 | 8 Feb 1958 | 22 Nov 1958 | **Academic** |
| (MSI 2) | CAPE | 56/136 | 5 Apr 1958 | 27 Feb 1959 | **Academic** |

| | |
|---|---|
| Builders: | Bethlehem Steel Co, Bellingham, Wash. |
| Displacement: | 120 tons light |
| | 240 tons full load |
| Length: | 105 feet (32 m) oa |
| Beam: | 22 feet (6.7 m) |
| Draft: | 10 feet (3 m) |
| Propulsion: | diesel (General Motors); 650 bhp; 1 shaft |
| Speed: | 12 knots |
| Complement: | |
| Guns: | removed |

These were prototype inshore minesweepers. After several years of service in the MSI role they were assigned to research tasks. Both are now operated by the Johns Hopkins Applied Physics Laboratory.

Additional MSIs have been built specifically for foreign transfer.

CONSTITUTION (U.S. Navy)

CAPE as MSI 2 (1968, U.S. Navy)

## 1 EXPERIMENTAL SURFACE EFFECT SHIP: BELL AEROSYSTEMS DESIGN

| Number | Name | Launched | Commissioned | Status |
|--------|------|----------|--------------|--------|
| SES-100 B | (unnamed) | 6 Mar 1971 | Feb 1972 | **Test** |

| | |
|---|---|
| Builders: | Bell Aerosystems, Michoud, La. |
| Displacement: | 100 tons gross |
| Length: | 77¾ feet (23.7 m) oa |
| Beam: | 35 feet (10.7 m) |
| Draft: | |
| Propulsion: | 3 gas turbines (Pratt & Whitney); 13,500 shp, 2 semi-submerged super-cavitating propellers |
| Lift: | 3 gas turbines (United Aircraft of Canada); 1,500 shp; 8 horizontal fans |
| Speed: | 80+ knots |
| Complement: | 4 + 6 observers |
| Armament: | none |

The SES-100B was built as a competitive prototype with the SES-100A to test surface-effect-ship concepts for the Navy in preparation for the large, 2,000–3,000-ton SES (see page 104). The 100-ton SES program was initiated in January 1969 as a joint Navy–Maritime Administration effort; however, MarAd withdrew in 1971, partly because it could not provide the required funding.

The SES-100B was developed by the Bell Aerosystems Division of the Textron Corporation and constructed at Bell Aerosystem's Michoud facility (a part of the National Aeronautics and Space Administration's assembly complex). The launch date above is the date of formal christening.

Cost: Estimated cost to construct the SES-100B is $14 million.

Design: The craft is constructed of aluminum and has a 10-ton cargo capacity. No SCB number is assigned.

Missiles: During April 1976 the SES-100B was used to test vertical launch techniques for the use of the Standard SM-1 missile in a surface-to-surface role. A successful launch was made at a speed of 60 knots.

Propulsion: The SES has three FT12A-6 propulsion engines and three ST6J-70 lift engines. The craft reached a speed of 82.3 knots during trials in 1975, and has sustained speeds in excess of 50 knots in sea state 3.

SES-100B (1976, U.S. Navy, Dave Wilson)

## 1 EXPERIMENTAL SURFACE EFFECT SHIP: AEROJET-GENERAL DESIGN

| Number | Name | Launched | Completed | Status |
|--------|------|----------|-----------|--------|
| SES-100A | (unnamed) | 24 July 1971 | May 1972 | **Test** |

| | |
|---|---|
| Builders: | Tacoma Boatbuilding Co, Wash. |
| Displacement: | 72.8 tons light<br>100 tons gross |
| Length: | 81¹¹⁄₁₂ feet (24.9 m) oa |
| Beam: | 41¹¹⁄₁₂ feet (21.7 m) |
| Draft: | 10⅓ feet (3.22 m) hullborne |
| Propulsion: | 4 gas turbines (Avco-Lycoming); 12,000 shp; 2 waterjets |
| Lift: | 3 horizontal fans (interconnected to propulsion engines) |
| Speed: | 80 + knots (designed) |
| Complement: | 4 + 6 observers |
| Armament: | none |

The SES-100A was developed by the Aerojet-General Corporation as a competitive prototype with the SES-100B. The launch date above is the christening date.

Cost: Estimated construction cost was $18 million.

Design: The SES-100A is constructed of aluminum. The craft has a 10-ton cargo capacity. Protruding outboard from each sidewall just below the displacement condition waterline are a stabilizer (forward, directly under "SES-100A") and a steering skeg (amidships, abaft the after end of the cabin). No SCB number is assigned.

Propulsion: The craft is fitted with TF-35 engines which are marine versions of the T55-L-11A aircraft engine. The SES-100A reached 76 knots on trials in 1973.

SES-100A (1976, Aerojet—General Corp)

# 19 Service Craft

The U.S. Navy operates several hundred service craft, both self-propelled and non-self-propelled, at bases in the United States and overseas. These craft perform a variety of Fleet support services.

Only the self-propelled craft are described here, with several "different" service craft being listed separately: the unclassified miscellaneous (IX) ships and craft are described under auxiliary ships, while the submersibles and floating dry docks are listed in separate chapters.

All service craft are Navy-manned with a few having all-woman crews.

Armament: Service craft are usually unarmed. The seamanship training craft (YP) can be armed with light weapons and used as harbor patrol craft.

Classification: The service craft "Y" designations were initiated when they were considered "yard" craft. A few "odd" craft without designations are listed on p. 234.

### 1 MOBILE LISTENING BARGE: CONVERTED WATER BARGE

| Number | Name |
|--------|------|
| YAG 61 | Monob 1 |

| | |
|---|---|
| Builders: | Zenith Dredge Co, Duluth, Minn. |
| Displacement: | 1,390 tons full load |
| Length: | 174 feet (53 m) oa |
| Beam: | 32 feet (9.75 m) |
| Draft: | |
| Propulsion: | diesel; 560 bhp; 1 shaft |
| Speed: | 7 knots |
| Complement: | 23 |

YAG 61 was originally completed in 1943 as a self-propelled water barge (YW 87). She was converted to a Mobile Noise Barge (MONOB) for acoustic research in 1969 and placed in service at Port Everglades, Florida, conducting research for the Naval Ship Research and Development Center.

Classification: As the Monob 1 the craft was initially classified in 1969 as IX 309, and changed to YAG 61 on 1 July 1970.

Monob 1 (U.S. Navy)

## Miscellaneous Auxiliary Disposals

The GEORGE EASTMAN (YAG 39), converted "Liberty" ship employed in nuclear effects research, was stricken on 1 December 1975.

### 3 COVERED LIGHTERS

| Number | Name |
|--------|------|
| YF 862 | (unnamed) |
| YF 866 | KODIAK |
| YF 885 | KEYPORT |

| | |
|--------|------|
| Builders: | YF 862, 866 Missouri Valley Bridge and Steel Co, Evansville, Ind. |
| | YF 885    Defoe Shipbuilding Co, Bay City, Mich. |
| Displacement: | 650 tons full load |
| Length: | 132 feet (40.2 m) oa |
| Beam: | 30 feet (9.1 m) |
| Draft: | |
| Propulsion: | diesel; 600 bhp; 2 shafts |
| Speed: | 10 knots |
| Complement: | 11 (EM) |

These are small coastal supply ships with a 250-ton cargo capacity constructed during World War II. The unnamed YF 862 is laid up; the two others are active. Disposals since Tenth Edition: LYNNHAVEN (YF 328) of an earlier design, stricken in 1977.

### 2 FERRYBOATS

| Number | Number |
|--------|--------|
| YFB 83 | YFB 87 |

| | |
|--------|--------|
| Builders: | |
| Displacement: | 773 tons full load |
| Length: | 180 feet (54.9 m) oa |
| Beam: | 59 feet (18 m) |
| Draft: | |
| Propulsion: | diesels; 2 shafts |
| Speed: | |
| Complement: | |

These are small, built-for-the-purpose ferryboats which service naval bases. Both are active.

YFB 87 (1970, U.S. Navy)

YF-type service craft laid up in reserve (1975, A. D. Baker)

### 4 FERRYBOATS: CONVERTED "LCU 1610" CLASS

| Number | Number | Number | Number |
|--------|--------|--------|--------|
| YFB 88 | YFB 89 | YFB 90 | YFB 91 |

| | |
|--------|--------|
| Builders: | |
| Displacement: | ~390 tons full load |
| Length: | 134¾ feet (41 m) oa |
| Beam: | 29¾ feet (9 m) |
| Draft: | 6 feet (1.8 m) |
| Propulsion: | geared diesels (Detroit); 2,000 bhp; 2 shafts |
| Speed: | 11 knots |
| Complement: | 6 (EM) |

These are former LCU 1610-class landing craft, modified for use as ferryboats.

Classification: Formerly LCU 1636 and 1638–1640, respectively; all were changed to YFB on 1 September 1969.

YFB 88 (ex-LCU 1636) (U.S. Navy)

## Ferryboat Disposals

The AQUIDNECK (YFB 14) was transferred to the State of Washington on 23 December 1975.

## 1 REFRIGERATED COVERED LIGHTER

| Number |
| --- |
| YFR 888 |

| | |
| --- | --- |
| Builders: | Defoe Shipbuilding Co, Bay City, Mich. |
| Displacement: | 610 tons full load |
| Length: | 132 feet (40.2 m) oa |
| Beam: | 30 feet (9.1 m) |
| Draft: | |
| Propulsion: | diesel; 600 bhp; 2 shafts |
| Speed: | 10 knots |
| Complement: | 11 (EM) |

This craft is of the same design as the Navy's surviving covered lighters (YF), but is provided with refrigerated cargo space. She is now laid up in reserve.

## 5 COVERED LIGHTERS (RANGE TENDER)

| Number | Number | Number | Number |
| --- | --- | --- | --- |
| YFRT 287 | YFRT 451 | YFRT 520 | YFRT 523 |
| YFRT 418 | | | |

| | | |
| --- | --- | --- |
| Builders: | YFRT 287 | Norfolk Navy Yard |
| | YFRT 418, 520, 523 | Erie Concrete and Steel Supply Co, Erie, Pa. |
| | YFRT 451 | Basalt Rock Co, Napa, Calif. |
| Displacement: | 650 tons full load | |
| Length: | 132½ feet (40.4 m) oa | |
| Beam: | 30 feet (9.1 m) | |
| Draft: | | |
| Propulsion: | diesel (Union except Cooper-Bessemer in YFRT 287); 600 bhp; 2 shafts | |
| Speed: | 10 knots | |
| Complement: | 11 (EM) | |

These craft are used for miscellaneous support purposes. They are YF-type craft, all completed during 1941–1945 (with some originally employed in the YF role). Cargo capacity was 250 tons. The YFRT 418 is laid up in reserve; the other units are active.

Classification: The YRFT 287 and 418 originally were classified as YF, with the same hull numbers; the YFRT 523 was the YF 852.

YFRT 520 (1969, U.S. Navy)

## 7 HARBOR UTILITY CRAFT: CONVERTED "LCU 1610" CLASS

| Number | Number | Number | Number |
| --- | --- | --- | --- |
| YFU 83 | YFU 97 | YFU 100 | YFU 102 |
| YFU 93 | YFU 98 | YFU 101 | |

| | |
| --- | --- |
| Builders: | |
| Displacement: | ~390 tons full load |
| Length: | 134¾ feet (41 m) oa |
| Beam: | 29¾ feet (9 m) |
| Draft: | 6 feet (1.8 m) |
| Propulsion: | geared diesels (Detroit); 2,000 bhp; 2 shafts |
| Speed: | 11 knots |
| Complement: | 6 (EM) |

Six of these craft are converted landing craft, with the YFU 83 having been built to the same design, specifically as a YFU. They carry cargo in coastal and harbor areas. All are active except the YFU 93 and 97, which are in reserve.

Class: YFU 99 was stricken on 15 November 1976.

Classification: Formerly LCU 1625, 1611, 1615, 1610, 1612, and 1642, respectively.

YFU 83 (1971, Defoe Shipbuilding Co)

## 10 HARBOR UTILITY CRAFT: "YFU 71" CLASS

| Number | Number | Number | Number |
| --- | --- | --- | --- |
| YFU 71 | YFU 74 | YFU 77 | YFU 82 |
| YFU 72 | YFU 75 | YFU 79 | |
| YFU 73 | YFU 76 | YFU 81 | |

| | |
| --- | --- |
| Builders: | Pacific Coast Engineering Co, Alameda, Calif. |
| Displacement: | |
| Length: | 125 feet (40.9 m) oa |
| Beam: | 36 feet (11.8 m) |
| Draft: | 7½ feet (2.4 m) |
| Propulsion: | diesels; 2 shafts |
| Speed: | 8 knots |
| Complement: | |

These craft were constructed specifically for use as coastal cargo craft in Vietnam. They were built to a modified commercial design, with 12 units (YFU 71–82) being completed in 1967–1968. Their cargo capacity is 300 tons. The YFU 71–77 and 80–82 were transferred to the U.S. Army in 1970 for use in South Vietnam; they were returned to the Navy in 1973. The YFU 82 is being modified for use as a research platform for the Naval Ocean System Center's facility at Long Beach, California. She will be mated forward with the barge YFN 816. The new craft probably will be assigned an IX classification. The YFU 73 and 81–82 are active; the others are laid up in reserve.

Guns: During their Vietnam service, these craft each had two or more .50-cal MG.

YFU 75 (1968, U.S. Navy)

### 1 HARBOR UTILITY CRAFT: CONVERTED "LCU 1466" CLASS

| Number |
| --- |
| YFU 50 |

| | |
| --- | --- |
| Builders: | |
| Displacement: | ~360 tons full load |
| Length: | 119 feet (39 m) oa |
| Beam: | 34 feet (10.4 m) |
| Draft: | 6 feet (1.8 m) |
| Propulsion: | geared diesels (Gray Marine); 675 bhp; 3 shafts |
| Speed: | 8 knots |
| Complement: | 6 (EM) |

The YFU 50 is a converted landing craft (formerly LCU 1486) employed in coastal and harbor cargo operations. The craft is in reserve.

### Harbor Utility Craft Disposals

Of the converted LCU 501 class, the YFU 55 (ex-LCU 637) was stricken on 1 July 1977; the YFU 44 (ex-LCU 1398), modified for research work, has been stripped and will be stricken (see YFU 82 listing for replacement).

### 16 FUEL OIL BARGES

| Number | Number | Number | Number |
| --- | --- | --- | --- |
| YO 106 | YO 202 | YO 223 | YO 241 |
| YO 129 | YO 203 | YO 224 | YO 257 |
| YO 171 | YO 205 | YO 225 | YO 264 |
| YO 174 | YO 219 | YO 228 | |
| YO 200 | YO 220 | YO 230 | |

| | |
| --- | --- |
| Builders: | YO 106, 174 Albina Engine and Machine Works, Portland, Ore. |
| | YO 129        Pensacola Shipyard and Engine Co, Fla. |
| | YO 171        R.T.C. Shipbuilding Co, Camden, N.J. |
| | YO 200–203 Manitowoc Shipbuilding Co, Wisc. |
| | YO 205        Smith Shipyards, Pensacola, Fla. |
| | YO 219–230 Jeffersonville Boat and Machinery Co, Ind. |
| | YO 241        John H. Mathis Co, Camden, N.J. |
| | YO 257        Puget Sound Navy Yard |
| | YO 264        Leatham D. Smith Co., Sturgeon Bay, Wisc. |
| Displacement: | 1,400 tons full load |
| Length: | 174 feet (53 m) oa |
| Beam: | 32 feet (9.8 m) |
| Draft: | 13⅓ feet (4.06 m) |
| Propulsion: | diesels; 560 shp; 1 shaft |
| Speed: | 10.5 knots |
| Complement: | 11 (EM) |

These are coastal and harbor tankers with a cargo capacity of 6,570 barrels. Thirteen of these craft are active, and five are in reserve (YO 171, 174, 228, 230, and 241).

Class: YO 205 was stricken on 15 June 1977; YO 219 stricken on 1 July 1977.

Classification: Three craft were originally classified as gasoline barges: YO 241 ex-YOG 5, YO 257 ex-YOG 72, and YO 264 ex-YOG 105.

YO-type service craft (1970, U.S. Navy)

## 1 FUEL OIL BARGE

| Number |
| --- |
| YO 153 |

| | |
| --- | --- |
| Builders: | Ira S. Bushey and Sons, Brooklyn |
| Displacement: | 1,076 tons full load |
| Length: | 156¼ feet (47.6 m) oa |
| Beam: | 30⁷/₁₂ feet (9.3 m) |
| Draft: | 11¾ feet (3.6 m) |
| Propulsion: | diesels (Fairbanks-Morse); 525 bhp; 1 shaft |
| Speed: | 10 knots |
| Complement: | 15 (EM) |

The YO 153 is the only survivor in U.S. service of a class of coastal and harbor tankers. Her cargo capacity is 6,000 barrels. The craft is laid up in reserve.

## 1 FUEL OIL BARGE

| Number | Name |
| --- | --- |
| YO 47 | CASING HEAD |

| | |
| --- | --- |
| Builders: | YO 47 Lake Superior Shipbuilding Co, Superior, Wisc. |
| Displacement: | 1,731 tons full load |
| Length: | 235 feet (71.6 m) oa |
| Beam: | 37 feet (11.3 m) |
| Draft: | 16½ feet (5 m) |
| Propulsion: | diesels (Enterprise); 2 shafts |
| Speed: | 9 knots |
| Complement: | |

This is a coastal gasoline carrier built in 1941. Its cargo capacity is 10,000 barrels. The CASING HEAD is in reserve.

Class: The CROWNBLOCK (YO 48) was stricken on 1 March 1977.

## 8 GASOLINE BARGES

| Number | Number | Number | Number |
| --- | --- | --- | --- |
| YOG 58 | YOG 78 | YOG 87 | YOG 93 |
| YOG 68 | YOG 79 | YOG 88 | YOG 196 |

| | |
| --- | --- |
| Builders: | YOG 58, 87–93 R.T.C. Shipbuilding Co, Camden, N.J. |
| | YOG 68 George Lawley and Sons, Neponset, Mass. |
| | YOG 78–79 Puget Sound Navy Yard |
| | YOG 196 Manitowoc Shipbuilding Co, Wisc. |
| Displacement: | |
| Length: | 174 feet (53 m) oa |
| Beam: | 32 feet (9.8 m) |
| Draft: | |
| Propulsion: | diesels; 640 bhp; 1 shaft |
| Speed: | |
| Complement: | |

These are self-propelled gasoline barges with a cargo capacity of 6,570 barrels. Four units are active and four are in reserve (YOG 58, 68, 79, 93).

Classification: The YOG 196 was originally classified YO 196.

## 19 + 3 SEAMANSHIP TRAINING CRAFT: "YP 654" CLASS

| Number | Number | Number | Number |
| --- | --- | --- | --- |
| YP 654 | YP 660 | YP 666 | YP 672 |
| YP 655 | YP 661 | YP 667 | (YP 673) |
| YP 656 | YP 662 | YP 668 | (YP 674) |
| YP 657 | YP 663 | YP 669 | (YP 675) |
| YP 658 | YP 664 | YP 670 | |
| YP 659 | YP 665 | YP 671 | |

| | |
| --- | --- |
| Builders: | YP 654–663 Stephen Brothers, Stockton, Calif. |
| | YP 664–665 Elizabeth City Shipbuilders, N.C. |
| | YP 666–672 Peterson Builders, Sturgeon Bay, Wisc. |
| Displacement: | 69.5 tons full load |
| Length: | 80⅓ feet (26.4 m) oa |
| Beam: | 18¾ feet (6.1 m) |
| Draft: | 5⅓ feet (1.7 m) |
| Propulsion: | diesels (General Motors); 660 bhp; 2 shafts |
| Speed: | 13.5 knots |
| Complement: | |

These craft are used for seamanship and navigation training at the Naval Academy in Annapolis, Maryland (YP 654–668) and at the Naval Officer Candidate School and Naval Surface Warfare Officers School, both in Newport, Rhode Island (YP 669–672). All could be armed with machine guns and employed as harbor patrol craft. There was $6 million provided for three additional YPs in FY 1977.

Design: These craft are wood with aluminum deckhouses. The YP 655 has oceanographic research equipment installed for instructional purposes. This design is SCB-139 (later SCB-800).

YP 659 (U.S. Navy)

YOG 196 (1977, Giorgio Arra)

## 8 SEAPLANE WRECKING DERRICKS: "YSD 11" CLASS

| Number | Number | Number | Number |
|--------|--------|--------|--------|
| YSD 34 | YSD 53 | YSD 63 | YSD 74 |
| YSD 39 | YSD 60 | YSD 72 | YSD 77 |

| | | |
|---|---|---|
| Builders: | YSD 34 | Charleston Navy Yard |
| | YSD 39 | Norfolk Navy Yard |
| | YSD 53 | Gulfport Boiler and Welding Works, Port Arthur, Texas |
| | YSD 60, 63 | Sonle Steel Co |
| | YSD 72 | Omaha Steel Works |
| | YSD 74 | Pearl Harbor Navy Yard |
| | YSD 77 | Missouri Valley Bridge and Iron Co, Leavenworth, Kansas |
| Displacement: | 270 tons full load | |
| Length: | 104 feet (31.7 m) oa | |
| Beam: | 31⅙ feet (9.5 m) | |
| Draft: | | |
| Propulsion: | diesels; 640 bhp; 1 shaft | |
| Speed: | 10 knots | |
| Complement: | 13–15 (EM) | |

These are small, self-propelled floating cranes completed in 1943–1944. They have 10-ton-capacity cranes. All are active. YSDs are called "Mary Anns."

YSD 63 (1977, Giorgio Arra)

KETCHIKAN (YTB-795) (U.S. Navy)

## 75 LARGE HARBOR TUGS: "YTB 760" CLASS

| Number | Name | Number | Name |
|--------|------|--------|------|
| YTB 760 | NATICK | YTB 800 | EUFAULA |
| YTB 761 | OTTUMWA | YTB 801 | PALATKA |
| YTB 762 | TUSCUMBIA | YTB 802 | CHERAW |
| YTB 763 | MUSKEGON | YTB 803 | NANTICOKE |
| YTB 764 | MISHAWAKA | YTB 804 | AHOSKIE |
| YTB 765 | OKMULGEE | YTB 805 | OCALA |
| YTB 766 | WAPAKONETA | YTB 806 | TUSKEGEE |
| YTB 767 | APALACHICOLA | YTB 807 | MASSAPEQUA |
| YTB 768 | ARCATA | YTB 808 | WEMATCHEE |
| YTB 769 | CHESANING | YTB 809 | AGAWAN |
| YTB 770 | DAHLONEGA | YTB 810 | ANOKA |
| YTB 771 | KEOKUK | YTB 811 | HOUMA |
| YTB 774 | NASHUA | YTB 812 | ACCOMAC |
| YTB 775 | WAUWATOSA | YTB 813 | POUGHKEEPSIE |
| YTB 776 | WEEHAWKEN | YTB 814 | WAXAHATCHIE |
| YTB 777 | NOGALES | YTB 815 | NEODESHA |
| YTB 778 | APOPKA | YTB 816 | CAMPTI |
| YTB 779 | MANHATTAN | YTB 817 | HYANNIS |
| YTB 780 | SAUGUS | YTB 818 | MECOSTA |
| YTB 781 | NIANTIC | YTB 819 | IUKA |
| YTB 782 | MANISTEE | YTB 820 | WANAMASSA |
| YTB 783 | REDWING | YTB 821 | TONTOGANY |
| YTB 784 | KALISPELL | YTB 822 | PAWHUSKA |
| YTB 785 | WINNEMUCCA | YTB 823 | CANONCHET |
| YTB 786 | TONKAWA | YTB 824 | SANTAQUIN |
| YTB 787 | KITTANNING | YTB 825 | WATHENA |
| YTB 788 | WAPATO | YTB 826 | WASHTUCNA |
| YTB 789 | TOMAHAWK | YTB 827 | CHETEK |
| YTB 790 | MENOMINEE | YTB 828 | CATAIIEOAGGA |
| YTB 791 | MARINETTE | YTB 829 | METACOM |
| YTB 792 | ANTIGO | YTB 830 | PUSHMATAHA |
| YTB 793 | PIQUA | YTB 831 | DEKANAWIDA |
| YTB 794 | MANDAN | YTB 832 | PETALESHARO |
| YTB 795 | KETCHIKAN | YTB 833 | SHABONEE |
| YTB 796 | SACO | YTB 834 | NEGWAGON |
| YTB 797 | TAMAQUA | YTB 835 | SKENANDOA |
| YTB 798 | OPELIKA | YTB 836 | POKAGON |
| YTB 799 | NATCHITOCHES | | |

| | |
|---|---|
| Builders: | Marinette Marine Corp, Wisc. |
| | Southern SB Corp, Slidell, La. |
| | Mobile Ship Repair Inc., Mobile, Ala. |
| Displacement: | 350–400 tons full load |
| Length: | 109 feet (35.7 m) oa |
| Beam: | 30½ feet (9.3 m) |
| Draft: | 13½ feet (4.1 m) |
| Propulsion: | diesels; 2,000 bhp; 2 shafts |
| Speed: | 12.5 knots |
| Complement: | 11–12 (EM) |

These tugs were completed during 1961–1975. (The similar YTB 837–838 were transferred to Saudi Arabia in 1975.) All of these tugs are in active service.

Design: SCB-147A. These and other Navy harbor tugs are used for towing and maneuvering ships in harbors and coastal waters. Their masts fold down to facilitate working alongside large ships. The tugs are also equipped for firefighting.

WATHENA (YTB 825) (1975, Giorgio Arra)

NASHUA (YTB 774) (1977, Giorgio Arra)

## 6 LARGE HARBOR TUGS: "YTB 752" CLASS

| Number | Name | Number | Name |
|--------|------|--------|------|
| YTB 752 | EDENSHAW | YTB 757 | OSHKOSH |
| YTB 753 | MARIN | YTB 758 | PADUCAH |
| YTB 756 | PONTIAC | YTB 759 | BOGALUSA |

| | |
|--|--|
| Builders: | YTB 752–753 Christy Corp, Sturgeon Bay, Wisc. |
| | YTB 756–759 Southern Shipbuilding Corp, Slidell, La. |
| Displacement: | 341 tons full load |
| Length: | 85 feet (25.9 m) oa |
| Beam: | 24 feet (7.3 m) |
| Draft: | 13¼ feet (4 m) |
| Propulsion: | diesel; 1 shaft |
| Speed: | |
| Complement: | 10–12 (EM) |

These tugs were completed in 1960–1961. Their design is SCB-147. All are active.

MASCOUTAH (YTM 760), left, and BOGALUSA (YTB 759) (1971, U.S. Navy, PH2 C. Velasquez)

PADUCAH (YTB 758) with JOHN F. KENNEDY (CV 67) (U.S. Navy)

## 9 SMALL HARBOR TUGS: "YTL 422" CLASS

| Number | Number | Number | Number |
|---|---|---|---|
| YTL 422 | YTL 435 | YTL 558 | YTL 588 |
| YTL 431 | YTL 438 | YTL 583 | YTL 602 |
| YTL 434 | | | |

| | | |
|---|---|---|
| Builders: | YTL 422, 431, 434, 558 | Everett-Pacific Shipbuilding and DD, Wash. |
| | YTL 435, 583, 588 | Bellingham Iron Works, Wash. |
| | YTL 438, 602 | Robert Jacob, Inc., City Island, N.Y. |
| Displacement: | 80 tons full load | |
| Length: | 66⅛ feet (20.2 m) oa | |
| Beam: | 17 feet (5.2 m) | |
| Draft: | 4¹¹/₁₂ feet (1.5 m) | |
| Propulsion: | diesel; 300 bhp; 1 shaft | |
| Speed: | 10 knots | |
| Complement: | 5 (EM) | |

These are the survivors of several hundred small tugs built during World War II. Six are active and three are in reserve (YTL 422, 435, 583).

Classification: These craft originally were classified as YT with the same hull numbers. YTL originally was "little" harbor tug.

## 1 MEDIUM HARBOR TUG: FORMER ARMY TUG

| Number | Name |
|---|---|
| YTM 748 | YUMA |

| | |
|---|---|
| Builder: | National Steel and Shipbuilding Co, San Diego |
| Displacement: | 470 tons full load |
| Length: | 107 feet (32.6 m) oa |
| Beam: | 26½ feet (8 m) |
| Draft: | 14⅚ feet (4.5 m) |
| Propulsion: | diesel; 1,200 bhp; 1 shaft |
| Speed: | 12 knots |
| Complement: | 8 (EM) |

The YUMA is the former Army tug LT 2078. The craft is in reserve.

Class: The former Army tug LT 2077 was acquired as the YTM 759; she was changed to IX 505 on 1 November 1975 to support research activities; and was stricken on 1 December 1977. No name was assigned to her during her Navy service.

## 2 MEDIUM HARBOR TUGS: "YTM 760" CLASS

| Number | Name | Number | Name |
|---|---|---|---|
| YTM 760 | MASCOUTAH | YTM 761 | MENASHA |

| | |
|---|---|
| Builders: | Jacobson Shipyard, Oyster Bay, N.Y. |
| Displacement: | ~200 tons full load |
| Length: | 85 feet (25.9 m) oa |
| Beam: | 24 feet (7.3 m) |
| Draft: | 11 feet (3.4 m) |
| Propulsion: | diesels; 2 cycloidial propellers |
| Speed: | 12 knots |
| Complement: | 12 (EM) |

These tugs were built to an experimental design with cycloidial propellers which provide a high degree of maneuverability and enable them to turn 360° within their length. Both units are active.

Classification: These tugs were built as YTB 772–773, respectively; they were changed to YTM 760–761 in September 1965.

MENASHA (YTM 761) (1976, U.S. Navy, Richard A. Banks)

## 7 MEDIUM HARBOR TUGS: "YTM 174" CLASS

| Number | Name | Number | Name |
|---|---|---|---|
| YTM 176 | JUNALUSKA | YTM 381 | CHEPANOC |
| YTM 252 | DEKANISORA | YTM 382 | COATOPA |
| YTM 359 | PAWTUCKET | YTM 383 | COCHALI |
| YTM 380 | CHANAGI | | |

| | |
|---|---|
| Builders: | Gulfport Boiler and Welding Works, Port Arthur, Texas |
| Displacement: | ~200 tons full load |
| Length: | 102 feet (31.1 m) oa |
| Beam: | 25 feet (7.6 m) |
| Draft: | 10 feet (3 m) |
| Propulsion: | diesel; 1,000 bhp; 1 shaft |
| Speed: | 12 knots |
| Complement: | 8 (EM) |

Three units of this class are active (YTM 252, 359, 380); the others are in reserve.

Classification: These tugs were originally classified YT; changed to large harbor tugs (YTB) in 1944 and reclassified as YTM on 1 February 1962.

## 55 MEDIUM HARBOR TUGS: "YTM 138" CLASS

| Number | Name | Number | Name |
|---|---|---|---|
| YTM 149 | TOKA | YTM 417 | TACONNET |
| YTM 151 | KONOKA | YTM 496 | CHAHAO |
| YTM 178 | DEKAURY | YTM 519 | MAHOA |
| YTM 180 | MADOKAWANDO | YTM 521 | NABIGWON |
| YTM 189 | NEPANET | YTM 522 | SAGAWAMICK |
| YTM 265 | HIAWATHA | YTM 523 | SENASQUA |
| YTM 268 | RED CLOUD | YTM 524 | TUTAHACO |
| YTM 359 | PAWTUCKET | YTM 526 | WAHAKA |
| YTM 364 | SASSABA | YTM 527 | WAHPETON |
| YTM 366 | WAUBANSEE | YTM 534 | NADLI |
| YTM 390 | GANADOGA | YTM 536 | NAHOKE |
| YTM 391 | ITARA | YTM 542 | CHEGODOEGA |
| YTM 392 | MECOSTA | YTM 543 | ETAWINA |
| YTM 393 | NAKARNA | YTM 544 | YATANOCAS |
| YTM 394 | WINAMAC | YTM 545 | ACCOHANOC |
| YTM 395 | WINGINA | YTM 546 | TAKOS |
| YTM 397 | YANEGUA | YTM 547 | YANABA |
| YTM 398 | NATAHKI | YTM 548 | MATUNAK |
| YTM 399 | NUMA | YTM 549 | MIGADAN |
| YTM 400 | OTOKOMI | YTM 701 | ACOMA |
| YTM 402 | PANAMETA | YTM 702 | ARAWAK |
| YTM 403 | PITAMAKAN | YTM 704 | MORATOC |
| YTM 404 | COSHECTON | YTM 768 | APOHOLA |
| YTM 405 | CUSSETA | YTM 770 | MIMAC |
| YTM 406 | KITTATON | YTM 776 | HIAMONEE |
| YTM 409 | ANAMOSA | YTM 777 | LELAKA |
| YTM 413 | POROBAGO | YTM 779 | POCASSET |
| YTM 415 | SECOTA | | |

Builders:       Defoe Boiler & Machine Works, Bay City, Mich.; Gibbs Gas Engine Co, Jacksonville, Fla.; Pacific Coast Engineering Co, Oakland, Calif.; Gulfport Boiler & Welding Works, Port Arthur, Texas; Consolidated SB Corp, Morris Heights, N.Y.; Ira S. Bushey & Sons, Brooklyn, N.Y.; Coast Guard Yard, Curtis Bay, Md.; Bethlehem Steel Co, San Pedro, Calif.; Commercial Iron Works, Portland, Ore.
Displacement:
Length:         100 feet (30.5 m) oa
Beam:           25 feet (7.6 m)
Draft:          9⁷/₁₂–10 feet (2.9–3 m)
Propulsion:     diesel; 805–1,200 bhp; 1 shaft
Speed:          11–14 knots
Complement:

These are harbor tugs employed at most U.S. naval bases. Plans to construct additional YTMs (initially YTM 800–802, authorized in FY 1973) were dropped in favor of additional YTB construction. Most units are active; the following ten are in reserve: YTM 265, 268, 390, 392, 393, 398, 403, 496, 532, and 546. All were built in 1940–1945.

Classification: These craft originally were classified as harbor tugs, with those through YTM 704 retaining their original YTB hull number. The YTM 768 and later units were numbered sequentially from YTB 501 onward.

## 11 WATER BARGES

| Number | Number | Number | Number |
|---|---|---|---|
| YW 83 | YW 101 | YW 119 | YW 127 |
| YW 86 | YW 108 | YW 123 | YW 128 |
| YW 98 | YW 113 | YW 126 | |

Builders:       YW 83           John H. Mathis Co, Camden, N.J.
                YW 86, 108      Zenith Dredge Co, Duluth, Minn.
                YW 98           George Lawley and Sons, Neponset, Mass.
                YW 101          Mare Island Navy Yard
                YW 113          Marine Iron and Shipbuilding Co, Duluth, Minn.
                YW 119          Henry C. Grebe and Co, Chicago
                YW 123, 126–128 Leathem D. Smith Shipbuilding Co, Sturgeon Bay, Wisc.
Displacement:   1,235 tons full load
Length:         174 feet (53 m) oa
Beam:           32 feet (9.7 m)
Draft:          15 feet (4.6 m)
Propulsion:     diesel; 560 bhp; 1 shaft
Speed:          8 knots
Complement:

These craft are similar to the YO/YOG types, but are employed to carry fresh water. Cargo capacity is 200,000 gallons. Three craft are active (YW 113, 119, 123); the remainder are in reserve.

ETAWINA (YTM 543) (1975, Giorgio Arra)

YW 119 (1976, Giorgio Arra)

## 2 RESEARCH CRAFT: "ASHEVILLE CLASS"

| Number | Name | Launched | PGM Commission | Status |
|--------|------|----------|----------------|--------|
| (ex-PG 94) | ATHENA | 8 June 1968 | 8 Nov 1969 | **AA** |
| (ex-PG 98) | ex-GRAND RAPIDS | 4 Apr 1970 | 5 Sep 1970 | **AA** |

| | |
|---|---|
| Builders: | Tacoma Boatbuilding Co, Wash. |
| Displacement: | ~245 tons full load |
| Length: | 164½ feet (50.1 m) oa |
| Beam: | 23¾ feet (7.3 m) |
| Draft: | 9½ feet (2.9 m) |
| Propulsion: | 2 diesels (Cummins), 1,750 bhp; 1 gas turbine (General Electric), 14,000 shp; 2 shafts (controllable-pitch propellers) |
| Speed: | 16 knots on diesels; 40+ knots on gas turbine |
| Complement: | |
| Armament: | removed |

These are former ASHEVILLE-class patrol combatants/gunboats. They were transferred to the Naval Ship Research and Development Center on 21 August 1975 and 3 October 1977, respectively, for use in towing high-speed underwater shapes in research and development programs. The ATHENA is based at Panama City, Florida.

Classification: No hull classifications are assigned in their current role.

Names: The ATHENA was renamed in 1975; she was formerly the CHEHALIS.

ATHENA (U.S. Navy)

## 1 DRONE RECOVERY CRAFT: FORMER MOTOR TORPEDO BOAT

| Number | Name | Launched | PT in Service | Status |
|--------|------|----------|---------------|--------|
| (ex-PT 809) | DR-1 | 7 Aug 1950 | 1950 | **AA** |

| | |
|---|---|
| Builders: | Electric Boat Co, Groton, Conn. |
| Displacement: | |
| Length: | 98 feet (29.9 m) oa |
| Beam: | 26 feet (7.9 m) |
| Draft: | 6 feet (1.8 m) |
| Propulsion: | 4 gasoline engines (Packard); 10,000 hp; 4 shafts |
| Speed: | 40+ knots |
| Complement: | |
| Armament: | removed |

The DR-1 was originally one of four experimental torpedo boats (PT 809–812) built as possible prototypes for post-World War II PT-boats (see Chapter 16). After extensive trials and limited service, the PT 809 was laid up in reserve. She was subsequently reactivated and employed to carry Secret Service agents screening the Presidential yacht on the Potomac River (based at the Washington Navy Yard); the craft was named the GUARDIAN in that role.

In December 1974 the craft was transferred to Fleet Composite Squadron 6 at Little Creek, Virginia, for operation as a recovery boat for aerial drones and a control boat for surface target drone craft. She was named DR-1 (for Drone Recovery) on 1 July 1975.

Design: The DR-1 is all-aluminum construction.

DR-1 (1975, Giorgio Arra)

## 1 RANGE SUPPORT SHIP: SWATH DESIGN

| Number | Name | Launched | In service | Status |
|--------|------|----------|------------|--------|
| (SSP) | KAIMALINO | 7 Mar 1973 | 1973 | **PA** |

| | |
|---|---|
| Builders: | Coast Guard Yard, Curtis Bay, Md. |
| Displacement: | 190 tons full load |
| Length: | 88 feet (26.8 m) oa |
| Beam: | 45 feet (13.7 m) |
| Draft: | |
| Propulsion: | 2 gas turbines (General Electric); 4,200 shp; 2 shafts |
| Speed: | 25 knots |
| Complement: | 5–7 |
| Armament: | none |

The Stable Semi-submerged Platform (SSP) KAIMALINO is an experimental design craft employed in the range support role at the Naval Ocean Surveillance Center's underwater test range in Hawaii.

Aircraft: The KAIMALINO has been used extensively to test the feasibility of landing helicopters on an SSP/SWATH-type ship in high seas at speeds up to 25 knots.

Design: The SSP is a Small Waterplane Area Twin-Hull (SWATH) craft developed to test this hull concept with craft of about 200 tons. The SWATH has two fully submerged torpedo-shaped hulls with struts penetrating the water surface to support the superstructure and flight deck. This concept differs from that of a catamaran which has two conventional ship hulls. The SWATH design provides a comparatively large deck area with a minimum of heave, pitch, and roll. In a sea state 4 the ship acts about the same as a conventional destroyer would in a sea state 6. Tests indicate the SWATH design will be suitable for ships up to about 20,000 tons. Ship motion in seas up to state 10 is considered minimal.

The KAIMALINO has a hull-stabilizing fin connecting her two submerged hulls and two small canard fins forward, one inboard on each hull. There is an opening in the craft's main deck for lowering research and recovery devices. This opening was covered over for the helicopter tests. The beam listed is the maximum over both torpedo-shape hulls.

Engineering: She is fitted with T64 aircraft-type gas turbines.

KAIMALINO under construction (1973, U.S. Navy)

KAIMALINO with SH-2 LAMPS (1976, U.S. Navy)

KAIMALINO (1973, U.S. Navy)

# 20 Submersibles

Several submersibles are operated by the U.S. Navy to support search, rescue, research, and deep-ocean recovery programs. These craft also have been used to maintain sea-floor test range and surveillance equipment, according to published reports of their activities.

Except for the NR-1 and the ALVIN, all of the Navy-operated Deep Submergence Vehicles (DSV) are assigned to Submarine Development Group 1 at Point Loma (San Diego), California. SubDevGru-1 was established on 12 August 1967 from the former Deep Submergence Group which had operated the TRIESTE.

## 1 NUCLEAR-PROPELLED RESEARCH SUBMERSIBLE: "NR-1"

| Number | Name | Launched | Completed | Status |
|--------|------|----------|-----------|--------|
| NR-1 | (none) | 25 Jan 1969 | 1969 | **AA** |

| | |
|---|---|
| Builders: | General Dynamics (Electric Boat) |
| Displacement: | |
| | 400 tons submerged |
| Length: | 136⁵/₁₂ feet (41.6 m) oa |
| Beam: | 12⁵/₁₂ feet (3.8 m) |
| Draft: | 12 feet (3.7 m) |
| Propulsion: | electric motors; 2 shafts |
| Reactors: | 1 pressurized-water |
| Speed: | |
| Operating depth: | ~3,000 feet (914.4 m) |
| Complement: | 5 (2 O + 3 EM) + 2 scientists |

The NR-1 was built as a test platform for a small submarine nuclear power plant. The craft has a deep-ocean research and recovery capability. The craft was funded from nuclear-propulsion

In addition to DSVs, SubDevGru-1 is assigned the research submarine DOLPHIN (AGSS 555), the TRIESTE support ship POINT LOMA (AGDS 2), the research submarine SEAWOLF (SSN 575), the attack submarine PARCHE (SSN 683), and the submarine rescue ships FLORIKAN (ASR 9) and PIGEON (ASR 21). The range-diving support ship ELK RIVER (IX 501), which supports SubDevGru-1 activities, is assigned to the Naval Ocean Systems Center on Point Loma.

The NR-1 is operated by Submarine Squadron 2 at New London, Connecticut, and the ALVIN by the Woods Hole Oceanographic Institution in Massachusetts.

research funds and was laid down on 10 June 1967. She is commanded by an officer-in-charge rather than a commanding officer.

Classification: NR-1 indicates Nuclear Research vehicle.

Costs: The estimated cost of the NR-1 in 1965 was $30 million, using "state of the art" equipment. Subsequently, specialized equipment had to be developed and a hull larger than the one originally intended was designed, with Congressional approval of a cost of $58 million being given in 1967. The final estimated cost of the NR-1 was $67.5 million plus $19.9 million for oceanographic equipment and sensors, and $11.8 million for research and development, associated mainly with the nuclear plant.

Design: The NR-1 does not have periscopes but instead has a fixed mast with a top-mounted television camera. The craft is fitted with external lights, a remote-control manipulator, and recovery devices.

Engineering: The NR-1 is propelled by twin propellers driven by electric motors outside of the pressure hull. Four ducted thrusters, two horizontal and two vertical, give the NR-1 a capability for precise maneuvering.

NR-1 (1976, U.S. Navy, Jean Pellegrino)

NR-1 at launching (1969, General Dynamics/Electric Boat)

NR-1 at launching (1969, General Dynamics/Electric Boat)

## 2 DEEP SUBMERGENCE RESCUE VEHICLES

| Number | Name | Launched | Completed | Status |
|--------|------|----------|-----------|--------|
| DSRV-1 | MYSTIC | 24 Jan 1970 | 6 Aug 1971 | **PA** |
| DSRV-2 | AVALON | 1 May 1971 | 28 July 1972 | **PA** |

| | |
|---|---|
| Builders: | Lockheed Missiles and Space Co, Sunnyvale, Calif. |
| Weight: | 37 tons |
| Length: | 49⅔ feet (15 m) oa |
| Diameter: | 8 feet (2.4 m) |
| Propulsion: | electric motor; 1 propeller-mounted in control shroud (see Engineering notes) |
| Speed: | 4 knots |
| Operating depth: | 5,000 feet (1,524 m) |
| Complement: | 3 + 24 rescuees |

These submersibles were developed after the loss of the submarine THRESHER (SSN 593) in 1963, to provide a capability for rescuing survivors from submarines disabled on the ocean floor above their hull-collapse depth. Initially 12 rescue vehicles were planned, each capable of carrying 12 survivors. Subsequently, their capacity was increased to 24 survivors and the proposed number of DSRVs was reduced to six. Only two have been built and no additional units are planned. After extensive tests and evaluation, both DSRVs were declared fully operational in late 1977.

Costs: The estimated construction cost of the DSRV 1 was $41 million, and DSRV-2 cost $23 million. The total development, construction, test, and support for these craft have cost in excess of $220 million.

Design: Each DSRV consists of three interconnected personnel spheres, each 7½ feet in diameter, constructed of HY-140 steel, encased in a fiberglass-reinforced plastic shell. The forward sphere contains the vehicle's controls and is manned by the pilot and copilot; the center and after spheres can accommodate 24 survivors and a third crewman.

The DSRV is configured to be launched and recovered by a submerged attack submarine or by a PIGEON-class (ASR 21) submarine rescue ship. After launching, the DSRV can descend to the disabled submarine, "mate" with one of the submarine's escape hatches, take on board up to 24 survivors, and return to the "mother" submarine or ASR. The submersible can be air-transported in C-141 aircraft, and ground-transported by a special trailer. It is fitted with a remote control manipulator.

Electronics: The DSRV is fitted with elaborate search and navigation sonars, closed-circuit television, and optical viewing devices for locating a disabled submarine and mating with the hatches.

Engineering: The DSRVs have a single propeller driven by a 15 hp electric motor for forward propulsion. The propeller is in a rotating control shroud which alleviates the need for rudders and diving planes (which could interfere with a rescue mission). Four ducted thrusters, two vertical and two horizontal, each powered by a 7½ hp electric motor, provide precise maneuvering. The craft has an endurance of five hours at a speed of 4 knots.

Names: Names were assigned in 1977.

AVALON, with "mating skirt" removed, on air-road transportable trailer (U.S. Navy)

MYSTIC on the HAWKBILL (SSN 666) (1971, U.S. Navy)

## 2 RESEARCH SUBMERSIBLES: MODIFIED "ALVIN" CLASS

| Number | Name | Launched | Completed | Status |
|--------|------|----------|-----------|--------|
| DSV-3 | TURTLE | 11 Dec 1968 | 1969 | **PA** |
| DSV-4 | SEA CLIFF | 11 Dec 1968 | 1969 | **PA** |

| | |
|---|---|
| Builders: | General Dynamics (Electric Boat) |
| Weight: | 21 tons |
| Length: | 26 feet (7.9 m) oa |
| Beam: | 8 feet (2.4 m); 12 feet (3.7 m) over propeller pods |
| Propulsion: | electric motor; 1 propeller (see Engineering notes) |
| Speed: | 2.5 knots |
| Operating depth: | 6,500 feet (1,980 m) |
| Complement: | 2 + 1 scientist |

These are small submersibles used for deep-ocean research. They were constructed using a test sphere and replacement sphere originally built for the ALVIN program.

Classification: These craft were designated DSV-3 and -4 on 1 June 1971.

Design: These craft have a single, 7-foot-diameter pressure sphere made of HY-100 steel. They are fitted with closed-circuit television, external lights, sonars, cameras, and two hydraulic remote-control manipulators.

The TURTLE's sphere is scheduled to be modified in 1979 for 10,000 foot operations and the SEA CLIFF is scheduled to be fitted with a titanium sphere for 20,000-foot operations in 1981–1982.

Engineering: A single stern propeller is fitted for ahead propulsion and two pod-mounted external electric motors rotate for maneuvering. (No thrusters are fitted.) Endurance is one hour at 2.5 knots and eight hours at 1 knot.

Names: During construction these submersibles were named the AUTEC I and II, respectively, because they were to be on the Atlantic Undersea Test and Evaluation Center. The names TURTLE and SEA CLIFF were assigned at launching.

SEA CLIFF (U.S. Navy)

SEA CLIFF being loaded in C-5A transport (U.S. Navy)

## 1 RESEARCH SUBMERSIBLE: "ALVIN"

| Number | Name | Launched | Completed | Status |
|--------|------|----------|-----------|--------|
| DSV-2 | ALVIN | 1964 | 1965 | **Academic** |

| | |
|---|---|
| Builders: | General Mills Inc, Minneapolis, Minn. |
| Weight: | 16 tons |
| Length: | 22½ feet (6.9 m) oa |
| Beam: | 8 feet (2.4 m); 12 feet (3.7 m) over propeller pods |
| Propulsion: | electric motor; 1 propeller (see Engineering notes) |
| Speed: | 2 knots |
| Operating depth: | 12,000 feet (3,658 m) |
| Complement: | 1 + 2 scientists |

The ALVIN is operated by the Woods Hole Oceanographic Institution for the Office of Naval Research, which sponsored construction of the craft.

The ALVIN accidentally sank in 5,051 feet of water on 16 October 1968 and her sphere was flooded (there were no casualties). She was raised in August 1969 and refurbished from May 1971 to October 1972, and became operational in November 1972.

Classification: Classified DSV-2 on 1 June 1971.

Design: As built, the ALVIN had a single, 7-foot-diameter pressure sphere made of HY-100 steel, which gave her a 6,000-foot operating depth. She was refitted with a titanium sphere in 1971–1972, which increased her capabilities. She is fitted with a remote-control manipulator.

Engineering: See the TURTLE and SEA CLIFF for propulsion and maneuvering arrangement.

ALVIN (U.S. Navy)

## 1 BATHYSCAPH RESEARCH VEHICLE: "TRIESTE"

| Number | Name | Launched | Completed | Status |
|--------|------|----------|-----------|--------|
| DSV-1 | TRIESTE II | (see comments) | 1966 | **PA** |

| | |
|---|---|
| Builders: | Mare Island Naval Shipyard |
| Displacement: | 84 tons surface (empty) |
| | 300 tons submerged |
| Length: | 78 feet (23.8 m) oa |
| Beam: | 15 feet (4.6 m); 18¾ feet (5.7 m) over propeller pods |
| Propulsion: | electric motors; 3 propeller pods aft |
| Speed: | 2 knots |
| Operating depth: | 20,000 feet (6,096 m) |
| Complement: | 2 + 1 scientist |

The TRIESTE is the U.S. Navy's only "bathyscaph" (from the Greek for "deep boat") designed to travel straight up and down in the water rather than maneuver like a submarine.

The original TRIESTE was built by August Piccard in Italy and launched on 1 August 1953. That vehicle was acquired by the Navy in 1958 and, piloted by Lieutenant Don Walsh, USN, and Jacques Piccard, reached a depth of 35,800 feet on 23 January 1960. The craft was rebuilt in 1963–1964 at the Mare Island Naval Shipyard, with a new sphere replacing the deep-dive Krupp chamber and a new float provided. In this configuration the craft was renamed TRIESTE II. The craft was again rebuilt in 1965–1966 and modified in 1967, all at Mare Island. Thus, the current vehicle is the "third generation–plus" bathyscaph.

The TRIESTE II is transported and supported by the POINT LOMA (AGDS 2).

Classification: The TRIESTE originally was classified as an unnumbered "submersible craft." She was assigned the hull number

TRIESTE II (U.S. Navy)

X-2 on 1 September 1969 and was subsequently changed to DSV-1 on 1 June 1971. (The X-1 was an unnamed midget submarine, the only craft of this type built for the U.S. Navy. The X-1 was stricken on 16 February 1973.)

Design: The TRIESTE II has a single, 7-foot-diameter pressure sphere, made of HY-120 steel. Originally rated for 12,000 feet, with the updating of certain subsystems the sphere and vehicle are now capable of 20,000-foot operations. The sphere is mounted at the bottom of a float-like hull which is filled with aviation gasoline to provide buoyancy. External lights, sonars, cameras, and a remote-control manipulator are fitted to the bottom of the float. "Leg"-like structures on each side of the sphere prevent it from sinking into the ocean floor and blocking the viewport (forward).

Engineering: The craft has three 6.5-hp electric motor pods at her stern for propulsion and limited maneuvering, and one 6.5-hp bow thruster for holding position in currents and for precise maneuvering. Her endurance is eight hours at two knots.

Names: The TRIESTE was Piccard's name for the original craft.

TRIESTE II (U.S. Navy)

# 21 Floating Dry Docks

The Navy operates floating dry docks at several bases in the United States and overseas for the repair and maintenance of ships. These are non-self-propelled docks, but all have generating plants to produce electricity for their equipment. Normally they operate with a flotilla of non-self-propelled barges that provide specialized services, including messing and berthing for the dry docks' crews when necessary.

The floating dry docks are arranged in this chapter in alphabetical order according to their classification. Technically they are considered service craft. Sectional docks are indicated by an asterisk (*). Unless otherwise indicated, all sectional docks are assembled.

These docks in active Navy service have their locations indicated; several others are operated by commercial firms under lease from the Navy, and the Coast Guard has one Navy dock at its shipyard. The docks on commercial lease are not included in type totals. The Army has one section of a multi-section dock employed at a Pacific island facility.

Guns: No floating dry docks are armed, although several types were designed to mount light antiaircraft guns.

Names: Several dry docks are named; those which support strategic missile submarines at four Polaris/Poseidon bases have been named for locations related to atomic energy development, as have some other docks.

## 6 LARGE AUXILIARY FLOATING DRY DOCKS

| Number | Name | Completed | Lengtha | Width | Capacity | Constructic | Status | Notes |
|--------|------|-----------|---------|-------|----------|-------------|--------|-------|
| AFDB 1* | | 1943 | 927 ft (282.5 m) | 256 ft (78 m) | 40,000 tons | steel | Subic Bay, Philippines | 6 sections; ex-ABSD 1 |
| AFDB 1* | | 1943 | | | 60,000 tons | steel | reserve | 4 sections |
| AFDB 2* | | 1944 | 927 ft (282.5 m) | 256 ft (78 m) | 90,000 tons | steel | reserve | 10 sections; ex-ABSD 2 |
| AFDB 3* | | 1944 | 844 ft (257.3 m) | 256 ft (78 m) | 81,000 tons | steel | reserve | 9 sections; ex-ABSD 3 |
| AFDB 4* | | 1944 | 825 ft (251.5 m) | 240 ft (73.2 m) | 55,000 tons | steel | reserve | 7 sections; ex-ABSD 4 |
| AFDB 5* | | 1944 | 825 ft (251.5 m) | 240 ft (73.2 m) | 55,000 tons | steel | reserve | 7 sections; ex-ABSD 5 |
| AFDB 7* | | 1944 | 825 ft (251.5 m) | 240 ft (73.2 m) | 20,000 tons | steel | reserve | 2 sections; ex-ABSD 7 |
| AFDB 7* | Los Alamos | 1945 | | | 40,000 tons | steel | Holy Loch, Scotland | 4 sections |

aall sections assembled

These docks formerly were classified as Advanced Base Sectional Docks (ABSD). They consist of 256- or 240-feet sections, about 80 feet wide with wing walls 83 feet high. The walls house accommodations, machinery, and storage spaces, and fold down for towing. The docks are assembled by the sections being connected side by side. The overall length of the assembled docks include a 50-foot outrigger at each end.

Names: Only one AFDB is named.

WHITE PLAINS (AFS 4) in AFDB 1 (1975, U.S. Navy, PH1 R. H. Green)

ABRAHAM LINCOLN (SSBN 602) in AFDB 7 at Holy Loch, Scotland (U.S. Navy)

## 9 SMALL AUXILIARY FLOATING DRY DOCKS

| Number | Completed | Length | Width | Capacity | Construction | Status | Notes |
|---|---|---|---|---|---|---|---|
| AFDL 1 | 1943 | 200 ft (61 m) | 64 ft (19.5 m) | 1,000 tons | steel | Guantanamo Bay, Cuba | ex-AFD 1 |
| AFDL 2 | 1943 | 200 ft (61 m) | 64 ft (19.5 m) | 1,000 tons | steel | lease | ex-AFD 2 |
| AFDL 6 | 1944 | 200 ft (61 m) | 64 ft (19.5 m) | 1,000 tons | steel | Little Creek, Va. | ex-AFD 6 |
| AFDL 7 | 1944 | 288 ft (87.8 m) | 64 ft (19.5 m) | 1,900 tons | steel | reserve | |
| AFDL 8 | 1943 | 200 ft (61 m) | 64 ft (19.5 m) | 1,000 tons | steel | lease | ex-AFD 8 |
| AFDL 9 | 1943 | 200 ft (61 m) | 64 ft (19.5 m) | 1,000 tons | steel | lease | ex-AFD 9 |
| AFDL 10 | 1943 | 200 ft (61 m) | 64 ft (19.5 m) | 1,000 tons | steel | Subic Bay, Philippines | ex-AFD 10 |
| AFDL 12 | 1943 | 200 ft (61 m) | 64 ft (19.5 m) | 1,000 tons | steel | lease | ex-AFD 12 |
| AFDL 15 | 1943 | 200 ft (61 m) | 64 ft (19.5 m) | 1,000 tons | steel | lease | ex-AFD 15 |
| AFDL 16 | 1943 | 200 ft (61 m) | 64 ft (19.5 m) | 1,000 tons | steel | lease | ex-AFD 16 |
| AFDL 19 | 1944 | 200 ft (61 m) | 64 ft (19.5 m) | 1,000 tons | steel | lease | ex-AFD 19 |
| AFDL 21 | 1944 | 200 ft (61 m) | 64 ft (19.5 m) | 1,000 tons | steel | Guam, Marianas | ex-AFD 21 |
| AFDL 23 | 1944 | 288 ft (87.8 m) | 64 ft (19.5 m) | 1,900 tons | steel | Subic Bay, Philippines | |
| AFDL 25 | 1944 | 200 ft (61 m) | 64 ft (19.5 m) | 1,000 tons | steel | reserve | ex-AFD 25 |
| AFDL 29 | 1943 | 200 ft (61 m) | 64 ft (19.5 m) | 1,000 tons | steel | lease | ex-AFD 29 |
| AFDL 30 | 1944 | 200 ft (61 m) | 64 ft (19.5 m) | 1,000 tons | steel | lease | ex-AFD 30 |
| AFDL 35 | 1944 | 389 ft (118.6 m) | 84 ft (25.6 m) | 2,800 tons | concrete | reserve | ex-ARDC 2 |
| AFDL 37 | 1944 | 389 ft (118.6 m) | 84 ft (25.6 m) | 2,800 tons | concrete | lease | ex-ARDC 4 |
| AFDL 38 | 1944 | 389 ft (118.6 m) | 84 ft (25.6 m) | 2,800 tons | concrete | lease | ex-ARDC 5 |
| AFDL 40 | 1944 | 389 ft (118.6 m) | 84 ft (25.6 m) | 2,800 tons | concrete | lease | ex-ARDC 7 |
| AFDL 41 | 1944 | 389 ft (118.6 m) | 84 ft (25.6 m) | 2,800 tons | concrete | lease | ex-ARDC 8 |
| AFDL 43 | 1944 | 389 ft (118.6 m) | 84 ft (25.6 m) | 2,800 tons | concrete | lease | ex-ARDC 10 |
| AFDL 45 | 1944 | 389 ft (118.6 m) | 84 ft (25.6 m) | 2,800 tons | concrete | lease | ex-ARDC 12 |
| AFDL 47 | 1946 | | | 6,500 tons | steel | lease | |
| AFDL 48 | 1956 | | | 4,000 tons | concrete | Long Beach | |

Most of these docks originally were classified as Auxiliary Floating Docks (AFD) or Auxiliary Repair Docks—Concrete (ARDC).

Class: AFDL 26 stricken 1 September 1976 (transferred to Paraguay).

AFDL 21 under tow (U.S. Navy)

AFDL 6 (1976, Giorgio Arra)

AFDL 7 in reserve (U.S. Navy)

Strategic missile submarine base in action: In foreground the floating dry dock OAK RIDGE (ARDM 1) docks an SSBN; in the background the CANOPUS (AS 34), arriving, and the HOLLAND (AS 32) at Rota, Spain. Submarine Squadron 16, based at Rota, will shift to King's Bay, Georgia, in 1979. (1966, U.S. Navy)

**4 MEDIUM AUXILIARY FLOATING DRY DOCKS**

| Number | Name | Completed | Lengthª | Width | Capacity | Construction | Status | Notes |
|--------|------|-----------|---------|-------|----------|--------------|--------|-------|
| AFDM 1* | | 1942 | 544 ft (165.8 m) | 116 ft (35.4 m) | 15,000 tons | steel | lease | 3 sections; ex-YFD 3 |
| AFDM 2* | | 1942 | 544 ft (165.8 m) | 116 ft (35.4 m) | 15,000 tons | steel | lease | 3 sections; ex-YFD 4 |
| AFDM 3* | | 1943 | 552 ft (168.2 m) | 124 ft (37.8 m) | 18,000 tons | steel | lease | 3 sections; ex-YFD 6 |
| AFDM 5* | | 1943 | 552 ft (168.2 m) | 124 ft (37.8 m) | 18,000 tons | steel | reserve | 3 sections; ex-YFD 21 |
| AFDM 6* | | 1944 | 552 ft (168.2 m) | 124 ft (37.8 m) | 18,000 tons | steel | Subic Bay, Philippines | 3 sections; ex-YFD 62 |
| AFDM 7* | | 1945 | 552 ft (168.2 m) | 124 ft (37.8 m) | 18,000 tons | steel | Davisville, R.I. | 3 sections; ex-YFD 63 |
| AFDM 8* | RICHLAND | 1944 | 552 ft (168.2 m) | 124 ft (37.8 m) | 18,000 tons | steel | Guam, Marianas | 3 sections; ex-YFD 64 |
| AFDM 9* | | 1945 | 552 ft (168.2 m) | 124 ft (37.8 m) | 18,000 tons | steel | lease | 3 sections; ex-YFD 65 |
| AFDM 10* | | 1945 | 552 ft (168.2 m) | 124 ft (37.8 m) | 18,000 tons | steel | lease | 3 sections; ex-YFD 67 |

ªAll sections assembled

These docks all originally were classified as floating dry docks (YFD), informally known as yard floating dry docks.

Names: Only the AFDM 8 is named; she became the RICHLAND in 1968 (she had begun supporting SSBNs in 1964).

AFDM 6 (U.S. Navy)

## 4 AUXILIARY REPAIR DOCKS

| Number | Name | Completed | Length | Width | Capacity | Construction | Status |
|--------|------|-----------|--------|-------|----------|--------------|--------|
| ARD 5 | WATERFORD | 1942 | 485⅔ ft (148 m) | 71 ft (21.6 m) | 3,000 tons | steel | New London, Conn. |
| ARD 7 | WEST MILTON | 1943 | 485⅔ ft (148 m) | 71 ft (21.6 m) | 3,000 tons | steel | New London, Conn. |
| ARD 24 | | 1944 | 491⅔ ft (149.9 m) | 81 ft (24.7 m) | 3,000 tons | steel | reserve |
| ARD 30 | SAN ONOFRE | 1944 | 491⅔ ft (149.9 m) | 81 ft (24.7 m) | 3,000 tons | steel | Pearl Harbor |

Class: The ARCO (ARD 29) was stricken on 15 September 1976 (transferred to Iran 1977).

## 4 MEDIUM AUXILIARY REPAIR DOCKS

| Number | Name | Completed | Length | Width | Capacity | Construction | Status | Notes |
|--------|------|-----------|--------|-------|----------|--------------|--------|-------|
| ARDM 1 | OAK RIDGE | 1944 | 536 ft (163.4 m) | 81 ft (247 m) | 3,500 tons | steel | Rota, Spain | ex-ARD 19 |
| ARDM 2 | ALAMOGORDO | 1944 | | | 3,500 tons | steel | Charleston, S.C. | ex-ARD 26 |
| ARDM 3 | | 1944 | | | 5,500 tons | steel | Charleston, S.C. | ex-ARD 18 |
| ARDM 4 | SHIPPINGPORT | 1977 | 492 ft (150 m) | 96 ft (29.3 m) | 7,800 tons | steel | fitting out | FY 1975 program |

The ARDM 1–3 were extensively modified from Auxiliary Repair Docks (ARD) to support ballistic missile submarines. The SHIPPINGPORT was built specifically to support SSBNs. Launched on 2 September 1977, at Bethlehem, Sparrows Point, Md.

Names: The ARD 19 was commissioned as the ARDM 1 and named OAK RIDGE on 1 October 1963.

OAK RIDGE with SSBN (U.S. Navy)

**2 YARD FLOATING DRY DOCKS**

| Number | Completed | Length[a] | Width | Capacity | Construction | Status | Notes |
|---|---|---|---|---|---|---|---|
| YFD 7* | 1943 | 552 ft (168.2 m) | 124 ft (37.8 m) | 18,000 tons | steel | lease | 3 sections |
| YFD 8* | 1942 | 587¼ ft (180 m) | 132½ ft (40.4 m) | 20,000 tons | wood | lease | 3 sections |
| YFD 9* | 1942 | 489 ft (149 m) | 132½ ft (40.4 m) | 16,000 tons | wood | lease | 5 sections |
| YFD 23* | 1943 | 472 ft (143.9 m) | 114 ft (34.7 m) | 10,500 tons | wood | lease | 6 sections |
| YFD 54 | 1943 | 352 ft (107.3 m) | 90 ft (27.4 m) | 5,000 tons | wood | lease | |
| YFD 68* | 1945 | 528 ft (160.9 m) | 118 ft (36 m) | 14,000 tons | steel | lease | 3 sections |
| YFD 69* | 1945 | 528 ft (160.9 m) | 118 ft (36 m) | 14,000 tons | steel | lease | 3 sections |
| YFD 70* | 1945 | 528 ft (160.9 m) | 118 ft (36 m) | 14,000 tons | steel | lease | 3 sections |
| YFD 71* | 1945 | 528 ft (160.9 m) | 118 ft (36 m) | 14,000 tons | steel | San Diego, Calif. | 3 sections |
| YFD 83 | 1943 | 200 ft (61 m) | 64 ft (19.5 m) | 1,000 tons | steel | U.S. Coast Guard; Curtis Bay, Md. | ex-AFDL 31 |

[a]All sections assembled

**(4) BOW DRY DOCKS**

| Number | Completed | Length | Beam |
|---|---|---|---|
| YBD 1 | FY 1978 program | 104 ft (31.7 m) | 84 ft (25.6 m) |
| YBD 2 | FY 1978 program | 104 ft (31.7 m) | 84 ft (25.6 m) |
| YBD 3 | FY 1979 program | 104 ft (31.7 m) | 84 ft (25.6 m) |
| YBD 4 | FY 1979 program | 104 ft (31.7 m) | 84 ft (25.6 m) |

These docks are being built to permit maintenance, including replacement of the rubber dome "windows," on SQS-26/53 sonars without the necessity of docking the entire ship. The docks can be used while the ships are in full load condition (i.e., making it unnecessary to unload fuel or munitions to lighten the ship).

Two docks are provided in the FY 1978 program proposal at a total cost of $14,800,000, and two in FY 1979 for $19,200,000.

Design: The YBD light displacement is 2,286 tons, submerged displacement is 6,216 tons, and maximum operating draft 42 feet. The docks are entirely dependent upon shore support for crane, electric, air, and water services.

# 22 Naval Air Organization

U.S. Naval Aviation operates more aircraft than any of the world's air forces, except those of the United States, Soviet Union, and China. Included in the generic term "naval aviation" is the air arm of the U.S. Marine Corps, which is the only marine force in the world to have a major aviation component. (Britain's Royal Marines, which operates helicopters, is believed to be the only other marine force with an aviation component.)

The following table lists U.S. naval aircraft—including Marine and reserve components—as of mid-1978. "Pipeline" aircraft are those in major rework, overhaul, or en route to or from units.

| Fixed-wing aircraft | Fighter | 700 |
|---|---|---|
| | Attack | 1,070 |
| | Antisubmarine | 140 |
| | Patrol | 370 |
| | Early warning | 100 |
| | Observation | 50 |
| | Drone control | 13 |
| | Tanker | 40 |
| | Transport | 160 |
| | Utility | 55 |
| | Training | 840 |
| Helicopters (including training) | | 1,075 |
| Pipeline aircraft and helicopters | | 685 |
| Total active inventory | | ~5,300 |

Note the large number of fixed-wing training aircraft which are used to provide basic and advanced flight training to Navy, Marine Corps, and Coast Guard fliers as well as a few foreign aviators. In addition, first-line and training aircraft are assigned to Navy and Marine Corps "readiness" or combat-training squadrons which check out pilots and air crewmen on the aircraft they will fly in combat squadrons.

The following pages describe the organizational components of naval aviation. Naval aviation units are designated by two systems of abbreviations, pronounceable ones and simpler letter-number combinations. Thus, Training Squadron Eight is known both as TraRonEight and as VT-8.

The V prefix dates back to 1922, when V indicated heavier-than-air and Z meant lighter-than-air blimps or airships. The V and Z were used for ships as well as aircraft and air organizations, hence the CV for aircraft carriers, AV for seaplane tenders, AZ for airship tenders, VF for fighters and fighter squadrons, and ZP for patrol airships, etc. Subsequently, the prefix H was introduced for helicopters. (The last U.S. Navy airship, a ZPG-2W, was decommissioned in 1962.)

The following V and H squadron designations are in current use; for Marine Corps squadrons, an M is indicated immediately after the V or H. The T suffix added to Marine squadrons indicates training units.

| | | | | |
|---|---|---|---|---|
| HC | Helicopter Combat Support | | VQ | Fleet Air Reconnaissance (VQ-1, VQ-2) and |
| HCT | Helicopter Combat Support Training | | | Communication Support (VQ-3, VQ-4) |
| HM | Helicopter Mine Countermeasures | | VR | Fleet Logistics Support |
| HMA | (Marine) Attack Helicopter | | VRC | Fleet Logistics Support (COD) |
| HMH | (Marine) Heavy Helicopter | | VRF | Aircraft Ferry |
| HML | (Marine) Light Helicopter | | VS | Air Antisubmarine |
| HMM | (Marine) Medium Helicopter | | VT | Training |
| HMX | (Marine) Helicopter Development | | VX | Air Test and Evaluation |
| HS | Helicopter Antisubmarine | | VXE | Antarctic Development |
| HSL | Light Helicopter Antisubmarine | | VXN | Oceanographic Development |
| HT | Helicopter Training | | | |

Other major naval aviation organizational abbreviations include:

| | | | | |
|---|---|---|---|---|
| RVAH | Reconnaissance–Heavy Attack | | | |
| VA | Attack | | CVW | Carrier Air Wing |
| VAQ | Tactical Electronic Warfare | | CVWR | Reserve Carrier Air Wing |
| VAW | Carrier Airborne Early Warning | | RCVW | Readiness Carrier Air Wing |
| VC | Fleet Composite | | H&MS | (Marine) Headquarters & Maintenance Squadron |
| VF | Fighter | | MAW | Marine Aircraft Wing |
| VFP | Light Photographic | | MCAF | Marine Corps Air Facility (Quantico, Va.) |
| VMA | (Marine) Attack | | MCAS | Marine Corps Air Station |
| VMAQ | (Marine) Electronic Warfare | | NAEC | Naval Air Engineering Center (Lakehurst, N.J.) |
| VMFA | (Marine) Fighter–Attack | | NAF | Naval Air Facility |
| VMFP | (Marine) Photo Reconnaissance | | NARU | Naval Air Reserve Unit |
| VMGR | (Marine) Refueller–Transport | | NAS | Naval Air Station |
| VMO | (Marine) Observation | | PatWing | Patrol Wing |
| VP | Patrol | | | |

Three A-7E Corsairs from Attack Squadron 147 on the carrier CONSTELLATION (CV 64) streak low over snow-covered mountains during a training flight. Standard Navy markings are visible on these Corsairs: the 400-number on the nose, top right and lower left wing indicates the fourth squadron (normally the second VA) and the plane's number in the squadron; the "stars and bars" on the fuselage, top left and lower right wing has been a national insignia since 1947; after the fuselage markings are the name of the carrier, "Navy," and aircraft "bureau" (old Bureau of Aeronautics) number (156803 on nearest plane); and tail fin markings include squadron number, squadron insignia (sword and insignia of the "Argonauts"), wing code letters (NG), and aircraft number on the tip. The leading Corsair is flown by the air wing (CVW-9) commander; his aircraft is identified by 00 or, in this A-7E aircraft, by the number 100 and "OAG" on the fin tip for air group commander. Although attack carrier wings changed from air groups to air wings on 23 December 1963, their commanding officers are still referred to as air group commanders. (1975, U.S. Navy)

Aircraft markings generally include national insignia and name of service. Identification letters indicate either aircraft wing or squadron, whichever is appropriate. Most Navy aircraft additionally have individual aircraft identification numbers. For carrier-based aircraft there is a three-digit series, usually with the 100 and 200 series for fighters, 300, 400, and 500 for attack aircraft, and 600 for special-mission aircraft.

The following pages provide a description of the carrier air wings and squadrons of U.S. naval aviation—the tactical organization. The administrative organization is headed by the Deputy Chief of Naval Operations (Air Warfare), and extends through the Commanders Naval Air Force Atlantic (NavAirLant) and Pacific (NavAirPac), and several wing commanders, and down to the individual carrier wings and squadrons. There also are many organizational representatives and detachments in the naval air organization which are not included in this listing.

The following are the principal administrative wing organizations:

### Naval Air Force Atlantic Fleet

Tactical Air Wings Atlantic
    Fighter Wing 1
    Light Attack Wing 1
    Medium Attack Wing 1
    Reconnaissance Attack Wing 1
    Airborne Early Warning Wing 12
Sea-Based Air Antisubmarine Warfare Wings Atlantic
    Air Antisubmarine Wing 1
    Helicopter Antisubmarine Wing 1
    Helicopter Sea Control Wing 1
Patrol Wings Atlantic
    Patrol Wing 5
    Patrol Wing 11
Tactical Support Wing 1

### Naval Air Force Pacific Fleet

Fighter/Airborne Early Warning Wing Pacific
Light Attack Wing Pacific
Medium Attack/Tactical Electronic Warfare Wing Pacific
Antisubmarine Warfare Wing Pacific
Patrol Wings Pacific
    Patrol Wing 1
    Patrol Wing 2

AirLant and AirPac wings and squadrons have two-letter identification codes. The system was established on 11 July 1946 and revised on 1 June 1957 to the current fleet "split," with the first letter indicating the fleet assignment: A to M for NavAirLant and N to Z for NavAirPac. (The letters I and O are not used to avoid confusion with numerals; AF is no longer used, to avoid confusion with the Air Force.)

### CARRIER AIR WINGS (CVW)

| Wing | Code | Aircraft Carrier |
|---|---|---|
| Carrier Air Wing 1 | AB | JOHN F. KENNEDY |
| Carrier Air Wing 2 | NE | RANGER |
| Carrier Air Wing 3 | AC | SARATOGA |
| Carrier Air Wing 5 | NF | MIDWAY |
| Carrier Air Wing 6 | AE | AMERICA |
| Carrier Air Wing 7 | AG | INDEPENDENCE |
| Carrier Air Wing 8 | AJ | NIMITZ |
| Carrier Air Wing 9 | NG | CONSTELLATION |
| Carrier Air Wing 11 | NH | KITTY HAWK |
| Carrier Air Wing 14 | NK | ENTERPRISE |
| Carrier Air Wing 15 | NL | EISENHOWER |
| Carrier Air Wing 17 | AA | FORRESTAL |

An air wing's size and composition varies with the ship in which it is embarked. A "nominal" carrier air wing consists of:

| | | |
|---|---|---|
| 2 VF | 24 | F-4 Phantom or F-14 Tomcat |
| 2 VA | 24 | A-7 Corsair |
| 1 VA | 10-12 | A-6 Intruder; 4 KA-6 Intruder |
| 1 VAQ | 4 | EA-6B Prowler |
| 1 VAW | 4 | E-2 Hawkeye |
| 1 VS | 10 | S-3 Viking |
| 1 HS | 6 | SH-3 Sea King |
| 1 RVAH | 3 | RA-5C Vigilante |
| or | | or |
| 1 VFP detachment | 3 | RF-8G Crusader |
| or | | or |
| 1 VMFP detachment | 3 | RF-4B Phantom |

### FIGHTER SQUADRONS (VF)

| Wings | Code | Squadrons | | | |
|---|---|---|---|---|---|
| Carrier Air Wing 1 | AB | VF-14 | VF-32 | | |
| Carrier Air Wing 2 | NE | VF-21 | VF-154 | | |
| Carrier Air Wing 3 | AC | VF-31 | VF-103 | | |
| Carrier Air Wing 5 | NF | VF-151 | VF-161 | | |
| Carrier Air Wing 6 | AE | VF-142 | VF-143 | | |
| Carrier Air Wing 7 | AG | VF-33 | VF-102 | | |
| Carrier Air Wing 8 | AJ | VF-41 | VF-84 | | |
| Carrier Air Wing 9 | NG | VF-24 | VF-211 | | |
| Carrier Air Wing 11 | NH | VF-114 | VF-213 | | |
| Carrier Air Wing 14 | NK | VF-1 | VF-2 | | |
| Carrier Air Wing 15 | NL | VF-51 | VF-111 | | |
| Carrier Air Wing 17 | AA | VF-11 | VF-74 | | |
| Fighter Wing 1 | AD | VF-43 | VF-101 | VF-101 Detachment Key West | |
| Fighter/AEW Wing Pacific | NJ | VF-51 | VF-111 | VF-124 | VF-126 |

VF squadrons assigned to carrier air wings fly F-4 Phantoms or, increasingly, F-14 Tomcats. VF-43 is the east-coast air combat maneuvering squadron, using A-4E/TA-4J, F-5E/F Tiger II, and T-38A Talon aircraft to teach advanced air-to-air combat. The Navy's Fighter Weapons School (Top Gun) serves in that role for west-coast VF/VA pilots. VF-101 is the east-coast F-14 readiness squadron, while on the west coast VF-171 transitions pilots to the F-4 and VF-124 to the F-14.

## ATTACK SQUADRONS (VA)

| Wings | Code | Squadrons | | |
|---|---|---|---|---|
| Carrier Air Wing 1 | AB | VA-34 | VA-46 | VA-72 |
| Carrier Air Wing 2 | NE | VA-25 | VA-113 | VA-145 |
| Carrier Air Wing 3 | AC | VA-37 | VA-75 | VA-105 |
| Carrier Air Wing 5 | NF | VA-56 | VA-93 | VA-115 |
| Carrier Air Wing 6 | AE | VA-15 | VA-87 | VA-176 |
| Carrier Air Wing 7 | AG | VA-12 | VA-65 | VA-66 |
| Carrier Air Wing 8 | AJ | VA-35 | VA-82 | VA-86 |
| Carrier Air Wing 9 | NG | VA-146 | VA-147 | VA-165 |
| Carrier Air Wing 11 | NH | VA-52 | VA-192 | VA-195 |
| Carrier Air Wing 14 | NK | VA-27 | VA-97 | VA-196 |
| Carrier Air Wing 15 | NL | VA-22 | VA-94 | VA-95 |
| Carrier Air Wing 17 | AA | VA-81 | VA-83 | VA-85 |
| Light Attack Wing 1 | AD | VA-45 | VA-174 | VA-174 Detachment (Yuma, Ariz.) |
| Medium Attack Wing 1 | AD | VA-42 | | |
| Light Attack Wing Pacific | NJ | VA-122 | VA-127 | VA-122 Detachment (Fallon, Nev.) |
| Medium Attack/Tactical Electronic Warfare Wing Pacific | NJ | VA-128 | | |

Carrier air wings have two A-7 Corsair squadrons and one A-6 Intruder squadron. The A-6 units technically are rated as "medium" attack squadrons; most have four KA-6D tankers in addition to "straight" attack aircraft. VA-42 provides A-6 Intruder readiness training, while VA-45 continues A-4 Skyhawk training, and VA-174 A-7 Corsair training on the east coast. VA-122 is the west-coast A-7 readiness squadron, VA-128 the A-6 readiness squadron, and VA-127 the A-4 readiness squadron. Although there are no longer Skyhawk attack squadrons in Navy service, many Skyhawks remain in readiness, training, and utility service.

## TACTICAL ELECTRONIC WARFARE SQUADRONS (VAQ)

| Wings | Code | Squadrons | | | |
|---|---|---|---|---|---|
| Carrier Air Wing 9 | NG | VAQ-132 | | | |
| Carrier Air Wing 11 | NH | VAQ-131 | | | |
| Carrier Air Wing 14 | NK | VAQ-134 | | | |
| Tactical Support Wing 1 | GD | VAQ-33 | | | |
| Medium Attack/Tactical Electronic Warfare Wing Pacific | NJ | VAQ-129 | VAQ-130 | VAQ-133 | VAQ-135 |
| | | VAQ-136 | VAQ-137 | VAQ-138 | |

All VAQ squadrons except VAQ-33 fly the EA-6B Prowler and are based at Whidbey Island, Washington, along with all A-6 Intruders in a composite medium attack/electronic warfare wing.

Three VAQs are specifically assigned to carrier wings; the other squadrons are allocated to east-coast and west-coast carriers as required. VAQ-129 provides EA-6B readiness training.

VAQ-33, based at Norfolk, Virginia, provides electronic warfare support to the Atlantic and Pacific Fleets. The squadron flies F-4B/J Phantoms, ERA-3B Skywarriors, EA-4F Skyhawks, and the Navy's last EC-121K Warning Star. All are fitted to simulate Soviet ECM/EW/radar characteristics. The Skywarriors' landing weight is too great for carrier operations; their hooks have been removed and they operate from shore bases.

## AIRBORNE EARLY WARNING SQUADRONS (VAW)

| Wings | Code | Squadrons | | | |
|---|---|---|---|---|---|
| Carrier Air Wing 1 | AB | VAW-125 | | | |
| Carrier Air Wing 3 | AC | VAW-123 | | | |
| Carrier Air Wing 5 | NF | VAW-115 | | | |
| Carrier Air Wing 6 | AE | VAW-124 | | | |
| Carrier Air Wing 14 | NK | VAW-113 | | | |
| Airborne Early Warning Wing 12 | | RVAW-120(GE) | VAW-121 | VAW-122 | VAW-126 |
| Fighter/Airborne Early Warning Wing Pacific | NJ | RVAW-110(TT) | VAW-112 | VAW-114 | |

All VAW squadrons fly the E-2 Hawkeye, with the E-2C scheduled for eventual use by all squadrons. In the Pacific Fleet the VAW squadrons not specifically assigned to carrier wings are teamed with the Pacific Fleet's fighters in a single fighter/AEW wing based at Miramar, California. This is a functional teaming, with the E-2s being used largely to control ship-based fighter aircraft. The readiness squadrons are designated RVAW, with RVAW-110 at Miramar and RVAW-120 at Norfolk, Virginia, close to the east-coast fighter "capital" of Oceana, Virginia.

## AIR ANTISUBMARINE SQUADRONS (VS)

| Wings | Code | Squadrons | |
|---|---|---|---|
| Carrier Air Wing 1 | AB | VS-32 | |
| Carrier Air Wing 2 | NE | VS-29 | |
| Carrier Air Wing 3 | AC | VS-22 | |
| Carrier Air Wing 6 | AE | VS-28 | |
| Carrier Air Wing 7 | AG | VS-31 | |
| Carrier Air Wing 8 | AJ | VS-24 | |
| Carrier Air Wing 9 | NG | VS-21 | |
| Carrier Air Wing 11 | NH | VS-33 | |
| Carrier Air Wing 14 | NK | VS-38 | |
| Carrier Air Wing 17 | AA | VS-30 | |
| Air ASW Wing 1 | | (none assigned) | |
| ASW Wing Pacific | | VS-37 | VS-41(RA) |

All fixed-wing ASW squadrons fly the S-3A Viking, replacement for the long-serving S-2/S2F Tracker. All "large" carriers have a VS squadron assigned; the veteran MIDWAY (CV 41) is the only flattop without Vikings. ASW Wing Pacific controls west coast VS squadrons when not at sea, as Air ASW Wing 1 does for east-coast VS units. VS-41 provides readiness training for all Viking crews.

### HELICOPTER ANTISUBMARINE SQUADRONS (HS)

| Wings | Code | Squadrons | |
|---|---|---|---|
| Carrier Air Wing 1 | AB | HS-11 | |
| Carrier Air Wing 2 | NE | HS-4 | |
| Carrier Air Wing 3 | AC | HS-7 | |
| Carrier Air Wing 6 | AE | HS-15 | |
| Carrier Air Wing 7 | AG | HS-5 | |
| Carrier Air Wing 8 | AJ | HS-9 | |
| Carrier Air Wing 9 | NG | HS-6 | |
| Carrier Air Wing 11 | NH | HS-8 | |
| Carrier Air Wing 14 | NK | HS-2 | |
| Carrier Air Wing 17 | AA | HS-3 | |
| Helicopter Antisubmarine Wing 1 | | HS-1(AR) | |
| ASW Wing Pacific | | HS-10(RA) | HS-12 |

The SH-3 Sea King is flown by helicopter ASW squadrons. All carrier air wings except CVW-5 aboard the MIDWAY (CV 41) have an HS squadron on board. These squadrons were reduced in 1977 from eight helicopters to six at the direction of the Department of Defense. East-coast SH-3 readiness training is provided by HS-1 and on the west coast by HS-10.

### RECONNAISSANCE-HEAVY ATTACK SQUADRONS (RVAH)

| Wings | Squadrons | | |
|---|---|---|---|
| Reconnaissance Attack Wing 1 | RVAH 1(GH) | RVAH 3(GJ) | RVAH 6(GS) |
| | RVAH 7(GL) | RVAH 12(GP) | |

These squadrons fly the aging RA-5C Vigilante multi-sensor reconnaissance aircraft. RVAH squadrons are descendants of the VAH heavy attack squadrons formed from the late 1940s through 1956 for the nuclear-strike role. Four RVAH squadrons, each with a nominal strength of only three aircraft, deploy with carrier wings. RVAH-3 provides readiness training. All are based at Key West, Florida, although some squadrons deploy aboard Pacific Fleet carriers.

### LIGHT PHOTOGRAPHIC SQUADRONS (VFP)

| Wings | Squadrons |
|---|---|
| Fighter/Airborne Early Warning Wing Pacific | VFP-63(PP) |

VFP-63 provides three-plane detachments of RF-8G Photo Crusaders to carriers in both the Atlantic and Pacific. Carriers rely on RA-5C Vigilantes, or RF-8G Crusaders, or Marine RF-4B Phantoms for "recce." All are scheduled to be replaced by pod-carrying F-14 Tomcats in the 1980s. VFP-63 is assigned to the Pacific Fleet's fighter "type" commander.

### FLEET AIR RECONNAISSANCE SQUADRONS (VQ)

| Squadrons |
|---|
| VQ-1 (PR) |
| VQ-2 (JQ) |

The two fleet air reconnaissance squadrons, VQ-1 at Agana, Guam, and VQ-2 at Rota, Spain, fly EP-3B/E Orions and EA-3B Skywarriors on electronic surveillance missions. The latter aircraft periodically operate from forward-deployed aircraft carriers.

### COMMUNICATION SUPPORT SQUADRONS (VQ)

| Wings | Squadrons |
|---|---|
| — | VQ-3 (TC) |
| Tactical Support Wing 1 | VQ-4 (HL) |

The communication support squadrons fly EC-130G/Q Hercules to provide emergency VLF/LF communications relay to submerged Polaris and Poseidon strategic missile submarines. VQ-3 is based at Agana, Guam, and VQ-4 at Patuxent River, Maryland, where the latter squadron falls under the control of the Atlantic Fleet's support air wing.

### PATROL SQUADRONS (VP)

| Wings | Squadrons | | | |
|---|---|---|---|---|
| Patrol Wing 1 | (deployed squadrons assigned) | | | |
| Patrol Wing 2 | VP-1 (YB) | VP-4 (YD) | VP-6 (PC) | VP-17 (ZE) |
| | VP-22 (QA) | | | |
| Patrol Wing 5 | VP-8 (LC) | VP-10 (LD) | VP-11 (LE) | |
| | VP-23 (LJ) | VP-26 (LK) | VP-44 (LM) | |
| Patrol Wing 11 | VP-5 (LA) | VP-16 (LF) | VP-24 (LR) | VP-45 (LN) |
| | VP-49 (LP) | VP-56 (LQ) | | |
| Patrol Wings Atlantic | VP-30 (LL) | | | |
| Patrol Wings Pacific | VP-9 (PD) | VP-19 (PE) | VP-31 (RP) | VP-40 (QE) |
| | VP-46 (RC) | VP-47 RD) | VP-48 (SF) | VP-50 (SG) |

The Navy's 24 first-line patrol squadrons fly the P-3B/C Orion aircraft. The last active P-3A was shifted to a reserve squadron early in 1978. Of the east-coast squadrons VP-30 and Patrol Wing 11 are based at Jacksonville, Florida, and Patrol Wing 5 at Brunswick, Maine. Their Orion squadrons deploy to the Mediterranean and Atlantic area. On the west coast, Patrol Wings Pacific's squadrons are based at NAS Moffett near San Francisco; Patrol Wing 1 at

Kamiseya, Japan, directs VP squadrons which rotate to the western Pacific; and Patrol Wing 2's squadrons are at Barber's Point, Hawaii. VP-30 and VP-31 provide Orion readiness training.

## LIGHT HELICOPTER ANTISUBMARINE SQUADRONS (HSL)

| Wings | Squadrons | | | |
|---|---|---|---|---|
| Helicopter Sea Control Wing 1 | HSL-30 (HT) | HSL-32 (HV) | HSL-34 (HX) | HSL-36 (HY) |
| ASW Wing Pacific | HSL-31 (TD) | HSL-33 (TF) | HSL-35 (TG) | HSL-37 (TH) |

The HSL squadrons provide detachments with SH-2 LAMPS helicopters for deployments aboard cruisers, destroyers, and frigates. The first LAMPS were assigned to helicopter combat support squadrons, HC-4 and HC-5. They were reclassified as HSL-30 and HSL-31, respectively, on 1 March 1972. Those squadrons provide readiness LAMPS training for their respective fleets. Atlantic HSL and HC squadrons have the initial letter "H" in their letter codes.

## HELICOPTER MINE COUNTERMEASURES SQUADRON (HM)

| Wings | Squadrons |
|---|---|
| Helicopter Sea Control Wing 1 | HM-12 (DH) |

The U.S. Navy began experiments with helicopter mine countermeasures in 1952. However, not until 19 years later was a minesweeping helicopter put in service, when HM-12 was commissioned on 1 April 1971. Initially flying CH-53A Sea Stallion helicopters, the squadron swept mines off North Vietnam in 1972 and then at the northern end of the Suez Canal in 1973. The squadron now flies RH-53D helicopters and deploys aboard amphibious assault ships (LPH). Twenty-three helicopters are assigned to the Norfolk-based squadron.

## HELICOPTER COMBAT SUPPORT SQUADRONS (HC)

| Wings | Squadrons | | |
|---|---|---|---|
| Tactical Support Wing 1 | HC-6 (HW) | HC-16 (BF) | |
| ASW Wing Pacific | HC-1 (UP) | HC-3 (SA) | HC-11 |
| Helicopter Antisubmarine Wing 1 | HC-2 (HU) | | |

These squadrons provide helicopters for Search And Rescue (SAR) and Vertical Replenishment (VERTREP) operations in direct support of the fleet. UH-46 Sea Knights are flown in the VERTREP role, with one- or two-helicopter detachments being provided to AFS-, AOE-, and AOR-type replenishment ships. HC-16, formerly HCT-16, provides readiness training for Sea Knight crewmen.

## FLEET COMPOSITE SQUADRONS (VC)

| Wings | Squadrons | | | |
|---|---|---|---|---|
| Tactical Support Wing 1 | VC-2 (JE) | VC-6 (JG) | VC-8 (GF) | VC-10 (JH) |
| ASW Wing Pacific | VC-3 (UF) | | | |
| Fighter/AEW Wing Pacific | VC-1 (UA) | VC-7 (UH) | | |
| — | VC-5 (UE) | | | |

Composite squadrons provide a variety of utility services for the Fleet, including non-combat photography, target tow, radar calibration, and transport. Their aircraft include fighters, attack planes, patrol planes, helicopters, and utility types. Pacific "utility" squadrons have the initial letter "U" in their identification codes; Atlantic squadrons have a "J" from the old VJ symbol for utility squadrons. VC-10, based at Guantanamo Bay, Cuba, is the only VC squadron with a combat mission, being responsible for close air support in the event of a Cuban attack against the U.S. base. The squadron flies mainly TA-4J Skyhawks.

## FLEET LOGISTIC SUPPORT SQUADRONS (VR/VRC)

| Wings | Squadrons | |
|---|---|---|
| Tactical Support Wing 1 | VR-1 (JK) | VRC-40 (CD) |
| — | VH-24 (JM) | |
| — | VR-30 (RW) | |
| — | VRC-50 (RG) | |

These squadrons transport passengers and high-priority cargo in direct support of fleet operations. A variety of transport aircraft are flown, with the two Carrier-Onboard Delivery (COD) squadrons providing direct shore-to-ship transport. The VRC squadrons fly C-1 Trader and C-2 Greyhound COD aircraft, as well as larger transports.

## AIRCRAFT FERRY SQUADRONS (VRF)

| Wings | Squadrons |
|---|---|
| Tactical Support Wing 1 | VRF-31 |

VRF-31 provides pilots to transfer Navy and Marine Corps aircraft throughout the world.

## AIR TEST AND EVALUATION SQUADRONS (VX)

| Wings | Squadrons |
|---|---|
| Sea-Based Air ASW Wings Atlantic | VX-1 (JA) |
| Fighter/AEW Wing Pacific | VX-4 (XF) |
| Light Attack Wing Pacific | VX-5 (XE) |

These squadrons test and evaluate weapon systems. Squadron VX-1 at Patuxent River, Maryland, specializes in ASW systems;

VX-4 at Point Mugu, California, specializes in fighter warfare; and VX-5 at China Lake, California, supports weapon development. All fly a variety of combat and support aircraft.

## ANTARCTIC DEVELOPMENT SQUADRONS (VXE)

| Wings | Squadrons |
|---|---|
| ASW Wing Pacific | VXE-6 (XD) |

VXE-6, homeported at Point Mugu, California, operates ski-equipped LC-130F Hercules and UH-1 Huey helicopters in support of Antarctic research programs.

## OCEANOGRAPHIC DEVELOPMENT SQUADRONS (VXN)

| Wings | Squadrons |
|---|---|
| Tactical Support Wing 1 | VXN-8 (JB) |

VXN-8, at Patuxent River, Maryland, flies RP-3A and RP-3D Orions on world-wide research projects.

## TRAINING SQUADRONS (VT)

| Wings | Code | Squadrons | | |
|---|---|---|---|---|
| Training Wing 1 | A | VT-7(TA-4J) | VT-9 (T-2C) | VT-19 (T-2C) |
| Training Wing 2 | B | VT-21 (TA-4J) | VT-22 (TA-4J) | VT-23 (T-2C) |
| Training Wing 3 | C | VT-24 (TA-4J) | VT-25 (TA-4J) | VT-26 (T-2C) |
| Training Wing 4 | D | VT-27 (T-28B/C) | VT-28 and VT-31 (TS-2A, US-2B, T-44A) | |
| Training Wing 5 | E | VT-2 (T-28B/C) | VT-3 (T-28B/C) | VT-6 (T-28B/C) |
| Training Wing 6 | F | VT-4 (T-2C, TA-4J) | VT-10 (T-2C, T-39D) | VT-86 (TA-4J, T-39D) |

These wings and squadrons, under the Naval Air Training Command, provide training for Navy, Marine Corps, Coast Guard, and foreign pilots and air crewmen. The principal aircraft flown by each squadron are indicated in parentheses. Training wings have single-letter identification codes.

## HELICOPTER TRAINING SQUADRONS (HT)

| Wings | Code | Squadrons | |
|---|---|---|---|
| Training Wing 5 | E | HT-8 (TH-57A) | HT-18 (UH-1E/L, TH-1L) |

These squadrons provide basic and advanced helicopter training, respectively. Note that they are part of TraWingFive that also flies fixed-wing aircraft.

## MARINE CORPS AVIATION

There are three Marine Aircraft Wings (MAW), with one wing nominally assigned to support each of the three active Marine

divisions. Headquarters for the First MAW is at Kadena on Okinawa, with one air group at Kaneohe Bay (Oahu), Hawaii; for the Second MAW at Cherry Point, North Carolina; and for the Third MAW at El Toro, California.

Operationally the Marine air wings are subordinate to their respective Fleet Marine Forces (FMFLant and FMFPac) and, additionally, are under the technical direction of NavAirLant and NavAirPac.

Marine helicopters operate regularly from amphibious ships, and Marine fighter and attack squadrons, as well as detachments of special-mission aircraft, periodically are deployed aboard aircraft carriers. All Marine fighter and attack aircraft are capable of operating from aircraft carriers. Marine squadrons all have two-letter identification codes. Aircraft are also assigned to the Headquarters and Maintenance Squadrons (H&MS).

## FIGHTER ATTACK SQUADRONS (VMFA)

| Wings | Squadrons | | |
|---|---|---|---|
| First Marine Aircraft Wing | VMFA-115 (VE) VMFA-235 (DB) | VMFA-212 (WD) | VMFA-232 (WT) |
| Second Marine Aircraft Wing | VMFA-122 (DC) VMFA-333 (DN) | VMFA-251 (DW) VMFA-451 (VM) | VMFA-312 (DR) |
| Third Marine Aircraft Wing | VMFA-314 (VW) | VMFA-323 (WS) | VMFA-531 (EC) |

Each VMFA squadron flies 12 F-4 Phantoms. Plans to provide the F-14 Tomcat to the Marines were dropped in 1975 in favor of the less expensive F-18 fighter.

## ATTACK SQUADRONS (VMA)

| Wings | Squadrons | | |
|---|---|---|---|
| First Marine Aircraft Wing | VMA-211 (CF) | VMA-513 (WF) | VMA(AW)-533 (ED) |
| Second Marine Aircraft Wing | VMA(AW)-121 (VK) VMA-311 (WL) VMA-542 (CR) | VMA(AW)-224 (WK) VMA-331 (VL) | VMA-231 (CG) VMA(AW)-332 (EA) |
| Third Marine Aircraft Wing | VMA-214 (WE) | VMA-223 (WP) | VMA(AW)-242 (DT) |

Five Marine all-weather attack squadrons each fly 12 A-6E Intruders. Five "straight" VMA squadrons are each assigned 16 A-4M Skyhawks and three fly 20 AV-8A Harrier VSTOL aircraft. VMA-231 made the first carrier deployment of VSTOL aircraft in the U.S. Navy when the squadron embarked aboard the FRANKLIN D. ROOSEVELT (CV 42) with CVW-19 (code NM), a west-coast wing, on the ship's final Mediterranean cruise in 1976. Harriers from VMA-513 flew from the GUAM (LPH 9) during 1972 tests of the sea control ship concept.

## ELECTRONIC WARFARE SQUADRONS (VMAQ)

| Squadrons |
| --- |
| VMAQ-2 (CY) |

The Marine Corps' three composite reconnaissance squadrons (VMCJ) were decommissioned in 1975 and their aircraft allocated to VMAQ-2 and VMFP-3. VMAQ-2 flies primarily the two-seat EA-6A Intruder, with the more capable four-seat EA-6B Prowler entering service since March 1977. Detachments from the squadron serve with all three air wings, and periodically go aboard carriers to compensate for the Navy's EA-6B shortfall.

## PHOTO RECONNAISSANCE SQUADRONS (VMFP)

| Squadrons |
| --- |
| VMFP-3 (RF) |

The Marines fly the RF-4B Phantom in the photo "recce" role, with the single VMFP squadron providing detachments to the three Marine air wings and, on occasion, to Navy carriers. The recce version of the Phantom is one of the few aircraft flown by the Marine Corps but not the Navy, the RF-4C is flown by the U.S. Air Force and the RF-4E by foreign air forces.

## OBSERVATION SQUADRONS (VMO)

| Wings | Squadrons |
| --- | --- |
| Second Marine Aircraft Wing | VMO-1 (ER) |
| Third Marine Aircraft Wing | VMO-2 (UV) |

These observation squadrons fly the nimble OV-10A Bronco, with the OV-10D night-flying variant being provided in limited numbers. Unlike previous VO-type aircraft, the Bronco can be heavily armed. Eighteen aircraft are authorized for each squadron. The Navy's light attack squadrons (VAL) which flew Broncos during the Vietnam War have been decommissioned.

## REFUELLER-TRANSPORT SQUADRONS (VMGR)

| Wings | Squadrons |
| --- | --- |
| First Marine Aircraft Wing | VMGR-152 (QD) |
| Second Marine Aircraft Wing | VMGR-252 (BH) |
| Third Marine Aircraft Wing | VMGR-352 (QB) |

These squadrons, each with 12 KC-130F Hercules, provide tactical lift and in-flight refueling for Marine air wings and divisions. One Marine KC-130F is assigned to support the Navy's Blue Angels flight demonstration team.

## ATTACK HELICOPTER SQUADRONS (HMA)

| Wings | Squadrons |
| --- | --- |
| First Marine Aircraft Wing | HMA-369 (SM) |
| Second Marine Aircraft Wing | HMA-269 (HF) |
| Third Marine Aircraft Wing | HMA-169 (SN) |

These squadrons are each assigned 24 AH-1 SeaCobra gunships for close-air support of ground troops.

## HEAVY HELICOPTER SQUADRONS (HMH)

| Wings | Squadrons | |
| --- | --- | --- |
| First Marine Aircraft Wing | HMH-462 (YF) | HMH-463 (YH) |
| Second Marine Aircraft Wing | HMH-362 (YL) | HMH-461 (CJ) |
| Third Marine Aircraft Wing | HMH-361 (YN) | HMH-363 (YZ) |

The six HMH squadrons each fly 21 CH-53A/D helicopters.

## LIGHT HELICOPTER SQUADRONS (HML)

| Wings | Squadrons |
| --- | --- |
| First Marine Aircraft Wing | HML-367 (VT) |
| Second Marine Aircraft Wing | HML-167 (TV) |
| Third Marine Aircraft Wing | HML-267 (UV) |

Twenty-four UH-1N Iroquois/Huey helicopters are assigned to each HML squadron.

## MEDIUM HELICOPTER SQUADRONS (HMM)

| Wings | Squadrons | | |
| --- | --- | --- | --- |
| First Marine Aircraft Wing | HMM-164 (YT) | HMM-165 (YW) | HMM-262 (ET) |
| Second Marine Aircraft Wing | HMM-162 (YS) | HMM-261 (EM) | HMM-263 (EG) |
| | HMM-264 (EH) | | |
| Third Marine Aircraft Wing | HMM-161 (YR) | HMM-163 (YP) | |

The HMM squadrons each fly 18 CH-46D/F Sea Knight helicopters.

## HELICOPTER DEVELOPMENT SQUADRONS (HMX)

| Squadrons |
| --- |
| HMX-1 (MX) |

HMX-1 was commissioned on December 3, 1947, to develop helicopter assault tactics and doctrine for the Marine Corps. Based at Quantico, Virginia, the squadron still performs that role as well as carrying out logistic support flights for Marine Corps Headquarters (in Arlington, Virginia) and the White House. Several types of helicopters are flown by the squadron.

## REPLACEMENT TRAINING SQUADRONS

| Wings | Squadrons |
|---|---|
| Second Marine Aircraft Wing | VMAT(AW)-202 (KC)(A-6A/E) |
| | VMAT-203 (KD)(TA-4J, A-4M, TAV/AV-8A) |
| | HMT-204 (GX) (CH-46D/F, CH-53A/D) |
| Third Marine Aircraft Wing | VMFAT-101 (SH) (F-4N/J) |
| | VMAT-102 (SC)(TA-4J, A-4E/F/M) |
| | HMT-301 (SU)(CH-46D/F, CH-53A/D) |

These squadrons provide "readiness" training for Marine fliers.

## NAVAL AIR RESERVE

The Naval Air Reserve provides a combat force of 2 carrier air wings (CVWR), 13 patrol squadrons (VP), 7 combat helicopter squadrons (HS, HC, and HAL) plus several support squadrons and units. The Commander Naval Air Reserve is based at New Orleans, Louisiana; the support units are under the Reserve Tactical Support Wing at NAS New Orleans. Approximately 360 aircraft are flown by the Naval Air Reserve.

## FIGHTER SQUADRONS (VF)

| Wings | Code | Squadrons | | Location |
|---|---|---|---|---|
| Reserve Carrier Air Wing 20 | AF | VF-201 (F-4) | VF-202 (F-4) | NAS Dallas, Texas |
| Reserve Carrier Air Wing 30 | ND | VF-301 (F-4N) | VF-302 (F-4N) | NAS Miramar, Calif. |

## ATTACK SQUADRONS (VA)

| Wings | Code | Squadrons | | Location |
|---|---|---|---|---|
| Reserve Carrier Air Wing 20 | AF | VA-203 (A-7A) | | NAS Jacksonville, Fla. |
| | | VA-204 (A-7B) | | NAS Memphis, Tenn. |
| | | VA-205 (A-7B) | | NAS Atlanta, Ga. |
| Reserve Carrier Air Wing 30 | ND | VA-303 (A-7A) | VA-304 (A-7A) | NAS Alameda, Calif. |
| | | VA-305 (A-7A) | | NAS Point Mugu, Calif. |

## PHOTO RECONNAISANCE SQUADRONS (VFP)

| Wings | Code | Squadrons | Location |
|---|---|---|---|
| Reserve Carrier Air Wing 20 | AF | VFP-206 (RF-8G) | NAF Andrews, Washington, D.C. |
| Reserve Carrier Air Wing 30 | ND | VFP-306 (RF-8G) | NAF Andrews, Washington, D.C. |

## ELECTRONIC WARFARE SQUADRONS (VAQ)

| Wings | Code | Squadrons | Location |
|---|---|---|---|
| Reserve Carrier Air Wing 20 | AF | VAQ-208 (EKA-3B) | NAS Alameda, Calif. |
| | | VAQ-209 (EA-6A) | NAS Norfolk, Va. |
| Reserve Carrier Air Wing 30 | ND | VAQ-308 (EKA-3B) | NAS Alameda, Calif. |

## AIRBORNE EARLY WARNING SQUADRONS (VAW)

| Wings | Code | Squadrons | Location |
|---|---|---|---|
| Reserve Carrier Air Wing 20 | AF | VAW-78 (E-2B) | NAS Norfolk, Va. |
| Reserve Carrier Air Wing 30 | ND | VAM-88 (E-2B) | NAS Miramar, Calif. |

## PATROL SQUADRONS (VP)

| Squadrons | Code | Location |
|---|---|---|
| VP-60 | LS | NAS Glenview, Ill. |
| VP-62 | LT | NAS Jacksonville, Fla. |
| VP-64 | LU | NAS Willow Grove, Penna. |
| VP-65 | PG | NAS Point Mugu, Calif. |
| VP-66 | LV | NAS Willow Grove, Penna. |
| VP-67 | PL | NAS Millington, Tenn. |
| VP-68 | LW | NAS Patuxent River, Md. |
| VP-69 | PJ | NAS Whidbey Island, Wash. |
| VP-90 | LX | NAS Glenview, Ill. |
| VP-91 | PM | NAS Moffett (Sunnyvale), Calif. |
| VP-92 | LY | NAS South Weymouth, Maine |
| VP-93 | LH | NAF Detroit, Mich. |
| VP-94 | LZ | NAS New Orleans, La. |

Reserve VP squadrons fly P-3A/B Orions.

## HELICOPTER ANTISUBMARINE SQUADRONS (HS)

| Squadrons | Location |
|---|---|
| HS-74 | NAS South Weymouth, Maine |
| HS-75 | NAEC Lakehurst, N.J. |
| HS-84 | NAS North Island (San Diego), Calif. |
| HS-85 | NAS Alameda, Calif. |

These squadrons fly SH-3 Sea King ASW helicopters. All reserve helicopter squadrons are assigned to the Reserve Helicopter Wing (HWR) for administrative purposes with the letter code NW (formerly used by Reserve ASW Air Group 80).

## HELICOPTER COMBAT SEARCH AND RESCUE SQUADRONS (HC)

| Squadrons | Location |
|---|---|
| HC-9 | NAS North Island (San Diego), Calif. |

This squadron flies HH-3A helicopters which are armed and armored for combat search and rescue operations.

## LIGHT ATTACK HELICOPTER SQUADRONS (HAL)

| Squadrons | Location |
| --- | --- |
| HAL-4 | NAS Norfolk, Va. |
| HAL-5 | NAS Point Mugu, Calif. |

These squadrons fly HH-1K Iroquois/Huey helicopters. The Navy's lone active helicopter gunship squadron, HAL-3, was decommissioned after Vietnam service.

## FLEET LOGISTIC SUPPORT SQUADRONS (VR)

| Squadrons | Code | Location |
| --- | --- | --- |
| VR-51 | RV | NAS Glenview, Ill. |
| VR-52 | JT | NAS Willow Grove, Penna. |
| VR-53 | RT | NAS Memphis, Tenn. |
| VR-54 | JS | NAS New Orleans, La. |
| VR-55 | RU | NAS Alameda, Calif. |
| VR-56 | JU | NAS Norfolk, Va. |
| VR-57 | RX | NAS North Island (San Diego), Calif. |
| VR-58 | JV | NAS Jacksonville, Fla. |

## COMPOSITE SQUADRONS (VC)

| Squadrons | Codo | Location |
| --- | --- | --- |
| VC-12 | JY | NAF Detroit, Mich. |
| VC-13 | UX | NAS New Orleans, La. |

## NAVAL AIR RESERVE TRAINING UNITS (NARU)

| Code | Location |
| --- | --- |
| 6A | NARU Andrews (Washington, D.C.) |
| 6F | NARU Jacksonville, Fla. |
| 6G | NARU Alameda, Calif. |
| 6H | NARU North Island (San Diego), Calif. |
| 6M | NARU Memphis, Tenn. |
| 6S | NARU Norfolk, Va. |
| 6T/RU | NARU Whidbey Island, Wash. |
| 6U | NARU Point Mugu, Calif. |

Aircraft assigned to Naval Air Reserve Units and Naval Air Stations have number-letter identification codes. These are mostly administrative and transport aircraft.

## NAVAL AIR STATIONS

| Code | Location |
| --- | --- |
| 7B | NAS Atlanta, Ga. |
| 7D | NAS Dallas, Texas |
| 7V | NAS Glenview, Ill. |
| 7W | NAS Willow Grove, Penna. |
| 7X | NAS New Orleans, La. |
| 7Z | NAS South Weymouth, Maine |

## NAVAL AIR FACILITIES

| Code | Location |
| --- | --- |
| 7Y | NAF Detroit, Mich. |

## MARINE AIR RESERVE

The small Marine Air Reserve forms the Fourth Marine Aircraft Wing, assigned to support the reserve 4th Marine Division. Approximately 200 aircraft are assigned to the Wing's 20 squadrons.

### FIGHTER ATTACK SQUADRONS (VMFA)

| Squadrons | Location |
| --- | --- |
| VMFA-112 (MA) | NAS Dallas, Texas |
| VMFA-321 (MG) | NAF Andrews (Washington, D.C.) |

Both reserve fighter squadrons fly the F-4N Phantom.

### ATTACK SQUADRONS (VMA)

| Squadrons | Location |
| --- | --- |
| VMA-124 (QP) | NAS Memphis, Tenn. |
| VMA-131 (QG) | NAS Willow Grove, Penna. |
| VMA-133 (ME) | NAS Alameda, Calif. |
| VMA-134 (MF) | MCAS El Toro, Calif. |
| VMA-142 (MB) | NAS Jacksonville, Fla. |
| VMA-322 (QR) | NAS South Weymouth, Mass. |

These squadrons fly various models of the A-4 Skyhawk.

### OBSERVATION SQUADRONS (VMO)

| Squadrons | Location |
| --- | --- |
| VMO-4 (MU) | NAS Atlanta, Ga. |

This squadron flies the OV-10A Bronco.

### ATTACK HELICOPTER SQUADRONS (HMA)

| Squadrons | Location |
| --- | --- |
| HMA-773 (MP) | NAS Atlanta, Ga. |

AH-1G SeaCobra gunships are flown by this squadron.

### LIGHT HELICOPTER SQUADRONS (HML)

| Squadrons | Location |
| --- | --- |
| HML-776 (QL) | NAS Glenview, Ill. |
| HML-770 (MN) | NAS Whidley Island, Wash. |
| HML-771 (QK) | NAS South Weymouth, Mass. |

The squadron is assigned UH-1E Iroquois/Huey helicopters.

### MEDIUM HELICOPTER SQUADRONS (HMM)

| Squadrons | Location |
|---|---|
| HMM-764 (ML) | MCAS Santa Ana, Calif. |
| HMM-767 (MM) | NAS New Orleans, La. |
| HMM-774 (MQ) | NAS Norfolk, Va. |

These squadrons all fly CH-46D helicopters.

### HEAVY HELICOPTER SQUADRONS (HMH)

| Squadrons | Location |
|---|---|
| HMH-769 (MS) | NAS Alameda, Calif. |
| HMH-772 (MT) | NAS Willow Grove, Penna. |
| HMH-777 (QM) | NAS Dallas, Texas |

These heavy helicopter squadrons operate CH-53A Sea Stallion helicopters.

### REFUELLER-TRANSPORT SQUADRONS (VMGR)

| Squadrons | Location |
|---|---|
| VMGR-234 (QH) | NAS Glenview, Ill. |

KC-130F Hercules transports are flown by this squadron.

An E-2 Hawkeye AEW aircraft warms up on the flight deck of the NIMITZ (CVN 00) during Air Wing 0 (AJ) operations in the North Atlantic. In the background are F-4J Phantoms and A-7 Corsairs. (1975, U.S. Navy, JO1 Chris Christensen)

# 23 Naval Aircraft

This chapter describes the principal aircraft now flown by the U.S. Navy, Marine Corps, and Coast Guard.

All naval aircraft are assigned designations under a standard Department of Defense system adopted on 18 September 1962. This system replaced the Navy scheme that had been in use for naval aircraft since 29 March 1922. The older scheme identified the aircraft's mission, the manufacturer, and the model of that type by the manufacturer. The current mission and sequence designation system used for naval aircraft is similar to that long used by the U.S. Air Force and its predecessors. Where appropriate, the older aircrafts' former (pre-1962) designations are shown in parentheses.

*Explanation of symbols:*

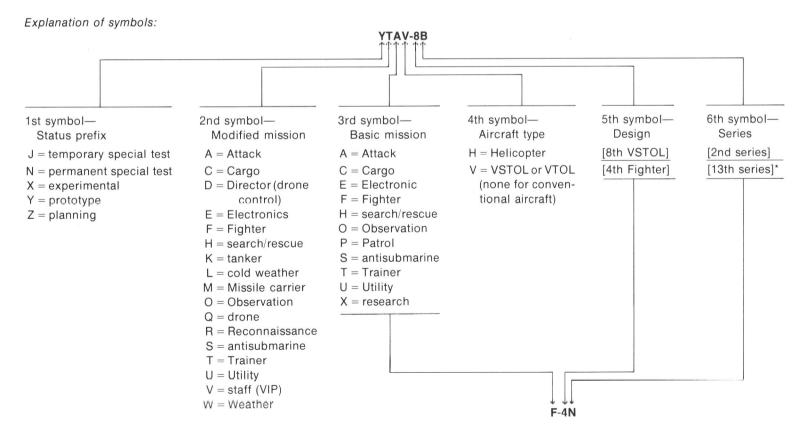

**YTAV-8B**

| 1st symbol— Status prefix | 2nd symbol— Modified mission | 3rd symbol— Basic mission | 4th symbol— Aircraft type | 5th symbol— Design | 6th symbol— Series |
|---|---|---|---|---|---|
| J = temporary special test | A = Attack | A = Attack | H = Helicopter | [8th VSTOL] | [2nd series] |
| N = permanent special test | C = Cargo | C = Cargo | V = VSTOL or VTOL (none for conventional aircraft) | [4th Fighter] | [13th series]* |
| X = experimental | D = Director (drone control) | E = Electronic | | | |
| Y = prototype | E = Electronics | F = Fighter | | | |
| Z = planning | F = Fighter | H = search/rescue | | | |
| | H = search/rescue | O = Observation | | | |
| | K = tanker | P = Patrol | | | |
| | L = cold weather | S = antisubmarine | | | |
| | M = Missile carrier | T = Trainer | | | |
| | O = Observation | U = Utility | | | |
| | Q = drone | X = research | | | |
| | R = Reconnaissance | | | | |
| | S = antisubmarine | | | | |
| | T = Trainer | | | | |
| | U = Utility | | | | |
| | V = staff (VIP) | | | | |
| | W = Weather | | | | |

**F-4N**

NOTE: *Letters I and O are not used to avoid confusion with numerals.

The following Navy, Marine Corps, and Coast Guard aircraft are described in this chapter.

| Mission/Type | Designation | Popular Name | Status[a] | Type[b] |
|---|---|---|---|---|
| Fighter | F-4 | Phantom II | N-NR-MC-MR | CV |
| | F-5E/F | Tiger II | N | L |
| | XFV-12A | — | development | VSTOL |
| | F-14 | Tomcat | N | CV |
| | F-18 | Hornet | development | CV |
| | Type B VSTOL | — | planning | VSTOL |
| Attack | A-4 | Skyhawk | N-NR-MC-MR | CV |
| | A-6 | Intruder | N-MC | CV |
| | A-7 | Corsair II | N-NR-MC | CV |
| | AV-8 | Harrier | MC | VSTOL |
| | AV-16 | Advanced Harrier | development | VSTOL |
| | A-18 | Hornet | development | CV |
| Antisubmarine | S-3 | Viking | N | CV |
| | Type A VSTOL | — | development | VSTOL |
| Patrol | P-2 | Neptune | NR | L |
| | P-3 | Orion | N-NR | L |
| | HU-16E | Albatross | CG | A |
| | HU-25A | Falcon | development | L |
| Electronic Warfare | E-2 | Hawkeye | N-NR | CV |
| | EA-3B | Skywarrior | N-NR | CV |
| | EA-6A | Intruder | MC | CV |
| | EA-6B | Prowler | N-MC | CV |
| | EB-47E | Stratojet | N | L |
| Reconnaissance | RA-5C | Vigilante | N | CV |
| | RF-8G | Crusader | N-NR | CV |
| Observation | OV-10 | Bronco | MC-MR | L-STOL |
| Cargo/transport/ utility | C-1A | Trader | N | CV |
| | C-2A | Greyhound | N | CV |
| | C-4 | Gulfstream I | N-MC-CG | L |
| | C-9B | Skytrain II | MC-NR | L |
| | VC-11A | Gulfstream II | CG | L |
| | C-117 | Skytrain | N-MC | L |
| | C-118B | Liftmaster | N | L |
| | C-130 | Hercules | N-NR-MC-MR-CG | L |
| | C-131 | Samaritan | N-CG | L |
| | CTX | — | development | L |
| Trainer | T-2C | Buckeye | N | CV |
| | TS-2/US-2 | Tracker | N | CV |
| | T-28 | Trojan | N | CV |
| | T-34C | Mentor | N | L |
| | T-38A | Talon | N | L |
| | T-39D | Sabreliner | N-MC | L |
| | T-44A | (King Air) | N | L |
| Helicopter | AH-1 | SeaCobra | MC-MR | |
| | UH-1 | Huey (Iroquois) | N-MC-MR | |
| | SH-2 | LAMPS | N | |
| | SH-3 | Sea King | N-NR | |
| | HH-3F | Pelican | CG | |
| | H-46 | Sea Knight | N-MC-MR | |
| | HH-52A | Sea Guard | CG | |
| | H-53 | Sea Stallion | N-MC-MR | |
| | CH-53E | Super Stallion | N-MC | |
| | TH-57A | Sea Ranger | N | |
| | SH-60B | LAMPS III | development | |

NOTE: a Primary users N = Navy, NR NR = Naval Air Reserve, MC = Marine Corps, MR = Marine Air Reserve, CG = Coast Guard
b Type CV = carrier-capable, L = land-based, VSTOL = Vertical and Short Take-Off and Landing, STOL = Short Take-Off and Landing (i.e. can operate from carrier-type ships under certain conditions)

## FIGHTER AIRCRAFT

### F-4 PHANTOM II (McDonnell Douglas)

The Phantom is an all-weather, multi-purpose fighter that has served in the U.S. Navy, Marine Corps, and Air Force since the early 1960s. It is now being replaced in the Navy by the F-14 Tomcat and in the Air Force by the F-15 Eagle. The Phantom is also flown by several foreign air forces. McDonnell-Douglas has produced about 5,000 Phantoms, and 158 of the F-4EJ model have been built by Mitsubishi in Japan.

Navy and Marine squadrons fly the F-4J/N/S variants, with 12 aircraft assigned to each squadron. The Marine Corps also has one reconnaissance squadron which is assigned 21 RF-4B photo aircraft. (These are unarmed, two-seat aircraft which have been lengthened to $62\frac{5}{6}$ feet to accommodate cameras, infrared detector, and side-looking radar).

The service life of the earlier Phantoms is being extended, with 228 F-4B aircraft being updated to the F-4N configuration and 260 F-4J aircraft being upgraded to the F-4S configuration. During the 1980s the surviving Navy and Marine Phantoms will be replaced by the F-18 Hornet.

### Characteristics (F-4J)

| | |
|---|---|
| Crew: | 1 pilot, 1 radar intercept officer |
| Weights: | 28,000 lbs empty; 46,000 lbs loaded clean; 54,600 lbs maximum |
| Dimensions: | length 58¼ ft (17.76 m), span 38⁵/₁₂ ft (11.71 m), height 16¼ ft (4.96 m) |
| Engines: | 2 GE J79-GE-10 turbojets; 17,900 lbst each with afterburner |
| Speeds: | 1,450 mph clean at 36,000 ft (Mach 2.2) |
| Ranges: | ~900-n.mile radius with AAMs; ~1,000-n.mile radius in ground attack role; 2,300-n.mile ferry range |
| Ceiling: | 71,000 ft |
| Guns: | no internal guns |
| Payload: | 4 Sparrow AAMs + 4 Sidewinder AAMs or 6 Sparrow AAMs + 18 750-lb bombs or 11 1,000-lb bombs or 1 Mk 28/43/57 nuclear weapon |

Two F-4J Phantoms from VMFA-451 assigned to the USS FORRESTAL (CV 59) (U.S. Navy)

F-4J Phantom with six Sparrow III AAMs and two 370-gallon fuel tanks (U.S. Navy)

**F-5E/F TIGER II** (Northrop)

The F-5E and F-5F are the latest aircraft in a long series of Northrop lightweight fighter and trainer aircraft of similar design, the F-5 Freedom Fighter and T-38 Talon, respectively. More than 3,000 of these aircraft have been built for the U.S. Air Force and 25 foreign air forces, with several hundred additional F-5E/F aircraft on order.

The Navy has taken delivery of 17 F-5E and six two-seat F-5F fighters to simulate Soviet fighter aircraft for combat training. These planes are flown by the Navy Fighter Weapons School (called "Top Gun") at Miramar, California, and two fighter squadrons. (The T-38A Talon and A-4E/F Skyhawk are also flown in this role.)

### Characteristics (F-5E)

| | |
|---|---|
| Crew: | 1 pilot (2 in F-5F) |
| Weights: | 9,588 lbs empty; 24,080 lbs maximum |
| Dimensions: | length 48⅓ feet (14.73 m), span 26⅔ ft (8.13 m), height 13⁵/₁₂ ft (4.08 m); F-5F length 51¾ ft (15.78 m) |
| Engines: | 2 GE J85-GE-21 turbojets; 5,000 lbst each |
| Speeds: | Mach 1.6 clean at 36,000 ft |
| Ranges: | 190-n.mile radius with maximum payload; 875-n.mile radius with 2 AAMs |
| Ceiling: | 54,000 ft |
| Guns: | 2 20-mm M39A2 (1 in F-5F) |
| Payload: | no bombs carried in Navy training role |

F-5E Tiger II from Navy Fighter Weapons School (U.S. Navy)

F-5E Tiger II from Navy Fighter Weapons School (Robert L. Lawson)

### XFV-12A (Rockwell International)

The XFV-12A is being developed as a high-performance VSTOL fighter for shipboard operation. The prototype XFV-12A was to begin flying in 1978 in an extensive NASA–Navy test program. There is no specific Navy acquisition plan; however, if successful the XFV-12A could be included in the Navy Type B VSTOL program (see later listing).

The aircraft has a thrust-augmented wing design to allow vertical and short take-offs and landings. The unusual configuration features a delta wing aft with vertical stabilizers and small canards forward. Engine exhaust is diverted through nozzles in the wing and canards to achieve vertical flight. To reduce cost and lead times, the prototype aircraft makes extensive use of F-4 Phantom and A-4 Skyhawk components, while the engine design is based on the F-14 Tomcat.

XFV-12A prototype (Rockwell International)

### Characteristics

| | |
|---|---|
| Crew: | 1 pilot |
| Weights: | 19,500 lbs maximum VTOL; 24,250 lbs maximum STOL |
| Dimensions: | length 43⅚ ft (13.3 m), span 28⅚ ft (8.8 m), height 10⁵/₁₂ ft (3.19 m) |
| Engines: | 1 P&W F401-PW-400 turbofan; 14,070 lbst; 21,800 lbst in lift configuration |
| Speeds: | Mach 2.2–2.4 |
| Ranges: | 575-n mile radius with AAMs |
| Ceiling: | |
| Guns: | 1 20-mm M61A1 rotary-barrel |
| Payload: | AAMs plus limited bomb and missile capacity |

XFV-12A prototype (Rockwell International)

Artist's concept of XFV-12A (Rockwell International)

### F-14 TOMCAT (Grumman)

The F-14 was developed specifically to carry the AWG-9 multi-target radar and the Phoenix long-range AAM. The radar can simultaneously track up to 24 targets and guide as many as six Phoenix missiles to targets more than 60 miles away.

The aircraft originally was intended for Navy and Marine use, but Marine procurement was cancelled in 1975. The Iranian Air Force is buying 80 F-14A aircraft. In 1978 the Navy had 14 fighter squadrons flying the F-14A with a total of 20 squadrons planned for the 1982–1984 period, after which time the number will decline to 18 squadrons for the next decade. Each squadron has 12 Tomcats. In addition, sufficient RF-14A reconnaissance variants carrying camera/infrared pods will be procured to form one squadron, with 12 three-plane detachments. The RF-14 will replace the RF-8G Crusader and RA-5C Vigilante in the carrier-based "recce" role.

The F-14 has variable-geometry wings which sweep automatically during high-speed maneuvers to provide the optimum wing form. They extend for long-range cruise, landing, and take-off, and sweep back for high-speed flight.

### Characteristics

| | |
|---|---|
| Crew: | 1 pilot, 1 radar intercept officer |
| Weights: | 37,500 lbs empty; 72,000 lbs maximum |
| Dimensions: | length 61⁵/₆ ft (18.86 m), span swept back 64¹/₁₂ ft (19.54 m), span extended 38¹/₆ ft (11.63 m), height 16 ft (4.88 m) |
| Engines: | 2 P&W TF30-P-412A turbofans; 20,900 lbst each with afterburner |
| Speeds: | Mach 2.34 |
| Ranges: | |
| Ceiling: | 60,000 ft |
| Guns: | 1 20-mm M61A1 rotary-barrel |
| Payload: | 4 Sidewinder AAMs + 4 Sparrow AAMs or 4 Sidewinder AAMs + 6 Phoenix AAMs |

F-14A Tomcat from VF-1 (Robert L. Lawson)

F-14A Tomcat from VF-1, landing on the ENTERPRISE (CVN 65) (U.S. Navy, PH3 Don W. Redden)

F-14A Tomcat in simulated combat with F-4 Phantom (Grumman Aircraft Corp)

F-14A Tomcat from VF-1 and A-6 Intruder from VA-196 ready for launch on the ENTERPRISE (CVN 65) (U.S. Navy, PH3 Harold Brown)

F-14A Tomcat from VF-1 in inverted flight (Robert L. Lawson)

**F-18 HORNET** (Northrop/McDonnell Douglas)

The F-18 is being developed as a replacement for the F-4 Phantom in Navy and Marine service. It is considered a lightweight aircraft, developed like the contemporary Air Force F-16 in an effort to reduce procurement and life-cycle costs, albeit with some loss in capability. The F-18 is the production model of the YF-17, which has been developed in competition with the F-16. Two YF-17 prototypes were evaluated by the Air Force, Navy, Marine Corps, and NASA.

Procurement of the F-18 fighter variant is planned for six Navy carrier squadrons and four reserve squadrons, and four Marine fighter squadrons and two reserve squadrons. Marine deliveries are scheduled to start in 1981 and Navy deliveries in 1982. A two-seat TF-18 is also planned. (See separate A-18 listing for attack variant.) Total F-18/A-18 procurement will be about 800 aircraft, plus 11 development aircraft, under current planning.

### Characteristics

| | |
|---|---|
| Crew: | 1 pilot |
| Weights: | 33,583 lbs maximum |
| Dimensions: | length 56 ft (17.1 m), span 37½ ft (11.4 m), height 15⅓ ft (4.7 m) |
| Engines: | 2 GE F404-GE-400 turbojets; 15,000 lbst each |
| Speeds: | Mach 1.8 |
| Ranges: | ~400-n.mile radius with AAMs; 2,000-n.mile ferry range |
| Ceiling: | 49,400 ft |
| Guns: | 1 20-mm M61A1 rotary-barrel |
| Payload: | 2 Sidewinder AAMs + 7 Sparrow AAMs |

YF-17A Hornet prototype with Sidewinder AAMs (Northrop)

YF-17A Hornet prototype with Sidewinder AAMs (Northrop)

**TYPE B VSTOL**

The Navy has begun preliminary planning for a supersonic VSTOL aircraft that would become operational about 1995 as a replacement for the F-14 Tomcat and A-6 Intruder. The first flight for competitive prototypes produced by two different firms would occur in 1988 under current plans.

The aircraft would have a gross take-off weight of some 35,000–45,000 lbs.

YF-17A Hornet prototype with Sidewinder AAMs (Northrop)

## ATTACK AIRCRAFT

### A-4 SKYHAWK (McDonnell Douglas)

The A-4 (originally A4D) was developed in the early 1950s as a lightweight, daylight-only nuclear strike aircraft for use in large numbers from aircraft carriers. The aircraft has evolved into a highly versatile strike aircraft with more than 2,600 being produced between the first Navy deliveries in 1954 through the mid-1970s.

Although this aircraft is no longer in first-line Navy service, the Marines have five Skyhawk squadrons (16 aircraft each), and it is flown by several foreign air forces. The last Navy attack squadrons with Skyhawks were disbanded in 1975 with the decommissioning of the carrier HANCOCK (CVA 16). The Navy continues to fly the aircraft in research, electronic, and training roles, with a few A-4E/Fs having been stripped down to simulate Soviet fighter aircraft, for use in advanced air combat training. (Those aircraft have been named "Mongoose" as a play on the system of designating Soviet training aircraft with names beginning with the letter "M.") The Navy's Blue Angels flight demonstration team flies the A-4F.

In addition to the five active and five Marine Reserve squadrons flying the A-4E/M in the attack role, each of the three active Marine Aircraft Wings has about ten TA-4F/J aircraft for tactical air control and proficiency flying.

A-4M Skyhawk from VMA-331 (U.S. Navy, Thomas Ackerman)

EA-4F Skyhawk from VAQ-33 (U.S. Navy)

### Characteristics (A-4M)

| | |
|---|---|
| Crew: | 1 pilot (2 in EA-4/TA-4) |
| Weights: | 10,465 lbs empty; 24,500 lbs maximum |
| Dimensions: | length 41⅓ ft (12.5 m), span 27½ ft (8.38 m), height 15 ft (4.57 m); length EA-4/TA-4 42⁷/₁₂ ft (12.99 m) |
| Engines: | 1 P&W J52-P-408A turbojet; 11,200 lbst |
| Speeds: | 670 mph clean at sea level (Mach 0.94); 645 mph with 4,000 lbs weapons |
| Ranges: | 335-n.mile radius with 4,000 lbs weapons; 2,055-n.mile ferry range |
| Ceiling: | |
| Guns: | 2 20-mm Mk 12 |
| Payload: | 2 Bullpup ASMs + 6 500-lb bombs + 12 250-lb bombs |
| | or 4 Bullpup ASMs |
| | or 3 2,000-lb bombs |
| | or 1 Mk 28/43/57 nuclear weapon |

A-4E Skyhawk from VC-1 fitted with in-flight refueling tanks (U.S. Navy, PHC C. C. Curtis)

TA-4J Skyhawk from VF-126 (U.S. Navy, Lieutenant J. F. Wantz)

**A-6 INTRUDER** (Grumman)

The A-6 (originally A2F) is an all-weather and night attack aircraft developed for conventional ground attack.

The Navy flies the A-6E in 12 carrier-based attack squadrons (10–12 aircraft each) and the Marines have five attack squadrons (12 aircraft each). In addition, four KA-6D tankers are assigned to most Navy carrier air wings. (Listed separately in this volume are the electronic warfare variants, the EA-6A Intruder and EA-6B Prowler).

The standard attack variant now in service, the A-6E, is being fitted with the TRAM package (Target Recognition Attack Multisensors) which includes a 20-inch diameter "turret" under the forward fuselage with infrared and laser targeting devices.

### Characteristics (A-6E)

| | |
|---|---|
| Crew: | 1 pilot, 1 bombardier/navigator |
| Weights: | 25,630 lbs empty; 60,400 lbs maximum |
| Dimensions: | length 54$^7$/$_{12}$ ft (16.67 m), span 53 ft (16.15 m), height 16$^1$/$_6$ ft (4.92 m) |
| Engines: | 2 P&W J52-P-8A/-8B turbojets; 9,300 lbst each |
| Speeds: | 685 mph at sea level (Mach 0.9); 482 mph cruise |
| Ranges: | |
| Ceiling: | 44,600 ft |
| Guns: | none |
| Payload: | 4 Bullpup ASMs |
| | or 20 500-lb bombs |
| | or 13 1,000-lb bombs |
| | or 5 2,000-lb bombs |
| | or 1 Mk 28/43/57 nuclear weapon |

A-6 Intruder landing aboard the ENTERPRISE (CVN 65) (U.S. Navy)

A-6E Intruder from VA-65 (Grumman Aerospace Corp)

**A-7 CORSAIR** (LTV-Vought)

The A-7 is a carrier-based, light attack aircraft. Originally developed as a replacement for the A-4 Skyhawk in the visual, daylight attack role, succeeding variants of the A-7 have incorporated improvements in navigation and sensors to provide a limited all-weather and night capability.

There are 24 carrier-based A-7 squadrons, each flying 12 A-7 A/B/C/E aircraft. An all A-7E force is being procured for first-line squadrons. In addition, 40 A-7B and 41 A-7C single-seat aircraft are being converted to the two-seat TA-7C variant for the training role. The two-seat aircraft will have the same electronics and weapons capabilities of the A-7E. Plans to procure an RA-7E using reconnaissance pods have been dropped in favor of using the RF-14 in the carrier-based "recce" role. The A-7E is similar to the U.S. Air Force A-7D variant, with the principal difference being the engine. Vought has proposed a twin-engine A-7 variant as an alternative to developing the A-18 light attack aircraft.

### Characteristics (A-7E)

| | |
|---|---|
| Crew: | 1 pilot (2 in TA-7C) |
| Weights: | 19,781 lbs empty; 42,000 lbs maximum |
| Dimensions: | length 46$^1$/$_6$ ft (14.06 m), span 38¾ ft (11.8 m), height 16$^1$/$_{12}$ ft (4.9 m) |
| Engines: | 1 Allison TF41-A-2 (Spey); 15,000 lbst |
| Speeds: | 690 mph at sea level (Mach 0.9) |
| Ranges: | ~700-n.mile radius with 4,000 lbs ordnance; 2,800-n.mile ferry range |
| Ceiling: | 42,600 ft |
| Guns: | 1 20-mm M61A1 rotary-barrel |
| Payload: | 2 Sidewinder AAMs + 12 250-lb bombs + 12 500-lb bombs |
| | or 2 Sidewinder AAMs + 20 500-lb bombs |
| | or 1 Mk 28/43/57 nuclear weapon |

Three A-7E Corsairs from VA-147 (Vought Aircraft)

A-7E Corsair from VA-52 (Vought Aircraft)

A-7E Corsair from VA-25 (U.S. Navy, PH2 Paul Burns)

**AV-8 HARRIER** (Hawker Siddeley/McDonnell Douglas)

The AV-8A was the first VSTOL aircraft to enter service with the U.S. armed forces. The British-developed Harrier and its experimental predecessor, the P.1127 Kestrel (XV-6A), flew test flights from several U.S. and foreign ships prior to its acceptance by the U.S. Marine Corps. The AV-8A variant, manufactured by McDonnell Douglas, entered Marine squadrons in 1972 (five years after squadron deliveries to the Royal Air Force).

The AV-8A is flown in the light attack role by three Marine squadrons (20 aircraft assigned to each), plus training formations. The improved, higher-performance AV-8B has been proposed, with two YAV-8B prototypes flying in 1978 and squadron deliveries to begin in 1984 as the replacement for all AV-8A Harriers and A-4 Skyhawks in Marine attack squadrons. (As an interim improvement to the light attack capability, the surviving AV-8A variants will be upgraded to a AV-8C configuration.) In addition to the 108 single-seat Harriers procured by the Marines, eight TAV-8A two-seat training aircraft were acquired.

In service the aircraft has suffered a high accident rate, with 21 aircraft destroyed in accidents and seven severely damaged through December 1977. Almost all of the losses occurred during conventional flight and not in the VSTOL flight mode.

The Harrier is powered by a vectored-thrust turbofan engine that exhausts through rotating nozzles. The nozzles are rotated for vertical and short take-offs and landings. The wings do not fold but the aircraft is fully carrier-capable.

Characteristics (AV-8A)

| | |
|---|---|
| Crew: | 1 pilot (2 in TAV-8A) |
| Weights: | 12,200 lbs empty; 17,500 lbs gross for VTOL; 21,489 lbs gross for STOL; 25,000+ lbs maximum with conventional take-off |
| Dimensions: | length 45½ ft (13.87 m), span 25¼ ft (7.7 m), height 11¼ ft (3.43 m) |
| Engines: | 1 Rolls-Royce Pegasus Mk 103 vectored-thrust turbofan; 21,500 lbst |
| Speeds: | 737 mph at 1,000 ft (Mach 0.95) |
| Ranges: | 200-n.mile radius with 2,500 lbs ordnance; 400-n.mile radius with 2 AAMs and 1 hour loiter |
| Ceiling: | 50,000+ ft |
| Guns: | none |
| Payload: | 2 Sidewinder AAMs + 3 3,000-lb bombs + 2 rocket pods |

AV-8A Harrier from VMA-513 with wheels retracted (U.S. Marine Corps)

AV-8A Harrier from VMA-513 aboard the USS Guam (LPH 9) (U.S. Navy)

AV-8A Harrier from VMA-231 being armed on the USS FRANKLIN D. ROOSEVELT (CV 42) (U.S. Navy, PH3 Greg Haas)

AV-8A Harrier from VMA-513 being refueled by an A-4M Skyhawk (U.S. Navy)

**AV-16 ADVANCED HARRIER** (Hawker Siddeley/McDonnell Douglas)

The Advanced Harrier is being developed as a VSTOL light-attack aircraft to supplement or replace the AV-8B.

The AV-16 design is based largely on the AV-8B.

### Characteristics (Tentative)

| | |
|---|---|
| Crew: | 1 pilot |
| Weights: | 21,100 lbs gross for VTOL; 28,000 lbs maximum |
| Dimensions: | length 46½ ft (14.18 m), span 30¼ ft (9.23 m), height 12 ft (3.66 m) |
| Engines: | 1 Rolls-Royce Pegasus 15 turbofan; 24,500 lbst |
| Speeds: | 720 mph |
| Ranges: | 345-n.mile radius with 2,000 lbs ordnance in VTOL mode; 345-n.mile radius with 4,000 lbs ordnance in STOL mode |
| Ceiling: | |
| Guns: | 1 20-mm |
| Payload: | 4,000 lbs ordnance |

AV-8A Harrier from VMA-513 (U.S. Marine Corps)

**A-18 HORNET** (Northrop/McDonnell Douglas)

The A-18 is the light-attack variant of the carrier-based F-18 Hornet fighter aircraft. Under current planning the Navy will begin squadron deliveries of the A-18 in 1983, with 24 attack squadrons (i.e., two per carrier air wing) and six reserve air squadrons scheduled to fly the aircraft in place of the current A-7 Corsair. No Marine procurement is planned for the A-18 variant.

### Characteristics

| | |
|---|---|
| Crew: | 1 pilot |
| Weights: | |
| Dimensions: | length 56 ft (17.1 m), span 37½ ft (11.4 m), height 15⅓ ft (4.7 m) |
| Engines: | 2 GE F404-GE-400 turbojets; 15,000 lbst each |
| Speeds: | |
| Ranges: | ~650 n.mile radius with 4,000 lbs bombs |
| Ceiling: | 49,400 ft |
| Guns: | 1 20-mm M61A1 rotary-barrel |
| Payload: | 4 1,000-lb bombs + 2 Sidewinder AAMs or 10 500-lb bombs + 2 Sidewinder AAMs |

AV-8A Harrier from VMA-231 on the USS FRANKLIN D. ROOSEVELT (CV 42) (PH3 Greg Haas)

## ANTISUBMARINE AIRCRAFT

### S-3 VIKING (Lockheed)

The S-3 is the Navy's carrier-based ASW aircraft, with one ten-plane squadron planned for each of the 12 carrier air wings. With 11 squadrons formed by 1978, the Viking has fully replaced the venerable S-2 Tracker in Navy first-line service (although Trackers continue to serve in the utility and training roles, and in several foreign air arms). About 180 are in U.S. service.

The aircraft carries a variety of ASW sensors with an on-board 65,000-word AYK-10 digital computer to process data for the sensors, communications, and navigation systems. The sensors include APS-116 high-resolution radar, ASQ-81 Magnetic Anomaly Detection (MAD), Forward-Looking Infrared (FLIR), Electronic Countermeasures (ECM), and fuselage tube launchers for 60 sonobuoys. The Viking's endurance is over nine hours.

Three variants of the S-3 are being proposed: The US-3A COD (Carrier On-Board Delivery), ES-3A TASES (Tactical Airborne Signal Exploitation System), and KS-3A tanker.

The COD variant will be able to carry up to 23 passengers or cargo in the fuselage compartment, and additional cargo in two underwing pods. The US-3A would replace the existing C-1 and C-2 COD aircraft.

The TASES aircraft will perform surveillance in direct support of fleet operations, using radar and electro-optical, electronic, and hydroacoustic (sonobuoy) systems. Each aircraft would have two pilots and three equipment operators. Sixteen ES-3A aircraft are planned to replace the EA-3B Skywarriors now flown by squadrons VQ-1 and -2, and provide additional pipeline aircraft.

The fifth production S-3A has been modified to a tanker demonstration aircraft which lacks certain ASW systems and is fitted with additional fuel tanks in the weapons bay and with a hose, reel, and drouge in the after fuselage. Two external fuel tanks also can be fitted. The aircraft can be configured to have twice the transfer fuel/time-on-station as the KA-6D Intruder.

### Characteristics (S-3A)

| | |
|---|---|
| Crew: | 2 pilots, 1 tactical coordinator, 1 systems operator |
| Weights: | 26,783 lbs empty; 52,539 lbs maximum |
| Dimensions: | length 53⅓ ft (16.26 m), span 68⅔ ft (20.93 m), height 22¾ ft (6.94 m) |
| Engines: | 2 GE TF34-GE-2 high by-pass ratio turbofans; 9,275 lbst each |
| Speeds: | 506 mph at sea level; 400+ mph cruise; 240 mph loiter at 20,000 ft |
| Ranges: | 2,300+ n.mile patrol range; 3,000+ n.mile ferry range |
| Ceiling | 40,000 ft |
| Guns: | none |
| Payload: | 4 Mk 46 torpedoes (weapons bay) + 6 500-lb bombs (wing pylons) or 4 500-lb bombs (weapons bay) + 6 500-lb bombs (wing pylons) |

S-3A Viking from VS-41 with MAD boom extended (U.S. Navy, PH1 B. L. Kuykendall)

S-3A Viking taking off from the USS FORRESTAL (CV 59) with practice mines on wing pylons (U.S. Navy, PH3 Terry C. Mitchell)

S-3A Vikings from VS-28; the fuselage openings aft of the wings are sonobuoy launch tubes (Robert L. Lawson)

## TYPE A VSTOL

The Navy is sponsoring contractor development of a Type A VSTOL aircraft which will serve in the carrier-based Antisubmarine Warfare (ASW) and Airborne Early Warning (AEW) roles and, in addition, possess certain secondary mission capabilities. Competitive prototypes will be built by two aircraft firms for flight tests in the early 1980s. The winner of that competition will produce the aircraft for squadron use by 1991.

Current planning calls for a "combat" configuration which would eventually replace the E-2 Hawkeye AEW aircraft and S-3 Viking ASW aircraft, and a cargo/utility configuration which would replace the KA-6 Intruder tanker, C-2 Hawkeye/US-3 Viking COD aircraft, and the CH-46 Sea Knight helicopter. A probable carrier air wing of the 1990s could include 10 Type A aircraft of the ASW configuration, 5 of the AEW type, and five COD/tanker aircraft. With spares, pipeline, and training aircraft, this would mean a total of about 235 Type A VSTOLs for a 12-carrier force.

Assuming about ten Type A VSTOLs would be assigned to each of 12 LHA/LPH amphibious ships for vertical assault, a total of some 170 troop and cargo carriers would be procured. Thus, some 400 to 500 Type A VSTOLs are anticipated in the Navy by the late 1990s if current planning is carried out.

The possibility exists of operating the ASW/AEW variants from cruisers and destroyers, and the troop and cargo carriers from LPD/LSD-type amphibious ships. This would result in a considerably larger Type A program. Flying from cruisers and destroyers, the Type A VSTOL presumably would also perform over-the-horizon targeting for cruise missiles. Frigates will probably be too small to operate this aircraft, which will have a gross weight of some 45,000–50,000 lbs.

## PATROL AIRCRAFT

### P-2 NEPTUNE (Lockheed)

The P-2 (originally P2V), the most advanced patrol and maritime reconnaissance aircraft developed during World War II, entered U.S. Navy squadron service in 1947. It is now flown by the Navy only in the utility role; reserve squadrons are phasing out the P-2H (P2V-7) variant. Several foreign navies and air forces still fly various Neptune models. Lockheed produced a total of 1,099 aircraft, and Kawasaki in Japan built an additional 89 P-2J variants. (Forty-eight Lockheed-produced P-2H aircraft were assembled in Japan.)

ASW sensors include APS-20E search radar, ASQ-8 MAD, and 72 sonobuoys. Early variants had a gun armament.

### Characteristics (P-2H)

| | |
|---|---|
| Crew: | 2 pilots, 1 navigator, 1 flight engineer, 3 observers/systems operators |
| Weights: | 49,935 lbs empty; 79,895 lbs maximum |
| Dimensions: | length 91⅔ ft (27.94 m), span 103¹¹/₁₂ ft (31.65 m), height 29⅓ ft (8.94 m) |
| Engines: | 2 Wright R-3550-32W radial piston; 3,500 hp each + 2 Westinghouse J34-WE-32W turbojet pods 3,400 lbst each |
| Speeds: | 356 mph at 10,000 ft (piston engines only); 173 mph patrol at 980 ft |
| Ranges: | 2,200-n.mile patrol range; 3,685-n.mile maximum range |
| Ceiling: | 22,000 ft |
| Guns: | none |
| Payload: | 4 2,000-lb bombs (weapons bay) + 16 5-inch rockets (wing pylons) or 8 Mk 46 torpedoes (weapons bay) + 16 5-inch rockets (wing pylons) |

P-2H Neptune (U.S. Navy)

Artist's concept of Grumman Aircraft Corporation's Type A VSTOL design (Grumman)

P-2H Neptune (U.S. Navy)

**P-3 ORION** (Lockheed)

The P-3 (formerly P3V) serves in all 24 Navy patrol squadrons and the 13 Naval Reserve VP squadrons. Several foreign navies and air forces also fly the Orion.

The aircraft was adopted from the commercial Electra airliner, with a succession of ASW/maritime-patrol variants being produced for the U.S. Navy. Most Navy squadrons now fly the P-3C variant, with the so-called A-NEW, UPDATE I, and UPDATE II programs providing improved sensors and data-handling capabilities to the basic P-3C.

The P-3C in its basic configuration has an on-board digital computer for ASW tactical calculations, APS-115 search radar, ASQ-10A MAD, Electronic Countermeasures (ECM), and other sensors, and tube launchers with storage for sonobuoys. Patrol endurance is up to 17 hours.

Three specialized configurations of the P-3 are in service, the EP-3B/E electronic reconnaissance variant, the RP-3A/D research aircraft, and WP-3D weather research aircraft.

The 12 EP-3B/E aircraft have radar pods faired into their upper and lower fuselage, and large radomes under the forward fuselage; they have 15-man crews and are employed in electronic surveillance missions.

The research aircraft are an RP-3A named the EL COYOTE used for environmental surveys, and RP-3A named the ARCTIC FOX for Arctic surveys, and an RP-3D named the ROADRUNNER for magnetic surveys.

Two WP-3D aircraft which have been modified for weather research are flown by the National Oceanic and Atmospheric Administration; they carry a crew of four plus 12 scientists.

### Characteristics (P-3C)

| | |
|---|---|
| Crew: | 1 command pilot, 2 pilots, 1 flight engineer, 1 navigator, 1 radio operator, 1 tactical coordinator, 3 systems operators; provisions for 2 additional observers |
| Weights: | 61,491 lbs empty; 135,000 lbs loaded; 142,000 lbs maximum |
| Dimensions: | length 116⅚ ft (35.61 m), span 99⅔ ft (30.37 m), height 33¾ ft (10.28 m) |
| Engines: | 4 Allison T56-A-14 turboprops; 4,910 ehp each |
| Speeds: | 473 mph at 15,000 ft; 378 mph cruise at 25,000 ft; 237 mph patrol at 1,500 ft |
| Ranges: | 2,380-n.mile patrol range; 4,500-n.mile ferry range |
| Ceiling: | 28,300 ft |
| Guns: | none |
| Payload: | 8 Mk 46 torpedoes (weapons bay) + 4 Mk 46 torpedoes (wing pylons) or 2 2,000-lb mines (weapons bay) + 4 Mk 46 torpedoes (wing pylons) or 4 1,000-lb mines (weapons bay) + 4 Mk 46 torpedoes (wing pylons) or 8 Mk 46 torpedoes (weapons bay) + 16 5-inch rockets (wing pylons) or 8 Mk 46 torpedoes (weapons bay) + 4 Bullpup ASMs (wing pylons) |

P-3C Orion from VP-24 with Bullpup ASMs under wing (U.S. Navy, PHC Arnold A. Clemons)

P-3 Orion (U.S. Navy)

EP-3E Orion from VQ-2; note fuselage electronics fairing and radome (U.S. Navy)

WP-3D Orion flown by National Oceanic and Atmospheric Administration; note projecting instrument probe on starboard side of aircraft. (NOAA)

## HU-16 ALBATROSS (Grumman)

The HU-16E (formerly designated UF) is flown by the U.S. Coast Guard in the Search And Rescue (SAR) role, and is the last seaplane in U.S. government service. (Several foreign navies and air forces continue to fly the Albatross in the SAR role, and a few ASW-configured Albatrosses are thought to be in foreign service.) The Navy's last HU-16D Albatross was retired in 1977. The aircraft has a SAR-mission endurance of up to 17 hours.

The Coast Guard plans to replace its Albatrosses with the land-based HU-25 Falcon (listed below).

### Characteristics (HU-16E)

| | |
|---|---|
| Crew: | 2 pilots, 1 navigator, 1 radio operator |
| Weights: | 23,025 lbs empty; 34,000 lbs maximum water takeoff; 37,500 lbs maximum runway takeoff |
| Dimensions: | length 62⅚ ft (19.17 m), span 96⅔ ft (29.48 m), height 25¹¹/₁₂ ft (7.9 m) |
| Engines: | 2 Wright R-1820-76A/B radial pistons; 1,425 hp each |
| Speeds: | 204 mph at 3,700 ft; 150 mph at 10,000 ft cruise; 135 mph at 1,500 ft search |
| Ranges: | 1,130-n.mile radius for SAR; 1,090-n.mile radius as transport |
| Ceiling: | 24,000 ft |
| Guns: | none |
| Payload: | 10 passengers or 12 litter patients |

HU-16E Albatross (U.S. Coast Guard)

## HU-25A FALCON (Falcon Jet)

The Coast Guard is procuring the HU-25A as a replacement for the aging HU-16E Albatross in the surveillance and Search And Rescue (SAR) roles. The aircraft is a modified commercial Falcon 20G business jet. Forty-one aircraft are being produced for the Coast Guard by the Falcon Jet Corporation, which is a jointly owned subsidiary of Dassault and Pan American. Deliveries are to begin in mid-1979 at the rate of one aircraft per month.

### Characteristics

| | |
|---|---|
| Crew: | 2 pilots, 2 observers, 1 surveillance systems operator |
| Weights: | 18,705 lbs empty; 30,500 lbs maximum |
| Dimensions: | length 56¼ ft (17.15 m), span 53½ ft (16.3 m), height 17⁵/₁₂ ft (5.32 m) |
| Engines: | 2 Garrett AiResearch ATF3-6 turbofans; 5,050 lbst each |
| Speeds: | 536 mph |
| Ranges: | 2,475 n.mile maximum range with 45 minutes on station |
| Ceiling: | |
| Guns: | none |
| Payload: | 3 passengers |

Artist's concept of HU-25A Falcon (Falcon Jet)

Artist's concept of HU-25A Falcon (Falcon Jet)

# ELECTRONIC WARFARE AIRCRAFT

**E-2 HAWKEYE** (Grumman)

The Hawkeye (formerly W2F) is a carrier-based Airborne Early Warning (AEW) aircraft which in its E-2C variant is generally considered the most capable electronic warning and control aircraft yet produced. (The E-2C had been offered as an alternative to the larger E-3 AWACS aircraft.) The Navy plans to procure enough E-2C aircraft to provide a four-plane detachment for each of 12 carrier air wings, with a total of 85 aircraft (including two prototype aircraft) planned for funding through FY 1982. One of the prototype aircraft was an E-2A modified to a YE-2C configuration, and now used as a trainer (designated TE-2C). Several E-2B aircraft (all updated E-2A) remain in service pending the availability of sufficient E-2C aircraft.

The E-2C has a 24-foot-diameter saucer-shaped radome, housing an APS-120 UHF radar. The dome revolves in the free airstream at the rate of six revolutions per minute. The radome can be retracted to reduce aircraft height to 16½ feet for carrier stowage. The aircraft has an on-board computer, ALR-59 passive detection system, and secure UHF and HF data links. Patrol endurance is six hours.

### Characteristics (E-2C)

| | |
|---|---|
| Crew: | 2 pilots, 1 combat information center (CIC) officer, 1 air controller, 1 radar operator or technician |
| Weights: | 37,678 lbs empty; 51,569 lbs maximum |
| Dimensions: | length $57^{7}/_{12}$ ft (17.56 m), span $80^{7}/_{12}$ ft (24.58 m), height $18^{1}/_{3}$ ft (5.59 m) |
| Engines: | 2 Allison T56-A-422 turboprops; 4,591 shp each |
| Speeds: | 375 mph; 310 mph cruise |
| Ranges: | 200-n.mile radius with up to six hours on station; 1,525-n.mile ferry range |
| Ceiling: | 30,800 ft |
| Guns: | none |
| Payload: | none |

E-2 Hawkeye landing aboard the carrier AMERICA (CV 66) (U.S. Navy)

E-2C Hawkeye from RVAW-120 (U.S. Navy, JOCS Dick Benjamin)

E-2B Hawkeye being catapulted from the carrier CONSTELLATION (CV 64) (U.S. Navy, PHCS Robert L. Lawson)

E-2B Hawkeye (U.S. Navy, PHCS Robert L. Lawson)

## EA-3B SKYWARRIOR (Douglas)

The Navy flies the EA-3B (formerly A3D-2Q) in the TASES (Tactical Airborne Signal Exploitation System) role in squadrons VQ-1 and -2. These aircraft are based ashore, but regularly go aboard carriers deployed in the Mediterranean and Western Pacific. The EA-3B began flying in the TASES role in 1960 and is expected to continue until about 1985 when it probably will be replaced by the ES-3 Viking. The TASES variant developed from the basic A-3(A3D) carrier-based heavy attack aircraft built in the late 1940s for the nuclear strike role.

The EA-3B is fitted with several electronic and communications-intercept systems, forward-looking and side-looking radars, infra-red sensors, and other specialized equipment. Fully loaded, the EA-3B is the heaviest carrier-based aircraft in service with any navy. In addition, ERA-3B aircraft, with cameras removed, are flown by VAQ-33 to support fleet exercises.

Two Naval Reserve squadrons fly the EKA-3B variant, which also has an in-flight refueling capability.

### Characteristics (EA-3B)

| | |
|---|---|
| Crew: | 1 pilot, 1 navigator/assistant pilot, 4 electronic systems operators, 1 additional crewman (optional); 4 crew in ERA-3B |
| Weights: | 41,193 lbs empty; 61,593 lbs loaded; 78,000 lbs maximum |
| Dimensions: | length 76⅓ ft (23.28 m), span 72½ ft (22.11 m), height 22⅚ ft (6.94 m) |
| Engines: | 2 P&W J57-P-10 turbojets; 12,400 lbst each |
| Speeds: | 640 mph at sea level (mach 0.84); 610 mph at 10,000 ft (Mach 0.83) 459 mph cruise |
| Ranges: | 1,100-n.mile radius |
| Ceiling: | 41,300 ft |
| Guns: | none |
| Payload: | none |

EA-3B Skywarrior from VQ-2; no identification markings are normally worn by EA-3B/EP-3 aircraft (U.S. Navy)

## EA-6A INTRUDER (Grumman)

The EA-6A (formerly A2F-1H) is a tactical Electronic Counter-measure (ECM) variant of the A-6A Intruder attack aircraft. The aircraft was developed specifically for the Marine Corps, and squadron VMAQ-2 was assigned 15 of the aircraft to provide detachments to the three Marine air wings. In addition, the VMAQ detachments periodically operate from aircraft carriers to compensate for the Navy's shortfall in EA-6B aircraft.

In 1977 the Marines took delivery of the first of the more capable EA-6B Prowlers which will replace the EA-6A aircraft by 1981.

Removal of the EA-6A jamming pods from the wing pylons permits the aircraft to operate in a limited attack mode.

### Characteristics (EA-6A)

| | |
|---|---|
| Crew: | 1 pilot, 1 electronic systems operator |
| Weights: | 27,769 lbs empty; 41,715 lbs loaded; 54,571 lbs maximum |
| Dimensions: | length 55½ ft (16.92 m), span 53 ft (16.15 m), height 15½ ft (4.72 m) |
| Engines: | 2 P&W J52-P-6 turbojets; 8,500 lbst each |
| Speeds: | 630 mph at sea level (Mach 0.83); 595 mph at sea level with five ECM pods |
| Ranges: | 825-n.mile radius with one ECM pod; 600-n.mile radius with three pods; 345-n.mile radius with five pods |
| Ceiling: | 37,800 ft |
| Guns: | none |
| Payload: | 5 ALQ-31B ECM pods (or various ordnance combinations up to 18,000 lbs, see A-6E Intruder listing) |

EA-6A Intruder being catapulted from a FORRESTAL-class carrier (U.S. Navy)

EA-6A Intruder from old VMCJ-2; now VMAQ-2 (U.S. Marine Corps)

**EA-6B PROWLER** (Grumman)

The EA-6B is an ECM variant of the A-6 Intruder attack aircraft which was developed for carrier operation. The aircraft differs from the EA-6A in having two more systems operators and more sophisticated jamming equipment. The EA-6B's name was changed from Intruder to Prowler in February 1972.

The Navy has nine EA-6B "squadrons" with 3 or 4 aircraft each, formed from about 60 aircraft delivered through early 1978 (the others being pipeline and training aircraft). The Navy plans to assign one such squadron to each of 12 carrier air wings. In addition, between 1977 and 1981 the Marine Corps will equip a 15-plane squadron with the EA-6B in place of the EA-6A.

Like the EA-6A, the Prowler has internal electronic equipment and can carry up to five jamming pods on wing and fuselage pylons. An APQ-129 search radar is also fitted.

EA-6B Prowler from VAQ-137 with wings folded; note two cockpits with side-by-side seating; ECM pods and drop tanks on wing and fuselage pylons (Robert L. Lawson)

## Characteristics (EA-6B)

| | |
|---|---|
| Crew: | 1 pilot, 3 electronic systems operators |
| Weights: | 34,581 lbs empty; 58,500 lbs maximum |
| Dimensions: | length 59⁵/₁₂ ft (18.11 m), span 53 ft (16.15 m), height 16¼ ft (4.95 m) |
| Engines: | 2 P&W J52-P-408 turbojets; 11,200 lbst |
| Speeds: | 660 mph at sea level; 477 mph cruise |
| Ranges: | 710-n.mile radius with four ECM pods |
| Ceiling: | |
| Guns: | none |
| Payload: | 5 ALQ-99 ECM pods |

EA-6B Prowler from VAQ-129 (Grumman)

EA-6B Prowler from VAQ-129 (Grumman)

**EB-47E STRATOJET** (Boeing)

The Navy operates two EB-47E aircraft to provide electronic warfare training and evaluation of fleet defenses. These are the only aircraft still flying of some 2,060 produced during the 1950s for the strategic bombing and reconnaissance roles. The last B-47s were discarded by the U.S. Air Force in 1965. Two B-47E aircraft were reactivated from storage by the Navy to serve in the electronic role; these are flown under contract by McDonnell Douglas flight personnel.

The EB-47E aircraft have been used extensively in support of test and evaluation of the Aegis radar and air defense system.

## Characteristics (EB-47E)

| | |
|---|---|
| Crew: | |
| Weights: | ~200,000 lbs maximum |
| Dimensions: | length 108 ft (32.92 m), span 116 ft (35.36 m), height 28 ft (8.53 m) |
| Engines: | 6 GE J47-GE-25 turbojets; 7,200 lbst |
| Speeds: | 606 mph at 16,300 ft; 557 mph at 38,500 ft |
| Ranges: | ~2,000-n.mile combat radius |
| Ceiling: | 40,500 ft |
| Guns: | removed |
| Payload: | no ordnance capability |

EB-47E Stratojet; note ECM pod on wing between twin and single engine nacelles (McDonnell Douglas)

## RECONNAISSANCE AIRCRAFT

### RA-5C VIGILANTE (North American)

The RA-5C is a multi-sensor reconnaissance aircraft developed from the short-lived A-5(A3J) heavy attack aircraft. The aircraft can operate under virtually all weather conditions and can be employed in the strike role. One hundred forty aircraft were delivered from 1961 to 1970.

There are four Navy reconnaissance–heavy attack squadrons (RVAH) which deploy aboard carriers. Each squadron normally operates three aircraft. (Navy RF-8G Crusaders and Marine RF-4B Phantoms provide reconnaissance capabilities aboard other carriers.) The surviving RA-5C aircraft are expected to be retired about 1980, with pod-carrying RF-14 Tomcat fighters now scheduled to replace them.

Reconnaissance equipment is carried in the internal weapons bay and in an elongated "canoe" faired into the lower fuselage. Reconnaissance equipment includes Side-Looking Aircraft Radar (SLAR), infrared sensors, active and passive ECM devices, and several cameras. The ASB-12 intertial bomb and navigation system is fitted. When the aircraft is used in the "recce" role, pods containing chaff, strobe flashers, or fuel tanks are carried on four wing pylons; however, bombs or nuclear weapons could still be loaded.

### Characteristics

| | |
|---|---|
| Crew: | 1 pilot, 1 navigator/systems operator |
| Weights: | 37,498 lbs empty; 55,617 lbs loaded; 79,588 lbs maximum |
| Dimensions: | length 76½ ft (23.32 m), span 53 ft (16.15 m), height 19⅓ ft (5.89 m) |
| Engines: | 2 GE J79-GE-8A/B turbojets; 10,900 lbst each; 17,000 lbst each with afterburner |
| Speeds: | 1,385 mph at 40,000 ft (Mach 2.1); 569 mph cruise |
| Ranges: | 1,330-n.mile radius with four 400-gal drop tanks |
| Ceiling: | 64,000 ft |
| Guns: | none |
| Payload: | 4 500-lb bombs (wing pylons) |
| | or 4 1,000-lb bombs |
| | or 4 2,000-lb bombs |

RA-5C Vigilante from RVAH-9 (U.S. Navy)

### RF-8G CRUSADER (LTV)

The Crusaders that remain in first-line Navy service are all RF-8G photo reconnaissance aircraft. From the mid-1950s into the late 1960s the F-8 (formerly F8U) Crusader was the standard carrier-based day fighter. Several "straight" F-8s remain in service in the utility role. One active Navy squadron and two reserve squadrons fly the RF-8G variant which is a "remanufactured" RF-8A (formerly F8U-1P) aircraft. The active Navy squadron, VFP-63, provides three-plane detachments to carriers. Under current plans the last RF-8G detachment will be disbanded in 1980 when the reconnaissance pod-fitted RF-14 Tomcats become available.

The aircraft carries several cameras fitted in the forward fuselage. No other reconnaissance sensors are provided.

### Characteristics

| | |
|---|---|
| Crew: | 1 pilot |
| Weights: | 16,796 lbs empty; 23,752 lbs loaded; 27,822 lbs maximum |
| Dimensions: | length 54½ ft (16.61 m), span 35⅔ ft (10.87 m), height 15¾ ft (4.8 m) |
| Engines: | 1 P&W J57-P420 turbojet; 11,440 lbst; 18,000 lbst with afterburner |
| Speeds: | 983 mph at 35,000 ft; 673 mph at sea level |
| Ranges: | 640-n.mile radius |
| Ceiling: | 51,800 ft |
| Guns: | none |
| Payload: | no ordnance capability |

RA-5C Vigilante from RVAH-9 being catapulted from the carrier NIMITZ (CVN 68) (U.S. Navy)

RF-8G Crusader from VFP-63; note camera port under star insignia and on bottom of fuselage (U.S. Navy)

## OBSERVATION AIRCRAFT

### OV-10 BRONCO (Rockwell International)

The OV-10 is a multi-purpose light attack aircraft developed by the Navy and Marine Corps for the counterinsurgency role. It is designed for rough field operation, and has operated in the STOL mode from LHA/LPH-type amphibious ships (without the use of arresting wires or catapults). The aircraft was flown by the U.S. Navy in the Vietnam War; it is now flown by three Marine VMO squadrons, each with 18 aircraft, and one Marine Reserve squadron. (The OV-10 is also flown by several foreign air forces.)

With removal of the second seat, the OV-10 can carry 3,200 pounds of cargo, or five paratroopers, or two litter patients and an attendant.

Two OV-10A aircraft have been modified to the YOV-10D Night Observation Gunship System (NOGS) configuration for evaluation by the Marines. They have Forward-Looking Infrared (FLIR) and laser target designator systems, and two 20-mm cannon mounted in an under fuselage turret. The aircraft has been lengthened 2½ feet. Another 18 conversions are planned with improved engines (OV-10D).

### Characteristics (OV-10A)

| | |
|---|---|
| Crew: | 1 pilot, 1 observer |
| Weights: | 6,969 lbs empty; 9,908 lbs loaded; 14,466 lbs maximum |
| Dimensions: | length 41⁷/₁₂ ft (12.67 m), span 40 ft (12.19 m), height 15¹/₆ ft (4.63 m) |
| Engines: | 2 Garrett AiResearch T76-G-10/10A/12/12A turboprops; 715 shp each |
| Speeds: | 281 mph clean at sea level |
| Ranges: | 228-n.mile radius in attack role; 1,430-n.mile ferry range |
| Ceiling: | |
| Guns: | 2 7.62-mm MG |
| Payload: | 1 1,100-lb bomb + 4 600-lb bombs |

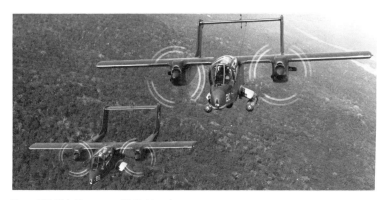

Two OV-10A Broncos (U.S. Navy)

## CARGO/TRANSPORT/UTILITY AIRCRAFT

### C-1A TRADER (Grumman)

The Trader is a Carrier On-board Delivery (COD) aircraft developed to carry high-priority freight and passengers to and from carriers at sea. The aircraft was developed from the S-2(S2F) Tracker ASW aircraft. Formerly designated TF-1, a small number of C-1As remain in Navy service. A few have been configured as electronic training aircraft (EC-1A formerly TF-1Q).

### Characteristics

| | |
|---|---|
| Crew: | 2 pilots |
| Weights: | 27,000 lbs loaded |
| Dimensions: | length 42 ft (12.8 m), span 69⅔ ft (21.23 m), height 16⅓ ft (4.98 m) |
| Engines: | 2 Wright R1820-82 radial pistons; 1,525 hp each |
| Speeds: | 334 mph |
| Ranges: | 1,200-n.mile range |
| Ceiling: | |
| Guns: | none |
| Payload: | 9 passengers |

Two OV-10A Broncos from now-disbanded VAL-4 (U.S. Navy)

C-1A Trader assigned to the carrier CONSTELLATION (CV 64) (U.S. Navy, PHCS Robert L. Lawson

**C-2A GREYHOUND** (Grumman)

The Greyhound is a second-generation COD aircraft derived from the E-2 Hawkeye AEW aircraft. The C-2A uses the same wings, power plant, and tail, but has a larger fuselage and rear loading ramp. The C-2A, as well as the surviving C-1A aircraft, will be replaced in the COD role by the US-3 Viking.

### Characteristics

| | |
|---|---|
| Crew: | 2 pilots, 1 flight engineer |
| Weights: | 31,250 lbs empty; 54,382 lbs loaded |
| Dimensions: | length 56⅔ ft (17.27 m), span 80⁷/₁₂ ft (24.57 m), height 15¹¹/₁₂ ft (4.85 m) |
| Engines: | 2 Allison T56-A-8A turboprops; 4,050 shp each |
| Speeds: | 352 mph at 30,000 ft; 296 mph cruise at 30,000 ft |
| Ranges: | 1,440-n.mile range |
| Ceiling: | 28,800 ft |
| Guns: | none |
| Payload: | 39 passengers or 20 litter patients |

C-2A Greyhound (U.S. Navy)

C-2A Greyhound from VRC-50 (U.S. Navy)

**C-4 GULFSTREAM I** (Grumman)

The Coast Guard operates one Gulfstream I as an executive transport (VC-4A) while the Navy and Marine Corps fly eight TC-4C trainers. The latter aircraft have their after cabin configured as an A-6 cockpit for training bombardier/navigators.

### Characteristics VC-4A

| | |
|---|---|
| Crew: | 2 pilots, 1 crewman |
| Weights: | 36,000 lbs loaded |
| Dimensions: | length 63¾ ft (19.34 m), span 78⅓ ft (23.87 m), height 23½ ft (7.11 m) |
| Engines: | 2 Rolls-Royce Dart Mk 529-8 turboprops; 2,210 shp each |
| Speeds: | 403 mph |
| Ranges: | 2,621-n.mile range |
| Ceiling: | |
| Guns: | none |
| Payload: | |

VC-4A Gulfstream I (U.S. Coast Guard)

TC-4C from VA-128 configured for training bombardier/navigators in the A-6 Intruder weapon system. VA-128, the Navy's Intruder readiness training squadron, flies three of the eight Gulfstreams in the TC-4C configuration. The elongated nose houses an A-6 nose radome; aft the TC-4C has a simulated Intruder cockpit with three repeater consoles for bombardier/navigators. (U.S. Navy)

**C-9B SKYTRAIN II** (McDonnell Douglas)

The C-9B is a military version of the DC-9 commercial transport which is convertible to the cargo or transport role. The aircraft is flown by the Marine Corps and the Naval Reserve. The U.S. Air Force flies the C-9A Nightingale for aeromedical airlift. (None are flown by active Navy squadrons.)

### Characteristics

| | |
|---|---|
| Crew: | 2 pilots, 1 crew chief, 2 attendants |
| Weights: | 59,706 lbs empty in cargo configuration; 65,283 lbs empty in transport configuration; 110,000 lbs maximum |
| Dimensions: | length 119⅓ ft (36.37 m), span 93⁵/₁₂ ft (28.47 m), height 27½ ft (8.38 m) |
| Engines: | 2 P&W JT8D-9 turbofans; 14,500 lbst each |
| Speeds: | 576 mph; 504 mph cruise |
| Ranges: | 2,538-n.mile range with 10,000 lbs cargo |
| Ceiling: | 37,000 ft |
| Guns: | none |
| Payload: | 90 passengers or 32,444 lbs cargo (8 standard type 463L cargo pallets) |

C-9B Skytrain II (U.S. Navy)

C-9B Skytrain II from VR-1 (U.S. Navy)

**C-11A GULFSTREAM II** (Grumman)

The Coast Guard flies one Gulfstream II in the executive transport role.

### Characteristics

| | |
|---|---|
| Crew: | 2 pilots, 2 crewmen |
| Weights: | 59,500 lbs loaded |
| Dimensions: | length 79¹¹/₁₂ ft (24.35 m), span 68⁵/₆ ft (21 m), height 24½ ft (7.47 m) |
| Engines: | 2 Rolls-Royce Mk 511-8 turbofans; 11,400 lbst each |
| Speeds: | 588 mph |
| Ranges: | 2,930-n.mile range |
| Ceiling: | |
| Payload: | 12 passengers |

The Coast Guard's two executive aircraft in flight: the turbofan VC-11A Gulfstream II followed by the turboprop VC-4A Gulfstream I. They were acquired in 1969 and 1963, respectively, and fly out of the Coast Guard Air Station at Washington (D.C.) National Airport. The Coast Guard aircraft identification scheme, adopted in 1967, provides for orange identification stripe on the fuselage with a smaller blue stripe and the CG emblem. Wing and tail panels are also painted orange. (U.S. Coast Guard, PA2 T. Nakata)

**C-117D SKYTRAIN** (Douglas)

The Navy and Marine Corps still fly several of the venerable C-117D (formerly R4D-8) "gooney birds" in the transport and utility roles. The C-117D was converted from earlier R4D (C-47) models, with their wings and fuselage being strengthened, and new engines and tail surfaces installed. The aircraft is no longer flown by the Air Force, although some are flown by the Federal Aviation Agency.

The Skytrain is probably the oldest aircraft design still in U.S. military service, with its prototype, the DC-3, having first been flown in late 1935. More than 10,000 military DC-3s were built, most being C-47 Dakotas for U.S. and allied air forces.

Some Skytrains are VC-117Ds configured as executive transports with provisions for 16 passengers.

## Characteristics

| | |
|---|---|
| Crew: | 2 pilots, 1 flight engineer |
| Weights: | 19,500 lbs empty; 31,000 lbs loaded, 36,800 lbs maximum |
| Dimensions: | length 67¾ ft (20.65 m), span 90 ft (27.43 m), height 18¼ ft (5.56 m) |
| Engines: | 2 Wright R-1820-80 radial piston; 2,800 hp each |
| Speeds: | 268 mph at 4,900 ft |
| Ranges: | 1,100-n.mile range with 6,000 lbs cargo; 3,000+ n.mile ferry range maximum |
| Ceiling: | 25,000 ft |
| Payload: | 30 passengers |
| | or 35 troops |
| | or 27 litter patients |
| | or 12,900 lbs cargo |

TC-117D Skytrain assigned to VT-28; since replaced (U.S. Navy)

C-118B Liftmaster from VR-1. Transport aircraft normally are identified by the last three digits of their ''bureau'' number, in this instance 426 having the bureau number 128426. The Bureau of Aeronautics, established in July 1921, directed naval air development until December 1959 when BuAer merged with the Bureau of Ordnance to form the Bureau of Naval Weapons, and subsequently changed on 1 May 1966 to the current Naval Air Systems Command. (U.S. Navy)

### C-118B LIFTMASTER (Douglas)

The Navy flies several C-118B (formerly R6D-1) aircraft in the transport role. These are military versions of the DC-6A commercial transport.

## Characteristics

| | |
|---|---|
| Crew: | 2 pilots, 1 navigator, 1 flight engineer, 1 attendant |
| Weights: | 54,995 lbs empty; 103,000 lbs loaded; 112,000 lbs maximum |
| Dimensions: | length 107 ft (32.61 m), span 117½ ft (35.81 m), height 28⅔ ft (8.74 m) |
| Engines: | 4 P&W R-2800-52W radial piston; 2,500 hp each |
| Speeds: | 303 mph at 16,700 ft |
| Ranges: | 2,000-n.mile range with maximum cargo |
| Ceiling: | 21,900 ft |
| Payload: | 76 passengers |
| | or 60 litter patients and 6 attendants |
| | or 31,611 lbs cargo |

### C-130 HERCULES (Lockheed)

The Navy, Marine Corps, and Coast Guard all fly several variants of the C-130 (formerly designated GV) in a variety of mission configurations. This cargo aircraft, capable of rough-field operations, has carried out landing and take-off trials from the aircraft carrier FORRESTAL (CV 59) without arresting gear or rocket/catapult assistance.

The Navy flies "straight" C-130 cargo aircraft, LC-130 cargo aircraft fitted with skis for Arctic or Antarctic operations, DC-130 drone control aircraft, and EC-130 strategic communications aircraft. The last are flown by squadrons VQ-3 and -4 and provide a communications relay to strategic missile submarines at sea, under a program known as TACAMO (Take Charge And Move Out). These planes have powerful VLF transmitters and can remain aloft up to

DC-130A Hercules from VC-3 carrying BQM-34 Firebee target drones (U.S. Navy, PHCS Robert L. Lawson)

13 hours. (Fourteen EC-130G/Q aircraft are in service with the two squadrons.)

The Marine Corps has a KC-130 squadron of 12 aircraft assigned to each air wing to provide tactical transport and in-flight refueling services.

The Coast Guard flies one EC-130E aircraft for the calibration of LORAN (Long Range Navigation) transmitters and several HC-130B/H aircraft used in the search and rescue role.

The Hercules aircraft is also flown by Navy and Marine reserve squadrons. As a transport, it can carry up to 92 passengers or 74 litter patients. (More than 40 nations fly the Hercules in military and civil service.)

### Characteristics (HC-130H)

| | |
|---|---|
| Crew: | 2 pilots, 1 navigator, 2 flight engineers, 1 radio operator, 2 load-masters, 2 para-rescue technicians; also 1 additional pilot and 1 additional navigator for long-duration missions |
| Weights: | 75,331 lbs empty; 155,000 lbs loaded; 175,000 lbs maximum |
| Dimensions: | length 98¾ ft (30.1 m), span 132⁷/₁₂ ft (40.41 m), height 38¼ ft (11.66 m) |
| Engines: | 4 Allison T56-A-15 turboprops; 4,500 ehp each |
| Speeds: | 366 mph; 345 mph cruise |
| Ranges: | 2,160-n.mile range; 4,460-n.mile range with external fuel tanks |
| Ceiling: | 33,000 ft |
| Guns: | none |
| Payload: | rescue equipment and 4 6-man rafts |

DC-130A Hercules from VC-3 carrying BQM-34 Firebee target drones (U.S. Navy, PHCS Robert L. Lawson)

**C-131 SAMARITAN** (Convair)

The Navy flies a small number of C-131F/G (formerly R4Y) aircraft in the transport role. A few are configured as VIP transports (VC-131).

### Characteristics (C-131G)

| | |
|---|---|
| Crew: | 2 pilots, 1 flight engineer |
| Weights: | 53,200 lbs loaded |
| Dimensions: | length 79¹/₆ ft (24.14 m), span 105⅓ ft (32.08 m), height 28 ft (8.53 m) |
| Engines: | 2 P&W R-2800-52W radial piston; 2,500 hp each |
| Speeds: | 316 mph |
| Ranges: | 2,000-n.mile range |
| Ceiling: | |
| Guns: | none |
| Payload: | 44 passengers or 21 litter patients and 3 attendants |

HC-130B Hercules (U.S. Coast Guard)

**CTX**

The Navy has initiated the CTX program to procure an available commercial aircraft for the cargo/utility role to support Navy and Marine operational requirements as well as certain research efforts. The aircraft will not be carrier-capable. About 60 aircraft will be procured from 1979 to 1981.

### Characteristics

| | |
|---|---|
| Crew: | 2 pilots |
| Weights: | ~20,000 lbs maximum |
| Dimensions: | |
| Engines: | 2 turboprop or turbojet |
| Speeds: | ~270 mph cruise |
| Ranges: | 1,000-n.mile range with 1,000 lbs cargo |
| Ceiling: | |
| Guns: | none |
| Payload: | 8–18 passengers |

HC-130B Hercules (U.S. Coast Guard, CWO N. Ruenzel)

## TRAINER AIRCRAFT

### T-2C BUCKEYE (North American Rockwell)

The T-2C (formerly T2J) is a carrier-capable jet trainer flown by the Navy for strike aircraft training. Wing-tip fuel tanks are normally fitted.

### Characteristics

| | |
|---|---|
| Crew: | 1 pilot + 1 student |
| Weights: | 8,115 lbs empty; 13,179 lbs maximum |
| Dimensions: | length 38⅓ ft (11.67 m), span 38⅙ ft (11.62 m), height 14⅚ ft (4.51 m) |
| Engines: | 2 GE J85-GE-4 turbojets; 2,950 lbst each |
| Speeds: | 522 mph at 25,000 ft |
| Ranges: | 909-n.mile range |
| Ceiling: | 40,400 ft |
| Guns: | none |
| Payload: | up to 640 lbs of bombs or rockets (wing pylons) |

T-2B Buckeye assigned to Naval Air Test Center (U.S. Navy)

### TS-2/US-2 TRACKER (Grumman)

These are former S-2 (S2F) antisubmarine aircraft modified for training and utility (primarily target tow) roles, respectively. Both aircraft are used in training pending the availability of sufficient numbers of the new T-44A aircraft. In addition, some US-2B aircraft are fitted as utility transports with five passenger seats added.

The last U.S. Navy ASW Trackers were retired late in 1976 after the aircraft had served in that role for 22 years. Over 1,000 were built by Grumman, and 100 by de Havilland of Canada; they are still flown in the ASW role by several foreign navies and air forces.

### Characteristics (TS-2A)

| | |
|---|---|
| Crew: | 1 pilot + 3 students |
| Weights: | 17,357 lbs empty; 24,500 lbs loaded; 26,300 lbs maximum |
| Dimensions: | length 42 ft (12.8 m), span 69⅔ ft (21.23 m), height 16⅓ ft (4.98 m) |
| Engines: | 2 Wright R-1820-82W radial piston; 1,525 hp each |
| Speeds: | 287 mph at sea level; 172 mph cruise at 5,000 ft |
| Ranges: | 900-n.mile range |
| Ceiling: | 23,000 ft |
| Guns: | none |
| Payload: | 2 Mk 44/46 torpedoes (weapons bay) + 6 5-inch rockets (wing pylons) |

### T-28 TROJAN (North American Rockwell)

The T-28 is a widely used piston-engine training aircraft. The Navy T-28B/C variants are carrier-capable.

### Characteristics (T-28B)

| | |
|---|---|
| Crew: | 1 pilot + 1 student |
| Weights: | 6,424 lbs empty; 8,500 lbs loaded |
| Dimensions: | length 33 ft (10.06 m), span 40¹/₁₂ ft (12.22 m), height 12⅔ ft (3.86 m) |
| Engines: | 1 Wright R-1820-86 radial piston; 1,425 hp |
| Speeds: | 343 mph; 310 mph cruise at 30,000 ft |
| Ranges: | 922-n.mile range |
| Ceiling: | 35,500 ft |
| Guns: | none |
| Payload: | |

TS-2A Tracker from VT-28 (U.S. Navy)

T-28 Trojan (U.S. Navy)

**T-34C MENTOR** (Beechcraft)

The T-34C Mentor is being introduced in the Naval Air Training Command as a replacement for the T-28 Trojan. The T-34C is an improved version of the long-serving Navy T-34B. The most significant improvement is provision of a turboprop engine. One hundred sixteen of these aircraft are planned for Navy use, with student training in the aircraft beginning in 1978.

Characteristics

| | |
|---|---|
| Crew: | 1 pilot + 1 student |
| Weights: | 2,630 lbs empty; 4,274 lbs maximum |
| Dimensions: | length 28¾ ft (8.75 m), span 33⅓ ft (10.16 m), height 9¹¹/₁₂ ft (3.02 m) |
| Engines: | 1 P&W of Canada PT6A-25 turboprop; 400 shp |
| Speeds: | 257 mph at 5,335 ft; 247 mph cruise at 5,335 ft |
| Ranges: | 650 n.miles |
| Ceiling: | 30,000 ft |
| Guns: | none |
| Payload: | no ordnance capability |

T-34C Mentor (Beech)

**T-38A TALON** (Northrop)

The T-38 is a standard U.S. Air Force jet trainer used in limited numbers by the Navy for test-pilot proficiency flying and air combat maneuver training. The T-38 is closely related in design and flight characteristics to Northrop's F-5 Freedom Fighter/Tiger II aircraft.

Characteristics

| | |
|---|---|
| Crew: | 1 pilot + 1 student or pilot |
| Weights: | 7,594 lbs empty; 12,000 lbs maximum |
| Dimensions: | length 46⁵/₁₂ ft (14.13 m), span 25¼ ft (7.7 m), height 12¹¹/₁₂ ft (3.92 m) |
| Engines: | 2 GE J85-GE-5A/J turbojets; 2,680 lbst each; 3,850 lbst each with afterburner |
| Speeds: | ~Mach 1.3 at 36,000 ft |
| Ranges: | 1,140-n.mile range |
| Ceiling: | 53,500 ft |
| Guns: | none |
| Payload: | no ordnance capability |

**T-39D SABRELINER** (North American Rockwell)

The T-39D (formerly T3J) is fitted with APQ-94 for radar training of naval flight officers (i.e., bombardier/navigators and radar intercept officers). In addition, 18 CT-39E/G aircraft remain in use as light transports for carrying high-priority cargo and passengers. The cargo versions can be fitted with seats for six passengers in addition to a two-man crew.

Characteristics (T-39D)

| | |
|---|---|
| Crew: | 1 pilot, 1 pilot/instructor + 4 students |
| Weights: | 17,760 lbs loaded |
| Dimensions: | length 44 ft (13.41 m), span 44½ ft (13.59 m), height 16 ft (4.88 m) |
| Engines: | 2 P&W J60-P-3A turbojets; 3,000 lbst each |
| Speeds: | 432 mph |
| Ranges: | 2,500-n.mile range |
| Ceiling: | |
| Guns: | none |
| Payload: | no ordnance capability |

T-38A Talon assigned to VF-43; note absence of tail fin codes on aircraft used for air combat maneuver training (Robert L. Lawson)

CT-39G Saberliner (U.S. Navy, PHAN B. R. Trombecky)

### T-44A (Air King) (Beechcraft)

The T-44A is being procured as a replacement for the TS-2/US-2 Tracker aircraft employed in the training role. The T-44A is a military training version of the commercial Air King Model 90. It is also flown by the Air Force as the VC-6B executive transport. Sixty-one T-44A aircraft are being delivered to Training Wing 4 between 1977 and 1980. (No Navy name has been assigned.)

### Characteristics

| | |
|---|---|
| Crew: | 1 pilot + 2 students |
| Weights: | 5,640 lbs empty; 9,650 lbs maximum |
| Dimensions: | length 35½ ft (10.82 m), span 50¼ ft (15.32 m), height 14¼ ft (4.33 m) |
| Engines: | 2 P&W of Canada PT6A-34B turboprops; 550 shp each |
| Speeds: | 256 mph at 12,000 ft |
| Ranges: | 1,200 + n.mile range |
| Ceiling: | 31,000 ft |
| Guns: | none |
| Payload: | no ordnance capability; can be configured in transport role for 2 pilots + 3 passengers |

T-44A assigned to TraWing-4 (Beech)

## HELICOPTERS

### AH-1 SEACOBRA (Bell)

The SeaCobra is a specialized gunship helicopter that evolved from the widely used Huey series. The SeaCobra has a narrow (38-inch) fuselage providing a minimal cross section, stub wings for carrying rocket packs or gun pods, and a nose gun turret.

The Marines have three 18-helicopter SeaCobra squadrons with a total inventory of some 20 AH-1G and 60 AH-1J variants. The former have a single engine (they are also flown by the U.S. Army as the HueyCobra). Fifty-seven AH-1T gunships are being procured for the Marines to replace the AH-1G helicopters and increase squadron strength to 24 units. The AH-1T will have structural provisions for carrying the TOW (Tube-launched, Optically guided, Wire-controlled) anti-tank missile, although only the last 23 heli-

copters procured by the Marines will have the missile fitted upon delivery.

### Characteristics (AH-1J)

| | |
|---|---|
| Crew: | 1 pilot, 1 gunner |
| Weights: | 6,816 lbs loaded; 10,000 lbs maximum |
| Dimensions: | fuselage length 44$^{7}/_{12}$ ft (13.6 m), overall length 53⅓ ft (16.27 m), height 13⅔ ft (4.17 m), main rotor diameter 44 ft (13.42 m) |
| Engines: | 2 United Aircraft of Canada T-400-CP-400 turboshafts; 1,800 shp each |
| Speeds: | 207 mph |
| Ranges: | 360-n.mile range |
| Ceilings: | 10,500 ft; 12,450 ft hovering in ground effect |
| Guns: | 1 20-ml XM-197 |
| Payload: | 4 XM-159 rocket packs (19 2.75-inch rockets per pack) or 2 7.62-mm XM-18E1 minigun pods |

AH-1J SeaCobra assigned to Marine Headquarters and Maintenance Squadron 24 (EW) (U.S. Navy, PH1 Eugene L. Goligoski)

AH-1J SeaCobra assigned to HMM-165 (U.S. Navy, PH3 Daniel A. Fort)

**UH-1 HUEY (IROQUOIS)** (Bell)

The Huey series (formerly HU-1, with the name being derived from the sound of the HU-1E designation), is the most widely used helicopter in the world with more than 9,000 produced from the late 1950s onward. It was extensively used in the Vietnam War. Officially named Iroquois (from the U.S. Army scheme of Indian names for helicopters), UH-1 variants are today flown by about 40 nations.

The U.S. Marine Corps has four squadrons with an assigned strength of 21 helicopters each. These are being replaced by the improved UH-1N version, with a planned strength of three 24-helicopter squadrons. The Navy and the Marine Reserve also fly the Iroquois in utility, transport, and training roles (the last include Navy-flown UH-1 and TH-1 variants).

### Characteristics (UH-1N)

| | |
|---|---|
| Crew: | 1 pilot |
| Weights: | 5,549 lbs empty; 10,500 lbs maximum |
| Dimensions: | fuselage length $42^{5}/_{12}$ ft (12.93 m), overall length $57^{1}/_{4}$ ft (17.47 m) height $14^{5}/_{12}$ ft (4.39 m), main rotor diameter $48^{1}/_{6}$ ft (14.7 m) |
| Engines: | 2 United Aircraft of Canada PT6 turboshafts; 900 shp each |
| Speeds: | 126 mph |
| Ranges: | 250-n.mile range |
| Ceilings: | 15,000 ft; 12,900 ft hovering in ground effect |
| Guns: | (see payload) |
| Payload: | 16 troops or various combinations of troops, guns, and rockets |

UH-1N Huey assigned to VXE-6; note extended nose and other differences from earlier Hueys (U.S. Navy, PHCS Robert L. Lawson)

TH-1L Huey assigned to HT-8 (U.S. Navy)

UH-1E Huey assigned to Marine Headquarters and Maintenance Squadron 24 (EW) (U.S. Navy, PH1 Eugene L. Goligoski)

**SH-2 LAMPS** (Kaman)

The LAMPS (Light Airborne Multi-Purpose System) is a ship-based antisubmarine helicopter converted from the UH-2 (formerly HU2K) Seasprite utility helicopter. The U.S. Navy's need for a ship-based ASW helicopter in the early 1970s led to the conversion of 20 utility helicopters to the SH-2D configuration and another 85 to the SH-2F variant. Two additional Seasprites were experimentally converted to the YSH-2E configuration.

The Navy has six light ASW squadrons which deploy LAMPS detachments aboard cruisers, destroyers, and frigates, plus two readiness training squadrons. The SH-2 LAMPS will be succeeded in service during the early 1980s by the improved LAMPS III helicopter (SH-60B).

The SH-2D/F LAMPS are used to localize and attack submarine contacts detected by shipboard sonar. The helicopters are fitted with surface search radar, MAD (Magnetic Anomaly Detection), and sonobuoys.

### Characteristics (SH-2D)

| | |
|---|---|
| Crew: | 2 pilots, 1 systems operator |
| Weights: | 6,953 lbs empty; 12,800 lbs maximum |
| Dimensions: | fuselage length 38⅓ ft (11.69 m), overall length 52⁷/₁₂ ft (16.04 m), height 15½ ft (4.73 m), main rotor diameter 44 ft (13.42 m) |
| Engines: | 2 GE T58-GE-8F turboshafts; 1,350 shp each |
| Speeds: | 165 mph; 150 mph cruise |
| Ranges: | 420-n.mile range |
| Ceilings: | 22,500 ft; 18,600 ft hovering in ground effect |
| Guns: | none |
| Payload: | 2 Mk 46 ASW torpedoes |

SH-2D LAMPS from HSL-32; note MAD gear being streamed and Mk 44 practice torpedo on port side. Above the torpedo is the rectangular sonobuoy dispenser (U.S. Navy)

SH-2D LAMPS from HC-4, subsequently redesignated HSL-30, hovering over the cruiser WAINWRIGHT (CG 28) (U.S. Navy)

**SH-3 SEA KING** (Sikorsky)

The SH-3 (formerly HSS-2) has been the U.S. Navy's standard carrier-based ASW helicopter since entering service in 1961. It is also in Air Force and foreign service in the transport role, while the Coast Guard flies a specialized rescue variant, the HH-3F Pelican (listed separately).

The Navy has nine carrier-based ASW squadrons, each with six SH-3D/G/H helicopters, plus two readiness squadrons. The number of deployable squadrons is being increased to 12. Eventually all will fly the SH-3H variant, with 137 SH-3A/G helicopters being updated to that configuration (the SH-3G is an SH-3A with some of its ASW equipment removed for use in the utility role). A small number of VH-3A VIP variants are flown by the U.S. Army and Marine Corps to transport the President. Two Sea Kings have been modified to the YSH-3J configuration to test weapons and sensors for the LAMPS III helicopter.

The ASW variants are fitted with surface search radar, electronic sensors, dipping sonar, MAD, sonobuoys, and a chaff dispenser.

### Characteristics (SH-3D)

| | |
|---|---|
| Crew: | 2 pilots, 2 systems operators |
| Weights: | 11,865 lbs empty; 20,500 lbs maximum |
| Dimensions: | fuselage length 54¾ ft (16.7 m), overall length 72⅔ ft (22.16 m), height 16⅚ ft (5.13 m), main rotor diameter 62 ft (18.91 m) |
| Engines: | 2 GE T58-GE-10 turboshafts; 1,400 shp each |
| Speeds: | 166 mph; 136 mph cruise |
| Ranges: | 625-n.mile range |
| Ceilings: | 14,700 ft; 10,500 ft hovering in ground effect |
| Guns: | none |
| Payload: | 2 Mk 46 ASW torpedoes |

SH-3A Sea King from HS-6 with MAD gear streamed (U.S. Navy, PHCS Robert L. Lawson)

SH-3A Sea King lowering dipping sonar (U.S. Navy)

SH-3D Sea King from HS-4; note ASW torpedo under starboard landing gear housing (U.S. Navy, PH3 H. Burgess)

HH-3F Pelican (U.S. Coast Guard)

**HH-3F PELICAN** (Sikorsky)

The HH-3F is a transport/Search and Rescue (SAR) derivative of the SH-3 Sea King ASW helicopter flown by the Coast Guard. The CH-3C/E cargo and HH-3E Jolly Green Giant rescue helicopters flown by the U.S. Air Force are of the same design as the HH-3F.

Forty HH-3F variants were delivered to the Coast Guard from 1968 onward. They are fitted with surface-search radar and carry droppable rescue supplies.

### Characteristics

| | |
|---|---|
| Crew: | 2 pilots, 1 crewman |
| Weights: | 22,050 lbs maximum |
| Dimensions: | fuselage length 57¼ ft (17.45 m), overall length 73 ft (22.25 m), height 18¹/₁₂ ft (5.51 m), main rotor diameter 62 ft (18.9 m) |
| Engines: | 2 GE T58-GE-5 turboshafts; 1,500 shp each |
| Speeds: | 162 mph; 125 mph cruise |
| Ranges: | 400-n.mile range |
| Ceilings: | 11,100 ft; 4,100 ft hovering in ground effect |
| Guns: | none |
| Payload: | 30 passengers or 15 litter patients |

HH-3F Pelican (U.S. Coast Guard, CWO Joseph Greco, Jr.)

## H-46 SEA KNIGHT (Boeing Vertol)

The CH-46 (formerly HRB) is the principal assault helicopter of the U.S. Marine Corps, while the Navy flies the UH-46 in the Vertical Replenishment (VERTREP) role to carry cargo from Underway Replenishment (UNREP) ships to warships. Personnel, spare parts, and munitions are transferred by VERTREP, alleviating the need for the replenishing ship and warship to steam together, or supplementing conventional transfer methods when they are fueling alongside.

The Marine Corps has nine squadrons, each with a nominal strength of 18 CH-46A/D/E helicopters. All will be updated to the CH-46E configuration which has an automatic navigation system and armored crew seats. The Navy has four helicopter combat support squadrons flying the UH-46A/D in the VERTREP role plus one readiness squadron with UH-46 and HH-46 helicopters. A rear-loading ramp is fitted. The first CH-46E entered squadron service in October 1977.

Marines board a CH-46 aboard the helicopter carrier TARAWA (LHA 1) (U.S. Navy, PH2 G. A. Davis)

### Characteristics (CH-46D)

| | |
|---|---|
| Crew: | 2 pilots, 1 crewman |
| Weights: | 13,112 lbs empty; 23,000 lbs maximum |
| Dimensions: | fuselage length 44$\frac{5}{6}$ ft (13.67 m), overall length 84$\frac{1}{3}$ ft (25.72 m), height 16$\frac{2}{3}$ ft (5.08 m), main rotor diameter (both) 51 ft (15.56 m) |
| Engines: | 2 GE T58-GE-10 turboshafts; 1,400 shp each |
| Speeds: | 166 mph; 163 mph cruise |
| Ranges: | 206-n.mile range; 774-n.mile ferry range (with external tanks) |
| Ceilings: | 14,000 ft; 9,500 ft hovering in ground effect |
| Guns: | none |
| Payload: | 17 troops or 15 litter patients + 2 attendants or 3,000 lbs cargo internal or 10,000 lbs cargo on sling |

CH-46D Sea Knight from HMM-764 (U.S. Navy, PH1 W. J. Galligan)

CH-46A from HC-3 (U.S. Navy, PH1 A. E. Legare)

CH-46D Sea Knight from HC-3 (U.S. Navy, PHCS Robert L. Lawson)

**HH-52A SEA GUARD** (Sikorsky)

The HH-52A (formerly HU2S-1G) is a commercial helicopter adopted for Coast Guard SAR missions. Although flown by several foreign nations as well as commercial operators, the helicopter (Sikorsky S-62 design) is not flown by any U.S. service except the Coast Guard. Ninety-nine were built for the Coast Guard.

The name Sea Guard was informally assigned by the Coast Guard and is not used officially.

## Characteristics

| | |
|---|---|
| Crew: | 2 pilots, 1 crewman |
| Weights: | 5,083 lbs empty; 8,100 lbs maximum |
| Dimensions: | fuselage length 44$7/12$ ft (13.59 m), overall length 45½ ft (13.87 m), height 16 ft (4.88 m), main rotor diameter 53 ft (16.17 m) |
| Engines: | 1 GE T58-GE-8B turboshaft; 1,250 shp |
| Speeds: | 109 mph; 98 mph cruise |
| Ranges: | 475-n.mile range |
| Ceilings: | 11,200 ft; 12,200 ft hovering in ground effect |
| Guns: | none |
| Payload: | ~10 passengers |

HH-52A Sea Guard (U.S. Coast Guard, Dan Boyd)

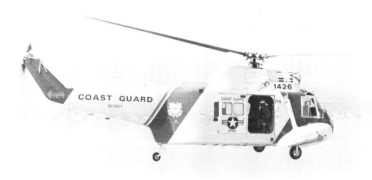

HH-52A Sea Guard (U.S. Coast Guard)

**H-53 SEA STALLION** (Sikorsky)

The CH-53 is a heavy assault helicopter developed specifically for use by the U.S. Marine Corps. The helicopter is a hybrid combining an enlarged CH-53 Sea King fuselage and the six-bladed rotor and power train systems from the Army's CH-54 Skytrain (Tarhe) helicopter. (The CH-53E heavy lift development of the helicopter is described separately, on p. 290.

The Marines fly six helicopter squadrons with 21 CH-53A/D helicopters assigned to each. In addition, the Navy has a single mine countermeasures squadron with 23 RH-53D helicopters.

The Navy's RH-53D aerial minesweepers are basic CH-53A/D helicopters with upgraded engines (T64-GE-415), strengthened fuselage, automatic flight control system, fittings for two swivel .50-cal MG, and attachment points for streaming minesweeping devices. The latter include the Mk-103 cutters for countering contact mines, the Mk-104 countermeasure for acoustic mines, the Mk-105 hydrofoil sled for magnetic mines, the Mk-106 (which is the Mk-105 sled with acoustic sweep equipment added), and the SPU-1 "Magnetic Orange Pipe" (MOP) for countering shallow-water mines. The sled weighs about 6,000 lbs, and is 27 feet long and 13 feet wide. The MOP is about 33 feet long and ten inches in diameter.

The helicopter is fitted with a rear loading ramp, cargo winches, and roller conveyors.

## Characteristics (CH-53D)

| | |
|---|---|
| Crew: | 2 pilots, 1 crewman (7 in RH-53D) |
| Weights: | 23,628 lbs empty; 34,958 lbs loaded; 42,000 lbs maximum |
| Dimensions: | fuselage length 67$1/6$ ft (20.48 m), overall length 88¼ ft (26.92 m), height 24$11/12$ ft (7.59 m), main rotor diameter 72¼ ft (22.04 m) |
| Engines: | 2 GE T64-GE-413 turboshafts; 3,925 shp each |
| Speeds: | 196 mph; 173 mph cruise |
| Ranges: | 540-n.mile range; 886-n.mile ferry range |
| Ceilings: | 21,000 ft; 13,400 ft hovering in ground effect |
| Guns: | none |
| Payload: | 38 troops or 24 litter patients + 4 attendants |
| | or 8,000 lbs cargo internal or external (an additional 4,000 lbs can be carried in overload condition) |

CH-53D from HMM-164 prepares to lift a 155 mm howitzer from the amphibious transport dock JUNEAU (LPD 10) (U.S. Navy, PH1 John R. Sheppard)

RH-53D Sea Stallion from HM-12 about to lift a Mk-105 mine countermeasure sled (U.S. Navy, PH2 E. L. Hawkins)

Prototype YCH-53E Super Stallion flying with a test payload of 16 tons (Sikorsky)

### CH-53E SUPER STALLION (Sikorsky)

The CH-53E, developed for Navy and Marine Corps use, is a heavy-lift derivative of the CH-53 Sea Stallion helicopter. Previously the most capable lift helicopter in U.S. production was the Army's CH-47 Chinook which can carry 11 tons of cargo; the CH-53E is rated at 16 tons of lift. The Soviet Union currently has over 500 Mi-10 Harke and Mi-6 Hook helicopters with a lift capability approaching or similar to that of the CH-53E.

The U.S. Navy and Marine Corps each have a requirement for 35 of the CH-53E helicopters. The CH-53E can lift 93 percent of all heavy equipment in a Marine division, compared to 38 percent for the CH-53D helicopter. In the aircraft recovery role the CH-53E can lift all Navy and Marine fighter, attack, and electronic warfare aircraft (with engines removed from the F-14 and partial disassembly of the E-2).

The CH-53E differs from the CH-53A/D helicopters in having a third engine, a seven-blade main rotor (instead of six), larger rotor blades, improved transmission, inflight refueling probe, provisions for 650-gallon fuel tanks on both landing gear housings, and improved tail configuration.

### Characteristics

| | |
|---|---|
| Crew: | 2 pilots, 1 crewman |
| Weights: | 31,915 lbs empty; 70,000+ lbs maximum |
| Dimensions: | fuselage length 91$^{7}/_{12}$ ft (27.94 m), overall length 99½ ft (30.35 m), height 27⅔ ft (8.44 m), main rotor diameter 79 ft (24.08 m) |
| Engines: | 3 GE T64-GE-415 turboshafts; 4,380 shp each |
| Speeds: | 196 mph |
| Ranges: | 50-n.mile radius with 32,000 lbs of cargo; 1,000+ n.mile ferry range |
| Ceilings: | |
| Guns: | none |
| Payload: | 56 troops or 32,000 lbs cargo |

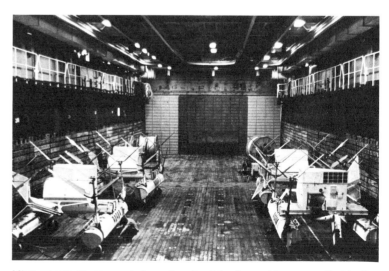

Mine countermeasure sleds and reels of towing cable are readied in the well deck of the amphibious transport dock DUBUQUE (LPD 8) for use by HM-12 helicopters (U.S. Navy, JOC Warren Grass)

**TH-57A SEA RANGER** (Bell)

The TH-57A is the Navy's training version of the U.S. Army's OH-58 Kiowa light observation helicopter. It is flown in large numbers by the U.S. Army and several foreign nations (more than 2,500 of this craft have been produced).

The TH-57A has dual controls. The Navy purchased 40 units for basic helicopter training, all delivered in 1968.

### Characteristics

| | |
|---|---|
| Crew: | 1 pilot +1–4 students |
| Weights: | 1,464 lbs empty; 3,000 lbs maximum |
| Dimensions: | fuselage length $32^{7}/_{12}$ ft (9.94 m), overall length 41 ft (12.5 m), height $9^{7}/_{12}$ ft (2.91 m), main rotor diameter $35^{1}/_{3}$ ft (10.78 m) |
| Engines: | 1 Allison T63-A-700 turboshaft; 317 shp |
| Speeds: | 138 mph; 117 mph cruise |
| Ranges: | 300-n.mile range |
| Ceilings: | 18,900 ft; 13,600 ft hovering in ground effect |
| Guns: | none |
| Payload: | none |

TH-57A Sea Ranger from HT-8 (U.S. Navy)

**SH-60B LAMPS III** (Sikorsky)

The LAMPS III (Light Airborne Multi-Purpose System) is primarily an antisubmarine helicopter being developed to operate from cruisers, destroyers, and frigates. The helicopter also will be fitted with EW equipment for threat detection and possibly jamming or decoying anti-ship cruise missiles. Six prototype aircraft are being built by Sikorsky with just over 200 service helicopters planned for delivery during the 1980s. The LAMPS design is based partially on the UH-60A, the U.S. Army's Utility Tactical Transport Aircraft System (UTTAS) now being produced by Sikorsky. The Army plans to procure some 1,100 of these helicopters.

(The LAMPS I helicopters were 105 UH-2 Seasprites converted to the SH-2D/F configurations. The LAMPS II, a proposed built-for-the-purpose light ASW helicopter, did not reach the advanced design stage.)

The LAMPS III will provide localization and kill against submarines initially detected by shipboard sensors. The helicopter will be fitted with surface-search radar, EW sensors, MAD gear, sonobuoys, and possibly other sensors. Chaff dispensers and other countermeasures against cruise missiles will be carried. Shipboard evaluation of the prototype will begin in 1979.

### Characteristics

| | |
|---|---|
| Crew: | 2 pilots, ~2 systems operators |
| Weights: | 20,800 lbs maximum |
| Dimensions: | fuselage length $50^{1}/_{12}$ (15.24 m), overall length $64^{5}/_{6}$ ft (19.76 m), height $17^{1}/_{2}$ ft (5.23 m), main rotor diameter $53^{2}/_{3}$ ft (16.36 m) |
| Engines: | 2 GE T700-GE-400 turboshafts |
| Speeds: | |
| Ranges: | 50-n.mile radius with 3 hrs on station; 150-n.mile radius with 1 hr on station |
| Ceilings: | |
| Guns: | none |
| Payload: | 2 Mk 46 ASW torpedoes |

Mockup of SH-60B LAMPS III (Sikorsky)

# 24 Weapons and Sensors

## MISSILES

*Explanation of symbols:*

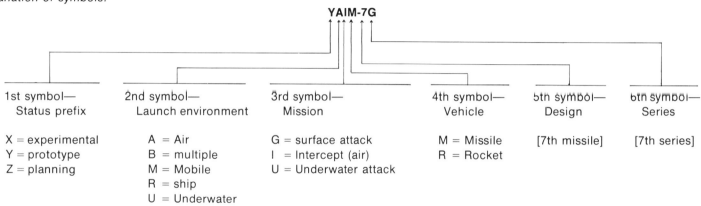

**YAIM-7G**

| 1st symbol—<br>Status prefix | 2nd symbol—<br>Launch environment | 3rd symbol—<br>Mission | 4th symbol—<br>Vehicle | 5th symbol—<br>Design | 6th symbol—<br>Series |
|---|---|---|---|---|---|
| X = experimental<br>Y = prototype<br>Z = planning | A = Air<br>B = multiple<br>M = Mobile<br>R = ship<br>U = Underwater | G = surface attack<br>I = Intercept (air)<br>U = Underwater attack | M = Missile<br>R = Rocket | [7th missile] | [7th series] |

| Type[a] | Desig-nation | Name | Manufacturer | Launch Platforms | Weight[b] | Length | Propulsion | Range (n.miles) | Notes[c] |
|---|---|---|---|---|---|---|---|---|---|
| SAM | RIM-2 | Terrier | General Dynamics | carriers cruisers destroyers | 3,000 lbs | 26$\frac{1}{6}$ ft (7.9 m) | solid-fuel rocket + booster | 20+ | to be replaced by Standard-ER |
| SAM | RIM-7 | Sea Sparrow | Raytheon | carriers destroyers amphibious ships auxiliary ships | ~500 lbs | 12 ft (3.7 m) | solid-fuel rocket | ~10 | for BPDMS/IPDMS |
| SAM | RIM-8 | Talos | Bendix | cruisers | 7,000 lbs | 33 ft (10.1 m) | solid-fuel rocket + booster | ~75 | nuclear or HE; being phased out |
| SAM | RIM-24 | Tartar | General Dynamics | cruisers destroyers frigates | 1,425 lbs | 14$\frac{5}{6}$ ft (4.5 m) | solid-fuel rocket | 10+ | to be replaced by Standard-MR |
| SAM | RIM-66B | Standard-MR/SM-1 | General Dynamics | cruisers destroyers frigates | 1,300 lbs | 14 ft (4.3 m) | solid-fuel rocket | ~25 | Tartar replacement |
| SAM | RIM-66C | Standard-MR/SM-2 | General Dynamics | cruisers | 1,300 lbs | 14 ft (4.3 m) | solid-fuel rocket | 25+ | for Aegis/Mk 26 launcher |

| Type[a] | Desig- nation | Name | Manufacturer | Launch Platforms | Weight[b] | Length | Propulsion | Range (n.miles) | Notes[c] |
|---|---|---|---|---|---|---|---|---|---|
| SAM | RIM-67 | Standard-ER/SM-1 | General Dynamics | cruisers destroyers | 2,900 lbs | 26⅙ ft (7.9 m) | solid-fuel rocket + booster | 30–40 | Terrier replacement |
| SAM | RIM-67 | Standard-ER/SM-2 | General Dynamics | cruisers destroyers | 2,900 lbs | 26⅙ ft (7.9 m) | solid-fuel rocket + booster | 75+ | Terrier/Talos replacement; nuclear warhead under consideration |
| AAM | AIM-7 | Sparrow III | Raytheon | VF aircraft | ~350 lbs | 12 ft (3.7 m) | solid-fuel rocket | 10–15 | 90-lb warhead |
| AAM | AIM-9 | Sidewinder | Raytheon | VF/VA aircraft | 185 lbs | 9½ ft (2.9 m) | solid-fuel rocket | 5+ | |
| AAM | AIM-54 | Phoenix | Hughes | F-14 | 985 lbs | 13 ft (4 m) | solid-fuel rocket | 60+ | 135-lb warhead |
| ASM | AGM-12C | Bullpup-B | Martin Maxson | VA/VP aircraft | 1,785 lbs | 13½ ft (4.1 m) | liquid-fuel rocket | 10 | 1,000-lb warhead |
| ASM | AGM-45 | Shrike | Texas Instrument UNIVAC | VA aircraft | 390 lbs | 10 ft (3 m) | solid-fuel rocket | ~10 | anti-radiation |
| ASM | AGM-62 | Walleye I | Martin Hughes | VA aircraft | 1,125 lbs | 11⅓ ft (3.5 m) | glide bomb | 16 | 825-lb warhead |
| ASM | AGM-62 | Walleye II | Martin Hughes | VA aircraft | 2,400 lbs | 13¼ ft (4 m) | glide bomb | 35 | 2,000-lb warhead |
| ASM | AGM-78 | Standard-ARM | General Dynamics | VA aircraft | 1,350 lbs | 15 ft (4.6 m) | solid-fuel rocket | 15+ | anti-radiation |
| ASM | AGM-84 | Harpoon | McDonnell Douglas | VA/VP aircraft | 1,168 lbs | 12½ ft (3.8 m) | turbojet | 60 | 510-lb warhead |
| ASM | AGM-88 | HARM | Naval Weapons Center | VF/VA aircraft | 780 lbs | 13⅔ ft (4.2 m) | solid-fuel rocket | | High-speed Anti-Radiation Missile |
| SSM | RGM-84 | Harpoon | McDonnell Douglas | cruisers destroyers frigates missile craft | 1,470 lbs[d] 1,530 lbs[e] | 15⅙ ft (4.6 m) | turbojet + booster | 60 | 510-lb warhead |
| SSM | UGM-84 | Harpoon | McDonnell Douglas | submarines | 1,530 lbs | 15⅙ ft (4.6 m) | turbojet + booster | 60 | 510-lb warhead |
| SSM | BGM-109 | Tomahawk | General Dynamics | cruisers destroyers submarines | 3,200 lbs 4,000 lbs[f] | 20½ ft (6.2 m) | turbofan | 300–500 | 1,000-lb warhead; nuclear option under consideration |
| ASW | RUR-5 | ASROC | Honeywell | cruisers destroyers frigates | 1,000 lbs | 15 ft (4.6 m) | solid-fuel rocket | 6 | Mk 17 nuclear depth charge or Mk 46 torpedo for warhead |
| ASW | UUM-44 | SUBROC | Goodyear | submarines | 4,000 lbs | 21 ft (6.4 m) | solid-fuel rocket | 25–30 | nuclear warhead; ballistic trajectory |
| SLBM | UGM-27 | Polaris A-3 | Lockheed | SSBN | 30,000 lbs | 32 ft (9.8 m) | solid-fuel rocket + booster | 2,500 | thermonuclear warhead; 3 Multiple Re-entry Vehicles (MRV) |
| SLBM | UGM-73 | Poseidon C-3 | Lockheed | SSBN | 65,000 lbs | 34 ft (10.4 m) | solid-fuel rocket + booster | ~2,500 | thermonuclear warhead; up to 14 Multiple Independently targeted Re-entry Vehicles (MIRV) |
| SLBM | UGM-96 | Trident C-4 | Lockheed | SSBN | 70,000 lbs | 34⅙ (10.4 m) | solid-fuel rocket + booster | ~4,000 | thermonuclear warhead; up to 24 MIRVs |
| Anti-Tank | MGM-71 | TOW | Hughes | helicopters (ground vehicles) | 47 lbs | 3⅔ ft (1.1 m) | solid-fuel rocket + booster | 2.3 | Tube-launched, Optically guided, Wire-controlled missile; 8-lb hollow-charge warhead |

a SAM = Surface-to-Air Missile; AAM = Air-to-Air Missile; ASM = Air-to-Surface Missile; SSM = Surface-to-Surface Missile; ASW = Antisubmarine Warfare; SLBM = Submarine-Launched Ballistic Missile. The Harpoon and Tomahawks are additionally considered as SLCM = Sea-Launched Cruise Missiles.
b In most instances weight and length are given for major production versions.
c All warheads are high explosive unless otherwise indicated.
d As carried in Tartar/Standard-MR missile magazine.
e As carried in multiple missile launch cannister.
f As encapsulated for submarine launch.

Terrier SAM on the WILLIAM H. STANDLEY (CG 32) (U.S. Navy)

Sea Sparrow SAM on the BLAKELY (FF 1072) (U.S. Navy)

Prototype Standard-MR SAM on the BUCHANAN (DDG 14) (U.S. Navy)

Talos SAM being launched by the LITTLE ROCK (CG 4) (U.S. Navy)

Standard-ER SAM being launched by the WAINWRIGHT (CG 28) U.S. Navy)

Sparrow III AAM experimentally fitted on UH-2C Sea Sprite helicopter (U.S. Navy)

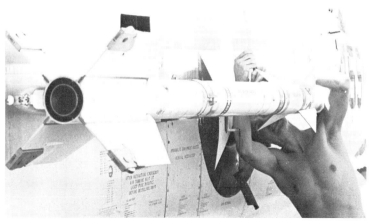

Sidewinder AAM being attached to "cheek" fuselage pylon of an F-8 Crusader fighter (U.S. Navy)

Six Phoenix AAMs on F-14A Tomcat (four on fuselage pylons and two on wing pylons) (U.S. Navy)

Modified Standard-MR (RIM-66A) interim SSM being fired from the ASROC launcher of the frigate VREELAND (FF 1068); the two end cells of this launcher have been modified for the Standard. (U.S. Navy)

Bullpup ASM being launched by P-3B Orion patrol aircraft. (U.S. Navy)

Walleye on A-4 Skyhawk attack aircraft (U.S. Navy)

Shrike ASM (outboard pylon) and Walleye ASM (inboard pylon) on JA-4M Skyhawk attack aircraft. (U.S. Navy, PHAN Randall Phillips)

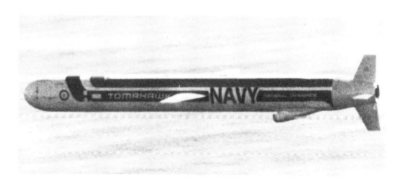

Tomahawk SSM in flight (test launch from an A-6 Intruder attack aircraft) (U.S. Navy)

Harpoon SSM launched from underwater; the fragment at left is from the disposable submarine launch canister. (U.S. Navy)

Harpoon SSM launch canisters during experimental installation on the Fox (CG 33) (U.S. Navy)

ASROC being fired by the destroyer BRINKLEY BASS (DD 887) (U.S. Navy)

Polaris A-3 missile launched from underwater (U.S. Navy)

Poseidon SLBM being launched from the submerged submarine JAMES MADISON (SSBN 627) (U.S. Navy)

Polaris A-3 missile being loaded in the submarine STONEWALL JACKSON (SSBN 634) at the Polaris loading facility in Bremerton, Washington. The missiles are stored, transported, and loaded in cannisters. As shown in this view, the cannister is lowered to the top of the open missile hatch and the missile is lowered into the tube. Another missile canister is on the pier. (U.S. Navy)

SUBROC launched from underwater (U.S. Navy)

Mockups of the Polaris A-3 (left) and Poseidon SLBMs. The latter missile is two feet longer and 1½ feet larger in diameter (6 feet rather than 4½ feet). Reportedly, the Poseidon can carry up to 14 independently targeted re-entry vehicles, although probably some ten are normally installed. (Lockheed Missiles and Space Co)

The first test launch of a Trident I SLBM from Cape Canaveral on 18 January 1977. The missile has the same length and diameter as the Poseidon, but has improvements in warhead and propellant, giving it better performance and accuracy. (U.S. Navy)

## MISSILE LAUNCHERS

| Designation | Missiles | Type | Operational | System Weight[a] | Ships |
|---|---|---|---|---|---|
| Mk 7 Mod 0 | 46 Talos | twin | 1960 | ~400,000 lbs | CG 5 |
| Mk 9 Mod 1 | 60 Terrier | twin | 1959 | ~500,000 lbs | CG 6–7 |
| Mk 10 Mod 0 | 40 Terrier/Standard-ER | twin | 1960 | 275,875 lbs | DDG 37–46 |
| Mk 10 Mod 1 | 40 Terrier/Standard-ER | twin | 1961 | 277,436 lbs | CGN 9 (forward) |
| Mk 10 Mod 2 | 80 Terrier/Standard-ER | twin | 1961 | 450,857 lbs | CGN 9 (forward) |
| Mk 10 Mod 3 | 40 Terrier/Standard-ER | twin | 1961 | 284,665 lbs | CV 63, 64, 66 (starboard) |
| Mk 10 Mod 4 | 40 Terrier/Standard-ER | twin | 1961 | 284,665 lbs | CV 63, 64, 66 (port) |
| Mk 10 Mod 5 | 40 Terrier/Standard-ER | twin | 1962 | 287,516 lbs | CG 16–24, CGN 25 (forward) |
| Mk 10 Mod 6 | 40 Terrier/Standard-ER | twin | 1962 | 274,938 lbs | CG 16–24, CGN 25 (aft) |
| Mk 10 Mod 7 | 60 Terrier/Standard-ER/ASROC | twin | 1964 | 361,994 lbs | CG 26–34, CGN 35 |
| Mk 10 Mod 8 | 60 Terrier/Standard-ER/ASROC | twin | 1967 | 364,197 lbs | CGN 35 |
| Mk 11 Mod 0 | 42 Tartar/Standard-MR/Harpoon | twin | 1962 | 165,240 lbs | DDG 2–14 |
| Mk 11 Mod 1 | 42 Tartar/Standard-MR | twin | 1962 | 165,240 lbs | CG 10–11 (starboard) |
| Mk 11 Mod 2 | 42 Tartar/Standard-MR | twin | 1962 | 165,240 lbs | CG 10–11 (port) |
| Mk 12 Mod 0 | 52 Talos | twin | 1961 | ~700,000 lbs | CGN 9 (aft) |
| Mk 12 Mod 1 | 52 Talos | twin | 1962 | ~700,000 lbs | CG 10–11 (forward and aft) |
| Mk 13 Mod 0 | 40 Tartar/Standard-MR | single | 1962 | 132,561 lbs | DDG 15–24 |
| Mk 13 Mod 1 | 40 Tartar/Standard-MR | single | 1967 | 135,079 lbs | DDG 31–34 |
| Mk 13 Mod 2 | 40 Tartar/Standard-MR | single | 1968 | 135,079 lbs | DDG 35–36 |
| Mk 13 Mod 3 | 40 Tartar/Standard-MR | single | 1974 | 135,012 lbs | CGN 36–37 |
| Mk 13 Mod 4 | 40 Tartar/Standard-MR/Harpoon | single | 1978 | 134,704 lbs | FFG 7 |
| Mk 16 Mods 1 to 6 | 8 ASROC[b] | 8-tube | | 47,782 lbs | cruisers, destroyers, frigates; some modified to launch Harpoon or Standard-ARM missiles (Mk 112 launcher "box") |
| Mk 22 Mod 0 | 16 Tartar/Standard-MR | single | 1966 | 92,395 lbs | FFG 1–6 |
| Mk 25 Mod 1 | 8 Sea Sparrow BPDMS | 8-tube | 1967 | 32,081 lbs | carriers, frigates, amphibious ships |
| Mk 26 Mod 0 | 24 Standard-MR/ASROC | twin | 1976 | 162,028 lbs | CGN 38–41, AVM 1 |
| Mk 26 Mod 1 | 44 Standard-MR/ASROC | twin | 1976 | 208,373 lbs | CGN 38–41, DDG 47 |
| Mk 26 Mod 2 | 64 Standard-MR/ASROC | twin | | 254,797 lbs | CGN 42 design |
| Mk 29 Mod 0 | 8 NATO Sea Sparrow IPDMS | 8-tube | 1974 | 24,000 or 28,000 lbs[c] | carriers, destroyers, frigates, amphibious ships, auxiliaries; NATO Sea Sparrow (Mk 132 launcher "box") |
| Mk 140 Mod 0[d] | 4 Harpoon | 4-tube | 1976 | 9,000 lbs | PHM 1, 3–6 |
| Mk 141 Mod 0[d] | 4 Harpoon | 4-tube | 1977 | 13,000 lbs | cruisers, destroyers |

a  Does not include missiles and hydraulic fluids; missiles are included for Mk 16, 25, 29, 140, 141 "box" launchers.
b  Does not include reloads available in some ships.
c  One director and two director systems, respectively.
d  These are launcher and not system designations (in same series as Mk 112 and 113, ASROC and IPDMS launchers).

Terrier/Standard-ER launcher Mk 10 Mod 5 in the cruiser LEAHY (CG 16) (U.S. Navy, PHCS Virgil McColley)

Sea Sparrow BPDMS launcher Mk 25 Mod 1 in frigate (Norman Polmar)

Talos launcher Mk 7 Mod 0 in a guided missile cruiser (Northern Ordnance)

Tartar/Standard-MR launcher Mk 11 Mod 0 in guided missile destroyer (General Dynamics/Pamona)

## GUNS

The U.S. Navy's shipboard gun firepower has declined considerably during the past decade and will not significantly increase in the near future. The decline has been due to (1) the disposal of almost all World War II-era cruisers and destroyers, and (2) the Navy's limited interest in developing and deploying gun systems in the 1950s and 1960s.

The following table indicates the decline of U.S. Navy shipboard guns over a ten-year period.

|  | 1970 | 1975 | 1980 (estimated) |
|---|---|---|---|
| 8-inch guns in active fleet | 18 | 1[a] | 1 |
| 6-inch guns in active fleet | 12 | 6 | 0 |
| 5-inch guns in active fleet | 657 | 267 | 212 |
| 5-inch guns in Naval Reserve Force | 164 | 132 | 33[b] |

a   Experimental Mk 71 Major Caliber Light-Weight Gun in the HULL (DD 945)
b   Assumes assignment of 14 SHERMAN-class (DD 931) destroyers to NRF (8 ships with 2 guns, 5 ships with 3 guns, and 1 ship with 2 guns plus the 8-inch MCLWG)

The only 8-inch gun in service is the experimental Mk 71 MCLWG in the destroyer HULL (DD 944). The Navy has proposed arming the CGN 42-class Aegis missile cruisers and the 30 SPRUANCE-class (DD 963) destroyers with the 8-inch gun during the 1980s. However, those plans are highly tentative.

The only 6-inch guns remaining in active service are three barrels in the cruiser flagship OKLAHOMA CITY (CG 5). All other gun-armed cruisers have been retired. (In comparison, the Soviet Navy maintains more than 100 guns of 6-inch caliber, which serve in up to ten SVERDLOV-class cruisers.)

The number of 5-inch guns available has been declining as the World War II-era FRAM destroyers, most with four guns, have been retired in favor of the KNOX-class (FF 1052) frigates with one 5-inch gun and the SPRUANCE-class destroyers with two guns. The 5-inch-gun levels will not increase with the current frigate construction program because the PERRY-class (FFG 7) ships have a 76-mm gun.

It is of considerable significance that the 5-inch guns will be provided with laser-guided and Rocket Assisted Projectiles (RAP). This ammunition will enhance the 5-inch guns' capabilities considerably.

The large number of 3-inch antiaircraft guns deployed from the early 1950s onward is being reduced to a minimal number in amphibious and auxiliary ships. These weapons have a limited effectiveness and are too difficult to maintain. A few are being kept for defense against small craft.

The Navy has belatedly obtained production approval for the Mk 15 Close-In Weapon System, a rotary-barrel "Gatling" gun for defense against anti-ship cruise missiles. The gun, which has been evaluated in destroyer-type ships, is planned for some 250 major combatant, amphibious, and auxiliary ships. It has built-in search and fire control radars, and can be operated fully automatically to react to short-warning attacks. The gun fires a "heavy" depleted uranium bullet of 12.75-mm diameter which is encased in a plastic "sabot," for an overall diameter of 20 mm. Bursts of several hundred rounds will be fired against incoming targets, and the fire control radar can track both target and "bullet stream" to make rapid corrections in aim.

(The Mk 15 CIWS will finally become available more than a decade after the sinking of the Israeli destroyer ELATH by Soviet cruise missiles—which alerted the West to the threat these weapons posed—and several years after the installation of 30-mm rapid-fire guns and 23-mm "Gatling" guns in Soviet ships.)

Classification: Guns are classified by the inside barrel diameter and gun-barrel length. Diameters traditionally were listed in inches for weapons larger than one inch, and in millimeters for smaller weapons. The Italian-designed OTO Melara 76-mm gun, however, retains its metric measurement in U.S. naval service.

Gun-barrel length is indicated by calibers. Thus, a 5-inch/38 caliber gun has a barrel length of approximately 190 inches (5 × 38).

Guns of 6-inch caliber and larger are installed in "turrets" and smaller-caliber guns in "mounts" under the former Bureau of Ordnance definitions. However, the unarmored, unmanned gun-house shield for the 8-inch Mk 71 MCLWG is more accurately considered a mount.

| Turret/Mount | Gun Barrel(s) | In Service[a] | Crew | Turret/Mount Weight | Rate of Fire[b] | Maximum Ranges[c] | Ammunition Weights[d] | Ships |
|---|---|---|---|---|---|---|---|---|
| 16"/50 cal (406 mm) triple turret | Mk 7 Mod 0 | 1943 | 79 | 1,700 tons | 2 rpm | 40,185 yds AP 41,622 yds HC | 2,700 lbs AP 1,900 lbs HC | BB 61 |
| 8"/55 cal (203 mm) triple turret | Mk 15 Mod 0 | 1943 | 40 | 297–304 tons | 4 rpm | 31,100 yds AP 31,350 yds HC @ 41° elevation | 335 lbs AP 260 lbs HC | CA 70, 73 |
| 8"/55 cal (203 mm) triple turret | Mk 16 Mod 0 | 1948 | 45 | 451 tons | 10 rpm | 30,100 yds AP 31,350 yds HC @ 41° elevation | 335 lbs AP 260 lbs HC | CA 134 |
| 8"/55 cal (203 mm) Mk 71 single mount (MCLWG) | Mk 30 Mod 2 | 1975 | 6 | 172,895 lbs | 12 rpm; guided projectiles 6 rpm | 31,408 yds | 260 lbs HC | DD 944 for evaluation |
| 6"/47 cal (152 mm) triple turret | Mk 16 Mod 1 | 1942 | 40 | 165–173 tons | 10–18 rpm | 26,118 yds AP 22,992 yds HC @ 47° elevation | 130 lbs AP 105 lbs HC | CG 4 |
| 5"/38 cal (127 mm) Mk 24 single mount | Mk 12 Mod 1 | | 15 | 33,100 lbs | 18 rpm | 17,306 yds @ 45° 32,250 ft @ 85° | 55 lbs | CV 9, 16, CG 10 |
| 5"/38 cal (127 mm) Mk 28 twin mount | Mk 12 Mod 1 | | 27 | 153,000– 169,000 lbs | 18 rpm | 17,306 yds @ 45° 32,250 ft @ 85° | 55 lbs | BB 61 |
| 5"/38 cal (127 mm) Mk 30 single mount | Mk 12 Mod 1 | | 17 | ~45,000 lbs | 20 rpm | 17,306 yds @ 45° 32,250 ft @ 85° | 55 lbs | CGN 9, FFG 1, FF 1040, AGFF 1, LKA, auxiliaries |
| 5"/38 cal (127 mm) Mk 32 twin mount | Mk 12 Mod 1 | | 27 | ~120,000 lbs | 18 rpm | 17,306 yds @ 45° 32,250 ft @ 85° | 55 lbs | CG 4, CA 134, 73, 70 |
| 5"/38 cal (127 mm) Mk 37 single mount | Mk 12 Mod 1 | | 11 | ~35,000 lbs | 15–18 rpm | 17,306 yds @ 45° 32,250 ft @ 85° | 55 lbs | auxiliaries |
| 5"/38 cal (127 mm) Mk 38 twin mount | Mk 12 Mod 1 | | 27 | 95,700– 105,600 lbs | 18 rpm | 17,306 yds @ 45° 32,250 ft @ 85° | 55 lbs | DD 710 |
| 5"/54 cal (127 mm) Mk 39 single mount | Mk 16 Mod 0 | 1945 | 17 | 73,900– 82,735 lbs | 18 rpm | 25,183 yds @ 45° 48,657 ft @ 85° | 70 lbs | CV 41 |
| 5"/54 cal (127 mm) Mk 42 single mount | Mk 18 Mod 0 | 1953 | 14 | Mod 1–6 ~145,000 lbs Mod 10 139,000 lbs | 20 rpm | 25,909 yds @ 47° 48,700 ft @ 85° | 70 lbs | Mod 1–6 in DDG 35, CC 1; Mod 7 and 10 in DD 931; Mod 10 in CGN 35, CG 26, DDG 37, 31, 2, FF 1952 |

(Table continued on page 302)

| Turret/Mount | Gun Barrel(s) | In Service[a] | Crew | Turret/Mount Weight | Rate of Fire[b] | Maximum Ranges[c] | Ammunition Weights[d] | Ships |
|---|---|---|---|---|---|---|---|---|
| 5"/54 cal (127 mm) Mk 45 single mount | | 1974 | 6 | 47,820 lbs | 16–20 rpm | 25,909 yds @ 47° 48,700 ft @ 85° | 70 lbs | CGN 38, CGN 36, DDG 47, DD 963, LHA |
| 3"/50 cal (76 mm) Mk 22 single mount | Mk 21 Mod 0 | | 11 | 7,510–8,310 lbs | 20 rpm | 14,041 yds @ 45° 29,367 ft @ 85° | 7 lbs | auxiliaries |
| 3"/50 cal (76 mm) Mk 26 single mount | Mk 21/22 | | 11 | 9,210–10,130 lbs | 20 rpm | 14,041 yds @ 45° 29,367 ft @ 85° | 7 lbs | auxiliaries |
| 3"/50 cal (76 mm) Mk 27 twin mount | Mk 22 | | 12 | 30,960–31,700 lbs | 50 rpm | 14,041 yds @ 45° 29,367 ft @ 85° | 7 lbs | CA 139, 134 |
| 3"/50 cal (76 mm) Mk 33 twin mount | Mk 22 | | 12 | ~33,000 lbs | 50 rpm | 14,041 yds @ 45° 29,367 ft @ 85° | 7 lbs | CA 139, 134, 73, 70; DD 931, FF 1037, AGF 3, amphibious ships, auxiliaries |
| 3"/50 cal (76 mm) Mk 34 single mount | Mk 22 | | 8 | | 50 rpm | 14,041 yds @ 45° 29,367 ft @ 85° | 7 lbs | PG 84 |
| 76 mm/62 cal Mk 75 single mount | Mk 75 | 1974 (FFG 4) | 4 | 13,680 lbs | 75–85 rpm | ~21,000 yds @ 45° ~39,000 ft @ 85° | 14 lbs | PHM 1, FFG 7 |
| 40 mm/60 cal Mk 1 twin mount | Mk 1 Mod 0 | | 5–9 | 13,000 lbs | 160 rpm | 11,000 yds @ 42° 22,800 ft @ 90° | 1.5 lbs 1.9 lbs | CC 2, LST |
| 40 mm/60 cal Mk 2 quad mount | Mk 1 Mod 0 | | 11 | 23,800–25,500 lbs | 160 rpm | 11,000 yds @ 42° 22,800 ft @ 90° | 1.5 lbs 1.9 lbs | BB 61, LSD, auxiliaries |
| 40 mm/60 cal Mk 3/M3 single mount | M1 | | 4–5 | 2,264 lbs | 160 rpm | 11,000 yds @ 42° 22,800 ft @ 90° | 1.5 lbs 1.9 lbs | LST, MSO, ARS |
| 20 mm/70 cal Mk 10 single mount | Mk 2/4 | | 2 | 700–1100 lbs | 450 rpm | 4,800 yds @ 35° 10,000 ft @ 90° | 0.2 lbs | MSO, auxiliaries |
| 20 mm Mk 67 single mount | Mk 16 Mod 5 | | 1 | | 800 rpm | 3,300 yds | 0.75 lbs | CGN 25, LHA 1, PTF, auxiliaries |
| 20 mm Mk 68 single mount | Mk 16 Mod 5 | | 1 | | 800 rpm | 3,300 yds | 0.75 lbs | MSO, auxiliaries |
| 20 mm/76 cal Mk 15 CIWS six-barrel Phalanx "Gatling" gun | M61A1 | 1973 (DDG 41) | — | ~12,000 lbs | 3,000 rpm | 1,625 yds | | DD 942 for evaluation |
| 81-mm mortar Mk 2[e] | | | 2 | | 10 rpm trigger mode; 18 rpm drop-fire mode | 3,940 yds | | PTF, PCF |
| 60-mm mortar Mk 4 | | | 2 | | 10 rpm trigger mode; 18 rpm drop-fire mode | 2,000 yds | | PBR |

a  Installed in combatant ship for evaluation or service.
b  Rounds-per-minute per barrel in multi-barrel mounts and turrets.
c  Maximum range at 45° elevation unless otherwise indicated.
d  AP = Armor-Piercing; HC = High Capacity (for shore bombardment).
e  Mk 2 Mod 0 mounted "piggy-back" with .50-cal MG.

The battleship New Jersey (BB 62) trains her forward 16-inch gun battery to port during firing exercises off the Virginia Capes. Amidships on both sides the Iowa-class dreadnoughts have twin 5-inch Mk 27 gun mounts. In her final period of active service, the New Jersey operated without the large 40-mm and 20-mm AA batteries that she and her sisters had during World War II.

The 8-inch Mk 71 MCLWG in the Hull (DD 945) (U.S. Navy)

Triple 6-inch gun turret and 5-inch Mk 32 twin gun mount in the Springfield (CG 7) (U.S. Navy)

Triple 6-inch gun turret and 5-inch Mk 32 twin gun mount in the Little Rock (CG 4) (U.S. Navy, Commander J. P. Mathews)

Triple 8-inch gun turrets in the BOSTON (CAG 1/CA 69) (U.S. Navy)

Twin 5-inch Mk 38 Mod 12 gun mount in the HENDERSON (DD 785) with SH-3A Sea King overhead. (U.S. Navy)

Single 5-inch Mk 39 Mod 0 gun mounts in the FRANKLIN D. ROOSEVELT (CV 42) (U.S. Navy)

Single 5-inch Mk 30 gun mounts in the PLATTE (AO 24) alongside the OKINAWA (LPH 3) (U.S. Navy)

Single 5-inch Mk 42 Mod 7/8 gun mount in the CHARLES F. ADAMS (DDG 2) (U.S. Navy)

Twin 3-inch Mk 33 Mod 0 gun mount in the TRUCKEE (AO 147) (Norman Polmar)

Single 5-inch Mk 42 Mod 9 gun mount (Northern Ordnance)

Single 5-inch Mk 45 Mod 0 gun mount in the SPRUANCE (DD 963) (U.S. Navy, PH1 Lonnie M. McKay)

Twin 3-inch Mk 33 Mod 0 gun mount in the CANBERRA (CAG 2/CA 70) (U.S. Navy)

Single 3-inch Mk 34 Mod 5 gun mount in the CLAUD JONES (DE 1033) (U.S. Navy, PH1 Joseph E. Higgins)

Single 76-mm Mk 75 Mod 0 gun mount in the PEGASUS (PHM 1) (U.S. Navy)

Quad 40-mm Mk 2 gun mounts (U.S. Navy)

Single 40-mm Mk 3 gun mount in the HARNETT COUNTY (LST 821) (U.S. Navy)

Phalanx 20-mm Mk 15 Close-In Weapons System (CIWS) (U.S. Navy)

Phalanx 20-mm Mk 15 Close-In Weapons System (CIWS) (General Dynamics/Pamona)

81-mm Mk 2 mortar mounted with .50-caliber machine gun (U.S. Navy)

## TORPEDOES

The U.S. Navy has three torpedoes in service use: the Mk 37 anti-submarine torpedo, Mk 46 antisubmarine torpedo, and Mk 48, which can be used against submarines and surface targets.

The Mk 37 is a medium-length torpedo that is being retained in Navy service as a submarine-launched, ASW weapon because of the high cost of its planned replacement, the Mk 48. Thus, U.S. submarines are armed with these two types of torpedoes. About 1,200 Mk 37 torpedoes are available.

The Mk 46 is a short torpedo which can be launched from surface ships (Mk 32 torpedo tubes or ASROC) or aircraft, and is fitted in the Mk 60 CAPTOR mine. The Mk 46 has fully replaced its predecessor, the Mk 44, in U.S. service. The Mk 46 Mod 1 torpedo is being improved under NEARTIP (Near Term Improvement Program), with improved acoustic guidance and countermeasure resistance features being fitted. The Mk 46 Mod 5 NEARTIP torpedo is scheduled to become operational during FY 1979.

The Mk 48 is a long torpedo that has been the subject of intense controversy, principally because of its high cost—currently about $625,000 per weapon. The Mk 48 was developed as a replacement for the Mk 14 and 16 torpedoes in the anti-ship role, and the Mk 37 and 45 ASTOR (Antisubmarine Torpedo) in the ASW role. However, because of the Mk 48's high cost, the Mk 37 has been retained for use against submarines.

In several respects the Mk 48 is probably the most capable torpedo in service with any navy. A number of advanced guidance features are provided, including a sophisticated passive-active acoustic search as well as wire guidance. Over 1,100 Mk 48 torpedoes have been delivered for fleet use, with another 619 programmed for funding in FY 1978–1979.

The availability of the Mk 48 has led to the phasing out of the Mk 45 ASTOR, the U.S. Navy's only torpedo with a nuclear warhead. The Mk 45 bodies have been mated with conventional warheads, while the discarded Mk 37 torpedoes are being fitted with improved engines and guidance, with both types provided to foreign navies as the Mk 45-F Freedom Torpedo and the NT-37C, respectively.

Although not technically a torpedo, the SUBROC (Submarine Rocket) must be mentioned in this section. This antisubmarine weapon is fired from standard 21-inch submarine torpedo tubes. It projects a nuclear depth charge to a distance of 25–30 miles from the launching submarine. SUBROC's limitations include the delays involved because of the need to obtain release authority for use of a nuclear weapon.

A Mk 46 torpedo is fired from the triple Mk 32 torpedo tubes in the Newman K. Perry (DD 883) (U.S. Navy)

| Designation | Launch Platforms | Operational | Weight | Length | Diameter | Propulsion | Guidance | Notes |
|---|---|---|---|---|---|---|---|---|
| Mk 37 Mod 2 | Submarines | 1967 | 1,690 lbs | 13½ ft (4.1 m) | 19 in (484.5 mm) | electric | wire; active-passive acoustic | range ~5 miles |
| Mk 37 Mod 3 | Submarines | 1967 | 1,430 lbs | 11¼ ft (3.4 m) | 19 in (484.5 mm) | electric | active-passive acoustic | range ~5 miles |
| Mk 46 Mod 0 | Aircraft | 1966 | 568 lbs | 8½ ft (2.6 m) | 12¾ in (324 mm) | solid-propellant | active-passive acoustic | |
| Mk 46 Mod 1/2 | Surface ships (Mk 32 tubes and ASROC); aircraft | 1967–1972 | 508 lbs | 8½ ft (2.6 m) | 12¾ in (324 mm) | liquid mono-propellant | active-passive acoustic | Mod 4 in CAPTOR mine; Mod 5 is NEARTIP |
| Mk 48 Mod 1/3 | Submarines | 1972 | 3,450 lbs | 19¹/₁₂ ft (5.8 m) | 21 in (533.6 mm) | liquid mono-propellant | wire; active-passive acoustic | range 20+ miles; deep diving |
| Mk XX | Surface ships (Mk 32 tubes and ASROC); aircraft | 1980s | ~500 lbs | ~8½ ft (2.6 m) | ~12¾ in (324 mm) | | active-passive acoustic | ASW Advanced Light-Weight Torpedo (ALWT); Mk 46 replacement |

A Mk 46 torpedo fitted on an SH-3 Sea King helicopter (U.S. Navy, Lorin Miller)

Mk 46 Mod 1 torpedoes in weapons bay of a P-3 Orion patrol aircraft; parachute packs are fitted at the tails of the torpedoes. (U.S. Navy)

## MINES

The U.S. Navy has only a slight interest in offensive or defensive mine warfare, and no surface ships are currently fitted for carrying mines. Minelaying exercises by carrier-based attack aircraft, land-based patrol aircraft, and submarines are carried out on a periodic basis; however, these exercises are severely limited in scope. The stowage of mines aboard aircraft carriers reduces the number of conventional bombs and missiles which can be embarked in those ships. Moreover, submarines do not carry mines when on peace-time patrols. To load mines they would have to first return to an allied port where the mines were available; offload their torpedoes and replace them with mines; steam to the target area, presumably at slow speed in order to plant the mines covertly; possibly return to base after planting the mines to embark a full load of torpedoes (or more mines); and then steam to the operational area. In view of the U.S. Navy's limited interest in mine warfare, it is un-likely that submarines would be diverted to minelaying operations in a sudden crisis situation or in the early days of actual conflict.

The U.S. Air Force has a secondary sea-control mission which includes minelaying. There are approximately 80 Air Force B-52D Stratofortress turbojet bombers in service which are configured to carry mines as well as nuclear or conventional bombs. However, their availability for minelaying in the event of a conflict with the Soviet Union or a major crisis is very questionable, in part because their use in the mine role could be interpreted by the Soviet leader-ship as a signal that the United States was either launching bomber strikes or, if the Soviets realized the nature of the operation, that the United States was reducing its nuclear-strike options. (Another 250 B-52G/H bombers are also in service and fully committed to the U.S. strategic attack plan.)

Most mines in the U.S. Navy inventory are obsolescent, with some having probably been recovered by North Vietnam and Soviet specialists—and thus "compromised"—after their use off North Vietnamese ports in 1972. Mines which are being discarded include the 1,110-lb Mk 36, the 2,025-lb Mk 39, and the 500-lb Mk 50 and Mk 53—all of which were air-laid mines.

The recently developed CAPTOR mine is now entering fleet service. This is a deep-moored mine which can detect passing sub-marines by their acoustic signature, and launch the Mk 46 homing torpedo. CAPTOR production was initiated in the FY 1978 budget with 550 mines funded, and an additional 1,000 are planned for FY 1979.

Other mine programs were initiated in the early 1970s to in-crease U.S. mine capabilities, including the Propelled-Rocket Ascent Mine (PRAM), Submarine-Launched Mobile Mine (SLMM), and Project Quickstrike. The last is an extension of the so-called Destructor program of fitting general-purpose bombs with a mine fuze.

The following table indicates the maximum mine-carrying capa-bility of various aircraft currently in service. The mines are identi-fied by "class" which indicates their approximate weight. Sub-marines can carry mines in place of torpedoes or SUBROCs. (The torpedo-carrying capacities of U.S. subs are classified.)

| Aircraft | Wing Pylons | | | Weapons Bay | | |
|---|---|---|---|---|---|---|
| A-6 Intruder | 5 | 2,000 lb | | | | |
| A-7 Corsair II | 6 | 2,000 lb | | | | |
| S-3 Viking | 2 | 2,000 lb | + | 4 | 500 lb | |
| P-2 Neptune | 8 | 500 lb | + | 8 | 1,000 lb | |
| | | | or | 4 | 2,000 lb | |
| P-3 Orion | 10 | 500 lb | + | 6 | 500 lb | |
| | | | or | | | |
| | 8 | 1,000 lb | + | 3 | 1,000 lb | |
| | | | or | | | |
| | 6 | 2,000 lb | + | 1 | 2,000 lb | |
| B-52D Stratofortress | 8 | 2,000 lb | + | 56 | 500 lb | |
| | | | or | | | |
| | 8 | 2,000 lb | + | 18 | 1,000 lb | |

Mk 36 mine fitted on A-7A Corsair attack aircraft (U.S. Navy)

| Designation | Launch Platforms | Class | Weight | Length ft (m) | Diameter in (mm) | Notes |
|---|---|---|---|---|---|---|
| Mk 25 | Aircraft | 2,000 lbs | 1,997 lbs | 7 (2.1) | 22½ (571.5) | ~1,200-lb warhead |
| Mk 52 | Aircraft | 1,000 lbs | 1,190 lbs | 7$^5/_{12}$ (2.3) | 13⅓ (337.8) | |
| Mk 55 | Aircraft | 2,000 lbs | 2,120 lbs | 9½ (2.9) | 23⅓ (591.8) | ~1,100-lb warhead |
| Mk 36 | Aircraft | 2,000 lbs | 2,000 lbs | 11¼ (3.5) | 22¾(591.9) | |
| Mk 57 | Submarines | 2,000 lbs | 2,059 lbs | 10$^1/_{12}$ (3) | 21⅓ (541) | |
| Mk 67 SLMM | Submarines | 1,600 lbs | 1,660 lbs | 13$^5/_{12}$ (4.1) | 19 (482.6) | Submarine-Launched Mobile Mine; converted Mk 37 torpedo |
| Mk 60 CAPTOR | Aircraft, Submarines | 2,000 lbs | | | | 98-lb warhead; enCAPsulated TORpedo (Mk 46 Mod 4) |
| PRAM | Aircraft, Submarines | | | | | Propelled Rocket Ascent Mine; under development; final characteristics not determined |

Mk 53 mine fitted on an A-4E Skyhawk attack aircraft (U.S. Navy)

Mk 56 mine fitted on an A-4 Skyhawk attack aircraft (U.S. Navy)

Mk 60 CAPTOR mine fitted with parachute pack (U.S. Navy)

Mk 56 mine (*Charleston News and Courier*)

## RADARS

*Explanation of symbols:*

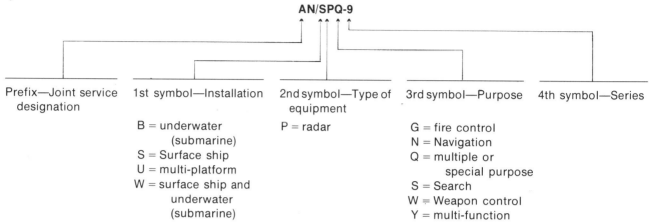

**AN/SPQ-9**

| Prefix—Joint service designation | 1st symbol—Installation | 2nd symbol—Type of equipment | 3rd symbol—Purpose | 4th symbol—Series |

1st symbol—Installation
B = underwater (submarine)
S = Surface ship
U = multi-platform
W = surface ship and underwater (submarine)

2nd symbol—Type of equipment
P = radar

3rd symbol—Purpose
G = fire control
N = Navigation
Q = multiple or special purpose
S = Search
W = Weapon control
Y = multi-function

Note: Major U.S. military electronic equipment is identified by the Joint Army-Navy Nomenclature System shown above. The prefix AN/ is omitted from electronic equipment listed in the ship and aircraft sections of this volume.

The SPG radars are in the same numerical series as the earlier Mark fire control radars; thus, the SPG-51 and Mk 26 radars are in the same numerical series.

In general, ship installations are identified by type of ship, except for new construction (e.g. DDG 47) and one-of-a-kind installations (e.g. BB 62).

| Designation | Purpose | Operational[a] | Band | Manufacturer | Ships | Notes |
|---|---|---|---|---|---|---|
| Mk 13 | radar for Mk 31 and Mk 38 gun directors (range and bearing) | | X | Western Electric | BB, CA, CG | mod 0; none in active ships |
| Mk 25 | radar for Mk 37 GFCS (conical scanning) | | X | Western Electric | CV, BB, CA, CG, DD | mod 3 |
| Mk 34/SPG-34 | radar for Mk 57 gun director and Mk 63 GFCS (conical scanning) | | X | Western Electric | BB, CA | mod 2/4/16; none in active ships |
| Mk 35 | radar for Mk 56 GFCS | | X | General Electric | CV, BB, CG, CGN, DD, FFG, FF, CC, LPD, LSD | mod 2 |
| Mk 90/91 | Aegis FCS illumination | | | Raytheon | CGN 42, DDG 47 | slaved to SPY-1 radars; see SPG-62 |
| BPS-5/11/14/15 | surface search | 1953 (BPS-5) | X | Lockheed Western Electric | submarines | primarily for surface navigation; retractable antennas |
| SG-6 | surface search | | | | CA | none in active ships |
| SPG-49 | Talos illumination and tracking | | C | Sperry | CGN, CG | mods A/B; used with SPW-2B |
| SPG-50 | radar for Mk 63 GFCS | | X | Western Electric | LPH | improved Mk 34 Mod 17 |
| SPG-51 | Tartar/Standard-MR illumination and tracking | 1960 | C/X | Raytheon | CGN, CG, DDG, FFG | mods B/C/D; pulse-doppler |
| SPG-52 | radar for Mk 70 GFCS | | | Lockheed | LPH | mod A |
| SPG-53 | radar for Mk 68 GFCS | | X | Western Electric | DDG, DD, FF | mods A/D/F; modified SPG-48 |

| Designation | Purpose | Operational[a] | Band | Manufacturer | Ship Type | Notes |
|---|---|---|---|---|---|---|
| SPG-55 | Terrier/Standard-ER illumination and guidance | | C | Sperry | CV, CGN, CG, DDG | mods A/B; successor to SPQ-5 |
| SPG-60 | Standard-MR/gun tracking and illumination for Mk 86 GFCS | | X | Lockheed | CGN, DD, LHA | see STIR (below); pulse-doppler |
| SPG-62 | Standard SM-2 illuminator (Aegis) | | X | Raytheon | CGN 42, DDG 47, AVM 1 | Mk 99 MFCS component; slaved to SPY-1 radar |
| SPQ-5 | Terrier illumination | | C | | CG | mod A; replaced by SPG-55 |
| SPQ-9 | surface search and weapons control for Mk 86 GFCS | 1970 | X | Lockheed | CGN, DD, LHA | mod A; high-resolution, short-range, track-while-scan; pulse-doppler |
| SPS-6 | air search | 1950 | L | Bendix Westinghouse | BB 62, CA, LSD 28-35, AOE 3-4 | mods B/C/E; mod C in active ships |
| SPS-8 | height-finding | 1955 (SPS-8A) | S | General Electric | BB, CA | mod A; none in active ships |
| SPS-10 | surface search | 1953 | C | Raytheon Sylvania | most combatant, amphibious, auxiliary ships | mods B-F; primarily for navigation |
| SPS-12 | air search | 1953 | L | RCA | CVN 65, CVT 16, CGN 9, CA 139 | mod C |
| SPS-29 | air search[b] | 1958 | P | Westinghouse | CA 148, DDG, DD | mods B/C/E |
| SPS-30 | long-range height-finding | 1962 | S | General Electric | CV, CG, DDG, CA | |
| SPS-32 | long-range air search | 1962 | P | Hughes | CVN 65, CGN 9 | fixed array (4 per ship); Frequency Scan (FRESCAN) in azimuth; 40 × 20 ft. panels |
| SPS-33 | 3-D multi-target tracking | 1962 | S | Hughes | CVN 65, CGN 9 | fixed array (4 per ship); Frequency Scan (FRESCAN) in elevation and phase scan in azimuth; 25 × 20 ft. panels |
| SPS-37 | long-range air search[b] | 1960 | P | Westinghouse | CGN, CG, CA, DDG, DD | mod A; antenna identical to SPS-29 |
| SPS-39 | 3-D search | | S | Hughes | CV 63, CGN 25, DDG 2, 42 | also mod A |
| SPS-40 | air search | 1961 | UHF | Lockheed | CGN, DDG, DD, FF, LCC, LHA, LPH | mods A through D |
| SPS-43 | long-range air search[b] | 1962 | P | Hughes Westinghouse | CVN, CV, CG, CA | mod A |
| SPS-48 | 3-D search | 1962 | S | ITT-Gilfillan | CVN, CV, CGN, CG, DDG, LCC | mods A through C; Frequency Scan (FRESCAN) in elevation and mechanical scan in azimuth |
| SPS-49 | long-range air search | 1965 | | Raytheon | CVN, CV, CGN 42, CG 19, DDG 47, FFG 7 | narrow-beam, very long-range |
| SPS-52 | 3-D search | 1963 | S | Hughes | CV, CGN 42, CGN DDG 47, DDG, FFG, LHA | mods A through C; improved SPS-39A; Frequency Scan (FRESCAN) in elevation and mechanical scan in azimuth |
| SPS-53 | surface search | 1967 | X | Sperry Marine | BB 62, PG, MSO, auxiliary ships | navigation |
| SPS-55 | surface search | | X | Cordion | BB 62, CGN 42, DDG 47, DD, FFG | slotted array; replacement for SPS-10 |
| SPS-58/65 | low-level threat detection | | L | Westinghouse | CV, CVN, FF, LCC, LHA, LPH, AOE, AOR | can be used with SPS-10 antenna; fed directly to NTDS; pulse-doppler |
| SPW-2 | Talos guidance | | C | Sperry | CGN 9, CG | mods A/B |
| SPY-1 | Aegis multi-function radar | | S | RCA | CGN 42, DDG 47, AVM 1 | mod A; fixed array (4 per ship); Frequency Scan (FRESCAN) in elevation and azimuth; 4,080 elements per 12 × 12 ft array; integrated search and fire control |
| STIR | Separate Target Illumination Radar | | X | | FFG | modified SPG-60 |

a   Includes first installation in combatant ship for at-sea evaluation.
b   The SPS-29/37/43 use the same antenna; the SPS-37A and SPS-43A use a larger antenna. The SPS-37A has an effective detection range of 300 miles, vice 233 miles for the SPS-37.

## RADAR FREQUENCY BANDS

| Band | Wavelength (centimeters) | Frequency (megacycles) | Notes |
|---|---|---|---|
| VHF | 1000–100 | 30–300 | |
| UHF | 100–30 | 300–1,000 | |
| P | 150–60 | 200–500 | P was original U.S. radar band; now part of UHF band |
| L | 30–15 | 1,000–2,000 | Long-wave signals used for air search radars |
| S | 15–7.5 | 2,000–4,000 | |
| C | 7.5–3.75 | 4,000–8,000 | Short-wave signals used for fire control, surface search, and height-finding (3-D) radars |
| X | 3.75–2.5 | 8,000–12,000 | |

The Mk 74 missile FCS for the Tartar/Standard-MR in U.S. cruisers, destroyers, and frigates uses the SPG-51 radar. Two SPG-51C radars are shown aft on the HENRY B. WILSON (DDG 7). An SPS-39A three-dimensional air search radar is mounted on the forward face of the funnel. Note the "E" for exercise competition excellence painted on both missile directors. (Giorgio Arra)

Twin SPG-55B radars are mounted atop Terrier/Standard-ER missile directors. This pair, shown aft on the cruiser HALSEY (CG 23), have an "E" and chevron, indicating two efficiency awards during a specific number of years. The twin 3-inch gun mount seen at left has been removed since this photo was taken in 1977. (Giorgio Arra)

This closeup view of the Mk 37 GFCS in the destroyer DAMATO (DD 871) shows the affixed Mk 25 Mod 3 radar. The 60-inch-diameter radar dish provides a maximum radar range of about 100,000 yards. Note the binoculars fixed to the director in front of the sailor at left. At right, the fire control symbol adorns the end of the Mk 37's optical sight. (U.S. Navy, PH2 Vincent R. Neaz)

The Mk 35 radar is affixed to the Mk 56 GFCS aboard the aircraft carrier MIDWAY (CV 41). The 48-inch-diameter dish provides acquisition and tracking for the Mk 56 which is employed for 3-inch and 5-inch gun control (U.S. Navy, AN G. Shreves)

The SPG-53A radar/Mk 68 GFCS is a feature of most destroyers and frigates built for the U.S. Navy since World War II. The radar/director is used with 3-inch and 5-inch guns. Note the optical rangefinder "ears" protruding from the director. (U.S. Navy)

This bow-on view of the CHICAGO (CG 11) shows the two large, "search-light" SPG-49B tracking radars, the SPS-48 3-D search antenna (square), and the SPS-43A air search antenna (rectangular). (Giorgio Arra)

Many U.S. missile ships, including the JULIUS A. FURER (FFG 6), use the SPS-52 three-dimensional radar. The planar array antenna is also used with the SPS-39/39A/42 radars. The SPS-52 can provide four-second data rates against small high-speed aircraft at ranges out to 60 miles and using longer radar pulses is effective to about 245 miles. Note the side panels or end plates; the SPS-48 has a single end plate. (Giorgio Arra)

The destroyer Bausell (DD 845) has SPS-29C and SPS-10 surface search radar antennas on the ship's tripod mast. The bar atop the −29 is for IFF (Identification Friend or Foe). The "mattress" antenna is similar to that of the discarded SPS-28 radar. The maximum range of the SPS-29 is about 270 miles. (Giorgio Arra)

Mounted atop the "mack"—combination mast and stack—of the frigate Lockwood (FF 1064) are an SPS-10 surface search/navigation antenna and an SPS-40D air search radar. The −10 is the most widely used radar in the Navy. Its nominal range is just over the horizon, although longer-range detections have been made. The −40 is rated as a medium-to-long-range radar. (Giorgio Arra)

**SONARS**
*Explanation of symbols:*

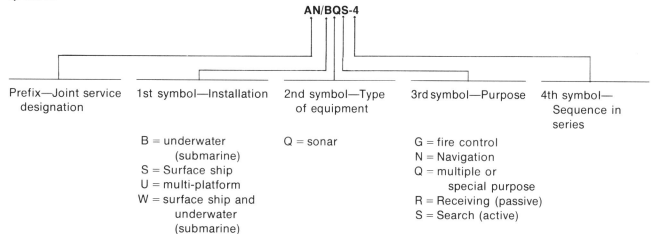

**AN/BQS-4**

| Prefix—Joint service designation | 1st symbol—Installation | 2nd symbol—Type of equipment | 3rd symbol—Purpose | 4th symbol—Sequence in series |
|---|---|---|---|---|
| | B = underwater (submarine)<br>S = Surface ship<br>U = multi-platform<br>W = surface ship and underwater (submarine) | Q = sonar | G = fire control<br>N = Navigation<br>Q = multiple or special purpose<br>R = Receiving (passive)<br>S = Search (active) | |

Note: See Radars (p. 312) for details of U.S. military electronic designation system.

| Designation | Purpose | Operational[a] | Manufacturer | Ships | Notes |
|---|---|---|---|---|---|
| BQG-4 PUFF | passive fire control | 1963 | Sperry | SS, SSN 597, LPSS 574 | three fin domes; Passive Underwater Fire control (Feasibility) |
| BQQ-2 | active/passive sonar system | 1960 | Raytheon | SSN 597, 594, 637, 685, 671 | includes BQR-7 and BQS-6; to be upgraded to BQQ-5 |
| BQQ-5 | active/passive sonar system | 1976 | IBM | SSN 688 | improved BQQ-2 system |
| BQQ-6 | passive sonar system | 1979 est. | IBM | SSBN 726 | passive BQQ-5 |
| BQR-2B | passive detection | 1955 | EDO | see BQS-4 | component of BQS-4 |
| BQR-7 | passive detection | 1955 | EDO Raytheon | see BQQ-2 | component of BQQ-2; conformal hydrophone array |
| BQR-15 | passive detection | 1974 | Western Electric | SSBN 608, 616 | towed array; includes BQR-23 signal processor |
| BQR-19 | short-range, rapid-scanning | 1970 | Raytheon | SSBNs | |
| BQR-21 DIMUS | passive detection | | Honeywell | SSBNs | Digital Multi-beam Steering |
| BQS-4 | active/passive sonar system | 1955 | EDO | SS, older SSNs | |
| BQS-8/14/20 | under ice/mine detection | 1960 | EDO Hazeltine | newer SSNs | |
| BQS-11/12/13 | active/passive detection | 1960 | Raytheon | newer SSNs | replaces BQS-6; component of BQQ-2/5; spherical array in bow dome |
| SQQ-14 | mine detection-classification | | EDO | MSOs, MCM (interim pending SMS) | Variable Depth Sonar (VDS); retracts into hull |
| SQQ-23 PAIR | active/passive detection | 1972 | Sperry | DDG 2 modernization | modified SQS-23; Passive/Active Integration Retrofit |
| SQR-17 | passive classification | 1975 | DRS | CG 26, DD 963, FFG 7, FF 1052 | acoustic precessor for LAMPS helicopters |
| SQR-18 TACTAS | passive long-range detection | 1978 | EDO | FF 1052 | employs winch, cable, towing body of SQS-35; Tactical Towed Array Sonar |
| SQR-19 TACTAS | passive long-range detection | | General Electric | CGN 42, DDG 47, DD 963, FFG 7 | improved TACTAS |
| SQS-23 | active/passive detection | 1958 | Sangamo | CV 66, CGN, CG, DDG, DD 931 | |
| SQS-26 | active/passive detection | 1962 | GE (AX/AXR/CX) EDO (BX) | CGN, CG 26, FFG 1, FF 1052, 1040, 1037, AGFF 1 | mods AX, AXR (AX update), BX, CX |

(Table continued on page 318)

| Designation | Purpose | Operational[a] | Manufacturer | Ships | Notes |
|---|---|---|---|---|---|
| SQS-35 | Independent Variable Depth Sonar | 1968 | EDO | FF 1052 | |
| SQS-53 | active/passive detection | 1975 | General Electric | CGN 38, DDG 47, DD 963 | SQS-26CX with digital interface for Mk 116 underwater FCS |
| SQS-56 | active/passive detection | 1977 | Raytheon | FFG 7 | improved SQS-23; digitalized; modular construction |
| SMS | Ship Minehunting Sonar | 1985 est. | | MCM design | replaces SQQ-14; multi-capability including volume search, high resolution, and side-looking features |
| WAA | Wide Aperture Array | | | future SSNs | submarine sonar system with three widely separated hull-mounted arrays on each side of the submarine; may be back-fitted to SSN 637 and 688 |

a   Includes first installation in combatant ship for at-sea evaluation.

Large bow sonar domes have become a key feature of U.S. surface combatants in the post-World War II period. The destroyer SPRUANCE (DD 963), shown here while fitting out, has the SQS-53 active sonar. The SQS-53 and its predecessor, the SQS-26, are the largest hull- or bow-mounted sonars in service with any navy. (Litton)

This is a rare view of a submarine sonar dome—in this view, a 15-foot-diameter BQS-6 sphere which was subsequently fitted with transducers and installed in an SSN. The complementary BQR-7 passive sonar consists of hydrophones in a conformal array along the forward sides of the submarine's hull. (U.S. Navy)

The SQS-35 Variable Depth Sonar (VDS) "fish" is lowered from the frigate FRANCIS HAMMOND (FF 1067) during dockside tests. The hoisting gear and "fish" retract into the open stern hangar. Towed arrays are larger and more complex. (U.S. Navy)

The McCLOY (FF 1038) is the smallest ship to have the SQS-26 bow-mounted sonar. The dome partially floods when at sea and has some dampening effects on ship motion. Unofficial sources credit the SQS-26/53 sonars with an effective range of about 35 miles using "convergence zone" techniques in the active mode. Passive "listening" use of the sonars can provide greater detection ranges against some targets. (U.S. Navy, Ed Dowling)

The submarine SALMON (SS 573) was one of several diesel submarines as well as one nuclear undersea craft, the TULLIBEE (SSN 597), to be fitted with the BQG-4 PUFF fire control sonar. Three sonar domes are provided: one forward, one just abaft of the sail structure, and one aft. The SALMON's fourth "fin" is her upper rudder. (Giorgio Arra)

# 25 Coast Guard

The U.S. Coast Guard is a separate military service under the Department of Transportation and is responsible for the enforcement of U.S. laws in coastal waters, and on high seas subject to the jurisdiction of the United States.

At the direction of the President the Coast Guard can become a part of the Navy (as it did during both world wars) or operate in a war zone while remaining an independent service (as during the Korean and Vietnam wars).

The Coast Guard was transferred to the newly established Department of Transportation on 1 April 1967. Previously, from 1790 to 1967, the service was a part of the Treasury Department. It was originally named the Revenue Marine, then the Revenue Cutter Service, and from 1915 onward the Coast Guard. The Lighthouse Service, established in 1789, was transferred to the Coast Guard in 1939.

## SHIPS

All Coast Guard ships are officially referred to as "cutters," and classes are identified by their length (e.g., the HAMILTON-class cutters are 378 feet). Cutter names are prefixed by USCGC.

The classifications of all Coast Guard ships and small craft are prefixed by the letter "W" (unofficially for White-painted ships). The larger cutters are numbered in a single, sequential series initiated in the 1940s. Cutters less than 100 feet in length have hull numbers whose first two digits indicate the ship's length overall.

The Coast Guard also operates several hundred small lifeboats and patrol boats. These are unnamed (and hence not considered cutters). Most are 44-, 40-, 30-, and 22-foot craft.

**COAST GUARD CUTTERS**

| Type | Class/Ship | Active | Building | Reserve | Commissioned | Notes |
|------|-----------|--------|----------|---------|--------------|-------|
| WHEC 715 | HAMILTON | 12 | — | — | 1967–1972 | |
| WHEC 379 | CASCO | 1 | — | — | 1943 | ex-U.S. Navy |
| WHEC 31 | "Secretary" | 6 | — | — | 1936–1937 | |
| WMEC 901 | BEAR | — | 4 | — | 1980– | 20+ planned |
| WMEC 615 | RELIANCE | 16 | — | — | 1964–1969 | 1 Ship is WTR |
| WMEC/WAGO | Oceangoing Tugs | 7 | — | — | 1940–1945 | ex-U.S. Navy |
| WPBH 1 | FLAGSTAFF | 1 | — | — | 1968 | ex-U.S. Navy |
| WPB 95300 | "Cape" | 26 | — | — | 1953–1959 | |
| WPB 82302 | "Point" | 53 | — | — | 1960–1970 | |
| WAGB 10 | "Polar" | 1 | 1 | — | 1976–1978 | |
| WAGB 4 | GLACIER | 1 | — | — | 1955 | ex-U.S. Navy |
| WAGB 281 | "Wind" | 2 | — | 1 | 1943–1946 | ex-U.S. Navy |
| WAGB 83 | MACKINAW | 1 | — | — | 1944 | |
| WAGB 38 | STORIS | 1 | — | — | 1942 | |
| WIX 327 | EAGLE | 1 | — | — | 1936 | ex-German |
| WIX 157 | CUYAHOGA | 1 | — | — | 1926 | |
| WLB/WAGO | Seagoing Buoy Tenders | 36 | — | — | 1942–1944 | |
| WLM | Coastal Buoy Tenders | 16 | — | — | 1943–1971 | |
| WLI | Inland Buoy Tenders | 17 | — | — | 1942–1969 | |
| WLIC | Construction Tenders | 12 | — | — | 1962–1976 | |
| WLR | River Buoy Tenders | 22 | — | — | 1940–1962 | |
| WLV | Lightships | 4 | — | — | 1950 | |

## AIRCRAFT

Search and rescue: 20 HC-130 B/H Hercules
17 C-131 Samaritan
19 HU-16E Albatross
38 HH-3F Pelican
79 HH-52A Sea Guard
Electronic: 1 EC-130E Hercules
Transport: 1 VC-4A Gulfstream I
1 VC-11A Gulfstream II

The Coast Guard air arm primarily provides search and rescue services. In addition, one electronic aircraft provides calibration for Coast Guard Loran navigation stations and two executive (VIP) transports provide transportation for senior officials of the Department of Transportation and Coast Guard.

The Coast Guard has on order 41 HU-25A Falcon medium-range surveillance aircraft as replacements for the Samaritan and Albatross aircraft and some of the Hercules. In addition, some 90 helicopters are to be procured to supplement and then replace the existing rotary-wing aircraft.

## PERSONNEL

The Coast Guard's strength in mid-1978 is approximately 4,500 officers, 1,300 warrant officers, and 32,000 enlisted men.

## 12 HIGH ENDURANCE CUTTERS: "HAMILTON" CLASS

| Number | Name | Builder | Laid down | Launched | Commissioned | Status |
|---|---|---|---|---|---|---|
| WHEC 715 | HAMILTON | Avondale Shipyards | 4 Jan 1965 | 18 Dec 1965 | 20 Feb 1967 | **AA** |
| WHEC 716 | DALLAS | Avondale Shipyards | 7 Feb 1966 | 1 Oct 1966 | 1 Oct 1967 | **AA** |
| WHEC 717 | MELLON | Avondale Shipyards | 25 July 1966 | 11 Feb 1967 | 22 Dec 1967 | **PA** |
| WHEC 718 | CHASE | Avondale Shipyards | 15 Oct 1966 | 20 May 1967 | 1 Mar 1968 | **AA** |
| WHEC 719 | BOUTWELL | Avondale Shipyards | 12 Dec 1966 | 17 June 1967 | 14 June 1968 | **PA** |
| WHEC 720 | SHERMAN | Avondale Shipyards | 13 Feb 1967 | 23 Sep 1967 | 23 Aug 1968 | **AA** |
| WHEC 721 | GALLANTIN | Avondale Shipyards | 17 Apr 1967 | 18 Nov 1967 | 20 Dec 1968 | **AA** |
| WHEC 722 | MORGENTHAU | Avondale Shipyards | 17 July 1967 | 10 Feb 1968 | 14 Feb 1969 | **AA** |
| WHEC 723 | RUSH | Avondale Shipyards | 23 Oct 1967 | 16 Nov 1968 | 3 July 1969 | **PA** |
| WHEC 724 | MUNROE | Avondale Shipyards | 18 Feb 1970 | 5 Dec 1970 | 10 Sep 1971 | **PA** |
| WHEC 725 | JARVIS | Avondale Shipyards | 9 Sep 1970 | 24 Apr 1971 | 30 Dec 1971 | **PA** |
| WHEC 726 | MIDGETT | Avondale Shipyards | 5 Apr 1971 | 4 Sep 1971 | 17 Mar 1972 | **PA** |

| | |
|---|---|
| Displacement: | 2,716 tons standard |
| | 3,050 tons full load |
| Length: | 350 feet (106.7 m) wl |
| | 378 feet (115.2 m) oa |
| Beam: | 42¾ feet (13 m) |
| Draft: | 20 feet (6.1 m) |
| Propulsion: | 2 gas turbines (Pratt & Whitney), 28,000 shp; 2 diesels (Fairbanks-Morse), 7,200 bhp; 2 shafts (controllable-pitch propellers) |
| Speed: | 29 knots |
| Range: | 9,600 n.miles at 19 knots; 2,300 n.miles at 29 knots |
| Complement: | 155 (15 O + 140 EM) |
| Helicopters: | 1 HH-3F Pelican or HH-52A Sea Guard |
| Guns: | 1 5-inch (127-mm) 54 cal DP Mk 30 (1 × 1) |
| | 2 81 mm mortars Mk 2 (2 × 1) |
| | 2 .50-cal MG |
| ASW weapons: | 6 12.75-inch (324-mm) torpedo tubes Mk 32 (2 × 3) |

Design: The superstructures of these ships are fabricated largely of aluminum. They are fitted with oceanographic and meteorological laboratories.

Electronics: The original SQS-36 sonar was replaced by SQS-38.

Engineering: These were the largest U.S. combat ships to have gas-turbine propulsion until completion of the SPRUANCE (DD 963) in 1975. The gas turbines are FT-4A, marine versions of the J75 aircraft engine. They are fitted with a 350-hp bow propeller pod.

Guns: The two 81-mm mortars, used primarily for illumination, are being removed from these ships and two 20-mm Mk 67 guns and two 40-mm Mk 64 grenade launchers are being installed.

Names: The first nine ships are named for Secretaries of the Treasury; the other three honor heroes of Coast Guard service.

These are the largest ships in Coast Guard service except for the new "Polar"-class icebreakers. During the fall of 1977 the GALLANTIN and MORGENTHAU each embarked two female officers and ten enlisted women to become the first U.S. combat ships to have regular female crewmen. Previously the ships carried female cadets from the Coast Guard Academy on summer cruises.

Aircraft: These are the only Coast Guard ships with helicopter hangars, except for icebreakers.

Antisubmarine: As completed, the earlier ships of this class had two ahead-firing hedgehogs. They have been removed and improved torpedo FCS has been provided.

CHASE (1976, Giorgio Arra)

## 1 HIGH ENDURANCE CUTTER: "CASCO" CLASS

| Number | Name | Builder | Laid down | Launched | AVP Comm. | Status |
|--------|------|---------|-----------|----------|-----------|--------|
| WHEC 379 | UNIMAK | Associated Shipbuilders, Seattle, Wash. | 15 Feb 1942 | 27 May 1942 | 31 Dec 1943 | **AA** |

| | |
|--|--|
| Displacement: | 1,766 tons standard |
| | 2,800 tons full load |
| Length: | 300 feet (91.4 m) wl |
| | 310¾ feet (94.7 m) oa |
| Beam: | 41 feet (12.5 m) |
| Draft: | 13½ feet (4.1 m) |
| Propulsion: | diesels (Fairbanks-Morse); 6,080 bhp; 2 shafts |
| Speed: | 18 knots |
| Complement: | ~152 (27 O + ~125 EM) |
| Guns: | 1 5-inch (127-mm) 38 cal DP Mk 30 (1 × 1) |
| ASW weapons: | removed |

The UNIMAK is the only survivor in U.S. service of 34 BARNEGAT-class (AVP 10) seaplane tenders built during World War II (four were completed as torpedo-boat tenders and one as an amphibious force flagship). The UNIMAK and 17 sister ships were transferred to the Coast Guard in 1946–1948 (WAVP/WHEC 370–387). She operated as a training cutter (WTR) from 1969 until her decommissioning in 1975. The ship had been scheduled for transfer to South Vietnam (as had other ships of this class), but with the fall of the Saigon government she was laid up in reserve; she was recommissioned as a WHEC in 1977 to support the 200-mile U.S. offshore resource zone.

Armament. The UNIMAK has carried a variety of armament during her Navy and Coast Guard service. An ASW hedgehog and two Mk 32 triple torpedo tubes had been removed prior to her decommissioning in 1975.

Classification: The ship was built as the Navy AVP 31. Her classification was changed to WAVP 31 upon transfer to the Coast Guard and to WHEC 379 on 1 May 1966. Subsequently it was changed to WTR 379 on 28 November 1969, but she was recommissioned in 1977 as WHEC.

Names: Seaplane tenders were named for bays and other bodies of water.

UNIMAK (1968, U.S. Coast Guard)

## 6 HIGH ENDURANCE CUTTERS: "SECRETARY" CLASS

| Number | Name | Builder | Laid down | Launched | Commissioned | Status |
|--------|------|---------|-----------|----------|--------------|--------|
| WHEC 31 | BIBB | Charleston Navy Yard | 18 May 1935 | 14 Jan 1937 | 19 Mar 1937 | **AA** |
| WHEC 32 | CAMPBELL | Philadelphia Navy Yard | 1 May 1935 | 3 June 1936 | 22 Oct 1936 | **PA** |
| WHEC 33 | DUANE | Philadelphia Navy Yard | 1 May 1935 | 3 June 1936 | 16 Oct 1936 | **AA** |
| WHEC 35 | INGHAM | Philadelphia Navy Yard | 1 May 1935 | 3 June 1936 | 6 Nov 1936 | **AA** |
| WHEC 36 | SPENCER | New York Navy Yard | 11 Sep 1935 | 3 Jan 1936 | 13 May 1937 | **AA** |
| WHEC 37 | TANEY | Philadelphia Navy Yard | 1 May 1935 | 3 June 1936 | 19 Dec 1936 | **AA** |

| | |
|--|--|
| Displacement: | 2,216 tons standard |
| | 2,414 tons full load |
| Length: | 308 feet (93.9 m) wl |
| | 327 feet (99.7 m) oa |
| Beam: | 41 feet (12.5 m) |
| Draft: | 15 feet (4.6 m) |
| Propulsion: | steam turbines (Westinghouse); 6,200 shp; 2 shafts |
| Boilers: | 2 (Babcock & Wilcox) |
| Speed: | 19.8 knots |
| Range: | 8,000 n.miles at 10.5 knots |
| Complement: | 143 (13 O + 130 EM) |
| Guns: | 1 5-inch (127-mm) 38 cal Mk 30 (1 × 1) |
| | 2 20-mm Mk 67 (2 × 1) |
| ASW weapons: | removed |

These were the largest ships in Coast Guard service until completion of the HAMILTON class.

Armament: These ships have carried a variety of armament during their service lives. Into the 1960s they carried an ASW armament of one hedgehog and two Mk 32 triple torpedo tubes. (Two 40-mm grenade launchers Mk 64 are to be installed.)

Class: Seven ships of this class were built; one ship, the ALEXANDER HAMILTON (WPG 34), was sunk by a German U-boat in 1942. Three additional ships were authorized, but their construction was deferred in 1941 in favor of the OWASCO class (WPG 39).

Classification: During World War II these ships initially were classified as gunboats (PG). In 1944–1945 six ships were reclassified during the war as amphibious force flagships and carried an AGC prefix with their Coast Guard hull numbers, except the DUANE, which was reclassified AGC 6 by the Navy. After the war all reverted to their gunboat configuration (WPG). All were changed to high endurance cutters (WHEC) on 1 May 1966.

Names: These ships were named for Secretaries of the Treasury. Originally full names were used, but they were shortened to surnames only in 1942; these ships were formerly GEORGE M. BIBB, GEORGE W. CAMPBELL, WILLIAM J. DUANE, SAMUEL D. INGHAM, JOHN C. SPENCER, and ROGER B. TANEY.

Radar: The TANEY has been fitted with an AN/WSR-S1 storm tracking radar atop the ship's bridge structure. (The ship operated on ocean weather station "Hotel" 200 miles northeast of Norfolk, Virginia, until late 1977, when an unmanned instrumented ocean buoy was placed on the ocean station.)

**High Endurance Cutter Disposals**

All surviving cutters of the OWASCO class (255 ft) have been stricken: the CHAUTAUQUA (WHEC 41), WINONA (WHEC 65), MINNETONKA (WHEC 67), MENDOTA (WHEC 69), and PONTCHARTRAIN (WHEC 70) in 1976.

BIBB (1975, U.S. Coast Guard)

CAMPBELL; note hangar aft of funnel for weather research balloons (1977, Giorgio Arra)

## (~20) MEDIUM ENDURANCE CUTTERS: "BEAR" CLASS

| Number | Name | FY | Launch | Commission | Status |
|--------|------|-----|--------|------------|--------|
| WMEC 901 | BEAR | 77 | 1979 est. | 1980 est. | Building |
| WMEC 902 | TAMPA | 77 | | | Building |
| WMEC 903 | HARRIET LANE | 78 | | | Building |
| WMEC 904 | NORTHLAND | 78 | | | Building |
| WMEC 905 | SENECA | | | | Planned |
| WMEC 906 | PICKERING | | | | Planned |
| WMEC 907 | ESCANABA | 79–83 | | | Planned |
| WMEC 908 | LEGARE | | | | Planned |
| WMEC 909 | ARGOS | | | | Planned |
| ~11 ships | | | | | Planned |

| | |
|---|---|
| Builders: | WMEC 901–904 Tacoma Boatbuilding Co, Wash. |
| Displacement: | 1,630 tons full load |
| Length: | 270 feet (82.3 m) oa |
| Beam: | 38⅓ feet (11.7 m) |
| Draft: | 13 feet (4 m) |
| Propulsion: | diesels; 7,000 bhp; 2 shafts |
| Speed: | 19.7 knots |
| Complement: | 103 (14 O + 89 EM) |
| Helicopters: | 1 |
| Guns: | 1 76-mm 62 cal AA Mk 75 (1 × 1) |
| ASW weapons: | (helicopter-delivered torpedoes; see notes) |

This class of medium endurance cutters is intended to replace the "Secretary"-class ships and complement the HAMILTON class. Approximately 20 ships are proposed for funding over a seven-year period.

ASW weapons: Although considered to be ASW-capable, these ships will have no ship-launched weapons, but could embark Navy LAMPS helicopters.

Design: These ships will be the only patrol cutters other than the HAMILTONs to have helicopter hangars. Fin stabilizers will be provided.

Electronics: The Mk 92 weapons control system will be fitted, as will an automated command and control center to enhance these ships' combat capabilities.

Guns: These ships will have the 76-mm OTO Melara rapid-fire gun which is also fitted in the PERRY-class (FFG 7) frigates and PEGASUS-class (PHM 1) patrol hydrofoils. Space and weight are reserved for provision of the 20-mm Phalanx Mk 15 gun during wartime.

Sonar: No hull-mounted sonar is provided. A containerized towed acoustic array can be embarked for ASW operations.

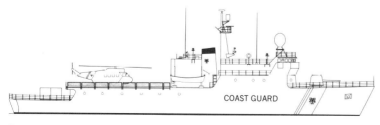

BEAR (U.S. Coast Guard)

## 16 MEDIUM ENDURANCE CUTTERS: "RELIANCE" CLASS

| Number | Name | Launched | Commissioned | Status |
|--------|------|----------|--------------|--------|
| WTR 615 | RELIANCE | 25 May 1963 | 20 June 1964 | **TRA-A** |
| WMEC 616 | DILIGENCE | 20 July 1963 | 26 Aug 1964 | **AA** |
| WMEC 617 | VIGILANT | 24 Dec 1963 | 3 Oct 1964 | **AA** |
| WMEC 618 | ACTIVE | 21 July 1965 | 17 Sep 1966 | **AA** |
| WMEC 619 | CONFIDENCE | 8 May 1965 | 19 Feb 1966 | **PA** |
| WMEC 620 | RESOLUTE | 30 Apr 1966 | 8 Dec 1966 | **PA** |
| WMEC 621 | VALIANT | 14 Jan 1967 | 28 Oct 1967 | **AA** |
| WMEC 622 | COURAGEOUS | 18 Mar 1967 | 10 Apr 1968 | **AA** |
| WMEC 623 | STEADFAST | 24 June 1967 | 25 Sep 1968 | **AA** |
| WMEC 624 | DAUNTLESS | 21 Oct 1967 | 10 June 1968 | **AA** |
| WMEC 625 | VENTUROUS | 11 Nov 1967 | 16 Aug 1968 | **PA** |
| WMEC 626 | DEPENDABLE | 16 Mar 1968 | 22 Nov 1968 | **AA** |
| WMEC 627 | VIGOROUS | 4 May 1968 | 2 May 1969 | **AA** |
| WMEC 628 | DURABLE | 29 Apr 1967 | 8 Dec 1967 | **AA** |
| WMEC 629 | DECISIVE | 14 Dec 1967 | 23 Aug 1968 | **AA** |
| WMEC 630 | ALERT | 19 Oct 1968 | 4 Aug 1969 | **AA** |

| | | |
|---|---|---|
| Builders: | WTR/WMEC 615–617 | Todd Shipyards, Houston, Texas |
| | WMEC 618 | Christy Corp, Sturgeon Bay, Wisc. |
| | WMEC 619, 625, 628–629 | Coast Guard Yard, Curtis Bay, Md. |
| | WMEC 620–624, 626–627, 630 | American Shipbuilding Co, Lorain, Ohio |
| Displacement: | 950 tons standard | |
| | 1,007 tons full load except WTR/WMEC 616–619 970 tons | |
| Length: | 210½ feet (64.2 m) oa | |
| Beam: | 34 feet (10.1 m) | |
| Draft: | 10½ feet (3.2 m) | |
| Propulsion: | 2 turbo-charged diesels (Alco); 5,000 bhp; WTR/WMEC 615–619 also have 2 gas turbines (Solar), 4,000 shp; 2 propellers (controllable pitch propellers) | |
| Speed: | 18 knots | |
| Range: | WTR/WMEC 615–619 5,000 n.miles at 13 knots; WMEC 620–630 5,000 n.miles at 14 knots | |
| Complement: | 61 ( 7 O + 54 EM) | |
| Guns: | 1 3-inch (76-mm) 50 cal AA Mk 22 (1 × 1) | |
| ASW weapons: | none | |

These are search and rescue ships. They can support an HH-52A Sea Guard helicopter, but no hangar is provided. The RELIANCE is a

VIGILANT (1976, Giorgio Arra)

reserve training ship at Yorktown, Virginia; she retains full operational capabilities.

Classification: These ships originally were classified as patrol craft (WPC); changed to WMEC with same hull numbers on 1 May 1966. The RELIANCE was changed to WTR on 27 June 1975 (the "TR" indicating training and reserves).

Design: The RELIANCE design features a small "island" superstructure with 360° visibility from the bridge to facilitate helicopter operations and towing. There is an engine exhaust vent in the stern in place of a conventional funnel.

**1 OCEANOGRAPHIC CUTTER**
**1 MEDIUM ENDURANCE CUTTER** } **FORMER SALVAGE SHIPS**

| Number | Name | Launched | Navy ARS Comm. | Status |
|--------|------|----------|----------------|--------|
| WAGO 167 | ACUSHNET | 1 Apr 1943 | 5 Feb 1944 | **PA** |
| WMEC 168 | YOCONA | 8 Apr 1944 | 3 Nov 1944 | **PA** |

| | |
|--|--|
| Builders: | Basalt Rock Co, Napa, Calif. |
| Displacement: | 1,557 tons standard |
| | 1,745 tons full load |
| Length: | 213½ feet (70 m) oa |
| Beam: | 39 feet (12.8 m) |
| Draft: | 15 feet (4.9 m) |
| Propulsion: | diesels; 3,000 bhp; 2 shafts |
| Speed: | 15.5 knots |
| Range: | 20,000 n.miles at 7 knots |
| Complement: | 64 (7 O + 57 EM) in WAGO 167; 72 (7 O + 65 EM) in WMEC 168 |

These are former Navy salvage ships transferred to the Coast Guard after World War II. The ACUSHNET was modified for handling environmental data buoys in 1969 and reclassified WAGO; the YOCONA was reclassified as WMEC on 1 May 1966; both were formerly classified as tugs (WAT 167–168).

Classification: The Navy classifications of these ships were ARS 9 and ARS 26, respectively.

Names: Renamed in Coast Guard service; former Navy names were the SHACKLE and SEIZE, respectively.

YOCONA (1970, U.S. Coast Guard)

**3 MEDIUM ENDURANCE CUTTERS: FORMER FLEET TUGS**

| Number | Name | Launched | Navy ATF Comm. | Status |
|--------|------|----------|----------------|--------|
| WMEC 153 | CHILULA | 1 Dec 1944 | 5 Apr 1945 | **AA** |
| WMEC 165 | CHEROKEE | 10 Nov 1939 | 26 Apr 1940 | **AA** |
| WMEC 166 | TAMAROA | 13 July 1943 | 9 Oct 1943 | **AA** |

| | |
|--|--|
| Builders: | WMEC 153 Charleston Shipbuilding and Dry Dock Co |
| | WMEC 165 Bethlehem Steel Co, Staten Island, N.Y. |
| | WMEC 166 Commercial Iron Works, Portland, Ore. |
| Displacement: | 1,731 tons full load |
| Length: | 205 feet (62.5 m) oa |
| Beam: | 38½ feet (11.7 m) |
| Draft: | 17 feet (5.2 m) |
| Propulsion: | diesel-electric (General Motors diesels); 3,000 shp; 1 shaft |
| Speed: | 16.2 knots |
| Range: | 15,000 n.miles at 8 knots |
| Complement: | 72 (7 O + 65 EM) |

These are former Navy fleet tugs which were transferred to the Coast Guard after World War II.

Classification: Navy classifications were ATF 153, 66, and 95, respectively. Upon transfer to the Coast Guard they became WAT 153, 165, and 166; all were changed to WMEC on 1 May 1966.

Names: The TAMAROA was named the ZUNI in Navy service.

CHEROKEE (1975, Giorgio Arra)

CHILULA (1970, U.S. Coast Guard)

## 2 MEDIUM ENDURANCE CUTTERS: FORMER AUXILIARY TUGS

| Number | Name | Launched | Navy ATA Comm. | Status |
|--------|------|----------|----------------|--------|
| WMEC 194 | MODOC | 4 Dec 1944 | 14 Feb 1945 | **PA** |
| WMEC 202 | COMANCHE | 10 Oct 1944 | 8 Dec 1944 | **PA** |

| | |
|--|--|
| Builders: | WMEC 194 Levingston Shipbuilding & Drydock Co, Orange, Texas |
| | WMEC 202 Gulfport Boiler & Welding Works, Port Arthur, Texas |
| Displacement: | 534 tons standard |
| | 860 tons full load |
| Length: | 143 feet (46.8 m) oa |
| Beam: | 33 ft (11 m) |
| Draft: | 14 feet (4.9 m) |
| Propulsion: | diesel-electric (General Motors diesels); 1,500 bhp; 1 shaft |
| Speed: | 13.5 knots |
| Range: | 12,000 n.miles at 8.5 knots |
| Complement: | 47 (5 O + 42 EM) |
| Guns: | 2 .50-cal MG |

These are former U.S. Navy steel-hulled tugs. The MODOC was stricken from the Navy Register after World War II and transferred to the Maritime Administration; she was acquired by the Coast Guard on 15 April 1959. The COMANCHE was transferred from the Navy to the Coast Guard on 25 February 1959 on loan; she was subsequently stricken from the Navy Register and transferred permanently on 1 June 1969.

Classification: As Navy tugs these ships were ATA 194 and ATA 202, respectively; as acquired by the Coast Guard they were classified WATA; both were reclassified as WMEC in 1968.

Names: These ships were assigned the Navy names BAGADUCE (ATA 194) and WAMPANOAG (ATA 202) in 1948; they were renamed upon being acquired by the Coast Guard.

MODOC (1970, U.S. Coast Guard)

## 1 HYDROFOIL PATROL GUNBOAT: "FLAGSTAFF"

| Number | Name | Launched | PGH in Service | Status |
|--------|------|----------|----------------|--------|
| WPBH 1 | FLAGSTAFF | 9 Jan 1968 | 14 Sep 1968 | **AA** |

| | |
|--|--|
| Builders: | Grumman Aircraft Corp, Stuart, Fla. |
| Displacement: | 56.8 tons full load |
| Length: | 73 feet (22.3 m) oa foils retracted |
| | 86½ feet (26.4 m) oa foils extended |
| Beam: | 21⁵/₁₂ feet (6.5 m) |
| Draft: | 4¼ feet (1.3 m) foils retracted |
| | 13¹¹/₁₂ feet (4.3 m) foils extended |
| Propulsion: | 2 diesels (Packard); 300 bhp; 2 waterjets hullborne |
| | 1 gas turbine (Rolls Royce); 3,620 shp; 1 supercavitating propeller pod (controllable pitch) |
| Speed: | 8 knots hullborne |
| | 40+ knots on foils |
| Complement: | 13 (1 O + 12 EM) |
| Armament: | none |

The FLAGSTAFF was constructed as a prototype hydrofoil gunboat for the Navy in competition with the TUCUMCARI (PGH 2). After extensive Navy trials and combat service in Vietnam, she was loaned to the Coast Guard for evaluation in 1974–1976; she was permanently transferred on 29 September 1976 and placed in Coast Guard commission on 2 March 1977.

Armament: In Navy service the FLAGSTAFF originally carried one 40-mm AA gun, four .50-cal MG, and one 81-mm mortar. She was used for evaluation of an Army 152-mm M551 howitzer during 1971. All armament has been removed in Coast Guard service.

Classification: The FLAGSTAFF was classified PGH 1 in Navy service, and was changed to PBH 1 in Coast Guard service.

Design: The FLAGSTAFF design provides for 70 percent of the craft's weight to be supported by the main foils and 30 percent by the stern foil when foilborne. Steering is accomplished with the stern foil strut which also serves as mounting for the propeller pod. The hull and superstructure are fabricated of aluminum.

Engineering: The gas turbine is a Rolls Royce Tyne Mk 621/10.

FLAGSTAFF (U.S. Coast Guard)

FLAGSTAFF (U.S. Coast Guard)

CAPE KNOX (top) and POINT BARNES; these two classes can be readily distinguished by their superstructures and first two digits of their hull numbers. (1972, U.S. Coast Guard)

## 26 PATROL BOATS: "CAPE" CLASS

| Number | Name | Number | Name |
|---|---|---|---|
| (A Series) | | | |
| WPB 95300 | CAPE SMALL | WPB 95313 | CAPE MORGAN |
| WPB 95301 | CAPE CORAL | WPB 95314 | CAPE FAIRWEATHER |
| WPB 95302 | CAPE HIGGON | WPB 95316 | CAPE FOX |
| WPB 95303 | CAPE UPRIGHT | WPB 95317 | CAPE JELLISON |
| WPB 95304 | CAPE GULL | WPB 95318 | CAPE NEWAGEN |
| WPB 95305 | CAPE HATTERAS | WPB 95319 | CAPE ROMAIN |
| WPB 95306 | CAPE GEORGE | WPB 95320 | CAPE STARR |
| WPB 95307 | CAPE CURRENT | (C Series) | |
| WPB 95308 | CAPE STRAIT | WPB 95321 | CAPE CROSS |
| WPB 95309 | CAPE CARTER | WPB 95322 | CAPE HORN |
| WPB 95310 | CAPE WASH | WPB 95324 | CAPE SHOALWATER |
| WPB 95311 | CAPE HEDGE | WPB 95326 | CAPE CORWIN |
| (B Series) | | WPB 95328 | CAPE HENLOPEN |
| WPB 95312 | CAPE KNOX | WPB 95332 | CAPE YORK |

| | |
|---|---|
| Builders: | Coast Guard Yard, Curtis Bay, Md. |
| Displacement: | A series 106 tons |
| | B series 105 tons |
| | C series 98 tons |
| Length: | 95 feet (29 m) oa |
| Beam: | 19 feet (5.8 m) |
| Draft: | 6 feet (1.8 m) |
| Propulsion: | 4 diesels (Cummins); 2,200 bhp; 2 shafts |
| Speed: | 20 knots |
| Range: | A series: 2,600 n. miles at 9 knots |
| | B series: 3,000 n. miles at 9 knots |
| | C series: 1,500 n. miles at 8 knots |
| Complement: | 14 (1 O + 13 EM) |
| Guns: | 2 .50-cal MG (2 × 1) |
| | or 1 81-mm mortar Mk 2/1 .50-cal MG M2 (1 × 1/1) |

These are 95-foot cutters employed in port security, search, and rescue. The A series was constructed in 1953, the B series in 1955–

CAPE CROSS (1969, U.S. Coast Guard)

1956, and the C series in 1958–1959. (Nine C-series cutters have been transferred to South Korea.)

Plans to scrap this class in favor of new construction patrol boats have been dropped in favor of modernizing the existing cutters. All are active.

Design: These are steel-hulled cutters. The principal difference in the three series is that the C series has less electronic equipment.

Guns: The weapons listed above are being removed in favor of small arms.

Modernization: All are being modernized from 1977 to 1980–1981, beginning with the CAPE UPRIGHT. They are being fitted with new engines, electronics, and deck equipment; their superstructures have been modified or replaced, and their accommodations improved.

## 62 PATROL BOATS: "POINT" CLASS

| Number | Name | Number | Name |
|---|---|---|---|
| (A Series) | | WPB 82353 | Point Monroe |
| WPB 82302 | Point Hope | WPB 82354 | Point Evans |
| WPB 82311 | Point Verde | WPB 82355 | Point Hannon |
| WPB 82312 | Point Swift | WPB 82356 | Point Francis |
| WPB 82314 | Point Thatcher | WPB 82357 | Point Huron |
| (C Series) | | WPB 82358 | Point Stuart |
| WPB 82318 | Point Herron | WPB 82359 | Point Steele |
| WPB 82332 | Point Roberts | WPB 82360 | Point Winslow |
| WPB 82333 | Point Highland | WPB 82361 | Point Charles |
| WPB 82334 | Point Ledge | WPB 82362 | Point Brown |
| WPB 82335 | Point Countess | WPB 82363 | Point Nowell |
| WPB 82336 | Point Glass | WPB 82364 | Point Whitehorn |
| WPB 82337 | Point Divide | WPB 82365 | Point Turner |
| WPB 82338 | Point Bridge | WPB 82366 | Point Lobos |
| WPB 82339 | Point Chico | WPB 82367 | Point Knoll |
| WPB 82340 | Point Batan | WPB 82368 | Point Warde |
| WPB 82341 | Point Lookout | WPB 82369 | Point Heyer |
| WPB 82342 | Point Baker | WPB 82370 | Point Richmond |
| WPB 82343 | Point Wells | (D Series) | |
| WPB 82344 | Point Estero | WPB 82371 | Point Barnes |
| WPB 82345 | Point Judith | WPB 82372 | Point Brower |
| WPB 82346 | Point Arena | WPB 82373 | Point Camden |
| WPB 82347 | Point Bonita | WPB 82374 | Point Carrew |
| WPB 82348 | Point Barrow | WPB 82375 | Point Doran |
| WPB 82349 | Point Spencer | WPB 82376 | Point Harris |
| WPB 82350 | Point Franklin | WPB 82377 | Point Hobart |
| WPB 82351 | Point Bennett | WPB 82378 | Point Jackson |
| WPB 82352 | Point Sal | WPB 82379 | Point Martin |

| | |
|---|---|
| Builders: | Coast Guard Yard, Curtis Bay, Md. |
| Displacement: | A series 67 tons |
| | C series 66 tons |
| | D series 69 tons |
| Length: | 83 feet (25.3 m) oa |
| Beam: | 17⅙ feet (5.2 m) |
| Draft: | 5¾ feet (1.8 m) |
| Propulsion: | 2 diesels; 1,600 bph; 2 shafts |
| Speed: | 23.5 knots except D series 22.6 knots |
| Range: | A series: 1,500 n. miles at 8 knots |
| | C series: 1,500 n. miles at 8 knots |
| | D series: 1,200 n. miles at 8 knots |
| Complement: | 8 (1 O + 7 EM; 8 EM only in some cutters) |
| Guns: | 2 .50-cal MG (2 × 1) |
| | or 1 81-mm mortar Mk 2/1 .50 cal MG (1 + 1/1), |
| | removed from some cutters |

These are 82-foot cutters used for port security, search, and rescue. The A series was constructed in 1960–1961, the C series in 1961–1967, and D series in 1970. (Twenty-six "Point"-class cutters were transferred to South Vietnam in 1969–1970.) All Coast Guard units are active.

Design: These are steel-hulled cutters with aluminum superstructures. There are no noticeable differences among the various series of the "Point" class.

Guns: The mortars and MGs are being replaced by small arms.

Names: The WPB 82301–82344 were assigned geographical point names in January 1964; later cutters were named as built.

Point Chico (1976, Giorgio Arra)

## 2 ICEBREAKERS: "POLAR" CLASS

| Number | Name | Launched | Commissioned | Status |
|---|---|---|---|---|
| WAGB 10 | Polar Star | 17 Nov 1973 | 17 Jan 1976 | **PA** |
| WAGB 11 | Polar Sea | 24 June 1975 | 23 Feb 1978 | **PA** |

| | |
|---|---|
| Builders: | Lockheed Shipbuilding Co, Seattle, Wash. |
| Displacement: | 13,190 tons full load |
| Length: | 399 feet (121.6 m) oa |
| Beam: | 83½ feet (25.5 m) |
| Draft: | 33½ feet (10.2 m) |
| Propulsion: | CODAG: 6 diesels (Alco), 18,000 bhp; 3 gas turbines (Pratt & Whitney), 60,000 shp; 3 shafts (controllable-pitch propellers) |
| Speed: | 21 knots |
| Complement: | 148 (13 O + 125 EM) + 10 scientists |
| Armament: | none |
| Helicopters: | 2 |

These are the largest icebreakers in service outside of the Soviet Union. Several ships were originally planned in this class as replacements for the "Wind"-class icebreakers. No additional ships are now planned, in part because of the higher-than-anticipated costs of these ships.

Design: These ships have conventional icebreaker hull forms. A hangar and flight deck are fitted aft and two 15-ton-capacity cranes are abaft the hangar. Arctic and oceanographic laboratories are provided.

Engineering: CODOG (Combination Diesel or Gas turbine) propulsion is provided, with diesel engines for cruising and rapid-reaction gas turbines available for surge-power requirements. The gas turbines are FT4A-12s. The controllable-pitch propellers allow propeller thrust to be reversed without reversing the direction of shaft rotation.

POLAR STAR (1976, U.S. Coast Guard)

## 1 ICEBREAKER: "GLACIER"

| Number | Name | Launched | AGB Comm. | WAGB Comm. | Status |
|--------|------|----------|-----------|------------|--------|
| WAGB 4 | GLACIER | 27 Aug 1954 | 27 May 1955 | 30 June 1966 | **PA** |

| | |
|---|---|
| Builders: | Ingalls Shipbuilding Corp, Pascagoula, Miss. |
| Displacement: | 8,449 tons full load |
| Length: | 309½ feet (94.4 m) oa |
| Beam: | 74 feet (6.9 m) |
| Draft: | 29 feet (8.8 m) |
| Propulsion: | diesel-electric (10 Fairbanks-Morse diesels, 2 Westinghouse electric motors); 21,000 shp; 2 shafts |
| Speed: | 17.6 knots |
| Range: | 29,000 n. miles at 12 knots |
| Complement: | 229 (14 O + 215 EM) |
| Guns: | removed |
| Helicopters: | 2 |

The GLACIER was the largest icebreaker constructed in the United States until completion of the POLAR STAR. She was active in the U.S. Navy as AGB 4 from 1955 until she was transferred to the Coast Guard in 1966 (stricken from the Navy List on 1 July 1966, the day after transfer to the Coast Guard).

Guns: As built the GLACIER mounted two 5-inch DP guns, six 3-inch AA guns, and four 20-mm AA guns. The lighter weapons were removed prior to transfer to the Coast Guard, and the 5-inch guns were removed in 1969.

GLACIER (top) and BURTON ISLAND (1975, U.S. Coast Guard)

**3 ICEBREAKERS: "WIND" CLASS**

| Number | Name | Launched | AGB Comm. | WAGB Comm. | Status |
|---|---|---|---|---|---|
| WAGB 281 | WESTWIND | 31 Mar 1943 | — | 1951 | **AA** |
| WAGB 282 | NORTHWIND | 25 Feb 1945 | — | 1947 | **PA** |
| WAGB 283 | BURTON ISLAND | 31 Dec 1945 | 28 Dec 1946 | 15 Dec 1966 | **PA** |

| | |
|---|---|
| Builders: | Western Pipe and Steel Co, San Pedro, Calif. |
| Displacement: | 3,500 tons standard |
| | 6,515 tons full load |
| Length: | 269 feet (82 m) oa |
| Beam: | 63½ feet (19.4 m) |
| Draft: | 29 feet (8.8 m) |
| Propulsion: | diesel-electric (Fairbanks-Morse diesels in WAGB 283; Enterprise in WAGB 281–282); 10,000 shp; 2 shafts |
| Speed: | 16 knots |
| Range: | 38,000 n. miles at 10.5 knots |
| Complement: | ~135 |
| Guns: | removed |
| Helicopters: | 1 |

The "Wind"-class ships were the principal U.S. icebreakers for more than three decades. Originally seven ships were built in two similar classes, five for the Coast Guard and two for the Navy; three of the former served the Soviet Navy from 1945 to 1950 1951.

The WESTWIND served as the Soviet SEVERNI POLIUS from 1945 to 1951; the NORTHWIND entered Coast Guard service upon completion; and the BURTON ISLAND served in the U.S. Navy as AGB 1 from 1946 to 1966.

Class: The EASTWIND (WAG 279/WAGB 279) was stricken in 1972; the SOUTHWIND (WAG 280/KAPITAN BELUSOV/AGB 3 ATKA/WAGB 280) stricken in 1974; the EDISTO (AG 89/AGB 2/WAGB 284), and NORTHWIND (WAG 278/SEVERNI VETER/AGB 5 STATEN ISLAND/WAGB 278) stricken in 1976.

Classification: The BURTON ISLAND was originally classified AG 88; she was changed to AGB 1 in 1949. The WESTWIND carried the Navy classification AGB 6 briefly after her return from the U.S.S.R., but she was never in Navy service.

Design: The ex-WAG 278–282 were built with ASW weapons, space for a floatplane, cargo space for 400 tons or 117 troops, and certain other features which were deleted in the ex-AG 88–89. The latter ships, built for Navy service, had certain post-war features including a helicopter platform, among the first provided in U.S. ships.

Engineering: As built, these ships had a third propeller shaft forward (3,300 shp) for backing down in heavy ice. The bow shafts were removed because of propeller losses in heavy ice. All were built with Fairbanks-Morse diesels; the two ships noted above were re-engined in the mid-1970s.

Guns: As built, some of the Coast Guard design ships had up to four 5-inch DP guns, 12 40-mm AA guns, and several 20-mm AA guns. The post-war-built Navy ships were equipped with one 5-inch gun and lighter weapons. Into the 1960s the NORTHWIND had two 5-inch guns and the other ships each had one 5-inch gun; all were removed 1969–1970

The WESTWIND is one of three survivors of a class of highly versatile and capable icebreakers that served in the U.S. and Soviet navies as well as the Coast Guard. Note the absence of guns forward, HH-52A Sea Guard on helicopter platform and expandable hangar. The WESTWIND and NORTHWIND had taller funnels provided when they were re-engined in 1973–1974 and 1974–1975, respectively.

## 1 ICEBREAKER: "MACKINAW"

| Number | Name | Launched | Commissioned | Status |
|---|---|---|---|---|
| WAGB 83 | MACKINAW | 4 Mar 1944 | 20 Dec 1944 | **GL** |

| | |
|---|---|
| Builders: | Toledo Shipbuilding Co, Ohio |
| Displacement: | 5,252 tons full load |
| Length: | 290 feet (88.4 m) oa |
| Beam: | 75 feet (22.9 m) |
| Draft: | 19 feet (5.8 m) |
| Propulsion: | diesel-electric (Fairbanks-Morse diesels, Westinghouse electric motors); 10,000 shp aft + 3,000 shp forward; 2 shafts aft + 1 shaft forward |
| Speed: | 18.7 knots |
| Range: | 41,000 n. miles at 9 knots |
| Complement: | 127 (10 O + 117 EM) |
| Armament: | none |
| Helicopters: | 1 |

The MACKINAW was designed and constructed specifically for Coast Guard use on the Great Lakes.

Classification: The ship originally was classified WAG 83; she was changed to WAGB on 1 May 1966.

Design: The MACKINAW has many of the features of the "Wind" class; however, being designed for the Great Lakes, the ship is longer and wider than the oceangoing ships, but has significantly less draft. Two 12-ton-capacity cranes are fitted. The ship has a clear deck aft for a helicopter, but no hangar is provided.

## 1 ICEBREAKER: "STORIS"

| Number | Name | Launched | Commissioned | Status |
|---|---|---|---|---|
| WAGB 38 | STORIS | 4 Apr 1942 | 30 Sep 1942 | **PA** |

| | |
|---|---|
| Builders: | Toledo Shipbuilding Co, Ohio |
| Displacement: | 1,715 tons standard |
| | 1,925 tons full load |
| Length: | 230 feet (70.1 m) oa |
| Beam: | 43 feet (13.1 m) |
| Draft: | 15 feet (4.6 m) |
| Propulsion: | diesel-electric (Cooper Bessemer diesels); 1,800 shp; 2 shafts |
| Speed: | 14 knots |
| Range: | 22,000 n. miles at 8 knots |
| Complement: | 106 (10 O + 96 EM) |
| Guns: | 1 3-inch (76-mm) 50 cal AA Mk 22 (1 × 1) |
| | 2 .50-cal MG (2 × 1) |

The STORIS was built specifically for offshore icebreaking and patrol. She is employed in Alaskan service for search, rescue, and law enforcement.

Classification: The STORIS originally was classified WAG 38; she was changed to WAGB 38 on 1 May 1966. Subsequently she was reclassified as a medium endurance cutter (WMEC) on 1 July 1972 to emphasize her role in law enforcement off the Alaskan fishing grounds.

Guns: As built, the STORIS carried two 3-inch guns and four 20-mm guns.

Names: The ship was initially named the ESKIMO.

MACKINAW (U.S. Coast Guard)

STORIS and Soviet fisheries support ship LAMUT off the coast of Alaska (1972, U.S. National Marine Fisheries Service)

STORIS (1975, U.S. Coast Guard)

## 1 TRAINING BARK: "EAGLE"

| Number | Name | Launched | Coast Guard Comm. | Status |
|--------|------|----------|-------------------|--------|
| WIX 327 | EAGLE | 13 June 1936 | 1946 | **TRA-A** |

| | |
|---|---|
| Builders: | Blohm and Voss, Hamburg, Germany |
| Displacement: | 1,816 tons full load |
| Length: | 231 feet (90 m) wl |
| | 295 feet (89.9 m) over bowsprit |
| Beam: | 39⅙ feet (11.9 m) |
| Draft: | 17 feet (5.2 m) |
| Masts: | fore and main 150⅓ feet (45.7 m) |
| | mizzen 132 feet (40.2 m) |
| Propulsion: | 2 auxiliary diesels (M.A.N.); 740 bhp; 1 shaft |
| Speed: | up to 18 knots under sail; 10.5 knots on auxiliary diesels |
| Complement: | 65 (19 O + 46 EM) + 195 cadets) |
| Armament: | none |

The EAGLE is the former German naval training bark HORST WESSEL. Taken by the United States as a war reparation, she was taken over in January 1946 at Bremerhaven and assigned to the Coast Guard. Based at New London, Connecticut, she is employed to carry Coast Guard Academy cadets on summer practice cruises.

Class: The ALBERT LEO SCHLAGETER (launched 1937) was also taken over by the United States in 1945, but was sold to Brazil in 1948 and re-sold to Portugal in 1962; a third ship of this basic design, the GORCH FOCK (1933) was taken over by the Soviet Union in 1946, and renamed the TOVARISH. A later ship of the same general design, also named the GORCH FOCK, was built at the same German yard for the West German Navy (launched 1958).

Design: The EAGLE is steel-hulled. She carries up to 21,350 square feet of sail.

## 1 TRAINING CUTTER: "CUYAHOGA"

| Number | Name | Launched | Commissioned | Status |
|--------|------|----------|--------------|--------|
| WIX 157 | CUYAHOGA | 27 Jan 1927 | 3 Mar 1927 | **TRA-A** |

| | |
|---|---|
| Builders: | Brown Bovari Electric Corp, Camden, N.J. |
| Displacement: | ~200 tons full load |
| Length: | 125 feet (38.1 m) oa |
| Beam: | 24 feet (7.3 m) |
| Draft: | 8 feet (2.4 m) |
| Propulsion: | diesels; 600 bhp; 2 shafts |
| Speed: | 13 knots |
| Complement: | 11 (1 O + 10 EM) |
| Guns: | removed |

The CUYAHOGA is the last of 33 ACTIVE-class steel patrol boats completed in 1926–1927 for the Coast Guard. She was transferred to the Navy and commissioned on 1 April 1935 (classified AG 26) and assigned as a tender and escort for the Presidential yacht; she was returned to the Coast Guard and recommissioned on 17 May 1941 as WPC 157.

Except for the relic CONSTITUTION, the CUYAHOGA is the oldest ship in U.S. government service. She is employed as a training ship for officer candidates at Yorktown, Virginia.

Classification: The CUYAHOGA's classification was changed from WSC 157 to medium endurance cutter (WMEC 157) on 1 May 1966; she was later changed to WIX 157.

EAGLE (1976, U.S. Navy)

CUYAHOGA (1974, U.S. Coast Guard)

**1 OCEANOGRAPHIC CUTTER** } **"BALSAM" CLASS**
**35 SEAGOING BUOY TENDERS**

| Number | Name | Number | Name |
|--------|------|--------|------|
| WLB 62 | BALSAM | WLB 389 | BITTERSWEET |
| WLB 277 | COWSLIP | WLB 390 | BLACKHAW |
| WLB 290 | GENTIAN | WLB 391 | BLACKTHORN |
| WLB 291 | LAUREL | WLB 392 | BRAMBLE |
| WLB 292 | CLOVER | WLB 393 | FIREBRUSH |
| WAGO 295 | EVERGREEN | WLB 394 | HORNBEAM |
| WLB 296 | SORREL | WLB 395 | IRIS |
| WLB 297 | IRONWOOD | WLB 396 | MALLOW |
| WLB 300 | CITRUS | WLB 397 | MARIPOSA |
| WLB 301 | CONIFER | WLB 399 | SAGEBRUSH |
| WLB 302 | MADRONA | WLB 400 | SALVIA |
| WLB 303 | TUPELO | WLB 401 | SASSAFRAS |
| WLB 305 | MESQUITE | WLB 402 | SEDGE |
| WLB 306 | BUTTONWOOD | WLB 403 | SPAR |
| WLB 307 | PLANETREE | WLB 404 | SUNDEW |
| WLB 308 | PAPAW | WLB 405 | SWEETBRIER |
| WLB 309 | SWEETGUM | WLB 406 | ACACIA |
| WLB 388 | BASSWOOD | WLB 407 | WOODRUSH |

| | |
|--|--|
| Builders: | WLB 62, 290–291, 296, 302–303, 389, 392–393, 395–397, 399–400, 406–407 Zeneth Dredge Co, Duluth, Minn. |
| | WLB 277, 292, 295, 300–301, 305–309, 388, 390–391, 394, 401–405 Marine Iron and Shipbuilding Co, Duluth, Minn. |
| | WLB 297 Coast Guard Yard, Curtis Bay, Md. |
| Displacement: | 935 tons standard |
| | 1,025 tons full load |
| Length: | 180 feet (59 m) oa |
| Beam: | 37 feet (12.1 m) |
| Draft: | 13 feet (4.2 m) |
| Propulsion: | diesel-electric; 1,000 shp in WLB 62–303 series except WLB 297, others 1,200 shp; 1 shaft |
| Speed: | WLB 62–303 series (except WLB 297) 12.8 knots; others 15 knots |
| Complement: | 53 (6 O + 47 EM) |
| Guns: | 1 3-inch (76-mm) 50 cal AA Mk 22 (1 × 1) in WLB 277, 296, 300, 394 |
| | 2 20-mm AA Mk 67 (2 × 1) in WLB 297, 389, 393, 402, 405 |
| | 2 .50-cal MG in some tenders |
| | some ships are unarmed |

These tenders service navigation buoys and other aids to navigation in coastal waters. They were completed in 1942–1945 with several sub-types. Twenty-nine ships are active; eight are in reserve (WLB 62, 277, 290, 296–297, 303, 308, 394).

Class: The EVERGREEN was refitted as an oceanographic cutter in 1973 and reclassified WAGO.

Design: The WLB 62, 296, 300, 390, 392, 402–404 have strengthened hulls for icebreaking.

Engineering: The WLB 277, 295, 389, 394 are fitted with controllable-pitch, bow-thrust propellers.

Guns: As completed, these tenders had one 3-inch AA gun and two or four 40-mm AA guns. Most are now unarmed.

Names: The ACACIA originally was named the THISTLE.

**5 COASTAL BUOY TENDERS: "RED" CLASS**

| Number | Name | Number | Name |
|--------|------|--------|------|
| WLM 685 | RED WOOD | WLM 688 | RED CEDAR |
| WLM 686 | RED BEECH | WLM 689 | RED OAK |
| WLM 687 | RED BIRCH | | |

| | |
|--|--|
| Builders: | Coast Guard Yard, Curtis Bay, Md. |
| Displacement: | 471 tons standard |
| | 512 tons full load |
| Length: | 157 feet (51.5 m) oa |
| Beam: | 33 feet (10.8 m) |
| Draft: | 6 feet (1.9 m) |
| Propulsion: | diesels; 1,800 bhp; 2 shafts (controllable-pitch propellers) |
| Speed: | 12.8 knots |
| Complement: | 31 (4 O + 27 EM) |

These buoy and navigation aid tenders have strengthened steel hulls for light icebreaking, and are fitted with bow thrusters. WLM 685–686 were launched in 1964, WLM 687 in 1965, WLM 688 in 1970, and WLM 689 in 1971.

Coast Guard buoy tenders are painted black except for the EVERGREEN, modified for use as an oceanographic research ship. She has a built-up amidships structure, laboratories, a stern hoise, and additional electronic equipment. (1973, U.S. Coast Guard)

RED CEDAR (1975, Giorgio Arra)

## 7 COASTAL BUOY TENDERS: "WHITE" CLASS

| Number | Name | Number | Name |
|---|---|---|---|
| WLM 540 | White Sumac | WLM 545 | White Heath |
| WLM 542 | White Bush | WLM 546 | White Lupine |
| WLM 543 | White Holly | WLM 547 | White Pine |
| WLM 544 | White Sage | | |

| | |
|---|---|
| Builders: | Petersen and Haecker, Blair, Neb. |
| Displacement: | 435 tons standard |
| | 600 tons full load |
| Length: | 133 feet (43.6 m) oa |
| Beam: | 31 feet (10.1 m) |
| Draft: | 9 feet (2.9 m) |
| Propulsion: | diesels (Union); 600 bhp; 2 shafts |
| Speed: | 9.8 knots |
| Complement: | 21 (1 O + 20 EM) |

White Bush (1969, U.S. Coast Guard)

These tenders are converted Navy self-propelled lighters (YF). All were launched in 1943.

## 1 COASTAL BUOY TENDER: "JUNIPER"

| Number | Name |
|---|---|
| WLM 224 | Juniper |

| | |
|---|---|
| Builders: | John H. Mathis, Camden, N.J. |
| Displacement: | 794 tons full load |
| Length: | 177 feet (58 m) oa |
| Beam: | 32 feet (9.75 m) |
| Draft: | 9$^1/_6$ feet (3 m) |
| Propulsion: | diesel-electric; 900 shp; 2 shafts |
| Speed: | 10.8 knots |
| Complement: | 38 (4 O + 34 EM) |

Juniper (1971, U.S. Coast Guard, Lieutenant M. Robinson)

The Juniper, previously classified as WAGL, was changed to WLM on 1 January 1965. She was launched on 18 May 1940.

## 3 COASTAL BUOY TENDERS: "HOLLYHOCK" CLASS

| Number | Name | Number | Name |
|---|---|---|---|
| WLM 212 | Fir | WLM 252 | Walnut |
| WLM 220 | Hollyhock | | |

| | |
|---|---|
| Builders: | |
| Displacement: | 989 tons full load |
| Length: | 175 feet (57.4 m) oa |
| Beam: | 34 feet (10.9 m) |
| Draft: | 12 feet (3.9 m) |
| Propulsion: | diesels; 1,350 bhp; 2 shafts |
| Speed: | 12 knots |
| Complement: | 40 (5 O + 35 EM) |

These tenders originally were classified as WAGL; they were changed to coastal tenders (WLM) on 1 January 1965. WLM 220 was launched in 1937; others in 1939.

Fir (1969, U.S. Coast Guard)

## 1 INLAND BUOY TENDER: "BUCKTHORN"

| Number | Name |
|--------|------|
| WLI 642 | BUCKTHORN |

| | |
|--------|------|
| Builders: | Mobile Ship Repair, Ala. |
| Displacement: | 200 tons full load |
| Length: | 100 feet (32.8 m) oa |
| Beam: | 24 feet (7.8 m) |
| Draft: | 4 feet (1.3 m) |
| Propulsion: | 2 diesels; 600 bhp; 2 shafts |
| Speed: | 7.3 knots |
| Complement: | 14 (1 O + 13 EM) |

The BUCKTHORN was launched in 1963.

BUCKTHORN (1970, U.S. Coast Guard)

## 1 INLAND BUOY TENDER: "TAMARACK"

| Number | Name |
|--------|------|
| WLI 248 | TAMARACK |

| | |
|--------|------|
| Builders: | Manitowoc Shipbuilding, Wisc. |
| Displacement: | 400 tons full load |
| Length: | 124 feet (40.6 m) oa |
| Beam: | 30 feet (9.8 m) |
| Draft: | 8 ft (2.6 m) |
| Propulsion: | diesel; 520 bhp; 1 shaft |
| Speed: | 10 knots |

The TAMARACK was launched in 1934. She is out of service.

## I INLAND BUOY TENDER: "AZALEA"

| Number | Name |
|--------|------|
| WLI 641 | AZALEA |

| | |
|--------|------|
| Builders: | Coast Guard Yard, Curtis Bay, Md. |
| Displacement: | 200 tons full load |
| Length: | 100 feet (32.8 m) oa |
| Beam: | 24 feet (7.8 m) |
| Draft: | 5 feet (1.6 m) |
| Propulsion: | 2 diesels; 440 bhp; 2 shafts |
| Speed: | 9 knots |
| Complement: | 14 (1 O + 13 EM) |

The AZALEA was launched in 1958.

## 2 INLAND BUOY TENDERS: IMPROVED "BERRY" CLASS

| Number | Name | Number | Name |
|--------|------|--------|------|
| WLI 65400 | BAYBERRY | WLI 65401 | ELDERBERRY |

| | |
|--------|------|
| Builders: | |
| Displacement: | 68 tons full load |
| Length: | 65 feet (21.3 m) oa |
| Beam: | 17 feet (5.6 m) |
| Draft: | 4 feet (1.3 m) |
| Propulsion: | 2 diesels; 400 bhp; 2 shafts |
| Speed: | 11.3 knots |
| Complement: | 5 (EM) |

Both tenders were launched in 1954.

BAYBERRY (1968, U.S. Coast Guard)

## 1 INLAND BUOY TENDER: "TERN"

| Number | Name |
|---|---|
| WLI 80801 | TERN |

| | |
|---|---|
| Builders: | Coast Guard Yard, Curtis Bay, Md. |
| Displacement: | 173 tons full load |
| Length: | 80 feet (24.4 m) oa |
| Beam: | 23 feet (7 m) |
| Draft: | 6 feet (1.8 m) |
| Propulsion: | diesels; 500 bhp; 2 shafts |
| Speed: | 10 knots |
| Complement: | 7 (EM) |

The TERN was a prototype inland buoy tender with a cutaway stern and moving gantry crane for handling buoys. She is fitted with a 125-hp bow thruster. The TERN was launched on 15 June 1968 and placed in service on 7 February 1969.

TERN (1969, U.S. Coast Guard)

## 3 INLAND BUOY TENDERS: "BERRY" CLASS

| Number | Name | Number | Name |
|---|---|---|---|
| WLI 65303 | BLACKBERRY | WLI 65305 | LOGANBERRY |
| WLI 65304 | CHOKEBERRY | | |

| | |
|---|---|
| Builders: | Dubuque Boat and Boiler Co, Iowa |
| Displacement: | 68 tons full load |
| Length: | 65 feet (21.3 m) oa |
| Beam: | 17 feet (5.6 m) |
| Draft: | 4 feet (1.2 m) |
| Propulsion: | diesel; 220 bhp; 1 shaft |
| Speed: | 9 knots |
| Complement: | 5 (EM) |

These tenders were launched in 1946.

## 6 INLAND BUOY TENDERS: "COSMOS" CLASS

| Number | Name | Number | Name |
|---|---|---|---|
| WLI 293 | COSMOS | WLI 315 | SMILAX |
| WLI 298 | RAMBLER | WLI 316 | PRIMROSE |
| WLI 313 | BLUEBELL | WLI 317 | VERBENA |

| | |
|---|---|
| Builders: | |
| Displacement: | 178 tons full load |
| Length: | 100 feet (32.8 m) oa |
| Beam: | 24 feet (7.8 m) |
| Draft: | 5 feet (1.6 m) |
| Propulsion: | 2 diesels; 600 bhp; 2 shafts |
| Speed: | 10.5 knots |
| Complement: | 15 (1 O + 14 EM) |

WLI 293 was launched in 1942, the others in 1944, except WLI 313 in 1945.

### Inland Buoy Tender Disposals

The CLEMATIS (WLI 74286), SHADBUSH (WLI 74287), BLUEBERRY (WLI 65302) were stricken in 1976.

## 2 + 1 CONSTRUCTION TENDERS: "PAMLICO" CLASS

| Number | Name | Number | Name |
|---|---|---|---|
| WLIC 800 | PAMLICO | WLIC 802 | . . . . . . |
| WLIC 801 | HUDSON | | |

| | |
|---|---|
| Builders: | Coast Guard Yard, Curtis Bay, Md. |
| Displacement: | |
| Length: | 160 feet (52.4 m) oa |
| Beam: | |
| Draft: | |
| Propulsion: | diesels |
| Speed: | |
| Complement: | 13 |

The first two tenders were launched in 1975 and 1976, respectively, with a third unit provided in FY 1977.

## 1 RIVER BUOY TENDER: "SUMAC"

| Number | Name |
|---|---|
| WLR 311 | SUMAC |

| | |
|---|---|
| Builders: | Peterson and Haecker, Blair, Neb. |
| Displacement: | 404 tons full load |
| Length: | 115 feet (37.7 m) oa |
| Beam: | 30 feet (9.8 m) |
| Draft: | 6 feet (1.9 m) |
| Propulsion: | diesels; 960 bhp; 3 shafts |
| Speed: | 10.6 knots |
| Complement: | 23 (1 O + 22 EM) |

The SUMAC was launched in 1943.

## 10 INLAND CONSTRUCTION TENDERS: 75-FT CLASS

| Number | Name | Number | Name |
|---|---|---|---|
| WLIC 75301 | ANVIL | WLIC 75306 | CLAMP |
| WLIC 75302 | HAMMER | WLIC 75307 | WEDGE |
| WLIC 75303 | SLEDGE | WLIC 75308 | SPIKE |
| WLIC 75304 | MALLET | WLIC 75309 | HATCHET |
| WLIC 75305 | VISE | WLIC 75310 | AXF |

Builders:
Displacement: 145 tons full load
Length: 75 feet (22.7 m) oa except WLIC 75306–75310 are 76 feet (23.2 m)
Beam: 22 feet (7.2 m)
Draft: 4 feet (1.3 m)
Propulsion: diesels; 600 bhp; 2 shafts
Speed: 10 knots
Complement: 9–10 (1 O in some tenders + 9 EM)

These tenders were launched in 1962–1965.

## 9 RIVER BUOY TENDERS: 75-FT CLASS

| Number | Name | Number | Name |
|---|---|---|---|
| WLR 75401 | GASCONADE | WLR 75406 | KICKAPOO |
| WLR 75402 | MUSKINGUM | WLR 75407 | KANAWHA |
| WLR 75403 | WYACONDA | WLR 75408 | PATOKA |
| WLR 75404 | CHIPPEWA | WLR 75409 | CHENA |
| WLR 75405 | CHEYENNE | | |

Builders:
Displacement: 145 tons full load
Length: 75 feet (24.5 m) oa
Beam: 22 feet (7.2 m)
Draft: 4 feet (1.3 m)
Propulsion: diesels; 600 bhp; 2 shafts
Speed: 10.8 knots
Complement: 12 (EM)

These tenders were launched in 1964–1971

WEDGE with crane barge (1971, U.S. Coast Guard)

CHEYENNE with buoy barge (1971, U.S. Coast Guard)

## 1 RIVER BUOY TENDER: "FOXGLOVE"

| Number | Name |
|---|---|
| WLR 285 | FOXGLOVE |

Builders: Dubuque Boat and Boiler Co, Iowa
Displacement: 350 tons full load
Length: 114 feet (37.4 m) oa
Beam: 30 feet (9.8 m)
Draft: 6 feet (1.9 m)
Propulsion: diesels; 8,500 bhp; 3 shafts
Speed: 13.5 knots
Complement: 21 (1 O + 20 EM)

The FOXGLOVE was launched in 1945.

## 1 RIVER BUOY TENDER: 80-FT CLASS

| Number | Name |
|---|---|
| WLR 80310 | LANTANA |

Builders: Peterson and Haecker, Blair, Neb.
Displacement: 235 tons full load
Length: 80 feet (26.2 m) oa
Beam: 30 feet (9.8 m)
Draft: 6 feet (1.9 m)
Propulsion: diesels; 10,000 bhp; 3 shafts
Speed: 10 knots
Complement: 20 (1 O + 19 EM)

The LANTANA was launched in 1943.

## 3 RIVER BUOY TENDERS: "DOGWOOD" CLASS

| Number | Name | Number | Name |
|---|---|---|---|
| WLR 259 | DOGWOOD | WLR 268 | SYCAMORE |
| WLR 263 | FORSYTHIA | | |

| Builders: | |
|---|---|
| Displacement: | 230 tons full load except WLR 263 280 tons |
| Length: | 114 feet (37.4 m) oa |
| Beam: | 26 feet (8.5 m) |
| Draft: | 4 feet (1.3 m) |
| Propulsion: | diesels; 2,800 bhp; 2 shafts |
| Speed: | 11 knots |
| Complement: | 21 (1 O + 20 EM) |

The WLR 259 and 268 were launched in 1940 and the WLR 263 in 1943.

## 1 RIVER BUOY TENDER: 73-FT CLASS

| Number | Name |
|---|---|
| WLR 73264 | OLEANDER |

| Builders: | Jeffersonville Boat and Machinery Co, Ind |
|---|---|
| Displacement: | 90 tons full load |
| Length: | 73 feet (23.9 m) oa |
| Beam: | 18 feet (5.9 m) |
| Draft: | 5 feet (1.6 m) |
| Propulsion: | diesels; 300 bhp; 2 shafts |
| Speed: | 12 knots |
| Complement: | 10 (EM) |

The OLEANDER was launched in 1940.

## (10) MEDIUM HARBOR TUGS: "BAY" CLASS

| Number | Name | Number | Name |
|---|---|---|---|
| WYTM 101 | KATMAI BAY | WYTM 103 | MOBILE BAY |
| WYTM 102 | BRISTOL BAY | WYTM 104 | BISCAYNE BAY |

| Builders: | Tacoma Boatbuilding Co, Wash. |
|---|---|
| Displacement: | 660 tons full load |
| Length: | 140 feet (45.9 m) oa |
| Beam: | 30 feet (9.8 m) |
| Draft: | 12½ feet (4 m) |
| Propulsion: | diesel-electric; 2,500 shp; 1 shaft |
| Speed: | 14 knots |
| Complement: | 17 (3 O + 14 EM) |

These are the largest tugs ever to be constructed specifically for Coast Guard use. They will replace the 110-foot tugs. They are strengthened for light icebreaking. Three tugs were funded in FY 1977 and one in FY 1978; ten are planned.

Names: The following tentative names have been assigned for future tugs of this class: the NEAH BAY (105), MORRO BAY (106), PENOBSCOTT BAY (107), THUNDER BAY (108), and STURGEON BAY (109).

## 6 RIVER BUOY TENDERS: 65-FT CLASS

| Number | Name | Number | Name |
|---|---|---|---|
| WLR 65501 | OUACHITA | WLR 65504 | SCIOTO |
| WLR 65502 | CIMARRON | WLR 65505 | OSAGE |
| WLR 65503 | ORION | WLR 65506 | SANGAMON |

| Builders: | |
|---|---|
| Displacement: | 139 tons full load |
| Length: | 65½ feet (21.5 m) oa |
| Beam: | 21 feet (6.9 m) |
| Draft: | 5 feet (1.6 m) |
| Propulsion: | diesels; 600 bhp; 2 shafts |
| Speed: | 12.5 knots |
| Complement: | 10 (EM) |

These tenders were launched in 1960–1962.

OSAGE with buoy barge; note square bow and stern of river and inland buoy tenders. The 65-foot class tenders have twin funnels. (1971, U.S. Coast Guard)

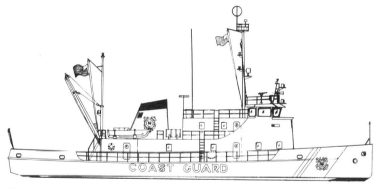

KATMAI BAY (U.S. Coast Guard)

## 13 MEDIUM HARBOR TUGS: "MANITOU" CLASS

| Number | Name | Number | Name |
|--------|------|--------|------|
| WYTM 60 | MANITOU | WYTM 92 | NAUGATUCK |
| WYTM 61 | KAW | WYTM 93 | RARITAN |
| WYTM 71 | APALACHEE | WYTM 96 | CHINOOK |
| WYTM 72 | YANKTON | WYTM 97 | OJIBWA |
| WYTM 73 | MOHICAN | WYTM 98 | SNOHOMISH |
| WYTM 90 | ARUNDEL | WYTM 99 | SAUK |
| WYTM 91 | MAHONING | | |

Builders:
Displacement: 370 tons full load
Length: 110 feet (36 m) oa
Beam: 27 feet (8.8 m)
Draft: 11 feet (3.6 m)
Propulsion: diesel-electric; 1,000 shp; 1 shaft
Speed: 11.2 knots
Complement: 20 (1 O + 19 EM)

The YTM 90–93 were launched in 1939, the others in 1943.

MESSENGER (1969, U.S. Coast Guard)

## 15 SMALL HARBOR TUGS: 65-FT CLASS

| Number | Name | Number | Name |
|--------|------|--------|------|
| WYTL 65601 | CAPSTAN | WYTL 65609 | SHACKLE |
| WYTL 65602 | CHOCK | WYTL 65610 | HAWSER |
| WYTL 65603 | SWIVEL | WYTL 65611 | LINE |
| WYTL 65604 | TACKLE | WYTL 65612 | WIRE |
| WYTL 65605 | TOWLINE | WYTL 65613 | BITT |
| WYTL 65606 | CATENARY | WYTL 65614 | BOLLARD |
| WYTL 65607 | BRIDLE | WYTL 65615 | CLEAT |
| WYTL 65608 | PENDANT | | |

Builders:
Displacement: 72 tons full load
Length: 65 feet (21.3 m) oa
Beam: 19 feet (6.2 m)
Draft: 7 feet (2.3 m)
Propulsion: diesel; 400 bhp; 1 shaft
Speed: 10.5 knots except WYTL 65607–65615 9.8 knots
Complement: 10 (EM)

These tugs were launched in 1961–1967.

## 1 MEDIUM HARBOR TUG: 85-FT CLASS

| Number | Name |
|--------|------|
| WYTM 85009 | MESSENGER |

Builders:
Displacement: 230 tons full load
Length: 85 feet (27.8 m) oa
Beam: 23 feet (7.5 m)
Draft: 9 feet (2.9 m)
Propulsion: diesel; 700 bhp; 1 shaft
Speed: 9.5 knots
Complement: 10 (EM)

The MESSENGER was launched in 1944.

TOWLINE (U.S. Coast Guard)

MAHONING (1976, Stefan Terzibaschitsch)

**4 LIGHTSHIPS**

| Number | Name | Number | Name |
|--------|------|--------|------|
| WLV 604 | LIGHTSHIP COLUMBIA | WLV 612 | LIGHTSHIP NANTUCKET |
| WLV 605 | LIGHTSHIP RELIEF | WLV 613 | LIGHTSHIP RELIEF |

| | |
|---|---|
| Builders: | Coast Guard Yard, Curtis Bay, Md. |
| Displacement: | 617 tons full load except WLV 612–613 607 tons |
| Length: | 128 feet (41.9 m) oa |
| Beam: | 30 feet (9.8 m) |
| Draft: | 11 feet (3.8 m) |
| Propulsion: | diesel; 550 bhp; 1 shaft |
| Speed: | 10.7 knots WLV 612–613 11 knots |
| Complement: | |

All were launched in 1950 except WLV 613 in 1952. Coast Guard lightships exchange names according to location; their hull numbers remain constant. The WLV 604 is assigned to Astoria, Oregon, the WLV 612–613, Boston, Massachusetts, and the WLV 613 is near Nantucket Shoals, Massachusetts.

Design: These are steel-hulled ships with two 55-foot masts. The main lantern is displayed from the forward mast.

LIGHTSHIP NANTUCKET (U.S. Coast Guard)

41-foot "cutter" in service at Little Creek, Virginia; two "Point"-class cutters and the FORT SNELLING (LSD 30) are moored in the background. (1976, Giorgio Arra)

52-foot "cutter" in service at Seattle, Washington (1970, U.S. Coast Guard)

# 26 National Oceanic and Atmospheric Administration

The National Oceanic and Atmospheric Administration (NOAA) conducts ocean surveys and other research and surveying activities for the U.S. government. These activities are of a non-military nature. However, NOAA maps and charts are used by the armed forces, and during time of war or national crisis the NOAA research ships can be expected to operate with the Navy, either as a separate service or integrated into the Navy.

NOAA is an agency of the Department of Commerce. Prior to the establishment of NOAA in 1970, these ships were part of the National Ocean Survey, a division of the Environmental Services Science Administration from 1965 to 1970. Before that the ships were operated by the Coast and Geodetic Survey (since 1878, and the Coast Survey from 1834, and the Survey of the Coast from 1807).

## SHIPS

The larger research and survey ships are listed here. In addition, NOAA operates several fisheries research ships and a few smaller research craft. NOAA ships are classified by their "Horsepower Tonnage," the numerical sum of the vessel's shaft horsepower plus gross tonnage. Class I ships are 5501–9000 HPT, Class II are 3501–5500 HPT, Class III are 2001–3500 HPT, Class IV are 1001–2000 HPT, Class V are 501–1000 HPT, and Class VI are up to 500 HPT.

Individual ships are designated with a three-digit number pre-ceded by the letter "R" for Research or "S" for Survey. The first digit indicates the HPT class and the next two digits the ship's hull number.

## AIRCRAFT

NOAA operates four aircraft for aerial photographic surveying:

> 1 Cessna Skymaster
> 1 de Haviland of Canada Buffalo
> 1 Rockwell International Turbo-Commander
> 2 WP-3D Orion

The Orions are former Navy weather-reconnaissance aircraft which were transferred to NOAA in 1975.

## PERSONNEL

The National Ocean Survey which operates NOAA ships has approximately 225 commissioned officers, plus 250 licensed and 2,250 unlicensed Civil Service personnel. Another 125 commissioned officers serve elsewhere in NOAA. Several Navy officers also are assigned to NOAA.

## 1 OCEANOGRAPHIC RESEARCH SHIP: "RESEARCHER"

| Number | Name | Launched | Commissioned | Status |
|---|---|---|---|---|
| R103 | RESEARCHER | 5 Oct 1968 | 8 Oct 1970 | **AA** |

| | |
|---|---|
| Builders: | American Shipbuilding Co, Lorain, Ohio |
| Displacement: | 2,875 tons light |
| Length: | 278¼ feet (84.7 m) oa |
| Beam: | 51 feet (15.5 m) |
| Draft: | 16¼ feet (4.9 m) |
| Propulsion: | 2 diesels; 3,200 bhp; 2 shafts (controllable-pitch propellers) |
| Speed: | 16 knots |
| Complement: | 66 (11 O + 55 EM) + 13 scientists |

Design: Maritime Administration S2-MT-MA74à design.

Engineering: The RESEARCHER is fitted with a 450-hp, 360° retractable bow thruster for precise maneuvering and "creeping" speeds up to seven knots.

RESEARCHER (NOAA)

## 2 OCEANOGRAPHIC RESEARCH SHIPS: "OCEANOGRAPHER" CLASS

| Number | Name | Launched | Commissioned | Status |
|---|---|---|---|---|
| R101 | OCEANOGRAPHER | 18 Apr 1964 | 13 July 1966 | **PA** |
| R102 | DISCOVERER | 29 Oct 1964 | 29 Apr 1967 | **AA** |

| | |
|---|---|
| Builders: | Aerojet-General Corp, Jacksonville, Fla. |
| Displacement: | 3,959 tons light |
| Length: | 303⅓ feet (92.4 m) oa |
| Beam: | 52 feet (15.8 m) |
| Draft: | 18½ feet (5.6 m) |
| Propulsion: | diesel-electric (4 diesels); 5,000 bhp; 2 shafts |
| Speed: | 18 knots |
| Complement: | 92 (14 O + 78 EM) + 18 scientists |

Design: Maritime Administration S2-MET-MA62a design.

Engineering: These ships have a 400-hp through-bow thruster.

OCEANOGRAPHER (NOAA)

DISCOVERER (NOAA)

## 1 HYDROGRAPHIC SURVEY SHIP: "SURVEYOR"

| Number | Name | Launched | Commissioned | Status |
|--------|------|----------|--------------|--------|
| S132 | SURVEYOR | 25 Apr 1959 | 30 Apr 1960 | **PA** |

| | |
|---|---|
| Builders: | National Steel Co, San Diego |
| Displacement: | 3,150 tons light |
| Length: | 292⅓ feet (88.8 m) oa |
| Beam: | 46 feet (14 m) |
| Draft: | 18 feet (5.5 m) |
| Propulsion: | steam turbine (De Laval); 3,200 shp; 1 shaft |
| Boilers: | 2 |
| Speed: | 16 knots |
| Complement: | 120 (14 O + 106 EM) + 9 scientists |

Design: Maritime Administration S2-S-RM28a design. A helicopter platform has been fitted aft.

SURVEYOR (NOAA)

## 2 HYDROGRAPHIC SURVEY SHIPS: "McARTHUR" CLASS

| Number | Name | Launched | Commissioned | Status |
|--------|------|----------|--------------|--------|
| S330 | McARTHUR | 15 Nov 1965 | 15 Dec 1966 | **PA** |
| S331 | DAVIDSON | 7 May 1966 | 10 Mar 1967 | **PA** |

| | |
|---|---|
| Builders: | Norfolk Shipbuilding and Dry Dock Co, Va. |
| Displacement: | 995 tons light |
| Length: | 175 feet (53 m) oa |
| Beam: | 38 feet (11.5 m) |
| Draft: | 11½ feet (3.5 m) |
| Propulsion: | diesels; 1,600 bhp; 2 shafts (controllable-pitch propellers) |
| Speed: | 13 knots |
| Complement: | 40 (8 O + 32 EM) |

Design: Maritime Administration S1-MT-MA70a design.

## 3 HYDROGRAPHIC SURVEY SHIPS: "FAIRWEATHER" CLASS

| Number | Name | Launched | Commissioned | Status |
|--------|------|----------|--------------|--------|
| S220 | FAIRWEATHER | 15 Mar 1967 | 2 Oct 1968 | **PA** |
| S221 | RAINIER | 15 Mar 1967 | 2 Oct 1968 | **PA** |
| S222 | MT. MITCHELL | 29 Nov 1966 | 23 Mar 1968 | **AA** |

| | |
|---|---|
| Builders: | Aerojet-General Corp, Jacksonville, Fla. |
| Displacement: | 1,798 tons light |
| Length: | 231 feet (70.2 m) oa |
| Beam: | 42 feet (12.8 m) |
| Draft: | 13⅚ (4.2 m) |
| Propulsion: | 2 diesels; 2,400 bhp; 2 shafts (controllable-pitch propellers) |
| Speed: | 14.5 knots |
| Complement: | 76 (12 O + 64 EM) + 2 scientists |

Design: Maritime Administration S1-MT-MA72a design.

Engineering: These ships have a 200-bhp diesel through-bow thruster.

MT. MITCHELL (NOAA)

"McARTHUR" class; NOAA has published this same photograph with the hull numbers retouched to both CSS 30 and CSS 31. (NOAA)

**2 HYDROGRAPHIC SURVEY SHIPS: "PEIRCE" CLASS**

| Number | Name | Launched | Commissioned | Status |
|--------|------|----------|--------------|--------|
| 6328 | PEIRCE | 15 Oct 1962 | 6 May 1963 | **AA** |
| 3329 | WHITING | 20 Nov 1962 | 8 July 1963 | **AA** |

| | |
|---|---|
| Builders: | Marietta Manufacturing Co, Point Pleasant, W.Va. |
| Displacement: | 760 tons light |
| Length: | 164 feet (50 m) oa |
| Beam: | 33 feet (10 m) |
| Draft: | 10 ft (3.1 m) |
| Propulsion: | diesels; 1,600 bhp; 2 shafts (controllable-pitch propellers) |
| Speed: | 12.5 knots |
| Complement: | 40 (8 O + 32 EM) |

Design: Maritime Administration S1-MT-59a design.

PEIRCE (NOAA)

**1 CURRENT SURVEY VESSEL: "FERREL"**

| Number | Name | Launched | Commissioned | Status |
|--------|------|----------|--------------|--------|
| ASV 92 | FERREL | 4 Apr 1968 | 4 June 1968 | **AA** |

| | |
|---|---|
| Builders: | Zeigler Shipyard, Jennings, La. |
| Displacement: | 363 tons light |
| Length: | 133¼ feet (40.5 m) oa |
| Beam: | 32 feet (9.7 m) |
| Draft: | 7 feet (2.1 m) |
| Propulsion: | diesels; 750 bhp; 2 shafts |
| Speed: | 10.6 knots |
| Complement: | 16 (3 O + 13 EM) |

The FERREL conducts near-shore and estuarine-current surveys. She employs data collection buoys in her work, hence there is a large open buoy stowage area aft as well as a comprehensive workshop.

Design: Maritime Administration S1-MT-MA83a design.
Engineering: Fitted with a 100-hp through-bow thruster.

FERREL (NOAA)

# Ship Names Index

(Service and yard craft and buoy tenders are not listed)

# Addenda

**Submarines** (pages 17–46)

SSBN 731-732: Authorized FY 1978; ordered 27 Feb 1978 from Electric Boat.

SSN 691: MEMPHIS commissioned 17 Dec 1977. **AA**

SSN 692: OMAHA commissioned 11 Mar 1978. **AA**

SSN 711: Named SAN FRANCISCO; laid down 26 May 1977.

SSN 571: NAUTILUS will be decommissioned beginning in July 1979; consideration is being given to laying her up at the U.S. Naval Academy, Annapolis.

**Aircraft Carriers** (pages 47–60)

CV 60: SARATOGA to be the first carrier modernized under the Service Life Extension Program (SLEP), from late 1980 to early 1983 at Newport News. The FORRESTAL and other ships of the class to follow, probably at Philadelphia Naval Shipyard. SLEP to cost approximately $500 million and include general updating—SPS-48C, SPS-49, and SPS-65 radars; NATO Sea Sparrow; and Phalanx CIWS.

CV 66: AMERICA has 4 steam C13 catapults (correction).

CV 43: CORAL SEA has 3 steam C11 catapults (correction); she will operate as a contingency and training carrier through 1980, after which she may be deployed briefly when the SARATOGA enters SLEP.

CVT 16: LEXINGTON to decommission and be stricken May 1979.

LHA 6: Has been proposed for construction, to permit one or two of the smaller IWO JIMA class (LPH 2) ships to be converted to ASW and sea control carriers operating VSTOL aircraft and ASW helicopters.

**Cruisers** (pages 64–83)

CG 26: BELKNAP being rebuilt at Philadelphia Naval Shipyard through early 1980.

**Destroyers** (pages 84–103)

DD 997H: Assigned to air-capable destroyer (DD 997 previously assigned to Iranian ship); current Navy planning provides for a standard DD 963 with enlarged hangar for four LAMPS.

DDG 35: MITSCHER decommissioned and stricken 1 June 1978.

DDG 36: JOHN S. MCCAIN decommissioned and stricken 29 Apr 1978.

DD 972: OLDENDORF commissioned 4 Mar 1978. **PA**

DD 975: O'BRIEN commissioned 3 Dec 1977. **PA**

DD 976: MERRILL commissioned 11 Mar 1978. **PA**

**Frigates** (pages 104–117)

3,000-ton Surface Effect Ship: Early in 1978, Secretary of Defense Harold Brown again cancelled construction of the prototype frigate SES. However, the future of the program is uncertain because of Navy and Congressional efforts to continue with the ship.

FFG 7: OLIVER HAZARD PERRY reportedly reached 31 knots on trials.

FFG 11: Named CLARK.

FFG 12: Named GEORGE PHILIP.

FFG 27, 30, 33: Ordered from Todd Shipyards (San Pedro).

FFG 28, 31: Ordered from Todd Shipyards (Seattle).

FFG 29, 32, 34: Ordered from Bath Iron Works.

**Amphibious Warfare Ships** (pages 122–143)

LHA 4: NASSAU launched 28 Jan 1978. Speed: ~22 knots (sustained: ~24 knots maximum).

LHA 5: DA NANG renamed PELELIU 15 Feb 1978.

**Patrol Ships and Craft** (pages 151–160)

PHM 2, 6: To be completed 1981; PHM 3-5 completed 1981.

#### Naval Aircraft (pages 259–291)

AV-8 Harrier: An additional aircraft destroyed in a crash on 1 Feb 1978; there have now been 23 destroyed and 6 severely damaged (change in assessment).

NKC-135A Stratotanker: Two aircraft planned for acquisition as replacements for EB-74E in electronic role.

CTX: Beech C-12A selected by Navy for CTX role, but procurement delayed by Congressional opposition; 66 aircraft planned.

TS-2/US-2 Tracker: Three ES-2D aircraft are used by Pacific Missile Range Facility in Hawaii for visual and radar surveillance, radar calibration, etc.

#### Coast Guard (pages 320–340)

WHEC 715: HAMILTON 36,000 shp (correction).

WAGB 11: POLAR SEA commissioned 23 Feb 1978

WAGB: New class of icebreakers under design, length approximately 300 feet; authorization in FY 1981 and completion of lead ship by 1985.

#### National Oceanic and Atmospheric Administration (pages 341–344)

Personnel (correction): NOAA has approximately 380 commissioned officers, of which 145 are assigned to the National Ocean Survey for duty aboard ship; another 95 officers serve elsewhere in the National Ocean Survey. One hundred thirty-five licensed civil service personnel and 540 unlicensed personnel are assigned to NOAA ships.

Aircraft: NOAA also operates 1 WC-130B Hercules and 4 helicopters.